A-Z LANCASH

CW00706936

CONTENTS

REFERENCE

Motorway	M6
Proposed	
A Road	A59
Under Construction	
Proposed	
B Road	B5269
Dual Carriageway	
One Way Street Traffic flow on A Roads is indicated by a heavy line on the driver's left.	→
Restricted Access	
Pedestrianized Road	
Track / Footpath	
Residential Walkway	
Railway	Tunnel / Station / Heritage Sta. / Level Crossing
Tramway	Tram Stop
Built Up Area	ALMA STREET
Local Authority Boundary	— · — · —
National Park Boundary	
Posttown Boundary	
Postcode Boundary	— — — —

Map Continuation	80 / Small Scale Pages 34
Car Park (Selected)	P
Church or Chapel	†
Fire Station	■
House Numbers (A & B Roads only)	13 8
Hospital	Ⓗ
Information Centre	𝒊
National Grid Reference	360
Police Station	▲
Post Office	★
Toilet	▽
with facilities for the Disabled	♿
Viewpoint	✳ ✴
Educational Establishment	
Hospital or Hospice	
Industrial Building	
Leisure or Recreational Facility	
Place of Interest	
Public Building	
Shopping Centre or Market	
Other Selected Buildings	

SCALE

Map Pages numbered in blue are
1:19000 3⅓ inches to 1 mile

0	¼	½ Mile
0	250	500	750 Metres

5.26 cm to 1 km   8.47 cm to 1 mile

Map Pages numbered in green are
1:38000 1⅔ inches to 1 mile

0	½	1 Mile
0	500 Metres	1 Kilometre

2.63 cm to 1 km   4.23 cm to 1 mile

Copyright of Geographers' A-Z Map Company Ltd.

Head Office:
Fairfield Road, Borough Green, Sevenoaks, Kent, TN15 8PP
Telephone: 01732 781000 (Enquiries & Trade Sales)
01732 783422 (Retail Sales)
www.a-zmaps.co.uk

Ordnance Survey This product includes mapping data licensed from Ordnance Survey® with the permission of the Controller of Her Majesty's Stationery Office.
© Crown Copyright 2004. Licence number 100017302

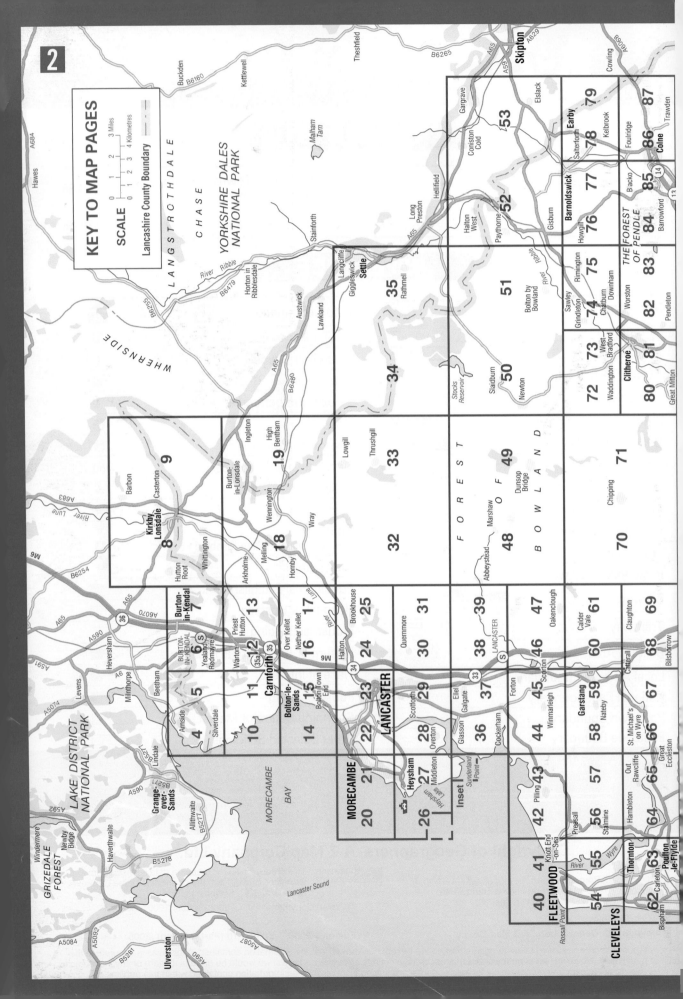

2

KEY TO MAP PAGES

SCALE

0   1   2   3 Miles
0 1 2 3 4 Kilometres

Lancashire County Boundary --------

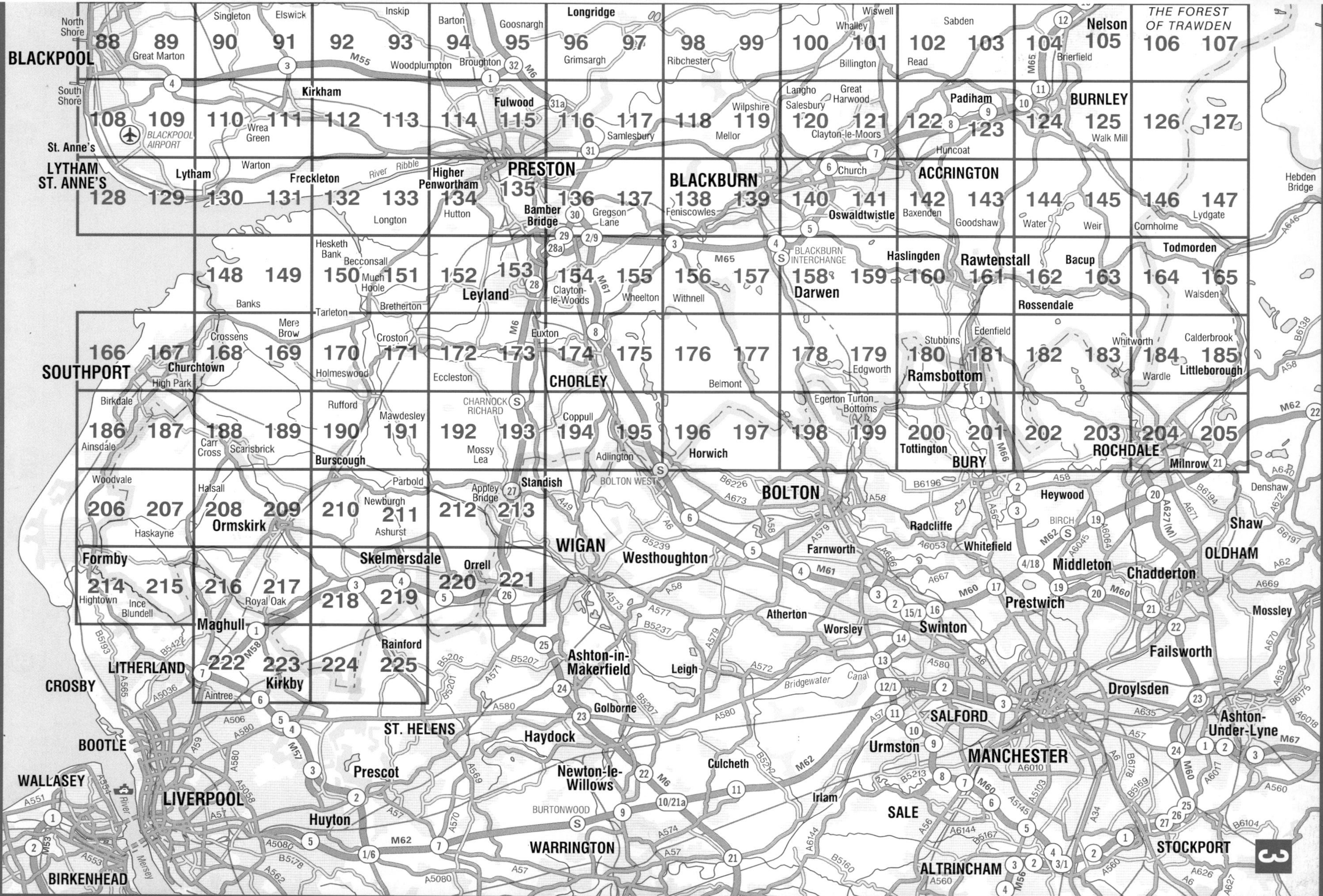
BLACKPOOL
North Shore
South Shore
St. Anne's
LYTHAM ST. ANNE'S
Singleton
Elswick
Inskip
Barton
Goosnargh
Longridge
Grimsargh
Ribchester
Whalley
Wiswell
Billington
Sabden
Read
Nelson
Brierfield
THE FOREST OF TRAWDEN
Great Marton
Woodplumpton
Broughton
Kirkham
Fulwood
Wrea Green
BLACKPOOL AIRPORT
Samlesbury
Mellor
Wilpshire
Langho
Salesbury
Great Harwood
Clayton-le-Moors
Padiham
Huncoat
BURNLEY
Walk Mill
Lytham
Warton
Freckleton
River Ribble
Higher Penwortham
PRESTON
Hutton
Longton
Bamber Bridge
Gregson Lane
BLACKBURN
Feniscowles
Church
Oswaldtwistle
ACCRINGTON
Baxenden
Goodshaw
Water
Weir
Cornholme
Lydgate
Hebden Bridge
Hesketh Bank
Becconsall
Much Hoole
Bretherton
Banks
Tarleton
Leyland
Clayton-le-Woods
Wheelton
Withnell
BLACKBURN INTERCHANGE
Darwen
Haslingden
Rawtenstall
Bacup
Rossendale
Todmorden
Walsden
SOUTHPORT
Crossens
Churchtown
High Park
Mere Brow
Croston
Holmeswood
Eccleston
Euxton
CHORLEY
Belmont
Edgworth
Stubbins
Edenfield
Ramsbottom
Whitworth
Calderbrook
Wardle
Littleborough
Birkdale
Ainsdale
Carr Cross
Scarisbrick
Rufford
Mawdesley
Burscough
CHARNOCK RICHARD
Mossy Lea
Coppull
Adlington
Horwich
Egerton
Turton Bottoms
Tottington
BURY
ROCHDALE
Milnrow
Woodvale
Haskayne
Halsall
Ormskirk
Parbold
Newburgh
Ashurst
Appley Bridge
Standish
BOLTON WEST
BOLTON
Heywood
Denshaw
Shaw
OLDHAM
Formby
Hightown
Ince Blundell
Royal Oak
Maghull
Skelmersdale
Orrell
WIGAN
Westhoughton
Farnworth
Radcliffe
Whitefield
BIRCH
Middleton
Chadderton
Prestwich
Mossley
Rainford
Kirkby
Aintree
LITHERLAND
CROSBY
BOOTLE
WALLASEY
LIVERPOOL
River Mersey
BIRKENHEAD
Ashton-in-Makerfield
Leigh
Atherton
Worsley
Swinton
Failsworth
Bridgewater Canal
Golborne
ST. HELENS
Haydock
Prescot
Huyton
Newton-le-Willows
BURTONWOOD
WARRINGTON
Culcheth
Irlam
SALFORD
Urmston
MANCHESTER
Droylsden
Ashton-Under-Lyne
SALE
ALTRINCHAM
STOCKPORT
M55
M6
M65
M61
M58
M57
M62
M60
M66
M56
M53
M67
A627(M)
3

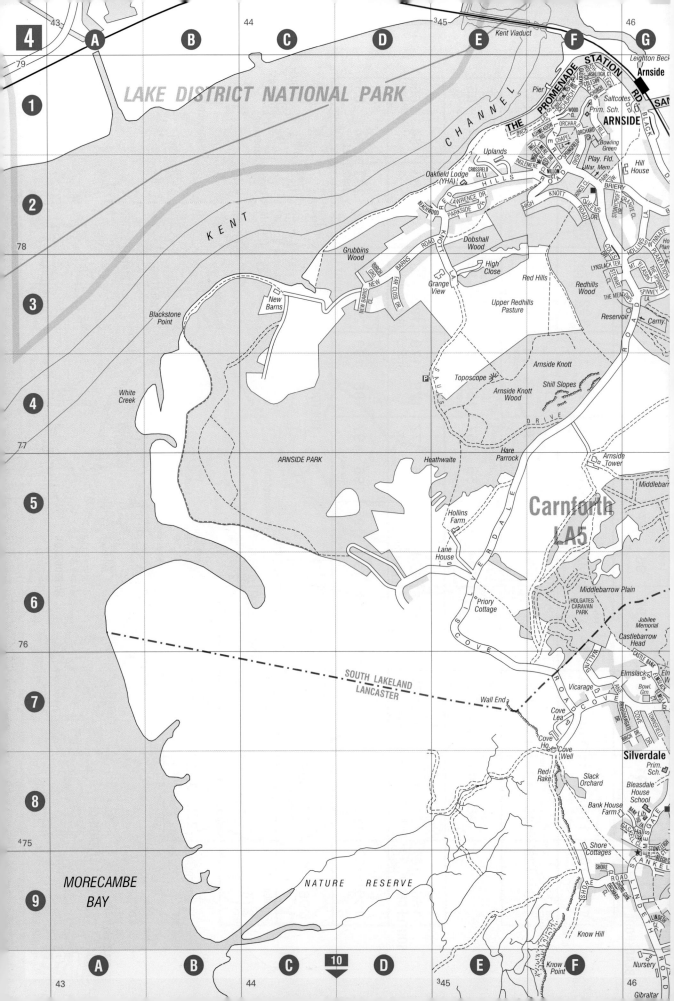

4

LAKE DISTRICT NATIONAL PARK

KENT

CHANNEL

THE PROMENADE

STATION RD

Arnside

ARNSIDE

Kent Viaduct

Pier

Uplands

Oakfield Lodge (YHA)

Crossfield Ct. L.

Grubbins Wood

Dobshall Wood

High Close

Red Hills

Redhills Wood

New Barns

Blackstone Point

Grange View

Upper Redhills Pasture

Reservoir

White Creek

Toposcope

Arnside Knott

Shill Slopes

Arnside Knott Wood

ARNSIDE PARK

Heathwaite

Hare Parrock

Arnside Tower

Middlebar

DRIVE

Carnforth LA5

Hollins Farm

Lane House

Middlebarrow Plain

HOLGATES CARAVAN PARK

Jubilee Memorial

Castlebarrow Head

SOUTH LAKELAND
LANCASTER

Priory Cottage

Wall End

Vicarage

Cove Lea

Cove Ho.

Cove Well

Silverdale
Prim. Sch.

Bleasdale House School

Red Rake

Slack Orchard

Bank House Farm

Shore Cottages

MORECAMBE BAY

NATURE RESERVE

Know Point

Shore

Know Hill

Know Hill

Nursery

Gibraltar

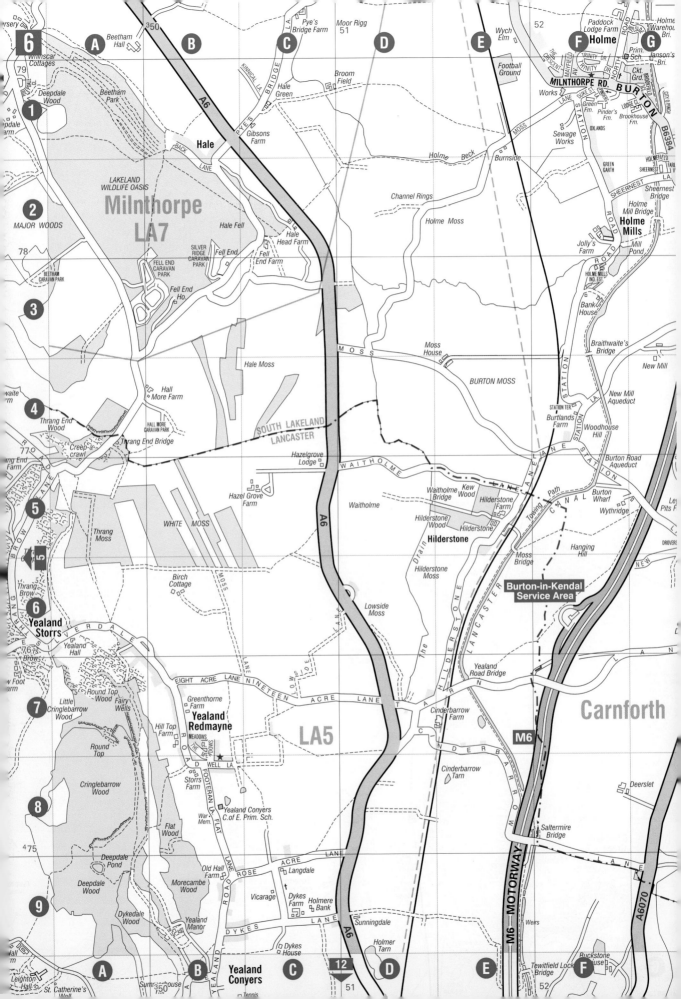

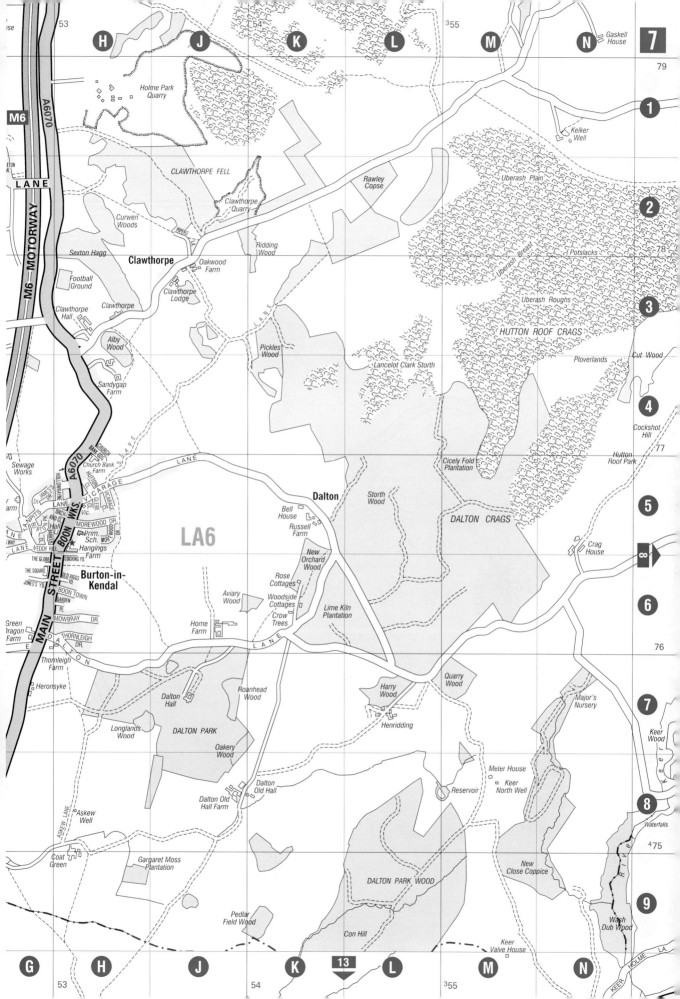

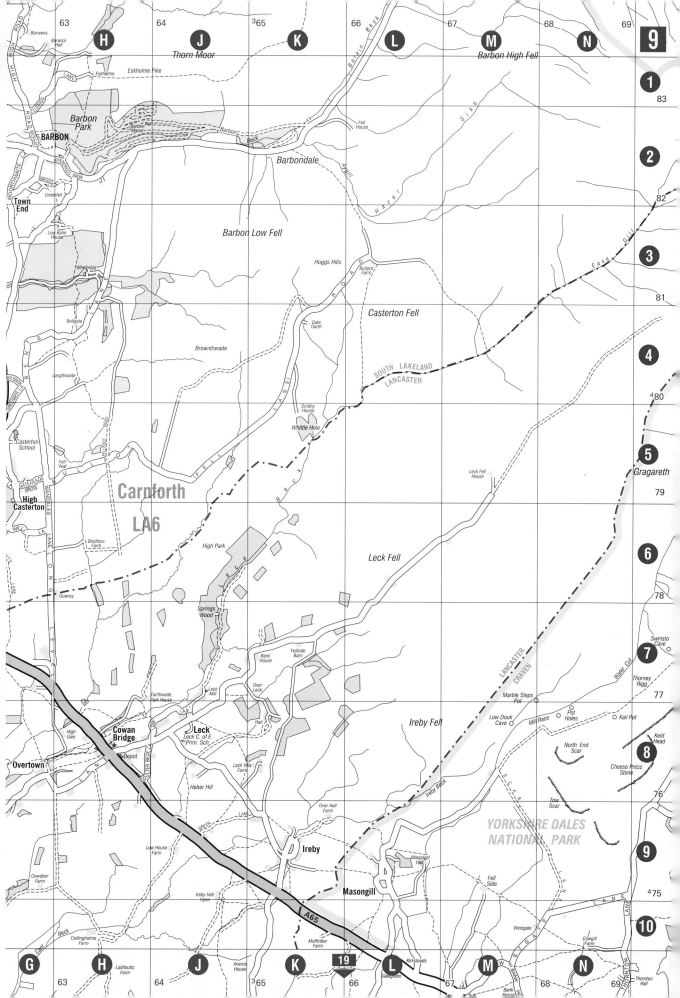

43 A 44 B 345 C 4 D E 945 F ow Hill 46 G

Know End
Point

Gibraltar
Farm

Nursery

Lindeth
Tower

Gibral
Cotta

74

Cow Close
Wood

Grey
Walls

Jack
Scout Cave

Hillside
Cottage

Jenny Brown's
Point

Quicksand

Pool

73

WARTON   SANDS

72

MORECAMBE

BAY

71

KENT

470

CHANNEL

43 A 44 B 345 C 14 D E 945 F 46

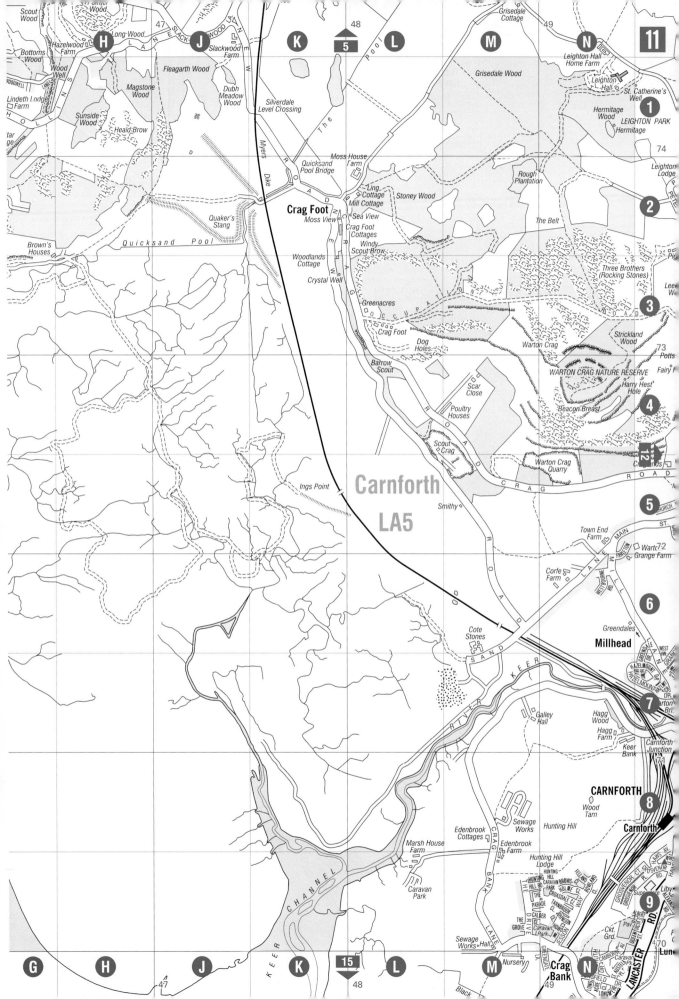

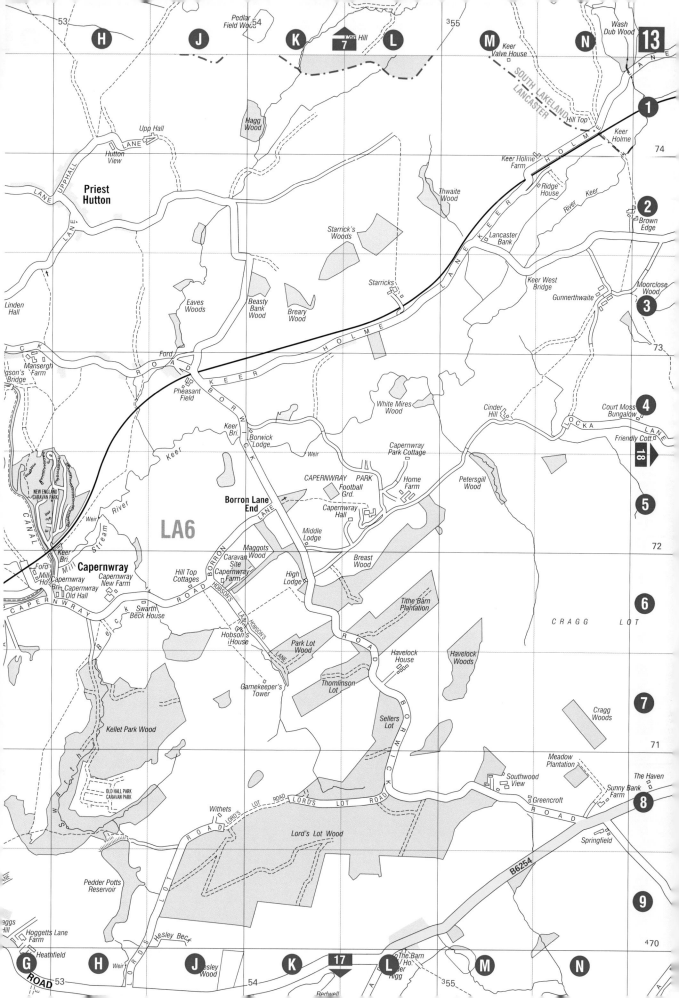

H J K L M N

G H J K L M N

Priest Hutton

LA6

Capernwray

Borron Lane End

CAPERNWRAY PARK

Wash Dub Wood

Keer Valve House

Hill Top

Keer Holme

Keer Holme Farm

Ridge House

Brown Edge

Thwaite Wood

Lancaster Bank

River Keer

Keer West Bridge

Gunnerthwaite

Moorclose Wood

Starrick's Woods

Starricks

White Mires Wood

Cinder Hill

Court Moss Bungalow

Friendly Cott.

Hagg Wood

Pedlar Field Wood

Upp Hall

Hutton View

Linden Hall

Mansergh Farm

Higson's Bridge

Ford

Eaves Woods

Beasty Bank Wood

Breary Wood

Pheasant Field

Keer Bri.

Borwick Lodge

Weir

Capernwray Park Cottage

Petersgill Wood

Home Farm

Football Grd.

Capernwray Hall

Middle Lodge

Maggots Wood

Caravan Site Capernwray Farm

High Lodge

Breast Wood

Tithe Barn Plantation

CRAGG LOT

Cragg Woods

Havelock House

Havelock Woods

Meadow Plantation

The Haven

Sunny Bank Farm

Southwood View

Greencroft

Springfield

Hill Top Cottages

Capernwray New Farm

Keer Bri.

Ford

Mill Ho.

Capernwray Bri.

Capernwray Old Hall

Swarth Beck House

Hobson's House

Park Lot Wood

Gamekeeper's Tower

Thomlinson Lot

Sellers Lot

Kellet Park Wood

Old Hall Park Caravan Park

Withets

Lord's Lot Wood

Pedder Potts Reservoir

Hoggetts Lane Farm

Heathfield

New England Caravan Park

Weir

Weir

Wesley Wood

The Barn Ho.

Lower Rigg

Redwell

NEW ENGLAND

CANAL

River Keer

Mill Stream

Beck

Swarth Beck

Hobson's Lane

Borron Lane

Borwick Road

Keer

Road

Borwick Road

Lord's Lot Road

Lord's Lot Road

Lord's Lot Road

B6254

Road

LANE

HOLME

KEER LANE

KEER LANE HOLME

UPHALL LANE

LOCKA LANE

HOLM LANE

SOUTH LAKELAND

LANCASTER

1

2

3

4

5

6

7

8

9

18

17

7

53

54

355

74

73

72

71

70

355

53

54

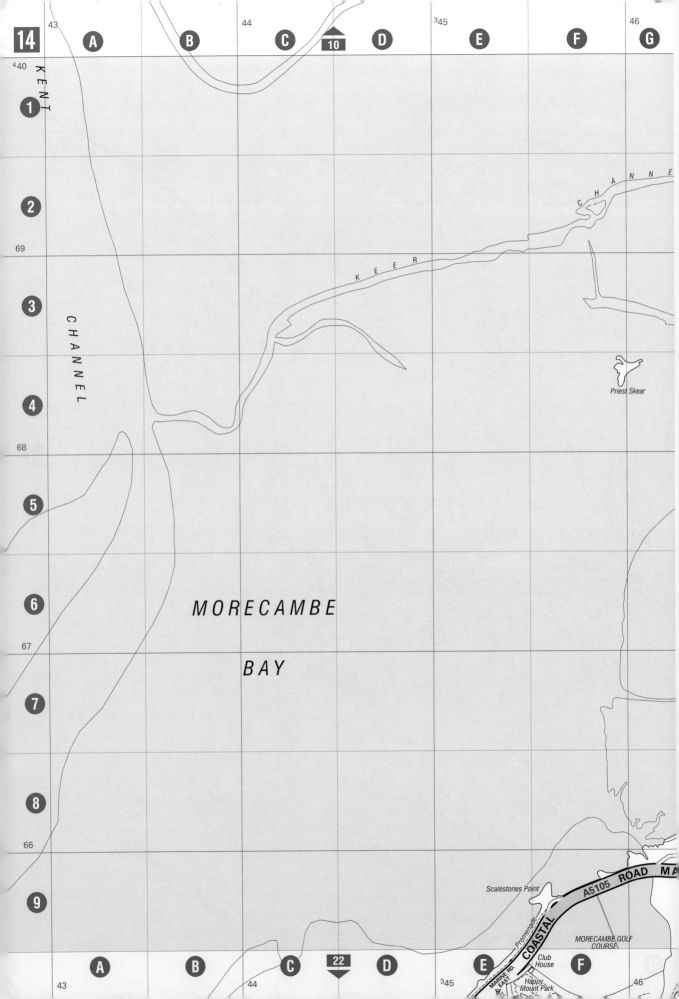

KENT

CHANNEL

CHANNEL

KEER

Priest Skear

MORECAMBE

BAY

Scalestones Point

A5105 ROAD MA

Promenade

COASTAL

MARINE RD. EAST

Club House

MORECAMBE GOLF COURSE

Happy Mount Park

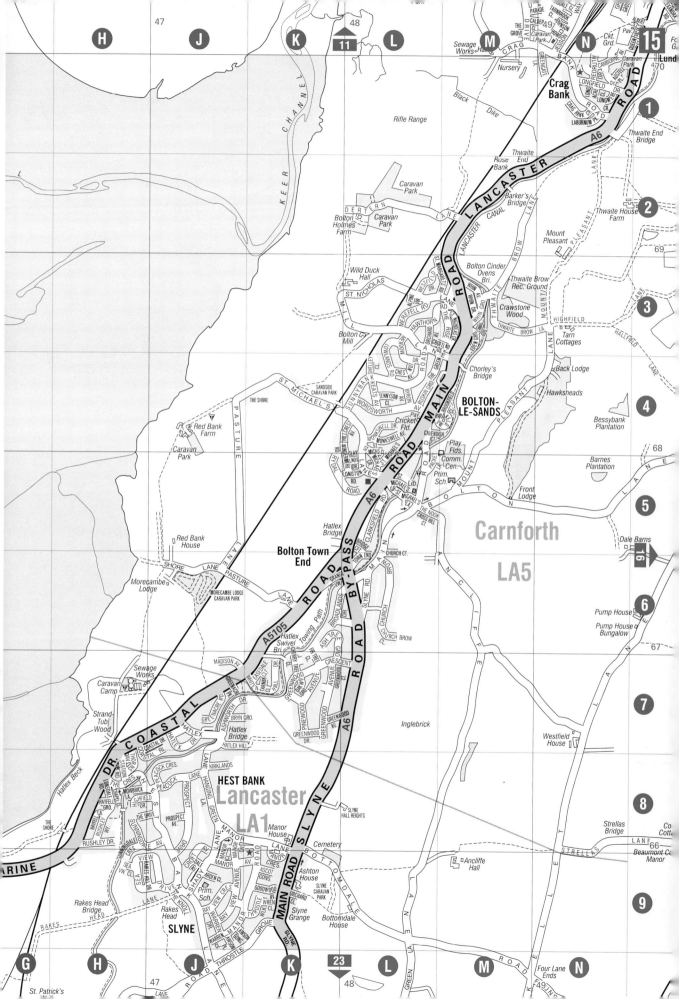

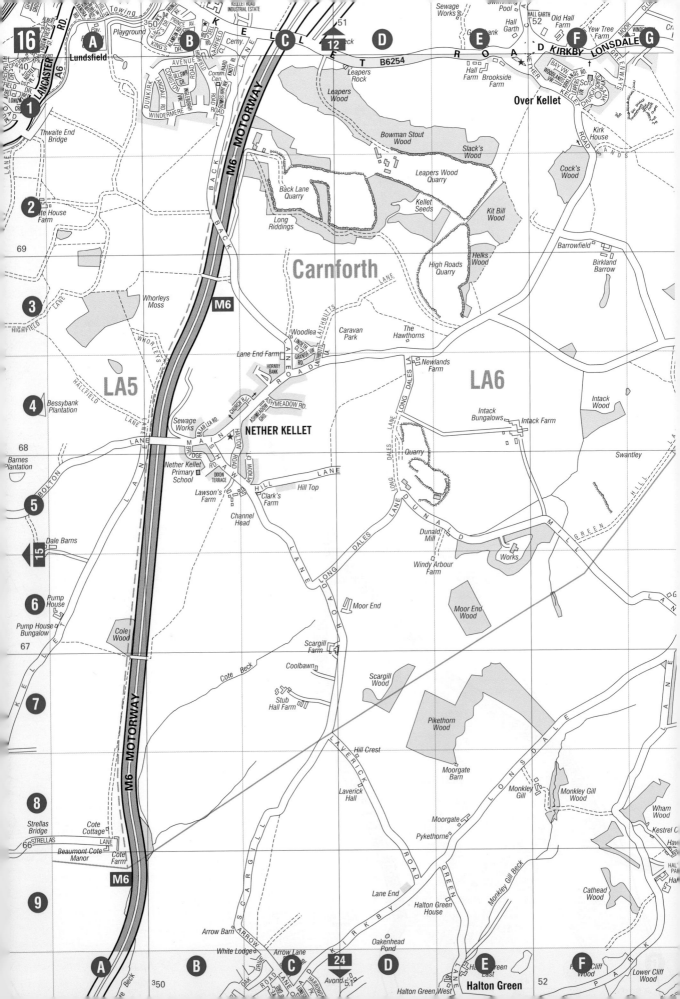

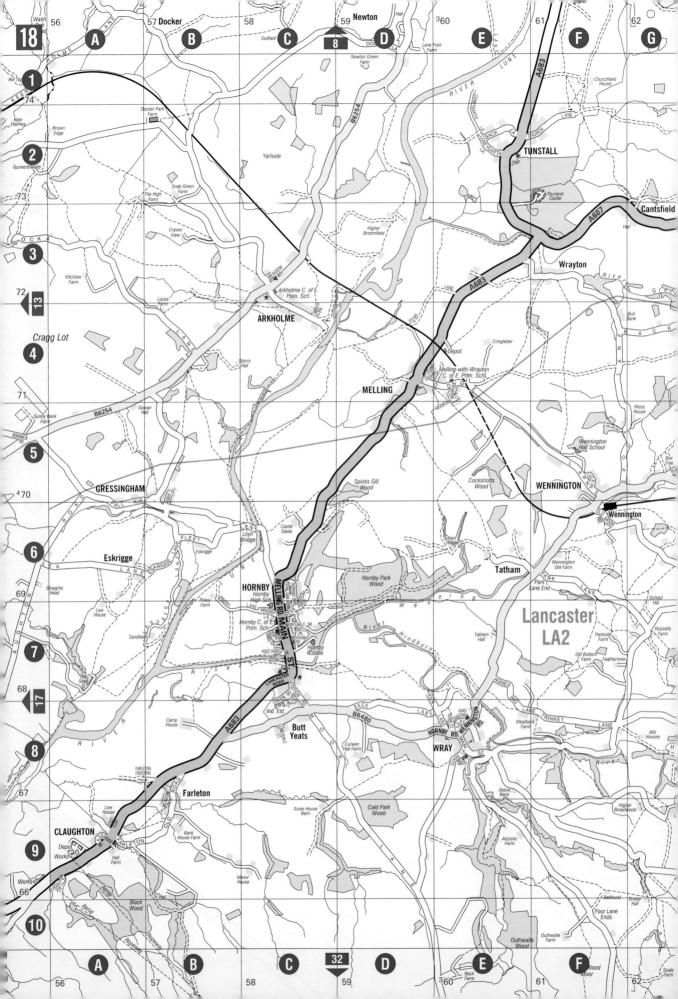

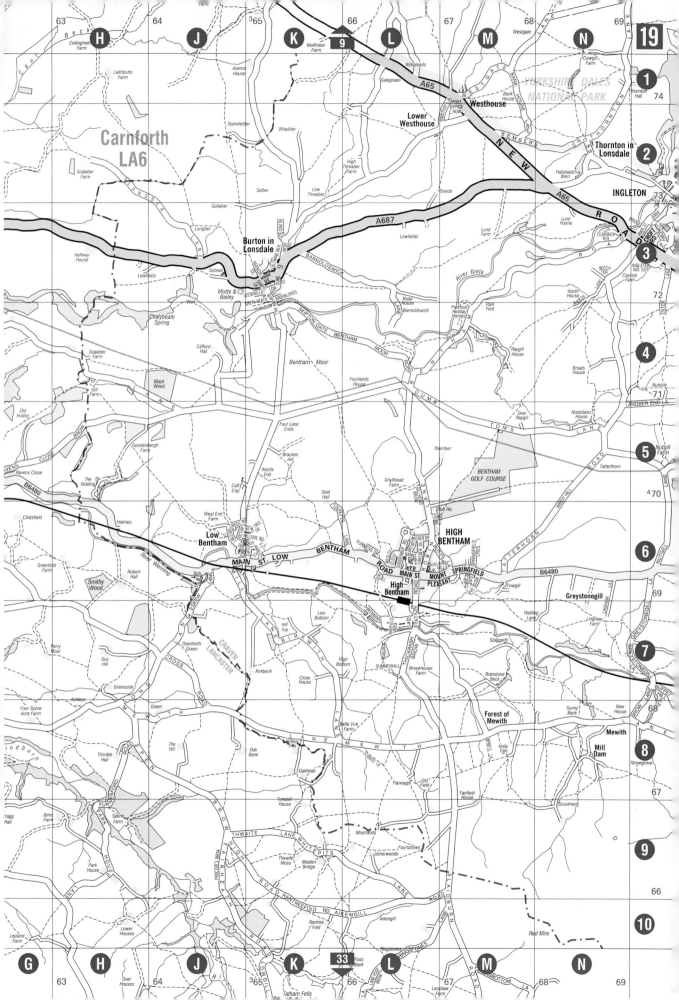

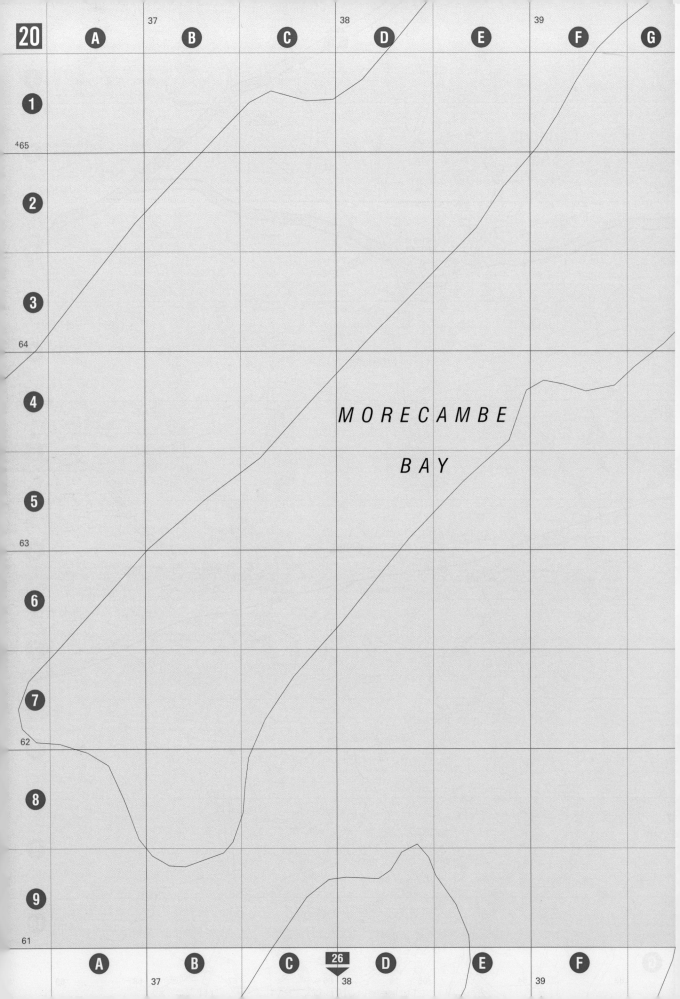

1

465

2

3

64

4

M O R E C A M B E

B A Y

5

63

6

7

62

8

9

61

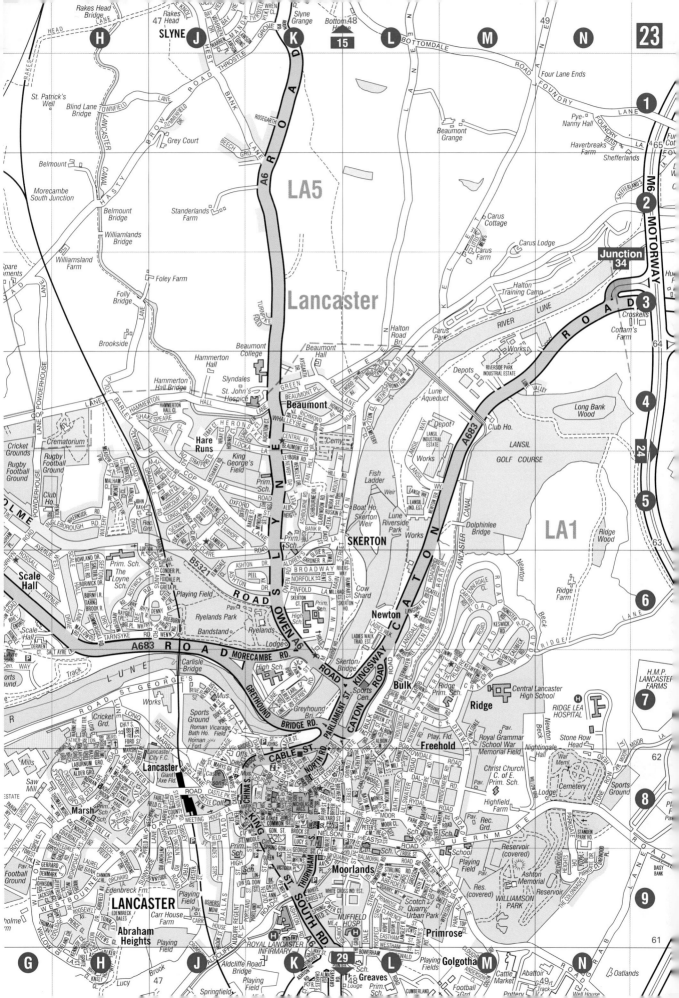

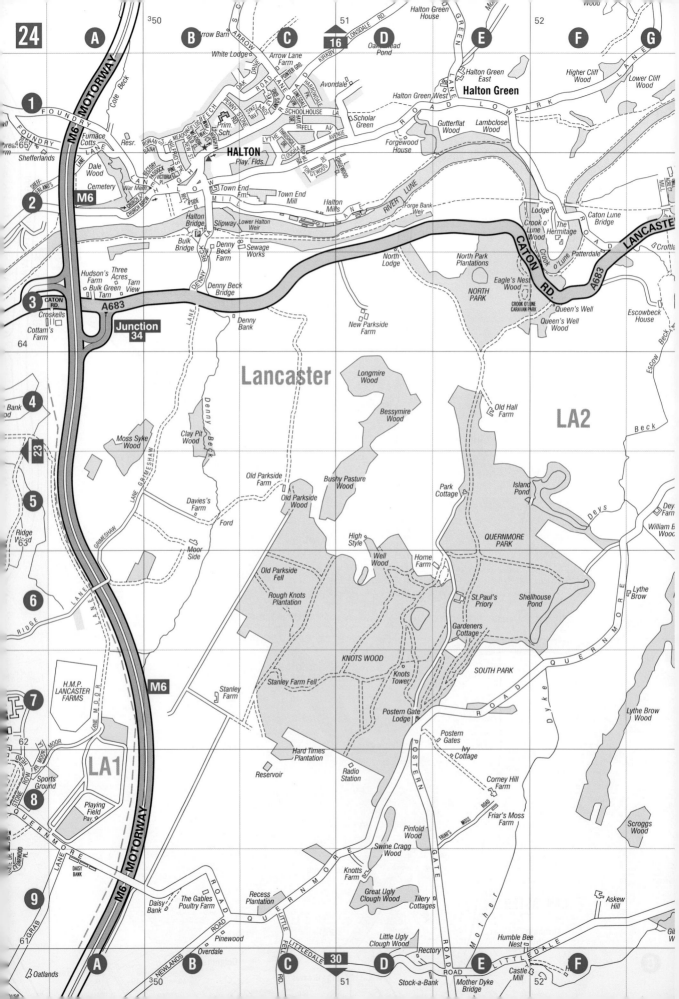

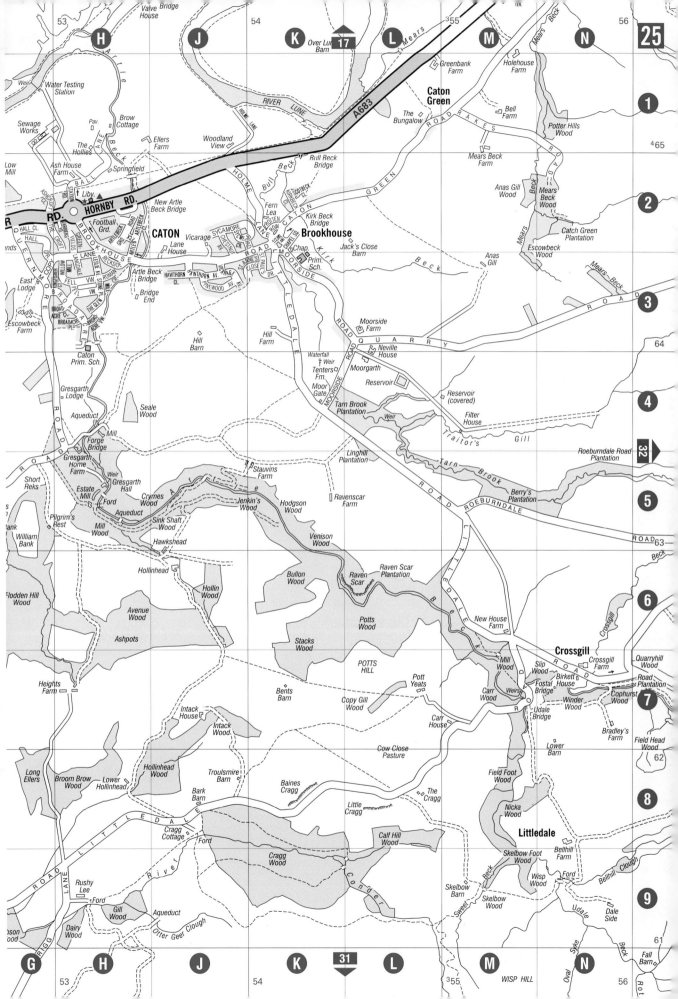

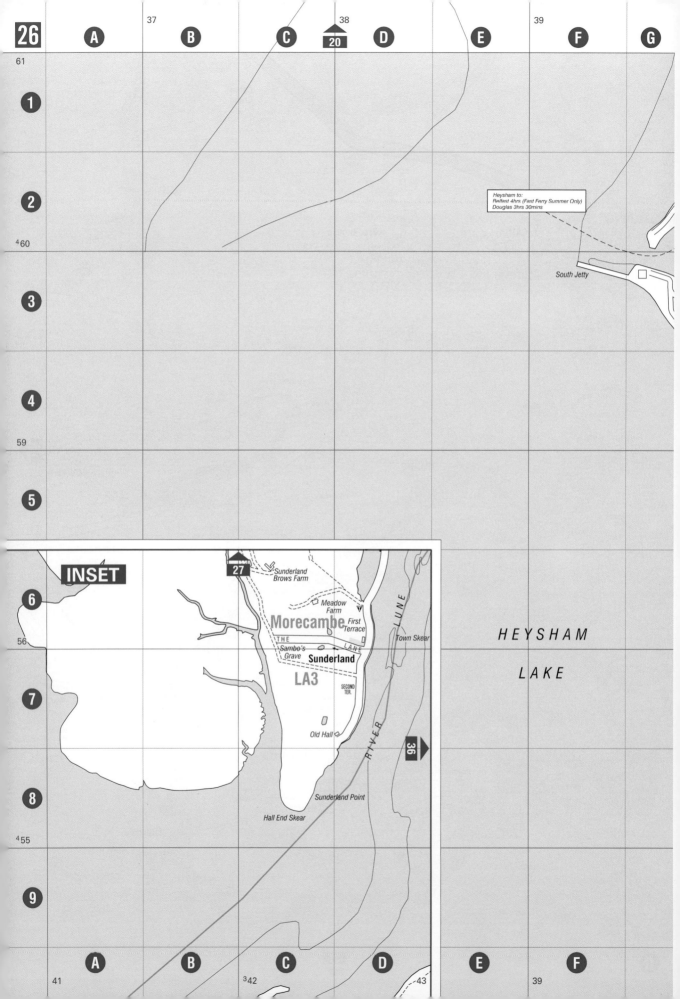

A　**B**　**C**　**D**　**E**　**F**　**G**

37　38　39

20

61

1

2

⁴60

Heysham to:
Belfast 4hrs (Fast Ferry Summer Only)
Douglas 3hrs 30mins

South Jetty

3

4

59

5

INSET

27

Sunderland
Brows Farm

6

Meadow
Farm

Morecambe First
Terrace

56

THE

Sambo's
Grave

Sunderland

LA3

SECOND
TER.

H E Y S H A M

L A K E

Town Skear

7

Old Hall

36

8

Sunderland Point

⁴55

Hall End Skear

9

A　**B**　**C**　**D**　**E**　**F**

41　³42　43　39

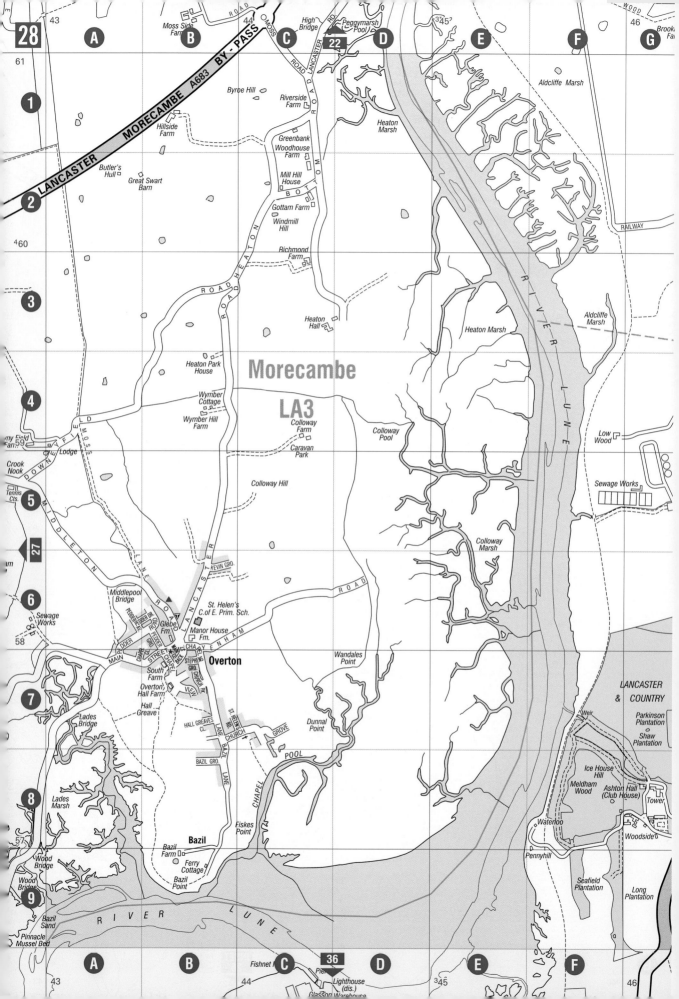

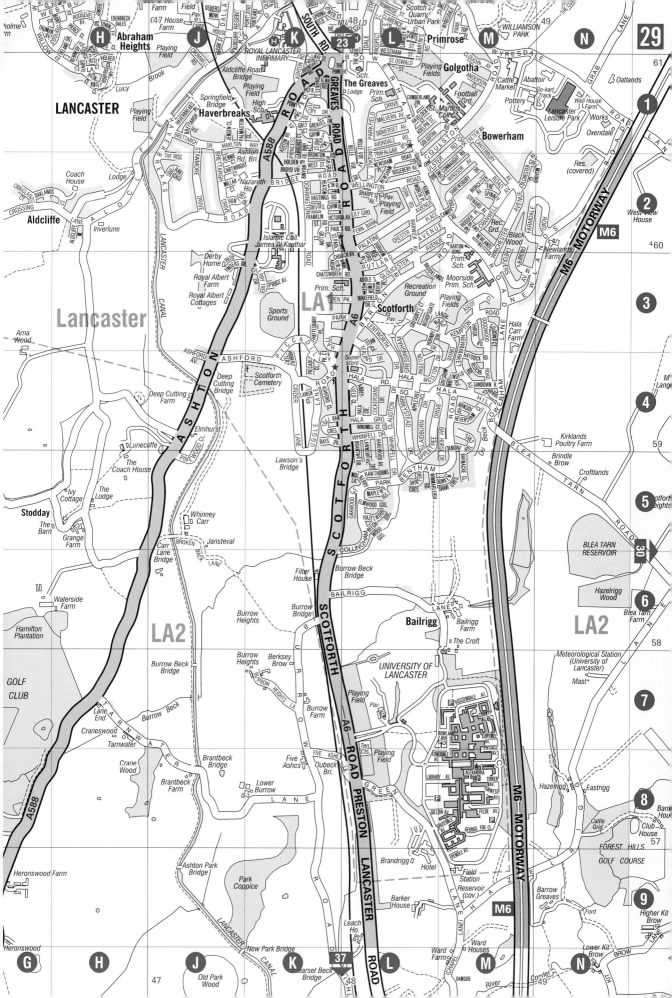

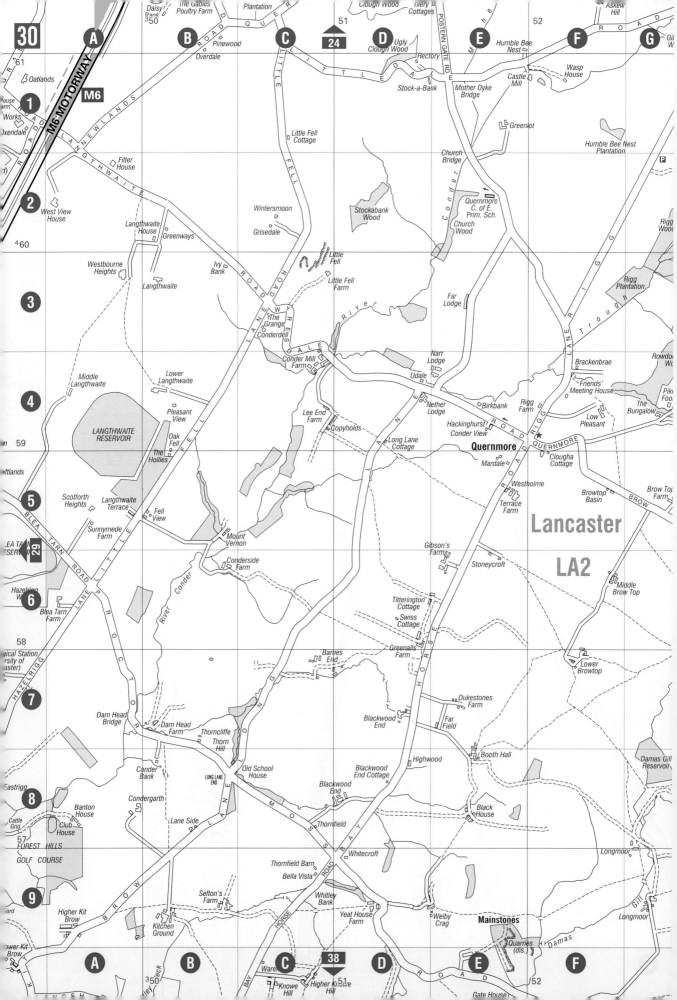

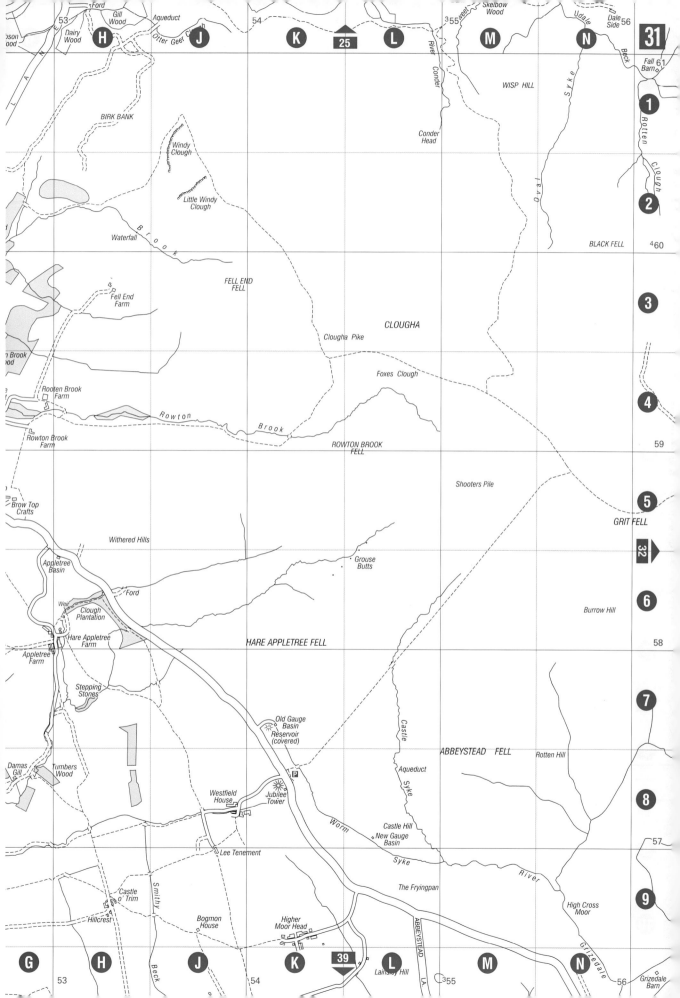

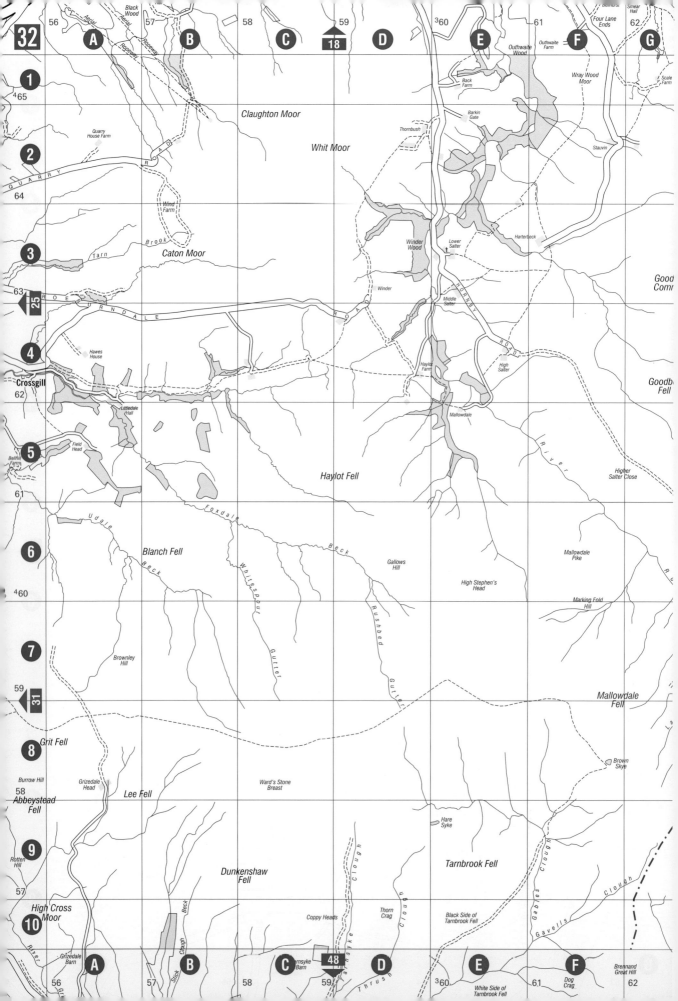

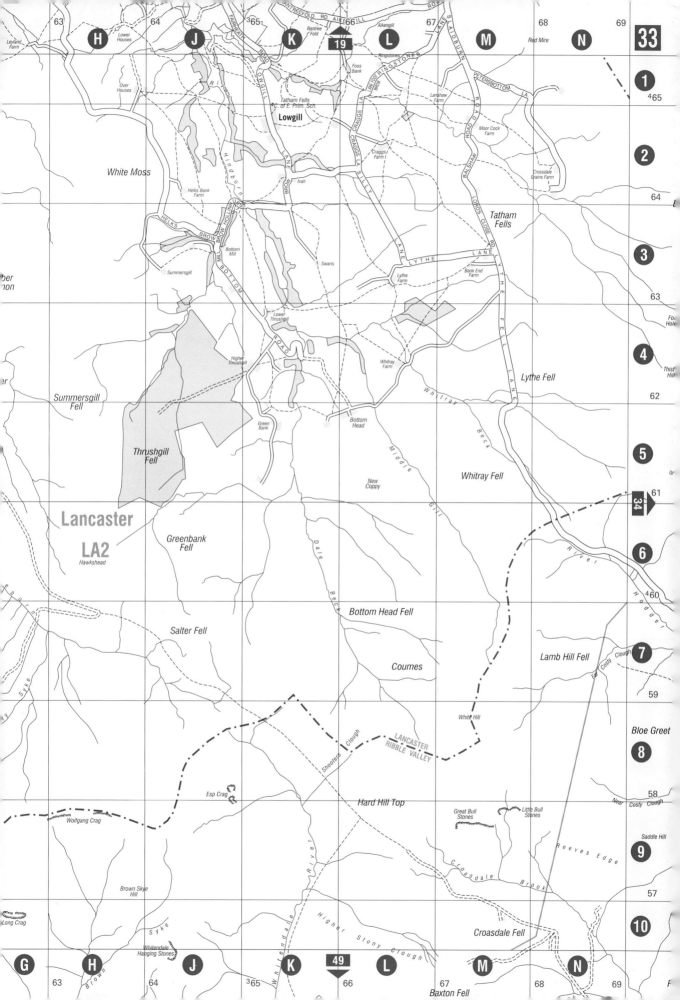

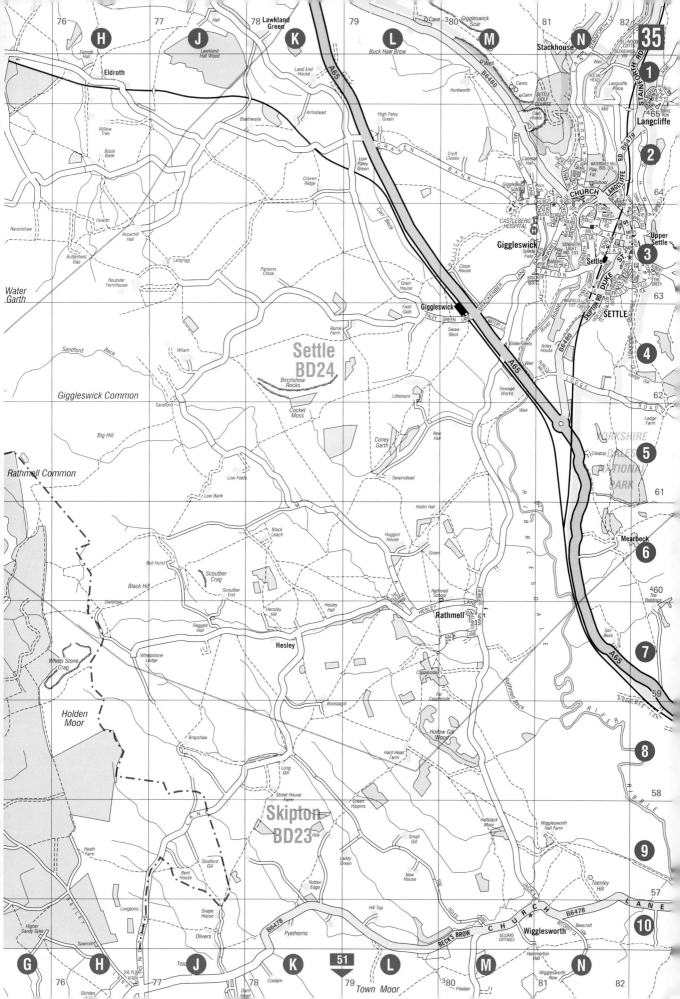

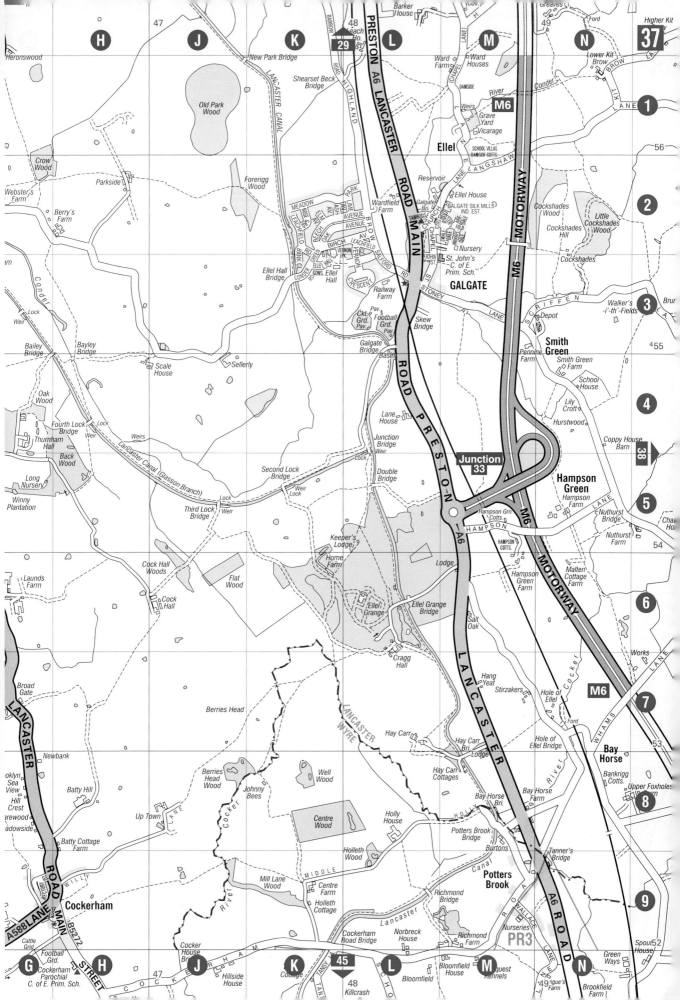

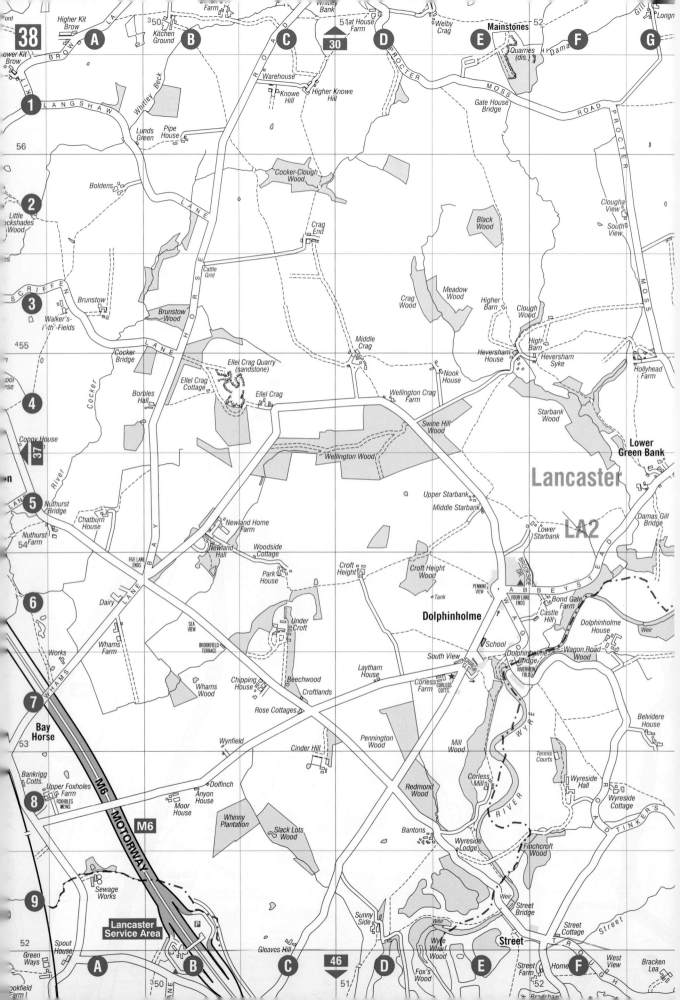

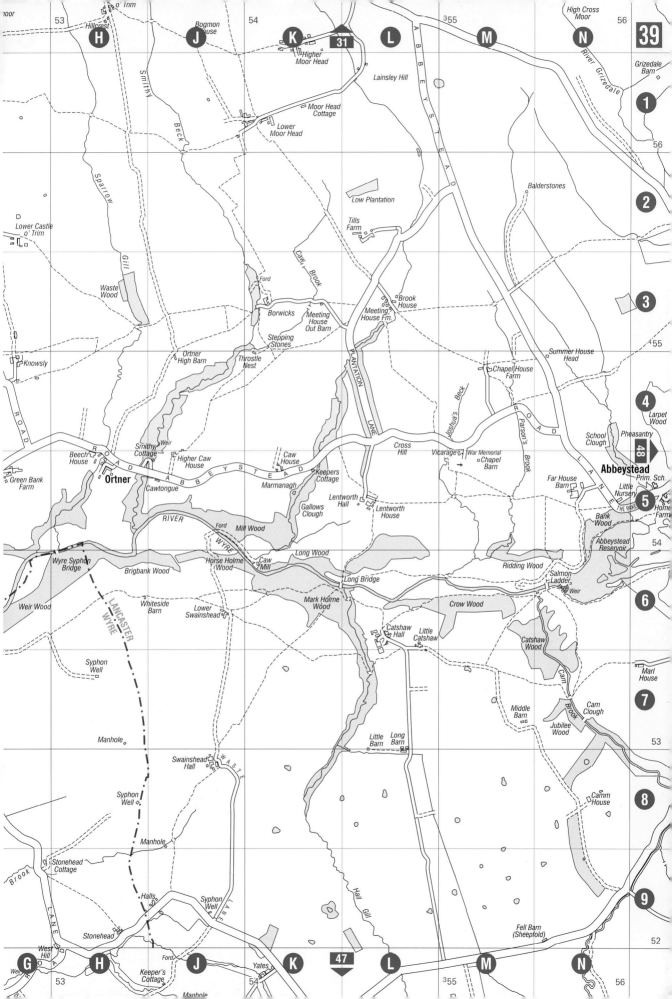

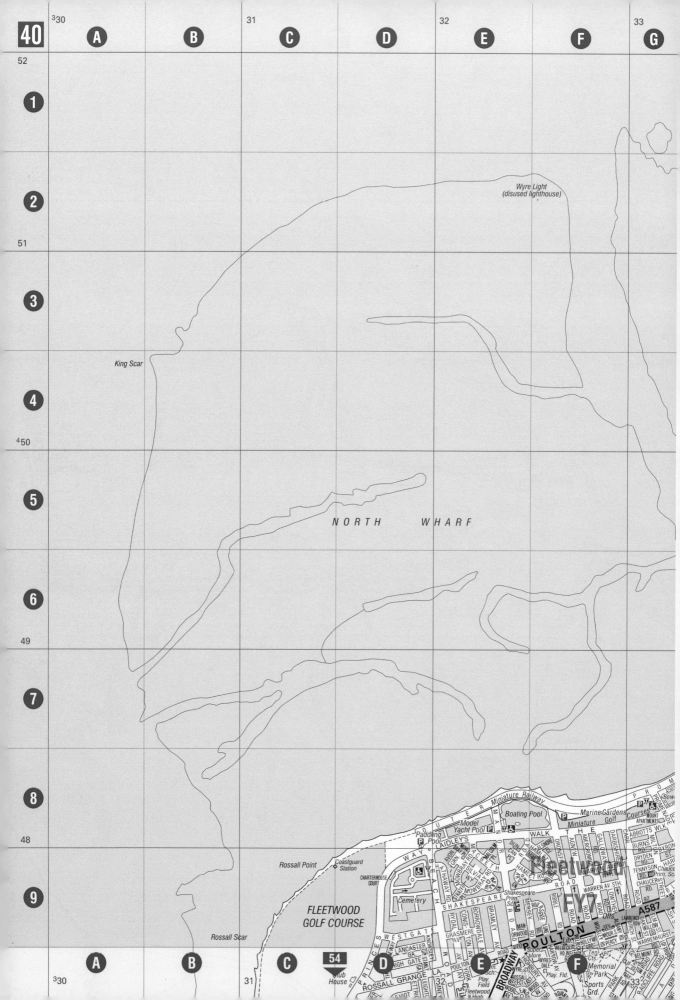

40

³30   A   B   31   C   ▽   D   32   E   F   33   G

52

1

2   Wyre Light
                                                                (disused lighthouse)

51

3

King Scar

4

⁴50

5   N O R T H   W H A R F

6

49

7

8   Miniature Railway
                                              Boating Pool   Marine Gardens
                                          Model   Miniature Golf
                                          Yacht Pool
                                     Paddling
                                     Pool
48

Rossall Point   Coastguard
                 Station

Cemetery

9   FLEETWOOD
            GOLF COURSE

Rossall Scar

A   B   31   C   **54**   D   E   F

³30   31   Club
                                            House

42

A　37　B　38　C　D　E　39　F　G

52

1

2

51

3

4

4 50

41

P R E E S A L L　S A N D S

Pilling Sands

Fluke Hall

Shillow Bridge

Seafield

Windy Ridge Cottages

New Ridge

Sandfield Cottage

Cocker's Dyke Houses

Ridge Farm

Pilling Ridge

Old Ridge

Sandside Farm

Marsh Side Farm

W h e e l　W a t e r

Carter's Charity Prim. Sch.

Thornton House Farm

BEACH ROAD

LANE

GREEN

Cocker's Dyke

Beech House

Seaspray Nurseries

Bond's Farm

DUCK ST.

Springfield Cottages

Bibbys Farm

Jacksons Farm

Middle Dyke

Proctors Farm

Carr House Farm

Chestnut House Farm

Nursery

Springfield House

PILLING LANE

Aberdeen Cottage

Muffy's Platt

Bimson's Cottage

Wheel Foot Watercourse

TONGUES

LANE

EIGHT ACRE LANE

Chapel House

Townson Hill

7

ROSSLYN

Muffy's Platt Farm

Parker's Close

WHEEL LANE

Works

Smithson's Farm

Hooles Farm

Smallwood Hey

ROSSLYN AVENUE

ROSSLYN CR. EAST

Tongues Farm

DICKS

SMALLWO

LA.

SMALLWOOD

8

Willows Farm

Little Tongues Lane

Bibby's Farm

Holme's Farm

Pasture House Farm

Wyresdale

Brookfield Farm

Smallwood Holme Hey Fm.

Poulton-le-Fylde

FY6

Camping Site

Sandy Lane Farm

SANDICROFT PL.

Winmore Fold

BOURBLES

Bourbles Farm

Greenlands

NED'S

LANE

Grange Cottages

HOOLES LANE

Shaw Fm.

SANDY LANE

SANDY LANE

Hampson av.

Jubilee

Forestone

Evimwoo

The Shaws

Hillside

B5270

LITTLE TONGUES LANE

Nickson's La.

Greenlands

LAMB'S LANE

Shaw Cottage

9

PREESALL

Nickson's Farm

Crossing Cottage

Adkinson's Wood

The Crossing Cottage

Ford Stones Bridge

PARK 5377 LANE

GAULTER'S

LANE

New England Cottage

56

SHAWS

Baldwin's Wood

Bowling Green

Old Vicarage Farm

A

SHADE ROW

Gaulter's Farm

B

Lane Ends Farm

C

D

38

Lyndale

E

39

F

Bennet's

Preesall Hill

37

LANC

ROA

Pointer

Throstle's

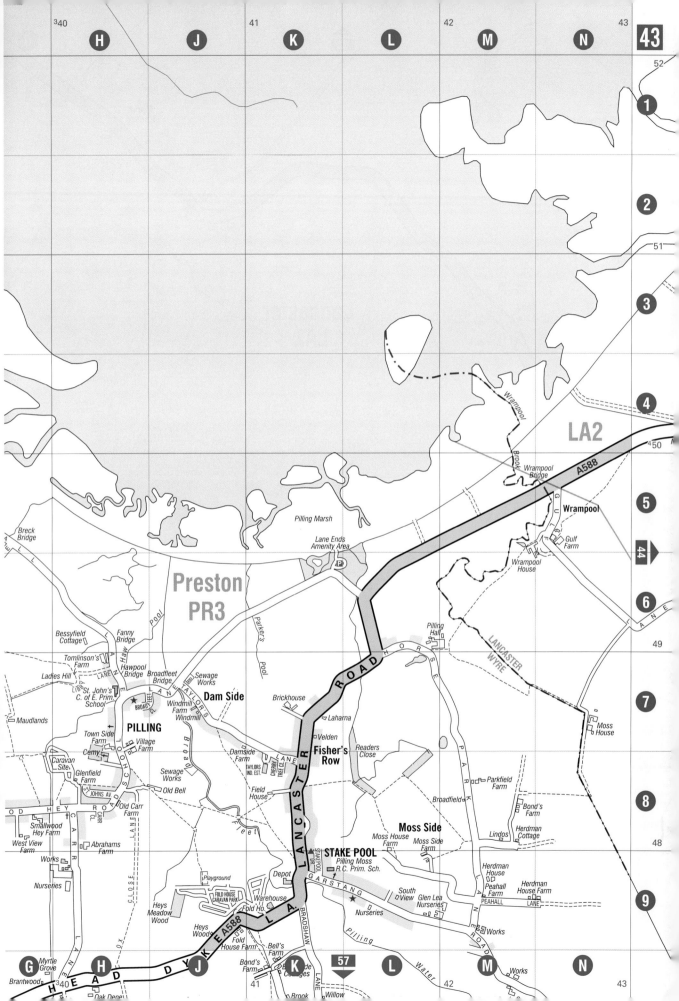

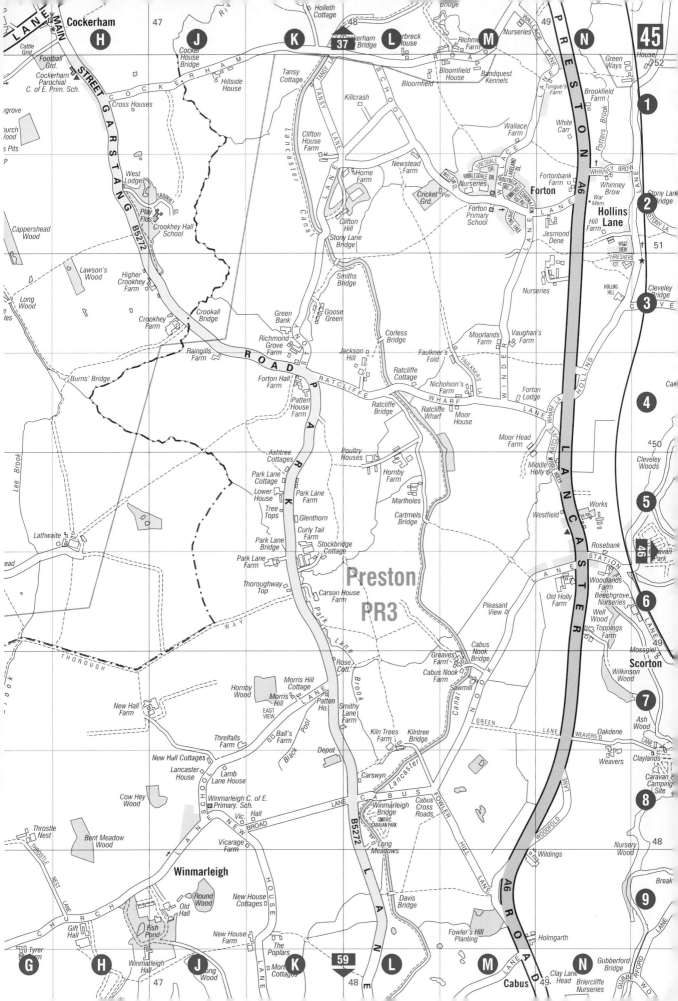

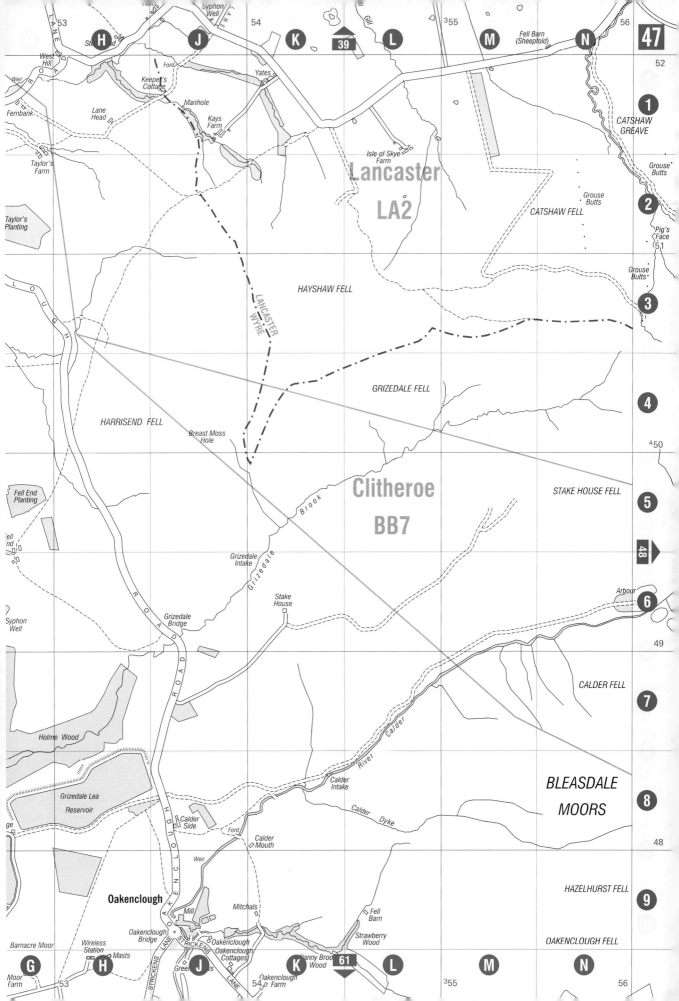

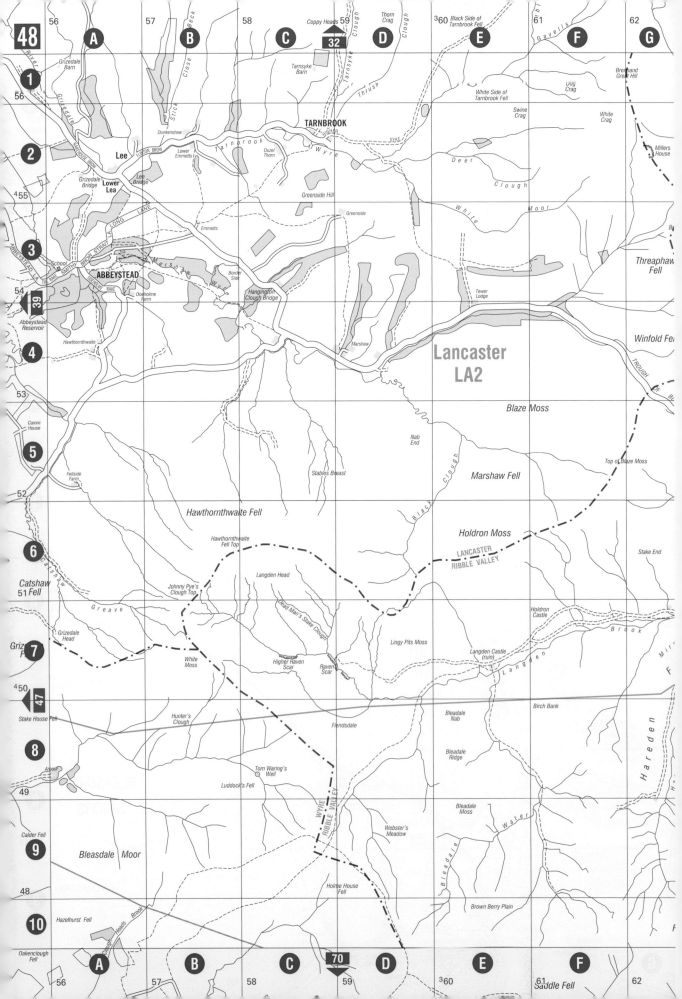

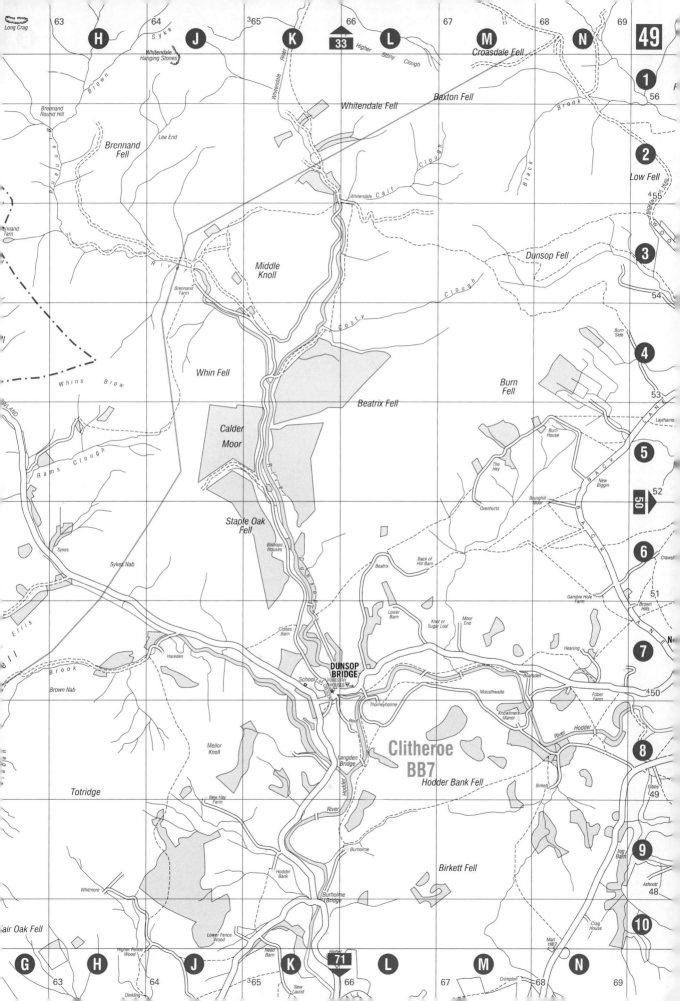

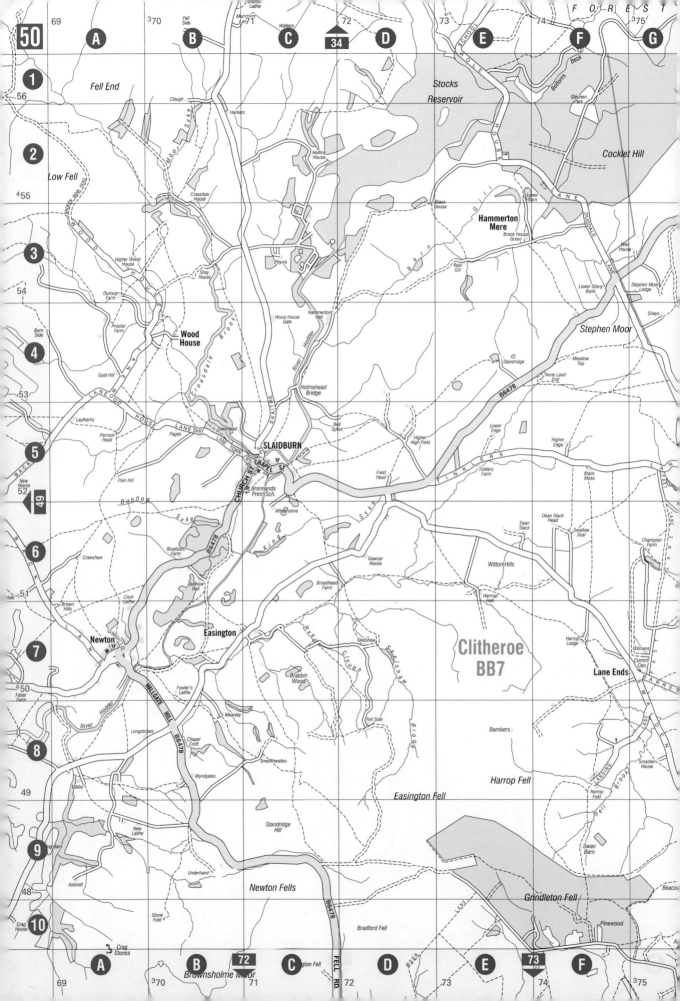

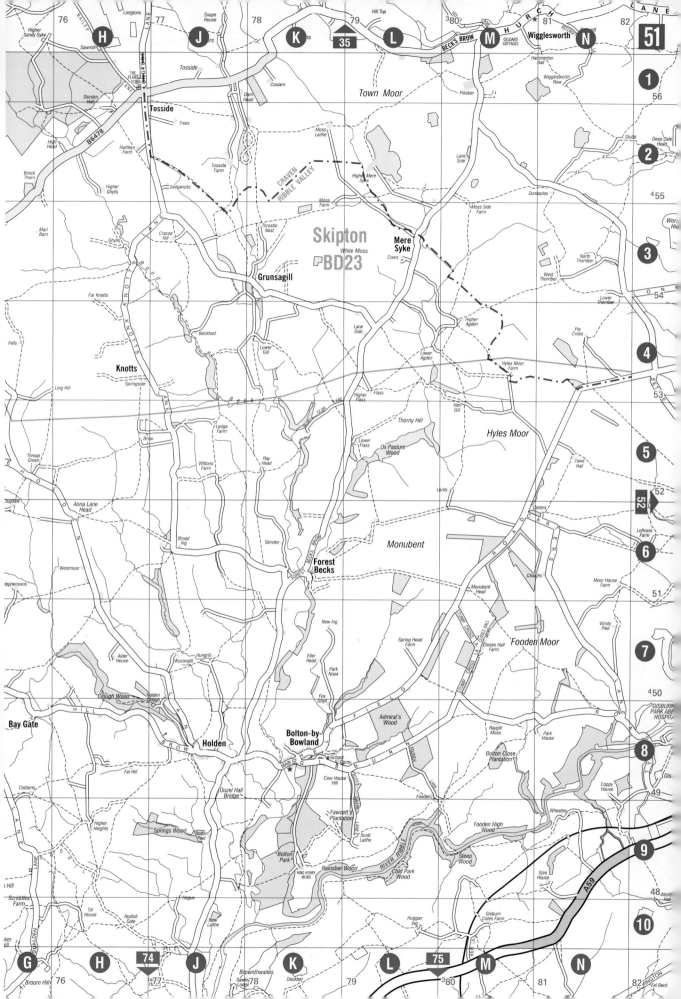

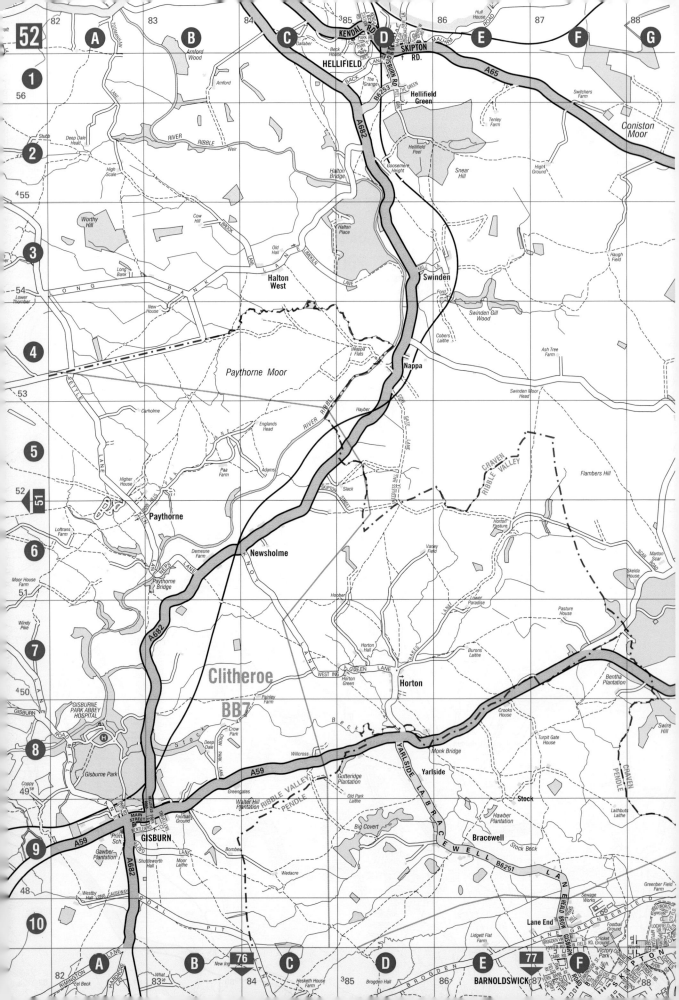

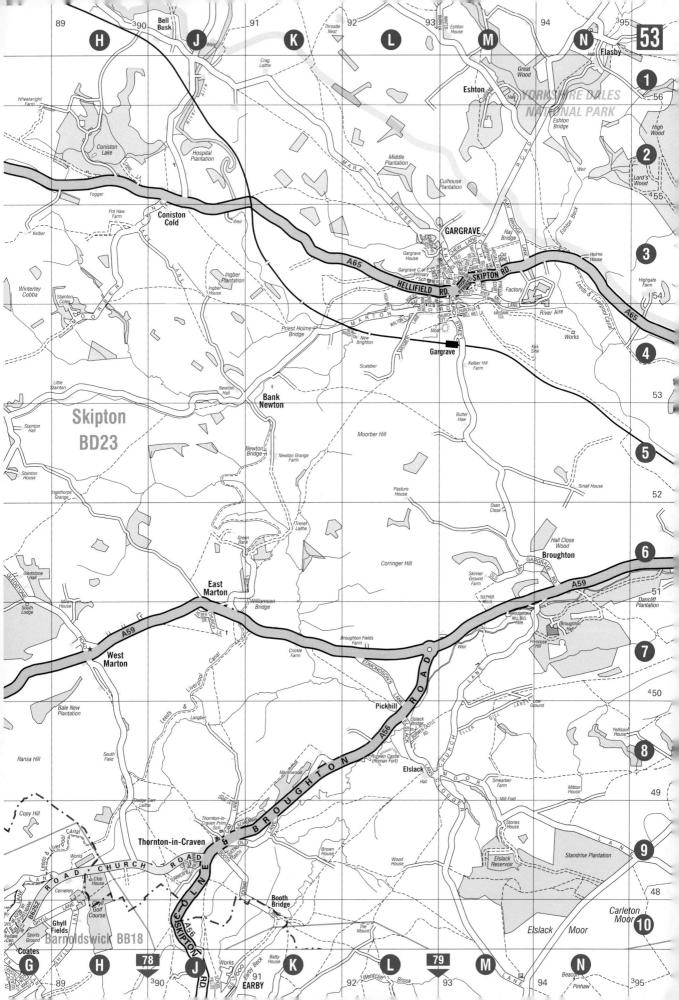

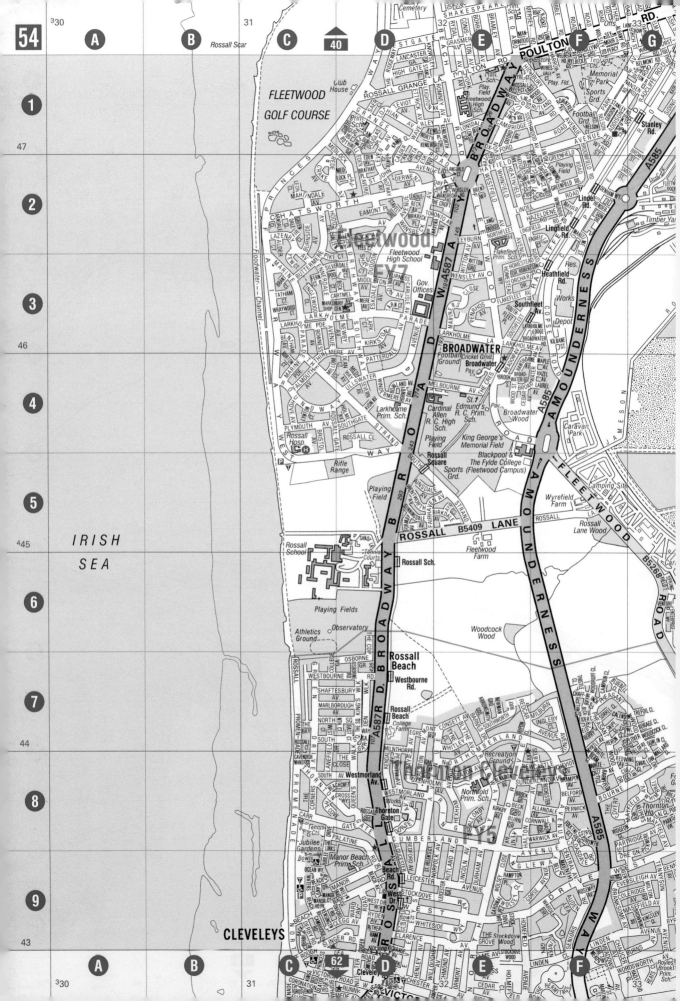

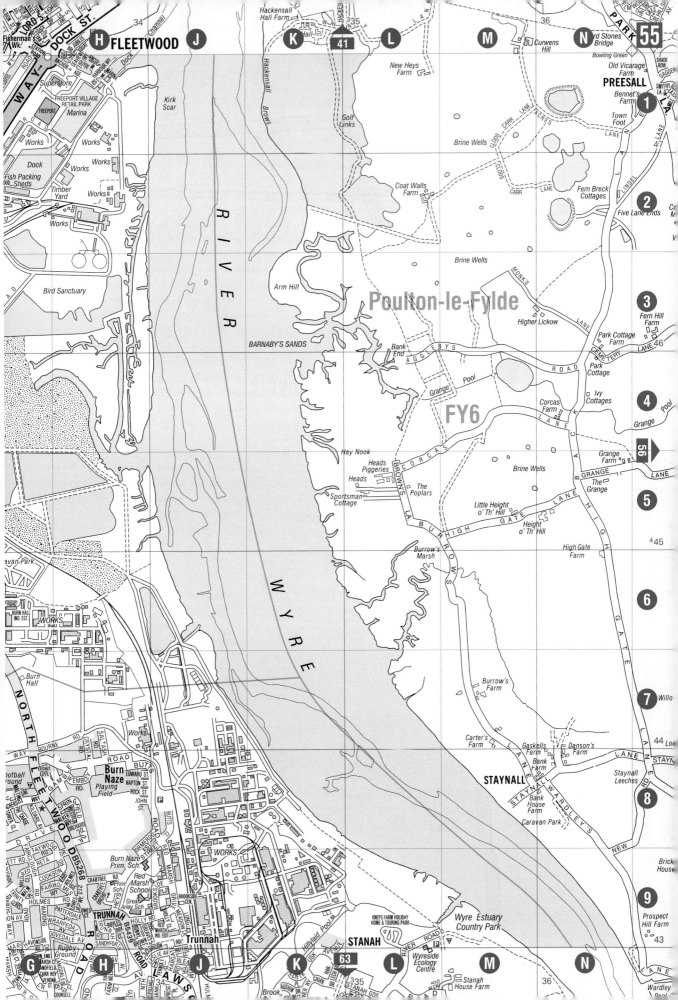

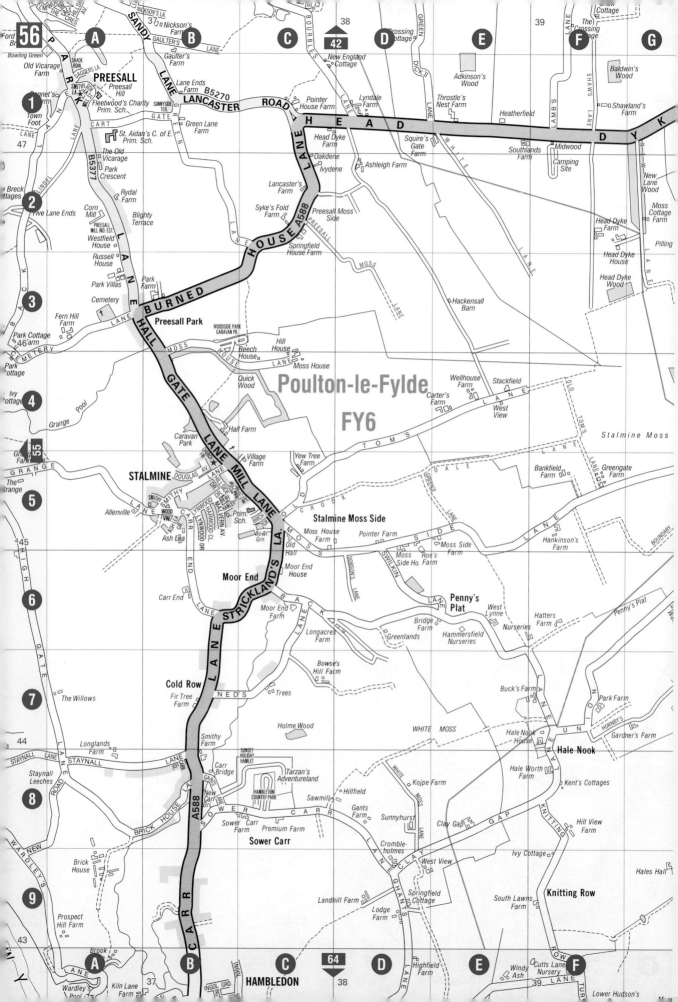

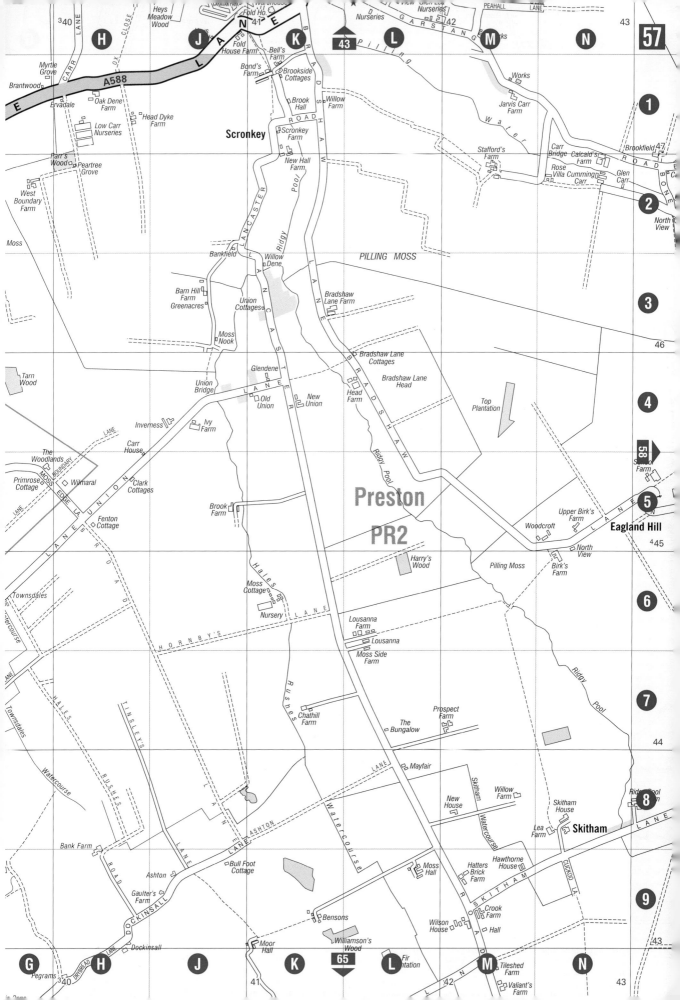

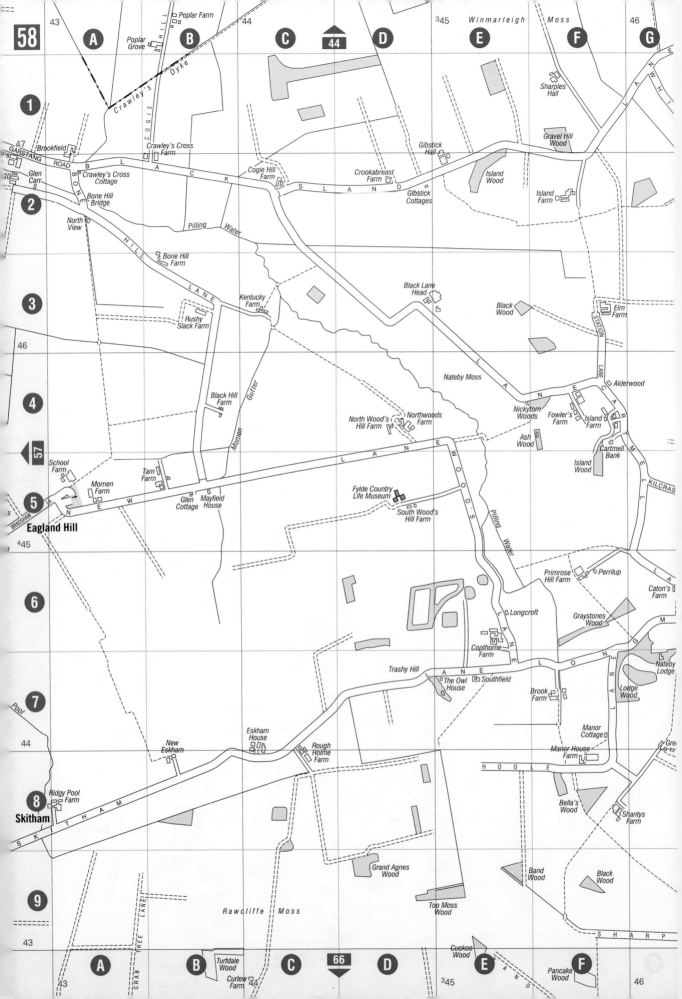

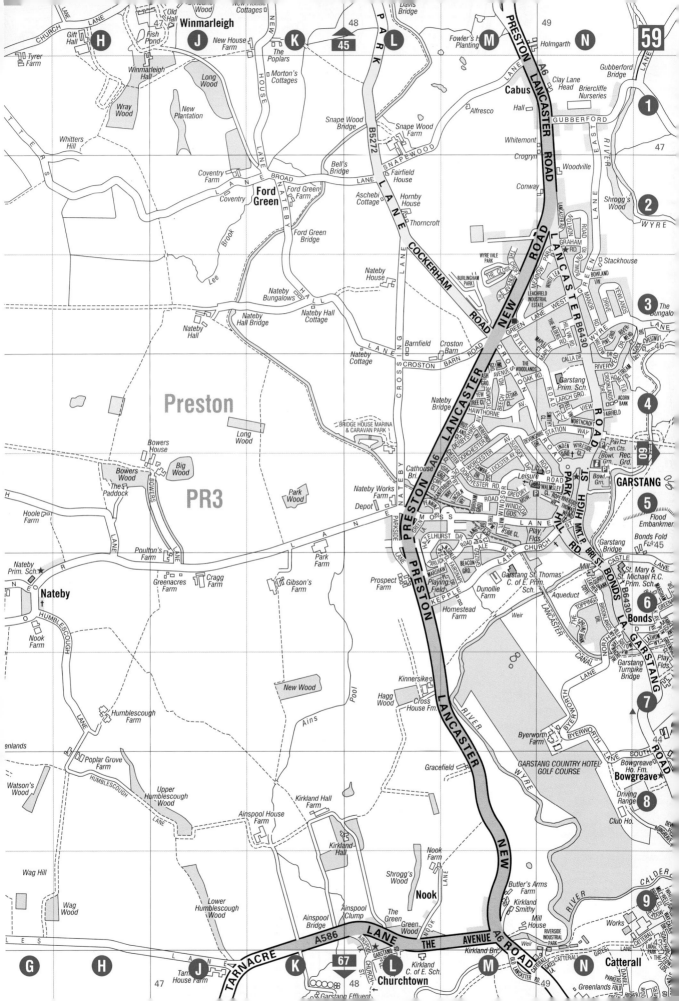

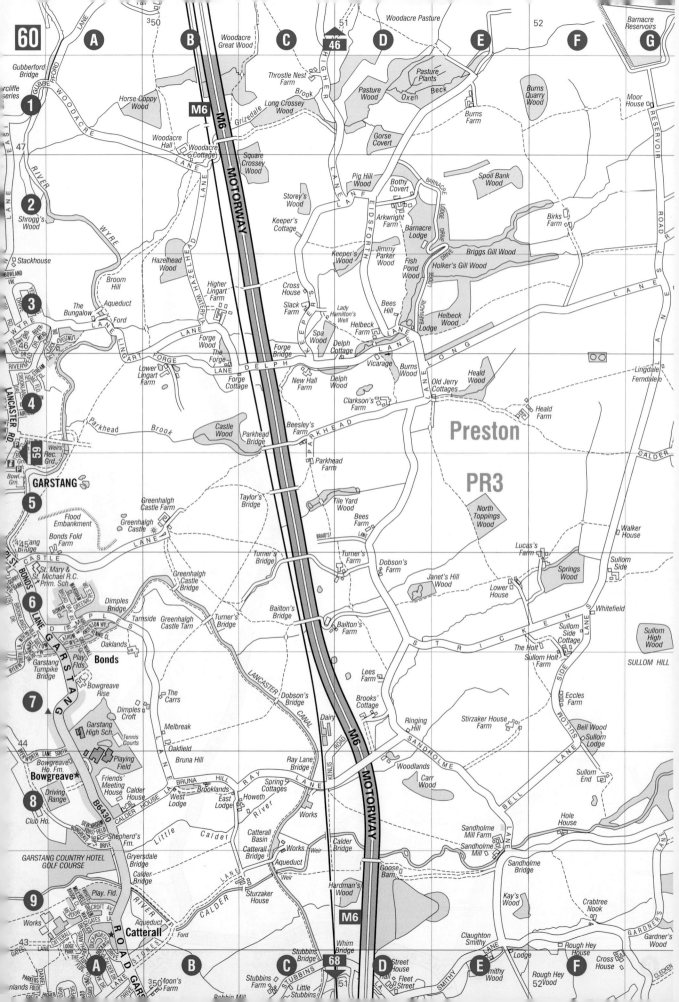

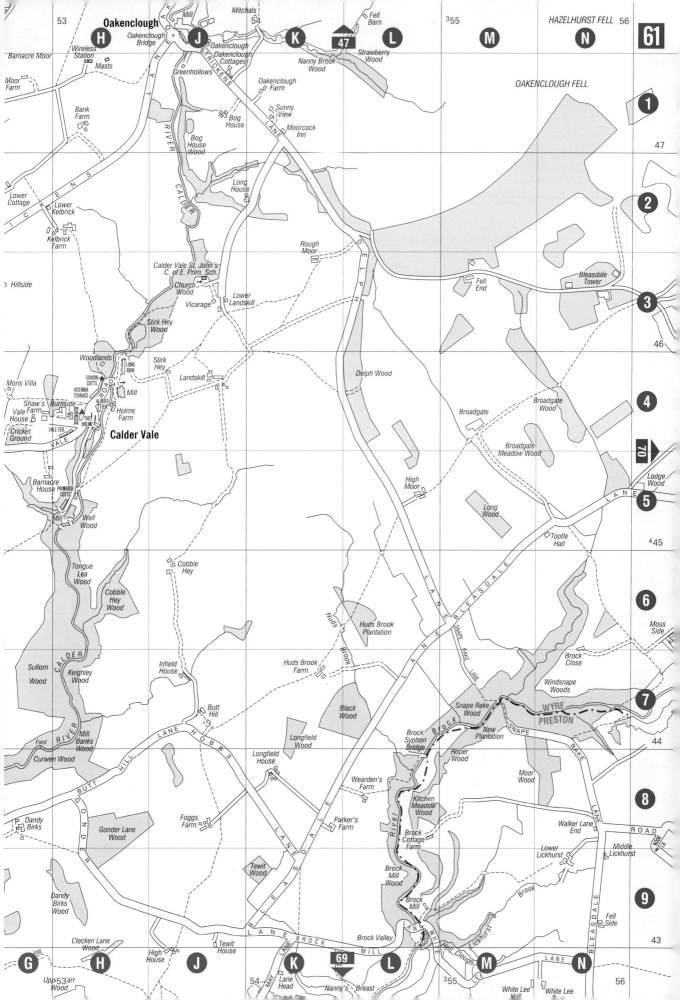

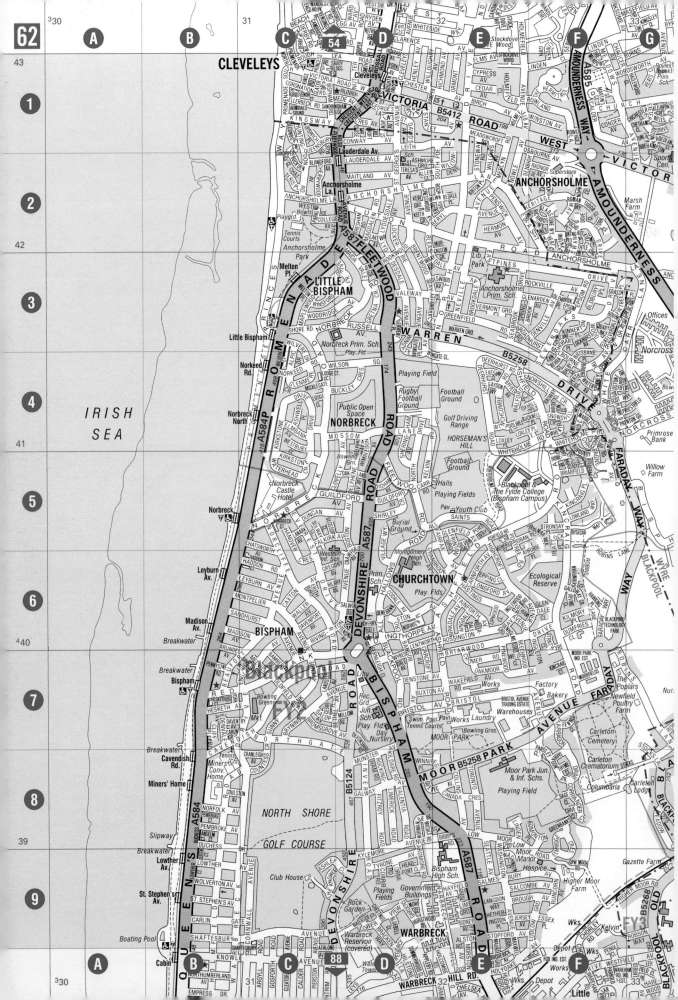

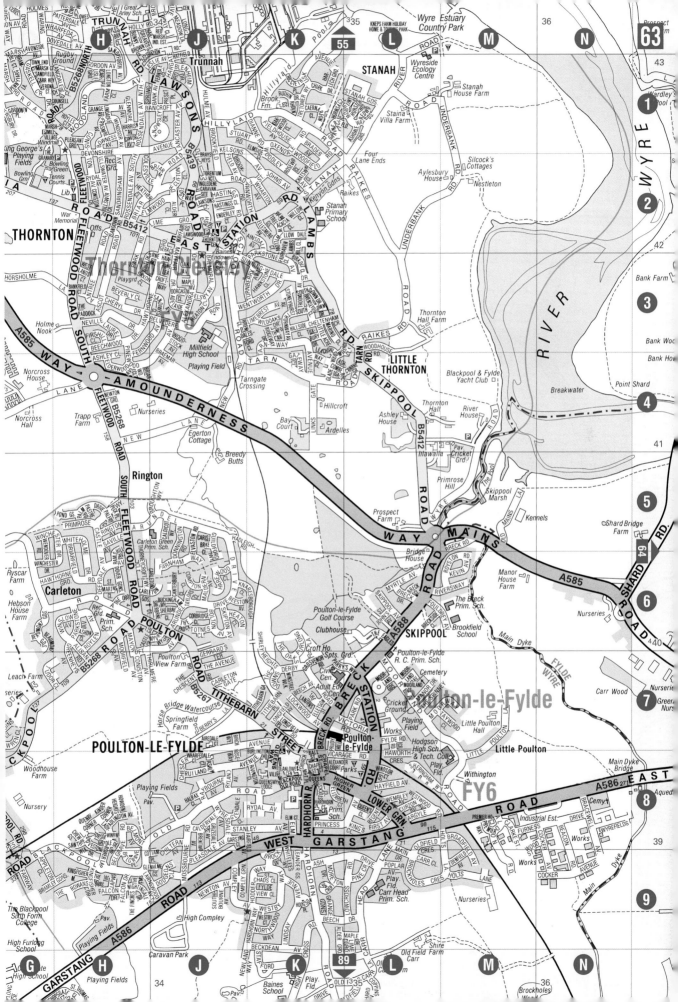

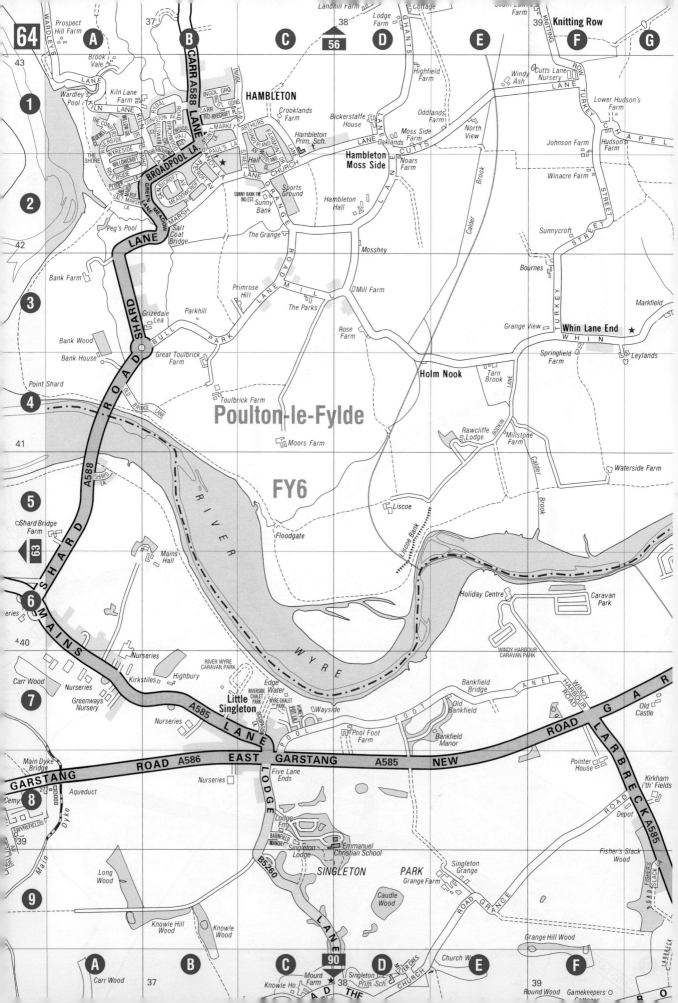

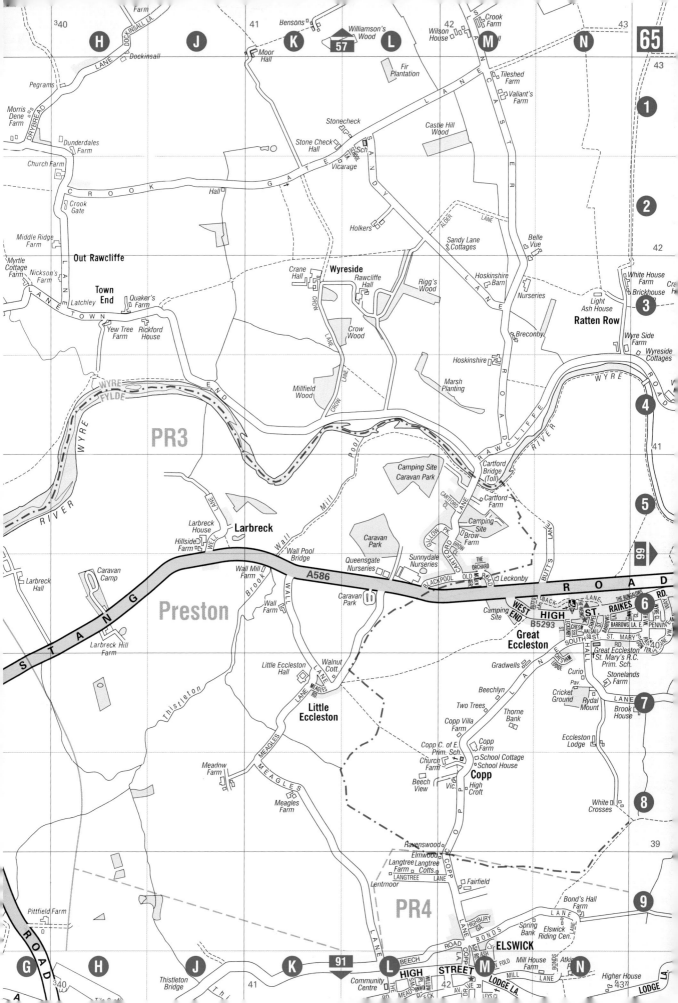

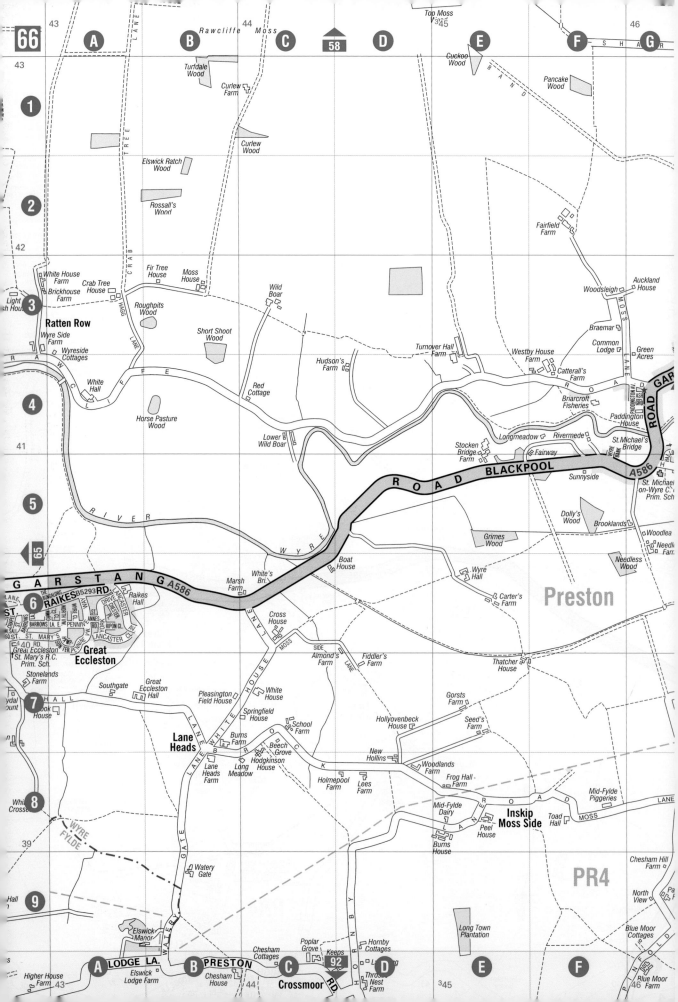

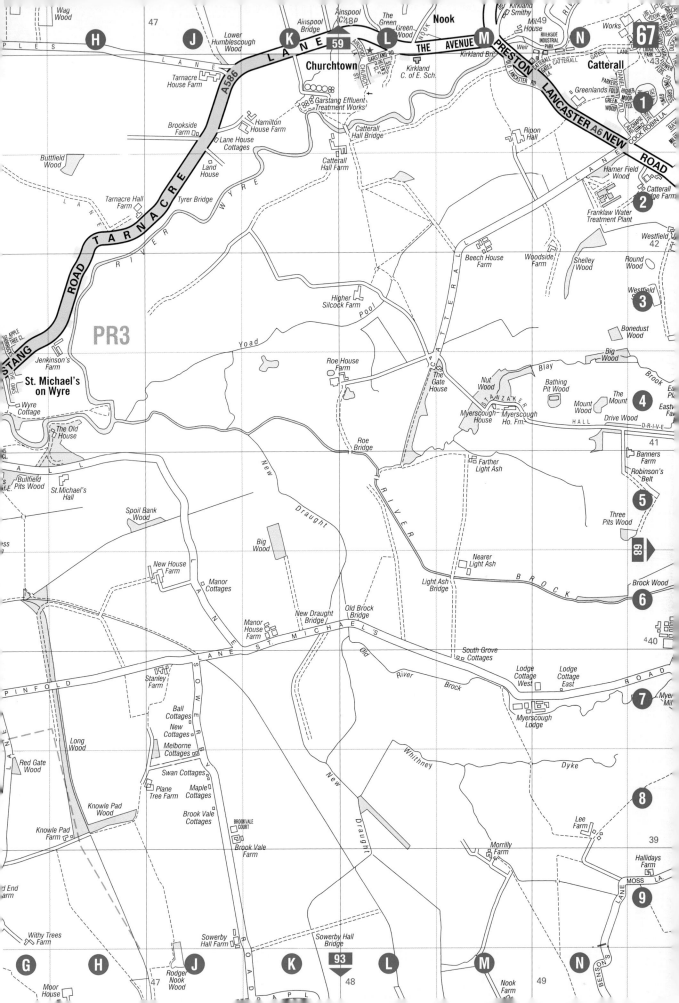

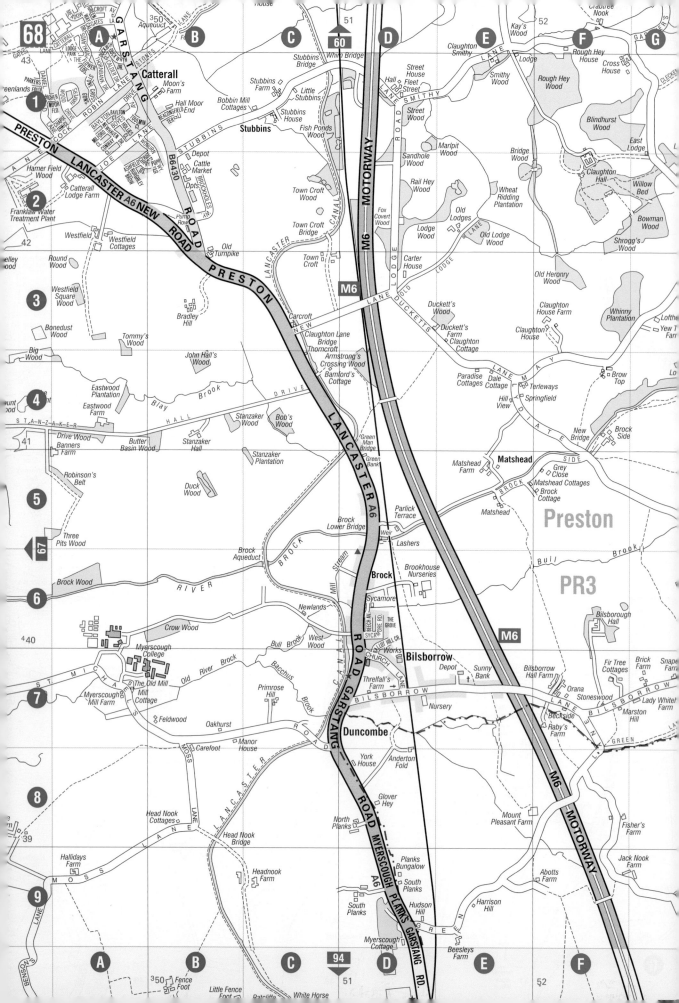

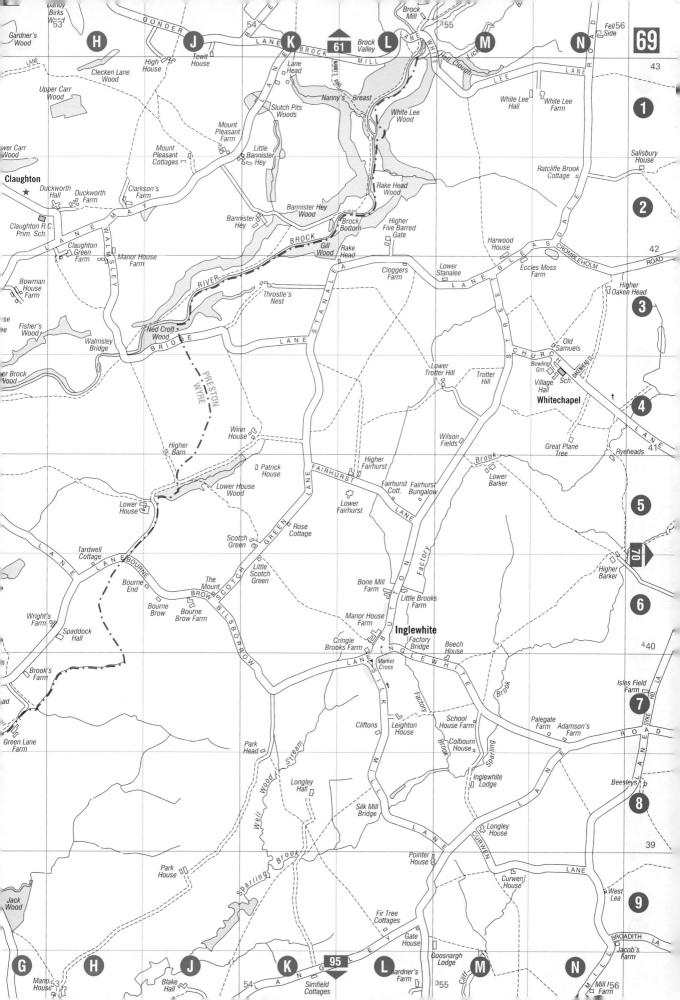

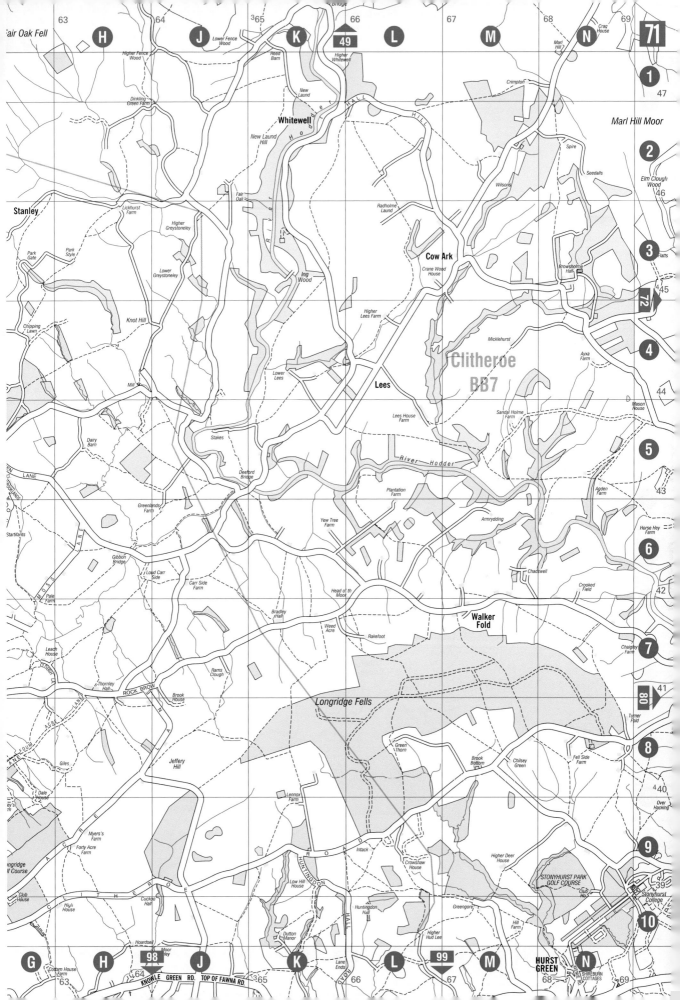

72

A · B · C · D · E · F · G

Crag Stones

Browsholme Tarn

Stony Hill

50

White Stone Cliff

Tittrington Clough

1

69

370

71

72

WADDINGTON FELL

BROWSHOLME MOOR

Cabin Hill

Tittrington Brow

47

FELL

B6478

Waddington Brook

2

MARL HILL MOOR

Cob Castle

Pye Copy

Moorcock House

Holt Well

Hare Clough Barn

Dribble Wood

Robin Barn

Jolly Croft

3

Elm Clough Wood

Hare Clough

Bashall Brook

Summit House

New-o-Nook

Ringley Hey

Rese (covere

46

Marls Clough

Hodgson Moor

BROWSHOLME

ROAD

Mitchells

Clitheroe

BB7

4

Flatts

Hare Clough

Birch Hill

Daisy Hill

Rushy Well

71

Braddup Clough

Braddup Moss Wood

Buckstall

WHINNY LANE

FREEHOLDS

Leemings

5

Braddup Wood

Burbles Hill

LANE FREEHOLDS

Thornbers

445

Blackhill Wood

T Plantation

Bashall Moor Wood

Reservoir (covered)

6

RABBIT

LANE

Moor Piece

Braddup Wood

Braddup Farm

Reservoir

Colthurst Bungalows

Hollins Clough

Talbot Bridge

Braddup House

Peter Barn

Colthurst Hall

Gannies Farm

Hollins Wood

Hollin

7

Kitchens

Talbot Bri.

CROSS LANE

Sandy Ford Brook

WHINNY

CROSS

New Page Fold

King Henry Grov

44

Bashall Brook

COW HEY Brook

Ridge Page Fold

Lower New House

8

Mason House

Clough Bottom

Page Fold

Sandy Ford

9

Bashall Eaves ★

The Bungalow

Saddle Bridge

Rugglesmire

Ford

Cow Hey

Backridge Plantation

Twitter Bridge Farm

Wetters Bridge

43

69

370

80

71

Bashall Brook

72

A · B · C · D · E · F · G

Horse Hey Farm

Backridge Farm

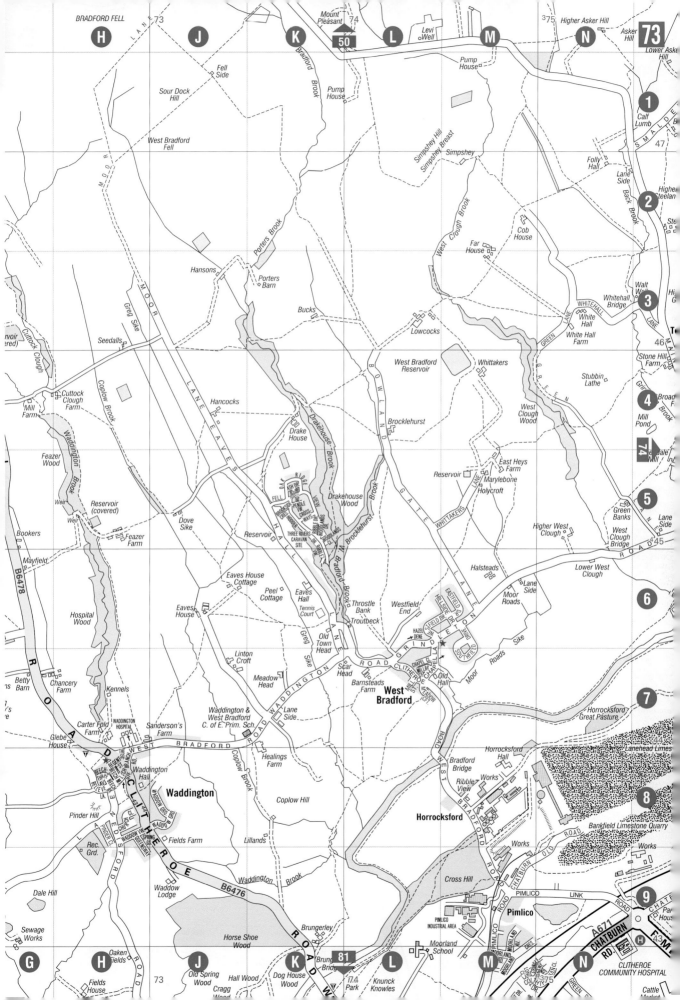

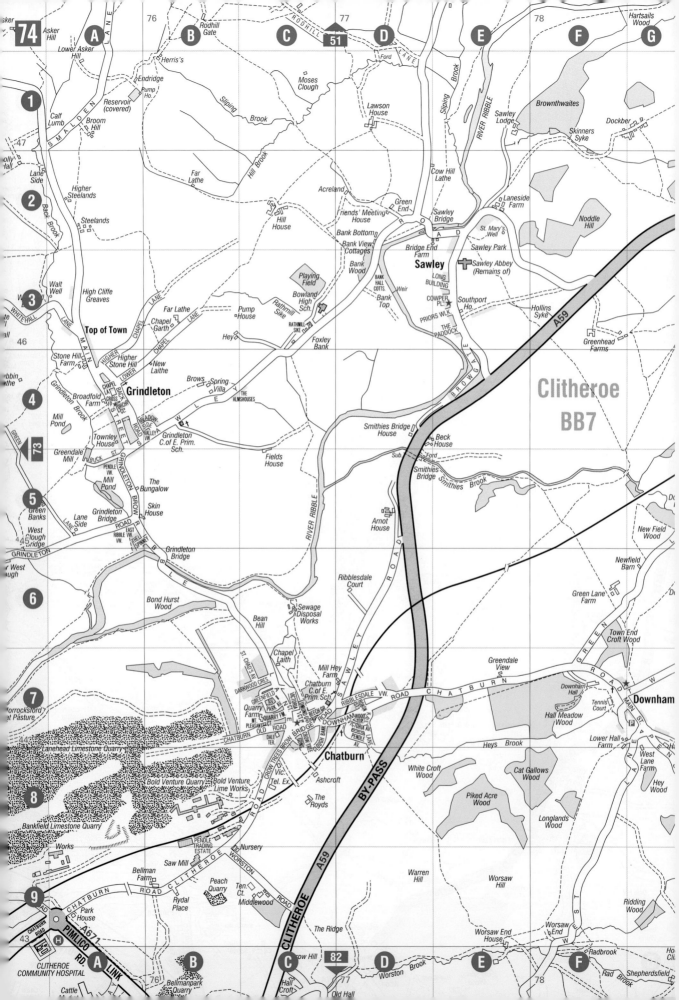

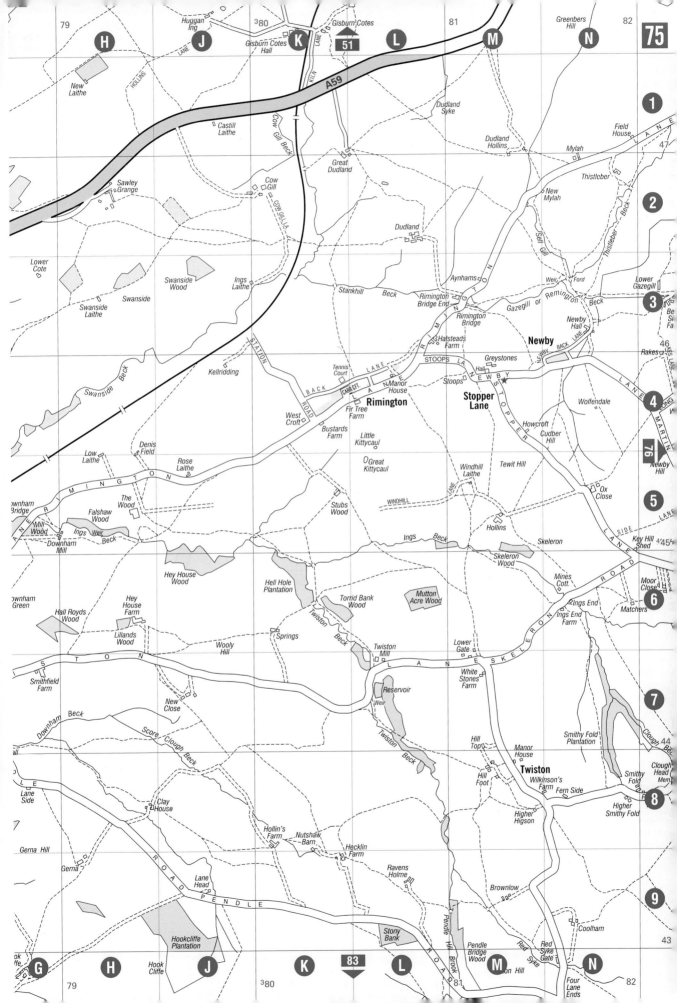

H J K 51 L M N

79 380 81 82

Greenbers Hill
Huggan Ing
Gisburn Cotes
Gisburn Cotes Hall
New Laithe
HOLLINS LANE
KILN LANE
A59
Castill Laithe
Cow Gill Beck
Dudland Syke
Field House
LANE
47
Dudland Hollins
Mylah
Thistleber
New Mylah
Sawley Grange
Cow Gill
COW GILLA
Self Gill
Lower Gazegill
Lower Cote
Swanside Wood
Ings Laithe
Stankhill Beck
Dudland
Weir Ford
Be Si Fa
Swanside Laithe
Swanside
Aynhams
Gazegill or Remington Beck
Rakes
46
STATION
Rimington Bridge End
Rimington Bridge
Newby Hall
KES LANE
Kellridding
Swanside Beck
BACK
Rimington Bridge
Halsteads Farm
Newby
Greystones
LONG MARTIN LANE
45
Tennis Court
CARR CFT
Manor House
STOOPS LANE
Hall
Stoops
NEWBY BACK LANE
76
Rimington
Fir Tree Farm
West Croft
Bustards Farm
Little Kittycaul
Stopper Lane
Wolfendale
Newby Hill
Denis Field
Low Laithe
Rose Laithe
Great Kittycaul
Howcroft
Cudber Hill
Tewit Hill
Ox Close
Downham Bridge
RIMINGTON
The Wood
Falshaw Wood
Windhill Laithe
LANE
5
Mill Wood
Ings Weir
Downham Mill
Beck
Stubs Wood
WINDHILL
Hollins
Skeleron
Key Hill Shed
445
Hey House Wood
Ings Beck
Skeleron Wood
Mines Cott.
SKELERON ROAD
Moor Close
6
Downham Green
Hey House Farm
Hall Royds Wood
Lillands Wood
Hell Hole Plantation
Torrid Bank Wood
Mutton Acre Wood
Ings End
Ings End Farm
Matchers
Wooly Hill
Springs
Twiston Beck
Twiston Mill
Lower Gate
White Stones Farm
7
Smithfield Farm
LANE
STON
New Close
Reservoir
Weir
Smithy Fold Plantation
Clough Beck
44
Downham Beck
Score Clough Beck
Twiston Beck
Hill Top
Manor House
Twiston
Clough Head Mem
Smithy Fold
8
Lane Side
Clay House
Hill Foot
Wilkinson's Farm
Fern Side
Higher Smithy Fold
Gerna Hill
Gerna
Hollin's Farm
Nutshaw Barn
Hecklin Farm
Higher Higson
Brownlow
9
ROAD
Lane Head
PENDLE
Ravens Holme
Coolham
43
Hookcliffe Plantation
Stony Bank
Pendle Hill Brook
Pendle Bridge Wood
Red Syke Gate
Hook Cliffe
PENDLE ROAD
Four Lane Ends

G H J K 83 L M N

79 380 81 82

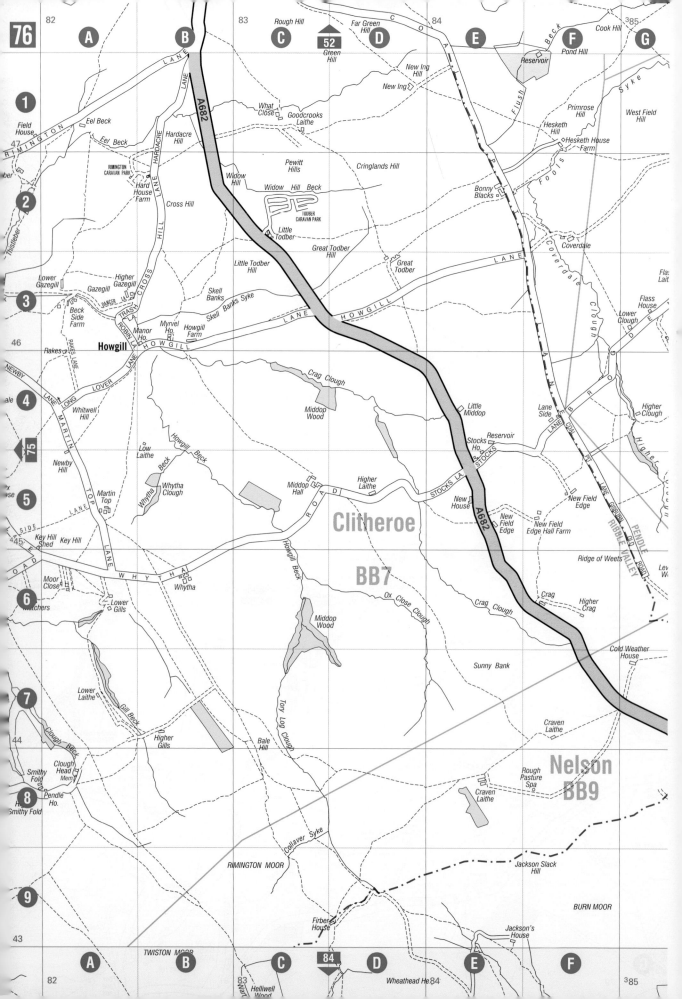

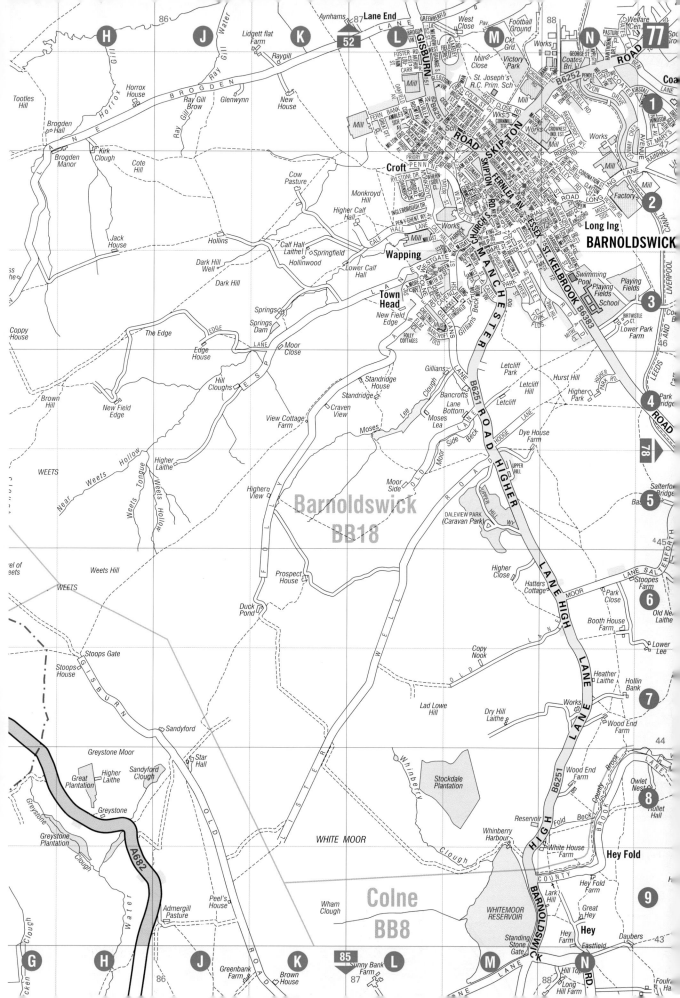

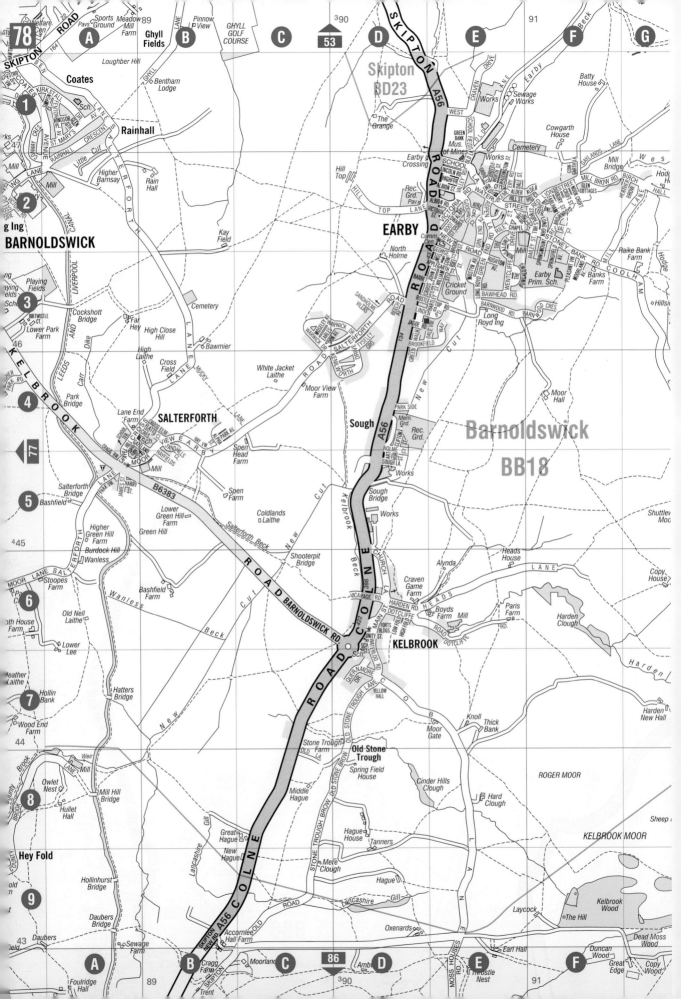

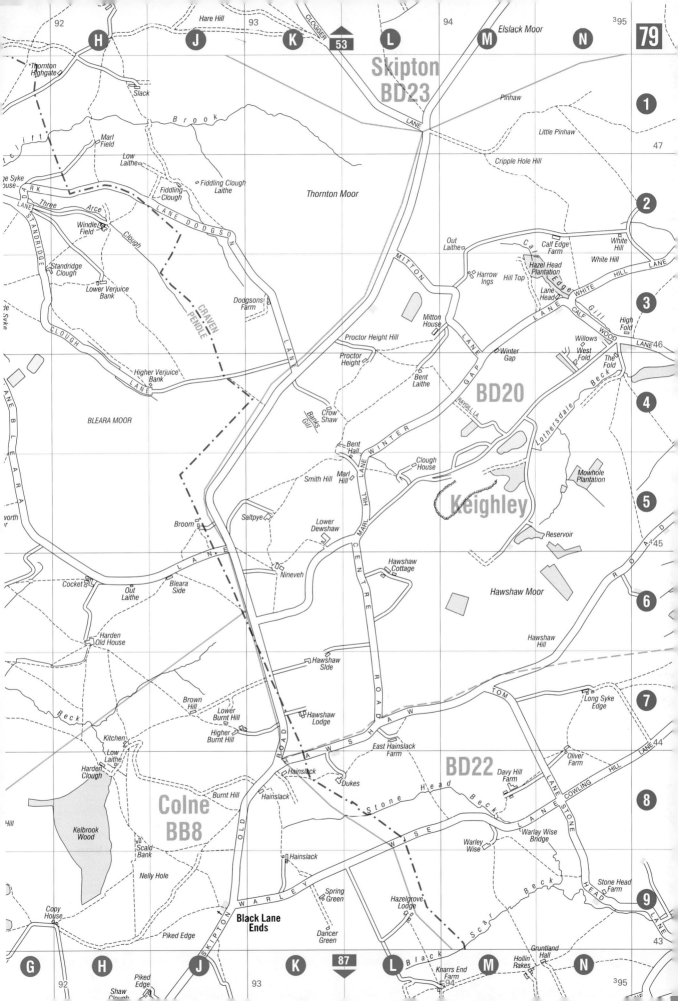

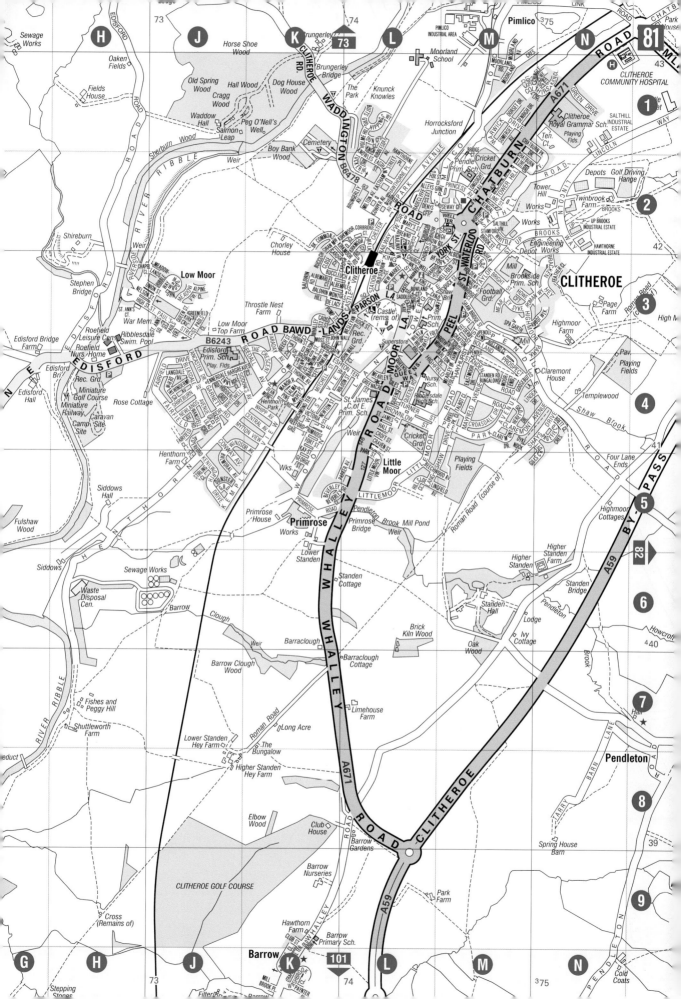

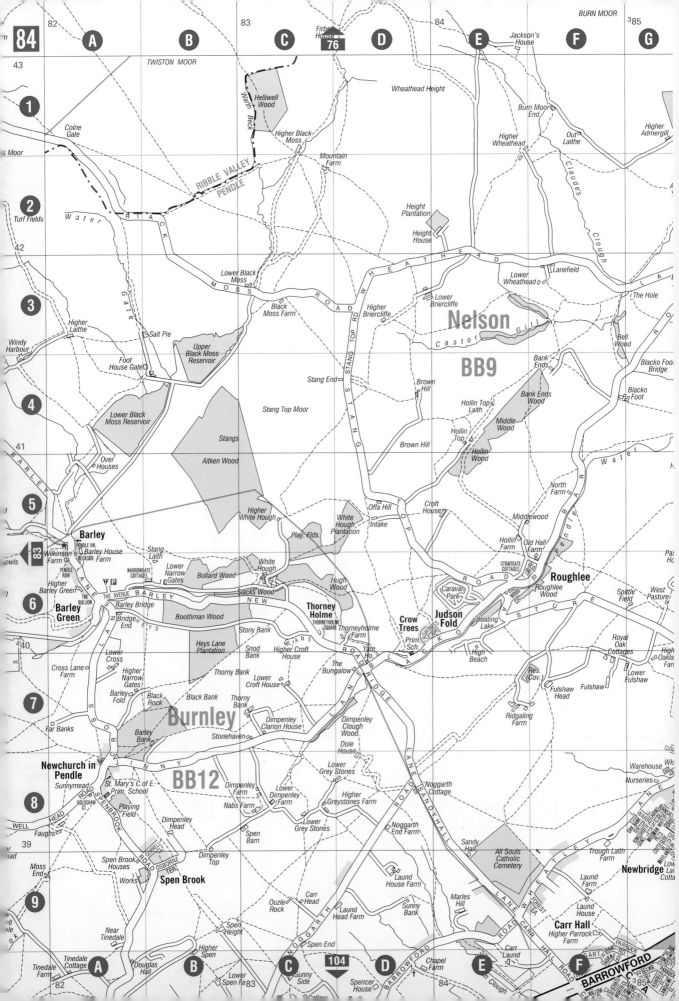

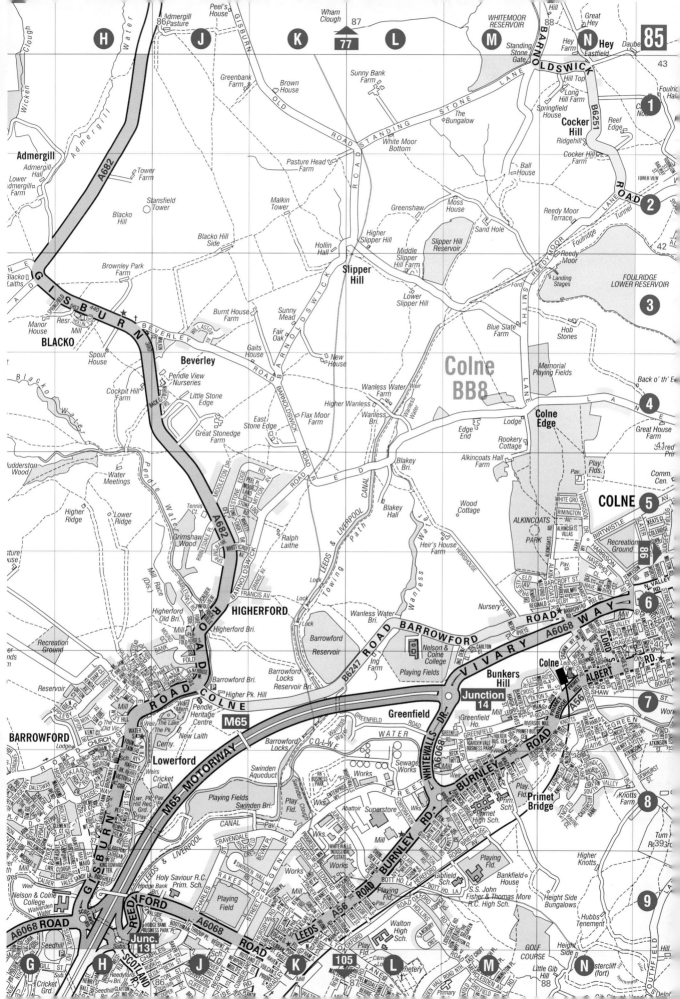

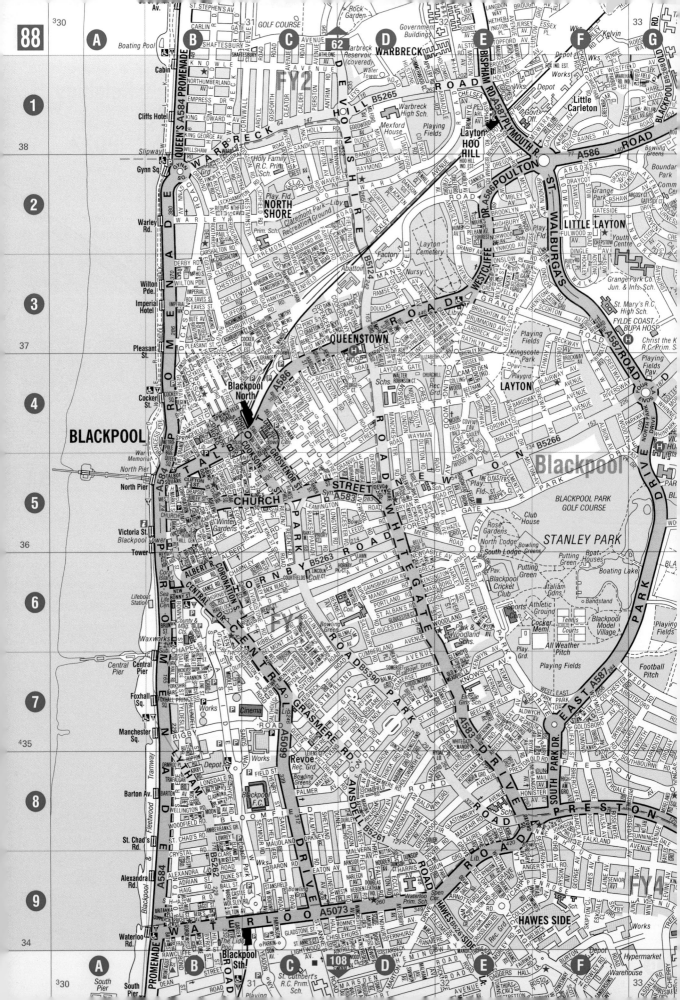

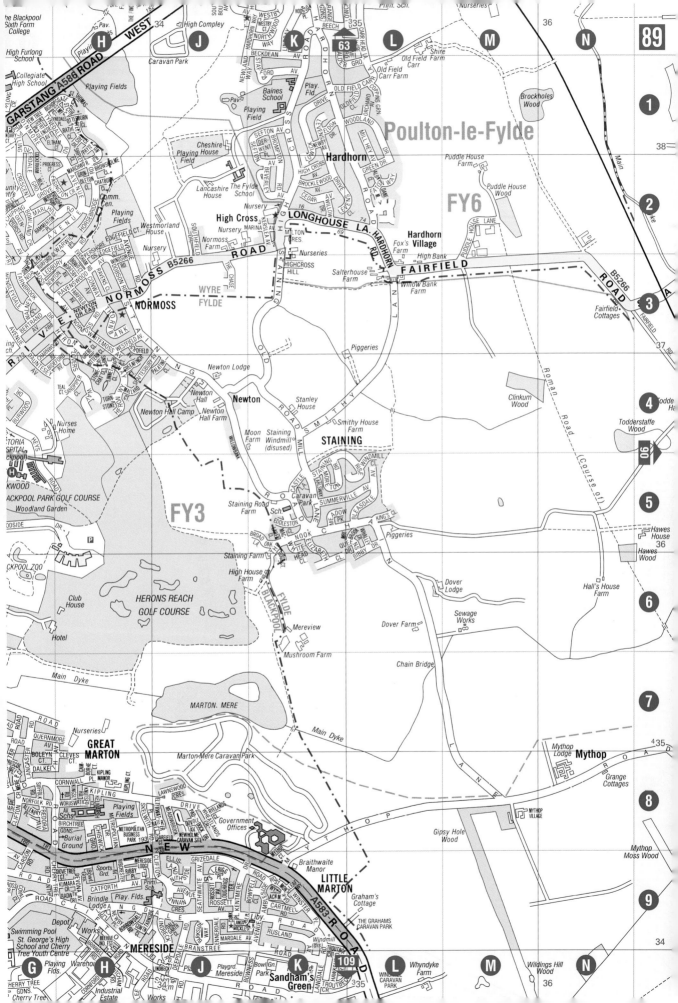

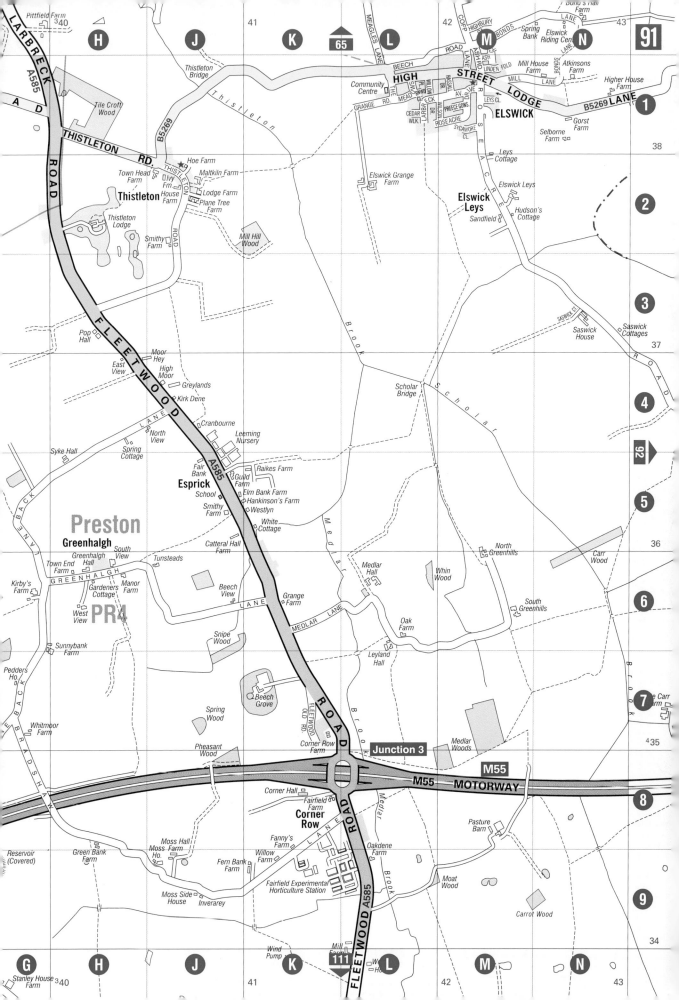

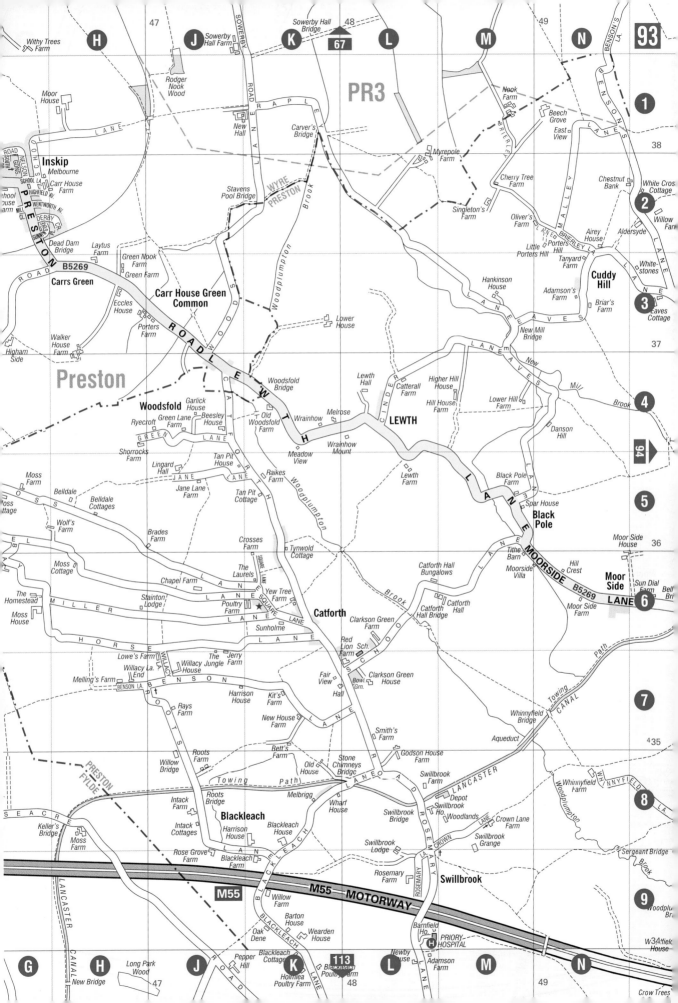

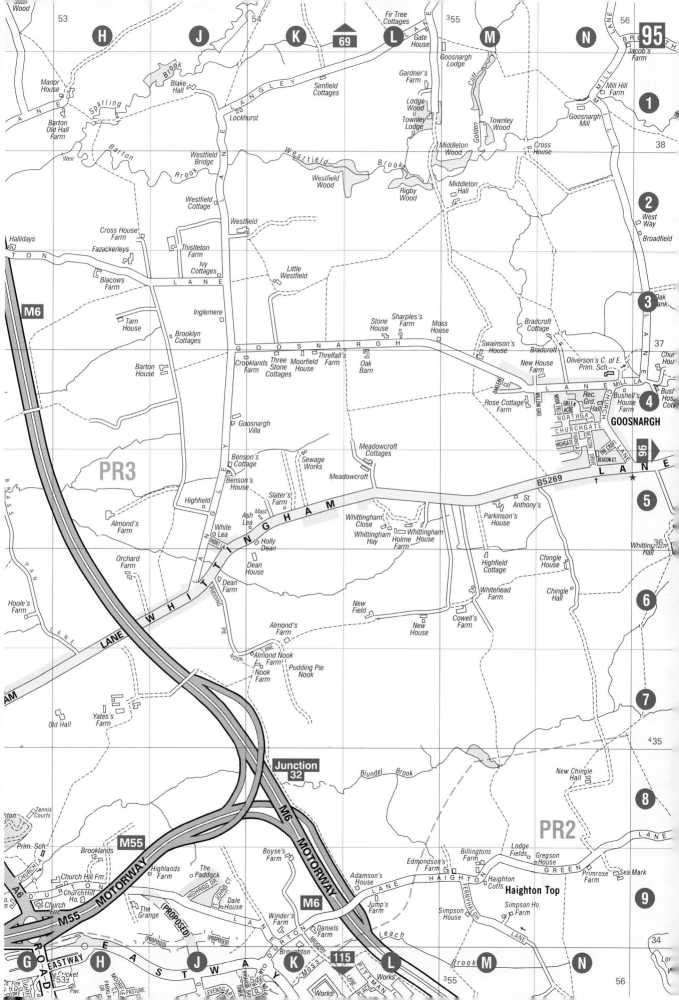

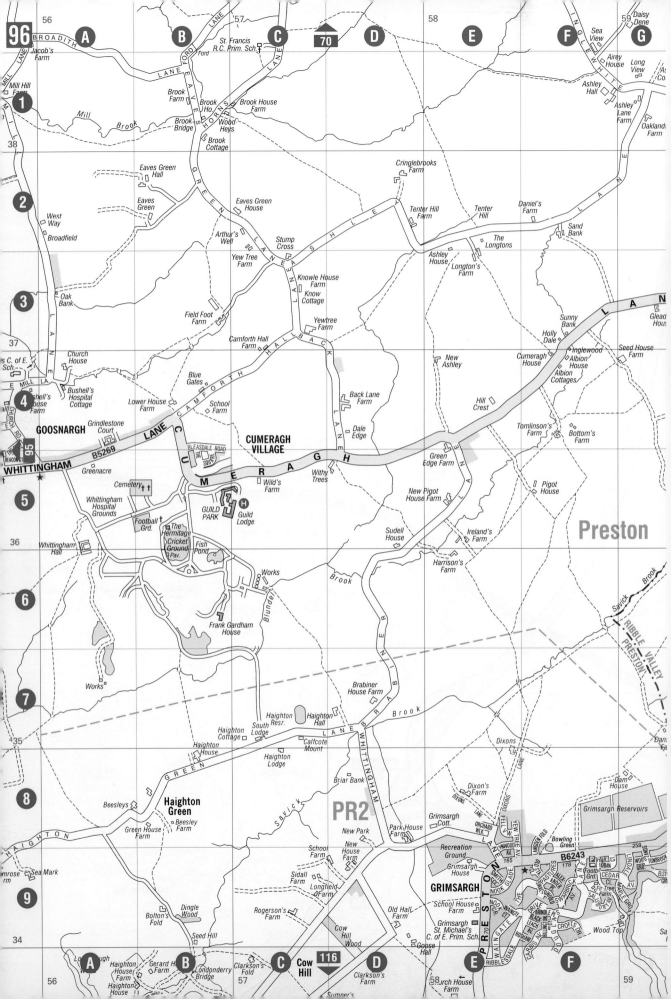

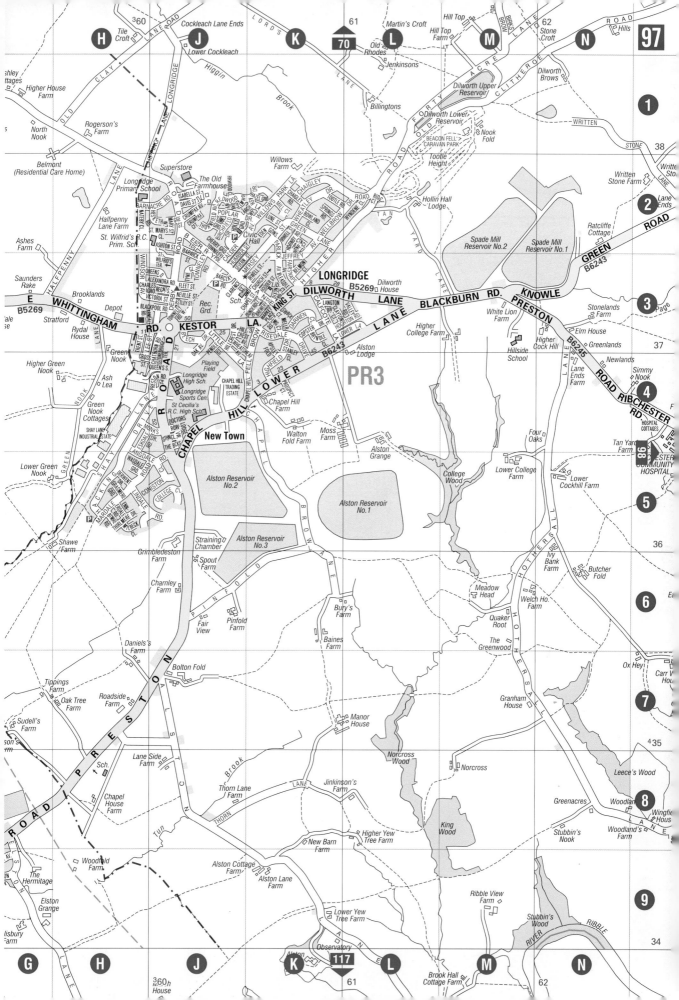

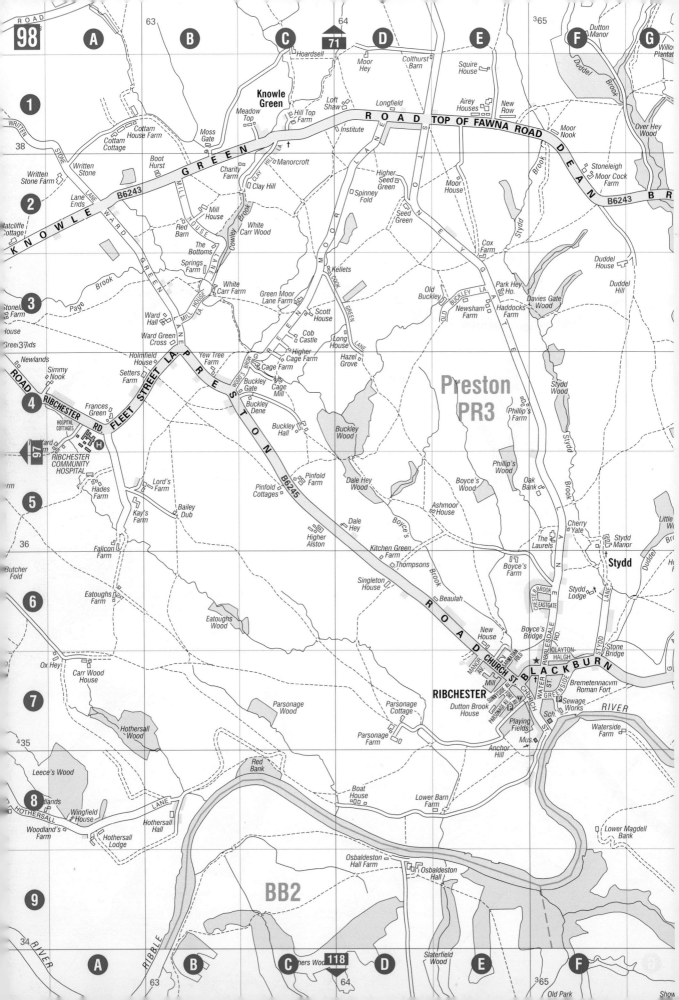

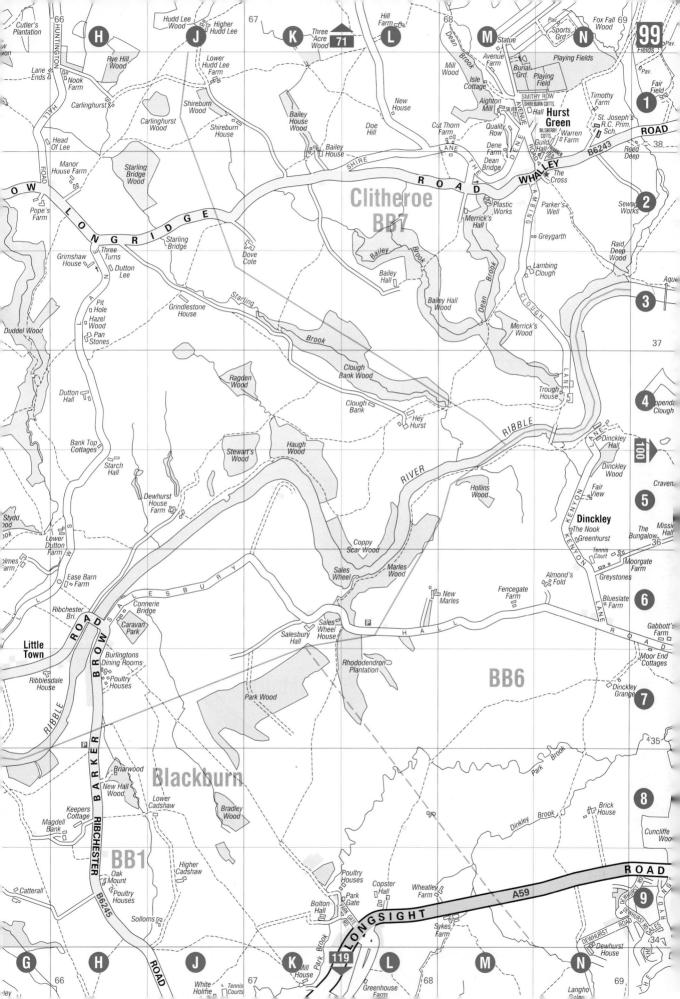

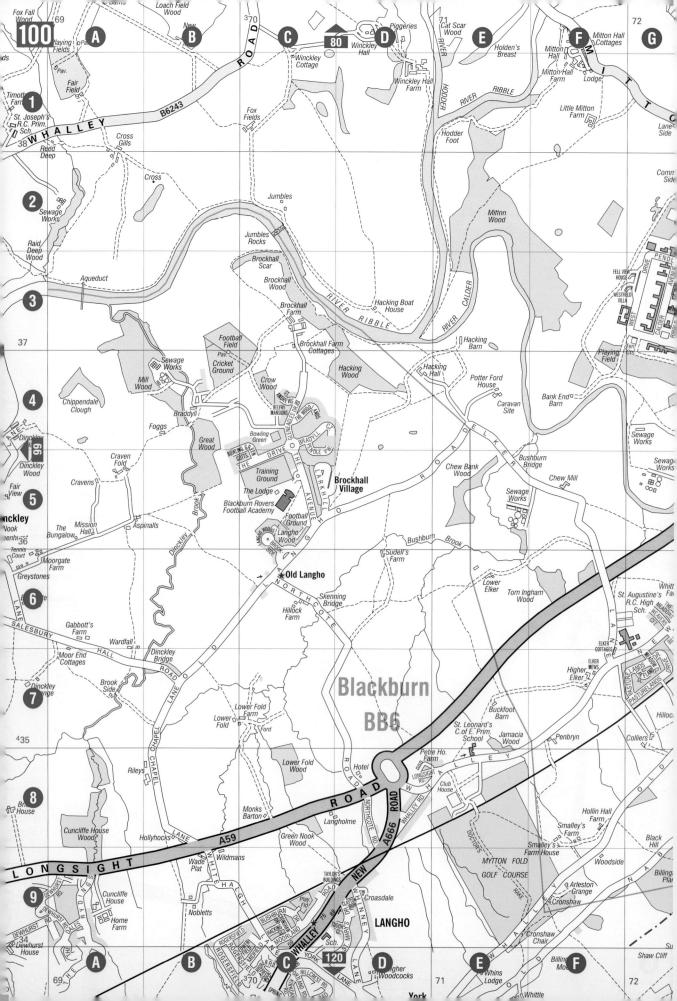

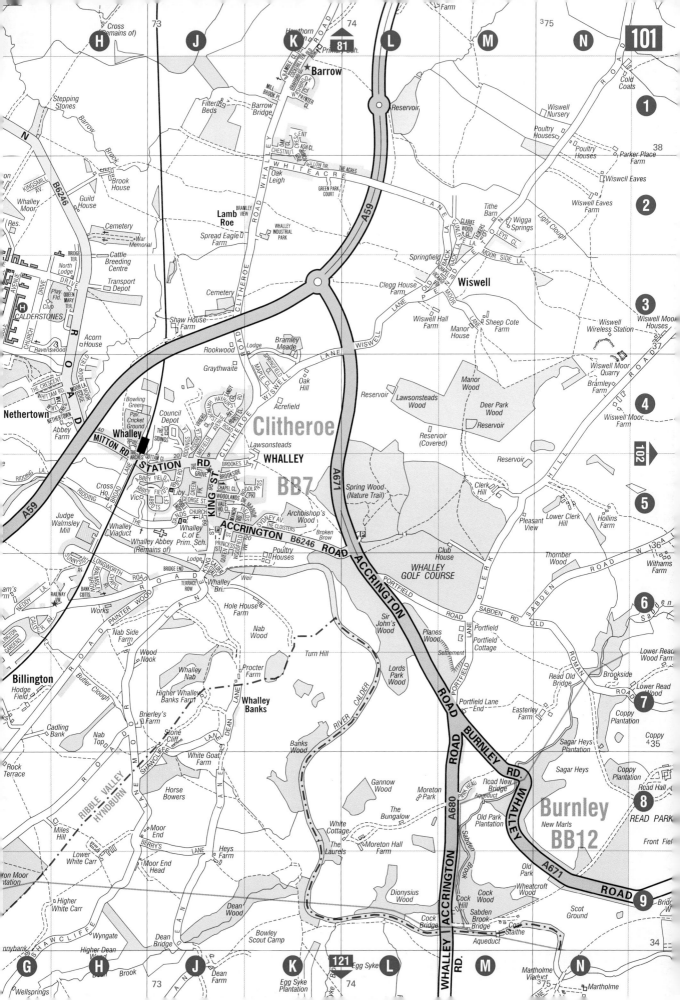

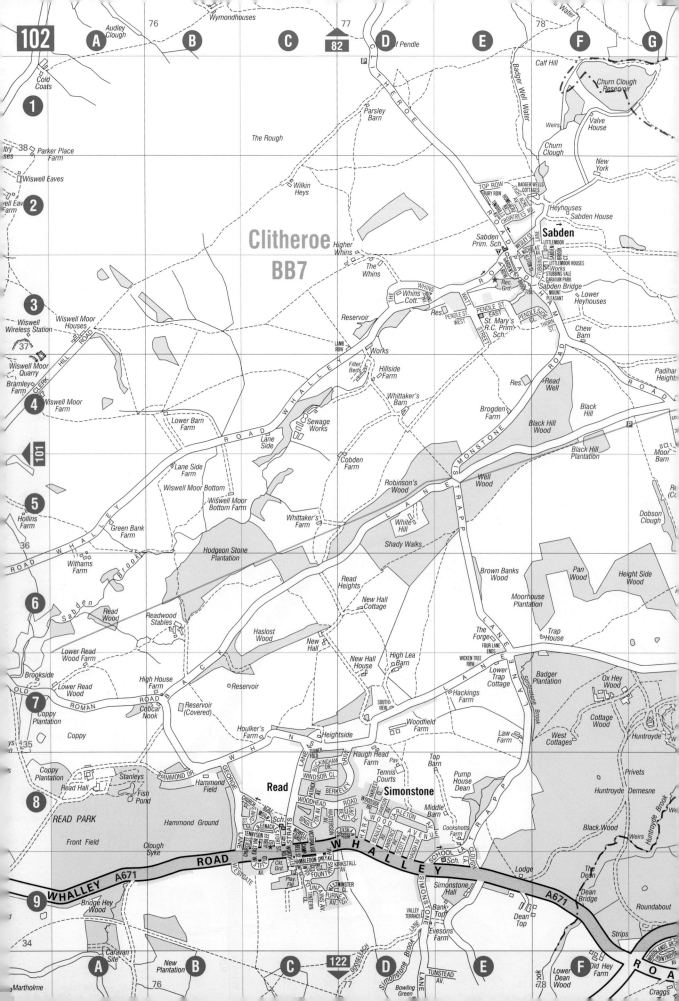

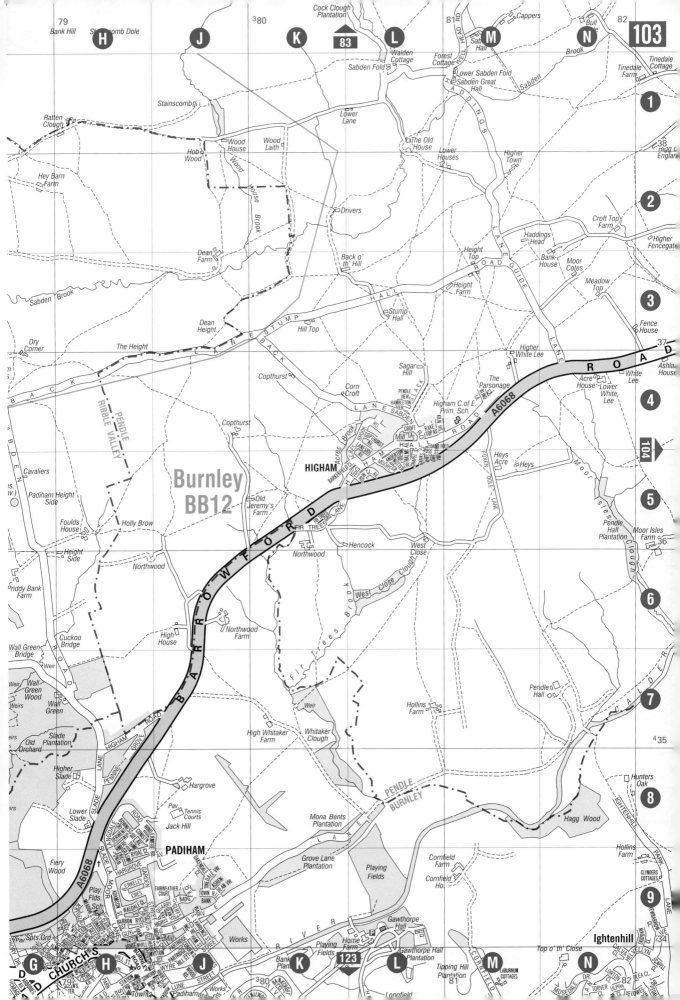

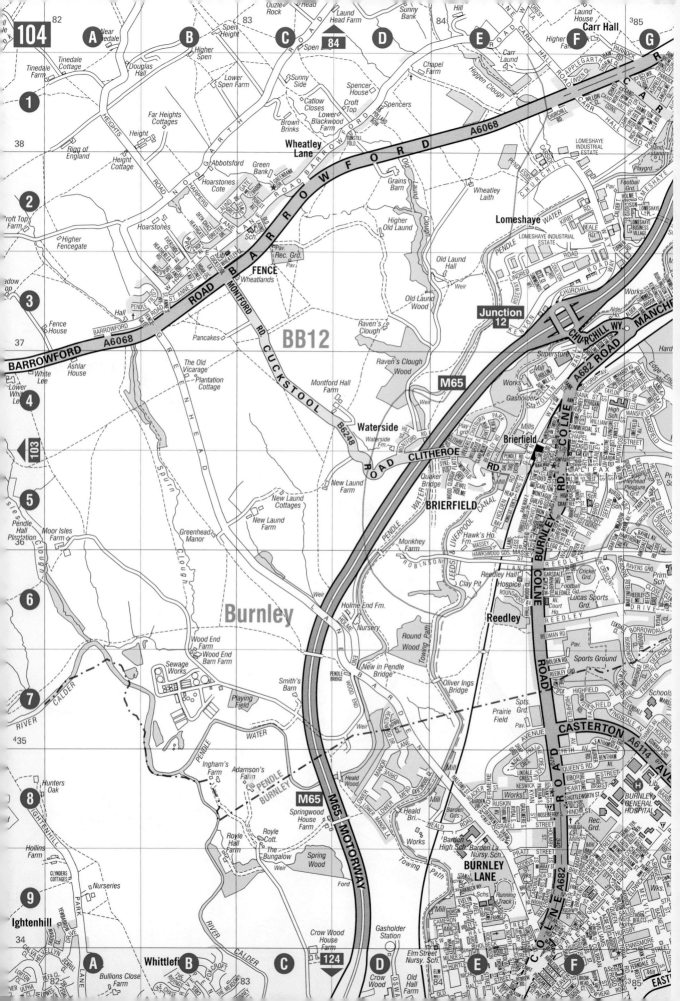

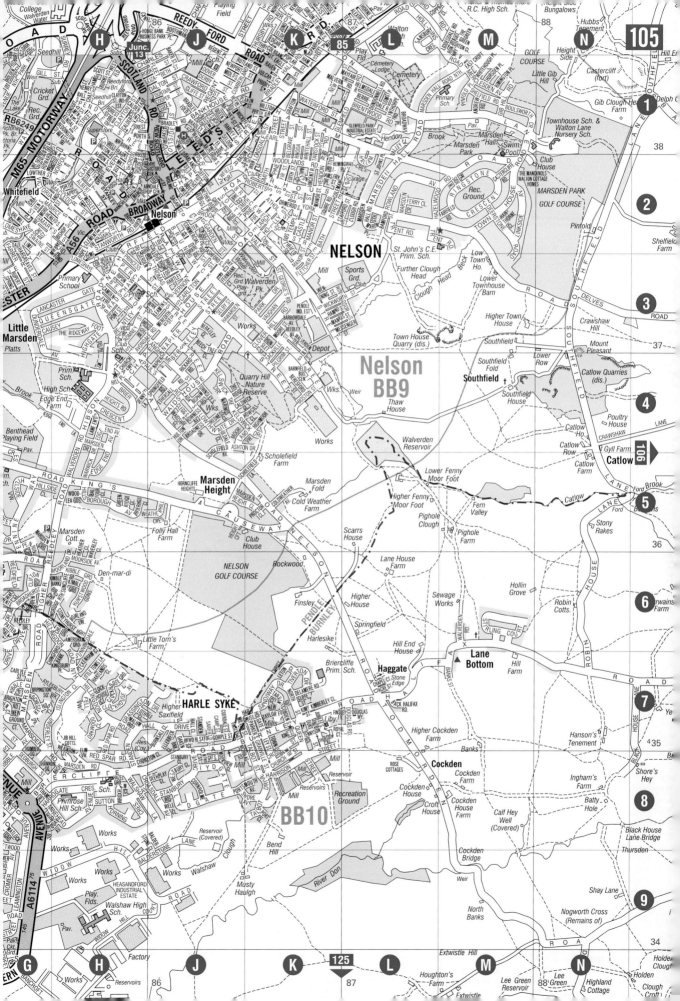

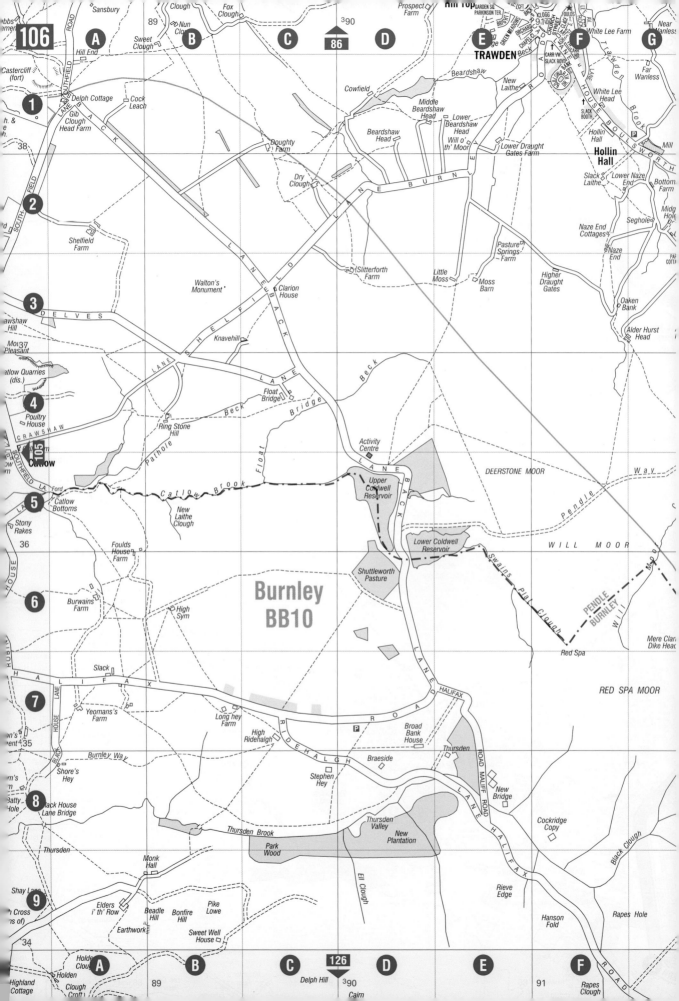

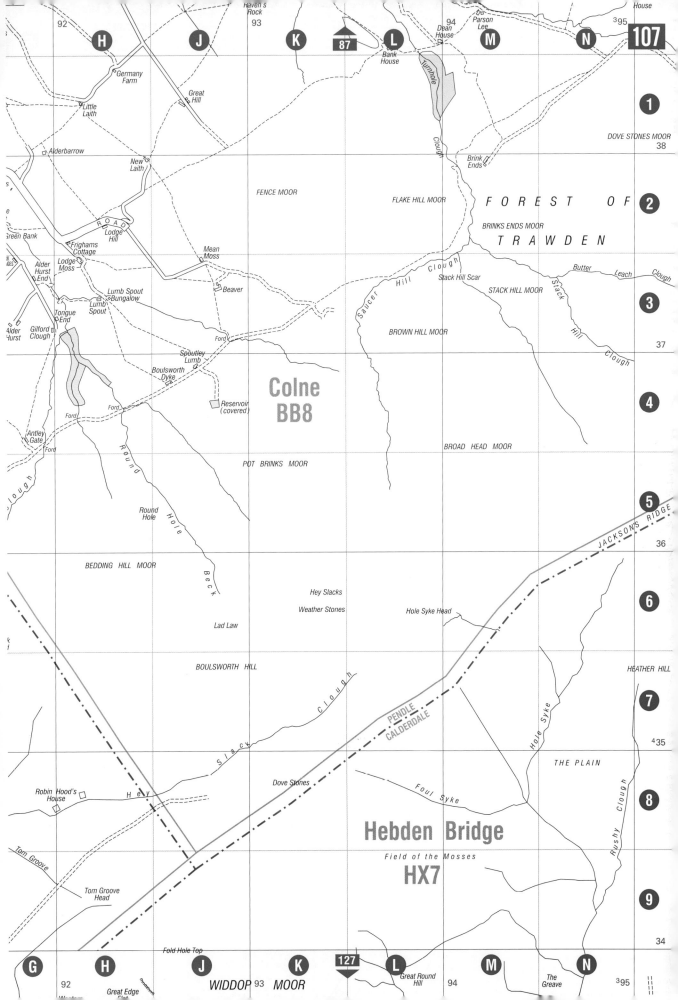

**Colne
BB8**

Hebden Bridge

Field of the Mosses

HX7

FOREST OF

TRAWDEN

FENCE MOOR

FLAKE HILL MOOR

BRINKS ENDS MOOR

DOVE STONES MOOR

Brink Ends

Stack Hill Scar

STACK HILL MOOR

Butter Leach Clough

Saucer Hill Clough

Stack Hill Clough

BROWN HILL MOOR

BROAD HEAD MOOR

POT BRINKS MOOR

Reservoir (covered)

BEDDING HILL MOOR

Round Hole

Round Hole Beck

JACKSON'S RIDGE

Hey Slacks

Weather Stones

Hole Syke Head

HEATHER HILL

Lad Law

BOULSWORTH HILL

Slack Clough

PENDLE
CALDERDALE

Hole Syke

THE PLAIN

Robin Hood's House

Hey

Dove Stones

Foul Syke

Rushy Clough

Tom Groove

Tom Groove Head

Fold Hole Top

WIDDOP MOOR

Great Round Hill

The Greave

Germany Farm

Little Laith

Haven's Rock

Great Hill

Bank House

Dean House

Parson Lee

House

Turnhole

Clough

Alderbarrow

New Laith

Green Bank

ROAD

Lodge Hill

Frighams Cottage

Lodge Moss

Mean Moss

Alder Hurst End

Lumb Spout Bungalow

Beaver

Lumb Spout

Tongue End

Gilford Clough

Alder Hurst

Spoutley Lumb

Boulsworth Dyke

Ford

Ford

Antley Gate

Ford

Ford

Great Edge Clough

92

93

94

395

38

37

36

35

34

87

127

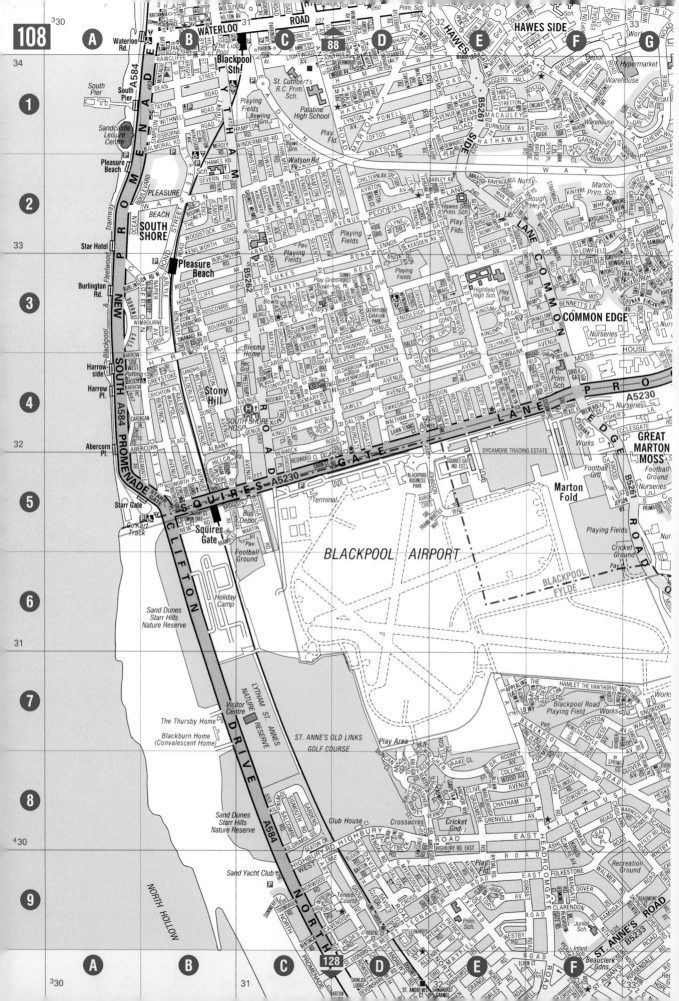

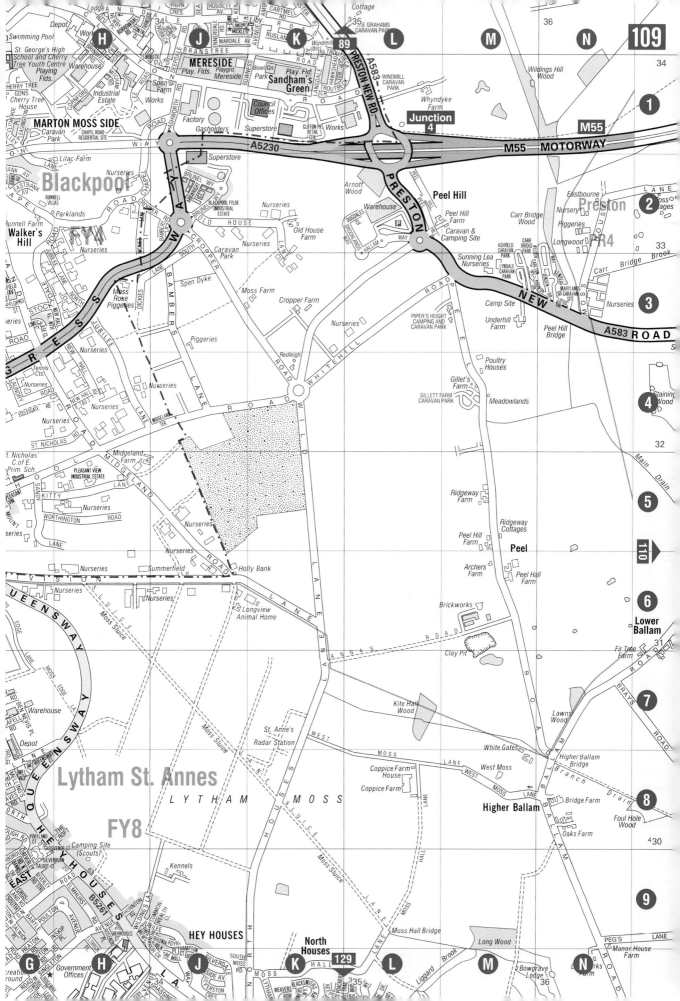

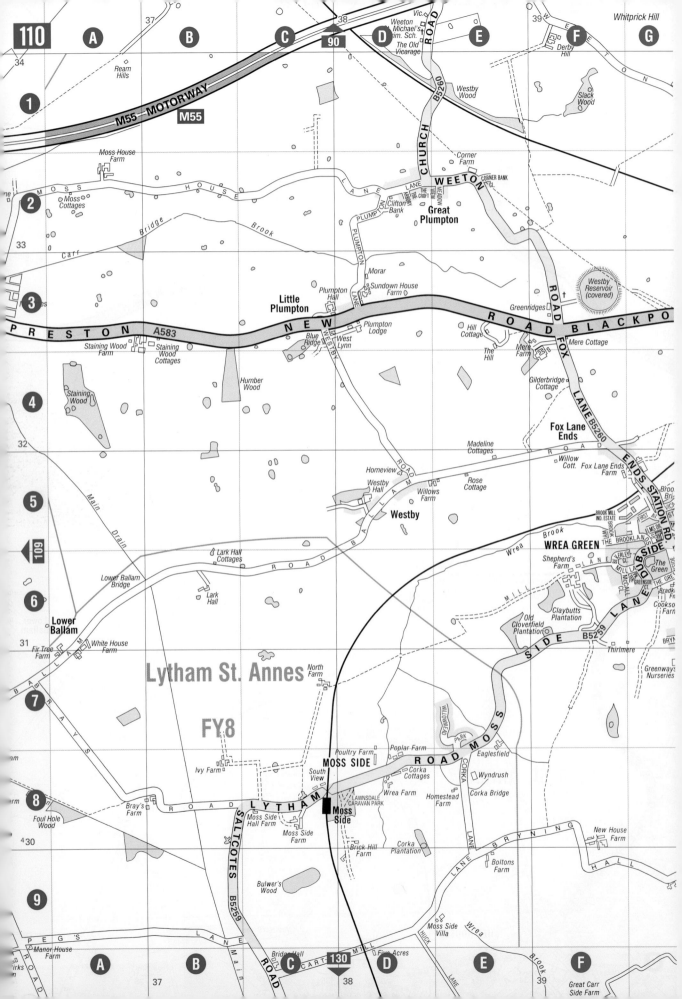

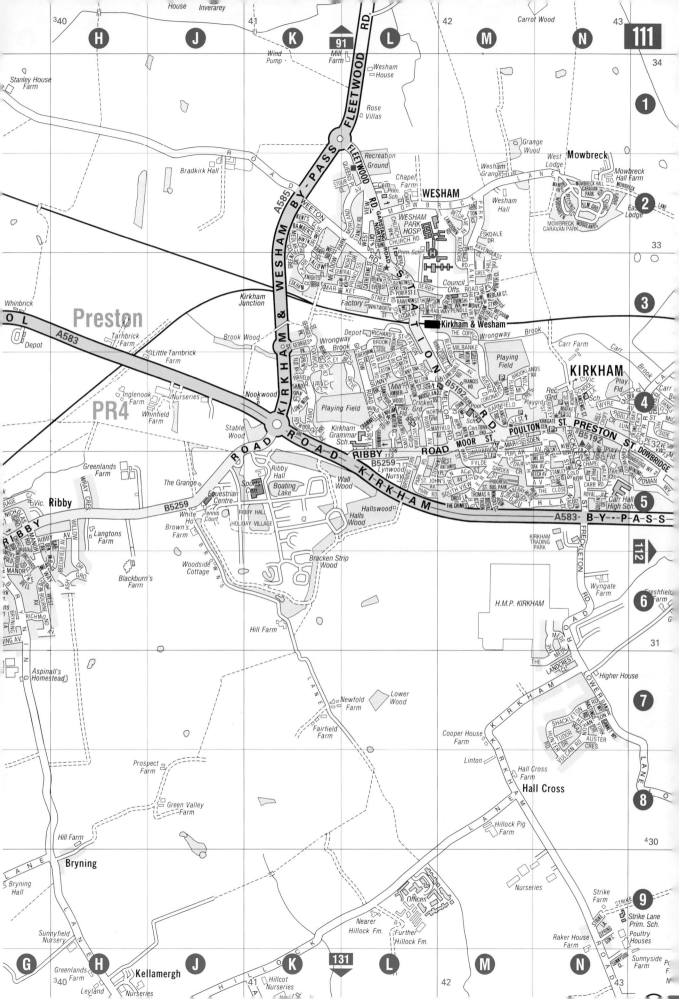

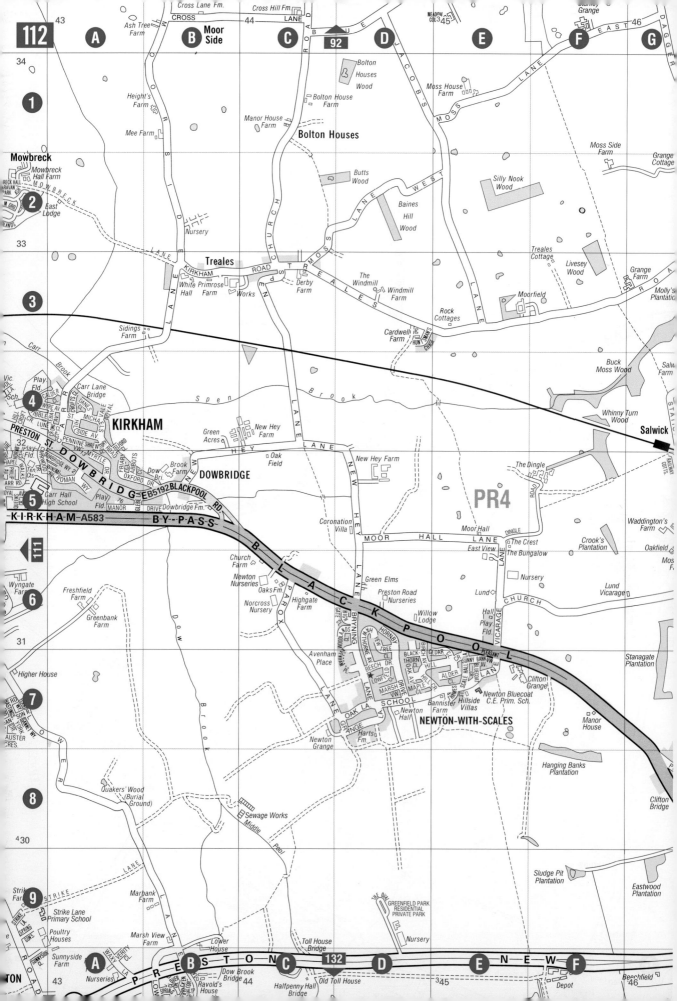

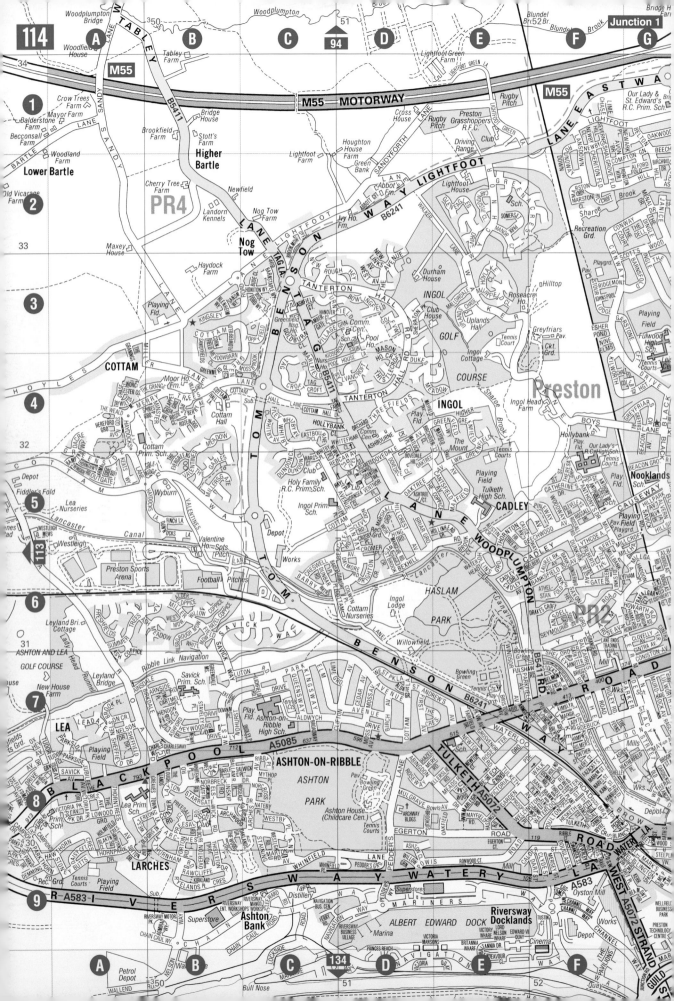

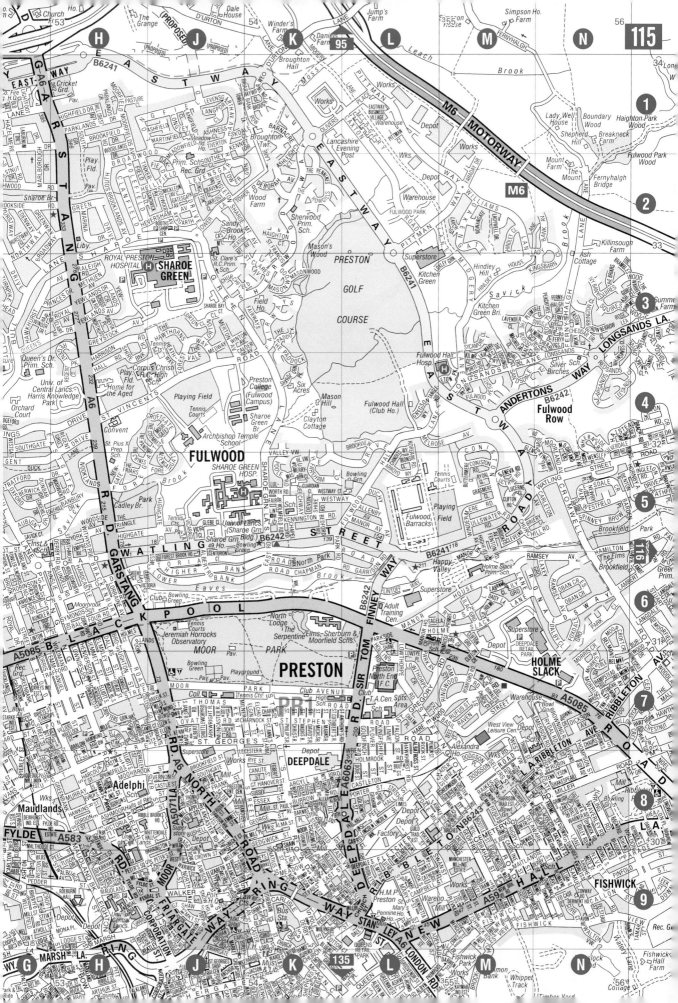

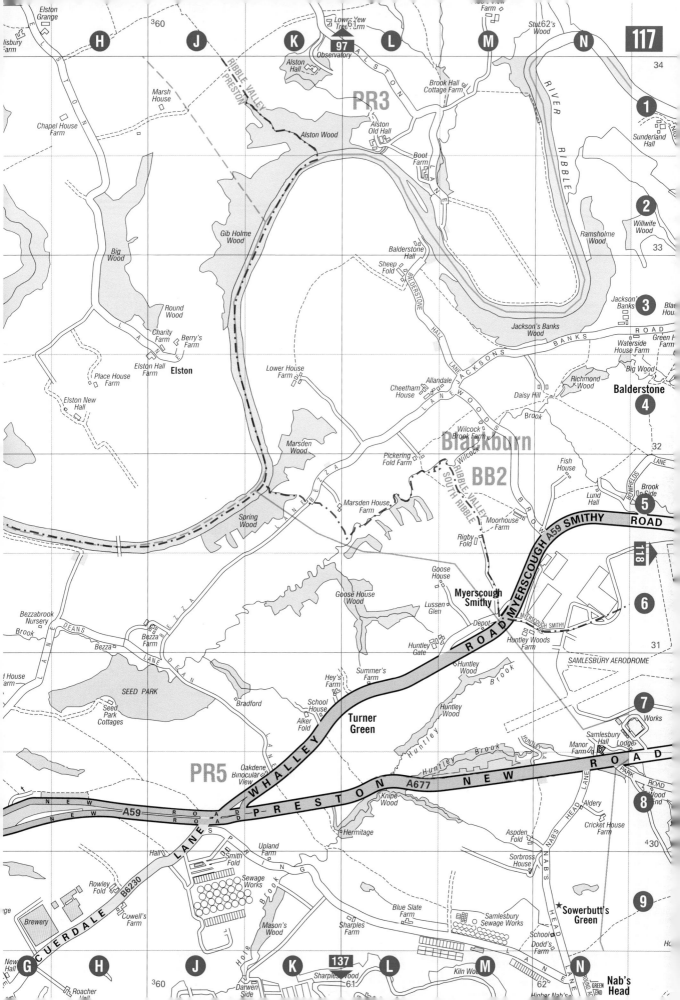

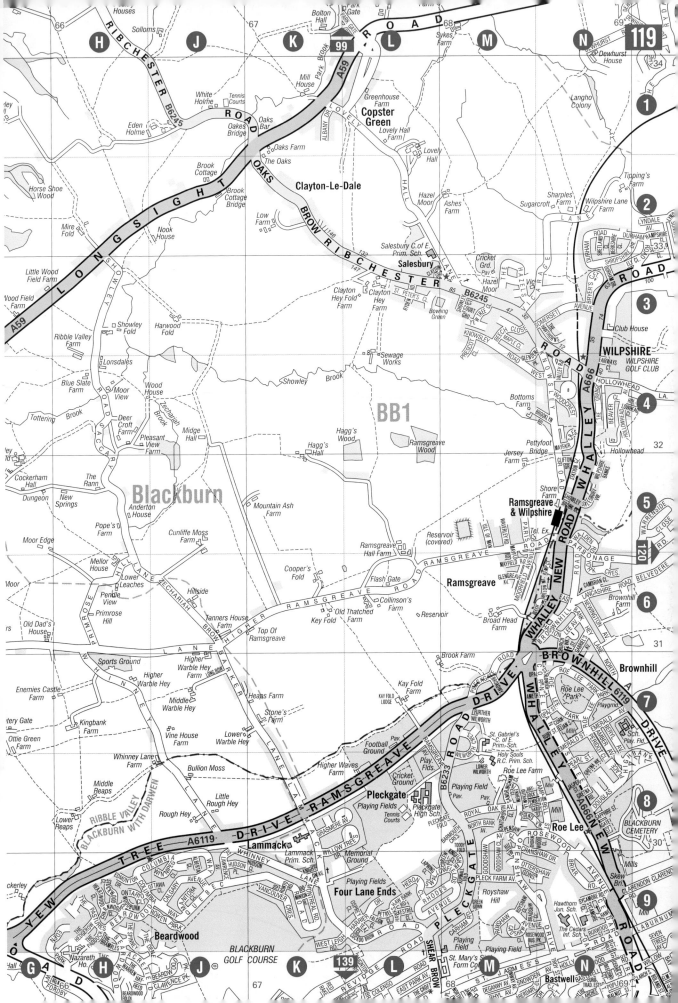

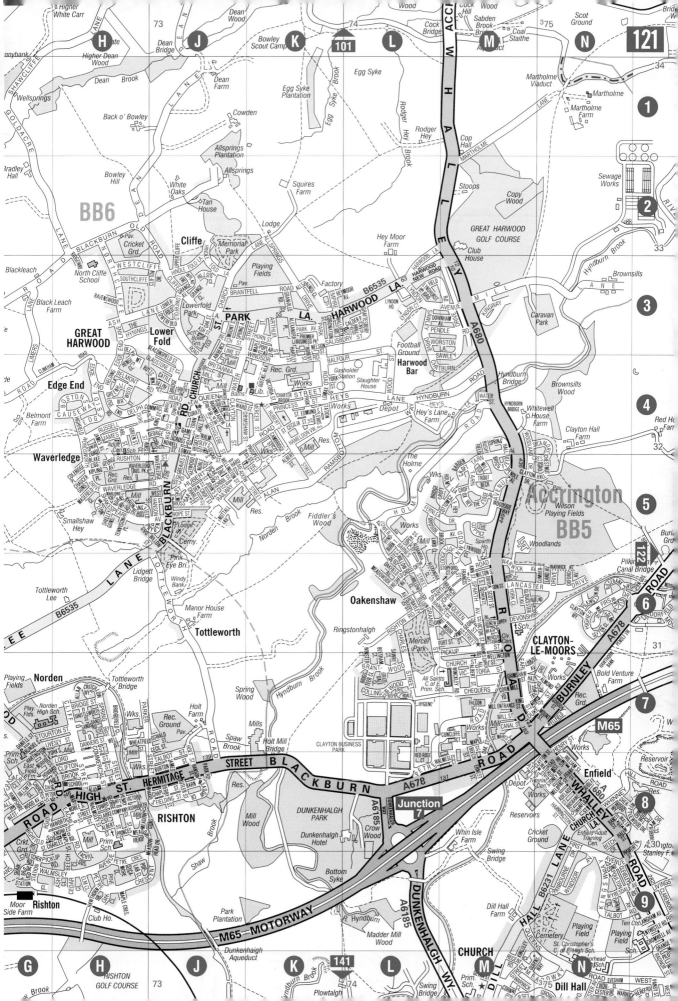

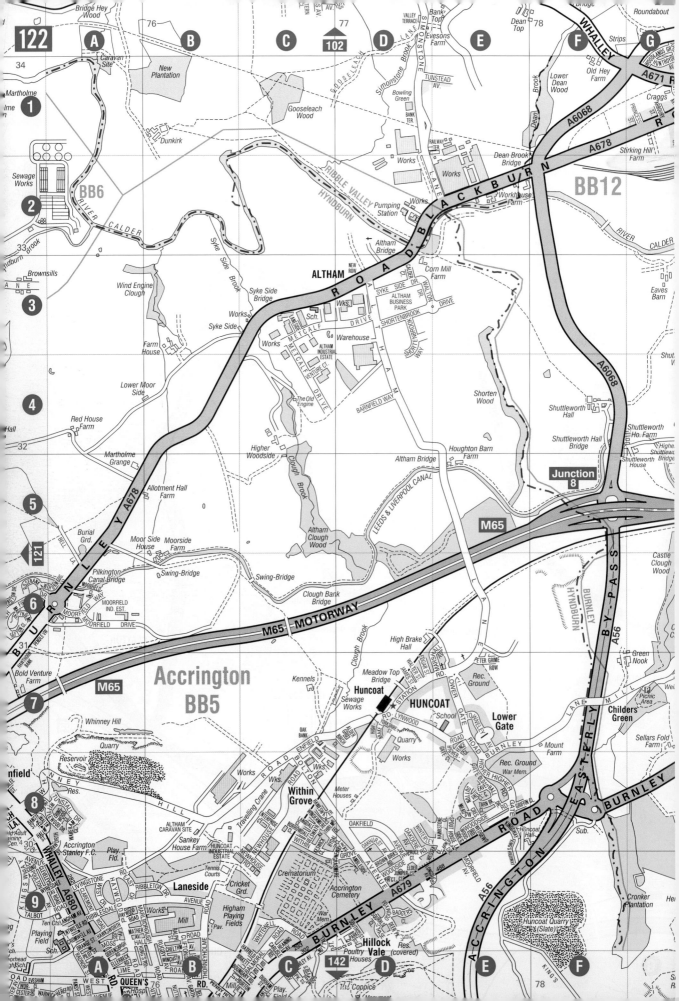

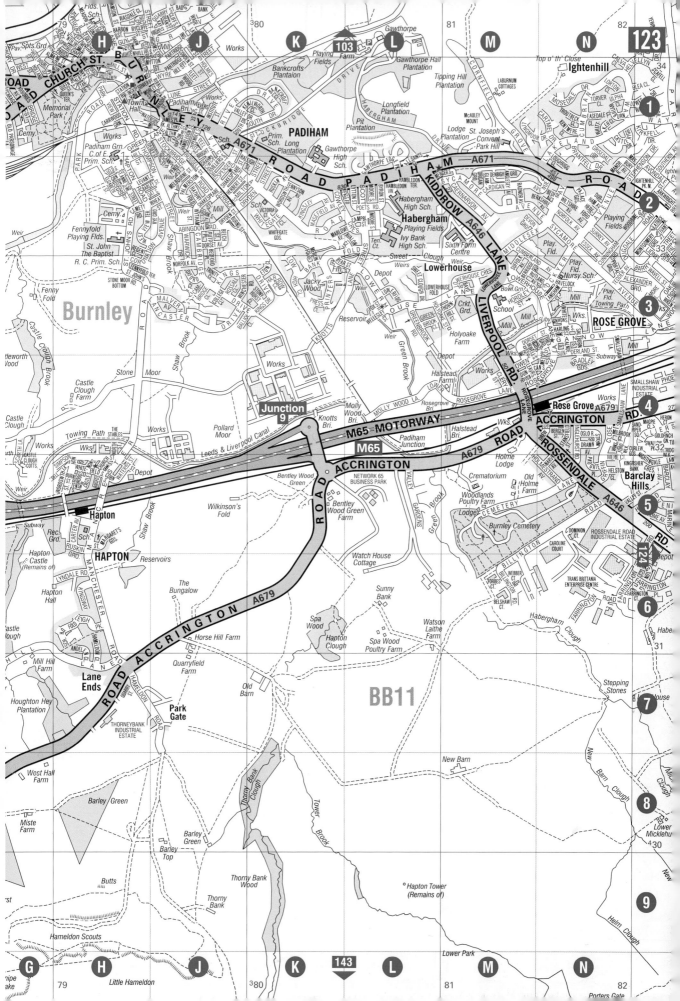

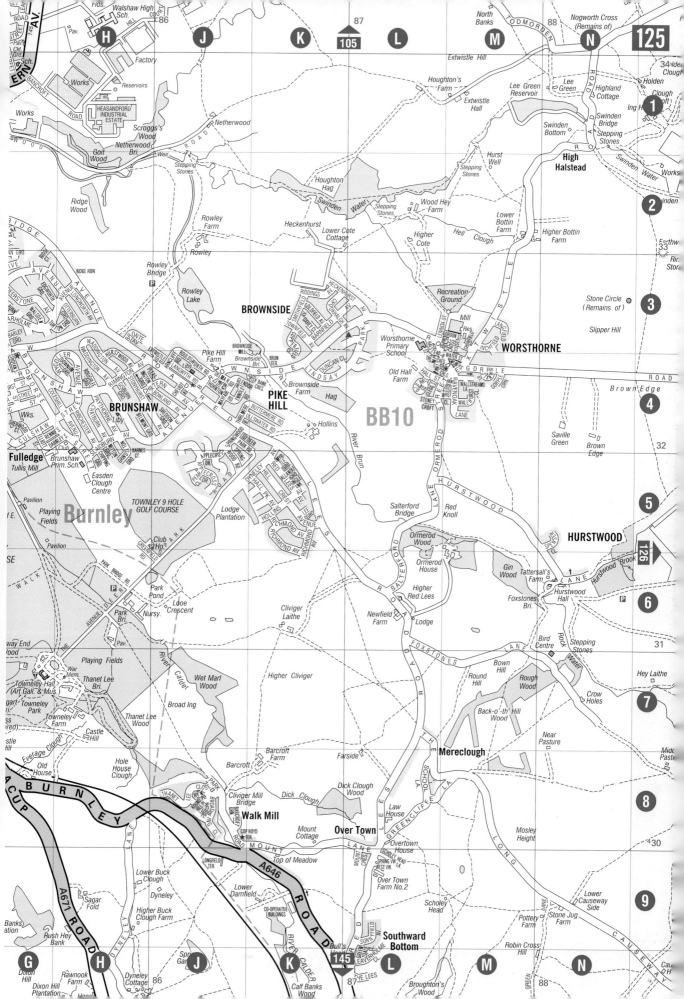

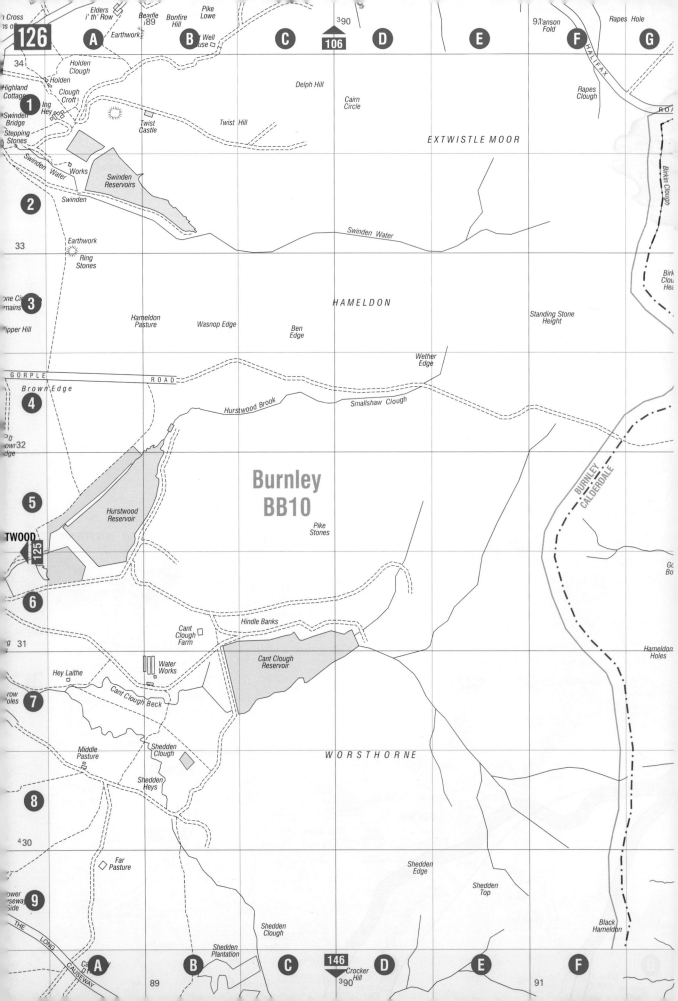

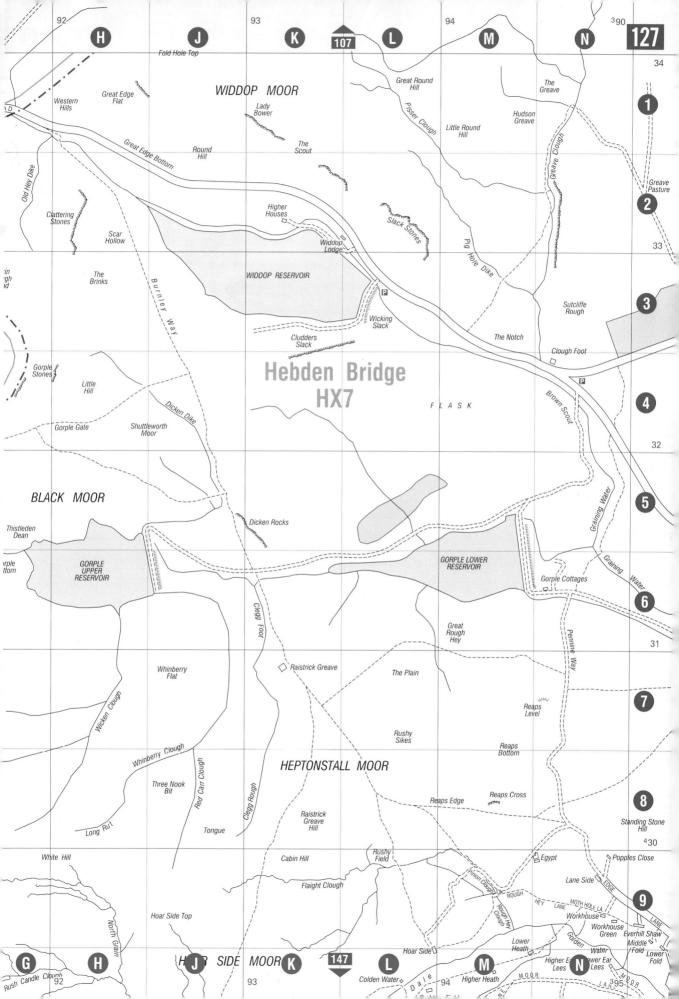

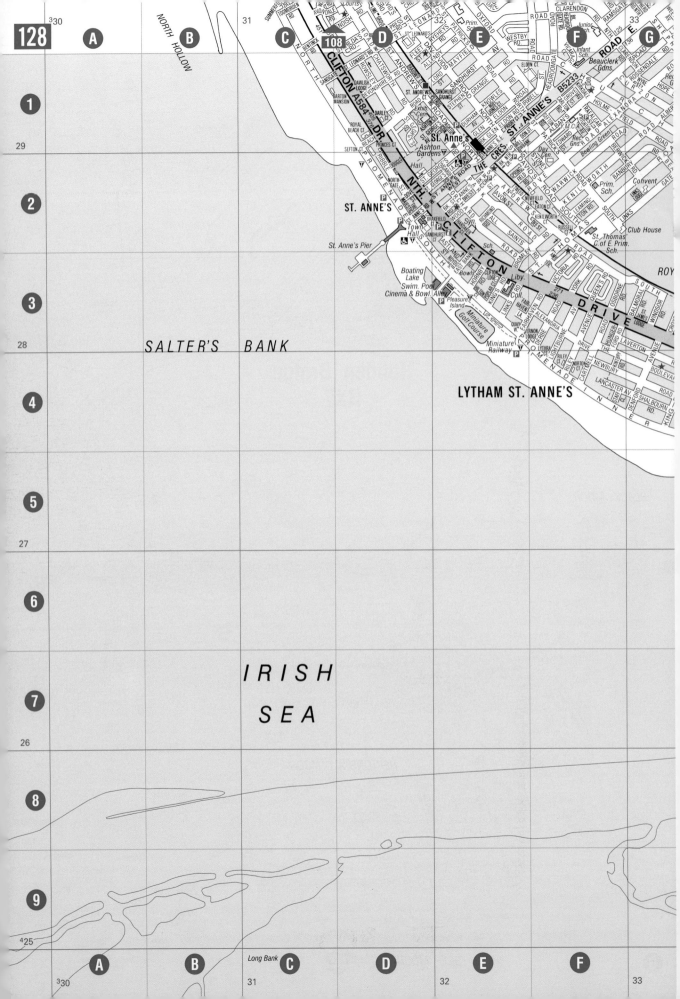

A   NORTH HOLLOW   **B**   **C**   108   **D**   **E**   **F**   **G**

1

29

2

ST. ANNE'S

St. Anne's Pier

3

28

SALTER'S BANK

Boating Lake
Swim. Pool
Cinema & Bowl. Alley
Pleasure Island
Miniature Golf Course
Miniature Railway

LYTHAM ST. ANNE'S

4

5

27

6

I R I S H

S E A

7

26

8

9

425

A   **B**   Long Bank   **C**   **D**   **E**   **F**

330   31   32   33

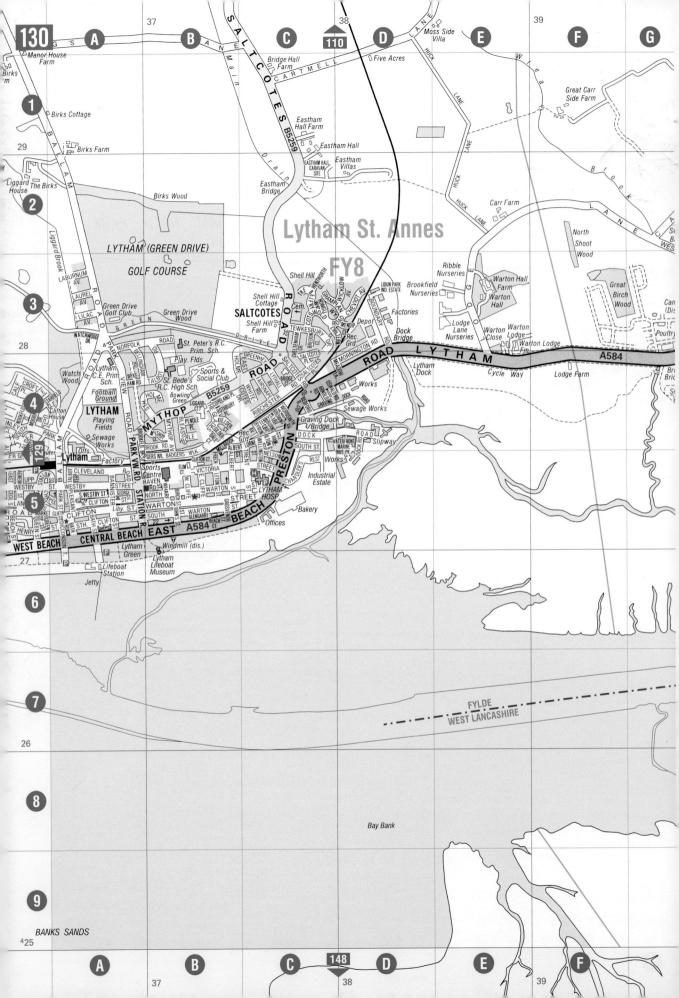

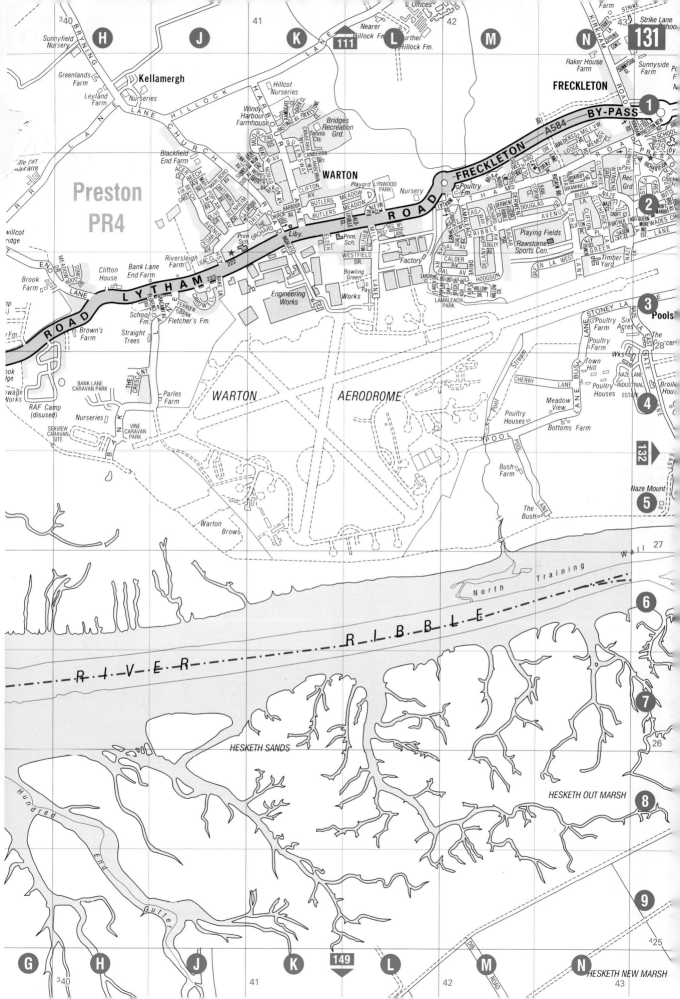

Preston
PR4

FRECKLETON

Kellamergh

WARTON

WARTON AERODROME

HESKETH SANDS

RIVER RIBBLE

North Training Wall

HESKETH OUT MARSH

HESKETH NEW MARSH

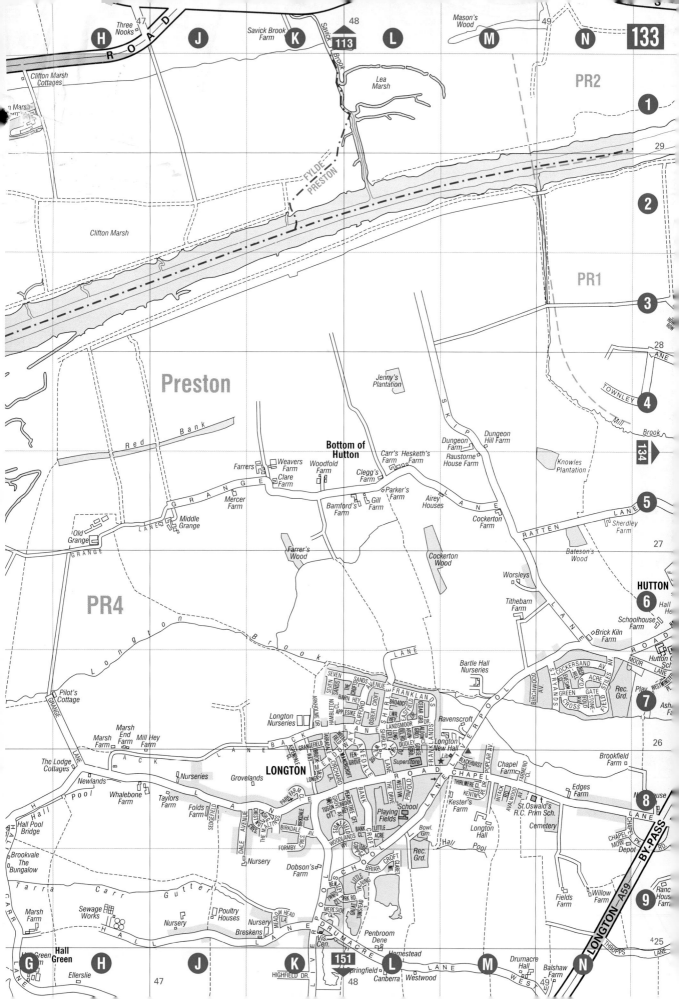

H   J   K   113   L   M   N

PR2
PR1
PR4
HUTTON

Three Nooks
Clifton Marsh Cottages
Clifton Marsh
Savick Brook Farm
Lea Marsh
Mason's Wood
FYLDE PRESTON

Preston

Red Bank
Farrers
Weavers Farm
Clare Farm
Woodfold Farm
Bottom of Hutton
Carr's Farm
Hesketh's Farm
Dungeon Farm
Dungeon Hill Farm
Raustorne House Farm
Knowles Plantation
Jenny's Plantation

GRANGE
Mercer Farm
Bamford's Farm
Clegg's Farm
Parker's Farm
Gill Farm
Airey Houses
Cockerton Farm
Sherdley Farm

Old Grange
Middle Grange
GRANGE LANES
Farrer's Wood
Cockerton Wood
Bateson's Wood
Worsleys
RATTEN LANE
Hall He

Tithebarn Farm
Schoolhouse Farm
Hutton Sch
Brick Kiln Farm
Rec. Grd.
Ash

Pilot's Cottage
Longton Brook
Bartle Hall Nurseries
COCKERSAND AV
BIRCHWOOD AV
STRANDS
MOOR LANE
CROSS
GREEN
GATE
ACRE
FIELD
STILES
STONE
Play
Rec. Grd.
WESTMINS

SEVEN SANDS
THE CROFTS
BROADC
EASTFIELD
LWR HEY
RED BEL
LONG
Ravenscroft

Longton Nurseries
BARN HEY
APPLESIKE
OSBERT CROFT
LANDSMOOR
DUDLEY
SHIRLEY
ARMHOLME DR
HAMBLETON CL
CLIFFORD

Marsh End Farm
Mill Hey Farm
BACK LANE
GRANGEFIELD
HARROWDALE
ASPINALL
FEN GROVE
LONGS
Longton New Hall
Superstore
Lib
CHAPEL
Chapel Farm
FARMEND CL
Brookfield Farm

The Lodge Cottages
Newlands
Whalebone Farm
Taylors Farm
Folds Farm
Nurseries
Grovelands
LONGTON
PARK FAR
ORCHARD
GROVE
BANK
THE DRIVE
WEST VW
School
THIRLMERE CL
KENTME
INTACK
AVONWOOD
St.Oswald's R.C. Prim Sch.
Cemetery
Edges Farm

Hall Pool Bridge
Brookvale
The Bungalow
SEDGEFIELD
DALE AVENUE
THE MALTINGS
BIRKDALE AV
FORMBY
PRES
Nursery
Dobson's Farm
TUSON CFT
BROOK CFT
STONEVFLD
WOODLANDS
BEAN CROFT
LITTLE ACRE
Bowl. Grn.
Playing Fields
Longton Hall
Kester's Farm
Longton Hall
Bowl. Grn.
Rec. Grd.
Fields Farm
Willow Farm
Ranc
Hous
Far

Marsh Farm
Tarra Carr Gutter
Sewage Works
Nursery
Poultry Houses
Nursery
Breskens
MEADOW HEAD
VIS Cen.
BRIAR
CROFT
MERESIDE
ELMSTEAD
PK RD
WHITS
Penbroom Dene
Homestead
Drumacre Hall Farm
Balshaw Farm
DRUMACRE

Hall Green
Ellerslie
HIGHFIELD DR
Springfield
Canberra
Westwood
LANE WEST
LONGTON A59
THROPPS

G   H   J   K   151   L   M   N

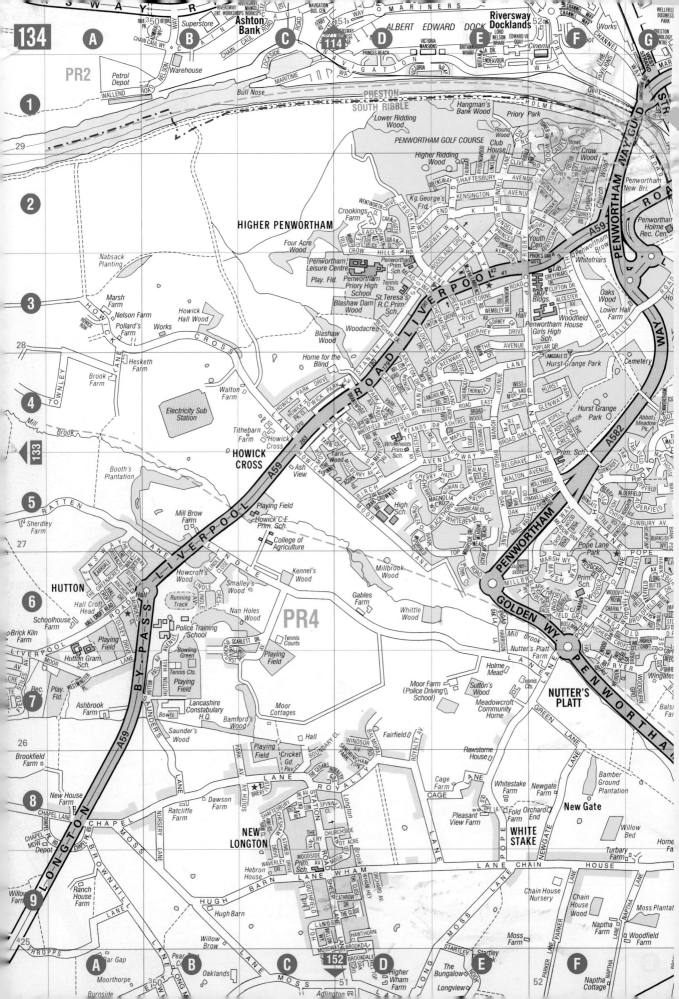

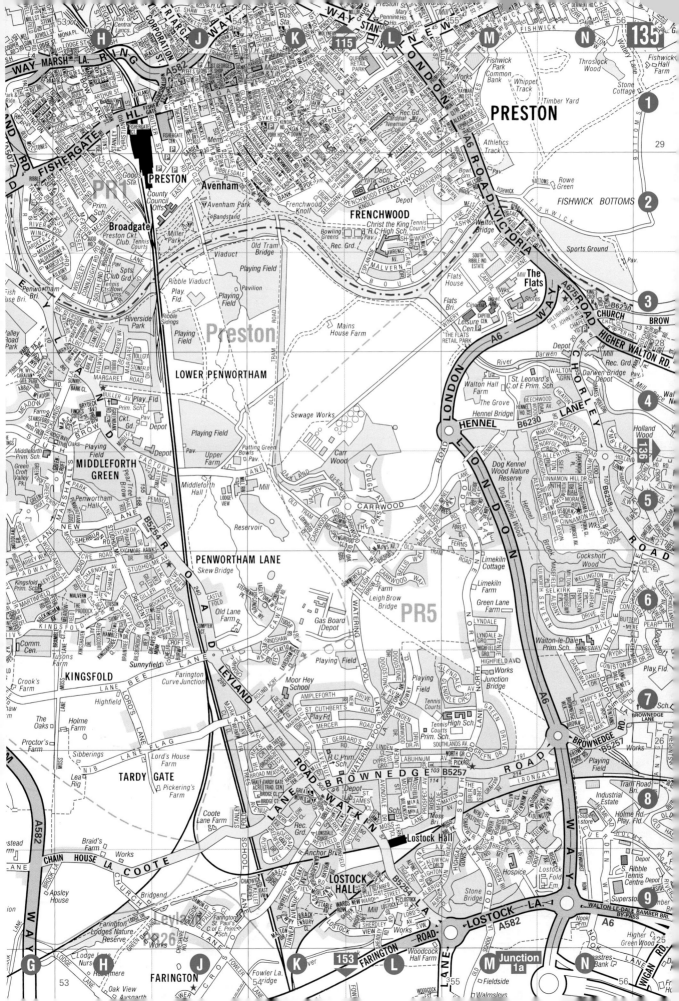

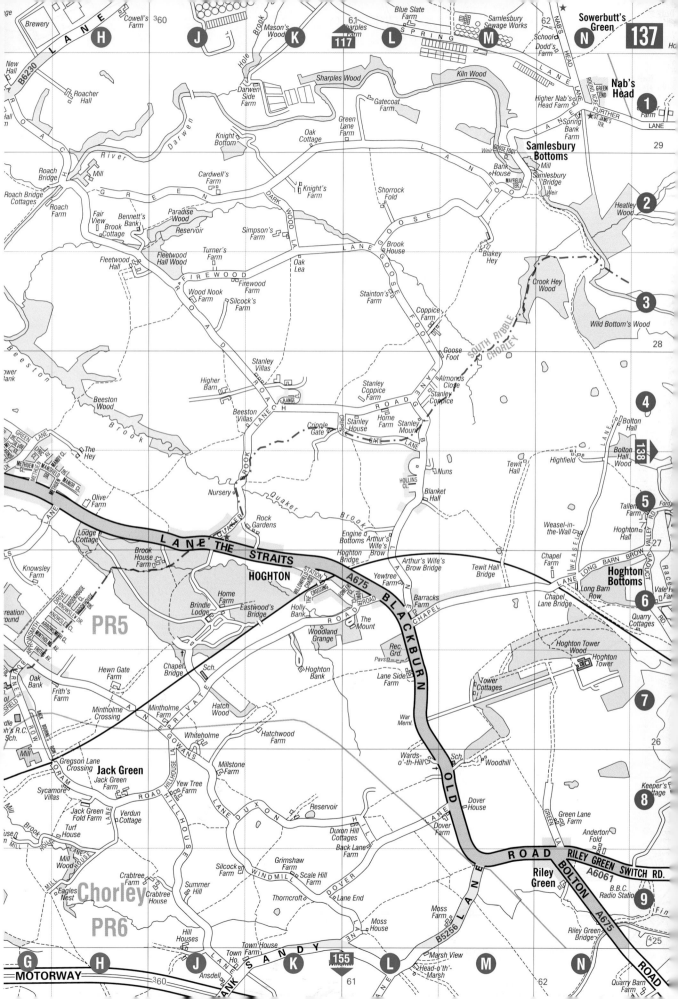

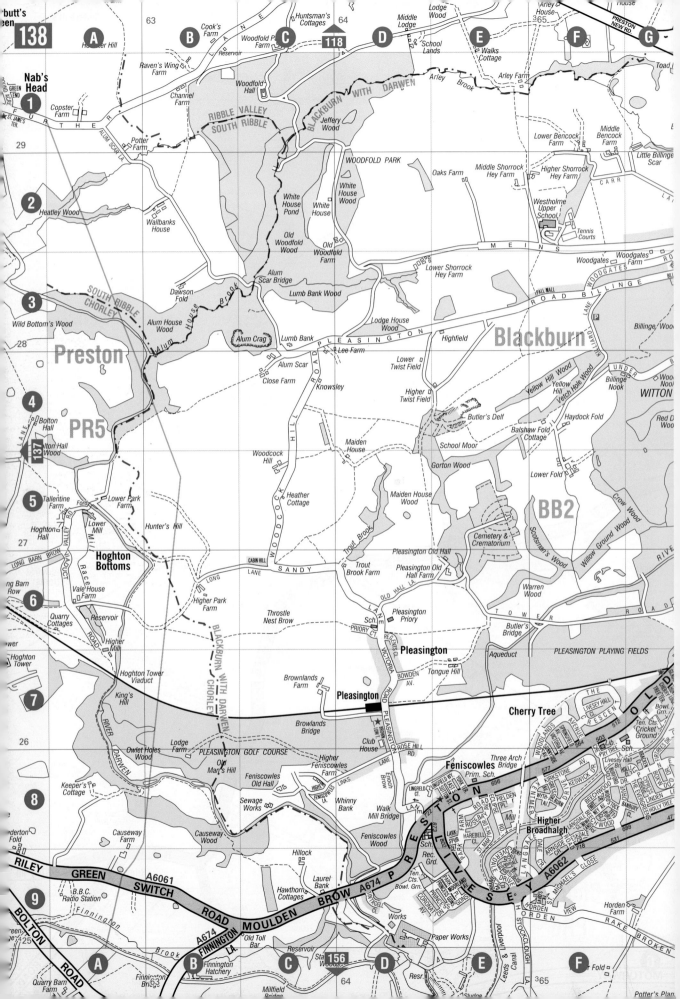

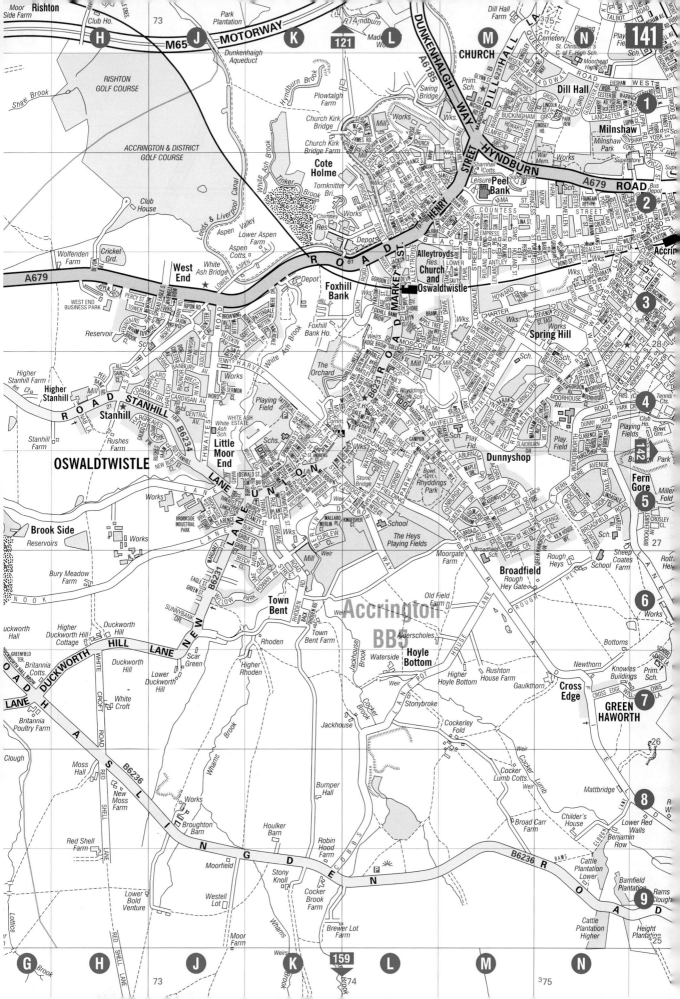

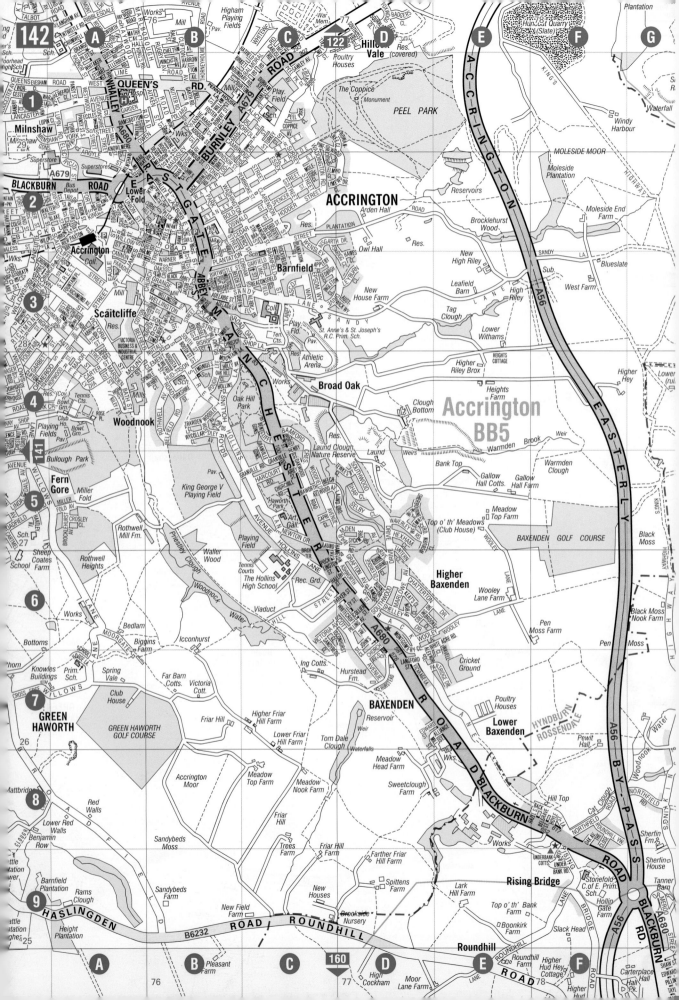

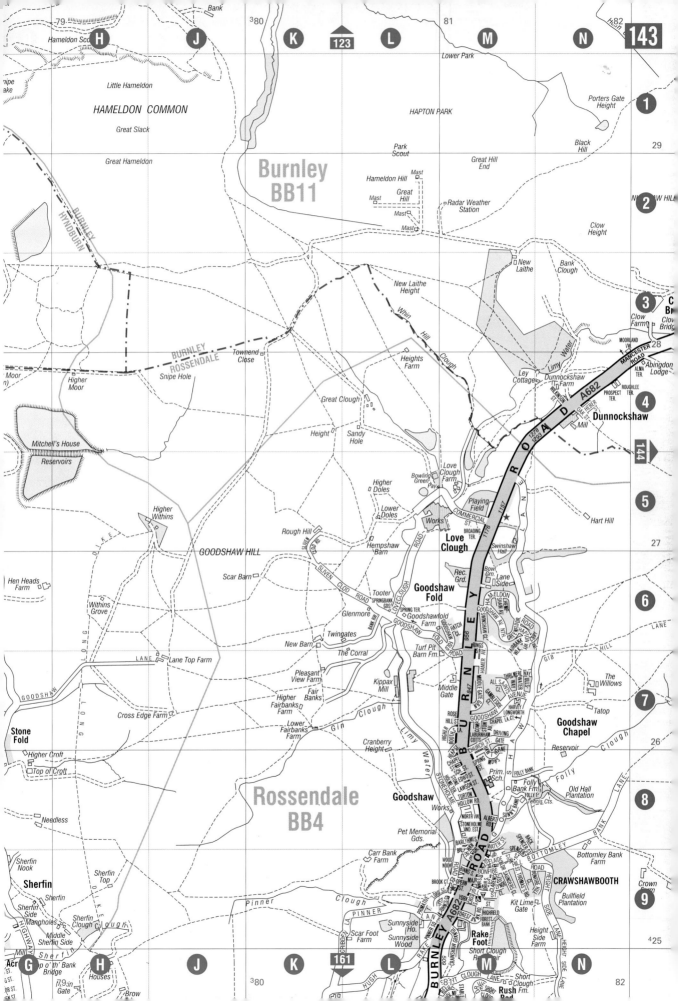

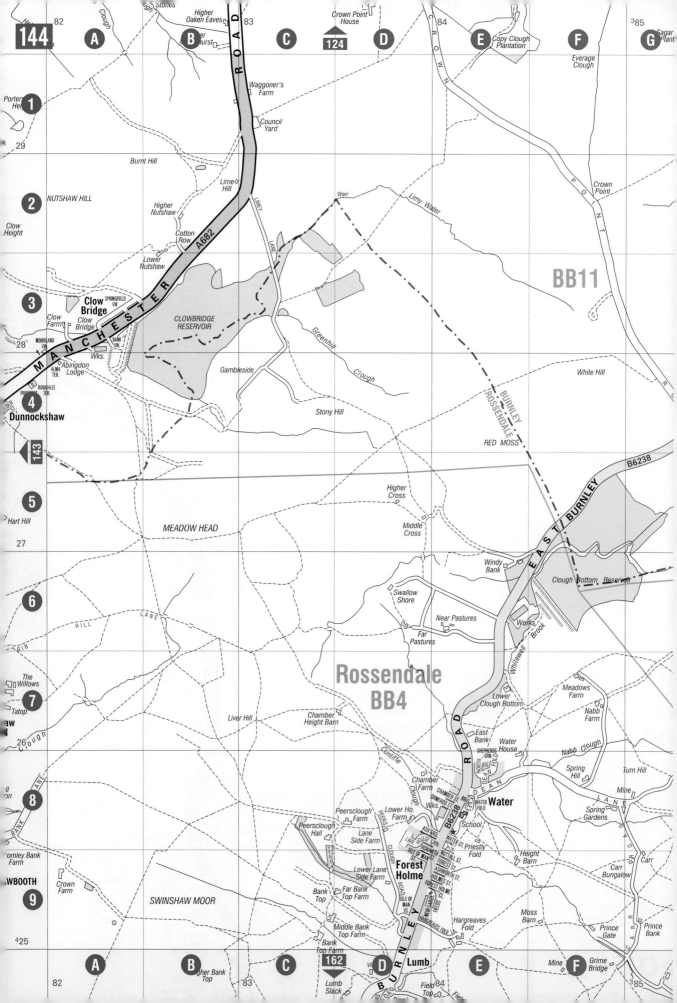

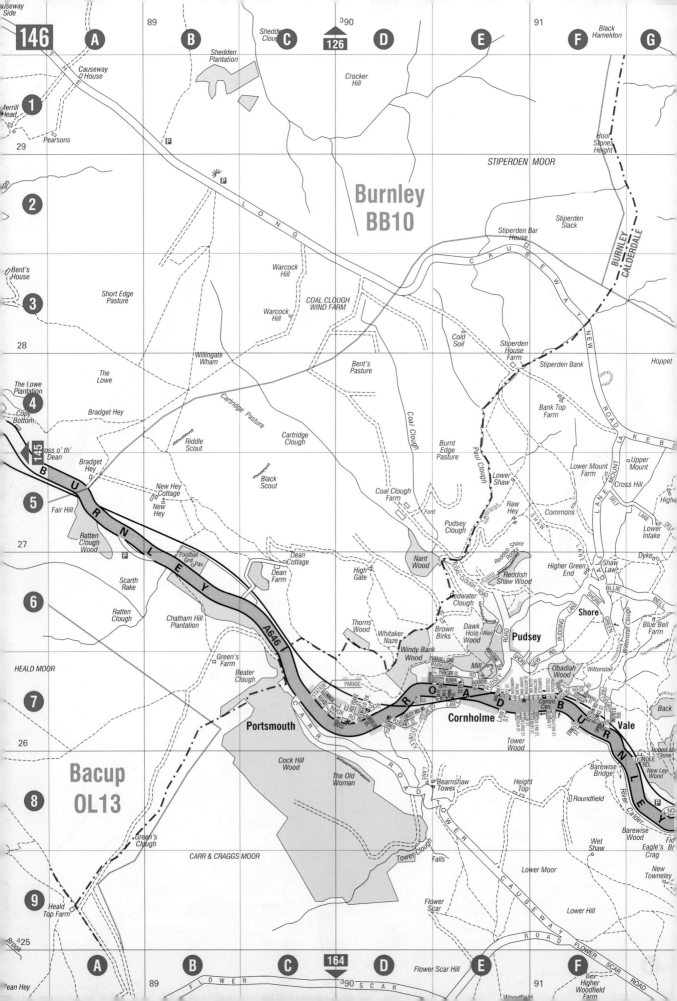

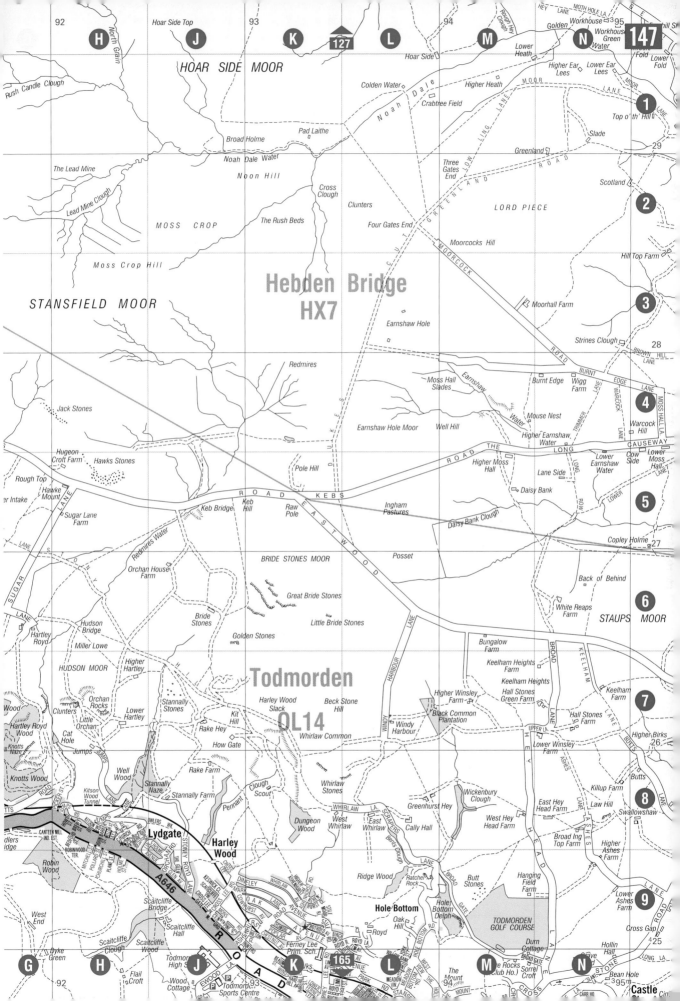

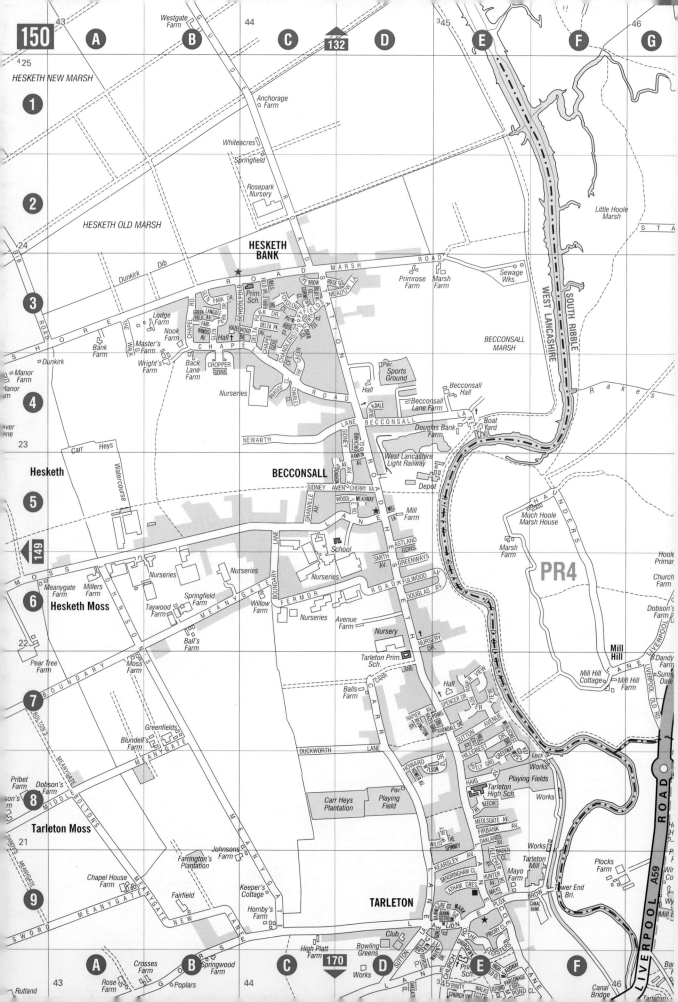

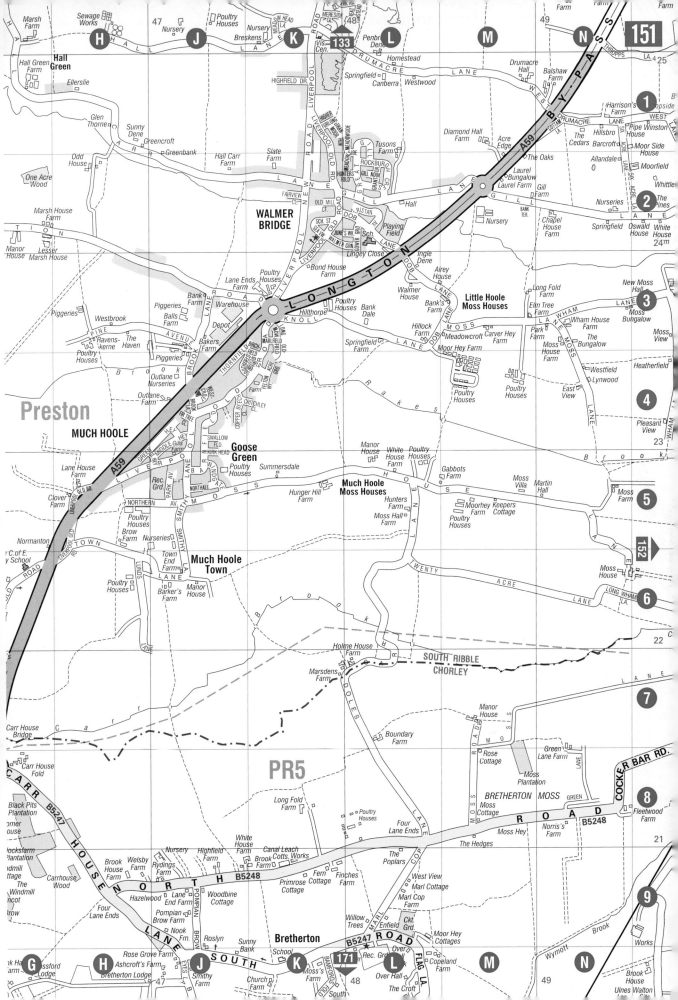

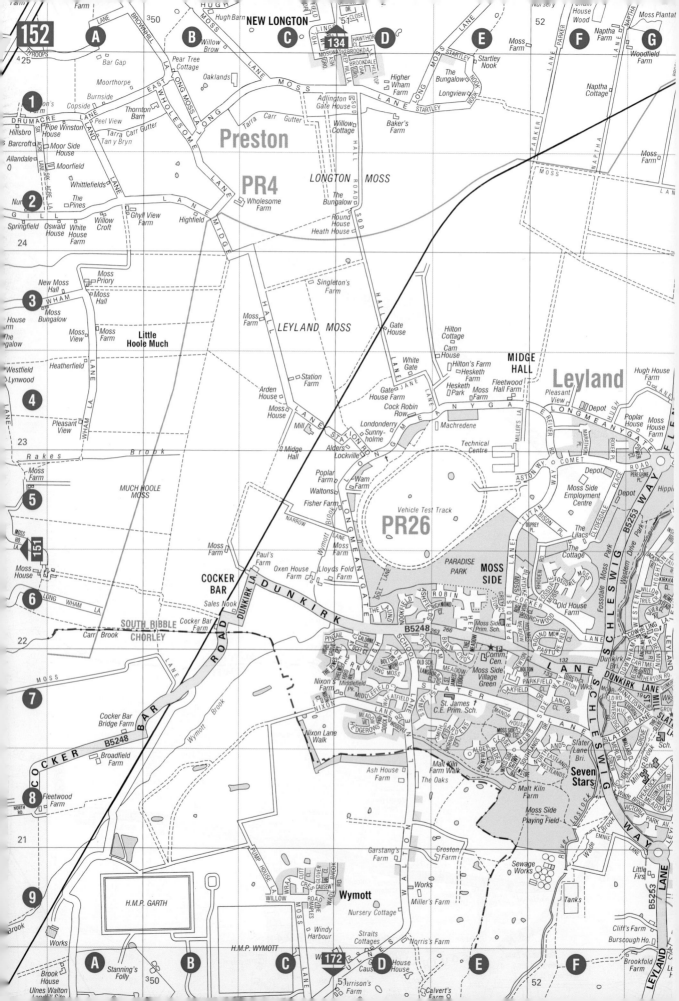

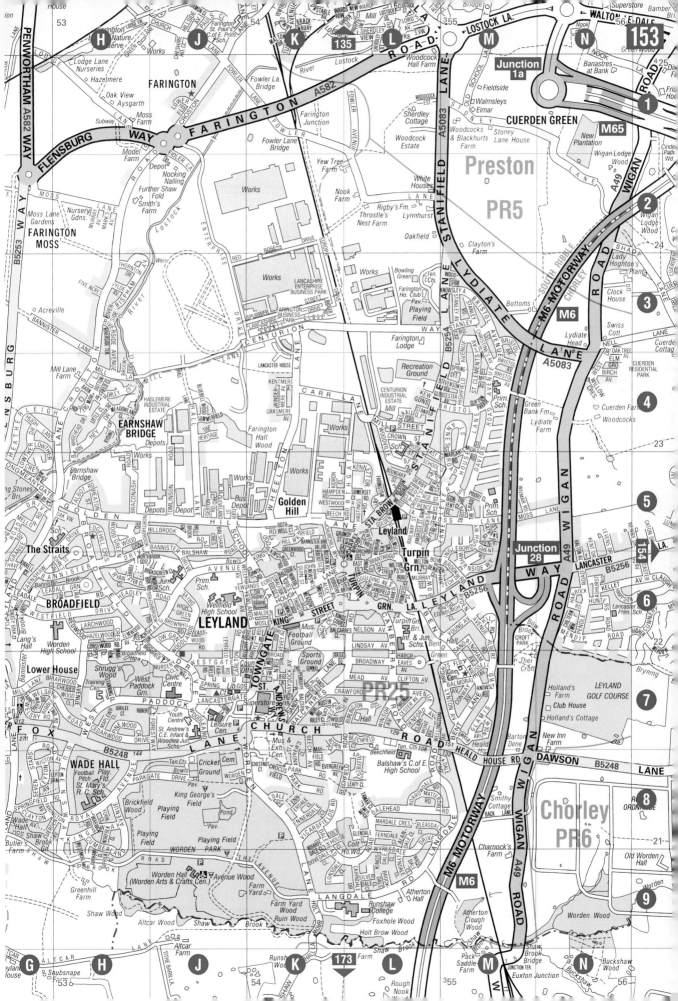

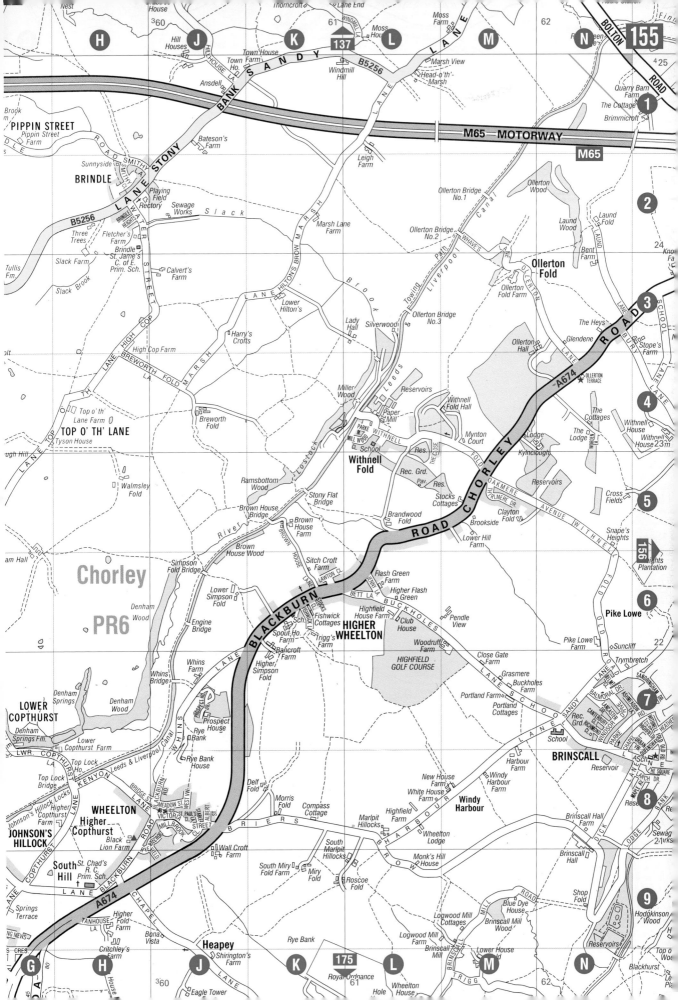

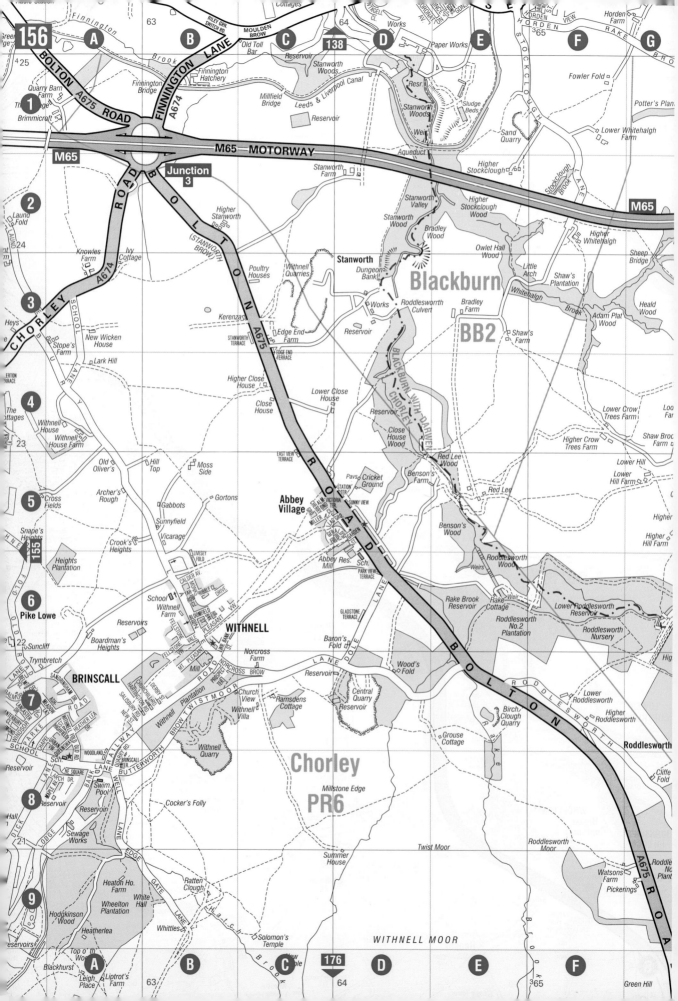

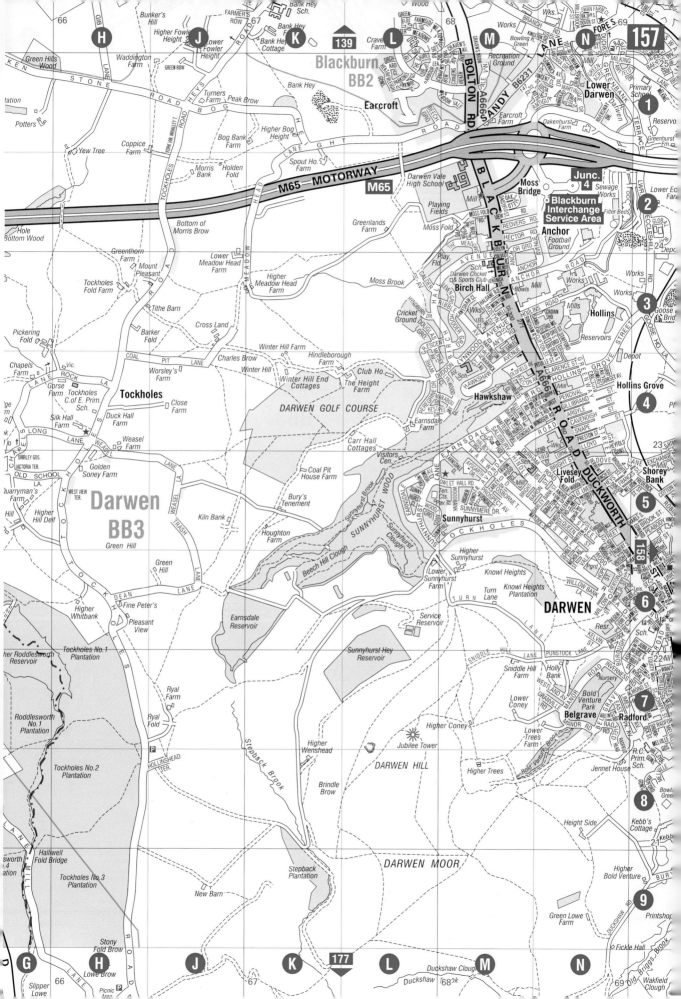

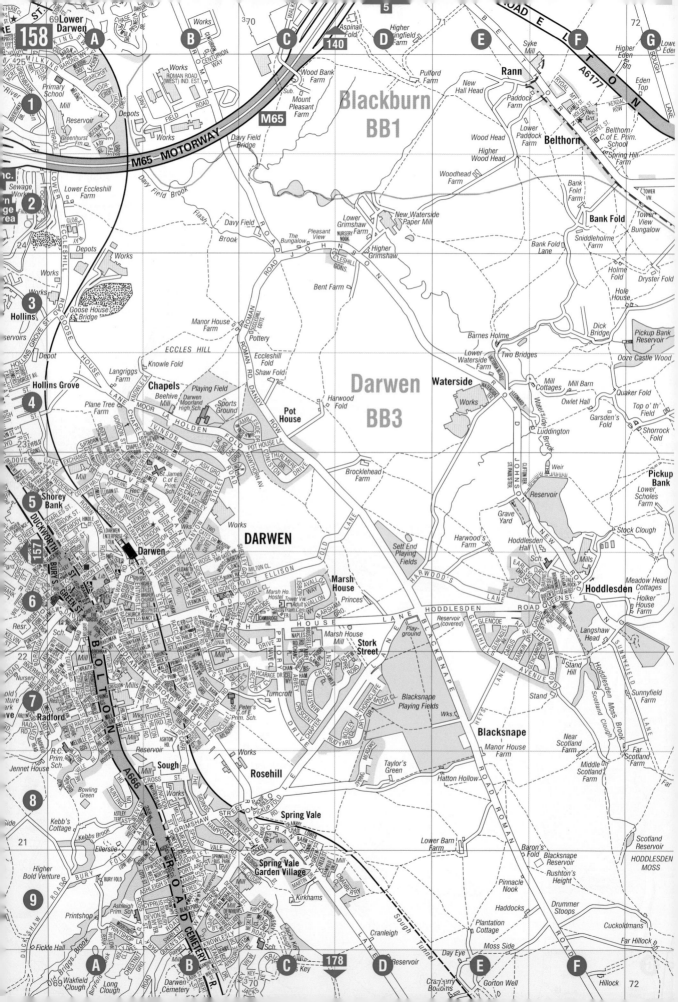

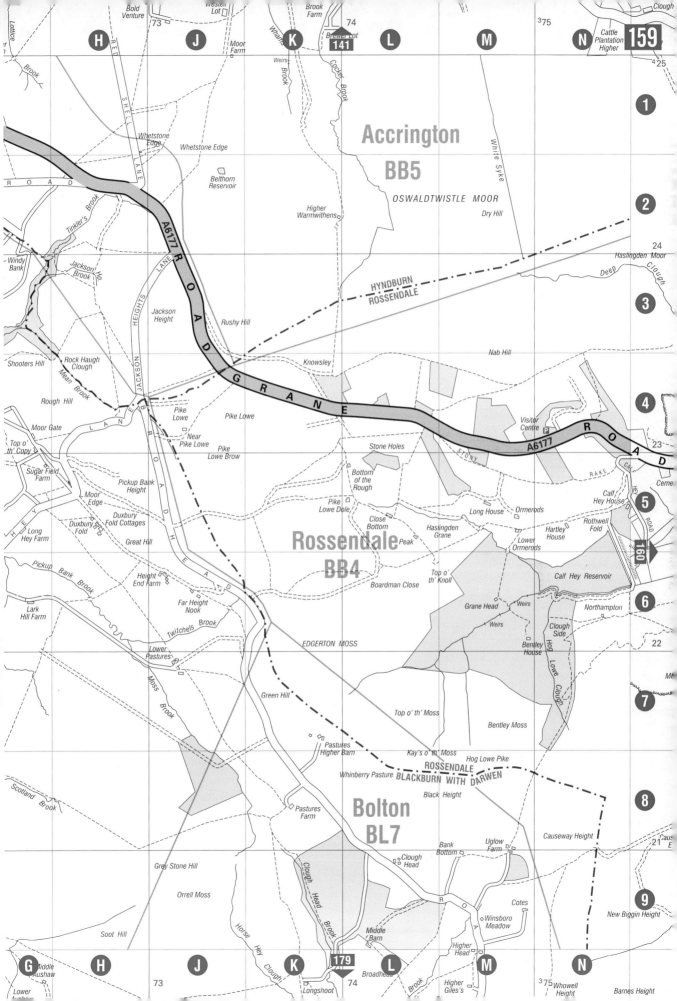

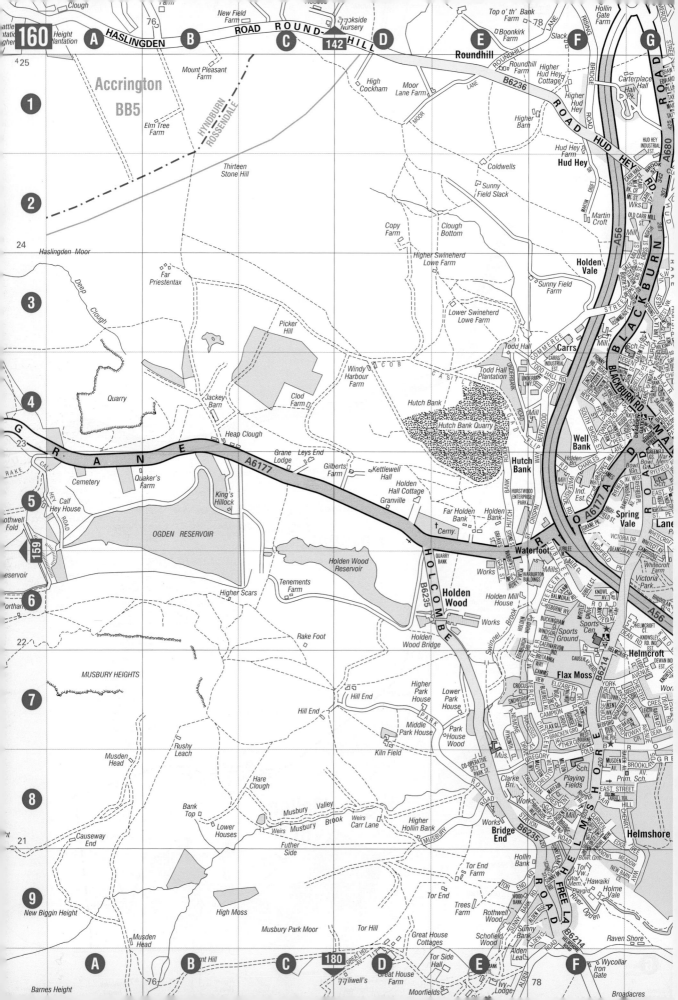

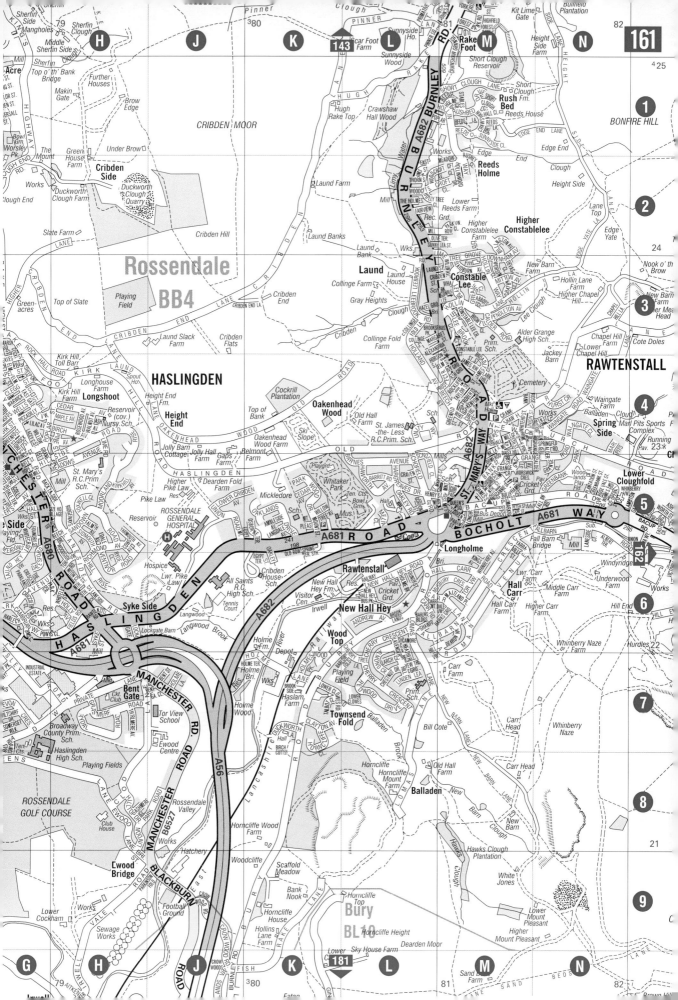

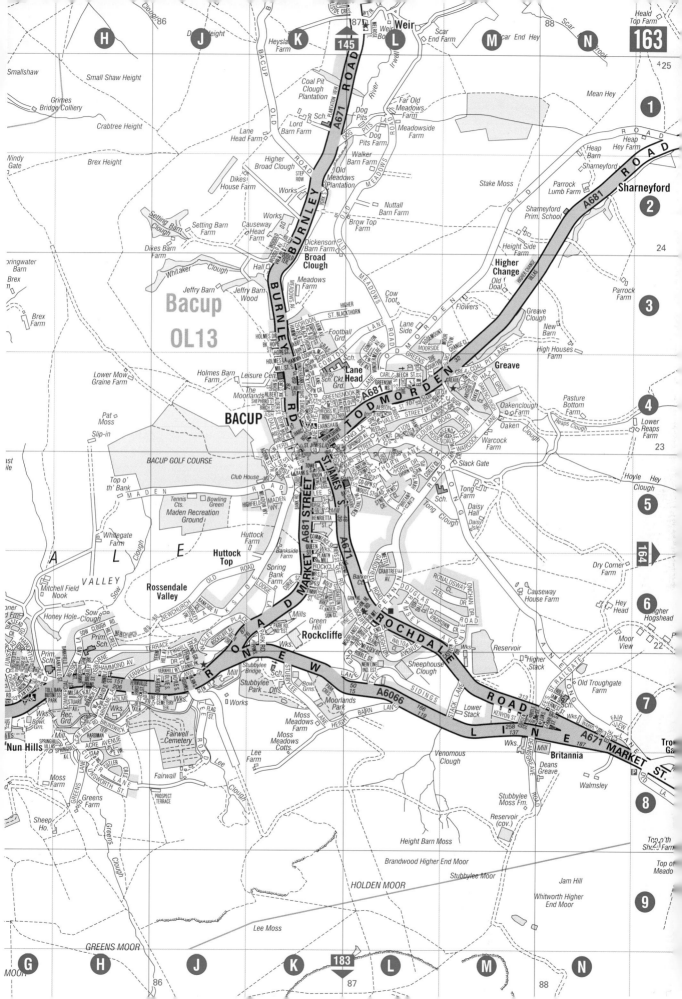

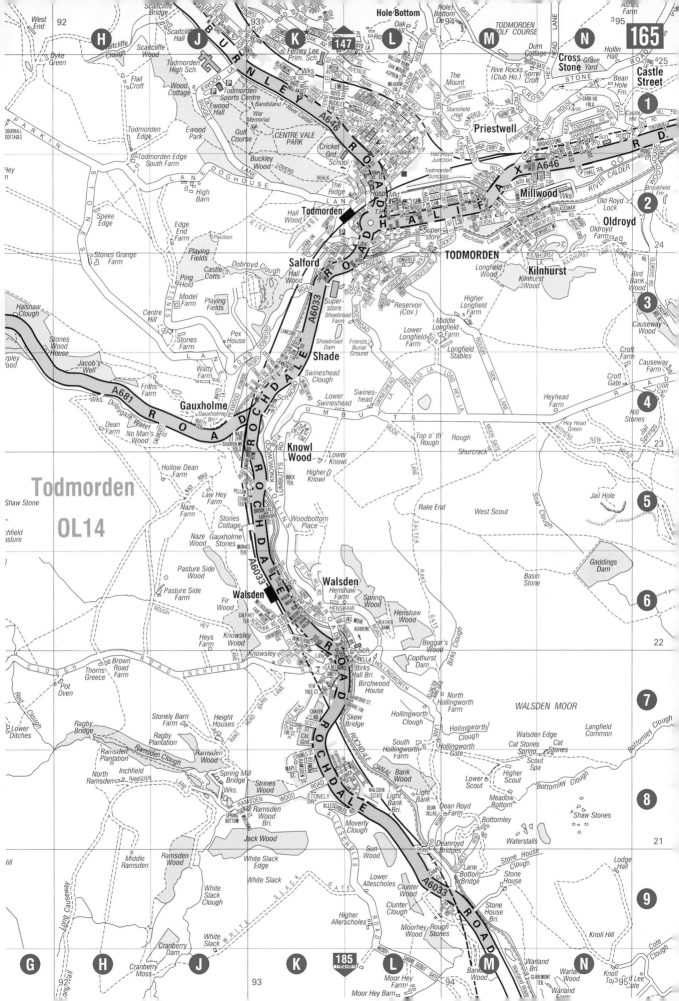

330
31
32
33

Horse Bank

1

SOUTHPORT SANDS

420

2

I R I S H

3

S E A

19

ANGRY BROW

4

5

Bog Hole

18

The Bog Breast

Pier

MARINE

Playgrou

Sea Bathing
Lake

Miniature
Golf Course

6

PRINCES PARK

Miniature
Railway

King
Garde

Southport
Zoo

Pleasureland

Coach
Park

Bowling
Greens

LOWER

7

Public
Baths

ESPLANADE

MARINE DR

MARINE

Road

KINGSWA

SOUTHPORT

VICTORIA

WAY

Superstore

17

Bowling
Greens

VICTORIA PARK

Bandstand

THE
BEACH

PRIORY GDNS

SANDS

Tennis
Courts

8

Dunes

Sunnymede
Sch.

ROAD

LORD ST WEST

CASTLE

BELMONT

TUDOR DONNINGTON
MANS. LODGE

ST PAULS

SOUTHERN

ROAD

WW
121

BEACH
MEWS

Kingswood
Sch.

PROMENADE

COASTAL

ROAD

HOLLY

NURSE

TWISTFIELD

GLOUCESTER

A565

CLAIRVILLE

B5209

9

BIRKDALE

WEST

CAMBERLEY CL

ASCOT

ROAD

WESTCLIFFE

BLANDFORD
RD

WARREN CT

PALATINE
RD

ROAD

GRENVO

ALIGHTON

ROAD

16

DUNES

PALACE

Sunshine
House
Sch.

OXFORD
RD

WESTBOURNE

DROITWICH

SAXON

PRINCE
CHARLES

SAXENHOLME

SOUTHERN

CARNE

PRIOR

330
31
32
33

186

WESTBOURNE
GDNS

COASTAL

LULWORTH

ROAD

ROAD

VICTORY
CT

ALMA S

OLIVE

Dunes

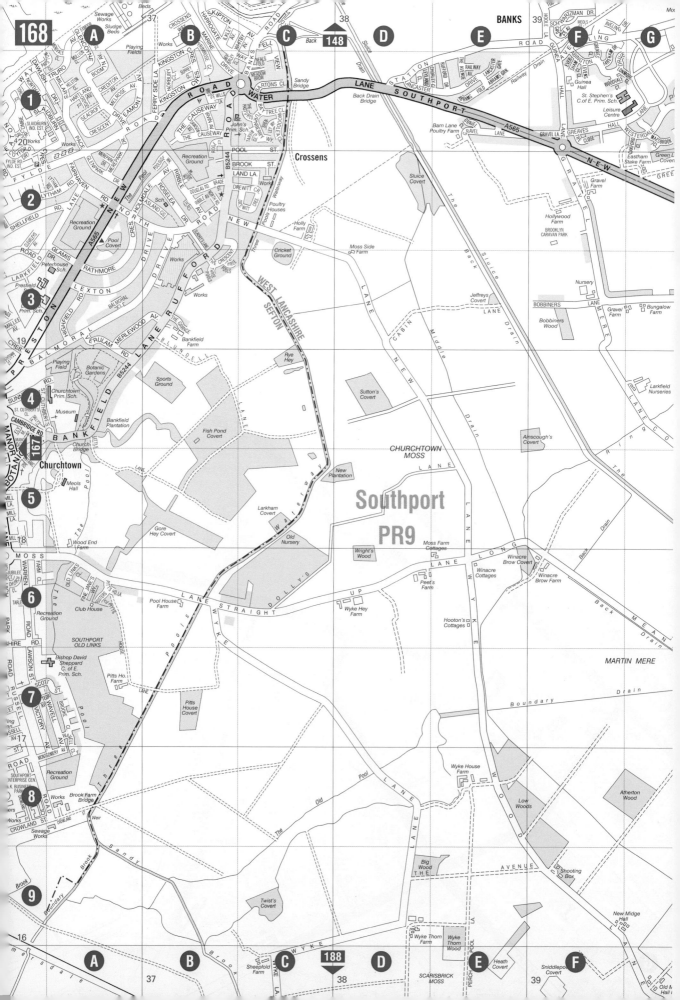

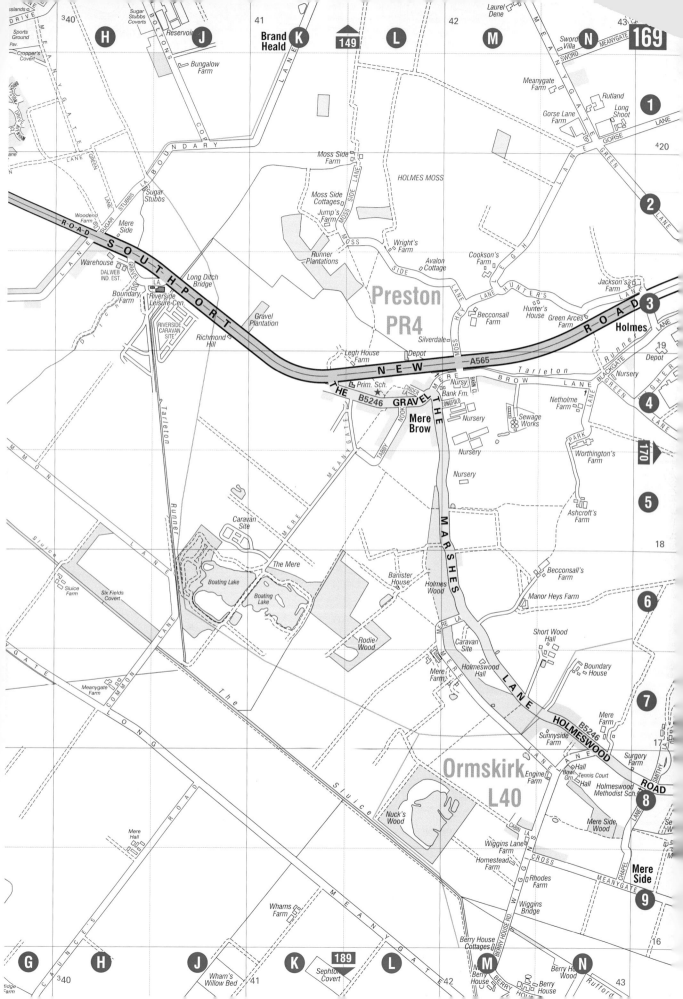

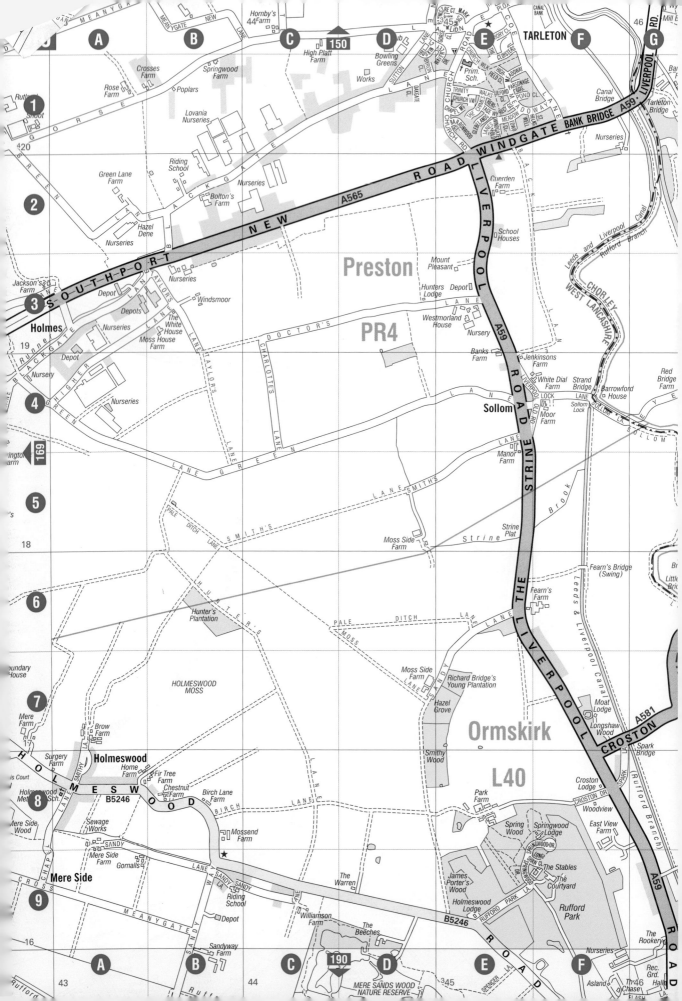

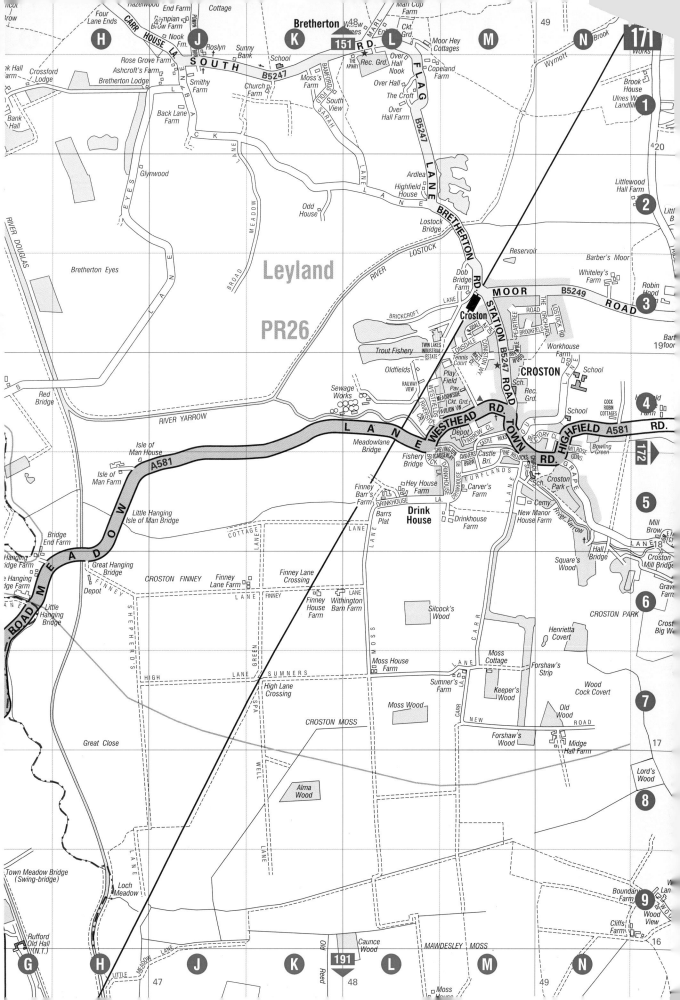

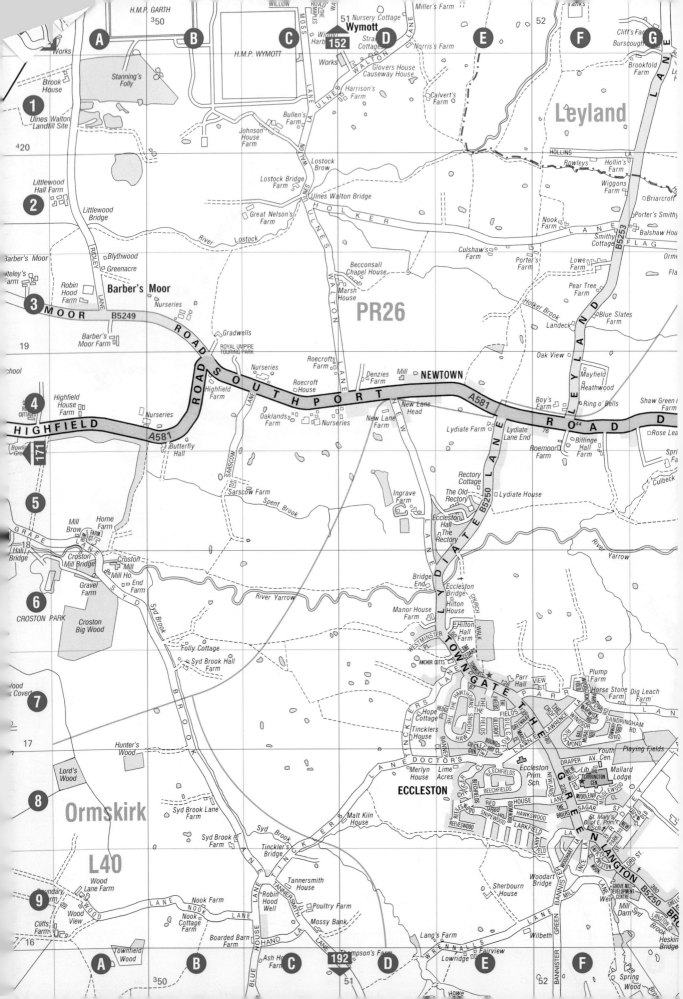

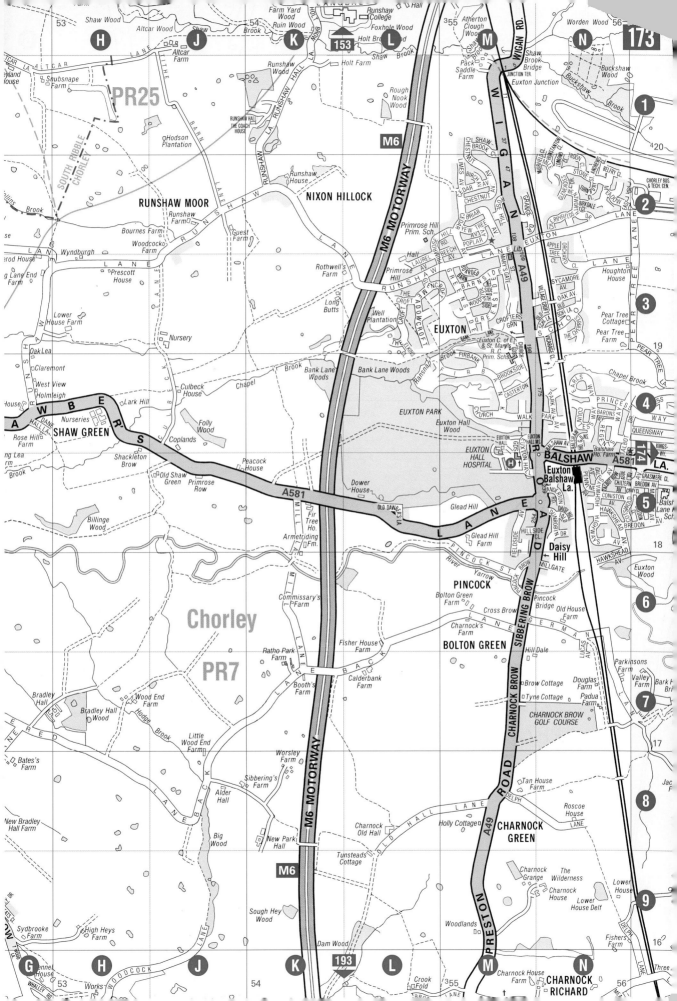

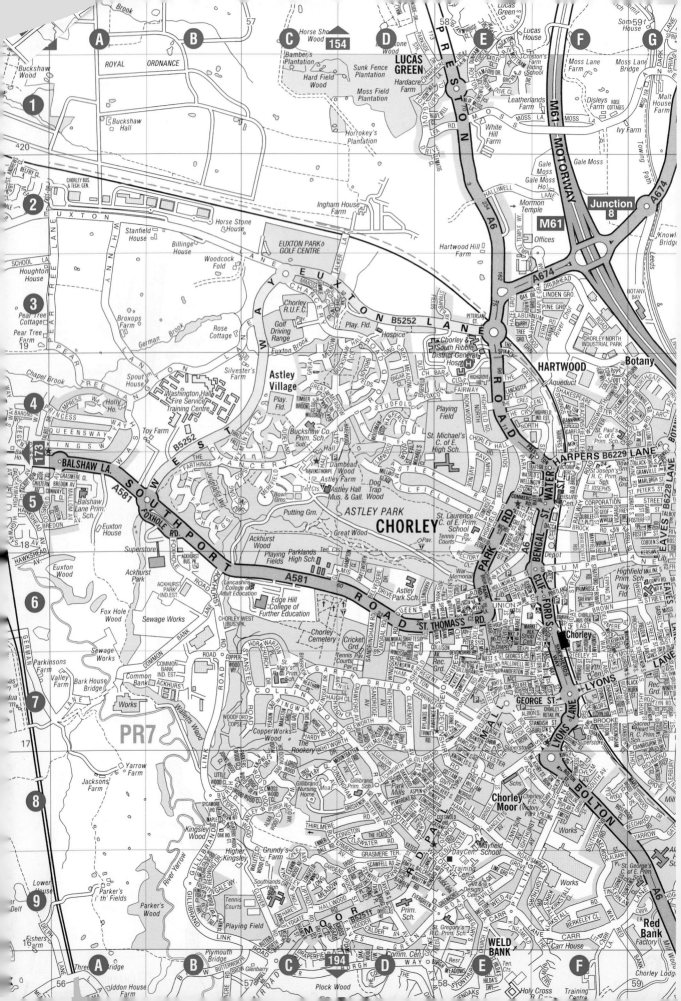

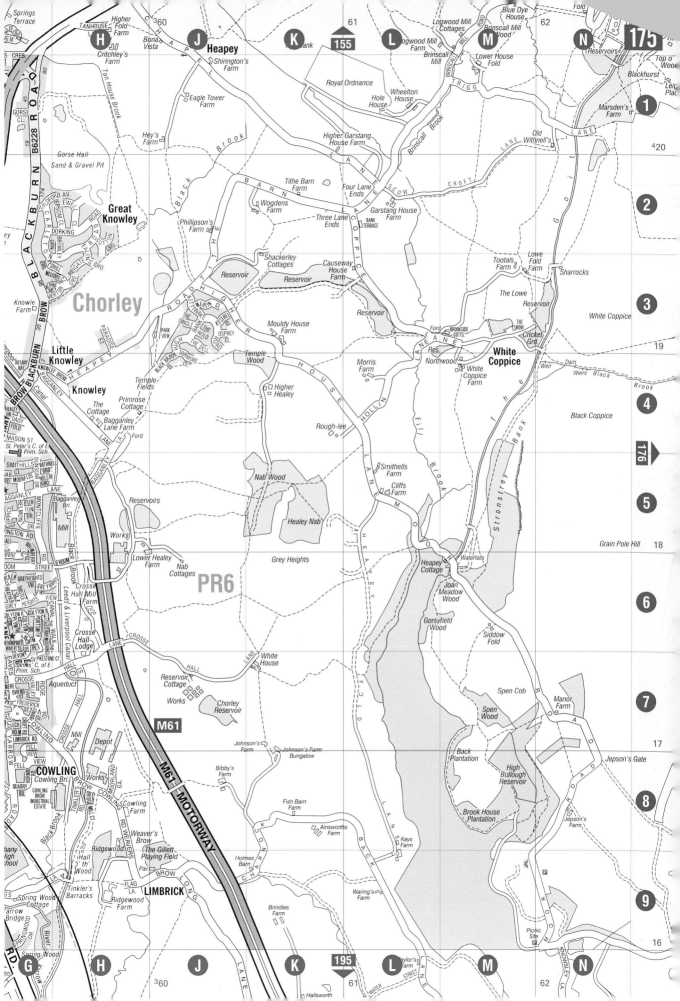

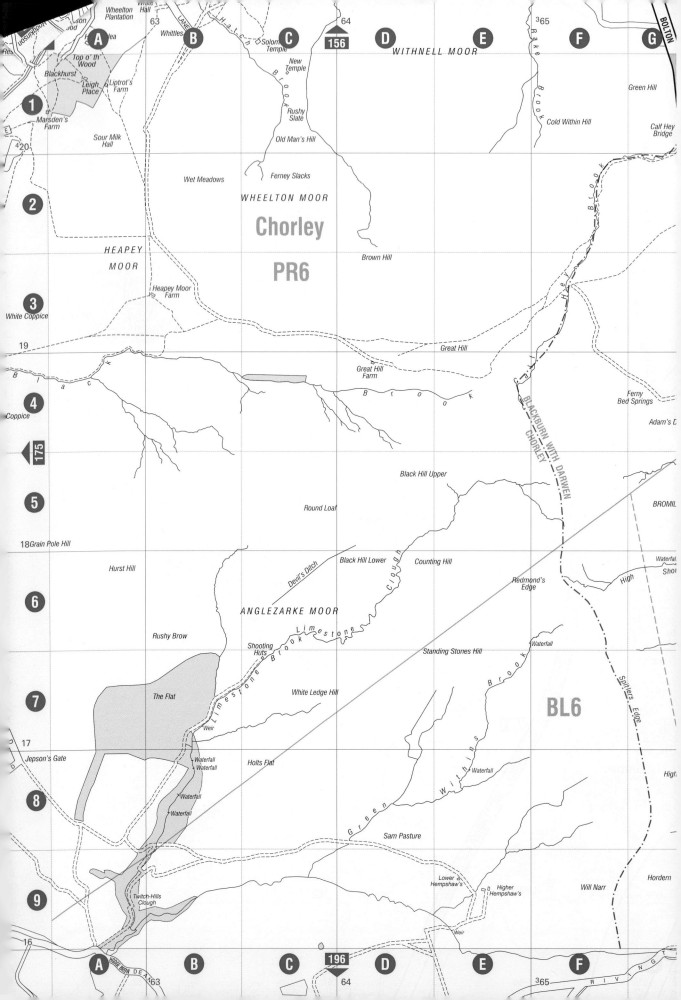

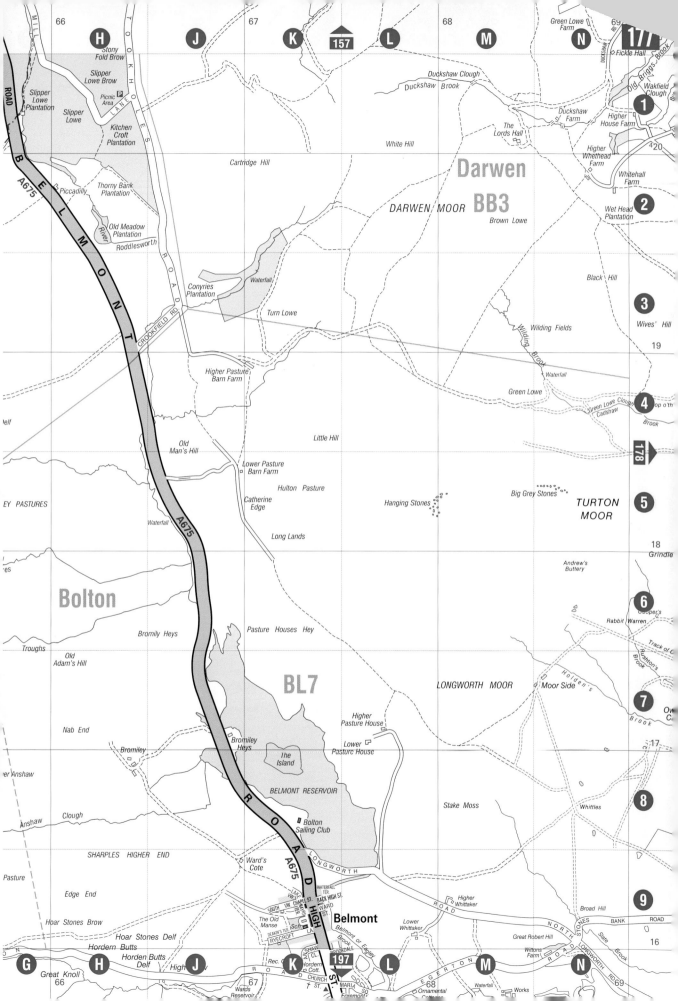

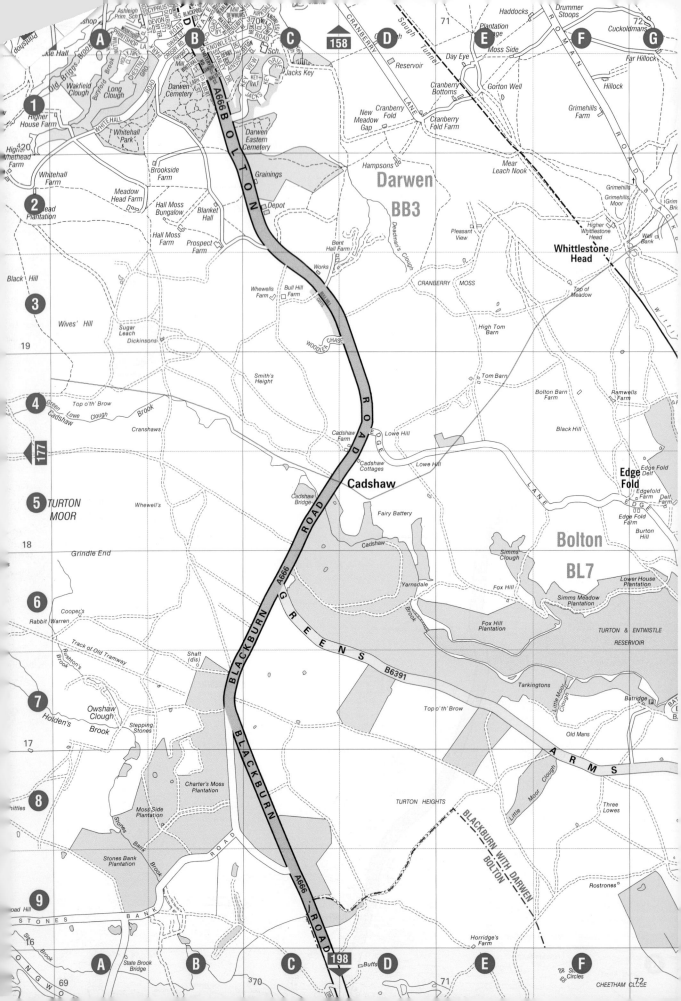

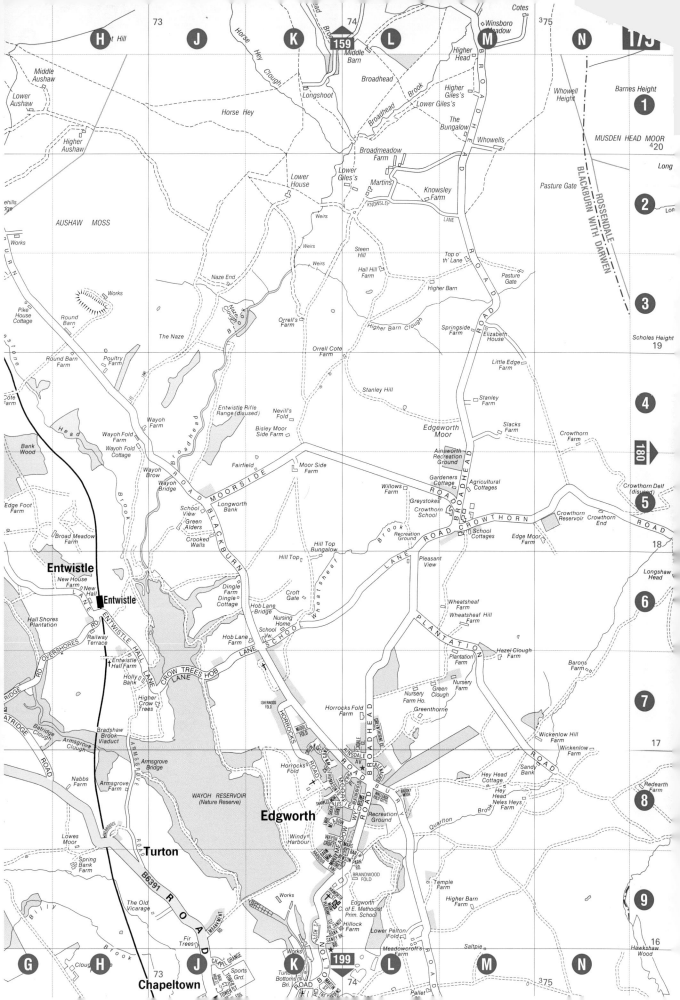

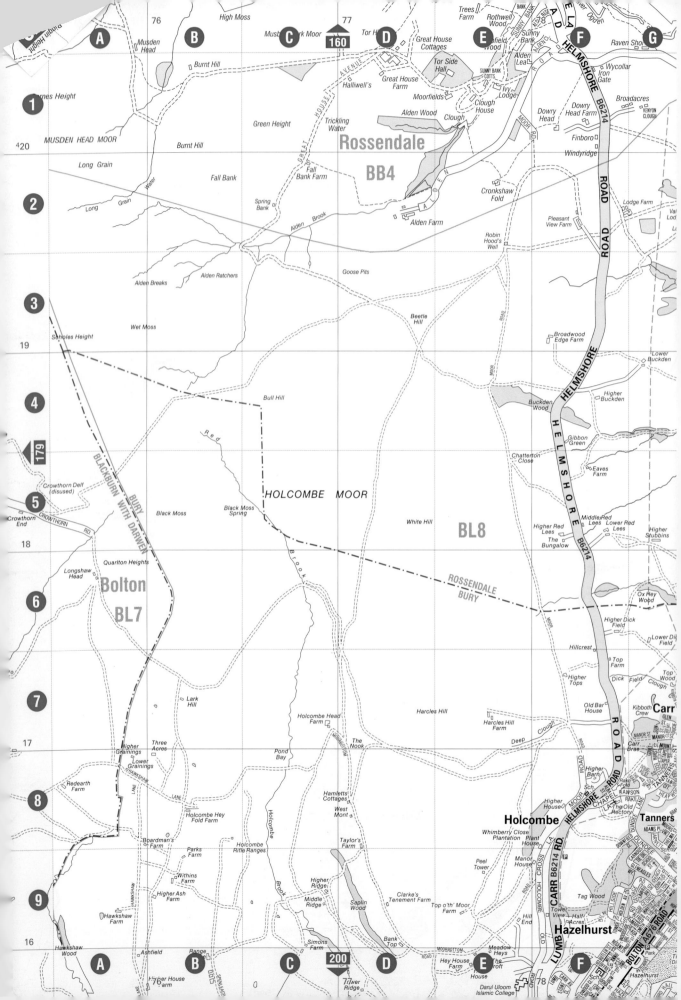

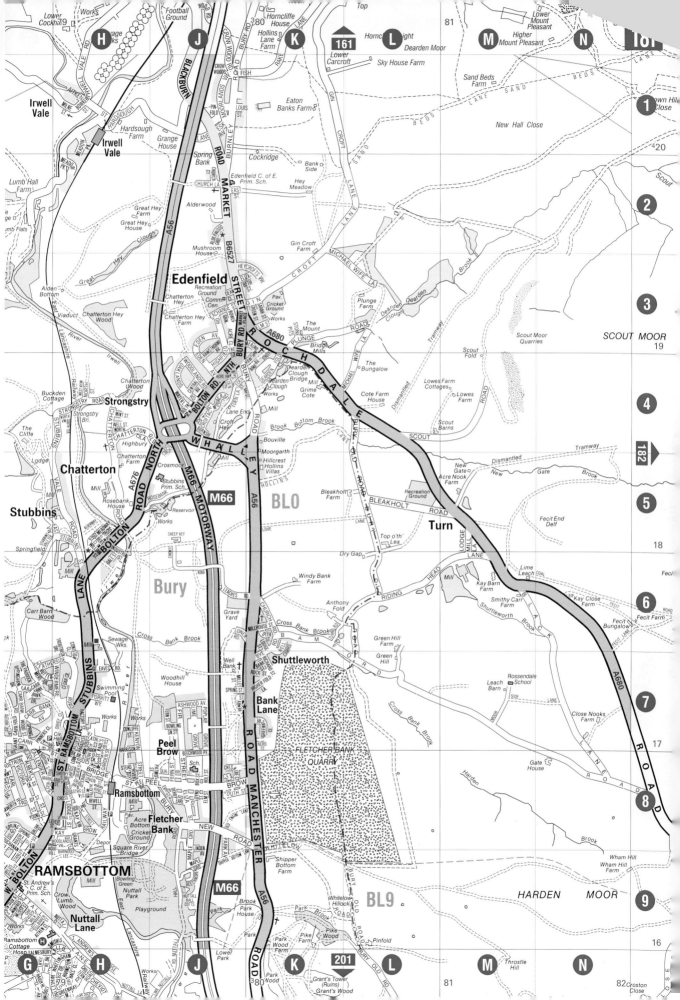

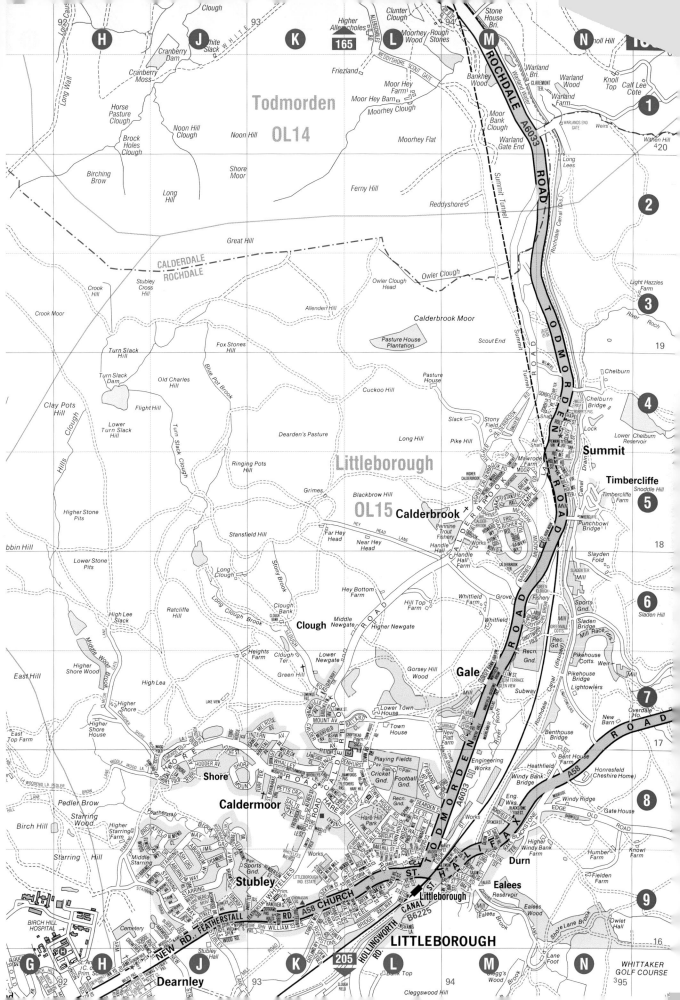

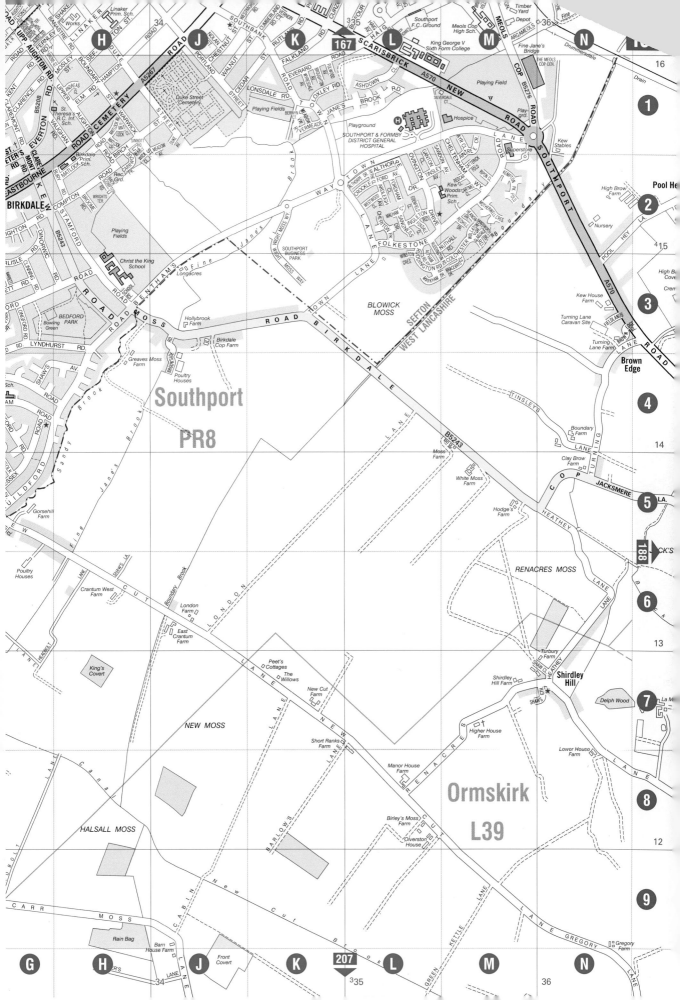

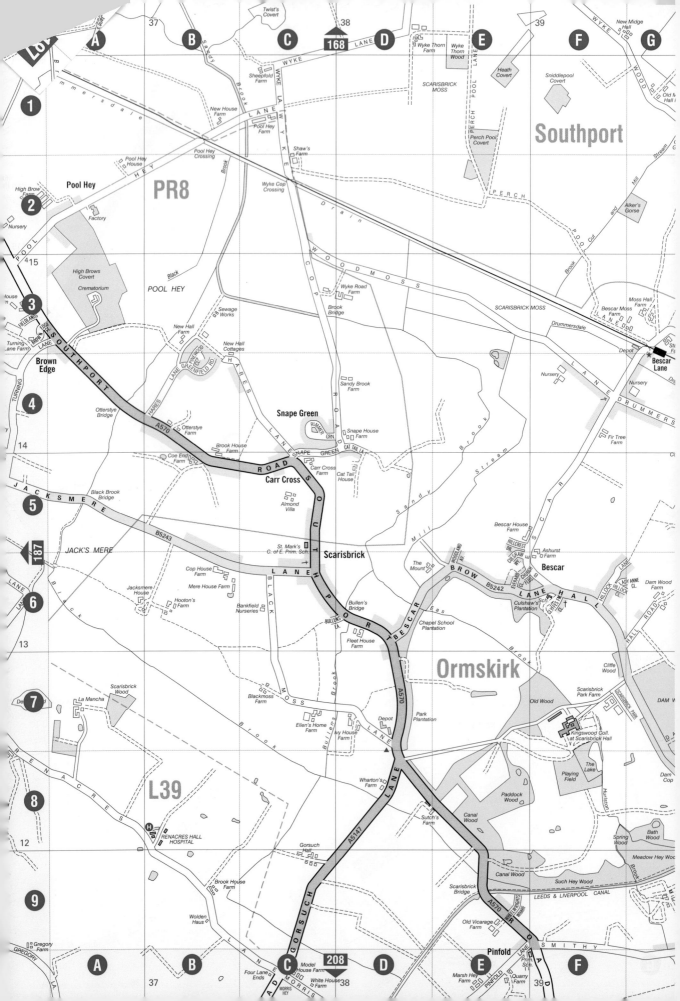

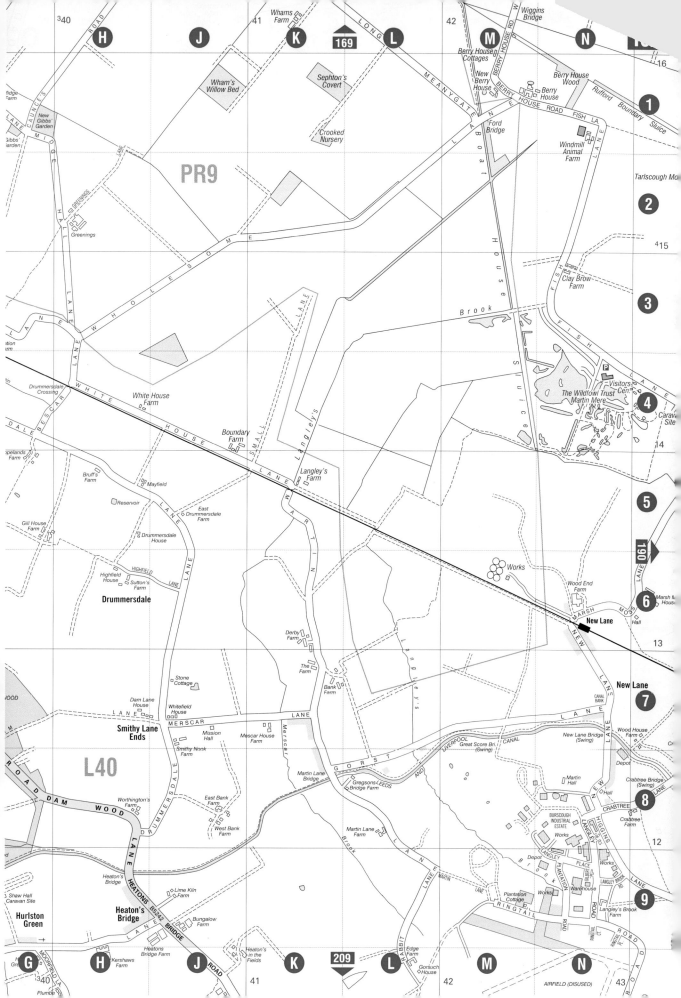

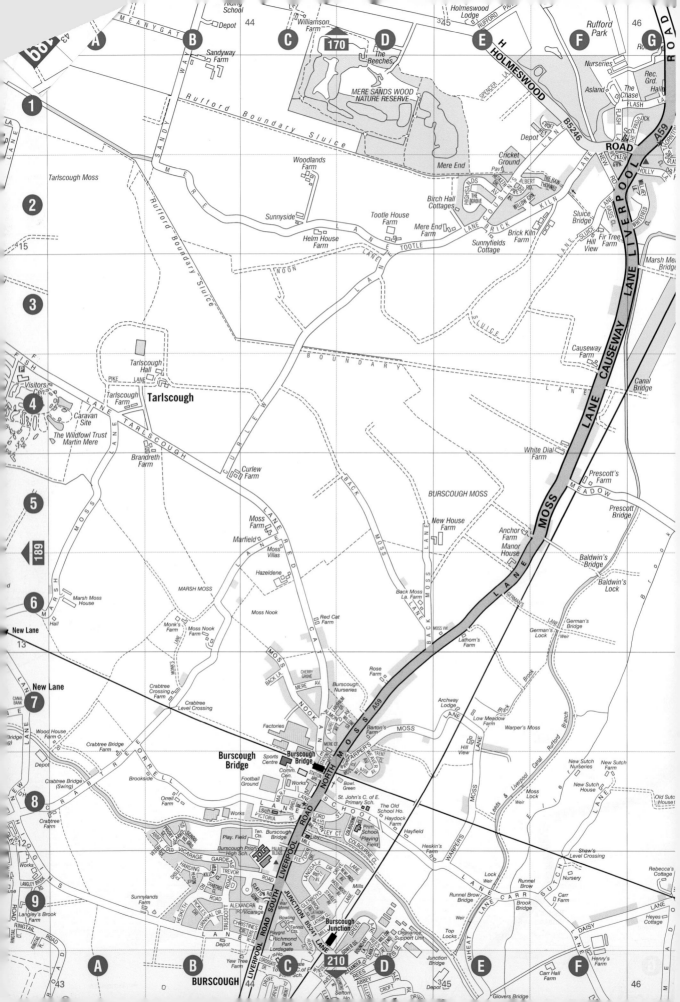

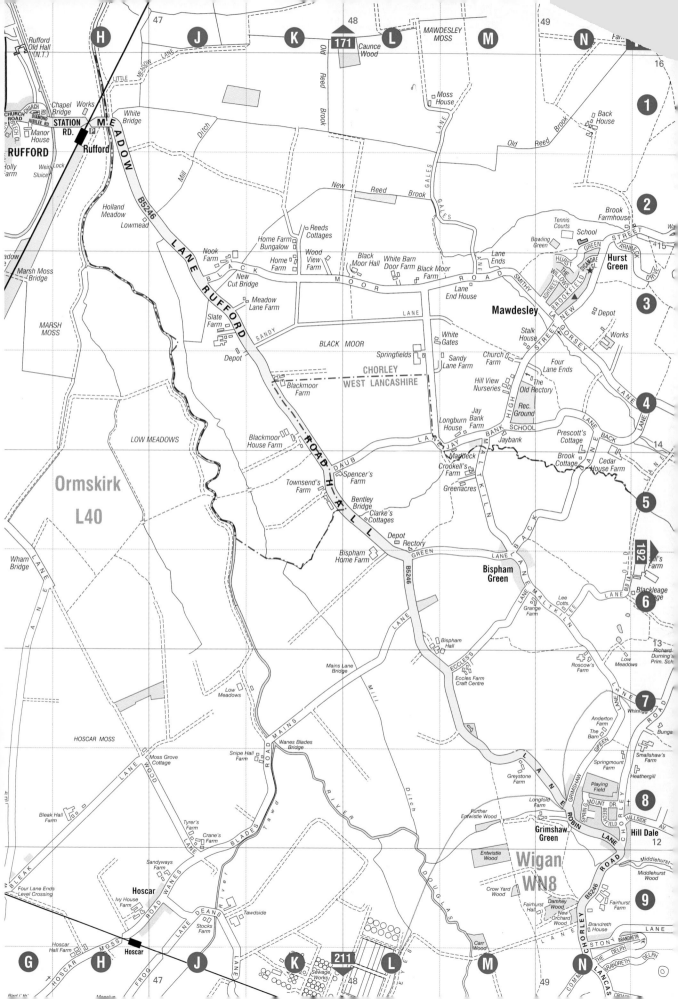

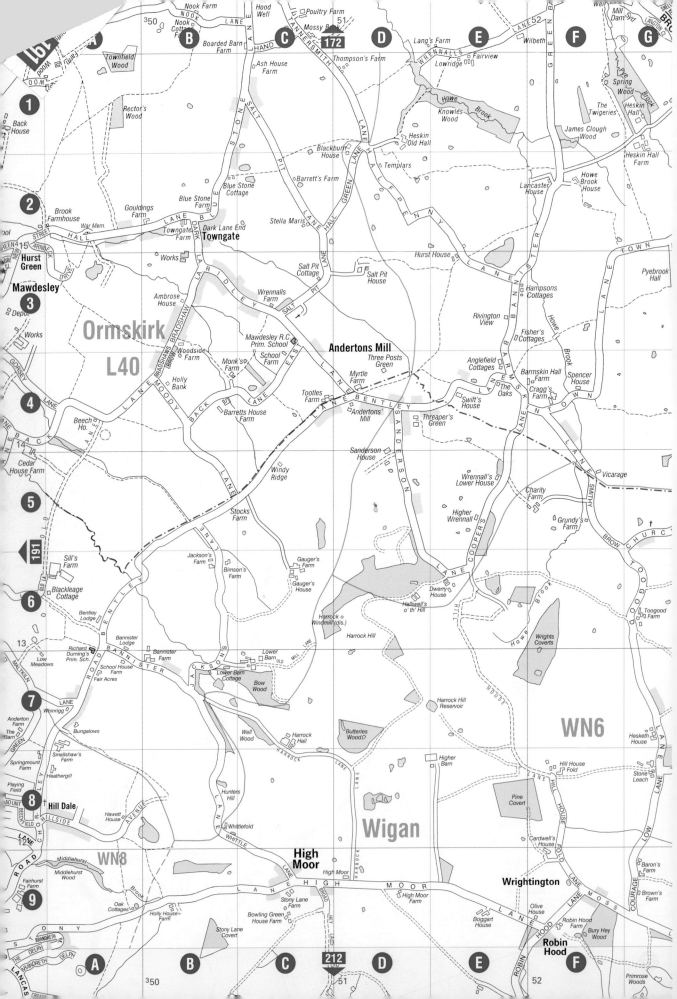

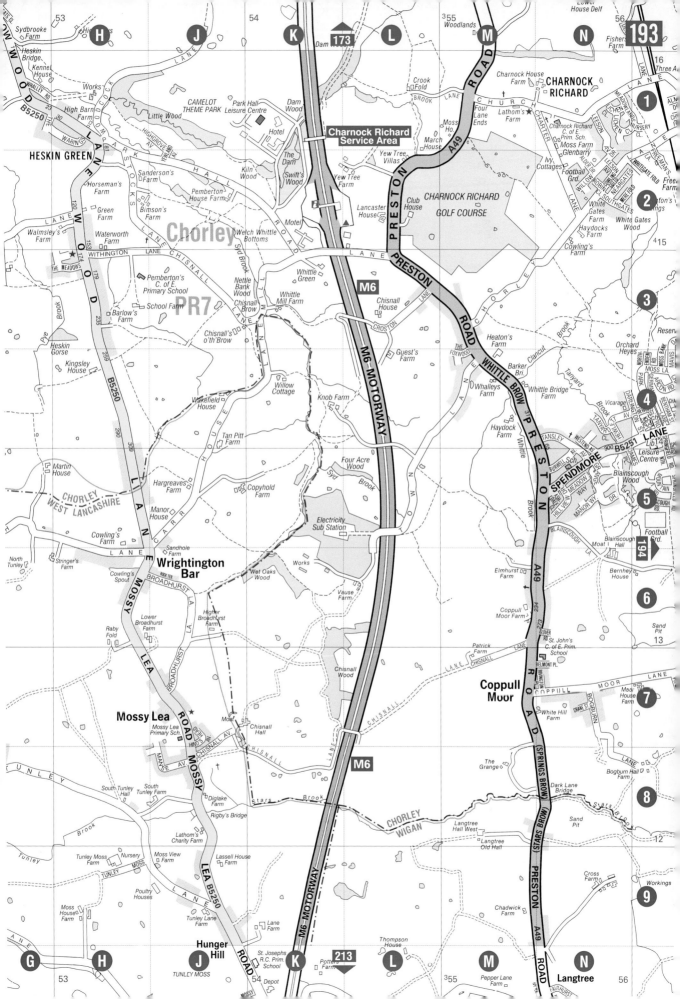

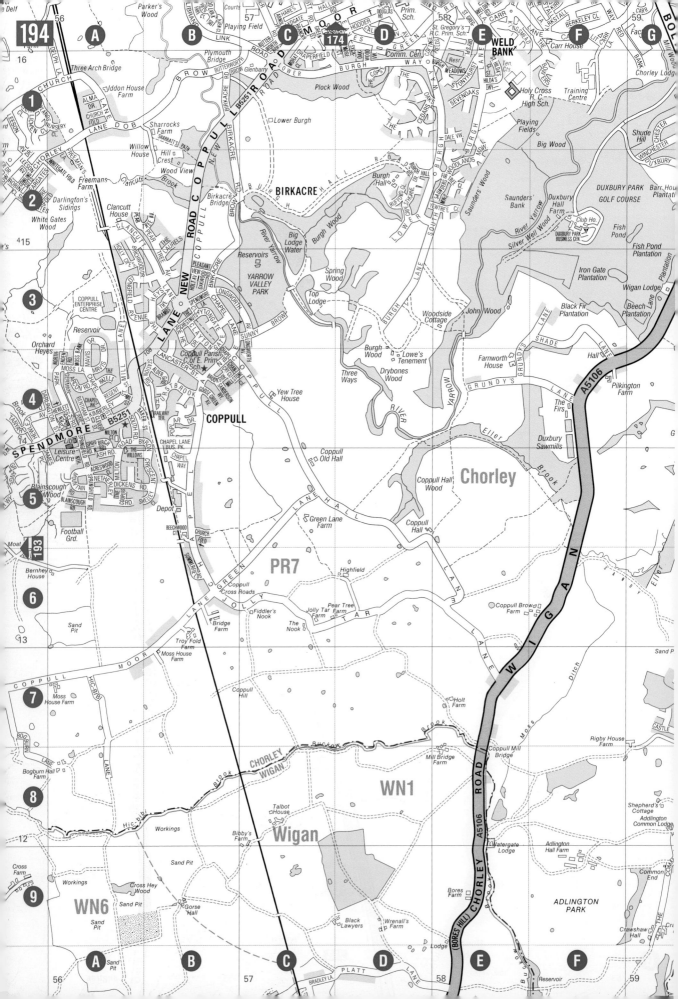

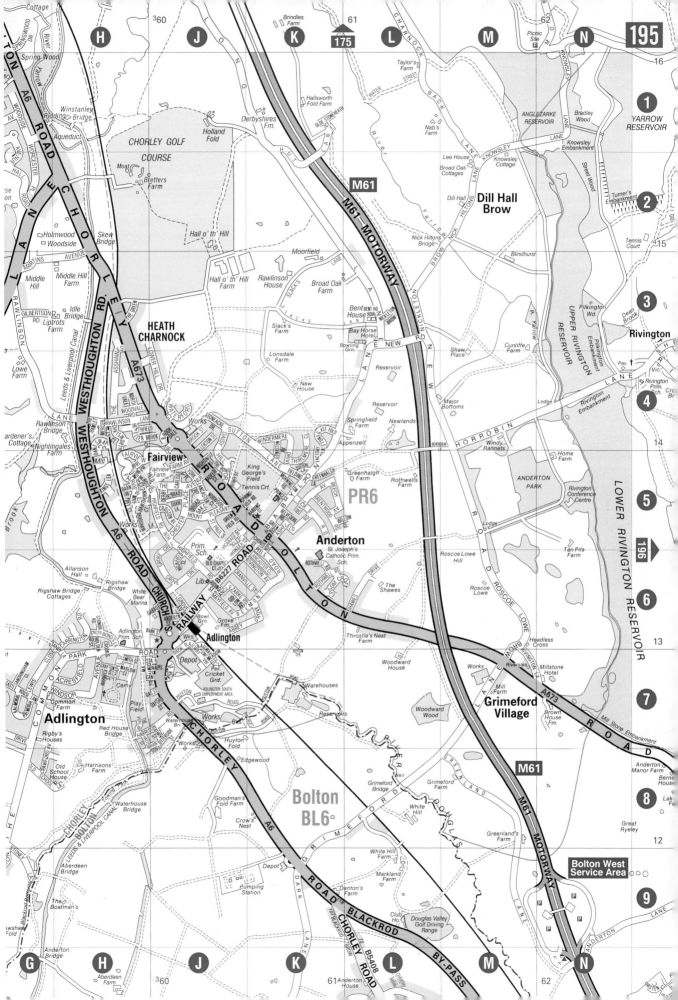

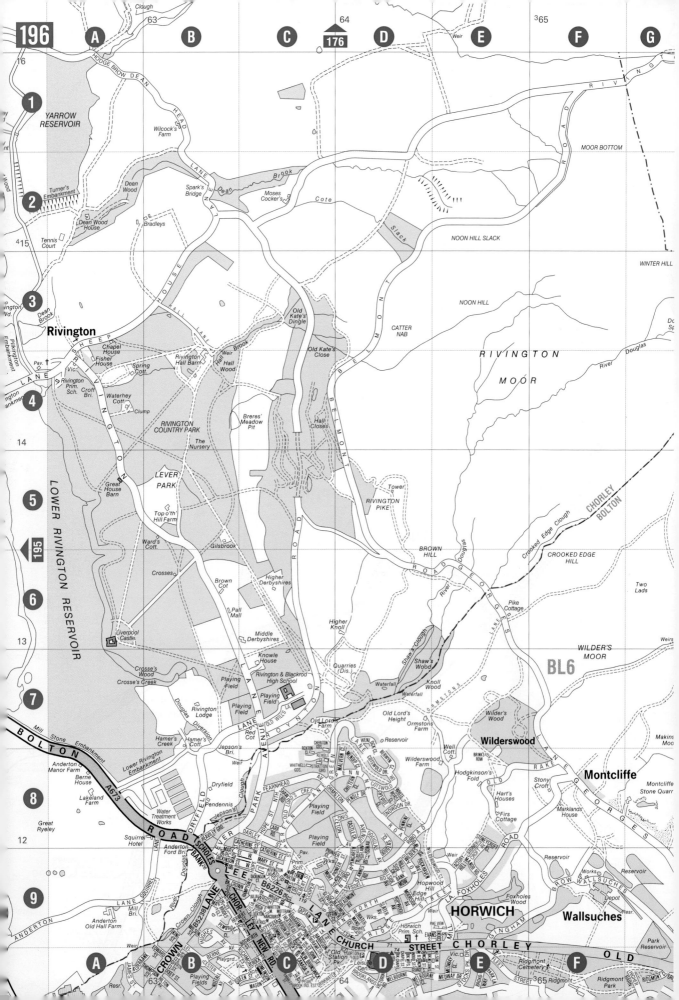

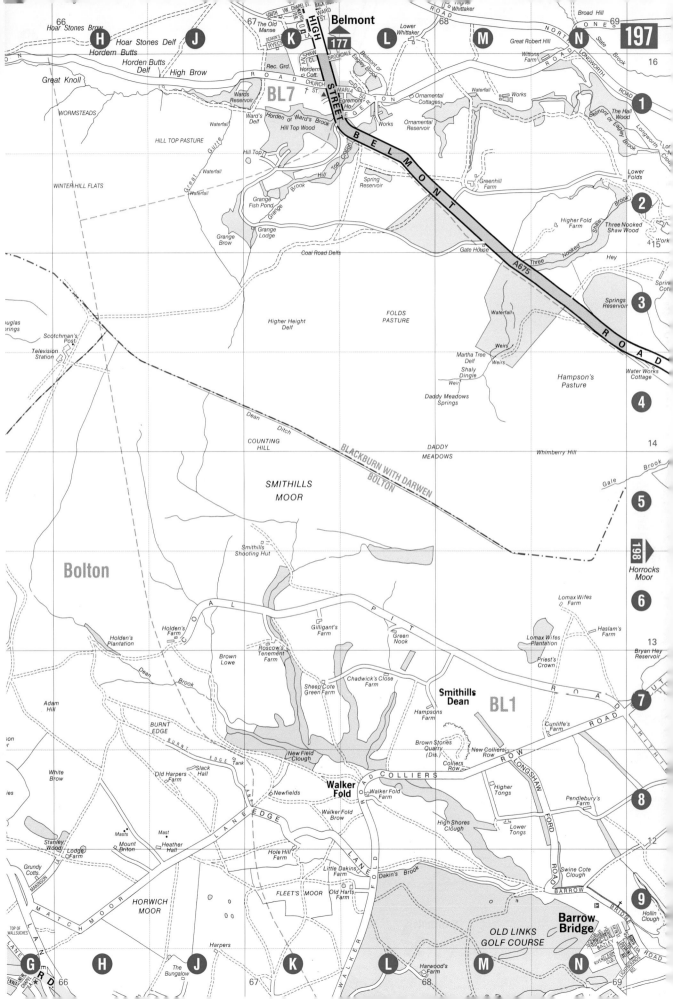

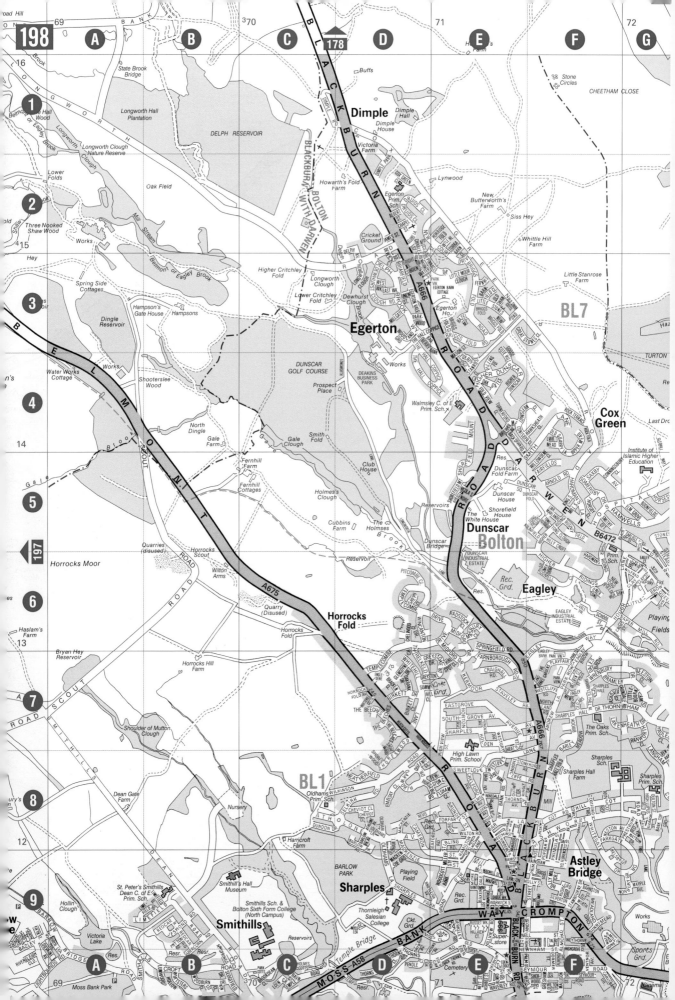

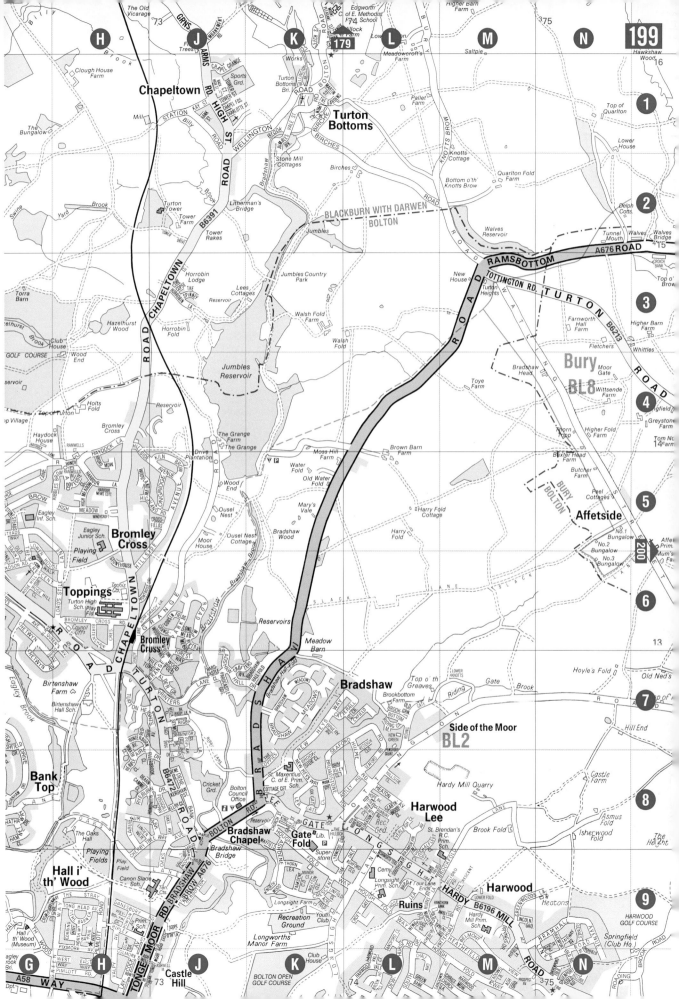

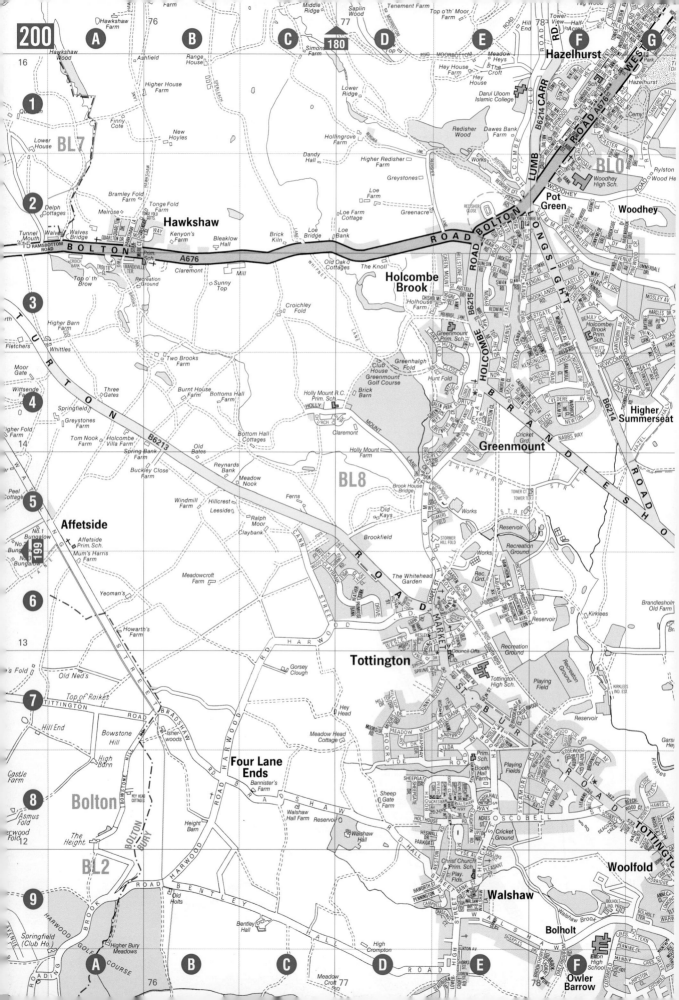

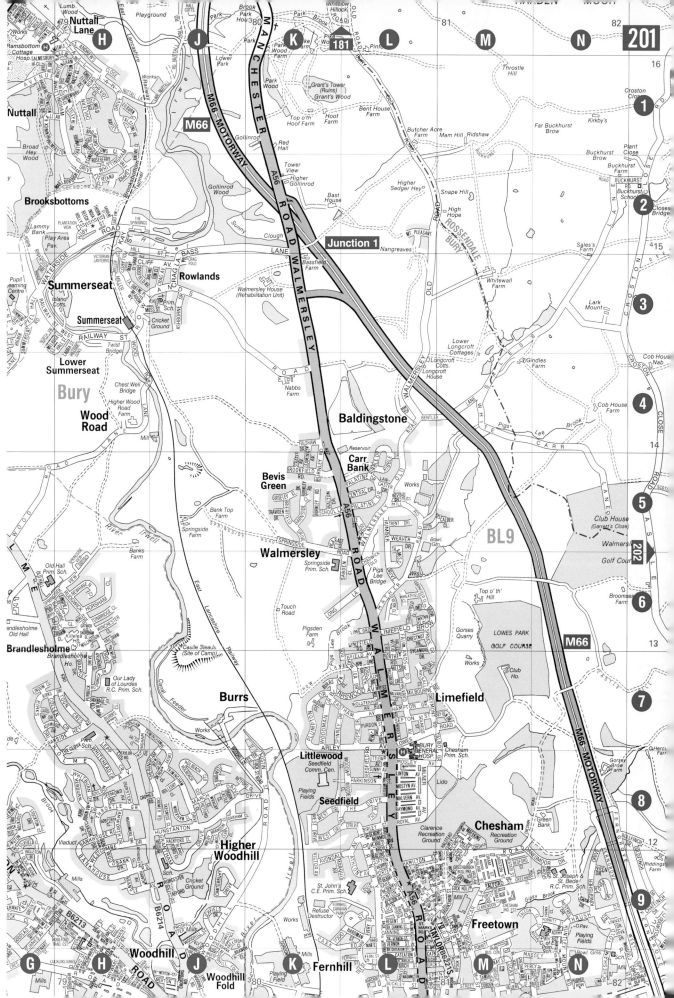

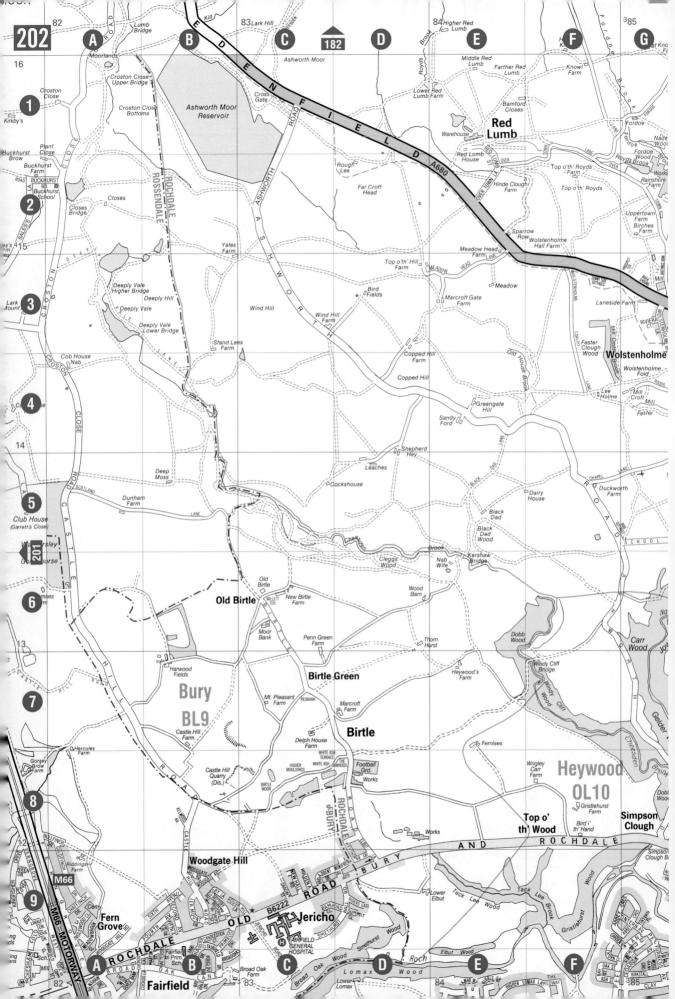

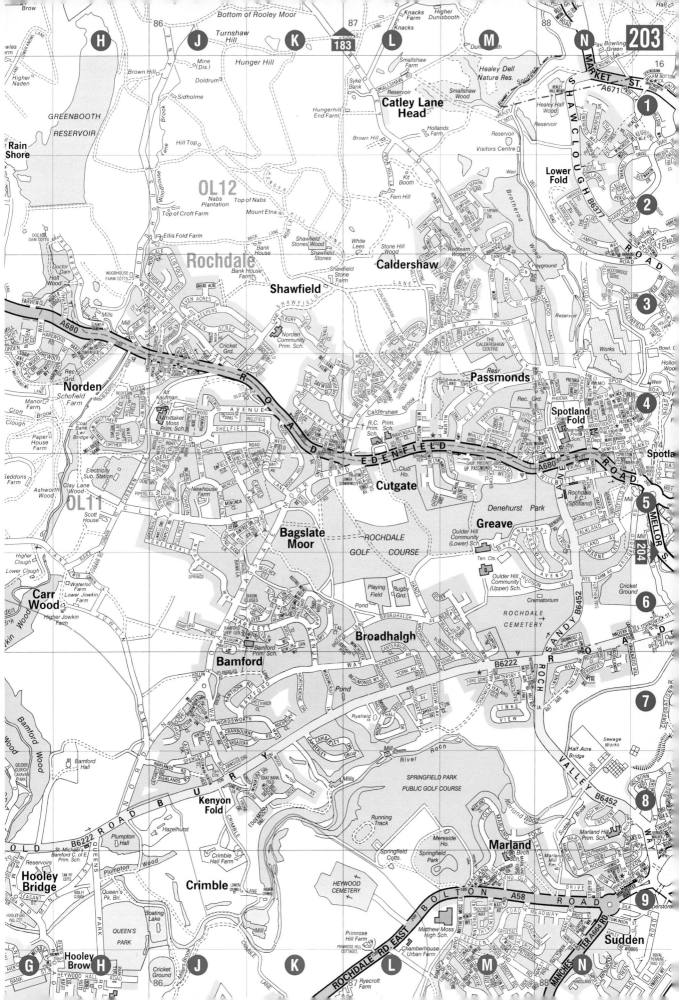

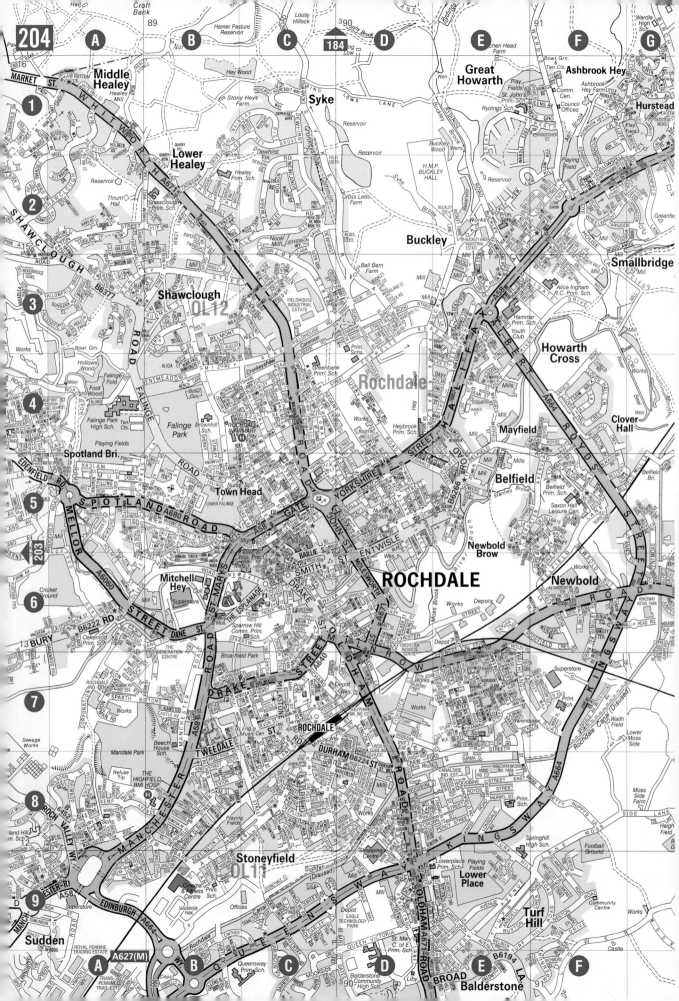

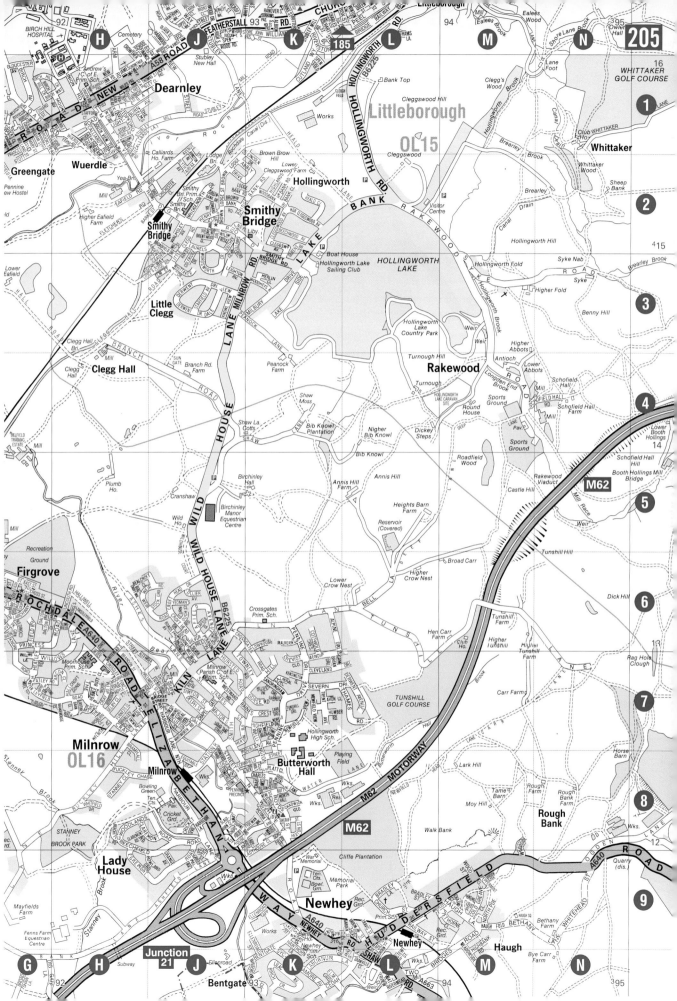

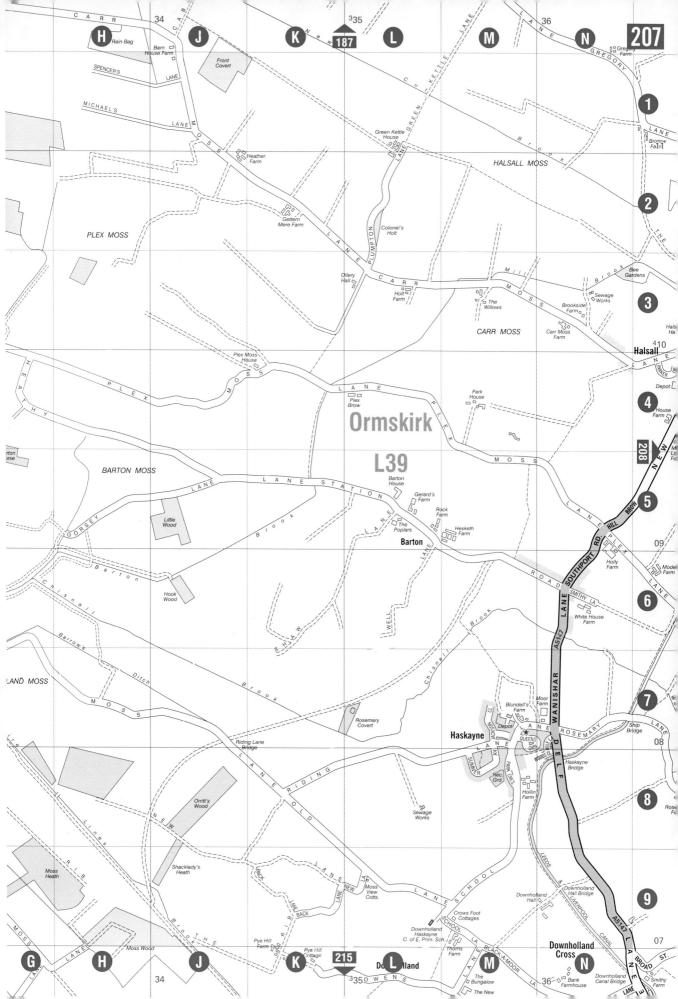

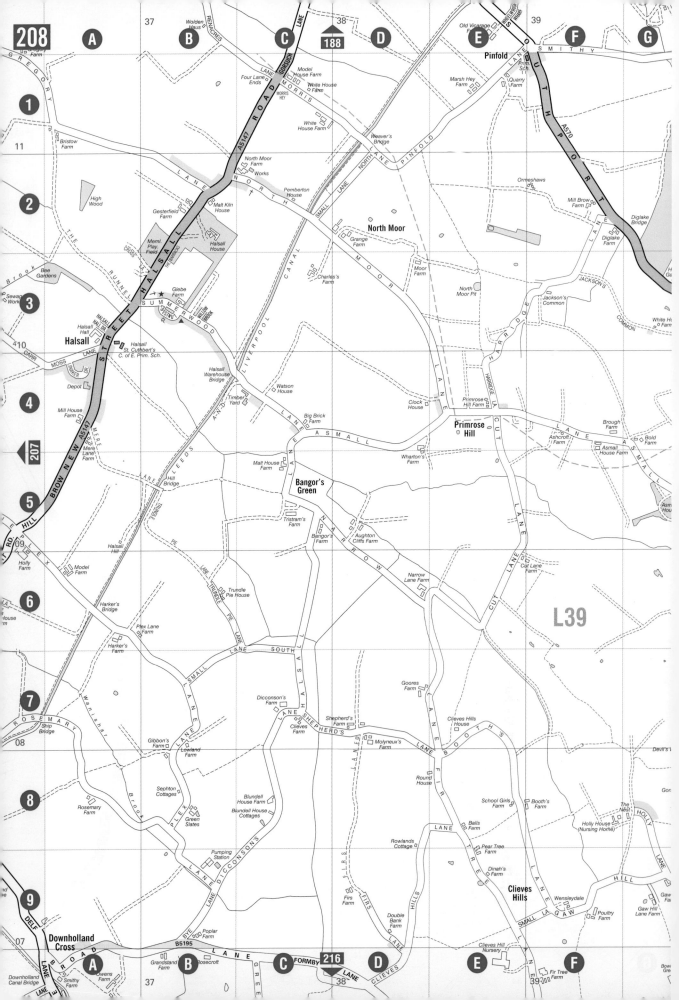

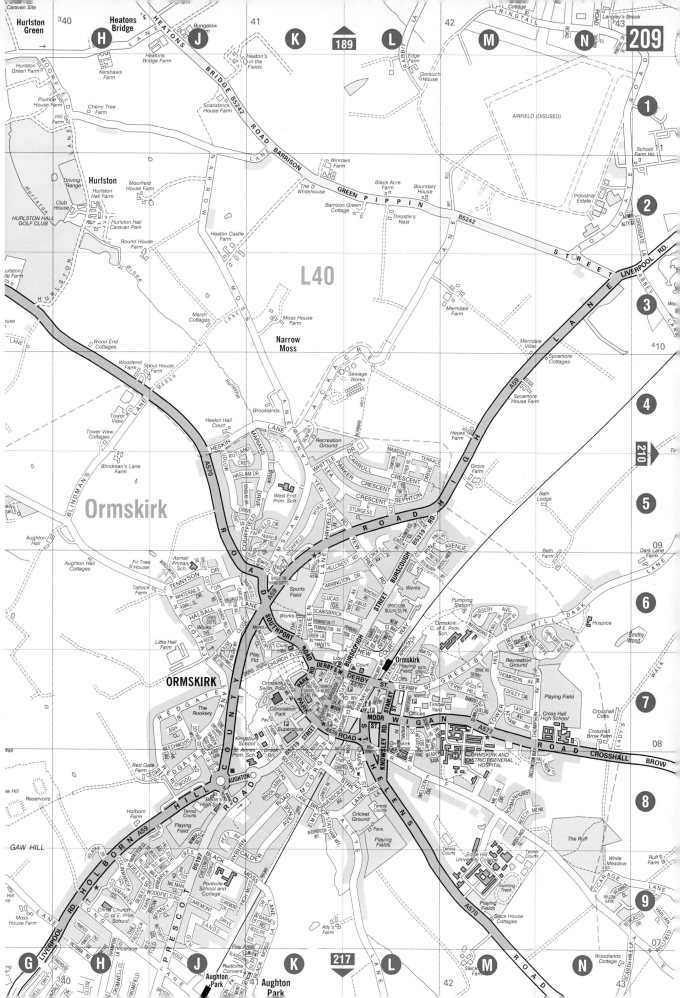

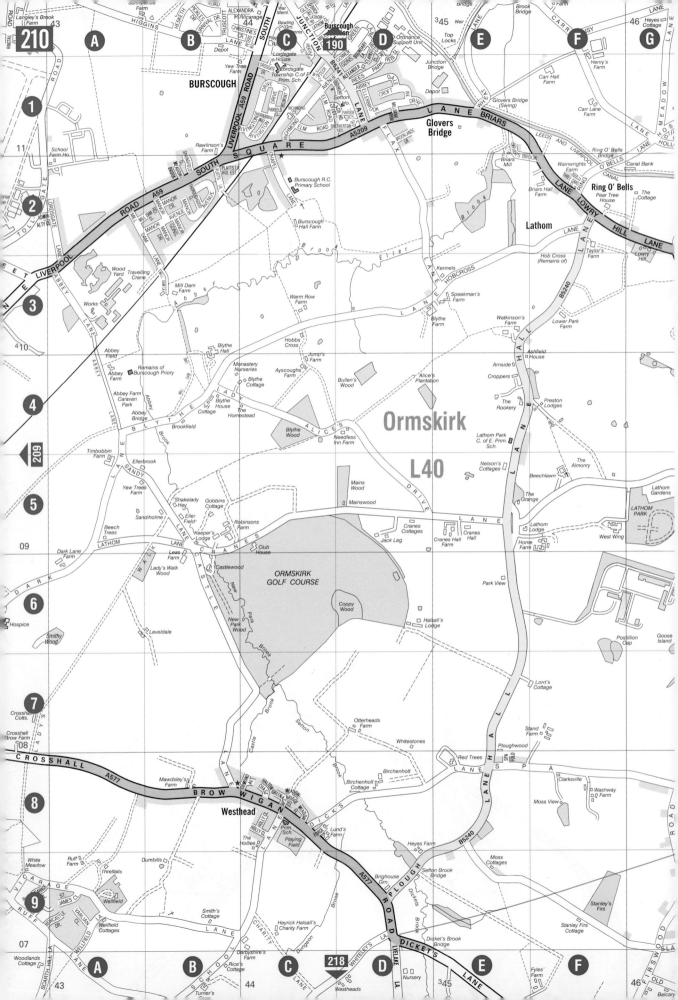

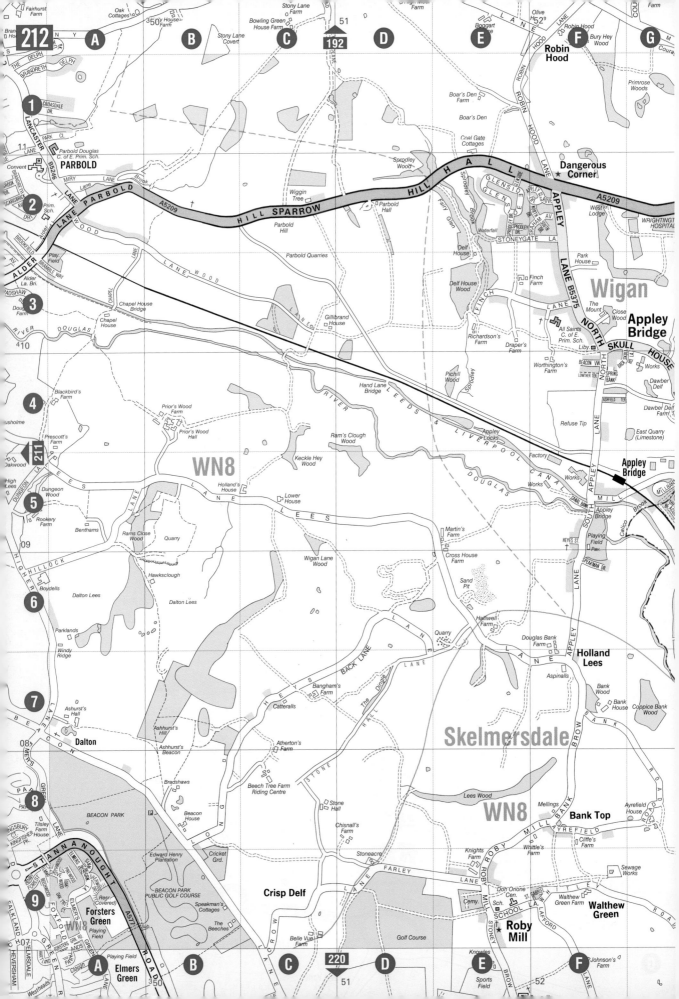

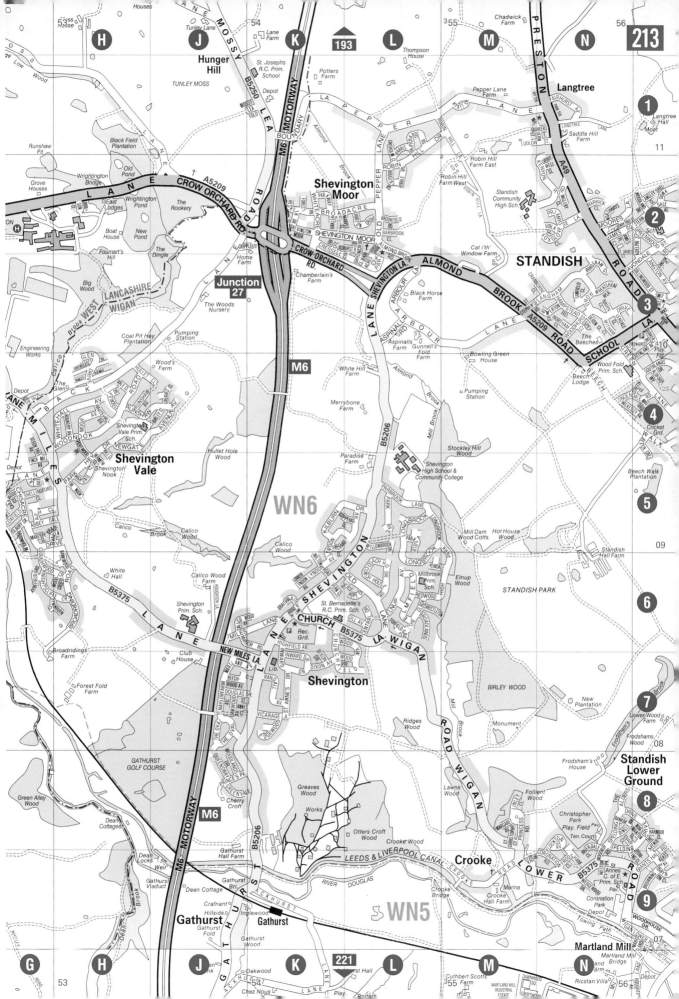

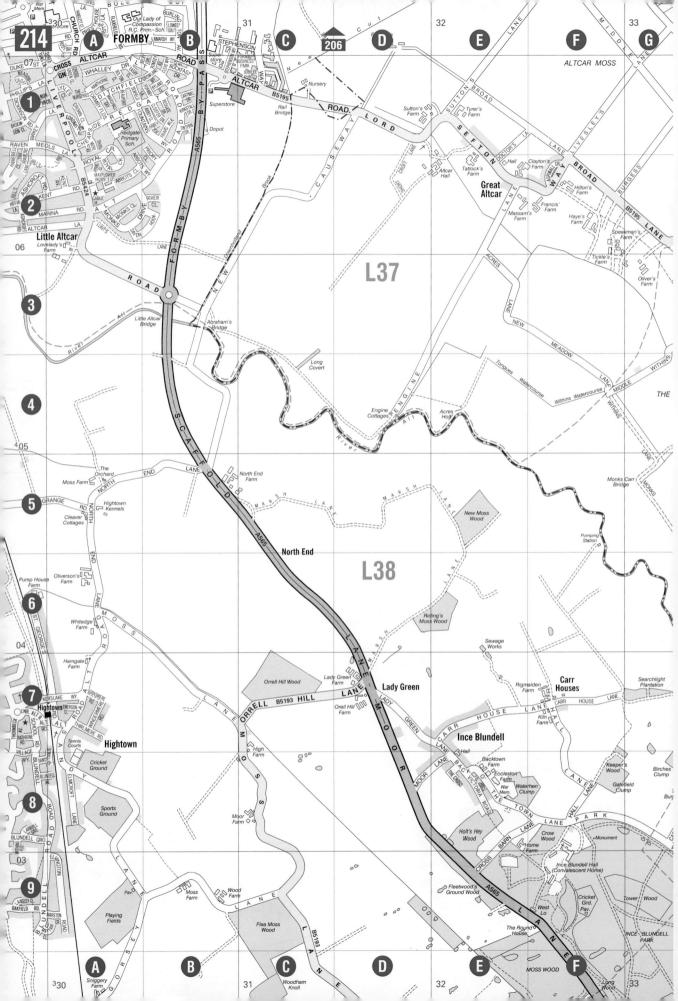

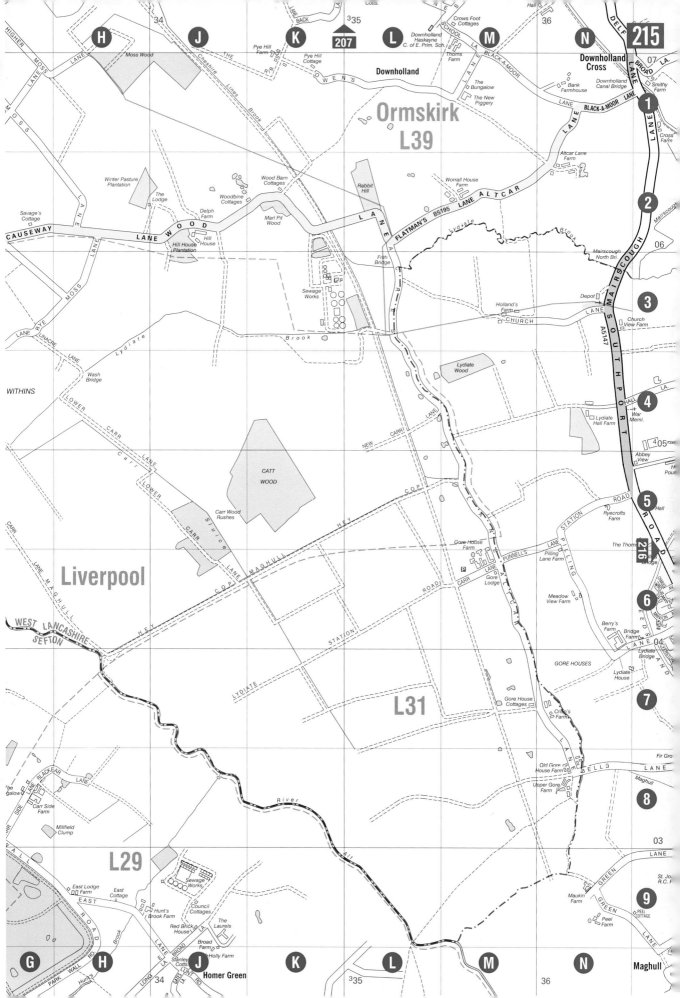

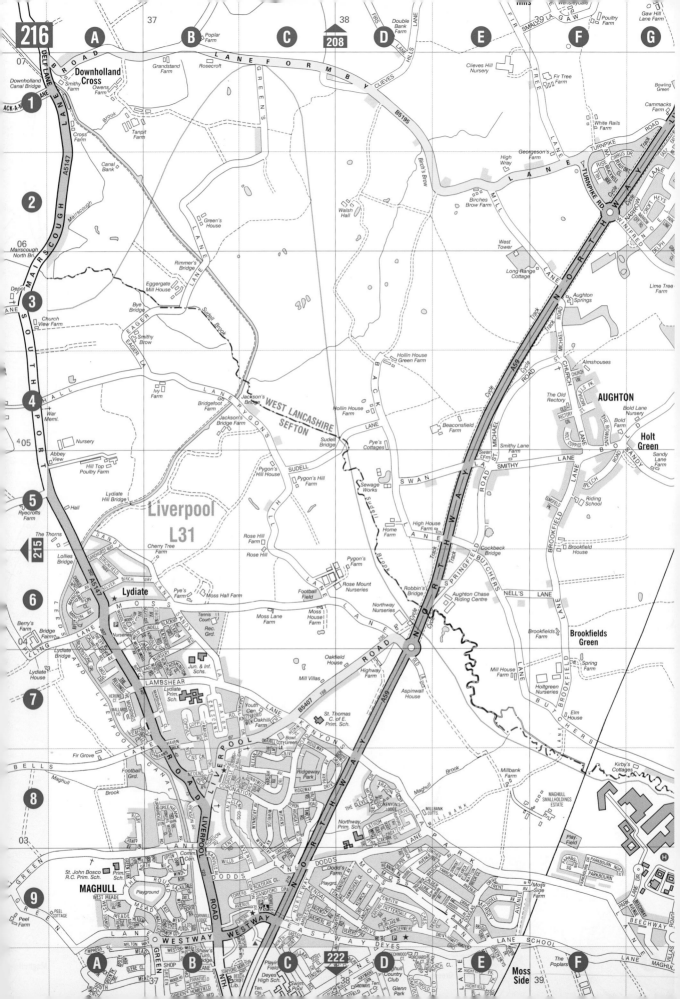

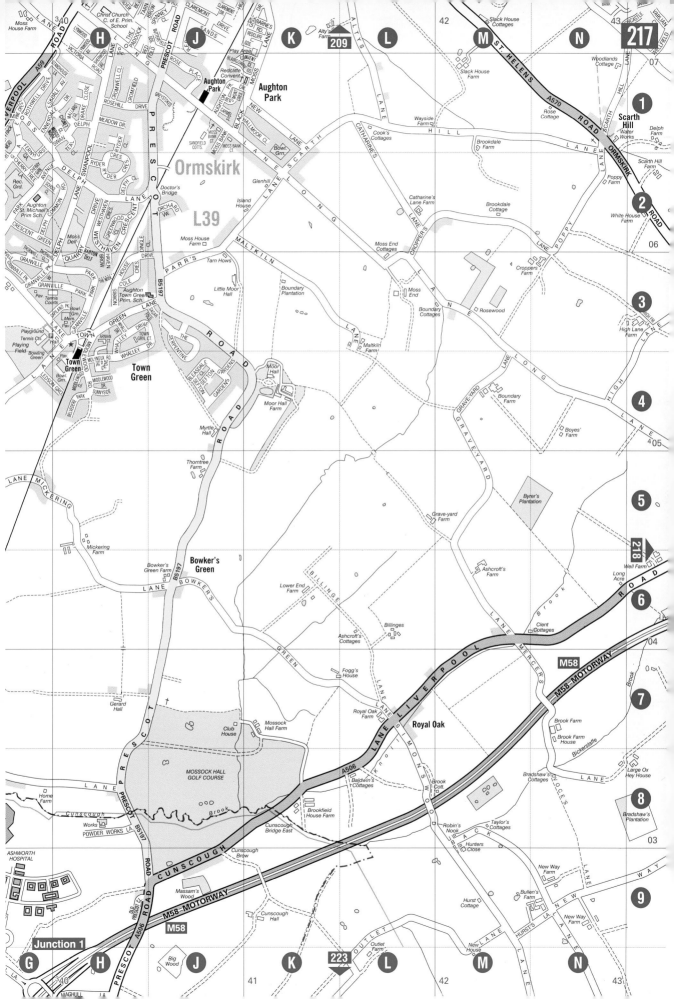

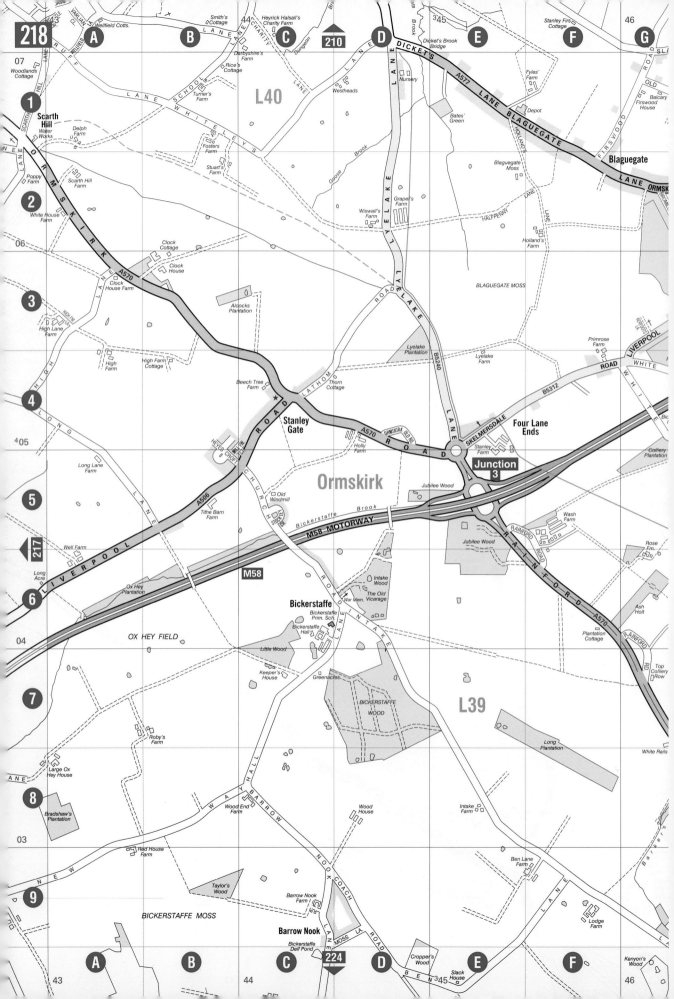

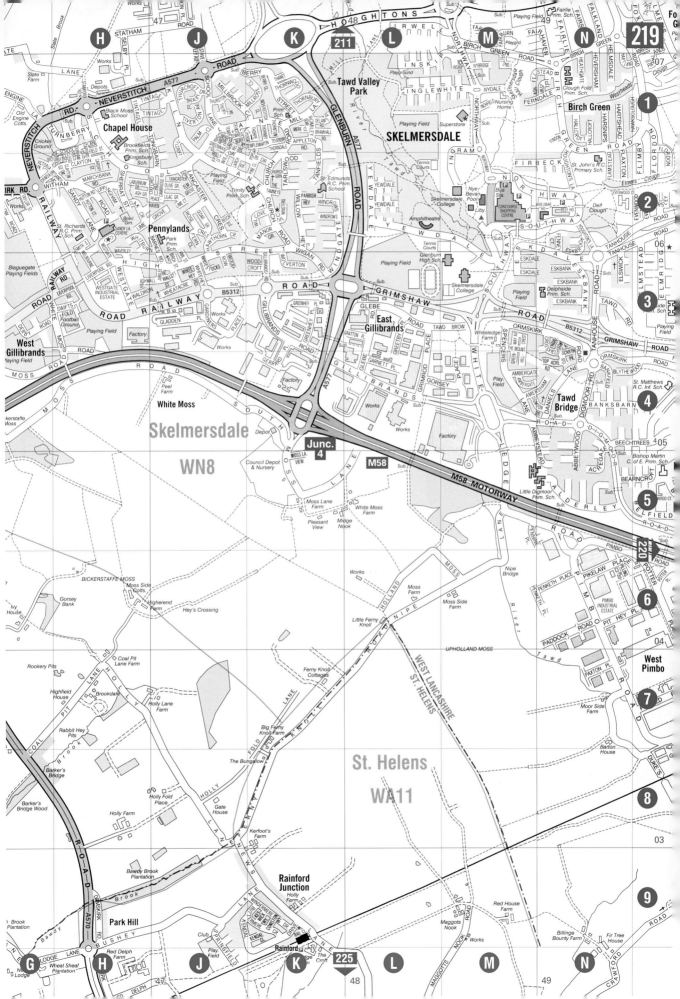

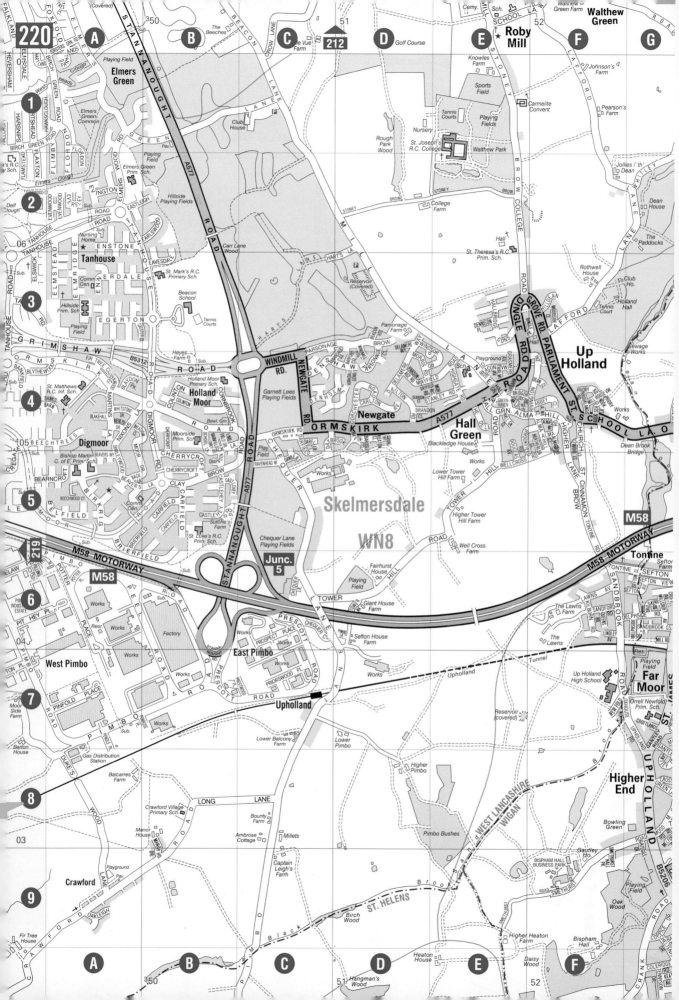

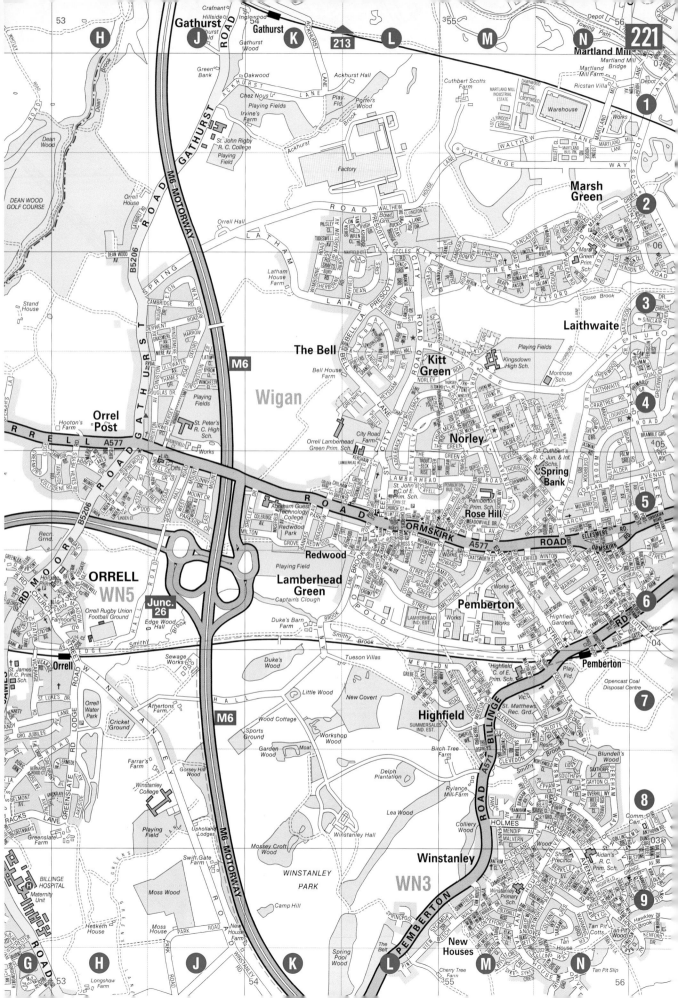

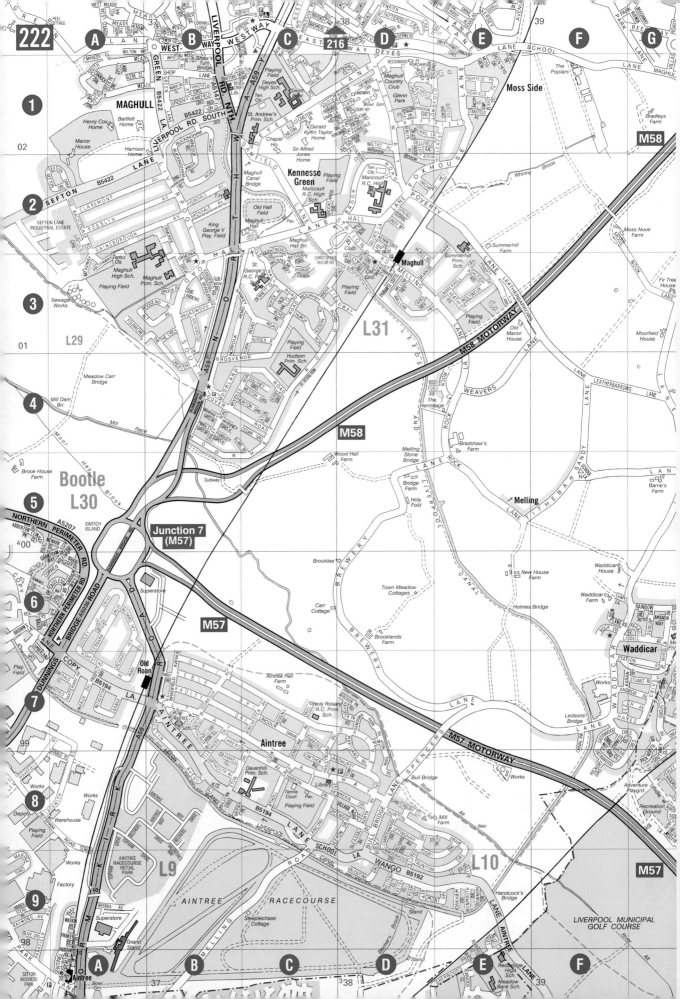

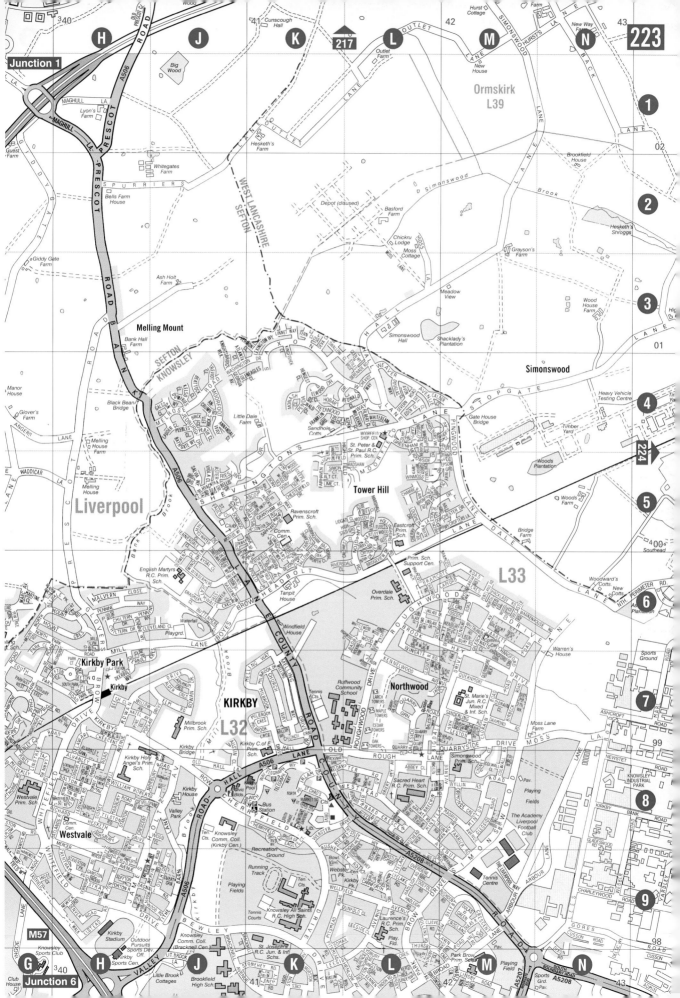

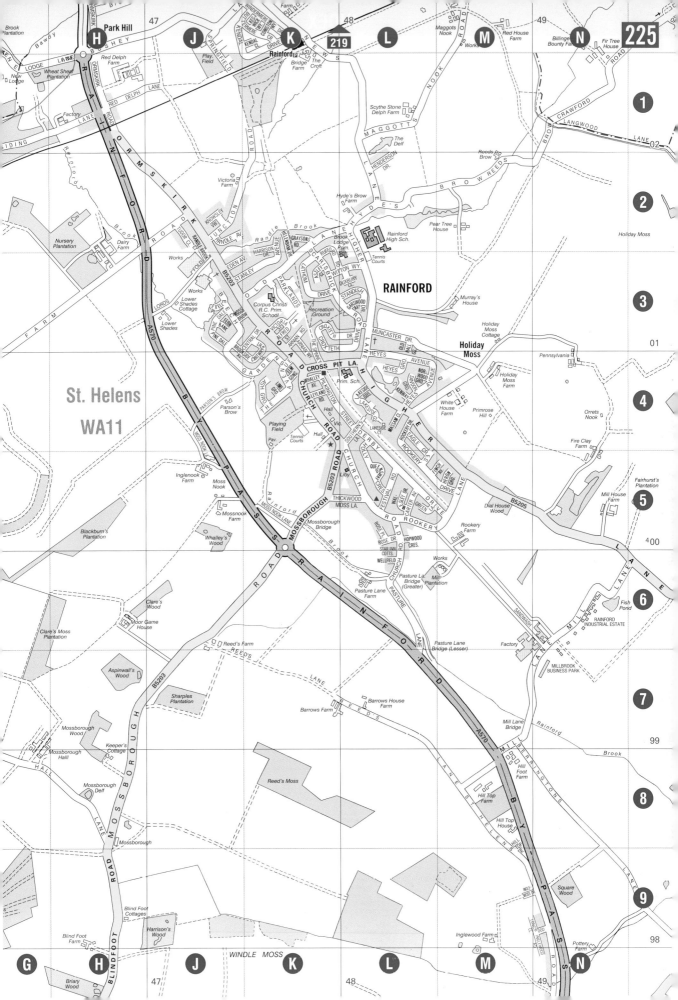

INDEX

Including Streets, Places & Areas, Industrial Estates, Selected Subsidiary Addresses
and Selected Places of Interest.

HOW TO USE THIS INDEX

1. Each street name is followed by its Posttown or Postal Locality and then by its map reference; e.g. Abbey Cres. *Dar* . . . .7C **158** is in the Darwen Posttown is to be found in square 7C on page **158**. The page number being shown in bold type.
   A strict alphabetical order is followed in which Av., Rd., St., etc. (though abbreviated) are read in full and as part of the street name; e.g. Acres Brook Rd. appears after Acresbrook Av. but before Acresbrook Wlk.

2. Streets and a selection of Subsidiary names not shown on the Maps, appear in the index in *Italics* with the thoroughfare to which it is connected shown in brackets; e.g. *Abbeydale. Roch* . . . .*5B* **204** (off Spotland Rd.)

3. Places and areas are shown in the index in **bold type**, the map reference referring to the actual map square in which the town or area is located and not to the place name; e.g. **Abbeystead** **3A 48**

4. An example of a selected place of interest is **Academy, The.** . . . **8M 223** (Liverpool F.C.)

GENERAL ABBREVIATIONS

All : Alley	Cir : Circus	Gt : Great	M : Mews	Sq : Square
App : Approach	Clo : Close	Grn : Green	Mt : Mount	Sta : Station
Arc : Arcade	Comn : Common	Gro : Grove	Mus : Museum	St : Street
Av : Avenue	Cotts : Cottages	Ho : House	N : North	Ter : Terrace
Bk : Back	Ct : Court	Ind : Industrial	Pal : Palace	Trad : Trading
Boulevd : Boulevard	Cres : Crescent	Info : Information	Pde : Parade	Up : Upper
Bri : Bridge	Cft : Croft	Junct : Junction	Pk : Park	Va : Vale
B'way : Broadway	Dri : Drive	La : Lane	Pas : Passage	Vw : View
Bldgs : Buildings	E : East	Lit : Little	Pl : Place	Vs : Villas
Bus : Business	Embkmt : Embankment	Lwr : Lower	Quad : Quadrant	Vis : Visitors
Cvn : Caravan	Est : Estate	Mc : Mac	Res : Residential	Wlk : Walk
Cen : Centre	Fld : Field	Mnr : Manor	Ri : Rise	W : West
Chu : Church	Gdns : Gardens	Mans : Mansions	Rd : Road	Yd : Yard
Chyd : Churchyard	Gth : Garth	Mkt : Market	Shop : Shopping	
Circ : Circle	Ga : Gate	Mdw : Meadow	S : South	

POSTTOWN AND POSTAL LOCALITY ABBREVIATIONS

Abb : Abbeystead	Burs : Burscough	Fort : Forton	Kno S : Knott End-on-Sea	Pend : Pendleton
Abb V : Abbey Village	Burs I : Burscough Ind. Est.	Foul : Foulridge	K Grn : Knowle Green	Pen : Penwortham
Acc : Accrington	Burt : Burton	Frec : Freckleton	Know I : Knowsley Ind. Pk.	Pick B : Pickup Bank
Adl : Adlington	Burt L : Burton in Lonsdale	Ful : Fulwood	Know N : Knowsley Ind. Pk. N.	Pil : Pilling
Aff : Affetside	Bury : Bury	Gal : Galgate	Lanc : Lancaster	Pleas : Pleasington
Ains : Ainsdale	Cabus : Cabus	Garg : Gargrave	Lane : Laneshawbridge	Poul I : Poulton Ind. Est.
Ain : Aintree	Cald V : Calder Vale	Gars : Garstang	L'clif : Langcliffe	Poul F : Poulton-le-Fylde
Ain R : Aintree Racecourse Retail &	Cap : Capernwray	Gigg : Giggleswick	Lang : Langho	Pre : Preesall
Bus. Pk.	Carn : Carnforth	Gis : Gisburn	Lan I : Lansil Ind. Est.	Pres : Preston
Airt : Airton	Carr B : Carr Bank	Glas D : Glasson Dock	Lar : Larbreck	P Hut : Priest Hutton
Ald : Aldcliffe	Cast : Casterton	Good : Goodshaw	Lath : Lathom	Queen I : Queensway Ind. Est.
Als : Alston	Catf : Catforth	Goos : Goosnargh	Lea : Lea	Quer : Quernmore
Alt : Altham	Cat : Caton	Gt Alt : Great Altcar	Lea T : Lea Town	Rainf : Rainford
Alt W : Altham West	Catt : Catterall	Gt Ecc : Great Eccleston	Leck : Leck	Ram : Ramsbottom
And : Anderton	Chai : Chaigley	Gt Har : Great Harwood	Ley : Leyland	Rams : Ramsgreave
Ang : Anglezarke	Char R : Charnock Richard	Gt Plu : Great Plumpton	L Grn : Lightfoot Green	Rath : Rathmell
Ans : Ansdell	Chat : Chatburn	G'hlgh : Greenhalgh	L'boro : Littleborough	Raw : Rawtenstall
App B : Appley Bridge	Cher T : Cherry Tree	G'mnt : Greenmount	L Ecc : Little Eccleston	Read : Read
Ark : Arkholme	Chip : Chipping	Grim V : Grimeford Village	L Hoo : Little Hoole	Red M : Red Marsh Ind. Est.
Arns : Arnside	Chor : Chorley	Grims : Grimsargh	Liv : Liverpool	Rdly : Reedley
Ash R : Ashton-on-Ribble	Chu : Church	Grin : Grindleton	Live : Livesey	Reed : Reedsholme
Ash S : Ashton with Stodday	Chur : Churchtown (Preston)	Guide : Guide	L'rdge : Longridge	Rib : Ribbleton
A'ton : Aughton (Lancaster)	Chtwn : Churchtown (Southport)	Haig : Haighton	Longt : Longton	Ribch : Ribchester
Augh : Aughton (Ormskirk)	Clau : Claughton	Hale : Hale	Los : Lostock	Rim : Rimington
Bacup : Bacup	Clau B : Claughton-on-Brock	Hals : Halsall	Los H : Lostock Hall	Rish : Rishton
Bail : Bailrigg	Claw : Clawthorpe	Halt : Halton	Loth : Lothersdale	Ris B : Rising Bridge
Bald : Balderstone	Clay D : Clayton le Dale	Halt W : Halton West	Love : Loveclough	Roby M : Roby Mill
Bam B : Bamber Bridge	Clay M : Clayton le Moors	Hamb : Hambleton	Low D : Low Dolphinholme	Roch : Rochdale
Banks : Banks	Clay W : Clayton-le-Woods	Hamp : Hampson	Lwr B : Lower Bartle	Ross : Rossendale
Barb : Barbon	Clie H : Clieves Hills	Hap : Hapton	L Bent : Lower Bentham	Rou : Roughlee (Burnley)
B'ley : Barley	Clif : Clifton (Preston)	Harw : Harwood	Lwr D : Lower Darwen	R'lee : Roughlee (Nelson)
Bncr : Barnacre	Clif : Clifton (Swinton)	Hask : Haskayne	Lowg : Lowgill	Ruf : Rufford
Barn : Barnoldswick	Clith : Clitheroe	Has : Haslingden	Lumb : Lumb	Sab : Sabden
Barr : Barrow	Cliv : Cliviger	Hawk : Hawkshaw	Lyd : Lydiate	St A : St Annes
Barfd : Barrowford	Clough : Cloughfold	Heal : Healey	Lytham : Lytham	St H : St Helens
Btle : Bartle	C'ham : Cockerham	H'pey : Heapey	Lyth A : Lytham St Annes	St M : St Michaels
Bar : Barton (Ormskirk)	C'den : Colden	Hth C : Heath Charnock	Mag : Maghull	Sale : Salesbury
Brtn : Barton (Preston)	Col : Colne	Heat O : Heaton with Oxcliffe	Man : Mansergh	Salt : Salterforth
Bas E : Bashall Eaves	Con C : Coniston Cold	Hell : Hellifield	Mart : Marton	Salw : Salwick
Bax : Baxenden	Cop : Coppull	Helm : Helmshore	Maw : Mawdesley	Sam : Samlesbury
Bay H : Bay Horse	Corn : Cornholme	Hept : Heptonstall	Mlng : Melling (Carnforth)	Saw : Sawley
Beet : Beetham	Cot : Cottam	Hesk B : Hesketh Bank	Mell : Melling (Liverpool)	Scar : Scarisbrick
Bel : Belmont	Crank : Crank	Hesk : Heskin	Mel : Mellor	Scor : Scorton
Belt : Belthorn	Craw : Crawshawbooth	Hest B : Hest Bank	Mel B : Mellor Brook	Scot : Scotforth
Ben : Bentham	Crook L : Crook o Lune	Hey : Heysham	Mere B : Mere Brow	Set : Settle
Bic : Bickerstaffe	Cros : Crosby	Heyw : Heywood	M'ton : Middleton	Shawf : Shawforth
Bil : Billinge	Crost : Croston	High : Higham	Midg H : Midge Hall	Shev : Shevington
Bill : Billington	Dal : Dalton	H Big : High Biggins	Mill : Millhead	Shir H : Shirdley Hill
Bils : Bilsborrow	Dar : Darwen	High B : Higher Bartle	Miln : Milnrow	Shore : Shore
Bkdle : Birkdale	Dink : Dinckley	High W : Higher Walton	Moor : Moorgate	Silv : Silverdale
Bis : Bispham	Doph : Dolphinholme	H Wltn : Higher Wheelton	More : Morecambe	S'stne : Simonstone
B'brn : Blackburn	D'ham : Downham	H'twn : Highton	Mos S : Moss Side (Lytham St Annes)	Sim : Simonswood
Black : Blacko	Down : Downholland	Hodd : Hoddlesden	M Side : Moss Side (Preston)	Sing : Singleton
Blac : Blackpool	Dunn : Dunnockshaw	Hogh : Hoghton	Much H : Much Hoole	Skel : Skelmersdale
Blac F : Blackpool & Fylde Ind. Est.	Dun B : Dunsop Bridge	Holc : Holcombe	Nate : Nateby	Sla H : Slack Head
B'rod : Blackrod	Dutt : Dutton	Hol M : Holland Moor	Nels : Nelson	Slai : Slaidburn
Blkhd : Blackshawhead	Eag H : Eagland Hill	Holme : Holme	Neth K : Nether Kellet	Slyne : Slyne
Blea : Bleasdale	Earby : Earby	H'wd : Holmeswood	N'bgn : Newbiggin	Smal : Smallbridge
Bolt : Bolton	E Mar : East Marton	Horn : Hornby	Newb : Newburgh	S'hills : Smithills
Bolt B : Bolton by Bowland	E'hill : Eccleshill	Hort : Horton	Newc : Newchurch	S'bri : Smithybridge
Bolt S : Bolton le Sands	E'ston : Eccleston	Hor : Horwich	Newc P : Newchurch-in-Pendle	Sough : Sough
Boot : Bootle	Eden : Edenfield	Hoth : Hothersall	New H : New Hall Hey	S'fld : Southfield
Borw : Borwick	Eger : Egerton	Hun : Huncoat	New L : New Longton	South : Southport
Bowg : Bowgreave	Ellel : Ellel	Hun I : Huncoat Ind. Est.	News : Newsholme	S'way : Southway
Brac : Bracewell	Elsl : Elslack	H End : Hundred End	Nwtn : Newton (Carnforth)	S'by : Sowerby
Brad : Bradshaw	Elsw : Elswick	Hur : Hurstead	Newt : Newton (Preston)	Stac : Stacksteads
Breth : Bretherton	E'tn : Eshton	Hur G : Hurst Green	Newt B : Newton in Bowland	Stainf : Stainforth
Brclf : Briercliffe	Esp : Esprick	Hut : Hutton	Old L : Old Langho	Stain : Staining
Brier : Brierfield	Eux : Euxton	Hut R : Hutton Roof	Old R : Old Roan	Stalm : Stalmine
Brin : Brindle	Fac : Facit	Ince B : Ince Blundell	Orm : Ormskirk	Stand : Standish
Brins : Brinscall	Far : Farington	I'ton : Ingleton	Orr : Orrell	Stand L : Standish Lower Ground
Brit : Britannia	Far M : Farington Moss	Ingle : Inglewhite	Osb : Osbaldeston	Stan I : Stanley Ind. Est.
Brom X : Bromley Cross	Farl : Farleton	Ing : Ingol	Osw : Oswaldtwistle	Stone : Stonefold
Brook : Brookhouse	Faz : Fazakerley	Ins : Inskip	Out R : Out Rawcliffe	Stony : Stonyhurst
Brough : Broughton (Preston)	Fence : Fence	Int : Intack	Over K : Over Kellet	S'seat : Summerseat
Brou : Broughton (Skipton)	Fen : Feniscowles	Ireby : Ireby	Over : Overton	Sun P : Sunderland Point
Bryn : Bryning	Firg : Firgrove	Kel : Kelbrook	Pad : Padiham	Tar : Tarleton
Burn T : Burnham Trad. Pk.	Fltwd : Fleetwood	Kirkby : Kirkby	Parb : Parbold	Tew : Tewitfield
Burn : Burnley	For H : Forest Holme	K Lon : Kirkby Lonsdale	Pay : Paythorne	This : Thistleton
Burr : Burrow	Form : Formby	K'ham : Kirkham	Pem : Pemberton	Thorn : Thornley

Thor : Thornton
T Clev : Thornton-Cleveleys
Thorn C : Thornton in Craven
Thur : Thurnham
Toc : Tockholes
Todm : Todmorden
Toss : Tosside
Tot : Tottington
Tow F : Townsend Fold
Traw : Trawden
Trea : Treales
Tun : Tunstall
Tur : Turton
Twis : Twiston
Uph : Upholland
Wadd : Waddington
Walm B : Walmer Bridge
Walm : Walmersley
W'den : Walsden
Wals : Walshaw
Walt D : Walton-le-Dale
Ward : Wardle
War : Warton (Carnforth)
W'ton : Warton (Preston)
Water : Water
Waterf : Waterfoot
Waters : Waterside
Weet : Weeton
Wenn : Wennington
Wesh : Wesham
W Brad : West Bradford
West : Westby
W'head : Westhead
W Mar : West Marton
Whal : Whalley
Whar : Wharles
Wheel : Wheelton
Whi I : Whitebirk Ind. Est.
W'chpl : Whitechapel
Whi L : White Lund Ind. Est.
Wstke : Whitestake
Whit I : Whitewalls Ind. Est.
White : Whitewell
Whit B : Whitewell Bottom
W'ham : Whittingham
Whit : Whittington
Whit W : Whittle-le-Woods
Whitw : Whitworth
Wig : Wigan
Wigg : Wigglesworth
Wilp : Wilpshire
Wind : Windle
Winm : Winmarleigh
Wins : Winstanley
Wis : Wiswell
W'gll : Withgill
Withn : Withnell
Wood : Woodplumpton
Wors : Worsthorne
Wray : Wray
W Grn : Wrea Green
Wrigh : Wrightington
Yeal C : Yealand Conyers
Yeal R : Yealand Redmayne

A

Aalborg Pl. Lanc 9K 23
Abberley Way. Wig 7L 221
Abberton Pk. Boot 5A 222
Abbey Clo. Form 1B 214
Abbey Clo. Kirkby 8L 223
Abbey Clo. Uph 4F 220
Abbey Cres. Dar 7C 158
Abbey Cres. Heyw 9F 202
Abbey Dale. App B 5G 213
Abbey Dale. Burs 1D 210
Abbeydale. Heat O 6B 22
Abbeydale. Roch 5B 204 (off Spotland Rd.)
Abbey Dri. L'boro 2J 205
Abbey Dri. Orr 5H 221
Abbeyfield. Burn 5F 124 (off Oxford Rd.)
Abbeyfield Clo. Lanc 4L 29
Abbeyfield Ho. Burn 4C 124 (off Harriet St.)
Abbey Fields. Whal 5H 101
Abbey Fold. Burs 8B 190
Abbey Gdns. South 1G 186
Abbey Gro. Adl 6J 195
Abbey La. Burs & Lath 3A 210
Abbey Pl. Dar 7C 158
Abbey Rd. Blac 3C 108
Abbey Rd. Whal 5J 101
Abbeystead 3A 48
Abbeystead. Skel 4M 219
Abbeystead Av. Boot 9A 222
Abbeystead Dri. Lanc 4L 29
Abbeystead Ho. Lanc 4L 29 (off Abbeystead Dri.)
Abbeystead La. Abb 9L 31
Abbeystead Rd. Doph 6E 38
Abbey St. Acc 2B 142
Abbey St. Ash R 9G 115
Abbey St. Bacup 3K 163
Abbey Village 5D 156
Abbeyville. Blac 3C 108
Abbey Wlk. Pen 6G 135
Abbeywood. Skel 5N 219
Abbot Mdw. Pen 4G 134
Abbots Clo. Form 2A 214
Abbots Clo. K'ham 5A 112
Abbots Clo. Ross 3M 161
Abbots Clough Av. B'brn 4E 140
Abbots Cft. Whal 5J 101
Abbotsford. Orm 7L 209
Abbotsford. Whitw 4A 184 (off Millfold)
Abbotsford Av. B'brn 7L 139
Abbotsford Rd. Blac 7F 88
Abbotsgate. K Lon 6E 8 (off Kendal Rd.)
Abbots Row. Lyth A 2K 129
Abbots Way. Form 2A 214
Abbots Way. Lanc 8G 22
Abbotsway. Pen 2F 134
Abbott Brow. Mel 5E 118
Abbott Clough Clo. B'brn 4E 140
Abbott Cft. Ful 2D 114
Abbott St. Hor 9C 196
Abbott St. Roch 9M 203
Abbotts Clo. Walt D 5B 136
Abbotts Wlk. Fltwd 8G 40
Abbot Wlk. Clith 3M 81
Abel St. Burn 9E 104
Abercorn Pl. Blac 4A 108
Abercorn Rd. Bolt 9B 198
Abercrombie Rd. Fltwd 8F 40
Aberdare Clo. B'brn 1M 139
Aberdeen Dri. B'brn 4A 140
Aberdeen Gdns. Roch 1A 204
Aberdeen Rd. Lanc 9L 23
Abingdon Clo. Roch 8B 204
Abingdon Dri. Ash R 8D 114
Abingdon Gro. Hey 9M 21
Abingdon Rd. Pad 2J 123
Abingdon St. Blac 4B 88
Abinger St. Burn 9G 104
Abington Dri. Banks 1F 168
Abner Row. Foul 2A 86 (off Warehouse La.)
Aboukir St. Roch 5E 204
Abraham Heights 9H 23
Abraham St. Acc 3A 142
Abraham St. B'brn 6M 139
Abraham St. Hor 9C 196
Abrams Fold. South 1E 168
Abrams Grn. Banks 1E 168
Acacia Clo. T Clev 2K 63
Acacia Rd. Rib 7A 116
Acacia Wlk. B'brn 3B 140 (off Longton St.)
Academy, The. 8M 223 (Liverpool F.C.)
Accrington 2C 142
Accrington & District Golf Course. 1J 141
Accrington Easterley By-Pass. Acc 9E 122
Accrington Rd. B'brn 3B 140
Accrington Rd. Burn & Hap 7H 123
Accrington Rd. Whal 5J 101
Accrington Stanley F.C. 9A 122 (Crown Ground)
Acer Clo. Roch 4H 203
Acer Gro. Rib 6B 116
Acker St. Roch 5C 204
Ackhurst Bus. Pk. Chor 6B 174
Ackhurst La. Orr 9K 213
Ackhurst Pk. Ind. Est. Chor 6B 174
Ackhurst Rd. Chor 6B 174
Ackroyd St. Todm 7E 146
Acorn Av. Osw 5M 141
Acorn Bank. Gars 4N 59
Acorn Clo. Ley 7K 153
Acorn Clo. Pen 6E 134
Acornfield Rd. Know I 9B 224
Acorn M. Blac 9K 89
Acorn St. Bacup 5K 163
Acorn St. B'brn 4B 140
Acott Ct. Ram 9G 180
Acre Av. Bacup 7H 163
Acre Clo. Ram 3J 181
Acrefield. Bam B 2E 154
Acrefield. B'brn 1H 139
Acre Fld. Bolt 9K 199
Acrefield. Newb 3L 211
Acrefield. Pad 9H 103
Acre Ga. Blac 2E 108
Acregate. Skel 5N 219
Acregate La. Pres 8N 115
Acre Gro. Much H 4K 151
Acre Gro. South 2F 186
Acre Mill Rd. Bacup 7H 163
Acre Moss La. More 4A 22
Acre Mt. Read 8C 102
Acresbrook Av. Tot 8E 200
Acres Brook Rd. High 5L 103
Acresbrook Wlk. Tot 8E 200
Acresfield. Adl 7H 195
Acresfield. Col 6D 86
Acres La. Gt Alt 3E 214
Acres La. Liv & Down 3L 215
Acres La. Pre 1N 55
Acres St. Tot 8E 200
Acres, The. Barr 2K 101
Acre St. Brclf 7L 105
Acre St. Burn 9F 104
Acre St. Whitw 5A 184
Acreswood Clo. Cop 5A 194
Acre Vw. Bacup 7H 163
Acre Vw. Eden 4J 181
Active Way. Burn 3D 124
Acton Rd. Blac 9E 88
Acton Rd. Liv 8H 223
Acton St. Roch 4D 204
Adams Dri. L'boro 9L 185
Adamson St. Burn 3A 124
Adamson St. Pad 9H 103
Adam St. Todm 1L 165
Ada St. B'brn 3K 139
Ada St. Burn 9F 104
Ada St. Nels 4J 105
Ada St. Ram 9G 180
Addington 4G 17
Addington Rd. Neth K 4G 17
Addington St. B'brn 3A 140
Addison Clo. B'brn 3K 139
Addison Ct. Kno S 8K 41 (off Esplanade)
Addison Cres. Blac 4D 88
Addison Rd. Fltwd 1F 54
Addison St. Acc 1B 142
Addison St. B'brn 3K 139 (in two parts)
Addle St. Lanc 3L 29
Adelaide Av. T Clev 3J 63
Adelaide Ct. Blac 5C 88 (off Regent Rd.)
Adelaide Ct. Roch 8A 204 (off Manchester Rd.)
Adelaide La. Acc 3B 142
Adelaide St. Acc 3B 142
Adelaide St. Adl 5J 195
Adelaide St. Blac 5B 88
Adelaide St. Burn 3B 124
Adelaide St. Clay M 8N 121
Adelaide St. Fltwd 8H 41
Adelaide St. Pres 9L 115
Adelaide St. Ram 1F 200
Adelaide St. Ross 9M 143
Adelaide St. Todm 1L 165
Adelaide St. W. Blac 6B 88
Adelaide Ter. B'brn 3K 139
Adelphi 8H 115
Adelphi Ho. Pres 8H 115 (off Adelphi St.)
Adelphi Pl. Pres 9J 115
Adelphi St. Blac 5B 88
Adelphi St. Burn 2E 124
Adelphi St. Lanc 1L 29
Adelphi St. Pres 8H 115
Adelphi St. Stand 2N 213
Aden St. Roch 4D 204
Adlington 6J 195
Adlington Av. Poul F 8H 63
Adlington S. Employment Area. Adl 7J 195
Adlington St. Burn 3E 124
Admergill 2G 84
Admin Rd. Know I 9A 224
Admiral Clo. Lyth A 8E 108
Admirals Sound. T Clev 1C 62
Admiral St. Burn 4F 124
Admiralty Clo. Burs 2N 209
Adrian St. Blac 9B 88
Adrian's Way. Liv 8K 223
Adrian Ter. Roch 7F 204
Adstone Av. Blac 3F 88
Affetside 5A 200
Agate St. B'brn 8N 119
Agglebys Rd. Poul F 4L 55
Agnes Ing La. Wray 7E 18
Agnes St. B'brn 5K 139
Agnes St. Pres 9K 115
Agnes St. Roch 7D 204
Agnew Rd. Fltwd 8F 40
Agnew St. Lyth A 5N 129
Aiken Ct. K'ham 4M 111
Aikengill Rd. Halt 10K 19
Ailsa Av. Blac 8F 88
Ailsa Clo. Brtn 2E 94
Ailsa Rd. B'brn 5D 140
Ailsa Wlk. Hey 9K 21
Ainscough Brook Ho. Rib 6B 116 (off Ribbleton Hall Cres.)
Ainsdale 8C 186
Ainsdale Av. Blac 6E 62
Ainsdale Av. Burn 5G 104
Ainsdale Av. Fltwd 5D 54
Ainsdale Av. T Clev 2K 63
Ainsdale Av. Tur 8L 179
Ainsdale Clo. Lanc 5H 23
Ainsdale Clo. Liv 9E 222
Ainsdale Dri. Ash R 7A 114
Ainsdale Dri. Dar 1B 178
Ainsdale Dri. Whitw 7A 184
Ainsdale-on-Sea 8A 186
Ainslie Clo. Gt Har 4H 121
Ainslie Rd. Ful 6G 115
Ainslie St. Burn 3A 124
Ainspool La. Chur 9L 59
Ainsworth Mall. B'brn 3M 139 (off Ainsworth St.)
Ainsworth St. B'brn 3M 139
Ainsworth St. Roch 7D 204
Aintree 7B 222
Aintree Ct. Liv 7B 222
Aintree Cres. South 1M 187
Aintree Dri. Lwr D 9A 140
Aintree Dri. Roch 5J 203
Aintree La. Faz 9E 222
Aintree La. Liv 7B 222
Aintree Racecourse 9B 222
Aintree Racecourse Retail Pk. Ain R 9A 222
Aintree Rd. Blac 1C 108
Aintree Rd. T Clev 3H 63
Aintree Way. Ain R 8B 222
Airdrie Cres. Burn 5B 124
Airdrie Pl. Blac 6E 62
Airebank Ter. Garg 4M 53
Aire Clo. More 6F 22
Airedale. Gal 2M 37
Airedale Av. Blac 7E 88
Airedale Av. Garg 3M 53
Airedale Ct. Poul F 7J 63
Aire Dri. Bolt 8H 199
Airegate. Liv 9A 216
Airey St. Acc 5C 142
Air Hill Ter. Roch 4N 203
Airton Gth. Barfd 8G 84
Aisthorpe Gro. Liv 3C 222
Aitken Clo. Ram 9G 181
Aitken St. Acc 1B 142
Aitken St. Ram 1H 181
Ajax St. Ram 9G 180
A.K. Bus. Cen. South 8N 167
Alamein Rd. Carn 9B 12
Alandale Clo. Ley 8L 153
Alan Gro. Hey 1L 27
Alan Haigh Ct. Col 5A 86
Alan Ramsbottom Way. Gt Har 5K 121
Alan's Way. Liv 6K 223
Alaska St. B'brn 6M 139
Albany Av. Blac 4B 108
Albany Clo. Poul F 2L 89
Albany Ct. Chor 6G 175 (off Devonport Way)
Albany Dri. Sale 1K 119
Albany Dri. Walt D 6N 135
Albany Rd. B'brn 2J 139
Albany Rd. Fltwd 9F 40
Albany Rd. Lyth A 2J 129
Albany Rd. More 4N 21
Albany Rd. South 5J 167
Albany St. Roch 8D 204
Alba St. Holc 8F 180
Albatross St. Pres 7L 115
Albemarle Ct. Clith 3K 81
Albemarle St. Clith 3K 81
Alberta Clo. B'brn 9J 119
Albert Ct. South 5K 167
Albert Hill. Set 3N 35
Albert La. Todm 1L 165
Albert Pl. Lwr D 9N 139
Albert Pl. South 6H 167
Albert Rd. Barn 2M 77
Albert Rd. Blac 6B 88
Albert Rd. Col 7N 85
Albert Rd. Ful 6J 115
Albert Rd. Lanc 7K 23
Albert Rd. Ley 6M 153
Albert Rd. Lyth A 1G 128
Albert Rd. More 4N 21
Albert Rd. Pres 7J 115
Albert Rd. Ross 8M 143
Albert Rd. Ruf 2E 190
Albert Rd. South 6J 167
Albert Royds St. Roch 3E 204
Albert Sq. Fltwd 8H 41
Albert St. Acc 3B 142
Albert St. B'brn 6K 139
Albert St. Brier 5F 104
Albert St. Burn 3F 124
Albert St. Carn 9A 12
Albert St. Chor 7F 174
Albert St. Chu 2L 141
Albert St. Clay M 7M 121
Albert St. Dar 1B 178
Albert St. Earby 2E 78
Albert St. Eger 2D 198
Albert St. Fltwd 9H 41
Albert St. Gt Har 5K 121
Albert St. Hodd 6F 158
Albert St. Hor 9C 196
Albert St. L'boro 9L 185
Albert St. Lyth A 4B 130
Albert St. Mill 7A 12
Albert St. Miln 8K 205
Albert St. Nels 2H 105
Albert St. Osw 4L 141
Albert St. Pad 1H 123
Albert St. Ram 8G 181
Albert St. Rish 8H 121
Albert St. Ross 2C 162
Albert St. Todm 1L 165
Albert St. Wesh 3L 111
Albert St. Wheel 8J 155
Albert St. Whitw 6N 183
Albert Ter. Bacup 4K 163
Albert Ter. Barfd 8H 85
Albert Ter. Cald V 4H 61
Albert Ter. Clough 5N 161
Albert Ter. High W 4D 136
Albert Ter. Pres 8K 115
Albert Ter. South 9G 167
Albion Av. Blac 4F 88
Albion Ct. Burn 5C 124
Albion M. Lanc 7L 23
Albion Rd. B'brn 7L 139
Albion Rd. Earby 2E 78
Albion Rd. Roch 7A 204
Albion Rd. Ind. Est. Roch 7A 204
Albion St. Acc 2A 142
Albion St. Bacup 4L 163
Albion St. B'brn 7K 139
Albion St. Brier 5F 104
Albion St. Burn 5C 124
Albion St. Chor 7E 174
Albion St. Clith 3M 81
Albion St. Earby 2E 78
Albion St. Lanc 7L 23
Albion St. L'boro 9K 185
Albion St. Nels 2H 105
Albion St. Pad 2J 123
Albion St. Stac 7G 163
Albion Ter. Burn 4D 124 (off Albion St.)
Albrighton Clo. Los H 9L 135
Albrighton Cres. Los H 9L 135
Albrighton Rd. Los H 9L 135
Albury Dri. Roch 3K 203
Albyn Bank Rd. Pres 1L 135
Albyn St. E. Pres 1L 135
Alcester Av. Pen 3F 134
Alconbury Cres. T Clev 1C 62
Aldate Gro. Ash R 7D 114
Aldcliffe 2G 29
Aldcliffe Ct. More 5B 22
Aldcliffe M. Ald 2H 29
Aldcliffe Pl. Lanc 9J 23
Aldcliffe Rd. Ash R 8B 114
Aldcliffe Rd. Lanc 2H 29
Alden Clo. Helm 9F 160
Alden Ri. Ross 9F 160
Alden Rd. Ross 2D 180
Alder Av. Ross 5N 161
Alder Av. Wig 5N 221
Alder Bank. B'brn 4J 139
Alderbank. Hor 9A 196
Alder Bank. Nels 3G 104
Alder Bank. Ross 4M 161
Alderbank. Ward 7F 184
Alderbrook Dri. Parb 2N 211
Alder Clo. Ley 7E 152
Alder Clo. Newt 7E 112
Alder Clo. T Clev 2J 63
Alder Coppice. Lea 6B 114
Alder Ct. Fltwd 2C 54
Alder Ct. Lanc 8H 23 (off Alder Gro.)
Alder Cres. Liv 7J 223
Alderdale Av. South 8A 186
Alder Dri. Char R 2N 193
Alder Dri. Hogh 7F 136
Alderfield. Pen 5G 134
Alderford Clo. Clith 4J 81
Alder Gro. Acc 7D 122
Alder Gro. Blac 3E 88
Alder Gro. Brom X 7J 199
Alder Gro. Cop 4B 194
Alder Gro. Lanc 8H 23
Alder Gro. Lyth A 4N 129 (in two parts)
Alder Gro. Poul F 9K 63
Alder Hill Ct. Earby 2F 78
Alder Hill St. Earby 2E 78
Alder La. Hals 5E 206
Alder La. Out R 2M 65
Alder La. Parb 3M 211
Alder Lee Clo. Wins 9N 221
Alderley. Skel 5N 219
Alderley Av. Blac 4B 108
Alderley Av. Bolt 8E 198
Alderley Heights. Lanc 5K 23
Alderman Foley Dri. Roch 3L 203
Alder Mdw. Clo. Roch 4L 203
Alderney Clo. B'brn 7J 139
Alder Rd. Rib 5C 116
Aldersleigh Cres. Hogh 7F 136
Alderson Cres. Liv 8A 206
Alders, The. Gars 3N 59
Alders, The. Stand L 8N 213
Alder St. Bacup 4K 163
Alder St. B'brn 1A 140
Alder St. Burn 3A 124
Alder St. Ross 4N 161
Alderville Clo. W'ton 2L 131
Alderway. Ram 5H 181
Alderwood Gro. Ram 2J 181
Aldfield Av. Lea 8N 113
Aldford Way. Stand 4N 213
Aldingham Ct. More 5B 22
Aldingham Wlk. More 3A 22
Aldon Gro. Longt 7L 133
Aldon Rd. Poul I 8M 63
Aldred St. Chor 7F 174
Aldren's La. Lanc 6K 23
Aldwych Av. Blac 7E 88
Aldwych Dri. Ash R 7C 114
Aldwych Dri. Los H 9L 135
Aldwych Pl. B'brn 7N 119
Aldykes. Liv 2D 222
Alert St. Ash R 8F 114
Alexander Clo. Acc 7D 142
Alexander Clo. Burs 1D 210
Alexander Ct. Poul F 8K 63
Alexander Dri. Liv 8C 216
Alexander Dri. Miln 7H 205
Alexander Gro. Burn 3N 123
Alexander Pl. Grims 9F 96
Alexander St. Nels 9L 85
Alexandra B'way. South 6K 167 (off Alexandra Rd.)
Alexandra Clo. Clay M 6L 121
Alexandra Ct. Blac 9B 88 (off Alexandra Rd.)
Alexandra Ct. South 6K 167
Alexandra Ho. B'brn 5B 140
Alexandra M. Orm 6K 209
Alexandra M. South 6J 167
Alexandra Pavilions. Pres 8K 115
Alexandra Pl. Gt Har 3K 121
Alexandra Rd. B'brn 2K 139
Alexandra Rd. Blac 9B 88
Alexandra Rd. Burs 9B 190
Alexandra Rd. Carn 9A 12
Alexandra Rd. Dar 5N 157
Alexandra Rd. Lanc 5K 23
Alexandra Rd. L'rdge 3J 97
Alexandra Rd. Lyth A 1F 128
Alexandra Rd. More 4M 21
Alexandra Rd. South 5J 167
Alexandra Rd. T Clev 3J 63
Alexandra Rd. Walt D 5N 135
Alexandra Rd. Wesh 2M 111
Alexandra Sq. Bail 8M 29
Alexandra St. Clay M 5L 121
Alexandra St. Pres 1M 135
Alexandra Vw. Dar 5N 157
Alexandria Dri. Lyth A 3F 128
Alexandria St. Ross 3L 161
Alford Fold. Ful 2G 114
Alfred's Ct. Chor 7E 174
Alfred St. Blac 5C 88
Alfred St. Dar 9B 158
Alfred St. Eger 2D 198
Alfred St. Lanc 8L 23
Alfred St. L'boro 8K 185
Alfred St. Rainf 3K 225
Alfred St. Ram 9G 180

Alfred St.—Ashford Clo.

Alfred St. Whitw 4A 184
Algar St. Nels 9K 85
Alice Av. Ley 6K 153
Alice Ingham Ct. Roch 4M 203
Alice Sq. Pres 8K 115
Alice St. Acc 1C 142
Alice St. Barn 2M 77
Alice St. Dar 7A 158
Alice St. More 3C 22
Alice St. Osw 5L 141
Alice St. Roch 4E 204
Alicia Ct. Roch 4B 204
Alicia Dri. Roch 4B 204
Alisan Rd. Poul F 6H 63
Alker La. Chor 3C 174
Alker St. Chor 7E 174
Alkincoats Rd. Col 6N 85
Alkincoats Vs. Col 5N 85
Allan Critchlow Way. Rish 7H 121
Allandale. Blac 4C 108
Allandale Av. T Clev 8F 54
Allandale Gro. Burn 5K 125
Allan St. Bacup 6K 163
Allenbury Pl. Blac 8G 89
Allenby Av. Ful 5L 115
Allenby Rd. Lyth A 1D 128
Allen Clo. Fltwd 2D 54
Allen Clo. T Clev 2D 62
Allen Ct. Burn 1E 124 (off Allen St.)
Allendale St. Burn 3N 123
Allendale St. Col 5C 86
Allengate. Ful 5J 115
Allen St. Burn 1E 124 (in two parts)
Allen St. Roch 7D 204
Allen Way. Fltwd 2C 54
Allerton Clo. Dar 5A 158
Allerton Dri. Burn 3B 124
Allerton Rd. South 5L 167
Allerton Rd. Walt D 5N 135
Allescholes Rd. Todm 8K 165
Alleys Grn. Clith 2L 81
Alleytroyds. 3L 141
Alleytroyds. Chu 3L 141
All Hallows Rd. Blac 6D 62
Alliance St. Acc 7E 142
Allington. Roch 7B 204
Allington Clo. Walt D 5B 136
Allison Gro. Col 5C 86
Allonby Av. T Clev 8E 54
All Saints Clo. Burn 2L 123
All Saints Clo. Osw 4H 141
All Saints Clo. Ross 7M 143
All Saints Rd. Lyth A 2E 128
All Saints Rd. T Clev 5E 62
All Saints Ter. Roch 3E 204
Allsprings Clo. Gt Har 3K 121
Allsprings Dri. Gt Har 2K 121
Alma Av. Foul 2A 86
Alma Clo. Uph 4F 220
Alma Ct. South 6F 186
Alma Ct. Uph 4F 220
Alma Dri. Char R 1A 194
Alma Grn. Uph 4E 220
Alma Hill. Uph 4E 220
Alma Ind. Est. Roch 4C 204
Alma Pde. Uph 4F 220
Alma Pl. Clith 4K 81
Alma Rd. Lanc 1K 29
Alma Rd. Lane 5G 86
Alma Rd. South 1G 186
Alma Rd. Todm 6K 165
Alma Rd. Uph 4F 220
Alma Row. Hogh 7G 136
Alma St. Bacup 5K 163
Alma St. B'brn 3L 139
Alma St. Clay M 6M 121
Alma St. Pad 9G 103
Alma St. Pres 8K 115
Alma St. Roch 4C 204
Alma St. Todm 6K 165
Alma Ter. Dunn 4A 144
Alma Wlk. Uph 4F 220
Alma Wood Clo. Chor 8C 174
Almond Av. Burs 7C 190
Almond Brook Rd. Stand 2L 213
Almond Clo. Abb V 5C 156
Almond Clo. Ful 3M 115
Almond Clo. L'boro 8J 185
Almond Clo. Pen 5E 134
Almond Cres. Ross 7L 161
Almond Gro. Bolt 9F 198
Almond Gro. Wig 5N 221
Almond St. Bolt 9F 198
Almond St. Dar 7A 158
Almond St. Pres 9L 115
Almshouse. Lanc 8J 23
Almshouses, The. Grin 4C 74
Alnwick Clo. Burn 2C 124
Alpha St. Dar 7B 158
Alpha St. Nels 9K 85
Alpha St. Salt 4B 78
Alpic Dri. T Clev 4C 62
Alpine Av. Blac 4E 108
Alpine Av. Los H 9L 135
Alpine Clo. Hodd 6E 158
Alpine Clo. Los H 9L 135
Alpine Dri. Ward 8F 184
Alpine Gro. B'brn 8J 139
Alpine Rd. Chor 3G 175
Alpine Vw. Bolt S 3L 15
Alscot Clo. Liv 2C 222
Alsop St. Pres 7J 115
Alston Av. T Clev 8D 54
Alston Clo. Sab 3E 102
Alston Dri. More 3F 22
Alston La. Als 7J 97
Alston Rd. Blac 9E 62
Alston St. Bury 9H 201
Alston St. Pres 8N 115
Alt Av. Liv 3B 222
Altcar La. Down 2M 215
Altcar La. Form 8C 206
Altcar La. Ley 1G 173
Altcar La. Liv 2A 214
Altcar La. Lyd 6M 215
Altcar Rd. Form 1A 214
Alt Ct. Liv 5K 223
Altham. 3D 122
Altham Bus. Pk. Alt 3D 122
Altham Cvn. Site. Acc 8B 122
Altham Ind. Est. Alt 3C 122
Altham La. Alt & Acc 3D 122
Altham Rd. More 4B 22
Altham Rd. South 3L 187
Altham St. Burn 1E 124
Altham St. Pad 1J 123
Altham Wlk. More 5C 22
Althorp Clo. Blac 3C 88
Althorpe Dri. South 2L 187
Altom St. B'brn 2M 139
Alton Clo. Liv 9A 214
Alt Rd. Form 1A 214
Alt Rd. H'twn 7A 214 (in two parts)
Altway. Liv 7B 222
Altway Ct. Liv 7B 222 (off Altway)
Altys La. Orm 8L 209
Alum Scar La. Sam 1A 138
Alvanley Clo. Wig 3M 221
Alvanley Grn. Liv 8H 223
Alvanley Rd. Kirkby 8H 223
Alvern Av. Ful 5G 114
Alvern Cres. Ful 5G 114
Alvina La. Kirkby 5L 223
Alwin St. Burn 4C 124
Alwood Av. Blac 4F 88
Amanda Way. Liv 6G 222
Amber Av. B'brn 7N 119
Amberbanks Gro. Blac 8B 88
Ambergate. Ing 3C 114
Ambergate. Skel 4M 219
Amberley St. B'brn 6K 139
Amberwood. K'ham 4L 111
Amberwood Dri. B'brn 7H 139
Ambledene. Bam B 1C 154
Ambleside. Wig 4M 221
Ambleside Av. Barn 1L 77
Ambleside Av. Eux 5N 173
Ambleside Av. Kno S 7M 41
Ambleside Av. Ross 5K 161
Ambleside Clo. Acc 9D 122
Ambleside Clo. B'brn 2A 140
Ambleside Clo. Bolt 9M 199
Ambleside Clo. Walt D 6A 136
Ambleside Dri. Dar 4C 158
Ambleside Rd. Blac 9K 89
Ambleside Rd. Lanc 7L 23
Ambleside Rd. Lyth A 8E 108
Ambleside Rd. Mag 9C 216
Ambleside Rd. Rib 4A 116
Ambleside Wlk. Rib 4A 116
Ambleway. Walt D 4N 135
Ambrose St. Ley 5L 153
Ambrose St. Roch 8C 204
Amelia St. B'brn 2B 140
Amersham. Skel 4M 219
Amersham Clo. New L 8C 134
Amersham Gro. Burn 6H 105
Amesbury Dri. Wig 9M 221
Amethyst St. B'brn 7M 119
Amounderness Ct. K'ham 5N 111
Amounderness Way.
Fltwd & T Clev 4F 54
Ampleforth Clo. Liv 9H 223
Ampleforth Dri. Los H 7K 135
Amy Johnson Way. Blac 4D 108
Amy St. Roch 4M 203
Amy Ter. Lyth A 3F 128
Ancenis Ct. K'ham 4N 111
Anchor. 2N 157
Anchorage Av. H End 6L 149
Anchorage M. Fltwd 1H 55
Anchorage Rd. Fltwd 1H 55
Anchor Av. Dar 3M 157
Anchor Cotts. E'ston 7D 172
Anchor Ct. Pres 1J 135
Anchor Dri. Hut 6A 134
Anchor Gro. Dar 3M 157
Anchor Retail Pk. Burn 3D 124
Anchor Rd. Dar 3M 157
Anchorsholme. 2F 62
Anchorsholme La. T Clev 3F 62
Anchorsholme La. E. T Clev 2D 62
Anchorsholme La. W. T Clev 2C 62
Anchor St. South 7H 167
Anchor St. Todm 2M 165
Anchor Way. Lyth A 8E 108
Ancliffe La. Bolt S 6M 15
Ancrum Rd. Liv 4J 223
Andelen Clo. Hap 6H 123
Anders Dri. Liv 5L 223
Anderson Clo. Bacup 6K 163
Anderson Clo. Lanc 1M 29
Anderson Rd. Wilp 2A 120
Anderson St. Blac 6C 88
Anderton. 5K 195
Anderton Clo. Ross 8D 162
Anderton M. More 3A 22
Anderton Rd. Eux 5N 173
Anderton Rd. High 5L 103
Andertons Mill. 3D 192
Anderton St. Adl 6J 195
Anderton St. Chor 7E 174
Andertons Way. Ful 4M 115
Anderton Way. Gars 6A 60
Andover Cres. Wig 9M 221
Andreas Clo. South 1H 187
Andrew Av. Liv 7F 222
Andrew Av. Ross 6L 161
Andrew Clo. B'brn 8J 139
Andrew Clo. G'mnt 4E 200
Andrew La. Bolt 7F 198
Andrew Rd. Nels 1M 105
Andrew's Ct. Burn 5E 124
Andrew St. Pres 8M 115
Anemone Dri. Has 7E 160
Angela St. B'brn 7J 139
Angel Way. Col 6B 86 (off King St.)
Anger's Hill Rd. Blac 9E 88
Angers La. Liv 4G 223
Anglesey Av. Burn 2M 123
Anglesey St. B'brn 8J 139
Angle St. Burn 1E 124
Anglezarke Rd. Adl 6J 195
Anglian Clo. Osw 3J 141
Angus St. Bacup 7G 162
Aniline St. Chor 6G 174
Annan Cres. Blac 9J 89
Annandale Clo. Liv 4J 223
Annandale Gdns. Skel 4C 220
Annarly Fold. Wors 4L 125
Annaside Clo. Blac 2E 108
Anna's Rd. Blac 7K 109
Anne Av. South 7E 186
Anne Clo. Burn 4F 124
Annecy Clo. Bury 9G 200
Anne Line Clo. Roch 8D 204 (off Wellfield St.)
Annesley Av. Blac 2E 88
Anne St. Burn 4F 124
Anne St. Lanc 9K 23
Annes Way. Lyth A 1K 129
Annie St. Acc 1B 142
Annie St. Ram 1F 200
Annie St. Ross 5M 161
Annis St. Pres 9M 115
Ann St. Barfd 8H 85
Ann St. Brier 4F 104
Ann St. Clay M 6M 121
Ann St. Roch 7C 204
Ann St. Skel 3J 219
Ansbro Av. Frec 2A 132
Ansdell. 4K 129
Ansdell Gro. Ash R 6F 114
Ansdell Gro. South 2N 167
Ansdell Rd. Blac 8D 88
Ansdell Rd. Hor 9D 196
Ansdell Rd. Wig 6N 221
Ansdell Rd. N. Lyth A 4K 129
Ansdell Rd. S. Lyth A 5K 129
Ansdell St. Pres 8M 115
Ansdell Ter. B'brn 7M 139
Anselm Ct. Blac 8B 62
Anshaw Clo. Bel 1K 197
Anson Clo. Lyth A 8D 108
Anson Pl. Wig 3M 221
Anson Rd. Frec 7N 111
Anstable Rd. More 3D 22
Anthony Rd. Lanc 9J 23
Anthorn Rd. Wig 8N 221
Antigua Dri. Lwr D 1N 157
Antrim Clo. Wig 9M 221
Antrim Rd. Blac 1C 88
Anvil Clo. Orr 6G 221
Anvil St. Bacup 7J 163
Anyon St. Dar 5B 158
Anzio Rd. Weet 5D 90
Apiary, The. Breth 1L 171
Apollo Cres. Liv 6K 223
Apostles Way. Kirkby 5J 223
Appealing La. Lyth A 7E 108
Appleby Clo. Acc 3C 142
Appleby Clo. Hogh 7G 136
Appleby Dri. Barfd 7H 85
Appleby Rd. Blac 1D 88
Appleby Rd. Liv 6J 223
Appleby St. B'brn 3A 140
Appleby St. Nels 2H 105
Appleby St. Pres 8J 115
Apple Clo. B'brn 4K 139
Apple Ct. B'brn 4K 139
Applecross Dri. Burn 5J 125
Applefields. Ley 8L 153
Applegarth. Barn 10G 52
Applegarth. Barfd 1F 104
Applegarth Rd. Hey 8M 21
Applegarth St. Earby 3E 78
Applesike. Longt 7L 133
Apple St. B'brn 4K 139
Appleton Clo. Poul F 9G 63
Appleton Rd. Skel 1K 219
Appletree Clo. Lanc 4L 29
Appletree Clo. Pen 6F 134
Apple Tree Clo. Eux 2N 173
Apple Tree Clo. St M 3G 67
Appletree Dri. Lanc 5L 29
Apple Tree Way. Osw 3L 141
Applewood Clo. Lyth A 5M 129
Appley Bridge. 5F 212
Appley Clo. App B 2E 212
Appley La. N. App B 2F 212
Appley La. S. Roby M 6F 212
Approach Way. Burn 7C 124
Apsley Brow. Liv 1A 222
Apsley Fold. L'rdge 3K 97
Aqueduct Mill Ind. Est. Pres 8G 115
Aqueduct Rd. B'brn 6K 139
Aqueduct St. Pres 8G 114
Aqueduct St. Ind. Est. Pres 8H 115
Aragon Clo. Liv 8D 216
Arago St. Acc 1B 142
Arbories Av. Pad 1G 123
Arbory Dri. Pad 9G 102
Arbory, The. Gt Plu 2D 110
Arbour Clo. Bury 7K 201
Arbour Dri. B'brn 1L 157
Arbour La. Liv 9M 223
Arbour La. Stand 3L 213
Arbour St. Bacup 4L 163
Arbour St. South 8J 167
Arboury St. Pad 1G 122
Arbury Av. Roch 8B 204
Arcade. Acc 3B 142 (off Church St.)
Arcade. South 7H 167
Arcadia. Col 6B 86 (off Market Pl.)
Arcadia Av. Liv 8C 216
Archer Hill. Carn 6A 12
Archery Av. Foul 2A 86
Arches, The. Whal 5H 101
Archibald All. Pres 9J 115
Arch St. Burn 3D 124
Arch St. Dar 6A 158
Archway Bldgs. Ash R 8D 114
Arcon Clo. Roch 7H 205
Arcon Rd. Cop 4A 194
Ardee Rd. Pres 2G 135
Arden Clo. Slyne 9J 15
Arden Clo. South 8A 186
Ardengate. Lanc 3K 29
Arden Grn. Fltwd 9E 40
Ardleigh Av. South 2L 187
Ardley Rd. Hor 9D 196
Ardmore Rd. Blac 9D 62
Ardwick St. Burn 9E 104
Argameols Clo. South 9M 167
Argosy Av. Blac 2F 88
Argosy Ct. Blac 2G 88
Argyle Pk. South 6K 167
Argyle Rd. Ley 7K 153
Argyle Rd. Poul F 8L 63
Argyle Rd. South 5K 167
Argyle St. Acc 2A 142
Argyle St. Bury 9L 201
Argyle St. Col 6A 86
Argyle St. Dar 4N 157
Argyle St. Lanc 9L 23
Argyle St. Roch 9D 204
Argyll Ct. Blac 1C 88 (off Argyll Rd.)
Argyll Rd. Blac 1C 88
Argyll Rd. Pres 8K 115
Ariel Way. Fltwd 9F 40
Arkholme. 4C 18
Arkholme Av. Blac 8D 88
Arkholme Clo. Carn 8B 12
Arkholme Ct. More 5B 22
Arkholme Dri. Longt 7K 133
Arkwright Ct. Blac F 2J 109
Arkwright Fold. B'brn 8K 139
Arkwright Rd. Pres 7J 115
Arkwright St. Burn 2A 124
Arley Av. Bury 7K 201
Arley Gdns. Burn 2D 124
Arley Ri. Mel 7F 118
Arley St. Chor 6F 174
Arley Wood Dri. Chor 8C 174
Arlington Av. Blac 2B 108
Arlington Clo. Bury 3H 201
Arlington Clo. South 8A 186
Arlington Rd. Dar 7N 157
Armadale Rd. Blac 1E 88
Armaside Rd. Cot 5A 114
Armitstead Ct. Fltwd 2F 54
Armitstead Way. Fltwd 2F 54
Arm Rd. L'boro 9H 185
Armsgrove Rd. Tur 7H 179
Armstrong Hurst Clo. Roch 2E 204
Armstrong St. Ash R 7E 114
Arncliffe Av. Acc 4M 141
Arncliffe Gro. Barfd 8G 85
Arncliffe Rd. Burn 4J 125
Arncliffe Rd. Hey 7L 21
Arncot Rd. Ram 8F 198
Arndale Cen. More 3A 22
Arndale Clo. Fltwd 2C 54
Arndale Rd. L'rdge 3H 97
Arndale Shop. Cen. Nels 2J 105
Arnhem Rd. Carn 9B 12
Arnhem Rd. Pres 9N 115 (in two parts)
Arnian Ct. Augh 3H 217
Arnian Rd. Rainf 3K 225
Arnian Way. Rainf 3K 225
Arnold Av. Blac 2C 108
Arnold Clo. Burn 7C 124
Arnold Clo. Rib 7A 116
Arnold Pl. Chor 9C 174
Arnold Rd. Eger 5F 198
Arnold Rd. Lyth A 4C 130
Arnold St. Acc 2B 142
Arno St. Pres 1L 135
Arnott Rd. Ash R 7F 114
Arnott Rd. Blac 9E 88
Arnside. 1F 4
Arnside Av. Blac 9D 88
Arnside Av. Lyth A 1J 129
Arnside Clo. Clay M 7L 121
Arnside Clo. Hogh 5G 137
Arnside Clo. Lanc 4M 29
Arnside Cres. B'brn 9F 138
Arnside Cres. More 3C 22
Arnside Dri. Roch 8J 203
Arnside Knott. 4F 4
Arnside Rd. Ash R 7B 114
Arnside Rd. Brough 8G 94
Arnside Rd. Orr 3L 221
Arnside Rd. South 7J 167
Arnside Ter. South 7J 167
Arnside Vw. Kno S 7L 41
Arran Av. B'brn 6D 140
Arran Clo. Hey 9K 21
Arran St. Burn 4B 124
Arrow La. Halt 9B 16
Arrowsmith Clo. Hogh 6G 137
Arrowsmith Dri. Hogh 7G 137
Arrowsmith Gdns. T Clev 7E 54
Arroyo Way. Ful 5L 115
Arthington St. Roch 5E 204
Arthur Pits. Roch 6K 203
Arthurs La. Hamb 1C 64
Arthur St. Bacup 4M 163
Arthur St. Barn 1L 77
Arthur St. B'brn 4K 139
Arthur St. Brier 5F 104
Arthur St. Burn 3C 124
Arthur St. Chor 7F 174
Arthur St. Clay M 6M 121
Arthur St. Fltwd 8H 41
Arthur St. Gt Har 3K 121
Arthur St. Nels 1J 105
Arthur St. Pres 1H 135
Arthur St. Roch 5A 204
Arthur St. Sough 5D 78
Arthur St. N. Fltwd 8H 41
Arthur Way. B'brn 4K 139
Artlebeck Clo. Cat 2H 25
Artlebeck Gro. Cat 2H 25
Artlebeck Rd. Cat 2H 25
Artle Pl. Lanc 6J 23
Arundel Av. Blac 6B 62
Arundel Av. Roch 9B 204
Arundel Clo. Bury 7H 201
Arundel Dri. Poul F 5H 63
Arundel Pl. Pres 1K 135
Arundel Rd. Longt 7L 133
Arundel Rd. Lyth A 4H 129
Arundel Rd. South 5F 186
Arundel St. Bolt 8E 198
Arundel St. Rish 7G 121
Arundel Way. Ley 7M 153
Ascot Clo. Lanc 3M 29
Ascot Clo. Roch 5J 203
Ascot Clo. South 9E 166
Ascot Dri. Liv 5K 223
Ascot Gdns. Slyne 9K 15
Ascot Rd. Blac 4D 88
Ascot Rd. T Clev 3H 63
Ascot Way. Acc 3C 142
Ash Av. Gal 2K 37
Ash Av. Has 4H 161
Ash Av. K'ham 5M 111
Ash Bank Clo. Brtn 2E 94
Ashbee St. Bolt 9E 198
Ashborne Dri. Bury 3J 201
Ashbourne Clo. Lanc 5K 23
Ashbourne Clo. Ward 8G 184
Ashbourne Cres. Ing 4D 114
Ashbourne Dri. Lanc 5K 23
Ashbourne Gro. More 6C 22
Ashbourne Rd. Lanc 5K 23
Ashbourne St. Roch 4J 203
Ashbrook Cres. Roch 2F 204
Ashbrook Hey. 1F 204
Ashbrook Hey La. Roch 1F 204
Ashbrook St. Lanc 8H 23
Ash Brow. Newb 3L 211
Ashburn Av. Liv 6K 223
Ashburnham Rd. Col 9L 85
Ashburton Ct. Blac 3B 88
Ashburton Rd. Blac 3B 88
Ashby St. Chor 8E 174
Ash Clo. App B 5G 213
Ash Clo. Barr 1K 101
Ash Clo. Elsw 1M 91
Ash Clo. Orm 7J 209
Ash Clo. Rish 9H 121
Ash Clo. Roch 1F 204
Ashcombe Ga. T Clev 4K 63
Ash Coppice. Lea 7A 114
Ash Ct. B'brn 1A 140 (off Plane St.)
Ash Ct. Clift 7H 113
Ash Cres. Frec 3M 131
Ashcroft. Hey 7M 21
Ashcroft. Roch 1G 205
Ashcroft Av. Orm 6L 209
Ashcroft Clo. Cat 2G 25
Ashcroft Rd. Form 2A 214
Ashcroft Rd. Know I 7N 223
Ashdale Gro. T Clev 1L 63
Ashdale Pl. Lanc 6J 23
Ashdene. Roch 1A 204
Ashdene. Todm 6L 165
Ashdene Cres. Bolt 8K 199
Ashdown Clo. Poul F 6H 63
Ashdown Clo. South 1L 187
Ashdown Dri. Clay W 4E 154
Ashdown M. Ful 3A 116
Ash Dri. Frec 3M 131
Ash Dri. Poul F 9K 63
Ash Dri. T Clev 2J 63
Ash Dri. W'ton 3J 131
Ash Dri. War 4B 12
Ash Dri. W Brad 5K 73
Asheldon St. Pres 8N 115
Ashendean Vw. Pad 9J 103
Ashenhurst Clo. Todm 9K 147
Ashenhurst Rd. Todm 9J 147
Ashes La. Miln 6H 205
Ashes La. Todm 8N 147
Ashfield. Clay W 4E 154
Ashfield. Ful 1J 115
Ashfield Av. Lanc 9H 23
Ashfield Av. More 2F 22
Ashfield Av. Roch 8C 204
Ashfield Cvn. Pk. Blac 2M 109
Ashfield Clo. Barfd 1G 104
Ashfield Ct. Blac 5E 62
Ashfield Ct. Ing 3C 114
Ashfield Gro. Bolt 7G 199
Ashfield Ho. Blac 5E 62
Ashfield Ho. Roch 8C 204
Ashfield La. Miln 9J 205
Ashfield Ri. Catt 2A 68
Ashfield Rd. And 5K 195
Ashfield Rd. Blac & T Clev 6E 62
Ashfield Rd. Burn 3D 124
Ashfield Rd. Chor 7D 174
Ashfield Rd. Roch 9B 204
Ashfields. Ley 6D 152
Ashfield Ter. App B 4F 212
Ashford Av. Lanc 4J 29
Ashford Clo. Bolt 9L 199
Ashford Clo. Lanc 4K 29

Ashford Cres.—Back La.

Ashford Cres. Brough 7F 94
Ashford Rd. Ash R 7B 114
Ashford Rd. Lanc 4J 29
Ashford St. Nels 3J 105
Ash Gro. Bam B 7B 136
Ash Gro. Barn 2M 77
Ash Gro. Chor 9E 174
Ash Gro. Dar 5B 158
Ash Gro. For H 8D 144
Ash Gro. Gars 4M 59
Ash Gro. Harw 9M 199
Ash Gro. Lanc 2K 29
Ash Gro. Longt 8K 133
Ash Gro. New L 1C 152
Ash Gro. Orr 5J 221
Ash Gro. Pre 9N 41
Ash Gro. Pres 8A 116
Ash Gro. Rainf 4K 225
Ash Gro. Ram 2E 200
Ash Gro. Raw 4M 161
(off Prospect Rd.)
Ash Gro. St M 4G 66
Ash Gro. Skel 2H 219
Ash Gro. Tot 8F 200
Ash Gro. Wesh 2N 111
Ash Gro. W Grn 6H 111
Ash Holme. Pres 6M 115
Ashia Clo. Roch 7D 204
Ashington Clo. Bolt 9B 198
Ashlands Clo. Ram 4J 181
(off Water La.)
Ash La. Clift 8H 113
Ash La. Gt Har 3H 121
Ash La. L'rdge 2K 97
Ashlea Gro. Stalm 5B 56
Ashleigh Ct. Arns 1F 4
Ashleigh Ct. Ful 2K 115
Ashleigh M. Blac 6E 88
(off Lever St.)
Ashleigh Rd. Arns 1F 4
Ashleigh Rd. Liv 3E 222
Ashleigh St. Dar 9B 158
Ashleigh St. Pres 1M 135
Ashley Clo. Blac 9C 62
Ashley Clo. Liv 5K 223
Ashley Clo. Roch 9N 203
Ashley Clo. T Clev 4H 63
Ashley Ct. Poul F 8J 63
Ashley Ct. Whitw 4A 184
Ashley La. Goos 3C 96
Ashley M. Ash R 8F 114
Ashley Rd. Lyth A 8F 108
Ashley Rd. South 7J 167
Ashley Rd. Uph 9M 211
Ashley St. Burn 2D 124
Ash Mdw. Lea 6A 114
Ashmeadow Gro. Neth K 4C 16
Ashmeadow La. Brins 7N 155
Ashmeadow Rd. Arns 1F 4
Ashmeadow Rd. Neth K 4C 16
Ashmead Rd. Uph 8L 211
Ashmere Clo. Has 8H 161
Ashmoor St. Pres 8H 115
Ashmore Gro. T Clev 2D 62
Ashmount Dri. Roch 3C 204
Ashmuir Hey. Liv 9L 223
Ashness Clo. Ful 1J 115
Ashover Clo. Bolt 7F 198
Ashridge Way. Orr 2L 221
Ash Rd. Cop 5A 194
Ash Rd. Elsw 9M 65
Ash St. Bacup 4K 163
Ash St. B'brn 1A 140
Ash St. Blac 3C 108
Ash St. Burn 4F 124
Ash St. Fltwd 9G 40
Ash St. Gt Har 3J 121
Ash St. Heyw 9F 202
Ash St. Nels 2K 105
Ash St. Osw 4K 141
Ash St. South 9J 167
Ash St. Traw 9F 86
Ashton & Lea Golf Course. . . . 7N 113
Ashton Av. Kno S 8K 41
Ashton Clo. Ash R 8D 114
Ashton Ct. Lyth A 1D 128
Ashton Dri. Lanc 6J 23
Ashton Dri. Nels 4J 105
Ashton Garden Ct. Lyth A 1E 128
Ashton Gardens. 1D 128
Ashton Gdns. Roch 8B 204
Ashtongate. Ash R 8B 114
Ashton Ho. Dar 7B 158
Ashton La. Dar 7A 158
Ashton La. Out R 8K 57
Ashton Memorial. 9M 23
Ashton on Ribble. 8B 114
Ashton Pk. Golf Course. 7G 28
Ashton Pl. South 8H 167
Ashton Rd. Blac 7C 88
Ashton Rd. Dar 7B 158
Ashton Rd. Lanc 4J 29
(in two parts)
Ashton Rd. More 3C 22
Ashton Rd. South 4F 186
Ashton St. Ash R 9G 115
Ashton St. L'rdge 2J 97
Ashton St. Lyth A 5N 129
Ashton St. Roch 8B 204
Ashton Wlk. Lanc 8K 23
(off Cheapside)
Ashtree Ct. Ful 5D 114
Ashtree Ct. High W 5E 136
Ash Tree Gro. Bolt S 6K 15
Ashtree Gro. Pen 4E 134
Ashtrees. Maw 3N 191
Ashtrees Way. Carn 8A 12
(off Pond St.)
Ashtrees Way. Carn 8A 12
(Market St.)
Ashtree Wlk. Barfd 9H 85
Ashurst. 8M 211
Ashurst Clo. Skel 1N 219
Ashurst Gdns. Skel 8M 211
Ashurst Rd. Ley 6N 153
Ashurst Rd. Skel 9M 211
Ashurst Rd. Stand 2L 213
Ashurst's Beacon. 8B 212
Ashville Ter. B'brn 8L 139
Ashwall St. Skel 3H 219
Ashwell M. Bolt 9J 199
Ashwell Pl. T Clev 4C 62
Ashwell St. Bolt 9H 199
Ashwood. Skel 9N 211
Ashwood Av. Ram 7J 181
Ashwood Clo. Kirkby 5K 223
Ashwood Clo. Lyth A 4L 129
Ashwood Ct. Longt 9L 133
(off Little Twining)
Ashwood Dri. Bury 7G 201
Ashwood Dri. L'boro 9J 185
Ashwood Rd. Ful 2G 114
Ashworth Clo. B'brn 3K 139
Ashworth Clo. L'boro 7K 185
Ashworth Ct. Blac 3D 88
Ashworth Ct. Pres 2L 135
Ashworth Dri. Hest B 7J 15
Ashworth Gro. Pres 2M 135
Ashworth La. Bolt 8F 198
Ashworth La. Pres 2L 135
Ashworth La. Ross 4D 162
Ashworth Rd. Blac 1J 109
Ashworth Rd. Roch & Heyw . . . 2C 202
Ashworth Rd. Ross 5D 162
Ashworth St. Acc 6D 142
Ashworth St. Bacup 4L 163
Ashworth St. Bam B 6B 136
Ashworth St. For H 9E 144
Ashworth St. Pres 1L 135
Ashworth St. Rish 8H 121
Ashworth St. Roch 5A 204
Ashworth St. Ross 5A 162
Ashworth St. Stac 7H 163
Ashworth St. Waterf 7D 162
(in two parts)
Ashworth Ter. Bacup 7F 162
Ashworth Ter. Bolt 9L 199
Ashworth Ter. Dar 7N 157
Ashworth Ter. Ross 5D 162
(off Burnley Rd.)
Askew La. Burt 8H 7
Askrigg Clo. Acc 2C 142
Askrigg Clo. Blac 2G 108
Asland Clo. Bam B 8D 136
Asland Gdns. South 2B 168
Asmall Clo. Orm 6J 209
Asmall La. Hals & Scar 4C 208
Asmall La. Orm 5G 208
Aspden St. Bam B 7A 136
Aspden St. Todm 1L 165
Aspels Cres. Pen 4F 134
Aspels Nook. Pen 4F 134
Aspels, The. Pen 4F 134
Aspen Clo. Kirkby 4L 223
Aspendale Clo. Longt 7K 133
Aspen Dri. Burn 2G 124
Aspen Fold. Osw 3H 141
Aspen Gdns. Chor 8D 174
Aspen Gdns. Roch 4L 203
Aspen La. Earby 2E 78
Aspen La. Osw 4H 141
Aspen Way. Skel 1J 219
Aspinall Clo. Pen 6G 134
Aspinall Cres. Liv 2F 214
Aspinall Fold. B'brn 9M 119
Aspinall Rd. Stand 3L 213
Aspley Gro. Traw 8F 86
(off Skipton Rd.)
Asshawes, The. Hth C 4H 195
Assheton Pl. Rib 5A 116
Assheton Rd. B'brn 3H 139
Asten Bldgs. Ross 8D 162
Aster Chase. Lwr D 9A 140
Aster Dri. Liv 5J 223
Astland Gdns. Tar 5D 150
Astland St. Lyth A 2E 128
Astley Bridge. 9F 198
Astley Clo. Rainf 3K 225
Astley Ct. Lanc 1H 29
Astley Cres. Frec 2A 132
Astley Ga. B'brn 3M 139
Astley Hall Mus. & Art Gallery. 5C 174
Astley Hill Dri. Ham 1H 201
Astley Rd. Bolt 8L 199
Astley Rd. Chor 5D 174
Astley St. Chor 5E 174
Astley St. Dar 8A 158
Astley St. L'rdge 3J 97
Astley Ter. Dar 8A 158
Astley Village. 4C 174
Aston Av. T Clev 1G 62
Aston St. Weet 4D 90
Aston Wlk. B'brn 8A 140
Aston Way. M Side 5E 152
Astra Bus. Cen. Rib 3E 116
Athelstan Fold. Ful 6F 114
Athens Vw. Burn 4G 125
(off Athletic St.)
Atherfield. Bolt 9L 199
Atherstone. Roch 5B 204
(off Spotland Rd.)
Atherstone Clo. Bury 9H 201
Atherton Rd. Lanc 7H 23
Atherton Rd. Ley 7G 152
Atherton St. Adl 7J 195
Atherton St. Bacup 7F 162
Atherton Way. Bacup 7F 162
Athletic St. Burn 4G 124
Athlone Av. Blac 9C 62
Athlone Av. Bolt 8C 198
Athlone Av. Bury 9L 201
Athole Gro. South 7M 167
Athol Gro. Chor 8G 174
Atholl Cres. Liv 8C 222
Atholl St. Pres 9G 115
Athol St. Nels 2K 105
Athol St. Ram 7H 181
Athol St. Roch 4E 204
Athol St. N. Burn 4B 124
Athol St. S. Burn 4B 124
Atkinson Art Gallery. 7H 167
(off Lord St.)
Atkinson St. Brclf 7K 105
Atkinson St. Col 8N 85
(in two parts)
Atlanta Ct. Liv 3J 223
Atlas Rd. Dar 6A 158
Atlas St. Clay M 8M 121
Atrium Ct. Burn 5F 124
Aubigny Dri. Ful 5G 115
Aubrey St. Roch 8C 204
Auburn Gro. Blac 8D 88
Auckland St. Dar 8B 158
Auden Lea. T Clev 9F 54
Audenshaw Rd. More 4C 22
Audley Clo. Lyth A 3K 129
Audley Clo. Nels 2J 105
(off Audley Ct.)
Audley Ct. Nels 2J 105
Audley La. B'brn 3A 140
Audley Range. B'brn 4N 139
Audley St. B'brn 3A 140
Aughton. 6M 17
(Lancaster)
Aughton. 4F 216
(Ormskirk)
Aughton Brow. A'ton 6M 17
Aughton Ct. Lanc 4K 23
Aughton M. South 9G 167
Aughton Park. 1J 217
Aughton Pk. Dri. Augh 1J 217
Aughton Rd. A'ton 6H 17
Aughton Rd. South 8F 166
Aughton St. Fltwd 8H 41
Aughton St. Orm 8J 209
(in two parts)
Aughton Wlk. Pres 8J 115
Augusta Clo. Roch 3B 204
(in two parts)
Augusta St. Acc 4B 142
Augusta St. Roch 4B 204
Austen Way. Blac 3N 109
Auster Cres. Frec 7N 111
Austin Clo. Ley 7K 153
Austin Clo. Liv 7J 223
Austin Cres. Ful 5E 114
Austin Gro. Blac 9B 88
Austin St. Bacup 5K 163
(off Union St.)
Austin St. Burn 4C 124
Austin St. Bury 8K 201
Austwick Rd. Lanc 6H 23
(in two parts)
Austwick Way. Acc 3D 142
Avallon Clo. Tot 6E 200
Avallon Way. Dar 6C 158
Avalon Clo. Burn 2L 123
Avalon Dri. Frec 1A 132
Avalwood Av. Longt 8M 133
Avebury Clo. B'brn 8A 140
Aveling Dri. South 9F 148
Avelon Clo. Liv 6A 216
Avenham. 2J 135
Avenham Clo. Banks 1G 169
Avenham Colonnade. Pres 2K 135
Avenham Ct. Pres 1K 135
Avenham Gro. Blac 4C 88
Avenham La. Pres 2K 135
Avenham Pl. Newt 7D 112
Avenham Pl. Pres 2K 135
Avenham Rd. Chor 7E 174
Avenham Rd. Pres 1K 135
Avenham St. Pres 1K 135
Avenham Ter. Pres 2K 135
Avenham Wlk. Pres 2K 135
Avenue Pde. Acc 2B 142
Avenue Rd. Blac 2H 89
Avenue Rd. Hur G 1M 99
Avenue, The. Adl 5J 195
Avenue, The. B'ley 6A 84
Avenue, The. Bil 8G 221
Avenue, The. Burn 7H 125
Avenue, The. Bury 8L 201
Avenue, The. Chur 9L 59
Avenue, The. Gars 3M 59
Avenue, The. Ing 3D 114
Avenue, The. Lea 8A 114
Avenue, The. Ley 9J 153
Avenue, The. Old L 5C 100
Avenue, The. Orm 6J 209
(Halsall La.)
Avenue, The. Orm 6K 209
(Southport Rd.)
Avenue, The. Pen 3E 134
Avenue, The. Poul F 7J 63
Avenue, The. Rainf 4K 225
Avenue, The. South 1E 168
(Station Rd.)
Avenue, The. South 9D 168
(Wyke La.)
Avenue, The. Stand L 8N 213
Aviemore Clo. B'brn 4A 140
Aviemore Clo. Ram 3F 200
Avocet Ct. Ley 6D 152
Avon Av. Fltwd 4D 54
Avon Bri. Ful 1F 114
Avon Clo. B'brn 5L 139
Avon Clo. Kirkby 4L 223
Avon Clo. Miln 7K 205
Avon Ct. Burn 2B 124
Avondale Av. B'brn 3E 140
Avondale Av. Burn 2A 124
Avondale Av. Bury 9K 201
Avondale Av. Liv 2B 222
Avondale Clo. Dar 5M 157
Avondale Cres. Blac 2F 108
Avondale Dri. Los H 8L 135
Avondale Dri. Ram 3E 200
Avondale Dri. Tar 7E 150
Avondale M. Dar 4M 157
Avondale Rd. Chor 7E 174
Avondale Rd. Dar 5M 157
Avondale Rd. Hey 5M 21
Avondale Rd. Lanc 1L 29
Avondale Rd. Lyth A 9C 108
Avondale Rd. Nels 3H 105
Avondale Rd. South 6H 167
Avondale Rd. N. South 5J 167
Avondale St. Col 6D 86
Avondale St. Stand 3N 213
Avon Dri. Barn 1N 77
Avon Dri. Bury 5L 201
Avon Gdns. Cot 4A 114
Avon Grn. Fltwd 9E 40
Avon Ho. Pres 9N 115
Avon Pl. Blac 2C 88
Avon Rd. Bil 4M 221
Avonside Av. T Clev 9G 55
Avon St. Lyth A 2E 128
Avonwood Clo. Dar 5M 157
Avroe Cres. Blac 5D 108
Aylesbury Av. Blac 9D 88
Aylesbury Wlk. Burn 7G 105
Ayr Clo. South 1M 187
Ayr Ct. Fltwd 5E 54
Ayrefield Gro. Shev 6G 213
Ayrefield Rd. Roby M 8F 212
Ayr Gro. Burn 6B 124
Ayr Rd. B'brn 5D 140
Ayr St. Bolt 9J 199
Ayr St. Lanc 9M 23
Ayrton Av. Blac 2D 108
Ayrton St. Col 6B 86
Aysgarth. Roch 4E 204
Aysgarth Av. Ful 2J 115
Aysgarth Ct. Blac 2F 108
Aysgarth Dri. Acc 2C 142
Aysgarth Dri. Dar 5M 157
Aysgarth Dri. Lanc 4K 23
Aysgarth Rd. Lanc 8H 23
Azalea Clo. Ful 3M 115
Azalea Clo. Ley 5A 154
Azalea Gro. More 3E 22
Azalea Rd. B'brn 2J 139

B

Babbacombe Av. Blac 3B 108
Baber Wlk. Burn 9E 198
Babylon La. Adl & And 5K 195
Babylon La. Hth C 4K 195
Bk. Albany St. Roch 8D 204
Bk. Albert Rd. Col 7A 86
(off Albert Rd.)
Bk. Albert St. Fltwd 9H 41
(off Albert St.)
Bk. Albert St. Pad 1H 123
(off Albert St.)
Bk. Albion Pl. Bury 9L 201
Bk. Alfred St. Ram 9G 180
(off Mary St.)
Bk. Altham St. Pad 1J 123
Bk. Argyle St. Bury 8L 201
Bk. Arthur St. Clay M 6M 121
Bk. Ashburton Rd. Blac 3C 88
Bk. Ashby St. Chor 8F 174
Bk. Atkinson St. Col 7N 85
Bk. Avondale Rd. E. Hey 5M 21
Bk. Avondale Rd. W. Hey 5M 21
Bk. Bath St. South 6H 167
Bk. Beehive Ter. Ross 2G 160
(off Blackburn Rd.)
Bk. Birch St. Bury 9L 201
(in two parts)
Bk. Blackburn Rd. W. Bolt 9E 198
(off Blackburn Rd.)
Bk. Bolton Rd. Dar 8B 158
Bk. Bond St. Col 6A 86
(off Bond St.)
Bk. Boundry St. Col 7A 86
Bk. Bourne's Row. Hogh 7G 137
Bk. Bradshaw St. Roch 5D 204
Bk. Bridge St. Ram 8H 181
Bk. Brook St. N. Bury 9M 201
(in two parts)
Back Brow. Uph 4F 220
Bk. Brown St. Col 7N 85
Bk. Burnley Rd. Acc 2B 142
Bk. Burnley Rd. Bury 5K 201
Bk. Byrom St. Bury 9G 201
(off Byrom St.)
Bk. Byrom St. Todm 1L 165
Bk. Byrom St. S. Bury 9G 201
Bk. Calton St. More 2B 22
Bk. Cambridge St. Col 7A 86
(off Cambridge St.)
Bk. Canada St. Hor 9C 196
Bk. Canning St. Bury 9L 201
Bk. Carr Mill St. Ross 2G 160
Bk. Carshalton Rd. Blac 3B 88
Bk. Cateaton St. Bury 9L 201
Bk. Cemetery Ter. Bacup 7J 163
Bk. Chapel St. Col 7A 86
(off Chapel St.)
Bk. Chapel St. Hor 9D 196
Bk. Chapel St. Tot 6E 200
Bk. Chapel St. Ward 7F 17
Bk. Chesham Rd. N. Bury 9M 201
(off Chesham Rd.)
Bk. Chesham Rd. S. Bury 9M 201
(off Chesham St.)
Bk. Chester St. Bury 9M 201
(off Chester St.)
Bk. Church St. Barn 2M 77
(off Church St.)
Bk. Church St. Barfd 8H 85
Bk. Church St. Blac 5B 88
Bk. Church St. Hap 5H 123
(off Church St.)
Bk. Church St. Newc 5C 162
Bk. Claremont. More 4N 21
(off Claremont Rd.)
Bk. Clarendon Rd. Blac 8B 88
Bk. Clarendon Rd. More 4N 21
(off Clarendon Rd. E.)
Bk. Clay St. Brom X 6G 198
Bk. Clay St. E. Brom X 6G 198
Bk. Clayton St. Nels 1H 105
(off Clayton St.)
Bk. Clifton St. Bury 9L 201
Bk. Colne Rd. Barn 3L 77
Bk. Colne Rd. Traw 9F 86
(off Colne Rd.)
Bk. Commercial St. Todm 2M 165
Bk. Commons. Clith 2K 81
Bk. Compton Rd. South 2H 187
Bk. Constablelee. Ross 3M 161
Bk. Cookson St. Blac 4C 88
Bk. Cop La. Fltwd 9G 41
Bk. Cowm La. Whitw 4N 183
Bk. Crescent St. More 3A 22
Bk. Crown St. Hor 9B 196
Bk. Dale St. Miln 8J 205
Bk. Darwen Rd. N. Eger 4E 198
Bk. Delamere St. S. Bury 8M 201
(off Delamere St.)
Bk. Denton St. Bury 9L 201
Bk. Derby Rd. T Clev 9C 54
Bk. Der St. Todm 2M 165
Bk. Dover St. Lwr D 9N 139
Bk. Drake St. Roch 7C 204
Bk. Drinkhouse La. Crost 5L 171
Bk. Duckworth St. Dar 6A 158
Bk. Duke St. Col 7A 86
(off Duke St.)
Bk. Duncan St. Hor 9D 196
Bk. Earl St. Col 7A 86
(off Earl St.)
Bk. East Bank. Barfd 7H 85
Bk. Eaves St. Blac 3B 88
Bk. Eden St. Ram 9E 198
Bk. Eldon St. Bury 9L 201
Bk. Emmett St. Hor 9C 196
Bk. Epsom Rd. T Clev 3F 62
Bk. Fazakerley St. Chor 6E 174
Bk. Forest Rd. South 8K 167
(in two parts)
Bk. Garston St. Bury 9M 201
(off Garston St.)
Back Ga. I'ton 3N 19
(off Croft Rd.)
Bk. George St. Hor 9E 196
(off George St.)
Bk. Gisburn Rd. Black 4J 85
Bk. Glen Eldon Rd. Lyth A 1E 128
Bk. Goodlad St. Bury 9G 201
(off Tottington Rd.)
Bk. Green St. More 2B 22
(in two parts)
Bk. Grimshaw St. Pres 1K 135
Bk. Grove Ter. More 4F 22
(off Kendal Dri.)
Bk. Halifax Rd. Brclf 7L 105
Bk. Hall St. Col 7A 86
(off Hall St.)
Bk. Hanson St. Bury 9L 201
Bk. Harry St. Barfd 8H 85
Bk. Haslam St. Bury 9M 201
Bk. Headroomgate Rd. Lyth A 9F 108
Bk. Hesketh St. Gt Har 4J 121
(off Blackburn Rd.)
Bk. Heys. Osw 5L 141
Bk. Heysham Rd. Hey 5M 21
Bk. High St. Bel 9K 177
Bk. High St. Blac 4B 88
Bk. High St. Tur 1J 199
Bk. Hill St. Brier 4D 104
(off Hill St.)
Bk. Hill St. Ross 9M 143
(off Hill St.)
Bk. Hilton St. Bury 9L 201
Bk. Holland St. Ram 9F 198
Bk. Hope St. Bacup 3K 163
Bk. Hornby St. Bury 8L 201
Bk. Hornby St. W. Bury 9L 201
(off Walmersley Rd.)
Backhouse St. Osw 4L 141
Bk. Hulme St. Bury 9J 201
(off Hulme St.)
Bk. Hunter St. Carn 8A 12
Bk. Huntley Mt. Rd. Bury 9N 201
Bk. Ivy Bank Rd. Ram 8E 198
Bk. King St. Acc 2A 142
Bk. Knowlys Rd. Hey 8L 21
Back La. Acc 6D 142
Back La. App B & Stand 4G 213
Back La. Arns 1E 4
Back La. Augh 4D 216
Back La. Bic 8M 217
Back La. Breth 1J 171
Back La. Brclf & S'fld 1A 106
Back La. Burs 7C 190
Back La. Carn 2B 16
Back La. Char R 8J 173
Back La. Clay W 5B 154
(in two parts)
Back La. Down 9K 207
(in two parts)
Back La. Goos 8B 70
Back La. Gt Ecc 6N 65
Back La. Hale 1B 6
Back La. Hell 1D 52
Back La. High 3K 103
Back La. Hol M 7D 212
Back La. K Lon 6F 8
(off Lunefield Dri.)

Barley Clo.—Belgrave Sq.

Barley Clo. B'brn 3L 139
Barley Cop La. Lanc 4G 22
Barleydale Rd. Barfd 6J 85
Barleyfield. Bam B 4E 154
Barley Green. 6A 84
Barley Gro. Burn 3G 125
Barley Holme Rd. Ross 9M 143
Barley Holme St. Ross 8M 143
Barley La. B'ley 3M 83
Barley La. B'brn 3L 139
Barley New Rd. B'ley & Rou 6B 84
Barley St. Pad 2H 123
Barley Way. B'brn 4L 139
Barlow Ct. Tur 9L 179
Barlow Cres. Blac 6E 88
Barlow Fold. Ross 7K 161
Barlow Moor Clo. Roch 3J 203
Barlow Pk. Av. Bolt 8D 198
Barlows Bldgs. Ross 6L 161
Barlow's La. Hals 8K 187
Barlow St. Acc 2N 141
Barlow St. Bacup 7G 162
Barlow St. Pres 7H 115
(Brook St., in two parts)
Barlow St. Pres 7J 115
(Garstang Rd.)
Barlow St. Roch 6D 204
Barlow St. Ross 4M 161
Barmouth Av. Blac 8G 88
Barmouth Cres. B'brn 8M 119
Barmskin La. Hesk 4E 192
Barnacre Clo. Ful 1K 115
Barnacre Clo. Lanc 5M 29
Barn Acre Lodge Dri. Bncr 2D 60
Barnacre Rd. L'rdge 2H 97
Barnard Clo. Osw 4J 141
Barn Clo. Boot 6A 222
Barn Clo. Mere B 4M 169
Barn Cft. Clith 4K 81
Barn Cft. Ley 6E 152
Barn Cft. Pen 3E 134
Barnes Av. Ross 5L 161
Barnes Clo. Ram 2F 200
Barnes Ct. Burn 5H 125
Barnes Dri. Liv 7B 216
Barnes Dri. T Clev 7E 54
Barnes Meadows. L'boro 5M 185
Barnes Rd. Augh 9K 209
Barnes Rd. Hey 5M 21
Barnes Rd. Skel 2J 219
Barnes Sq. Clay M 6M 121
Barnes St. Acc 2B 142
(in two parts)
Barnes St. Burn 3E 124
Barnes St. Chu 2L 141
Barnes St. Clay M 6L 121
Barnes St. Has 3G 160
Barnes St. Todm 6K 165
(off Rochdale Rd.)
Barnfield. 3C 142
Barnfield. K'ham 4M 111
Barnfield. L'boro 8N 185
Barnfield. Los H 8K 135
Barnfield. Much H 5J 151
Barnfield Av. Burn 3K 125
Barnfield Bus. Cen. Nels 4K 105
Barnfield Clo. Col 6D 86
Barnfield Clo. Eger 3E 198
Barnfield Clo. T Clev 8F 54
Barnfield Dri. Skel 4B 220
Barn Fld. La. Ward 7D 184
Barnfield Mnr. Sing 8C 64
Barnfield St. Acc 3C 142
Barnfield St. Roch 3C 204
Barnfield Way. Alt 4D 122
Barn Flatt Clo. High W 4C 136
Barn Gill Clo. B'brn 5N 139
Barn Hey. Longt 7L 133
Barn Hey Dri. Far M 4H 153
Barn Hey Rd. Liv 8M 223
Barn Mdw. Bam B 1D 154
Barn Mdw. Tur 9K 179
Barn Mdw. Cres. Rish 8J 121
Barnmeadow La. Gt Har 4J 121
Barnoldswick. 2M 77
Barnoldswick La. Burt L 3K 19
Barnoldswick Rd. Black 4K 85
Barnoldswick Rd. Foul 9M 77
Barnoldswick Rd. Kel 6C 78
Barnsfold. Ful 3G 114
Barnside. Eux 3M 173
Barnside. Whitw 6N 183
Barnside Clo. Bury 5K 201
Barns La. Goos 7B 70
Barnstaple Way. Cot 3C 114
Barnston Clo. Bolt 9F 198
Barn Vw. Hth C 5H 195
Barnwood Cres. Earby 3F 78
Barnwood Rd. Earby 3E 78
Baron Fold. Ross 7C 162
Baron Rd. Blac 9C 88
Barons Clo. Lwr D 9A 140
Baron St. Dar 5M 157
Baron St. Roch 6C 204
Baron St. Ross 6A 162
Barons Way. Eux 4N 173
Barons Way. Lwr D 1A 158
Barracks Rd. Burn 3B 124
Barracks, The. Hals 3B 208
Barrel Sykes. Set 2N 35
(off Langcliffe Rd.)
Barrel Hill Brow. Bolt B 7G 50
Barret St. Earby 3D 78
Barrett Av. South 3G 187
Barrett Rd. South 3G 186
Barrett St. Burn 1E 124
Barrie Way. Bolt 9H 199
Barrington Clo. Wins 9N 221
Barrington Dri. South 8B 186
Barrison Grn. Scar 1K 209
Barritt Rd. Ross 5L 161
Barronwood Ct. Tar 1E 170
Barrow. 1K 101
Barrow Bridge. 9N 197
Barrow Bri. Rd. Bolt 9N 197
Barrowdale Av. Nels 3K 105
Barrowford. 7H 85
Barrowford Rd. Col 6L 85
(in two parts)
Barrowford Rd. Pad & Fence 7J 103
(in two parts)
Barrow La. More 3F 22
Barrow Nook. 9C 218
Barrow Nook La. Bic 8C 218
Barrows La. Gt Ecc 6N 65
Barrows La. Hey 1J 27
Barrows La. E. Gt Ecc 6N 65
Barry Av. Ing 6C 114
Barry Gro. Hey 1L 27
Barry St. Burn 3A 124
Bar St. Burn 1F 124
Bar St. Todm 3K 165
Bar Ter. Whitw 7N 183
Bartholomew Rd. More 4C 22
Bartle La. Lwr B 2M 113
Bartle Pl. Ash R 8B 114
Bartle Rd. Lyth A 9G 109
Bartle St. Burn 4B 124
Barton. 5L 207
(Ormskirk)
Barton. 2E 94
(Preston)
Barton & Broughton. 5D 94
Barton Av. Blac 8B 88
Barton Av. Kno S 8L 41
Barton Gdns. Lanc 2M 29
Barton La. Brtn 2F 94
Barton Mansion. Lyth A 1C 128
Barton Rd. Lanc 3L 29
Barton Rd. Lyth A 9D 108
Bartons Clo. South 1C 168
Barton Sq. Kno S 8L 41
Barton St. B'brn 3M 139
Barton St. Pem 6L 221
Barwood Lee. Ram 9H 181
Bashal Eaves. 9B 72
Bashall Gro. Far 4L 153
Bashall Town. 2D 80
Bashful All. Lanc 8K 23
(off Sir Simons Arc.)
Basil Ct. Roch 7E 204
Basil St. Col 7A 86
Basil St. Pres 7M 115
Basil St. Roch 7E 204
Basnett St. Burn 9G 104
Bassenthwaite Av. Liv 6J 223
Bassenthwaite Rd. Blac 8J 89
Bassett Clo. Roch 2B 204
Bassett Gdns. Roch 2B 204
Bassett Gro. Wig 9M 221
Bassett Way. Roch 3B 204
Bass La. Bury 2J 201
Bastwell. 1N 139
Bastwell Rd. B'brn 1N 139
Bateman Gro. More 3B 22
Bateman Rd. More 3B 22
Bates St. Clay M 6L 121
Bathgate Way. Liv 4J 223
Bath Mill La. Lanc 8L 23
Bath Mill Sq. Lanc 8L 23
(off Woodville St.)
Bath Rd. Lyth A 5A 130
Bath Springs. Orm 7L 209
Bath Springs Ct. Orm 7L 209
Bath St. Acc 4A 142
Bath St. Ash R 8G 114
Bath St. Bacup 5L 163
Bath St. B'brn 4K 139
Bath St. Blac 9B 88
Bath St. Col 6B 86
Bath St. Dar 6A 158
Bath St. Lanc 8L 23
Bath St. Lyth A 5A 130
Bath St. More 3A 22
Bath St. Nels 2K 105
Bath St. Roch 4D 204
Bath St. South 6H 167
Bath St. Todm 2L 165
(off Dalton St.)
Bath St. N. South 6H 167
Bathurst Av. Blac 3G 88
Bathurst St. B'brn 3L 139
Batridge Rd. Tur 7G 178
Battersby St. Bury 9B 202
Battersby St. Roch 7M 203
Battismore Rd. More 3A 22
Battle Way. Liv 1B 214
Baum, The. Roch 5C 204
Bawdlands. Clith 3K 81
Bawhead Rd. Earby 3E 78
Baxendale St. Bolt 9E 198
Baxenden. 6D 142
Baxenden Golf Course. 5F 142
Baxter Ga. More 2B 22
Bayard St. Burn 3M 123
Baycliffe Cres. More 3A 22
Bay Clo. Hey 1J 27
Bay Gate. 8G 50
Bay Horse. 7N 37
Bay Horse Dri. Lanc 4M 29
Bay Horse La. Catf 5G 93
Bay Horse Rd. Bay H 6B 38
Bayley Fold. Clith 3L 81
Bayley St. Clay M 6L 121
Baylton Ct. Catt 1A 68
Baylton Dri. Catt 1A 68
Baynes St. Hodd 6F 158
Bay Rd. Hey 1J 27
Bay Rd. Rib 7A 116
Bayside. Fltwd 1H 55
Bay St. B'brn 1A 140
Bay St. Heyw 9F 202
Bay St. Roch 4D 204
Bayswater. Blac 7C 62
Bay, The. T Clev 7C 54
Baytree Clo. Los H 8M 135
Baytree Clo. South 1C 168
Bay Tree Farm. Lea 9A 114
Baytree Gro. Ram 3G 200
Bay Tree Rd. Clay W 4D 154
Baytree Wlk. Whitw 5N 183
Bay Vw. Over K 1F 16
Bay Vw. Av. Slyne 9J 15
Bay Vw. Cres. Slyne 9J 15
Bay Vw. Dri. Hey 8L 21
Baywood St. B'brn 1N 139
Bazil. 8B 28
Bazil Gro. Over 8B 28
Bazil La. Over 8B 28
Bazley Rd. Lyth A 5K 129
Bazley St. Bolt 9N 197
Beacham Rd. South 7L 167
Beach Av. Lyth A 5J 129
Beach Av. T Clev 9D 54
Beachcomber Dri. T Clev 9C 54
Beach Ct. Lyth A 5B 130
Beach Ct. T Clev 9C 54
Beachcroft. T Clev 8C 54
Beachley Rd. Ing 6D 114
Beachley Sq. Burn 2B 124
Beach M. South 8F 166
Beach Priory Gdns. South 8F 166
Beach Rd. Fltwd 9D 40
Beach Rd. Lyth A 1D 128
Beach Rd. Pre 6A 42
Beach Rd. South 8F 166
Beach Rd. T Clev 9C 54
Beach St. Lyth A 5N 129
Beach St. More 1E 22
Beachwood. Arns 2D 4
Beacon Av. Ful 4G 114
Beacon Clo. Col 8N 85
Beacon Ct. Goos 5N 95
Beacon Dri. Goos 4N 95
Beacon Fell Country Pk. 6A 70
Beacon Fell Cvn. Pk. L'rdge 1L 97
Beacon Fell Rd. Goos 6A 70
Beacon Gro. Ful 5G 114
Beacon Gro. Gars 6M 59
Beacon Heights. Uph 3D 220
Beacon La. Dal 6L 211
Beacon Pk. 8A 212
Beacon Pk. Public Golf Course. 9B 212
Beacon Rd. Poul I 8N 63
Beacon Rd. Stand 2L 213
Beaconsfield Av. Pres 8B 116
Beaconsfield Rd. South 8M 167
Beaconsfield St. Acc 3C 142
Beaconsfield St. Gt Har 3J 121
Beaconsfield St. Has 4G 160
Beaconsfield St. Todm 2M 165
Beaconsfield Ter. Catt 1B 68
Beaconsfield Ter. Chor 4F 174
Beacons, The. Form 9A 206
(off School La.)
Beacons, The. Shev 5G 212
Beacon St. Chor 7F 174
Beacon Vw. App B 4F 212
Beacon Vw. Dri. Uph 4E 220
Beaford Clo. Wig 6L 221
Beal Cres. Roch 4F 204
Bealcroft Clo. Miln 6H 205
Bealcroft Wlk. Miln 6H 205
Beale Rd. Nels 2F 104
Beal Ter. Miln 7J 205
Beamont Dri. Pres 9G 114
Bean Av. Blac 1E 108
Beardshaw Av. Blac 8D 88
Beardsworth St. B'brn 9A 120
Beardwood. 9H 119
Beardwood. B'brn 1H 139
Beardwood Brow. B'brn 1H 139
Beardwood Dri. B'brn 1H 139
Beardwood Fold. B'brn 1H 139
Beardwood Mdw. B'brn 1H 139
Beardwood Pk. B'brn 1J 139
Bearncroft. Skel 5N 219
Bear St. Burn 3K 123
Bearswood Cft. Clay W 5D 154
Beatie St. Brier 4F 104
Beatrice Av. Burn 2A 124
Beatrice M. Hor 9C 196
Beatrice Pl. B'brn 8A 140
Beatrice St. Roch 6A 204
Beatrice Ter. Dar 7B 158
Beattock Clo. Liv 4J 223
Beattock Pl. Blac 6F 62
Beatty Av. Chor 8D 174
Beatty Clo. Lyth A 8D 108
Beatty Rd. South 9L 167
Beauclerk Rd. Lyth A 2G 128
Beaufort. Liv 1A 214
Beaufort Av. Blac 7B 62
Beaufort Clo. Augh 2F 216
Beaufort Clo. Read 8D 102
Beaufort Gro. More 3D 22
Beaufort Rd. Bacup 9L 145
Beaufort Rd. More 3D 22
Beaufort St. Nels 3H 105
Beaufort St. Roch 4N 203
Beauley Av. S'stne 8D 102
Beauly Clo. Ram 3F 200
Beaumaris Av. B'brn 7H 139
Beaumaris Clo. Has 6G 161
Beaumaris Rd. Ley 7M 153
Beaumonds Way. Roch 7L 203
Beaumont. 4K 23
Beaumont Av. Hor 9D 196
Beaumont Clo. L'boro 9J 185
Beaumont Ct. Lyth A 9G 108
Beaumont Cres. Augh 1J 217
Beaumont Dri. Liv 9D 222
Beaumont Gdns. Poul F 6G 63
Beaumont Gro. Orr 3L 221
Beaumont Pl. Lanc 4K 23
Beaumont St. Lanc 4K 23
Beaumont St. Todm 1K 165
Beaver Clo. Wilp 4N 119
Beavers La. Skel 5A 220
Beavers Way. Skel 5A 220
Beaver Ter. Bacup 4L 163
Bebles Rd. Orm 9H 209
Becconsall. 5D 150
Becconsall La. Hesk B 4D 150
Bechers Dri. Ain R 8A 222
Beck Ct. Fltwd 3D 54
Beckdean Av. Poul F 9K 63
Beckenham Ct. Burn 7H 105
Beckett Clo. Liv 9A 224
Beckett Ct. Pres 8J 115
Beckett St. Dar 7A 158
Beckgate. Barb 2G 9
Beck Gro. T Clev 8E 54
Beck Head. K Lon 6F 8
(off Queen's Sq.)
Beck La. Man 2B 8
Beck's Brow. Wigg 10M 35
Beckside. B'ley 6A 84
Beckside. Cat 3H 25
Beckside Clo. Traw 8F 86
Beckside M. Borw 4G 12
Beck Vw. Scot 4L 29
(off Hala Sq.)
Beck Way. Col 8M 85
Beckway Av. Blac 3F 88
Bective Rd. K Lon 6F 8
(off New Rd.)
Bedale Pl. T Clev 2E 62
Bedale Wlk. Liv 6L 223
Beddington St. Nels 1H 105
Bede Clo. Liv 4K 223
Bedford Av. Liv 4D 222
Bedford Av. T Clev 8D 54
Bedford Clo. Osw 4J 141
Bedford M. Dar 3N 157
Bedford Pk. 3H 187
Bedford Pl. Lanc 3L 29
Bedford Pl. Pad 2J 123
Bedford Rd. Blac 2C 88
Bedford Rd. Ful 5K 115
Bedford Rd. Lyth A 4C 130
Bedford Rd. South 3G 186
Bedfordshire Av. Burn 2N 123
Bedford St. Barfd 1G 104
Bedford St. B'brn 6K 139
Bedford St. Bury 9M 201
Bedford St. Chor 8E 174
Bedford St. Dar 3N 157
Bedford St. Eger 3D 198
Bedford St. Pem 6M 221
Bedford St. Todm 8H 147
Bedford Ter. Has 7F 160
Beechacre. Ram 9J 181
Beecham St. More 2B 22
Beech Av. And 5K 195
Beech Av. Bils 6D 68
Beech Av. Blac 5E 88
Beech Av. Dar 5B 158
Beech Av. Earby 3D 78
Beech Av. Eux 2M 173
Beech Av. Gal 2K 37
Beech Av. K'ham 5N 111
Beech Av. Ley 7K 153
Beech Av. Mell 7F 222
Beech Av. Parb 3N 211
Beech Av. Poul F 7K 63
Beech Av. Todm 1L 165
Beech Av. W'ton 2J 131
Beech Bank. Wadd 8H 73
Beech Clo. Bacup 4L 163
Beech Clo. Bolt 7J 199
Beech Clo. Clay D 3M 119
Beech Clo. Clith 3K 81
Beech Clo. Garg 3L 53
Beech Clo. Kirkby 7H 223
Beech Clo. Osw 6J 141
Beech Clo. Rish 9H 121
Beech Clo. Ruf 1G 191
Beech Clo. Skel 2J 219
Beech Clo. Whitw 5N 183
Beech Ct. Hell 1D 52
(off Hammerton Dri.)
Beech Ct. Silv 9G 4
Beech Cres. Alt W 8N 121
Beech Cres. Stand 4N 213
Beechcroft. Liv 1B 222
Beech Dri. Frec 3M 131
Beech Dri. Ful 1G 114
Beech Dri. Has 5H 161
Beech Dri. L'rdge 3J 97
Beech Dri. Newt 7D 112
Beech Dri. Poul F 9K 63
Beeches, The. Bolt 7D 198
Beeches, The. Brin 4E 154
Beeches, The. Sing 1C 90
Beeches, The. Tar 8E 150
Beeches, The. Whitw 5N 183
Beechfield. Lanc 8H 23
Beechfield. Liv 1D 222
Beechfield. Parb 8N 191
Beechfield. Roch 7J 203
Beechfield Av. Blac 7E 88
Beechfield Av. Pre 8N 41
Beechfield Av. W Grn 6H 111
Beechfield Clo. Roch 7J 203
Beechfield Ct. Ley 7L 153
Beechfield Gdns. South 8F 166
Beechfield M. South 7H 167
Beechfield Rd. Ley 8K 153
Beechfield Rd. Miln 8H 205
Beechfields. E'ston 8E 172
Beech Gdns. Clay W 6D 154
Beech Gdns. Rainf 3J 225
Beech Gro. Acc 4N 141
Beech Gro. Ash R 8E 114
Beech Gro. Barn 2N 77
Beech Gro. Burn 6G 104
Beech Gro. Chat 7C 74
Beech Gro. Dar 1L 157
Beech Gro. G'mnt 4F 200
Beech Gro. Kno S 7L 41
Beech Gro. More 3F 22
Beech Gro. Slyne 1J 23
Beech Gro. South 7L 167
Beech Gro. War 5A 12
Beech Gro. Clo. Bury 9N 201
Beechill Clo. Walt D 5A 136
Beech Ind. Est. Bacup 4L 163
(off Vale St.)
Beeching Clo. Lanc 1K 29
Beech Mdw. Orm 8M 209
Beech Mt. Rams 6N 119
Beech Mt. Wadd 8H 73
Beech Rd. Augh 5F 216
Beech Rd. Elsw 1L 91
Beech Rd. Gars 4M 59
Beech Rd. Halt 1B 24
Beech Rd. Ley 5K 153
Beech St. Acc 3B 142
Beech St. Bacup 4L 163
Beech St. Barn 3M 77
Beech St. B'brn 1A 140
Beech St. Clay M 8M 121
Beech St. Clith 3K 81
Beech St. Gt Har 3J 121
Beech St. Lanc 8H 23
Beech St. Miln 9K 205
Beech St. Nels 1J 105
Beech St. Pad 2J 123
Beech St. Pres 2G 135
Beech St. Ross 4M 161
Beech St. S'seat 2H 201
Beech St. Tur 9K 179
Beech St. S. Pres 2H 135
Beech Ter. I'ton 3N 19
Beech Ter. Pres 2H 135
Beechthorpe Av. Wadd 8H 73
Beech Tree Av. App B 4G 213
Beech Tree Clo. Nels 3J 105
Beechtrees. Skel 4N 219
Beech Wlk. Wins 9M 221
Beech Walks. Stand 4N 213
Beechway. Ful 5K 115
Beechway. Liv 9G 216
Beechway. Pen 4E 134
Beechway Av. Liv 9G 216
Beechwood. Skel 9N 211
Beechwood. Wesh 2N 111
Beechwood Av. Acc 5C 142
Beechwood Av. Burn 6C 124
Beechwood Av. Clith 5L 81
Beechwood Av. Ful 5F 114
Beechwood Av. L'boro 2K 205
Beechwood Av. Ram 8J 181
Beechwood Av. Shev 7J 213
Beechwood Av. Walt D 4M 135
Beechwood Ct. B'brn 1N 139
Beechwood Ct. Liv 1D 222
Beechwood Ct. Skel 5A 220
Beechwood Ct. Tot 8G 200
Beechwood Cres. Orr 5H 221
Beechwood Cft. Clay W 4C 154
Beechwood Dri. B'brn 8F 138
Beechwood Dri. Orm 7J 209
Beechwood Dri. T Clev 3H 63
Beechwood Gdns. Lanc 5L 29
Beechwood Gro. Blac 6E 62
Beechwood M. B'brn 8A 140
Beechwood Rd. B'brn 1A 140
Beechwood Rd. Chor 8G 174
Beecroft La. Wigg 10N 35
Beehive Ind. Est. Blac 9H 89
Bee La. Pen 7G 134
Beenland St. Pres 8N 115
Beeston Av. Poul F 6J 63
Beeston Clo. Bolt 7G 198
Beeston Dri. Boot 5A 222
Beetham Cvn. Pk. Hale 3N 5
Beetham Ct. Clay M 7L 121
Beetham Pl. Blac 4E 88
Begonia St. Dar 6B 158
Beightons Wlk. Roch 1A 204
Bela Clo. Lanc 6G 22
Bela Gro. Blac 8C 88
Beldale Pk. Liv 6G 223
Belfield. 5F 204
Belfield. Skel 5A 220
Belfield Clo. Roch 5F 204
Belfield La. Roch 6G 204
Belfield Lawn. Roch 5G 204
Belfield Mill La. Roch 5F 204
Belfield Old Rd. Roch 5F 204
Belfield Rd. Acc 3A 142
Belfield Rd. Roch 5E 204
Belfield Trad. Est. Miln 4G 205
Belford Av. T Clev 8F 54
Belford St. Burn 2D 124
Belfry Clo. Eux 2N 173
Belfry Mans. Old L 4C 100
Belfry, The. Lyth A 3C 130
Belgarth Rd. Acc 1B 142
Belgium St. Roch 6J 203
Belgrave. 7N 157
Belgrave Av. Pen 5E 134
Belgrave Av. Wesh 2M 111
Belgrave Clo. B'brn 5J 139
Belgrave Clo. Lyth A 2K 129
Belgrave Clo. Wig 8N 221
Belgrave Ct. Burn 2D 124
(off Belgrave St.)
Belgrave Pl. Poul F 9H 63
Belgrave Pl. South 2F 186
Belgrave Rd. Blac 9E 88
Belgrave Rd. Col 5A 86
Belgrave Rd. Dar 7N 157
Belgrave Rd. Ley 7J 153
Belgrave Rd. Poul F 9H 63
Belgrave Rd. South 2F 186
Belgrave Sq. Dar 6A 158

Belgrave St.—Blackpool Airport

Belgrave St. Acc 8F 142
Belgrave St. Brier 5E 104
Belgrave St. Burn 2D 124
Belgrave St. Nels 2K 105
Belgrave St. Roch 4A 204
Bell-Aire Pk. Homes. Hey 2L 27
Bellamy Av. More 5A 22
Bell Busk. 1J 53
Belle Fld. Clo. Pen 6K 135
Belle Hill. Gigg 2N 35
Belle Isle Av. Roch 8N 183
Belle Vue Av. Lanc 1L 29
Belle Vue Dri. Lanc 1L 29
Belle Vue La. Wadd 8H 73
Belle Vue Pl. Blac 5D 88
Belle Vue Pl. Burn 3C 124
Belle Vue St. B'brn 3K 139
Belle Vue St. Burn 3C 124
Belle Vue St. Wig 6N 221
Belle Vue Ter. Lanc 1L 29
(off Belle Vue Dri.)
Bellfield La. Roch 6F 204
Bellfield Rd. More 3C 22
Bellflower Clo. Ley 4A 154
Bellingham Rd. Lyth A 4A 130
Bellis Av. South 4M 167
Bellis Gro. Liv 5J 223
Bellis Way. Walt D 6L 135
Bell La. Bncr 8E 60
Bell La. Clay M 5A 122
Bell La. Miln 6L 205
Bell La. Orr 3L 221
Bell Mdw. Dri. Roch 8K 203
Bells Arc. Burn 1E 124
(off Ardwick St.)
Bell's Clo. Liv 7A 216
Bellshill Cres. Roch 4F 204
Bells La. Hogh 6G 136
Bells La. Liv 8N 215
Bell St. Has 4G 160
Bell St. Roch 5C 204
Bell, The. 4L 221
Belmont. 9K 177
Belmont Av. Bil 8G 221
Belmont Av. Blac 6C 88
Belmont Av. Poul F 8H 63
Belmont Av. Rib 6N 115
Belmont Clo. B'brn 1H 139
Belmont Clo. Brins 7N 155
Belmont Clo. Burs 1C 210
Belmont Clo. Lanc 5H 23
Belmont Clo. Rib 7N 115
Belmont Ct. L'rdge 3K 97
Belmont Cres. Rib 7N 115
Belmont Dri. Chor 5G 175
Belmont Gro. Burn 4H 125
Belmont Pl. Cop 7N 193
Belmont Rd. Adl & Bel 2G 177
Belmont Rd. Ash R 7F 114
Belmont Rd. Bel & Bolt 1L 197
Belmont Rd. Bolt 6C 198
Belmont Rd. Fltwd 1G 54
Belmont Rd. Gt Har 4H 121
Belmont Rd. Hor 4D 196
Belmont Rd. Ley 6G 152
Belmont Rd. Lyth A 3J 129
Belmont St. Orr 5L 221
Belmont St. South 8G 166
Belmont Ter. Barfd 8H 85
(off Nora St.)
Belmont Ter. Foul 2A 86
(off Lowther La.)
Belmont Ter. Foul 2B 86
(off Skipton Old Rd.)
Belmont Vw. Bolt 9M 199
Belmont Way. Roch 3B 204
Belper St. B'brn 2A 140
Belsfield Dri. Hesk B 3C 150
Belshaw Ct. Burn 6M 123
Belthorn. 1F 158
Belthorn Rd. Guide 9D 140
(in two parts)
Belton Av. Roch 4F 204
Belton Hill. Ful 1G 114
Belvedere Av. G'mnt 4F 200
Belvedere Av. Ross 6E 162
Belvedere Dri. Chor 6D 174
Belvedere Pk. Augh 4H 217
Belvedere Rd. And 5K 195
Belvedere Rd. B'brn 6A 120
Belvedere Rd. Burn 3F 124
Belvedere Rd. Ley 5L 153
Belvedere Rd. South 8C 186
Belvedere Rd. T Clev 3J 63
Belverdale Gdns. Blac 4F 108
Belvere Av. Blac 4D 108
Belvoir Meadows. Roch 1H 205
Belvoir St. Roch 4A 204
Bember's Cross. I'ton 2M 19
Bembridge Ct. Wins 9N 221
Benbow Clo. Lyth A 7D 108
Bence Rd. Pres 1L 135
Bence St. Col 7B 86
Bench Carr. Roch 4B 204
Benenden Pl. T Clev 1G 62
Bengal St. Chor 6F 174
Bengarth Rd. South 6M 167
Ben La. Barn 1N 77
Ben La. Bic 1D 224
Bennett Av. Blac 6C 88
Bennett Dri. Orr 7G 221
Bennett Rd. T Clev 9G 54
Bennett's La. Blac 3F 108
Bennett St. Nels 9K 85
Bennett St. Roch 8D 204
Ben Nevis Pl. Queen I 7G 109
Bennington St. B'brn 5N 139
Benson Av. More 4D 22
Benson Ho. B'brn 1B 140
Benson La. Catf 7H 93
Benson Rd. Blac 1E 88
Benson's La. Wood 9N 67
Benson St. B'brn 1B 140
Benson St. Tur 9K 179
Bentcliffe Gdns. Acc 4C 142
Bent Est. Bacup 9L 145
Bentfield Cres. Miln 9K 205
Bent Gap La. B'brn 4K 139
Bentgate Clo. Has 7J 161
Bentgate Clo. Miln 9K 205
Bentgate St. Miln 9K 205
Bentham Av. Burn 7F 104
Bentham Av. Fltwd 3C 54
Bentham Clo. B'brn 7J 139
Bentham Golf Course. 5M 19
Bentham Ind. Est. Ben 7L 19
Bentham Moor Rd. I'ton 4K 19
Bentham Rd. B'brn 7J 139
Bentham Rd. Horn 7C 18
Bentham Rd. I'ton 4L 19
Bentham Rd. Lanc 5L 29
Bentham St. Cop 4A 194
Bentham St. South 9H 167
Bentham's Way. South 3H 187
Bentinck Av. Blac 4B 108
Bentinck Rd. Lyth A 9C 108
Bentinck St. Roch 4N 203
Bent La. Col 5E 86
Bent La. Ley 6L 153
Bentlea Rd. Gis 9A 52
Bentley Dri. Blac 3N 109
Bentley Dri. K'ham 4K 111
Bentley Hall Rd. Bury 9B 200
Bentley La. Bis 4D 192
Bentley La. Bury 4L 201
Bentley Pk. Rd. Longt 9K 133
Bentley St. Bacup 4K 163
Bentley St. B'brn 3C 140
Bentley St. Dar 8C 158
Bentley St. Nels 3H 105
Bentley St. Roch 3A 204
Bentmeadows. Roch 4B 204
Benton Rd. Rib 5N 115
Bents. 5E 86
Bents. Col 5E 86
Bents Farm Clo. L'boro 9J 185
Bents La. Cast 4G 9
Bent St. B'brn 4L 139
Bent St. Has 7J 161
Bent St. Osw 5K 141
Bentwood Rd. Has 4F 160
Benwick Rd. Liv 8G 223
Beresford Dri. South 3M 167
Beresford Gdns. South 4M 167
Beresford Rd. B'brn 1L 139
Beresford St. Blac 3C 88
Beresford St. Burn 4B 124
Beresford St. Miln 9L 205
Beresford St. Nels 4K 105
Bergen St. Burn 4N 123
Bergerac Cres. Blac 5F 62
Berkeley Av. Wig 9N 221
Berkeley Clo. Chor 9F 174
Berkeley Clo. Nels 3J 105
Berkeley Cres. Pad 9H 103
Berkeley Dri. Bam B 3A 154
Berkeley Dri. Read 8C 102
Berkeley Dri. Roch 9E 204
Berkeley Rd. Bolt 9E 198
Berkeley St. Brier 5E 104
Berkeley St. Nels 4J 105
Berkeley St. Pres 8H 115
Berkley Clo. K'ham 3K 111
Berkley Wlk. L'boro 9J 185
Berkshire Av. Burn 2M 123
Berkshire Clo. Wilp 2N 119
Bernard St. Roch 2B 204
Bernard Wood Ct. Bil 8G 221
Berne Av. Hor 9B 196
Berridge Av. Burn 3M 123
Berriedale Rd. Nels 1L 105
Berringtons La. Rainf 8M 225
Berry Clo. Skel 1K 219
Berry Fld. Pen 5F 134
Berry Ho. Rd. H'wd 1M 189
Berry La. L'rdge 2J 97
Berry's La. Gt Har 8H 101
Berry's La. Poul F 7J 63
Berry St. Adl 5J 195
Berry St. Brier 5F 104
Berry St. Burn 5D 124
Berry St. Los H 8K 135
Berry St. Pres 1K 135
Berry St. Skel 1K 219
Bertha Rd. Roch 6F 204
Bertha St. Acc 2C 142
Bertie St. Roch 9A 204
Bertram Av. More 4A 22
Bertrand Av. Blac 3G 89
Berwick Av. South 7C 186
Berwick Av. T Clev 8F 54
Berwick Dri. Burn 2C 124
Berwick Dri. Ful 5G 115
Berwick Rd. Blac 4C 108
Berwick Rd. Lyth A 1F 128
Berwick Rd. Pres 2K 135
Berwick St. Pres 8A 116
Berwick St. Roch 7E 204
Berwick Way. Hey 9K 21
Berwyn Av. More 2D 22
Berwyn Clo. Hor 8D 196
Berwyn Ct. South 1K 187
Beryl Av. B'brn 7N 119
Beryl Av. T Clev 2E 62
Beryl Av. Tot 6E 200
Beryl St. Ram 9F 198
Bescar. 6F 188
Bescar Brow La. Scar 6D 188
Bescar La. Scar 6F 188
Bescot Way. T Clev 4F 62
Bessie St. Barn 2M 77
Best St. K'ham 4L 111
Beswicke Royds St. Roch 4F 204
Beswicke St. L'boro 9M 185
Beswicke St. Roch 5B 204
Beswick St. Todm 8K 165
Bethany La. Miln 9M 205
Bethel Av. Blac 7C 62
Bethel Grn. L'boro 5M 185
(off Calderbrook Rd.)
Bethel Rd. B'brn 1A 140
Bethel St. Barn 1M 77
Bethel St. Col 7M 85
Bethesda Clo. B'brn 5L 139
Bethesda Rd. Blac 6B 88
Bethesda St. Barn 3M 77
Bethesda St. Burn 3D 124
Betony. More 2F 22
Betony Clo. Roch 2A 204
Bett La. Wheel 6L 155
Betty Nuppy's La. Roch 8F 204
Betula M. Roch 4H 203
Between Gates La. Barb 1G 8
Beulah Av. More 3D 22
Bevan Pl. Nels 9K 85
Beverley. 3J 85
Beverley Av. Poul F 2K 89
Beverley Clo. Ash R 8F 114
Beverley Clo. Clith 5K 81
Beverley Clo. South 1B 168
Beverley Clo. W Grn 6F 110
Beverley Ct. More 3D 22
Beverley Dri. Clith 5K 81
Beverley Gro. Blac 2C 108
Beverley Pl. Roch 5D 204
Beverley Rd. Black 3H 85
Beverley Rd. Wig 3L 221
Beverley Rd. N. Lyth A 9G 109
Beverley Rd. S. Lyth A 9G 109
Beverley St. B'brn 7J 139
Beverley St. Burn 4C 124
Beverley Ter. B'brn 7J 139
(off Broadway St.)
Beverly Clo. T Clev 3H 63
Beverston. Roch 7B 204
Bevington Clo. Burn 4C 124
Bevis Green. 5K 201
Bevis Grn. Bury 5L 201
Bewcastle Dri. W'head 9N 209
Bewley Dri. Liv 9J 223
Bexhill Rd. Ing 6D 114
Bexley Av. Blac 2D 88
Bexley Pl. Lyth A 3L 129
Bezza La. Sam & Bald 6J 117
Bibby Dri. Stain 6L 89
Bibby Rd. South 4N 167
Bibby's Rd. Blac 8E 62
Bickerstaffe. 6D 218
Bickerstaffe St. Blac 7B 88
Bickerton Rd. South 1F 186
Bicknell St. B'brn 2M 139
Bideford Av. Blac 4G 89
Bideford Way. Cot 3C 114
Bidston St. Pres 9A 116
Bigdale Dri. Liv 7L 223
Biggins La. H Big 7D 8
Biggins Rd. K Lon 6E 8
Bigholmes La. Wigg 7N 35
Bilberry St. Roch 7D 204
Billinge Av. B'brn 3H 139
Billinge Clo. B'brn 3J 139
Billinge End. B'brn 2H 139
Billinge End Rd. B'brn 3F 138
Billinge La. Bic 6K 217
Billinge Rd. Wig 8M 221
Billinge Side. B'brn 3G 138
Billinge St. B'brn 4A 140
Billinge Vw. B'brn 6G 139
Billington. 6G 101
Billington Av. Ross 2M 161
Billington Ct. Grims 9F 96
Billington Gdns. Bill 6G 100
Billington Rd. Burn 6M 123
Billington St. Wesh 3L 111
Billington St. E. Wesh 3L 111
Billsborrow La. Ingle 6J 69
Bill's La. Liv 2A 214
Bilsberry Cotts. Hur G 1N 99
Bilsborough Hey. Pen 7H 135
Bilsborough Mdw. Lea 6B 114
Bilsborrow. 7D 68
Bilsborrow La. Bils 7D 68
Bilson Sq. Miln 8K 205
Binbrook Pl. Chor 7C 174
Binfold Cft. K Lon 6F 8
(off Lunefield Dri.)
Bingley Av. Blac 4F 88
Bingley Clo. Clay W 5E 154
Bingley Rd. Roch 6F 204
Bingley Sq. Roch 6F 204
Bingley Ter. Roch 6F 204
Binns Nook Rd. Roch 3D 204
Binns St. Craw 9M 143
Binn's Ter. L'boro 8L 185
(off Barehill St.)
Binyon Ct. Lanc 1K 29
Binyon Rd. Lanc 2K 29
Birbeck Rd. Liv 7M 223
Birbeck Wlk. Liv 7M 223
Birchall Lodge. Rib 5B 116
(off Grange Av.)
Birch Av. Ash R 7D 114
Birch Av. Burs 9C 190
Birch Av. Eux 2M 173
Birch Av. Gal 2K 37
Birch Av. Has 4H 161
Birch Av. Ley 4N 153
Birch Av. Newt 6D 112
Birch Av. Pen 5D 134
Birch Av. T Clev 1E 62
Birch Av. Todm 9K 147
Birch Av. Tot 8F 200
Birchbank Gdns. B'brn 2N 139
Birch Clo. Acc 7D 122
Birch Clo. Mag 1E 222
Birch Clo. Whitw 8N 183
Birch Cotts. Ross 7K 161
Birch Cres. Hogh 7G 136
Birch Cres. Miln 9K 205
Birch Cres. Osw 5M 141
Birch Dri. Silv 7G 4
Birchen Bower Dri. Tot 8E 200
Birchen Bower Wlk. Tot 8E 200
Birchenlee La. Col 8A 86
Birches Rd. Tur 1K 199
Birches, The. Pres 8M 115
Birchfield. Bolt 7L 199
Birch Fld. Clay W 4D 154
Birchfield. Much H 3K 151
Birchfield Dri. L'rdge 2J 97
Birchfield Dri. Roch 8N 203
Birchfield Way. Liv 6A 216
Birch Green. 1N 219
Birch Grn. Rd. Uph 9M 211
Birch Gro. Arns 3D 4
Birch Gro. Barr 2K 101
Birch Gro. Lanc 8H 23
Birch Gro. Ram 2F 200
Birch Gro. Stalm 5C 56
Birch Hall. 3M 157
Birch Hall Av. Dar 3M 157
Birch Hall La. Earby 2G 78
Birch Hey Clo. Roch 1F 204
Birch Hill Cres. Roch 1G 205
Birch Hill La. Ward 8G 184
Birch Hill Wlk. L'boro 9H 185
Birchill Rd. Know I 8A 224
Birchin La. Whit W & Brin 6E 154
Birch La. Goos 7C 70
Birch La. H'wd 8B 170
Birch Mt. Roch 1G 205
Birchmuir Hey. Liv 9L 223
Birchover Clo. Ing 4D 114
Birch Rd. Chor 4F 174
Birch Rd. Cop 4A 194
Birch Rd. Gars 3M 59
Birch Rd. Ward & Roch 8F 184
Birch St. Acc 2A 142
Birch St. Bacup 4K 163
Birch St. Bury 9L 201
Birch St. Fltwd 9G 40
Birch St. Lyth A 5B 130
Birch St. Skel 3J 219
Birch St. South 1H 187
Birch St. Ward 8F 184
Birch Ter. Acc 5C 142
Birchtree Av. Hey 7M 21
Birchtree Gdns. Blac 8H 89
Birch Vs. Whitw 9N 183
Birch Wlk. B'brn 4B 140
Birch Way. Poul F 7J 63
Birchway Av. Blac 4E 88
Birchwood. Ley 6F 152
Birchwood Av. Hut 7M 133
Birchwood Clo. Lyth A 4L 129
Birchwood Clo. Set 3N 35
Birchwood Clo. Wins 9M 221
Birchwood Dri. Cop 3A 194
Birchwood Dri. Ful 2G 114
Birchwood Dri. Hamb 1B 64
Birchwood Way. Liv 5M 223
Bird i' th' Hand Cotts. Orm 6K 209
Bird St. Brier 5F 104
Bird St. Pres 2G 135
Birdy Brow. Chai 8N 71
Birkacre. 2C 194
Birkacre Brow. Cop 3B 194
Birkacre Rd. Chor 1B 194
Birkbeck Pl. Fltwd 2D 54
Birkbeck Way. Burn 9E 104
Birkdale. 1G 186
Birkdale Av. Blac 6E 62
Birkdale Av. Fltwd 5E 54
Birkdale Av. Longt 8K 133
Birkdale Av. Lyth A 8F 108
Birkdale Clo. Eux 1N 173
Birkdale Clo. Lanc 5H 23
Birkdale Clo. Longt 8K 133
Birkdale Clo. T Clev 3K 63
Birkdale Cop. South 3K 187
Birkdale Dri. Ash R 7A 114
Birkdale Hills Nature Reserve. 5B 186
Birkdale Rd. Roch 9F 204
Birkdale Trad. Est. South 3G 186
Birkett Clo. Bolt 7D 198
Birkett Dri. Bolt 7D 198
Birkett Dri. Rib 6C 116
Birkett Pl. More 2C 22
Birkett Pl. Rib 6C 116
Birkett Rd. Acc 1B 142
Birkey La. Liv 1A 214
Birklands Av. More 4C 22
Birkrig. Skel 5A 220
Birks Brow. Thorn 9F 70
Birks Dri. Bury 7G 201
Birkside Way. Blac 9J 89
Birks La. Todm 7L 165
Birk St. Pres 1H 135
Birkwith La. L Bent 7K 19
Birley Clo. App B 4J 213
Birley Pl. Burn 1E 124
Birley St. B'brn 2N 139
Birley St. Blac 5B 88
Birley St. Bolt 9E 198
Birley St. K'ham 4N 111
Birley St. Pres 9J 115
Birleywood. Skel 5A 220
Birnam Grn. Fltwd 9E 40
Birtenshaw Cres. Brom X 6H 199
Birtle. 7D 202
Birtle Green. 7C 202
Birtle Moor. Bury 8C 202
Birtle Rd. Bury 6C 202
Birtwistle Av. Col 5N 85
Birtwistle Clo. Brier 5F 104
Birtwistle Ct. Barn 3N 77
Birtwistle Fold. Col 6B 86
Birtwistle Hyde Pk. Col 6A 86
Birtwistle Standroyd Bungalows.
Col 6D 86
Birtwistle St. Acc 3B 142
Birtwistle St. Gt Har 4H 121
Birtwistle St. Los H 9L 135
Birtwistle Ter. Lang 9C 100
(off Whalley New Rd.)
Bisham Clo. Dar 7C 158
Bishopdale Clo. B'brn 9E 138
Bishopdale Clo. More 5F 22
Bishopdale Rd. Lanc 9H 23
Bishopgate. Pres 9K 115
Bishopsgate. Blac 1G 89
Bishopsgate. Lanc 3L 29
Bishops Ga. Lyth A 2K 129
Bishops Ga. Wlk. Roch 9F 204
Bishopstone Clo. B'brn 8A 140
Bishop St. Acc 3B 142
Bishop St. Burn 9F 104
Bishop St. Nels 2H 105
Bishop St. Roch 4E 204
Bishopsway. Pen 5G 134
Bison Pl. Ley 5F 152
Bispham. 7B 62
Bispham Av. Far M 3H 153
Bispham Green. 6M 191
Bispham Hall Bus. Pk. Orr 9F 220
Bispham Rd. Blac 7D 62
Bispham Rd. Nels 4J 105
Bispham Rd. South 7M 167
Bispham Rd. T Clev 1C 62
Bispham Rd. T Clev & Poul F 4F 62
Bispham St. Pres 9J 115
Bittern Clo. Blac 4H 89
Bittern Clo. Roch 6K 203
Bivel St. Burn 3B 124
Black Abbey St. Acc 3B 142
Blackacre La. Orm 4K 209
Blackamoor. 8B 140
Black-a-Moor La. Down 1M 215
Blackamoor Rd. Guide 9B 140
Blackberry Hall Cres. Hey 8M 21
Blackberry Way. Pen 6F 134
Blackbrook Clo. H'pey 4J 175
Black Bull La. Ful 4G 114
Blackburn. 3M 139
Blackburn Brow. Chor 4G 175
Blackburn Cathedral. 4M 139
Blackburn Golf Course. 1J 139
Blackburn Mus. & Art Gallery. 3M 139
Blackburn Old Rd. Eger 1C 198
Blackburn Old Rd. Gt Har 4E 120
Blackburn Old Rd. Hogh 6L 137
Blackburn Old Rd. Rish 7C 120
(in two parts)
Blackburn Rd. Acc 8E 142
Blackburn Rd. Alt & Pad 2D 122
Blackburn Rd. B'brn & Osw 3E 140
Blackburn Rd. Bolt 9E 198
Blackburn Rd. Chor & Whit W 3G 175
(in three parts)
Blackburn Rd. Chu 2L 141
Blackburn Rd. Clay M 8K 121
Blackburn Rd. Dar 2M 157
Blackburn Rd. Gt Har 5J 121
Blackburn Rd. Has 4F 160
Blackburn Rd. Has & Ram 9J 161
Blackburn Rd. High W 4D 136
Blackburn Rd. L'rdge 3L 97
Blackburn Rd. Ribch 7F 98
Blackburn Rd. Rish 1D 140
Blackburn Rd. Tur & Eger 7B 178
Blackburn Rovers F.C. 8L 139
(Ewood Pk.)
Blackburn Rovers Football Academy. 5C 100
Blackburn Shop. Cen. B'brn 3M 139
(off Church St.)
Blackburn St. B'brn 2M 139
Blackburn St. Burn 3D 124
Blackburn St. Chor 7G 174
Blackcroft. Clay W 4D 154
Black Dad La. Roch 5E 202
Black Dyke Rd. Arns 1G 4
Blackear La. Liv 8G 215
Blacker St. Burn 8E 104
Blackfen Pl. Blac 2D 88
Blackfield Rd. Frec 2N 131
Blackgate La. Tar 4N 169
(in two parts)
Black Horse St. Chor 8D 174
Black Ho. La. Bils 6E 70
Black Ho. La. Brclf 8A 106
Blackhurst Av. Hut 6B 134
Blackhurst Ct. Longt 8M 133
Blackhurst Rd. Liv 6B 216
Black La. Nate 2A 58
Black La. Ram 6M 181
Black La. Cft. Clith 2L 81
(off Railway Vw.)
Black La. Cft. Clith 2L 81
(Chester Av.)
Black Lane Ends. 9J 79
Blackleach. 8J 93
Blackleach Av. Grims 9F 96
Blackleach La. Btle & Lwr B 9K 93
Blackledge Clo. Orr 6H 221
Blackley Gro. Liv 5L 223
(off Carl's Way)
Black Moor Rd. Maw 3J 191
Black Moss La. Augh & Orm 9J 209
Black Moss La. Scar 6C 188
Black Moss Rd. Black 2A 84
Blacko. 3G 85
Blacko Bar Rd. R'lee & Black 7D 84
Blackpits Rd. Roch 4H 203
Black Pole. 5N 93
Blackpool. 5B 88
Blackpool Airport. 6D 108
Blackpool Airport. Blac 6D 108

Blackpool Bus. Pk.—Braintree Av.

Blackpool Bus. Pk. Blac 5D 108
Blackpool Cricket Club. 6E 88
Blackpool F.C. 8C 88
(Bloomfield Pk.)
Blackpool Fylde Ind. Est. Blac 2J 109
Blackpool Model Village. 6F 88
Blackpool Old Rd. Blac & Poul F 1G 88
Blackpool Old Rd. L Ecc 6L 65
Blackpool Pk. Golf Course. 5F 88
Blackpool Rd. Blac 7D 62
Blackpool Rd. Ful & Pres 6H 115
Blackpool Rd. K'ham 5B 112
Blackpool Rd. Lea & Pres 8M 113
Blackpool Rd. L'rdge 3J 97
Blackpool Rd. Lyth A 2K 129
Blackpool Rd. Poul F 8G 62
Blackpool Rd. St M 5E 66
Blackpool Rd. W Grn 3F 110
Blackpool Rd. N. Lyth A 7E 108
Blackpool St. Chu 3L 141
Blackpool St. Dar 9B 158
Blackpool Technology Pk. Blac 6F 62
Blackpool Tower. 5B 88
(Aquarium, Circus & Ballroom)
Blackpool Zoo. 6H 89
Blackrod Brow. Hor 9K 195
Blackrod By-Pass Rd. B'rod 9L 195
Blackshaw St. Todm 2N 165
Blacksmith La. Roch 9M 203
Blacksmiths Row. Lyth A 1K 129
Blacksnape. 7E 158
Blacksnape Rd. Hodd 6D 158
Blacksticks La. Chip 6C 70
Blackstone Av. Roch 5F 204
Blackstone Edge Ct. L'boro 8M 185
Blackstone Edge Old Rd. L'boro 8M 185
Blackstone Rd. Chor 5G 174
Blackthorn Clo. Lea 8A 114
Blackthorn Clo. Newt 7D 112
Blackthorn Clo. Roch 3B 204
Blackthorn Clo. T Clev 7F 54
Blackthorn Cres. Bacup 4K 163
Blackthorn Cft. Clay W 5C 154
Blackthorn Dri. Pen 5E 134
Blackthorn La. Bacup 3K 163
Blackwood Pl. Lanc 2M 29
Blackwood Rd. Bacup 8F 162
Blades St. Lanc 8J 23
Blaguegate. 2F 218
Blaguegate La. Skel 1E 218
Blainscough La. Cop 5N 193
Blainscough Rd. Cop 5A 194
Blairgowrie Gdns. Orm 1J 217
Blair Gro. South 7M 167
Blair St. Brom X 5F 198
Blairway Av. Blac 4F 88
Blake Av. Los H 9K 135
Blake Gdns. Gt Har 5H 121
Blakehall. Skel 4A 220
Blakeley Cres. Barn 10F 52
Blake St. Acc 2A 142
Blake St. Brom X 6G 199
Blake St. Roch 5D 204
Blakewater Rd. B'brn 1B 140
Blakey Moor. B'brn 3L 139
Blakey St. Burn 3E 124
Blakiston St. Fltwd 9G 40
Blanche St. Ash R 8F 114
Blanche St. Roch 3D 204
Blandford Av. T Clev 2C 62
Blandford Clo. Bury 8J 201
Blandford Clo. South 9F 166
Blannell St. Burn 3C 124
Blascomay Sq. Col 7A 86
(off Raglan St.)
Blashaw La. Pen 3D 134
Blaydike Moss. Ley 6E 152
Blaydon Av. T Clev 8E 54
Blaydon Pk. Skel 4A 220
Bleachers Dri. Ley 6H 153
Bleackley St. Bury 9H 201
Blea Clo. Burn 1A 124
Bleakholt Rd. Ram 5L 181
Bleak La. Lath 9G 191
Bleara Rd. Earby 4G 79
Bleasdale. 3A 70
Bleasdale Av. Clith 4J 81
Bleasdale Av. K'ham 3M 111
Bleasdale Av. Liv 8D 222
Bleasdale Av. Poul F 9J 63
Bleasdale Av. Stain 5L 89
Bleasdale Av. T Clev 2D 62
Bleasdale Clo. Augh 4J 217
Bleasdale Clo. Bam B 8B 136
Bleasdale Clo. Ley 8L 153
Bleasdale Ct. L'rdge 3K 97
Bleasdale Gro. Hey 7M 21
Bleasdale La. Blea 5N 61
Bleasdale La. Clau B 9K 61
Bleasdale Rd. Kno S 8K 41
Bleasdale Rd. Lyth A 4B 130
Bleasdale Rd. W'chpl 4B 96
Bleasdale Rd. W'ham 3M 69
Bleasdale St. E. Pres 8L 115
Blea Tarn Pl. More 4D 22
Blea Tarn Rd. Lanc 4M 29
Blelock St. Pres 1K 135
Blenheim Av. Blac 6D 88
Blenheim Av. K'ham 4L 111
Blenheim Clo. B'brn 8M 119
Blenheim Clo. Los H 8M 135
Blenheim Dri. T Clev 1J 63
Blenheim Dri. W'ton 2J 131
Blenheim Pl. Lyth A 8E 108
Blenheim Rd. South 7B 186
Blenheim Rd. Wig 3M 221
Blenheim St. Col 6D 86
Blenheim St. Roch 4N 203
Blenheim Ter. Foul 2B 86
(off Skipton Old Rd.)
Blenheim Way. Cot 3B 114
Blesma Ct. Blac 3C 108
(off Lytham Rd.)
Blindfoot Rd. Rainf & Wind 9H 225
Blind La. Burt L 3K 19
Blind La. Gis 9A 52
Blind La. Todm 1K 165
Blindman's La. Orm 5H 209
Blind La. High 4M 103
Bloomfield Ct. Pres 7H 115
Bloomfield Grange. Pen 6F 134
Bloomfield Pk. Carn 9A 12
Bloomfield Rd. Blac 8B 88
Bloomfield Rd. Withn 6B 156
Bloomfield St. Bolt 9E 198
Bloom St. Ram 1F 200
Blossom Av. Blac 2F 108
Blossom Pl. Roch 5C 204
Blossoms, The. Ful 3M 115
Blowick. 8L 167
Blucher St. Col 7B 86
Bluebell Av. Has 7F 160
Bluebell Clo. Hesk B 3C 150
Bluebell Clo. T Clev 7F 54
Bluebell Clo. Whit W 1D 174
Bluebell Dri. Roch 9M 203
Blue Bell La. Todm 6F 146
Bluebell Pl. Pres 9K 115
Blue Bell Way. Ful 3A 116
Bluebellwood. Ley 4J 153
Bluecoat Cres. Newt 7E 112
Blue Moor. Whar 9C 92
Blue Scar La. Bolt B 5K 51
Bluestone La. Liv 1D 222
Blue Stone La. Maw 2B 192
Blundell Av. H'twn 8A 214
Blundell Av. South 3F 186
Blundell Cres. South 3F 186
Blundell Dri. South 3F 186
Blundell Gro. Liv 8A 214
Blundell La. Pen 2E 134
Blundell La. South 3B 168
Blundell Links Ct. South 9C 186
Blundell M. Wig 7N 221
Blundell Rd. Ful 6H 115
Blundell Rd. Liv 8A 214
Blundell Rd. Lyth A 8F 108
Blundell St. Blac 7B 88
Blyth Av. L'boro 2J 205
Blythe Av. T Clev 7E 54
Blythe La. Lath 4B 210
Blythewood. Skel 4N 219
Boarded Barn. Eux 3M 173
Boardman Av. Blac 4B 88
Boardman St. Todm 1L 165
Board St. Burn 9E 104
Boarsgreave. 9E 162
Boarsgreave La. Ross 9D 162
Boathorse La. Burn 3B 124
Bobbin Clo. Acc 3N 141
Bobbiners La. South 3F 168
Bobbin Mill Clo. Todm 7E 146
Bobbin St. Todm 7E 146
Bocholt Way. Ross 5M 161
Bodiam Rd. G'mnt 4E 200
Bodkin La. Out R 4E 64
Bodmin Av. South 1A 168
Bodmin St. Pres 8N 115
Boegrave Av. Los H 8K 135
Bogburn La. Cop 7N 193
Bog Height Rd. Dar 1J 157
Boland St. B'brn 1A 140
Bold La. Augh 4F 216
Bold St. Acc 2B 142
Bold St. Bacup 6K 163
Bold St. B'brn 2M 139
Bold St. Col 7B 86
Bold St. Fltwd 8H 41
Bold St. Hey 4M 21
Bold St. Pres 7G 115
Bold St. South 6H 167
Bold St. Wig 6N 221
Boleyn Ct. Blac 8G 89
Boleyn, The. Liv 8D 216
Bolholt. 9F 200
Bolholt Ind. Pk. Bury 9F 200
Bolholt Ter. Bury 9G 200
Bolland Clo. Clith 3M 81
Bolland Prospect. Clith 3M 81
Bolland St. Barn 1M 77
Bolton Av. Acc 8C 122
Bolton Av. Lanc 4K 23
Bolton Av. Liv 8H 223
Bolton Av. Poul F 6J 63
Bolton-by-Bowland. 8K 51
Bolton Clo. Liv 1A 214
Bolton Cft. Ley 7E 152
Bolton Green. 6M 173
Bolton Gro. Barfd 8H 85
Bolton Houses. 1C 112
Bolton La. Bolt S 5M 15
Bolton-le-Sands. 4L 15
Bolton Mdw. Ley 7D 152
Bolton Rd. And & Hor 5K 195
Bolton Rd. B'brn 7L 139
Bolton Rd. Brad 8J 199
Bolton Rd. Dar 1B 178
(Cemetery Rd.)
Bolton Rd. Dar 6A 158
(Circus, The)
Bolton Rd. Hogh 9N 137
Bolton Rd. South 1G 186
Bolton Rd. Tur 1K 199
Bolton Rd. N. Ram 5H 181
Bolton Rd. W. Hawk & Ram 2E 200
Bolton's Cop. Banks 9H 149
Bolton's Ct. B'brn 3M 139
(off Exchange Ter.)
Bolton's Ct. Pres 1K 135
Boltons Cft. Salw 2J 113
Bolton's Meanygate. Tar 7N 149
Bolton St. Blac 9B 88
Bolton St. Chor 7E 174
Bolton St. Col 7M 85
Bolton St. Newc 6C 162
Bolton St. Ram 9G 181
Bolton Town Ends. 6L 15
Bolton Wlk. Liv 8H 223
Bombay Rd. Wig 3M 221
Bombay St. B'brn 5K 139
Bonchurch St. B'brn 4C 140
Bond La. Set 3N 35
Bonds. 7A 60
Bond's La. Adl 6H 195
Bond's La. Banks 8F 148
Bonds La. Elsw 9M 65
Bonds La. Gars 6N 59
Bond St. Acc 3N 141
Bond St. Blac 9B 88
Bond St. Burn 1E 124
Bond St. Col 6A 86
Bond St. Dar 4A 158
Bond St. Lanc 8L 23
Bond St. Nels 3H 105
Bond St. Ram 4K 181
Bond St. Todm 2L 165
Bone Cft. Clay W 4D 154
Bone Hill La. Winm 2A 58
Bonfire Hill Clo. Ross 9N 143
Bonfire Hill Rd. Ross 9M 143
Bonny Grass Ter. Bill 6G 101
(off Whalley New Rd.)
Bonny St. Blac 6B 88
Bonny St. T Clev 9H 55
Bonsall St. B'brn 6H 139
Boome St. Blac 3C 108
Boonfields. Brom X 5G 198
Boon Town. Burt 6H 7
Boon Walks. Burt 5H 7
Booth Bridge. 10K 53
Booth Bri. La. Thorn C 9J 53
Booth Clo. Tot 8F 200
Booth Ct. Burn 1E 124
(off Old Hall St.)
Booth Cres. Ross 6E 162
Boothfield Ho. Cvn. Pk. Pre 7N 41
Booth Hall Dri. Tot 8E 200
Boothley Rd. Blac 4C 88
Boothman Pl. Nels 9J 85
Boothman St. B'brn 6L 139
Booth Pl. Ross 6D 162
Booth Rd. Ross & Bacup 6D 162
Boothroyden. Blac 2B 88
Booth's La. Augh 7E 208
Booths Shop. Cen. Ful 2J 115
Booth St. Acc 3B 142
Booth St. Bacup 5K 163
Booth St. Carn 9A 12
Booth St. Has 3F 160
Booth St. Nels 2H 105
Booth St. Ross 7C 162
Booth St. South 6H 167
Booth St. Tot 7E 200
Booth Way. Tot 8D 200
Boothwood Stile. Holc 2E 200
Bootle St. Pres 8M 115
(in two parts)
Boot St. Earby 2E 78
Boot Way. Burn 4E 124
Borage Clo. T Clev 7G 54
Border Ct. Lanc 7H 23
Bores Hill. Wig 9E 194
Borough Rd. Dar 7N 157
Borron La. Cap 6J 13
Borron Lane End. 5K 13
Borrowdale Av. B'brn 5C 140
Borrowdale Av. Fltwd 9C 40
Borrowdale Clo. Acc 8C 122
Borrowdale Clo. Burn 7G 104
Borrowdale Dri. Burn 6G 104
Borrowdale Dri. Roch 9M 203
Borrowdale Gro. More 3D 22
Borrowdale Rd. Blac 5E 88
Borrowdale Rd. Lanc 7L 23
Borrowdale Rd. Ley 8L 153
Borrowdale Rd. Wig 4M 221
Borwick. 3G 12
Borwick Av. War 4B 12
Borwick Clo. War 5B 12
Borwick Ct. Borw 3F 12
Borwick Ct. More 5B 22
Borwick Dri. Lanc 6H 23
Borwick La. Borw 4F 12
Borwick La. War 4B 12
Borwick M. Borw 4F 12
Borwick Rd. Borw & Cap 3G 12
Bosburn Dri. Mel B 6D 118
Boscombe Av. Hey 6M 21
Boscombe Rd. Blac 3B 108
Bosley Clo. Dar 7D 158
Bostock St. Pres 1K 135
Boston Av. Blac 5D 62
Boston Rd. Bacup 4K 163
Boston Rd. Lyth A 2H 129
Bostons. Gt Har 4H 121
Boston St. Nels 4K 105
Boston Way. Blac 1F 108
Bosworth Dri. South 9B 186
Bosworth Pl. Blac 5B 108
Bosworth Sq. Roch 9A 204
Bosworth St. Hor 9C 196
Botanical Gardens & Mus. 4A 168
(Churchtown)
Botanic Rd. South 5N 167
Botany. 4G 174
Botany Bay. Chor 3G 174
(in two parts)
Botany Brow. Chor 4G 174
Bott Ho. La. Col 9L 85
(in two parts)
Bottomdale Rd. Slyne 9K 15
Bottomgate. B'brn 3B 140
Bottomley Bank La. Ross 9M 143
Bottomley Rd. Todm 9M 165
Bottomley St. Nels 2J 105
Bottom of Hutton. 5K 133
Bottom o' th' Moor. Hor 9G 197
Bottom Rd. Wray 3J 33
Bottoms La. Silv 7H 5
Bottom's Row. Ross 9D 162
Boulder St. Ross 9M 143
Bouldon Dri. Bury 8H 201
Bouldsworth Rd. Burn 4J 125
Boulevard. Pres 3L 135
Boulevard, The. B'brn 4M 139
Boulevard, The. Lyth A 3F 128
Boulsworth Cres. Nels 1M 105
Boulsworth Dri. Traw 1F 106
Boulsworth Gro. Col 6D 86
Boulsworth Rd. Traw 1F 106
Boulview Ter. Col 6D 86
Boundary Clo. E'ston 7E 172
Boundary Clo. New L 8C 134
Boundary Ct. Blac 1G 89
Boundary La. Burs 9D 190
Boundary La. Hesk B 6C 150
Boundary La. H End 2J 169
Boundary La. Kirkby 8C 224
Boundary La. Poul F & Pil 5G 56
Boundary La. Ruf 4C 190
Boundary La. Wrigh 1K 213
Boundary Meanygate. Hesk B 8L 149
Boundary Rd. Acc 1B 142
Boundary Rd. Ful 6G 115
Boundary Rd. Lanc 1K 29
Boundary Rd. Lyth A 3D 130
Boundary St. Burn 8G 104
Boundary St. Col 7A 86
Boundary St. Ley 5L 153
Boundary St. Roch 7B 204
Boundary St. South 1H 187
Boundary Wlk. Roch 8B 204
Bourbles La. Pre 9C 42
Bourne Brow. Ingle 6H 69
Bourne Cres. Blac 3A 108
Bourne May Rd. Kno S 8K 41
Bournemouth Rd. Blac 3B 108
Bourne Rd. T Clev 7G 55
Bournesfield. Hogh 7G 136
Bourne's Row. Hogh 7G 137
Bourne Way. T Clev 8F 54
Bouverie St. Pres 8A 116
Bouymasters. Lanc 7J 23
(off St Georges Quay)
Bovington Av. T Clev 3F 62
Bow Brook Rd. Ley 6L 153
Bowden Av. Pleas 7D 138
Bowen St. B'brn 6J 139
Bower Av. Roch 1G 204
Bower Clo. B'brn 6J 139
Bowerham. 1L 29
Bowerham La. Lanc 4M 29
Bowerham Rd. Lanc 1L 29
Bowerham Ter. Lanc 9L 23
(off Bowerham Rd.)
Bowers La. Nate 5J 59
Bowers, The. Chor 9F 174
Bower St. B'brn 6J 139
Bower St. Bury 9A 202
Bowes Clo. Bury 8G 200
Bowes Lyon Pl. Lyth A 1J 129
Bowfell Av. More 3D 22
Bowfell Clo. Blac 9K 89
Bowfield's La. Bald 5A 118
Bowgreave. 8N 59
Bowgreave Clo. Blac 3F 108
Bowgreave Dri. Bowg 8A 60
Bow Hills La. Pay 6B 52
Bowker Clo. Roch 4J 203
Bowker's Green. 6J 217
Bowker's Grn. La. Augh & Bic 6J 217
Bowker St. Ram 1H 181
Bowland Av. Burn 4J 125
Bowland Av. Chor 6F 174
Bowland Av. Fltwd 4D 54
Bowland Av. Lanc 7M 29
Bowland Clo. Carn 9N 11
Bowland Clo. L'rdge 2K 97
Bowland Ct. Clith 3L 81
Bowland Ct. South 6J 167
(off Gordon St.)
Bowland Cres. Blac 2G 89
Bowland Dri. Lanc 6H 23
Bowland Ga. La. W Brad 4L 73
Bowland Gro. Miln 9J 205
Bowland Ho. B'brn 2N 139
(off Primrose Bank)
Bowland Pl. Lyth A 2J 129
Bowland Pl. Rib 6C 116
Bowland Rd. Cabus 3N 59
Bowland Rd. Hey 8M 21
Bowland Rd. Rib 6C 116
Bowland Vw. Brier 6H 105
Bowland Vw. Cabus 3N 59
Bowland Vw. Glas D 1C 36
Bow La. Ley 6L 153
Bow La. Pres 1H 135
Bowlers Clo. Ful 4M 115
Bowlers Wlk. Roch 3C 204
Bowlingfield. Ing 3D 114
Bowling Grn. Ram 3J 181
Bowling Grn. Clo. Dar 9A 158
Bowling Grn. Clo. South 9M 167
Bowling Grn. Cotts. Old L 5B 100
Bowling Grn. Mobile Home Pk. Carn 9N 11
(off Queen St.)
Bowling Grn. St. Ram 7J 181
(in two parts)
Bowling Grn. Way. Roch 6K 203
Bowman Ct. B'brn 3N 139
(off Cleaver St.)
Bowness Av. Blac 1J 109
Bowness Av. Fltwd 3C 54
Bowness Av. Lyth A 7F 108
Bowness Av. Nels 4J 105
Bowness Av. Roch 4N 203
Bowness Av. South 1C 206
Bowness Av. T Clev 1H 63
Bowness Clo. B'brn 2A 140
Bowness Rd. Lanc 7L 23
Bowness Rd. Pad 8H 103
Bowness Rd. Pres 8C 116
Bowood Ct. Blac 3H 89
Bowran St. Pres 9H 115
Bowstone Hill Rd. Bolt 8A 200
Bow St. Ley 5L 153
Boxer Pl. Ley 4F 152
Box St. L'boro 9K 185
Box St. Ram 8J 181
Boxwood Dri. B'brn 8G 138
Boxwood St. B'brn 9N 119
Boyer Av. Liv 3C 222
Boyes Av. Catt 1A 68
Boyes Brow. Liv 6J 223
Boyle St. B'brn 2N 139
Boys La. Ful 4F 114
Brabazon Pl. Wig 3M 221
Brabiner La. Haig & W'ham 7D 96
Bracebridge Dri. South 3M 187
Bracewell. 9E 52
Bracewell Av. Poul I 8N 63
Bracewell Clo. Nels 2J 105
Bracewell La. Brac 9D 52
Bracewell Rd. Rib 4A 116
Bracewell St. Barn 1M 77
Bracewell St. Burn 9F 104
Bracewell St. Nels 2J 105
Brackenber Clo. Gigg 3M 35
Brackenber La. Gigg 4M 35
Brackenbury Clo. Los H 9K 135
Brackenbury Rd. Ful & Pres 6H 115
Brackenbury St. Pres 7J 115
Bracken Clo. B'brn 8G 138
Bracken Clo. Bolt 7D 198
Bracken Clo. Chor 6G 174
Bracken Dri. Frec 1B 132
Bracken Gro. Has 7F 160
Bracken Hey. Clith 3N 81
Brackenhurst Grn. Liv 8K 223
Brackenlea Fold. Roch 3M 203
Brackenthwaite Rd. Carr B 3L 5
Brackenway. Form 6A 206
Bracknell Av. Liv 9J 223
Bracknell Clo. Liv 9J 223
Bracknell Way. Augh 2F 216
Braconash Rd. Ley 5H 153
Bradda Rd. B'brn 7M 139
Braddocks Clo. Roch 1G 204
Braddon St. Pres 8N 115
Brades Av. T Clev 1K 63
Brades La. Frec 1B 132
Brade St. South 2B 168
Bradfield Av. Liv 7B 222
Bradford Gro. Hey 1L 27
Bradford St. Acc 2C 142
Bradkirk La. Bam B 8D 136
Bradkirk Pl. Bam B 9C 136
Bradley Fold. Nels 1J 105
Bradley Gdns. Burn 4N 123
Bradley Hall Rd. Nels 1K 105
Bradley La. E'ston 8F 172
Bradley La. Miln 9L 205
Bradley La. Stand 9C 194
Bradley Rd. Nels 1J 105
Bradley Rd. E. Nels 1J 105
Bradley Smithy Clo. Roch 3B 204
Bradley St. Col 6C 86
Bradley St. Miln 9L 205
Bradley St. South 6J 167
Bradley Vw. Nels 1J 105
Bradman Rd. Know I 7A 224
Bradshaw. 7K 199
Bradshaw Brow. Bolt 9J 199
Bradshaw Chapel. 8J 199
Bradshaw Clo. B'brn 9M 119
Bradshaw Clo. Nels 3J 105
Bradshaw Clo. Stand 3N 213
Bradshawgate Dri. Silv 7F 4
Bradshaw Hall Dri. Bolt 7J 199
Bradshaw Hall Fold. Bolt 7K 199
Bradshaw La. Adl 5H 195
Bradshaw La. G'hlgh 7G 91
Bradshaw La. Maw 3B 192
Bradshaw La. Parb 3N 211
Bradshaw La. Pil 9K 43
Bradshaw Meadows. Bolt 7K 199
Bradshaw Rd. Bolt & Tur 8K 199
Bradshaw Rd. Tot 7B 200
Bradshaw Row. Chu 2M 141
Bradshaws Brow. Maw 4B 192
Bradshaw's La. South 7D 186
Bradshaw St. Chu 2M 141
Bradshaw St. Lanc 9L 23
Bradshaw St. Nels 3H 105
Bradshaw St. Orr 5K 221
Bradshaw St. Roch 5D 204
Bradshaw St. E. Acc 2B 142
Bradshaw St. W. Acc 2M 141
Bradyll Ct. Old L 4C 100
Brady St. Hor 9B 196
Braefield Cres. Rib 7B 116
Braemar Av. South 4M 167
Braemar Av T Clev 4J 63
Braemar Ct. More 4D 22
Braemar Wlk. Blac 5F 62
Braemore Clo. Wig 9M 221
Braeside. B'brn 2K 139
Braganza Way. Lanc 8G 22
Braid Clo. Pen 7G 134
Braidhaven. Shev 5G 213
Braid's La. Bncr 5C 60
Braidwood Ct. Lyth A 1D 128
Braintree Av. Pen 7H 135

Chapman Rd.—Church St.

Chapman Rd. Hodd 6F 158
Chapter Rd. Dar 7C 158
Chardonnay Cres. T Clev 4F 62
Charity La. W'head 9C 210
Charlbury Gro. Hey 9M 21
Charles Av. South 7E 186
Charlesbye Av. Orm 6M 209
Charlesbye Clo. Orm 6N 209
Charles Clo. Hesk B 4C 150
Charles Ct. Blac 3D 88
Charles Ct. Lanc 1K 29
(off Charles St.)
Charles Ct. South 7J 167
Charles Cres. Hogh 5E 136
Charles Gro. L'rdge 3H 97
Charles La. Has 5F 160
Charles La. Miln 8K 205
Charles M. Miln 8K 205
Charles Pl. Todm 4K 165
Charles St. B'brn 6L 139
Charles St. Blac 5C 88
Charles St. Bury 9L 201
Charles St. Clay M 6L 121
Charles St. Col 6B 86
Charles St. Dar 5A 158
Charles St. Eger 2D 198
Charles St. Gt Har 5J 121
Charles St. Lanc 1K 29
Charles St. L'boro 9K 185
Charles St. More 3C 22
Charles St. Nels 1H 105
Charles St. Osw 5L 141
Charles St. Ross 5D 162
Charles St. Whitw 4A 184
Charleston Ct. Bam B 7A 136
Charles Way. Ash R 7B 114
Charlesway Ct. Lea 8B 114
Charles Whittaker St. Roch 4K 203
Charlesworth Clo. Liv 6A 216
Charleywood Rd. Know I 9N 223
Charlotte Dri. Wig 7N 221
Charlotte Pl. Pres 1K 135
Charlotte's La. Tar 3C 170
Charlotte St. B'brn 2M 139
Charlotte St. Burn 4D 124
Charlotte St. Pres 1K 135
Charlotte St. Ram 9G 180
Charlotte St. Roch 9D 204
Charlotte St. Tur 1J 199
Charnley Clo. Pen 6F 134
Charnley Fold. Walt D 5B 136
Charnley Fold Ind. Est.
Bam B 5B 136
Charnley Fold La. Bam B 5B 136
Charnley Rd. Blac 6B 88
Charnley's La.
Banks & South 7D 148
(in two parts)
Charnley St. B'brn 6K 139
Charnley St. Lanc 7H 23
Charnley St. Pres 1J 135
Charnock. Skel 5B 220
Charnock Av. Pen 6H 135
Charnock Bk. La. Hth C 9K 175
Charnock Brow. Char R 7M 173
Charnock Brow Golf Course. 7N 173
Charnock Fold. Pres 7K 115
Charnock Green. 8M 173
Charnock Ho. Chor 4E 174
(off Lancaster Ct.)
Charnock Richard. 2N 193
Charnock Richard Golf Course. 2M 193
Charnock St. Chor 7F 174
Charnock St. Ley 6K 153
Charnock St. Pres 7K 115
Charnock St. Wesh 3L 111
Charnock's Yd. Wig 6L 221
Charnwood Av. Blac 4G 89
Charnwood Clo. B'brn 9H 119
Charter Brook. Gt Har 4K 121
Charterhouse Ct. Fltwd 9D 40
Charterhouse Dri. Liv 8D 222
Charterhouse Pl. B'brn 5J 139
Charter La. Char R 1N 193
Charter St. Acc 3M 141
Charter St. Roch 9D 204
Chartwell Clo. Clay W 5E 154
Chartwell Ri. Los H 8M 135
Chartwell Rd. South 7B 186
Chasden Clo. Whit W 1E 174
Chase Clo. South 1F 186
Chase Heys. South 5M 167
Chaseley Rd. Roch 5B 204
Chase, The. Blac 3J 89
Chase, The. Burn 1B 124
Chase, The. Cot 4A 114
Chase, The. Ley 5M 153
Chase, The. Silv 9H 5
Chase, The. T Clev 8G 55
Chatburn. 7C 74
Chatburn Av. Burn 4H 125
Chatburn Av. Clith 2M 81
Chatburn Clo. Blac 2H 89
Chatburn Clo. Gt Har 4L 121
Chatburn Clo. Ross 3M 161
Chatburn Old Rd. Chat 7B 74
Chatburn Old Rd. Clith 9M 73
Chatburn Pk. Av. Brier 4E 104
Chatburn Pk. Dri. Brier 4E 104
Chatburn Pk. Dri. Clith 1M 81
Chatburn Rd. Chat 7E 74
Chatburn Rd. Clith 2M 81
Chatburn Rd. L'rdge 4J 97
Chatburn Rd. Rib 5A 116
Chatburn St. B'brn 3K 139
Chatham Av. Lyth A 8E 108
Chatham Cres. Col 5B 86
Chatham Pl. Chor 6G 175
Chatham Pl. Pres 7L 115
Chatham St. Col 5B 86
Chatham St. Nels 1H 105
Chatsworth Av. Blac 5C 62
Chatsworth Av. Fltwd 2C 54
Chatsworth Av. W'ton 2J 131
Chatsworth Clo. Barfd 1F 104
Chatsworth Clo. B'brn 8M 119
Chatsworth Clo. Chor 6D 174
Chatsworth Clo. T Clev 2K 63
Chatsworth Ct. Hth C 4H 195
Chatsworth Rd. Lanc 3K 29
Chatsworth Rd. Ley 6K 153
Chatsworth Rd. Lyth A 1D 128
Chatsworth Rd. More 5N 21
Chatsworth Rd. South 7A 186
Chatsworth Rd. Walt D 5N 135
Chatsworth St. Pres 9M 115
Chatsworth St. Roch 2B 204
Chatsworth St. Wig 6M 221
Chatteris Pl. T Clev 2C 62
Chatterton. 5H 181
Chatterton. Ram 4H 181
(off Well St. N.)
Chatterton Dri. Acc 6D 142
Chatterton Old La. Ram 4H 181
Chatterton Rd. Ram 4H 181
Chatwell Ct. Miln 9M 205
Chaucer Av. T Clev 9F 54
Chaucer Clo. E'ston 8E 172
Chaucer Gdns. Gt Har 5H 121
Chaucer Rd. Fltwd 9G 40
Chaucer St. Pres 7N 115
Cheam Av. Chor 8F 174
Cheapside. Blac 5B 88
Cheapside. Chor 7E 174
Cheapside. Form 1A 214
Cheapside. Lanc 8K 23
Cheapside. L Bent 6J 19
(off Doctor's Hill)
Cheapside. Pres 1J 135
Cheapside. Set 3N 35
(off High St.)
Cheddar Av. Blac 3D 108
Cheddar Dri. Ful 3N 115
Chedworth Av. Hey 9M 21
Cheesden. 9B 182
Cheesden Edge. Roch 9C 182
Cheetham Hill. Whitw 3A 184
Cheetham Mdw. Ley 6D 152
Cheetham St. B'brn 3K 139
Cheetham St. Roch 5C 204
Chelburn Gro. Burn 3G 124
Chelburn Vw. L'boro 5M 185
Chelford Av. Blac 2E 88
Chelford Av. Bolt 8E 198
Chelford Clo. Pen 7J 135
Chelmorton Gro. Wig 9M 221
Chelmsford Clo. Lanc 2M 29
Chelmsford Gro. Chor 7D 174
Chelmsford Pl. Chor 7D 174
Chelmsford Wlk. Ley 7D 152
Chelsea Av. Blac 1E 88
Chelsea Ct. Blac 1E 88
(off Chelsea Av.)
Chelsea M. Blac 1E 88
(off Bispham Rd.)
Chelsea St. Roch 8A 204
Chelston Dri. Ross 8F 160
Cheltenham Av. Acc 9B 122
Cheltenham Clo. Liv 9D 222
Cheltenham Cres. Lyth A 3C 130
Cheltenham Cres. T Clev 3K 63
Cheltenham Dri. Bil 9G 220
Cheltenham Rd. B'brn 3K 139
Cheltenham Rd. Blac 3B 88
Cheltenham Rd. Lanc 2K 29
Cheltenham St. Roch 9A 204
Cheltenham Way. South 1M 187
Chelwood Clo. Bolt 6D 198
Chennell Ho. Lanc 8J 23
(off Castle Pk. M.)
Chepstow Clo. Roch 5K 203
Chepstow Ct. Blac 2F 88
Chepstow Rd. Blac 2F 88
Chequer Clo. Uph 6C 220
Chequer La. Uph 4C 220
Chequers. Clay M 7M 121
Chequers Av. Lanc 3M 29
Cheriton Fld. Ful 2F 114
Cheriton Gdns. Hor 7C 196
Cheriton Pk. South 2L 187
Cherries, The. Eux 3N 173
Cherry Clo. B'brn 3B 140
Cherry Clo. Ful 3N 115
Cherry Clo. K'ham 4K 111
Cherryclough Way. B'brn 8H 139
Cherry Cres. Osw 6K 141
Cherry Cres. Ross 7L 161
Cherrycroft. Skel 4B 220
Cherrydale. Blac 6D 62
Cherryfield Cres. Liv 8K 223
Cherryfield Dri. Liv 8J 223
Cherryfields. Eux 2N 173
Cherry Gdns. Catt 2A 68
Cherry Grn. Augh 2G 217
Cherry Gro. Abb V 5C 156
Cherry Gro. Burs 7C 190
Cherry Gro. L'rdge 2J 97
Cherry Gro. Roch 5L 203
Cherry La. Frec 4M 131
Cherry Lea. B'brn 7G 139
Cherry Rd. South 2D 206
Cherry St. B'brn 3B 140
Cherry Tree. 7G 138
Cherrytree Clo. Bolt S 7K 15
Cherry Tree Clo. Hey 1K 27
Cherry Tree Clo. Pil 8K 43
Cherry Tree Ct. Blac 9H 89
(off Radworth Cres.)
Cherry Tree Ct. Fltwd 8H 41
Cherry Tree Ct. Stand 2N 213
Cherry Tree Dri. Lanc 3K 29
Cherry Tree Gdns. Blac 1G 108
Cherry Tree Gro. Chor 3E 174
Cherry Tree La. Augh 2G 217
Cherry Tree La. B'brn 8F 138
Cherry Tree La. Ross 6L 161
Cherry Tree M. Burn 6B 124
(off Bristol St.)
Cherry Tree Rd. Blac 1G 108
Cherry Tree Rd. N. Blac 9G 89
Cherry Trees. Los H 5M 135
Cherry Tree Ter. B'brn 7G 138
Cherry Tree Way. Bolt 9H 199
Cherry Tree Way. Ross 8F 160
Cherry Va. Hesk B 5D 150
Cherry Vw. Liv 5L 223
Cherry Wood. Pen 5D 134
Cherrywood Av. Lyth A 4L 129
Cherrywood Av. T Clev 2C 62
Cherrywood Clo. Ley 7H 153
Chervil Wlk. Wig 7M 221
Cheryl Dri. T Clev 3H 63
Chesham. 8M 201
Chesham Cres. Bury 9M 201
Chesham Dri. New L 8C 134
Chesham Fold Rd. Bury 9N 201
Chesham Ind. Est. Bury 9M 201
Chesham Lodge. Gt Ecc 7N 65
Chesham Rd. Bury 9L 201
Chesham St. Gt Ecc 6N 65
Cheshire Ct. Ram 8J 181
Cheshire Ho. Clo. Far M 9J 135
Chesmere Dri. Pen 3E 134
Chesnell Gro. Liv 5L 223
Chessington Grn. Burn 7H 105
(off Hillingdon Rd. N.)
Chester Av. Chor 1G 194
Chester Av. Clith 2L 81
Chester Av. Poul F 9J 63
Chester Av. Roch 7L 203
Chester Av. South 6L 167
Chester Av. T Clev 1D 62
Chesterbrook. Ribch 6F 98
Chester Clo. B'brn 5A 140
Chester Clo. Gars 5M 59
Chester Clo. Heat O 6B 22
Chester Cres. Has 7G 160
Chester Dri. Ram 1F 200
Chesterfield Clo. South 9B 186
Chesterfield Dri. Liv 5K 223
Chesterfield Rd. Blac 3B 88
Chesterfield Rd. South 9B 186
Chester Pl. Adl 5J 195
Chester Pl. Gt Ecc 6A 66
Chester Pl. Lanc 2L 29
Chester Rd. Blac 3D 88
Chester Rd. Pres 8M 115
Chester Rd. South 6M 167
Chester St. Acc 3N 141
Chester St. B'brn 4A 140
Chester St. Bury 9M 201
Chester St. Roch 7D 204
Chestnut Av. Blac 4F 108
Chestnut Av. Bolt S 4L 15
Chestnut Av. Brook 2J 25
Chestnut Av. Chor 4G 174
Chestnut Av. Eux 1M 173
Chestnut Av. Pen 4D 134
Chestnut Av. Todm 9K 147
Chestnut Av. Tot 8F 200
Chestnut Clo. Gars 3A 60
Chestnut Clo. Hals 3B 208
Chestnut Clo. K'ham 4N 111
Chestnut Clo. Walt D 6A 136
Chestnut Ct. Ley 8K 153
Chestnut Ct. Orm 6L 209
Chestnut Ct. South 6J 167
Chestnut Cres. Barr 1K 101
Chestnut Cres. Longt 8K 133
Chestnut Cres. Rib 7A 116
Chestnut Dri. Barn 3L 77
Chestnut Dri. Bury 6L 201
Chestnut Dri. Ful 2G 114
Chestnut Dri. More 2F 22
Chestnut Dri. Ross 7L 161
Chestnut Gdns. B'brn 1N 139
Chestnut Grange. Orm 9J 209
Chestnut Gro. Acc 4N 141
Chestnut Gro. Clay M 5N 121
Chestnut Gro. Dar 1A 178
Chestnut Gro. Lanc 8H 23
Chestnut Pl. Roch 5E 204
Chestnut Ri. Burn 5D 124
Chestnuts, The. Cop 3B 194
Chestnut St. South 1J 187
Chestnut Wlk. B'brn 3B 140
(off Longton St.)
Chestnut Way. L'boro 8J 185
Chethams Clo. T Clev 1G 62
Chetwyn Av. Brom X 6G 199
Chevassut Clo. Barfd 1G 104
Cheviot Av. Burn 4J 125
Cheviot Av. Lyth A 3D 130
Cheviot Av. T Clev 8F 54
Cheviot Clo. Bolt 8D 198
Cheviot Clo. Bury 9F 200
Cheviot Clo. Hor 8D 196
Cheviot Clo. Miln 7K 205
Cheviot Clo. Ram 1H 201
Cheviot Clo. Wig 9M 221
Cheviot St. Pres 9G 114
Cheviot Way. Liv 4L 223
Chew Gdns. Poul F 8H 63
Chew La. Garg 3M 53
Chichester Bus. Cen. Roch 6D 204
Chichester Clo. Burn 3F 124
Chichester Clo. L'boro 2J 205
Chichester Clo. T Clev 1G 62
Chichester St. Roch 6D 204
Chicken St. B'brn 4K 139
Chiddlingford Ct. Blac 7D 88
Childrey Wlk. B'brn 8A 140
(off Ridgeway Av.)
Chilham St. Orr 5K 221
Chiltern Av. Blac 2D 108
Chiltern Av. Burn 4H 125
Chiltern Av. Eux 5N 173
Chiltern Av. Poul F 8J 63
Chiltern Clo. Hor 8D 196
Chiltern Clo. Kirkby 6H 223
Chiltern Clo. Lyth A 3C 130
Chiltern Clo. Ram 1H 201
Chiltern Dri. Bury 9G 200
Chiltern Dri. Liv 6H 223
Chiltern Dri. Wig 8M 221
Chiltern Mdw. Ley 6N 153
Chiltern Rd. Ram 1H 201
Chiltern Rd. South 7A 186
Chilton Clo. Liv 1C 222
Chilton M. Liv 1C 222
Chimes, The. K'ham 5M 111
Chimes, The. Tar 1E 170
China St. Acc 2M 141
China St. Lanc 8K 23
Chindits Way. Ful 5L 115
Chines, The. Ful 5H 115
Chingford Bank. Burn 7G 105
Chingle Clo. Ful 3A 116
Chipping. 5G 70
Chipping Av. South 8A 186
Chipping Ct. Blac 2G 88
Chipping Fold. Miln 8J 205
Chipping Gro. Blac 2G 89
Chipping Gro. Burn 5H 125
Chipping La. L'rdge 2H 97
Chipping St. Pad 9J 103
Chirk Dri. T Clev 1K 63
Chisacre Dri. Shev 5G 213
Chisholm Clo. Stand 1L 213
Chisholme Clo. G'mnt 3D 200
Chislehurst Av. Blac 9C 88
Chislehurst Gro. Burn 6H 105
Chislehurst Pl. Lyth A 2K 129
Chislett Clo. Burs 9B 190
Chisnall Av. Wrigh 8J 193
Chisnall La. Cop 8K 193
(in two parts)
Chisnall La. Hesk 3J 193
Chiswell Gro. T Clev 3K 63
Chiswell St. Wig 6M 221
Chiswick Gro. Blac 8H 89
Chorley. 6E 174
Chorley Bus. & Technology Cen.
Eux 2A 174
Chorley Clo. South 1D 168
Chorley F.C. 8E 174
(Victory Pk.)
Chorley Golf Course. 1J 195
Chorley Hall Rd. Chor 4E 174
Chorley La. Char R 3M 193
Chorley Moor. 8E 174
Chorley New Rd. Hor & Los 9B 196
Chorley N. Ind. Pk. Chor 3F 174
Chorley Old Rd. Hor 9E 196
Chorley Old Rd.
Whit W & Brin 8E 154
Chorley Retail Pk. Chor 7F 174
Chorley Rd. Blac 9F 62
Chorley Rd. B'rod 7J 195
Chorley Rd. Hth C 2H 195
Chorley Rd. Parb 1N 211
Chorley Rd. Walt D 4N 135
Chorley Rd. Withn 5M 155
Chorley R.U.F.C. 3C 174
(Brookfields Chancery Rd.)
Chorley St. Adl 5K 195
Chorley W. Bus. Pk. Chor 6B 174
Chorlton Clo. Burn 8H 105
Chorlton Gdns. B'brn 2N 139
Chorlton St. B'brn 1N 139
Christchurch La. Bolt 9M 199
Christchurch Sq. Acc 3B 142
Christchurch St. Acc 3B 142
Christchurch St. Bacup 4L 163
Christ Chu. St. Pres 1H 135
Christian Rd. Pres 1H 135
Christie Av. More 4D 22
Christines Cres. Burs 9B 190
Christleton. Shev 6L 213
Christleton Clo. Brclf 7K 105
Christopher Acre. Roch 4J 203
Christopher Taylor Ho. Mag 5C 222
Church. 1M 141
Church All. Clay M 7M 121
Church and Oswaldtwistle. 3L 141
Church Av. Acc 7D 142
Church Av. Lanc 3K 29
Church Av. Pen 2F 134
Church Av. Pres 9A 116
Church Bank. Chu 1L 141
Church Bank. Over K 1F 16
Chu. Bank Gdns. Burt 4H 7
Chu. Bank St. Dar 6A 158
Church Brow. Bolt S 6L 15
Church Brow. Chor 6E 174
Church Brow. Clith 2L 81
Churchbrow. Halt 2A 24
Church Brow. Walt D 3N 135
Church Brow Clo. Bolt S 6L 15
Chu. Brow Gdns. Clith 2L 81
Church Clo. Clith 2L 81
Church Clo. Doph 7E 38
Church Clo. Frec 2M 131
Church Clo. Liv 9A 206
Church Clo. Mel 7F 118
Church Clo. Ram 9G 180
Church Clo. Read 8C 102
Church Clo. South 6N 167
Church Clo. Wadd 8H 73
Church Clo. Ct. Liv 9A 206
Church Ct. Bolt S 6L 15
Church Ct. Pres 7M 115
Church Ct. Ram 2J 181
Church Cft. Garg 4M 53
Church Dri. Lyth A 5M 129
Church Dri. Orr 6G 221
Church Dri. Whal 3G 101
Churchfield. Ful 3J 115
Churchfield. Shev 6K 213
Churchfield. Silv 8G 5
Church Fields. Orm 7K 209
Church Fields. Scar 6E 188
Churchfields. South 2F 186
Church Fold. Char R 1A 194
Church Fold. Cop 5B 194
Church Gdns. Eux 3M 173
Church Gdns. W'ton 2K 131
Churchgate. Goos 4N 95
Churchgate. South 5M 167
(in two parts)
Churchgate M. South 5N 167
Church Grn. Kirkby 7K 223
Church Grn. Skel 2K 219
Church Gro. Over 7B 28
Church Hall. Acc 1M 141
Church Hill. Arns 1F 4
Church Hill. Nether K 4B 16
Church Hill. Whit W 8D 154
Chu. Hill Av. War 5A 12
Church Hill Rd. Orm 6J 209
Churchill Av. Rish 9G 120
Churchill Av. South 4M 167
Churchill Clo. T Clev 1H 63
Churchill Ct. Blac 4D 88
Churchill M. Blac 5D 62
Churchill Rd. Acc 5C 142
Churchill Rd. Barfd 1F 104
Churchill Rd. B'brn 1A 140
Churchill Rd. Brins 7B 156
Churchill Rd. Ful 5M 115
Churchill St. Roch 4N 203
(in two parts)
Churchill St. Todm 9H 147
Churchill Way. Brier 2E 104
Churchill Way. Ley 5K 153
Church La. Augh 4F 216
Church La. Bils 7D 68
Church La. Brough 9G 95
Church La. Char R 1M 193
Church La. Clay M 8N 121
Church La. Clith 7E 80
Church La. E Mar 7J 53
Church La. Elsl & Brou 8M 53
Church La. Gal 2L 37
Church La. Garg 4M 53
Church La. Goos 4N 95
Church La. Gt Har 3J 121
Church La. Hamb 2C 64
Church La. Kel 6D 78
Church La. Lanc 8K 23
Church La. Lyd 3M 215
Church La. Mel 7F 118
Church La. More 2B 22
(Lord St.)
Church La. More 2C 22
(Marine Rd. E.)
Church La. Newc 6C 162
Church La. Newt & Clift 6E 112
Church La. Pad 9H 103
Church La. Ram 2J 181
Church La. Roch 6C 204
Church La. Shev 6K 213
Church La. Tun 2F 18
Church La. Whal 5J 101
Church La. W'chpl 3M 69
Church La. Wstke & Far M 9H 135
Church La. Wigg 10M 35
Church La. Winm 9G 45
Church La. Wrigh 5G 192
Church Meadows. Col 6A 86
Church Pad. Ross 5M 161
Church Pk. Lea T 6K 113
Church Pk. Over 7B 28
Church Path. Liv 7A 206
Church Raike. Chip 5G 70
Church Rd. Bam B 9A 136
(in three parts)
Church Rd. Barn 9H 53
Church Rd. Bic 5C 218
Church Rd. Form 8A 206
Church Rd. Gt Plu 2D 110
Church Rd. Ley 7K 153
Church Rd. Lytham 5L 129
Church Rd. Mag 3C 222
Church Rd. Rainf 4K 225
Church Rd. Ram 6K 181
Church Rd. Roch 7E 204
Church Rd. Ruf 1G 191
Church Rd. St A 1F 128
Church Rd. Sing 1D 90
Church Rd. Skel 2K 219
Church Rd. South 9F 148
Church Rd. Tar 1E 170
Church Rd. T Clev 1F 62
Church Rd. Todm 8H 147
Church Rd. Trea 2C 112
Church Rd. W'ton 1J 131
Church Rd. Wesh 2L 111
Church Row. Pres 9K 115
Church Row. W Grn 5G 111
Church Row Chambers.
Longt 8L 133
(off Franklands)
Churchside. New L 8C 134
Church Sq. Wors 4M 125
(off Ravenoak La.)
Church Stile. Roch 6C 204
Church St. Acc 3B 142
Church St. Adl 6J 195
Church St. Bacup 7G 163
Church St. Barn 2M 77
Church St. Barfd 7H 85
Church St. Bel 1K 197
Church St. B'brn 3M 139
Church St. Blac 5B 88
Church St. Bolt 8K 199
Church St. Brclf 8K 105
Church St. Brier 5F 104

238 A-Z Lancashire

Church St.—Cobden St.

Church St. Burn 2E 124
Church St. Chor 7E 174
Church St. Chu 1L 141
Church St. Chur 1L 67
Church St. Clay M 7M 121
Church St. Clith 3L 81
Church St. Col 6A 86
Church St. Crost 5M 171
Church St. Dar 6A 158
Church St. Fltwd 9H 41
Church St. Garg 3M 53
Church St. Gars 5M 59
Church St. Gigg 2N 35
(in two parts)
Church St. Good 7M 143
Church St. Gt Har 4J 121
Church St. Halt 2A 24
Church St. Hap 5H 123
Church St. Has 4G 160
Church St. High W 5D 136
Church St. Hor 9D 196
Church St. K Lon 6F 8
(off Market St.)
Church St. K'ham 4N 111
Church St. Lanc 8J 23
Church St. Ley 5L 153
Church St. L'rdge 3K 97
Church St. Miln 9L 205
Church St. More 2B 22
Church St. Newc 6C 162
Church St. Orm 7K 209
Church St. Orr 6G 221
Church St. Osw 5K 141
Church St. Pad 1G 123
Church St. Poul F 8K 63
Church St. Pres 1K 135
Church St. Ram 8H 181
Church St. Read 8C 102
Church St. Ribch 7E 98
Church St. Rish 8G 121
Church St. Roch 6B 204
Church St. Ross 7C 162
Church St. Slai 5B 50
Church St. South 7J 167
Church St. Todm 8H 147
Church St. Traw 9F 86
Church St. Uph 4F 220
Church St. Whit 8D 8
Church St. Whitw 6N 183
Church St. Wig 5L 221
Church Ter. Dar 6A 158
Church Ter. High W 5D 136
Church Ter. Miln 8K 205
Church Ter. Ward 7F 184
Churchtown 6D 62
(Blackpool)
Churchtown 1L 67
(Preston)
Churchtown 5N 167
(Southport)
Churchtown Ct. South 4N 167
Churchtown Cres. Bacup 6L 163
Church Vw. Arns 1F 4
Church Vw. Augh 4F 216
Church Vw. Gis 9B 52
(off Park La.)
Church Vw. Roch 3J 203
Church Vw. Stalm 5B 56
Church Vw. Tar 1E 170
Church Vw. Traw 9F 86
(off Ash St.)
Church Vw. Ct. Orm 7K 209
(off Burscough St.)
Church Wlk. B'brn 6N 119
Church Wlk. Clith 3L 81
Church Wlk. E'ston 6E 172
Church Wlk. Eux 4M 173
Church Wlk. G'mnt 4C 200
Church Wlk. More 2C 22
Church Wlk. Tar 9E 150
Church Wlk. Todm 6K 165
Church Wlk. Wesh 2L 111
Church Walks. Orm 7K 209
Church Way. Kirkby 7K 223
Church Way. Nels 4H 105
Churton Gro. Stand 2L 213
Cicely Ct. B'brn 4N 139
Cicely La. B'brn 3N 139
Cicely St. B'brn 4N 139
Cinderbarrow La. Yeal R 7D 6
Cinder Hill Rd. Todm 1N 165
Cinder La. Lanc 4K 29
Cinder La. Mere B 4L 169
Cinder La. Wood 4L 93
Cinnamon Brow. Uph 5F 220
Cinnamon Clo. Roch 5A 204
Cinnamon Ct. Pen 6F 134
Cinnamon Hill Dri. N. Walt D 5N 135
Cinnamon Hill Dri. S. Walt D 5N 135
Cinnamon St. Roch 5A 204
Cintra Av. Ash R 6G 114
Cintra Ter. Ash R 6G 114
Circus, The. Dar 6A 158
Cirrus Dri. Augh 2F 216
City Heights Clo. Lanc 8L 23
City o Pinch. Holme 1G 6
City Rd. Wig 3L 221
Clairane Av. Ful 3H 115
Clairville. South 9F 166
Clancut La. Cop 2A 194
Clanfield. Ful 2H 115
Clanwood Clo. Wig 9N 221
Clapgate Rd. Roch 4J 203
Clara Gorton Ct. Roch 7F 204
Clara St. Pres 1M 135
Clara St. Roch 8C 204
Clare Av. Col 9L 85
Clare Clo. Bury 8J 201
Claremont Av. Chor 7D 174
Claremont Av. Clith 4M 81
Claremont Av. Ley 7L 153
Claremont Av. Liv 2A 222
Claremont Av. South 1G 186
Claremont Ct. Blac 3C 88
Claremont Cres. More 4N 21
Claremont Dri. Augh 9J 209
Claremont Dri. Clith 4M 81
Claremont Pl. Lyth A 9E 108
Claremont Pl. Todm 1L 165
(off Stansfield Rd.)
Claremont Rd. Acc 9A 122
Claremont Rd. Blac 3C 88
Claremont Rd. Chor 9D 174
Claremont Rd. Miln 8H 205
Claremont Rd. More 4N 21
Claremont Rd. Roch 6N 203
Claremont Rd. South 1G 187
Claremont St. Brier 5E 104
Claremont St. Burn 3B 124
Claremont St. Col 6C 86
Claremont Ter. Nels 3H 105
Claremont Ter. Todm 1N 185
Clarence Av. Has 6F 160
Clarence Av. Kno S 8L 41
Clarence Av. T Clev 9D 54
Clarence Ct. Blac 9B 88
Clarence Pk. B'brn 1J 139
Clarence Rd. Acc 4N 141
Clarence Rd. South 1G 187
Clarence St. Barn 3N 77
Clarence St. B'brn 2L 139
Clarence St. Burn 5F 124
Clarence St. Chor 7F 174
Clarence St. Col 6D 86
Clarence St. Dar 4N 157
Clarence St. Lanc 9L 23
Clarence St. Ley 5L 153
Clarence St. L'rdge 3J 97
Clarence St. More 2B 22
Clarence St. Osw 5J 141
Clarence St. Roch 3A 204
Clarence St. Ross 9M 143
Clarence St. Traw 9F 86
Clarence St. Ind. Est. Chor 7F 174
(off Clarence St.)
Clarendon Gro. Liv 6B 216
Clarendon Rd. B'brn 9N 119
Clarendon Rd. Blac 8B 88
Clarendon Rd. Lanc 5K 23
Clarendon Rd. Lyth A 9F 108
Clarendon Rd. E. B'brn 9A 120
Clarendon Rd. E. More 4N 21
Clarendon Rd. N. Lyth A 9F 108
Clarendon Rd. W. More 5M 21
Clarendon St. Acc 2C 142
Clarendon St. Bury 9M 201
Clarendon St. Chor 7G 174
Clarendon St. Col 6E 86
Clarendon St. Pres 2K 135
Clarendon St. Roch 9E 204
Clare Rd. Lanc 5J 23
Clare St. Blac 9B 88
Clare St. Burn 3C 124
Claret St. Acc 3N 141
Clarke Holme St. Ross 5D 162
Clarke's La. Roch 5A 204
Clarke St. Poul F 8M 63
Clarke St. Rish 8H 121
Clarke St. Roch 3E 204
Clarke Wood Clo. Wis 2M 101
Clarkfield Clo. Burs 1D 210
Clarkfield Dri. More 3D 22
Clarksfield Rd. Bolt S 5L 15
Clark St. More 2B 22
Clarrick Ter. I'ton 3N 19
Claude St. Wig 5N 221
Claughton 9A 18
(Lancaster)
Claughton 2G 69
(Preston)
Claughton Av. Ley 6A 154
Claughton Dri. Lanc 4L 29
Claughton Rd. Wals 8E 200
Claughton St. Burn 9F 104
Claughton Ter. Clau 9A 18
Clawthorpe 3H 7
Claybank. Pad 9H 103
Claybank Dri. Tot 6C 200
Clay Bank St. Heyw 9G 202
Claybridge Clo. Wig 2L 221
Clay Brow Rd. Skel 5B 220
Clayburn Clo. Chor 4F 174
Clay Cft. Ter. L'boro 7K 185
Clayfield Dri. Roch 5K 203
Clay Gap La. Hamb & Out R 9D 56
Clay Hill La. L'rdge 2C 98
Claylands Dri. Bolt S 5L 15
Clay La. Hey 7N 21
Clay La. Roch 5H 203
Claymere Av. Roch 5J 203
Clay St. Brom X 6G 198
Clay St. Burn 4A 124
Clay St. L'boro 9J 185
Clayton Av. Ley 8G 153
Clayton Av. Ross 7K 161
Clayton Brook Rd. Bam B 2D 154
Clayton Bus. Pk. Clay M 7K 121
Clayton Clo. Nels 1H 105
Clayton Ct. L'rdge 3K 97
Clayton Cres. Blac 3D 108
Claytongate. Cop 3B 194
Claytongate Dri. Pen 6K 135
Clayton Green 4D 154
Clayton Grn. Bus. Pk.
Clay W 3D 154
Clayton Grn. Cen. Clay W 3D 154
Clayton Grn. Rd. Clay W 4C 154
Clayton Gro. Clay D 3L 119
Claytonhalgh. Ribch 7F 98
Clayton Hall Dri. Clay M 5M 121
Clayton Ho. Gdns. Burs 9C 190
Clayton-le-Dale 2K 119
Clayton-le-Moors 6M 121
Clayton-le-Woods 5B 154
Clayton M. Skel 2H 219
Clayton Row. Lang 9D 100
Clayton's Ga. Pres 9J 115
Clayton St. Bam B 7A 136
Clayton St. Barn 2N 77
Clayton St. B'brn 4M 139
Clayton St. Clay M 8N 121
Clayton St. Col 7B 86
Clayton St. Gt Har 4J 121
Clayton St. Nels 2H 105
(in two parts)
Clayton St. Osw 3L 141
Clayton St. Roch 3E 204
Clayton St. Skel 2H 219
Clayton St. Ind. Est. Nels 1H 105
Claytonvilla Fold. Clay W 4C 154
Clayton Way. Clay M 6N 121
Cleadon Dri. S. Bury 8H 201
Cleator Av. Blac 1C 88
Cleaver St. B'brn 3N 139
Cleaver St. Burn 1F 124
Cleavland Ter. Dar 7B 158
Clecken La. Clau B 1G 68
Clegg Av. T Clev 9D 54
Clegg Hall 4H 205
Clegg Hall Rd.
Roch & L'boro 3G 204
(in two parts)
Clegg's Av. Whitw 4N 183
(off Clegg St.)
Clegg's Ct. Whitw 4N 183
(off Clegg St.)
Clegg St. Bacup 7G 163
Clegg St. Brier 5F 104
Clegg St. Burn 1E 124
Clegg St. Has 4G 161
Clegg St. K'ham 4M 111
Clegg St. L'boro 7J 185
Clegg St. Miln 8K 205
Clegg St. Nels 4J 105
Clegg St. Skel 2H 219
Clegg St. Whitw 4N 183
Clegg St. Wors 4L 125
Clegg St. E. Burn 1E 124
(off Grey St.)
Cleggswood Av. L'boro 2K 205
Clematis Clo. Chor 3C 174
Clematis St. B'brn 3J 139
Clement Ct. Roch 7E 204
Clementina St. Roch 4C 204
(in two parts)
Clement Pl. L'boro 9M 185
Clement Pl. Roch 5B 204
Clement Royds St. Roch 5B 204
Clements Dri. Brier 6G 104
Clement St. Acc 4B 142
Clement St. Dar 7A 158
Clement Vw. Nels 2H 105
Clenger's Brow. South 4M 167
Clent Av. Liv 8B 216
Clent Gdns. Liv 8B 216
Clent Rd. Liv 8B 216
Clerk Hill Rd. Whal 6M 101
Clerkhill St. B'brn 3B 140
Clery St. Burn 4M 123
Clevedon Dri. Wig 7M 221
Clevedon Rd. Blac 3B 88
Clevedon Rd. Ing 5D 114
Cleveland Av. Ful 5M 115
Cleveland Av. Silv 7G 5
Cleveland Av. Wig 9M 221
Cleveland Clo. Liv 6H 223
Cleveland Clo. Ram 2H 201
Cleveland Dri. Lanc 1H 29
Cleveland Dri. Miln 7K 205
Cleveland Ho. Has 4G 160
(off Pleasant St.)
Cleveland Rd. Ley 5J 153
Cleveland Rd. Lyth A 5A 130
Clevelands Av. More 5N 21
Clevelands Gro. Burn 5C 124
Clevelands Gro. More 5N 21
Clevelands Mt. Burn 5D 124
(off Clevelands Gro.)
Clevelands Rd. Burn 5C 124
Cleveland St. Chor 6E 174
Cleveland St. Col 5C 86
Cleveland St. Cop 4A 194
Cleveland St. Todm 7E 146
Clevelands Wlk. More 5N 21
Cleveleys 1D 62
Cleveleys Av. Ful 5F 114
Cleveleys Av. Lanc 5G 22
Cleveleys Av. South 2N 167
Cleveleys Av. T Clev 1D 62
Cleveleys Rd. Acc 9N 121
Cleveleys Rd. B'brn 7N 139
Cleveleys Rd. Hogh 5G 136
Cleveleys Rd. South 3N 167
Clevely Bank La. Fort 3A 46
Cleves Ct. Blac 8H 89
Cleves, The. Liv 8D 216
Cleve Way. Liv 1B 214
Clieves Hills 9E 208
Clieves Hills La. Augh 1D 216
Clieves Rd. Liv 9L 223
Cliff Av. Bury 3H 201
Cliffe 3J 121
Cliffe Ct. Pres 9N 115
Cliffe Dri. Whit W 7D 154
Cliffe La. Gt Har 3J 121
Cliffe St. L'boro 4N 185
Cliffe St. Nels 1J 105
Cliff Mt. Ram 7G 180
Clifford Av. Longt 7L 133
Clifford Av. More 2D 22
Clifford Rd. Blac 3B 88
Clifford Rd. South 4G 186
Clifford St. Barn 2N 77
Clifford St. Chor 6F 174
Clifford St. Col 6B 86
Clifford St. Roch 8C 204
Cliff Pl. Blac 7B 62
Cliff Rd. South 4K 167
Cliffs, The. Hey 7L 21
Cliff St. Col 8M 85
Cliff St. Pad 9J 103
Cliff St. Pres 2H 135
Cliff St. Rish 7H 121
Cliff St. Roch 4E 204
Clifton 8H 113
Clifton Av. Acc 9B 122
Clifton Av. Ash R 7C 114
Clifton Av. Blac 9J 89
Clifton Av. Ley 7L 153
Clifton Av. W'ton 2K 131
Clifton Clo. T Clev 2J 63
Clifton Ct. Blac 3B 108
Clifton Ct. Lytham 5B 130
Clifton Cres. Blac 8G 89
Clifton Cres. Pres 7M 115
Clifton Dri. Blac 3A 108
Clifton Dri. Gt Har 3J 121
Clifton Dri. Liv 8C 222
Clifton Dri. Lyth A 4H 129
Clifton Dri. More 3E 22
Clifton Dri. Pen 3F 134
Clifton Dri. N. Lyth A 5B 108
Clifton Dri. S. Lyth A 2E 128
Clifton Gdns. Lyth A 2J 129
Clifton Grn. Clift 8G 113
Clifton Gro. Chor 7D 174
Clifton Gro. Pres 6M 115
Clifton Gro. Wilp 5N 119
Clifton Ho. Ful 5M 115
Clifton La. Clift 6G 113
Clifton Lodge. Lyth A 3E 128
Clifton Pde. Far 4M 153
Clifton Pk. Retail Cen. Blac 1K 109
Clifton Pl. Ash R 7E 114
Clifton Pl. Frec 2N 131
Clifton Rd. Blac 9H 89
Clifton Rd. Brier 6G 105
Clifton Rd. Burn 2A 124
Clifton Rd. Fltwd 1G 54
Clifton Rd. Form 7A 206
Clifton Rd. South 8M 167
Clifton Sq. Lyth A 5A 130
Clifton St. Acc 4N 141
Clifton St. B'brn 4M 139
Clifton St. Blac 5B 88
Clifton St. Burn 3C 124
Clifton St. Bury 9L 201
Clifton St. Col 6A 86
Clifton St. Dar 3N 157
Clifton St. Lyth A 5A 130
Clifton St. Miln 7J 205
Clifton St. Pres 2G 135
Clifton St. Rish 8H 121
Clifton St. Sough 4D 78
Clifton St. Traw 9E 86
Clifton Ter. Hodd 5E 158
Clinkham Rd. Gt Har 4F 120
Clinning Rd. South 3G 187
Clinton Av. Blac 6C 88
Clinton St. B'brn 2A 140
Clipper Quay. B'brn 5N 139
Clitheroe 3L 81
Clitheroe By-Pass. Clith 8L 81
Clitheroe Castle Mus. 3L 81
Clitheroe Clo. Heyw 9H 203
Clitheroe Golf Course 9J 81
Clitheroe Pl. Blac 1G 109
Clitheroe Rd. Brier 5D 104
Clitheroe Rd. Chat 9B 74
Clitheroe Rd. Lyth A 2J 129
Clitheroe Rd. Sab 9D 82
Clitheroe Rd. Wadd 8H 73
Clitheroe Rd. W Brad 7L 73
Clitheroe Rd. Whal 4J 101
Clitheroe's La. Frec 2N 131
Clitheroe St. Pad 9H 103
Clitheroe St. Pres 1M 135
Clive Av. Lyth A 8E 108
Clive Lodge. South 3F 186
Clive Rd. Pen 2E 134
Clive Rd. South 3F 186
Clive St. Burn 1D 124
Clockhouse Av. Burn 7H 105
Clockhouse Ct. Burn 7H 105
Clockhouse Gro. Burn 7H 105
Clod La. Has 8H 161
Clods Carr La. Pre 1M 55
Clogger La. Elsl 8L 53
Clogger La. Loth 10M 53
Clogg Head. Traw 9F 86
Cloister Dri. Dar 6B 158
Cloister Grn. Liv 1B 214
Cloisters. Heat O 6C 22
Cloisters, The. Ash R 9G 115
Cloisters, The. Blac 5E 88
Cloisters, The. Ley 5M 153
Cloisters, The. Roch 4E 204
Cloisters, The. Tar 9E 150
Cloisters, The. Whal 5K 101
Clorain Clo. Liv 7M 223
Clorain Rd. Liv 7M 223
Closebrook Rd. Wig 5N 221
Closes Hall M. Clith 7M 51
Close, The. Acc 8F 142
Close, The. Bury 7H 201
Close, The. Clay M 5M 121
Close, The. Ful 3A 116
Close, The. Gars 3M 59
Close, The. K'ham 5N 111
Close, The. New L 9D 134
(in two parts)
Close, The. South 1F 168
Close, The. T Clev 1D 62
(Conway Av.)
Close, The. T Clev 8D 54
(Queen's Wlk.)
Close, The. Weet 8D 90
Close, The. Withn 5L 155
Cloth Hall St. Col 6A 86
Clough 6K 185
Clougha Av. Lanc 1M 29
Clough Acre. Chor 4C 174
Clough Av. Walt D 5L 135
Clough Bank. Chat 7C 74
Clough Bank. L'boro 6K 185
Clough End Rd. Has 2G 160
Clough Fld. L'boro 1K 205
Cloughfield. Pen 7G 134
Cloughfold 5A 162
Clough Head. L'boro 4M 185
(off Higher Calderbrook Rd.)
Clough Ho. La. Ward 8E 184
Clough La. Halt 2C 24
Clough La. Heyw 9G 203
Clough La. S'stne 9E 102
Clough La. Thorn 7G 71
Clough Rd. Bacup 4L 163
Clough Rd. L'boro 6K 185
Clough Rd. Nels 2L 105
Clough Rd. Todm 6K 165
Clough St. Bacup 7H 163
Clough St. Burn 4B 124
(in two parts)
Clough St. Dar 9C 158
Clough St. Ross 6D 162
Clough St. Ward 8F 184
Clough Ter. Barn 3M 77
(off North St.)
Clough, The. Clay W 4C 154
Clough, The. Dar 9C 158
Cloughwood Cres. Shev 5G 213
Clovelly Av. Ash R 6G 114
Clovelly Av. T Clev 5C 62
Clovelly Dri. Newb 3L 211
Clovelly Dri. Pen 3D 134
Clovelly Dri. South 5E 186
Clovelly St. Roch 9M 203
Clover Av. Lyth A 8G 108
Clover Ct. Blac 5F 62
Clover Cres. Burn 1B 124
Clover Dri. Frec 1B 132
Clover Fld. Clay W 5D 154
Cloverfield. Pen 4E 134
Cloverfields. B'brn 2A 140
Clover Hall 4F 204
Clover Hall Cres. Roch 4F 204
Clover Hill Rd. Nels 3K 105
Clover M. Blac 4E 88
Clover Rd. Chor 9C 174
Clover St. Bacup 4L 163
Clover St. Roch 5B 204
Clover Ter. Dar 4A 158
Clover Vw. Roch 5F 204
Clow Bridge 3A 144
Club La. Chip 5G 70
Club St. Bam B 9A 136
Club St. Barr 9K 81
Club St. Todm 7E 146
Clucas Gdns. Orm 6K 209
Clyde Ct. Roch 7E 204
Clydesdale Pl. Ley 5F 152
Clyde St. Ash R 9F 114
Clyde St. B'brn 5J 139
Clyde St. Blac 3B 88
Clyffes Farm Clo. Scar 6F 188
Clynders Cotts. Burn 9A 104
Coach Ho. Ct. Burs 1D 210
Coach Ho. Dri. Shev 6L 213
Coach Ho., The. Eux 1J 173
Coach La. Roch 8J 203
Coach Rd. Bic 9D 218
Coach Rd. Chu 3L 141
Coach Rd. Liv 9F 224
Coach Rd. War 2A 12
Coal Clough La. Burn 4C 124
Coal Clough Rd. Todm 6E 146
Coal Hey St. Has 4G 160
(off Peel St.)
Coal Pit La. Acc 4M 141
Coal Pit La. Bacup 4M 163
Coal Pit La. Bic 7G 219
Coal Pit La. Col 7C 86
Coal Pit La. Gis 10A 52
Coal Pit La. Ross 4E 162
Coal Pit La. Toc 4H 157
Coal Pit Rd. S'hills 6J 197
Coal Rd. Ram 6N 181
Coal St. Burn 3D 124
Coastal Dri. Hest B 7J 15
Coastal Ri. Hest B 8H 15
Coastal Rd. Ains 7A 186
Coastal Rd. Hest B & Bolt S 7H 15
Coastal Rd. More & Hest B 1E 22
Coates 1N 77
Coates Av. Barn 1N 77
Coates Fields. Barn 10G 52
Coates La. Barn 10G 52
Cobb's Brow La. Newb 4L 211
Cobb's Clough Rd. Lath 7K 211
Cobbs La. Osw 9K 141
Cob Castle Rd. Has 4D 160
Cobden Ct. B'brn 3M 139
(off Blackburn Shop. Cen.)
Cobden Ho. Ross 6B 162
Cobden Pl. Traw 6E 86
(off Rosley St.)
Cobden Rd. South 8M 167
(in two parts)
Cobden St. Bacup 7M 163
Cobden St. Barn 3M 77
Cobden St. Brclf 7K 105
Cobden St. Burn 1F 124
Cobden St. Bury 9M 201
Cobden St. Chor 5G 174
Cobden St. Dar 7A 158
Cobden St. Eger 3D 198
Cobden St. Hap 5H 123
Cobden St. Nels 3H 105
Cobden St. Pad 9J 103
Cobden St. Todm 2L 165

Cobham Ct.—Courtfield Av.

Cobham Ct. *Ross* 6C **162**
Cobham Rd. *Acc* 3C **142**
Cob La. *Kel* 7D **78**
Cob Moor Rd. *Bil* 9G **221**
Cobourg Clo. *B'brn* 6N **139**
Cob Wall. 1A **140**
Cob Wall. *B'brn* 2A **140**
Cochran St. *Dar* 7A **158**
Cocker Av. *Poul I* 8N **63**
Cocker Bar. 6B **152**
Cocker Bar Rd. *Ley* 8N **151**
Cockerham. 9G **37**
Cockerham Rd. *C'ham* 1H **45**
Cockerham Rd. *Nate* 2L **59**
Cockerham Wlk. *Blac* 1G **89**
Cocker Hill. 1N **85**
Cockerill St. *Has* 3G **161**
Cockerill Ter. *Barr* 1K **101**
Cocker La. *Ley* 6E **152**
Cockermouth Clo. *B'brn* 9N **139**
Cocker Rd. *Bam B* 9C **136**
Cockersand Abbey. 6A **36**
Cockersand Av. *Hut* 7N **133**
Cockersand Dri. *Lanc* 4L **29**
Cocker Sq. *Blac* 4B **88**
Cocker St. *Blac* 4B **88**
Cocker St. *Dar* 8C **158**
Cocker Trad. Est. *Blac* 3C **88**
Cockhall La. *Whitw* 5N **183**
Cockhill La. *Col* 3E **86**
Cock Hollow. *Bury* 9M **201**
Cocking Yd. *Burt* 6H **7**
Cockle Dick's La. *South* 4L **167**
Cocklinstones. *Bury* 9H **201**
Cockridge Clo. *B'brn* 8J **139**
Cock Robin. *Crost* 4N **171**
Cock Robin La. *Catt* 1A **68**
Codale Av. *Blac* 6D **62**
Coddington St. *B'brn* 3B **140**
Coe La. *Tar* 9E **150**
Cogie Hill. *Winm* 1B **58**
Cog La. *Burn* 4A **124**
Cog St. *Burn* 4B **124**
Colbern Clo. *Liv* 1D **222**
Colbourne Clo. *Burs* 8D **190**
Colbran St. *Burn* 9F **104**
Colbran St. *Nels* 9K **85**
Colchester Av. *Lanc* 2M **29**
Colchester Dri. *T Clev* 8F **54**
Colchester Rd. *Blac* 7F **88**
Colchester Rd. *South* 3M **187**
Coldale Ct. *Blac* 3B **108**
Cold Bath St. *Pres* 9H **115**
Cold Greave Clo. *Miln* 9M **205**
Cold Row. 7B **56**
Coldstream Pl. *B'brn* 6M **139**
Coldwall St. *Roch* 5A **204**
Coldweather Av. *Nels* 5K **105**
Cold Well La. *Carr B* 2K **5**
Colebatch. *Ful* 4G **114**
Cole Cres. *Augh* 3H **217**
Coleman St. *Nels* 2K **105**
Colenso Rd. *Ash R* 7F **114**
Colenso Rd. *B'brn* 1L **139**
Coleridge Av. *Orr* 5K **221**
Coleridge Av. *T Clev* 9F **54**
Coleridge Clo. *Col* 5A **86**
Coleridge Clo. *Cot* 5B **114**
Coleridge Dri. *Acc* 6D **142**
Coleridge Dri. *L'boro* 3J **205**
Coleridge Pl. *Gt Har* 5H **121**
Coleridge Rd. *Bil* 9G **220**
Coleridge Rd. *Blac* 4D **88**
Coleridge Rd. *G'mnt* 3E **200**
Coleridge St. *B'brn* 5K **139**
Colerne Way. *Wig* 9N **221**
Colesberg Ct. *Arns* 1F **4**
Coles Dri. *Arns* 2F **4**
Coleshill Av. *Burn* 4G **125**
Coleshill Ri. *Wig* 9M **221**
Colesville Av. *T Clev* 2H **63**
Colinmander Gdns. *Orm* 9H **209**
Colin St. *Barn* 1M **77**
Colin St. *Burn* 4B **124**
Colinton. *Skel* 4B **220**
Colldale Ter. *Has* 5G **161**
College Av. *T Clev* 2C **62**
College Clo. *L'rdge* 5J **97**
College Clo. *Pad* 3J **123**
College Clo. *South* 2G **186**
College Ct. *Pres* 7H **115**
College Ga. *T Clev* 7C **54**
College Rd. *Roch* 6A **204**
College Rd. *Uph* 2E **220**
College St. *Acc* 2N **141**
College St. *Todm* 7F **146**
Collen Cres. *Bury* 7G **201**
Colley St. *Roch* 4D **204**
Collier Av. *Miln* 6J **205**
Collier's La. *Cast* 5G **8**
Collier's Row. *Guide* 7F **140**
Colliers Row Rd. *Bolt* 8L **197**
Colliers Sq. Acc 3L **141**
(off Colliers St.)
Colliers St. *Osw* 3L **141**
Collier St. *Osw* 6D **142**
Collinge Fold La. *Ross* 3L **161**
Collinge St. *Bury* 9G **201**
Collinge St. *Pad* 2H **123**
Collinge St. *Ross* 3L **161**
Collingham Pk. *Lanc* 5L **29**
Colling St. *Ram* 9G **180**
Collingwood. *Clay M* 7L **121**
Collingwood Av. *Blac* 4E **88**
Collingwood Av. *Lyth A* 8E **108**
Collingwood Pl. *Blac* 4E **88**
Collingwood Rd. *Chor* 7C **174**
Collingwood St. *Col* 7M **85**
Collingwood St. *Stand* 3N **213**
Collingwood Ter. Ben 6L **19**
(off Mt. Pleasant)
Collins Av. *Blac* 8E **62**
Collins Dri. *Acc* 6D **142**
Collin's Hill La. *Chip* 5E **70**
Collinson St. *Pres* 8M **115**
Collins Rd. *Bam B* 7A **136**
Collins Rd. N. *Bam B* 6B **136**
Collins St. *Wals* 9E **200**
Collisdene Rd. *Orr* 5G **221**
Collison Av. *Chor* 6E **174**
Collyhurst Av. *Blac* 3E **108**
Colman Ct. *Pres* 2G **135**
Colmoor Clo. *Liv* 4L **223**
Colmore Gro. *Bolt* 9H **199**
Colmore St. *Bolt* 9H **199**
Colnbrook. *Stand* 3L **213**
Colne. 6B **86**
Colne & Broughton Rd.
Thorn C 10J **53**
Colne Edge. 4N **85**
Colne Golf Course. 3E **86**
Colne La. *Col* 7B **86**
Colne Rd. *Barn* 3L **77**
Colne Rd. *Barfd & Col* 7J **85**
Colne Rd. *Brier* 4F **104**
(in two parts)
Colne Rd. *Burn* 6F **104**
Colne Rd. *Col* 9C **78**
Colne Rd. *Kel* 6D **78**
Colne Rd. *Traw* 9E **86**
Colonnades, The. *Lanc* 9N **23**
Colthirst Dri. *Clith* 1M **81**
Colt Ho. Clo. *Ley* 8K **153**
Coltsfoot Dri. *Chor* 4F **174**
Coltsfoot Wlk. *More* 6B **22**
Columbia Way. *B'brn* 9H **119**
Columbine Clo. *Chor* 3C **174**
Columbine Clo. *Roch* 2N **203**
Colville Av. *Blac* 4C **108**
Colville Rd. *Dar* 3M **157**
Colville St. *Burn* 1E **124**
Colwall Clo. *Liv* 8M **223**
Colwall Rd. *Liv* 8M **223**
Colwall Wlk. *Liv* 8M **223**
Colwyn Av. *Blac* 9E **88**
Colwyn Av. *More* 2D **22**
Colwyn Pl. *Ing* 6D **114**
Colyton Clo. *Chor* 6G **175**
Colyton Rd. *Chor* 6G **175**
Colyton Rd. E. *Chor* 6G **175**
Combermere Gro. *Hey* 2K **27**
Combermere Rd. *Hey* 1K **27**
Comer Gdns. *Liv* 8B **216**
Comet Rd. *M Side* 5F **152**
Comet Rd. *Wig* 3M **221**
Comet St. *Bacup* 9K **145**
Commerce St. *Bacup* 5K **163**
Commerce St. *Has* 4F **160**
(in two parts)
Commercial Rd. *Chor* 5E **174**
Commercial Rd. *Gt Har* 4J **121**
Commercial Rd. *Nels* 2J **105**
Commercial St. *Bacup* 7H **163**
Commercial St. *Barn* 2M **77**
Commercial St. *Blac* 9B **88**
Commercial St. *Brier* 4F **104**
Commercial St. *Chu* 2L **141**
Commercial St. *Gt Har* 4J **121**
Commercial St. *Osw* 5K **141**
Commercial St. *Rish* 7H **121**
Commercial St. *Ross* 5M **143**
Commercial St. *Set* 3N **35**
Commercial St. *Todm* 2M **165**
Commodore Pl. *Wig* 2N **221**
Comn. Bank Ind. Est. *Chor* 7B **174**
Comn. Bank La. *Chor* 7B **174**
Common Edge. 3F **108**
Comn. Edge Rd. *Blac* 3F **108**
Comn. Garden St. *Lanc* 8K **23**
Common La. *South* 4G **168**
Commonside. *Lyth A* 4K **129**
Commons La. *Bald* 3A **118**
Common, The. *Adl* 9G **194**
Common, The. *Parb* 1N **211**
Commonwealth Clo. *Lyth A* 9J **109**
Como Av. *Burn* 5A **124**
Company St. *Rish* 8H **121**
Compley Av. *Poul F* 9J **63**
Compley Grn. *Poul F* 9J **63**
Compression Rd. *Hey* 5K **27**
Compston Av. *Ross* 7M **143**
Compton Clo. *Poul F* 6J **63**
Compton Grn. *Ful* 2F **114**
Compton Rd. *South* 2H **187**
Comrie Cres. *Burn* 6B **124**
Concourse Shop. Cen. *Uph* 2M **219**
Conder Av. *T Clev* 1F **62**
Conder Brow. *Carn* 8B **12**
Conder Green. 1G **36**
Conder Grn. Rd. *Gal* 3K **37**
Conder Pl. *Lanc* 6J **23**
Conder Rd. *Ash R* 8B **114**
Condor Gro. *Blac* 8D **88**
Condor Gro. *Lyth A* 9D **108**
Condor Way. *Pen* 6K **135**
Conduit St. *Nels* 1H **105**
Coneygarth La. *Whit* 9E **8**
(in two parts)
Congleton Clo. *Blac* 9H **89**
Congress St. *Chor* 5E **174**
Conifer Clo. *Kirkby* 5K **223**
Conifers, The. *Brtn* 2E **94**
Conifers, The. *Hamb* 1A **64**
Conifers, The. *K'ham* 4N **111**
Conifers, The. *Liv* 8B **216**
Conisber Clo. *Eger* 4E **198**
Conisborough. *Roch* 7B **204**
Coniston Av. *Acc* 4M **141**
Coniston Av. *Adl* 5K **195**
Coniston Av. *Ash R* 7G **114**
Coniston Av. *Bacup* 3L **163**
Coniston Av. *Barn* 1L **77**
Coniston Av. *Eux* 5N **173**
Coniston Av. *Fltwd* 9E **40**
Coniston Av. *Hamb* 1B **64**
Coniston Av. *Kno S* 7L **41**
Coniston Av. *Lyth A* 7F **108**
Coniston Av. *Orr* 4J **221**
Coniston Av. *Pad* 8H **103**
Coniston Av. *Poul F* 7H **63**
Coniston Av. *T Clev* 1H **63**
Coniston Clo. *Kirkby* 6J **223**
Coniston Clo. *L'rdge* 5H **97**
Coniston Clo. *Ram* 6H **181**
Coniston Cold. 3J **53**
Coniston Ct. More 2C **22**
(off Marine Rd. E.)
Coniston Ct. *South* 1C **206**
Coniston Cres. *T Clev* 2H **63**
Coniston Dri. *Dar* 5C **158**
Coniston Dri. *Walt D* 6N **135**
Coniston Gro. *Col* 5D **86**
Coniston Rd. *B'brn* 1A **140**
Coniston Rd. *Blac* 1C **108**
Coniston Rd. *Bolt S* 5L **15**
Coniston Rd. *Carn* 1B **16**
Coniston Rd. *Chor* 8D **174**
Coniston Rd. *Ful* 4M **115**
Coniston Rd. *Lanc* 6L **23**
Coniston Rd. *Mag* 9C **216**
Coniston Rd. *More* 3C **22**
Coniston St. *Burn* 3A **124**
Coniston Way. *Crost* 3M **171**
Coniston Way. *Rainf* 9K **219**
Coniston Way. *Rish* 8F **120**
Connaught Rd. *Hey* 2J **27**
Connaught Rd. *Lanc* 2M **29**
Connaught Rd. *Pres* 3H **135**
Conningsbury Clo. *Brom X* 5F **198**
Consett Av. *T Clev* 7E **54**
Constable Av. *Burn* 6D **124**
Constable Av. *Los H* 9K **135**
Constable Lee Ct. Ross 3M **161**
(off Burnley Rd.)
Constable Lee Cres. *Ross* 3M **161**
Constable St. *Pres* 9K **115**
Constantine Rd. *Roch* 6C **204**
Constitution Hill. Set 3N **35**
(off Church St.)
Convent Clo. *Augh* 1K **217**
Convent Clo. *Bam B* 7N **135**
Convent Clo. *Ley* 5M **153**
Convent Cres. *Blac* 2G **88**
Convent Gro. *Roch* 8A **204**
Conway Av. *B'brn* 1M **139**
Conway Av. *Blac* 3H **89**
Conway Av. *Clith* 4J **81**
Conway Av. *Ley* 7M **153**
Conway Av. *Pen* 7K **135**
Conway Av. *T Clev* 1D **62**
Conway Clo. *Catt* 1A **68**
Conway Clo. *Eux* 5A **174**
Conway Clo. *Has* 6G **161**
Conway Clo. *Liv* 5J **223**
Conway Clo. *Ram* 8G **180**
Conway Ct. *Hogh* 6F **136**
Conway Cres. *Barn* 2N **77**
Conway Cres. *G'mnt* 3E **200**
Conway Dri. *Ful* 2F **114**
Conway Dri. *Osw* 4H **141**
Conway Gro. *Burn* 7G **104**
Conway Ho. *Pres* 9N **115**
Conway Rd. *E'ston* 7F **172**
Conway Rd. *Ross* 4A **162**
Conway St. *Wig* 6M **221**
Conyers Av. *South* 2F **186**
Cook Ct. *B'brn* 2H **139**
Cooke St. *Hor* 9E **196**
Cook Gdns. *B'brn* 4B **140**
Cook Grn. La. *K Grn* 3C **98**
Cook Ho. Rd. *Col* 5B **86**
Cookson Clo. *Frec* 2N **131**
Cookson Rd. *T Clev* 9G **55**
Cookson St. *Blac* 4C **88**
Cook St. *Roch* 4E **204**
Cook Ter. *Roch* 4E **204**
Coolham La. *Earby* 3F **78**
Coolidge Av. *Lanc* 9H **23**
Coombes, The. *Ful* 4J **115**
Cooperage, The. *Osw* 5K **141**
Co-operation St. *Bacup* 5L **163**
Co-operation St. *Craw* 9M **143**
Co-operation St. *Ross* 5N **161**
(Bacup Rd.)
Co-operation St. *Ross* 5D **162**
(Burnley Rd. E.)
Co-operative Bldgs. *Cliv* 9K **125**
Co-operative St. *Bam B* 8A **136**
Co-operative St. *Barn* 2M **77**
Co-operative St. *Ross* 8E **160**
Cooperative St. *Todm* 8K **165**
Cooper Ct. *T Clev* 9D **54**
Cooper Hill Clo. *Walt D* 3N **135**
Cooper Hill Dri. *Walt D* 3N **135**
Cooper Rd. *Pres* 9G **115**
Coopers Clo. Osw 5K **141**
(off Peel St.)
Cooper's La. *Hesk* 6E **192**
Coopers Row. *Lyth A* 1K **129**
Cooper St. *Bacup* 4K **163**
Cooper St. *Burn* 4E **124**
Cooper St. *Hor* 9C **196**
Cooper St. *Nels* 1J **105**
Cooper St. *Roch* 1G **205**
Coopers Wlk. *Roch* 3F **204**
Coopers Way. *Blac* 3C **88**
Cooper Ter. *Roch* 5E **204**
Coop St. *Blac* 6B **88**
Coop St. *Bolt* 9E **198**
Coop Ter. *Roch* 6G **205**
Coote La. *Wstke & Los H* 9H **135**
Copeland Pl. *Lyth A* 4B **130**
Copenhagen Sq. *Roch* 5D **204**
Copenhagen St. *Roch* 5D **204**
(in two parts)
Cop La. *Fltwd* 9G **41**
Cop La. *Pen* 3E **134**
Copp. 8M **65**
Copperas Clo. *Shev* 5K **213**
Copperas Ho. Ter. *Todm* 5J **165**
Copper Beech Clo. *Much H* 4J **151**
Copper Beeches. *Pen* 7G **134**
Copperfield Clo. *Burn* 3K **125**
Copperfield St. *B'brn* 5N **139**
Copperwood Way. *Chor* 7B **174**
Coppice Av. *Acc* 1C **142**
Coppice Brow. *Carn* 8C **12**
Coppice Clo. *Chor* 5G **175**
Coppice Clo. *Nels* 9L **85**
Coppice Dri. *Bil* 9G **220**
Coppice Dri. *Whitw* 7N **183**
Coppice La. *H'pey* 2L **175**
Coppice St. *Bury* 9A **202**
Coppice, The. *B'brn* 1H **139**
Coppice, The. *Bolt* 8K **199**
Coppice, The. *Clay M* 5M **121**
Coppice, The. *Ing* 5D **114**
Coppice, The. *K'ham* 3M **111**
Coppice, The. *Longt* 8L **133**
Coppice, The. *More* 3E **22**
Coppice, The. *Ram* 1F **200**
Coppingford Clo. *Roch* 3L **203**
Coppins Grn. *Poul F* 1L **89**
Copp La. *Gt Ecc & Elsw* 8M **65**
Coppull. 4A **194**
Coppull Enterprise Cen. *Cop* 3A **194**
Coppull Hall La. *Cop* 4C **194**
Coppull Moor. 7N **193**
Coppull Moor La. *Cop* 7N **193**
Coppull Rd. *Chor* 2B **194**
Coppull Rd. *Liv* 7B **216**
Cop Royd Ter. *Cliv* 8K **125**
Copse Dri. *Bury* 7L **201**
Copse Rd. *Fltwd* 3F **54**
Copse, The. *Acc* 3M **141**
Copse, The. *Chor* 1D **194**
Copse, The. *Tur* 3J **199**
Copse Vw. Bus. Pk. *Fltwd* 2F **54**
Copse Wlk. *L'boro* 9J **185**
Copster Dri. *L'rdge* 3K **97**
Copster Green. 1L **119**
Copster Hill Clo. *Guide* 8D **140**
Cop, The. *T Clev* 6D **54**
Copthorne Rd. *Liv* 8G **222**
Copthorne Wlk. *Liv* 8G **222**
Copthorne Wlk. *Tot* 8E **200**
Copthurst Av. *High* 4L **103**
Copthurst La.
H'pey & Whit W 9G **155**
Copthurst St. *Pad* 9H **103**
Coptrod Head Clo. *Roch* 1B **204**
Coptrod Rd. *Roch* 5A **204**
Copy La. *Boot* 6A **222**
Copy La. *Cat* 3G **25**
Copy Nook. *B'brn* 3A **140**
Copy St. *B'brn* 3A **140**
Coral Clo. *Blac* 9G **89**
Coral Island. 6B **88**
Corbet Clo. *Liv* 8H **223**
Corbett St. *Roch* 5E **204**
Corbet Wlk. *Liv* 8H **223**
Corbridge Clo. *Blac* 2G **108**
Corbridge Clo. *Poul F* 6J **63**
Corbridge Ct. *Clith* 2L **81**
Corcas La. *Stalm* 5L **55**
Corka La. *Lyth A* 8E **110**
Cork Rd. *Lanc* 1M **29**
Corlass St. *Barfd* 8H **85**
Corless Cotts. *Doph* 7E **38**
Cornall St. *Bury* 9H **201**
Cornbrook. *Skel* 4B **220**
Cornbrook Clo. *Ward* 8F **184**
Corncroft. *Pen* 5F **134**
Cornel Gro. *Burn* 5A **124**
Cornelian St. *B'brn* 7N **119**
Corner Bank Clo. *Gt Plu* 2E **110**
Corner Row. 8K **91**
Corners, The. *T Clev* 8C **54**
Cornfield. *Cot* 3B **114**
Cornfield Clo. *Bury* 6L **201**
Cornfield Gro. *Burn* 1M **123**
Cornfield St. *Dar* 5B **158**
Cornfield St. *Miln* 8J **205**
Cornfield St. *Todm* 1N **165**
Cornflower Clo. *Chor* 4F **174**
Cornflower Clo. *Hesk B* 3C **150**
Cornford Rd. *Blac* 1H **109**
Cornhill. *Acc* 2B **142**
Cornhill Arc. Acc 2B **142**
(off Cornhill)
Cornholme. 7E **146**
Cornholme. *Burn* 8J **105**
Cornholme Ter. Todm 7E **146**
(off Burnley Rd.)
Corn Mkt. Lanc 8K **23**
(off Comn. Gdns. St.)
Corn Mill Clo. *Roch* 1F **204**
Corn Mill La. Ross 4M **161**
(off Greenfield St.)
Cornmill Lodge. *Liv* 9B **216**
Cornmill Ter. *Barn* 1M **77**
Corn Mill Yd. *Clay M* 7M **121**
Cornthwaite Rd. *Ful* 6H **115**
Cornwall Av. *B'brn* 4E **140**
Cornwall Av. *Blac* 1C **88**
Cornwall Av. *T Clev* 8F **54**
Cornwall Pl. *Blac* 8H **89**
Cornwall Pl. *Chu* 1M **141**
Cornwall Pl. *Wig* 5M **221**
Cornwall Rd. *Rish* 8G **120**
Cornwall Way. *South* 1B **206**
Corona Av. *Liv* 6B **216**
Coronation Av. *B'brn* 9D **138**
Coronation Av. *Form* 1A **214**
Coronation Av. *Fort* 2M **45**
Coronation Av. *Pad* 3H **123**
Coronation Cres. *Pres* 1L **135**
Coronation Gro. *Ross* 6C **162**
Coronation Pk. 7K **209**
(Ormskirk)
Coronation Pk. 9N **213**
(Standish Lower Ground)
Coronation Pl. *Barfd* 8H **85**
Coronation Rd. *Brier* 5G **104**
Coronation Rd. *K'ham* 4M **111**
Coronation Rd. *Lyd* 8B **216**
Coronation Rd. *Lyth A* 4J **129**
Coronation Rd. *Stand L* 9N **213**
Coronation Rd. *T Clev* 1C **62**
Coronation Rock Company. 9G **89**
(off Cherry Tree Rd. N.)
Coronation St. *Barn* 2N **77**
Coronation St. *Blac* 5B **88**
Coronation St. *Gt Har* 3K **121**
Coronation Ter. Lang 9C **100**
(off Whalley New Rd.)
Coronation Vs. *Whitw* 4A **184**
Coronation Wlk. *South* 7G **167**
Coronation Way. *Lanc* 4L **23**
Corporation Rd. *Roch* 7A **204**
Corporation St. *Acc* 3N **141**
Corporation St. *B'brn* 3M **139**
Corporation St. *Blac* 5B **88**
Corporation St. *Chor* 5F **174**
Corporation St. *Clith* 3K **81**
Corporation St. *Col* 8L **85**
Corporation St. *Pres* 9J **115**
Corporation St. *South* 7H **167**
Corrib Rd. *Blac* 9D **62**
Corringham Rd. *More* 3B **22**
Corring Way. *Bolt* 9H **199**
Corwen Clo. *B'brn* 2M **139**
Corwen Dri. *Boot* 6A **222**
Cosford St. *Weet* 4D **90**
Cosgate Clo. *Orr* 6H **221**
Costessey Way. *Wig* 8M **221**
Cote Holme. 2L **141**
Cote La. *L'boro* 8J **185**
Cotford Rd. *Ram* 8F **198**
Coton Way. *Liv* 7H **223**
Cotswold Av. *Eux* 5N **173**
Cotswold Av. *Wig* 6L **221**
Cotswold Clo. *E'ston* 8G **172**
Cotswold Clo. *Ram* 1H **201**
Cotswold Cres. *Bury* 9F **200**
Cotswold Cres. *Miln* 6K **205**
Cotswold Dri. *Hor* 8D **196**
Cotswold Ho. *Chor* 8E **174**
Cotswold Ho. Has 4G **161**
(off Warwick St.)
Cotswold M. *B'brn* 8A **140**
Cotswold Rd. *Blac* 1D **88**
Cotswold Rd. *Chor* 8E **174**
Cotswold Rd. *Lyth A* 3C **130**
Cottage Clo. *Orm* 8J **209**
Cottage Cft. *Bolt* 8K **199**
Cottage Fields. *Chor* 1D **194**
Cottage La. *Bam B* 6B **136**
Cottage La. *Crost* 5J **171**
Cottage La. *Orm* 6J **209**
Cottage M. *Orm* 7J **209**
Cottage Wlk. *Roch* 1N **203**
Cottam. 4B **114**
Cottam Av. *Ing* 5C **114**
Cottam Clo. *Lyth A* 7F **108**
Cottam Clo. *Whal* 5J **101**
Cottam Grn. *Cot* 3B **114**
Cottam Hall La. *Cot* 4B **114**
Cottam La. *Ing & Ash R* 6D **114**
Cottam La. *Longt* 1N **151**
Cottam Pl. *Poul F* 9H **63**
Cottam St. *Bury* 9H **201**
Cottam St. *Chor* 8E **174**
Cottam Way. *Cot* 5N **113**
Cottesloe Pl. *Barfd* 8G **84**
Cottesmore Pl. *Blac* 4G **88**
Cottom Cft. *Clay M* 5M **121**
Cotton Ct. *Col* 8N **85**
Cotton Ct. *Pres* 9K **115**
Cotton Dri. *Orm* 6J **209**
Cotton Fold. *Roch* 7F **204**
Cotton Hall St. *Dar* 5A **158**
Cotton La. *Roch* 9N **203**
Cotton St. *Acc* 3A **142**
Cotton St. *Burn* 3B **124**
Cotton St. *Pad* 2H **123**
Cotton Tree. 6E **86**
Cotton Tree La. *Col* 6D **86**
Cottys Brow. *South* 3M **167**
Coudray Rd. *South* 5L **167**
Coulston Av. *Blac* 8B **62**
Coulston Rd. *Lanc* 2L **29**
Coultate St. *Burn* 3A **124**
Coulter Beck La. *Leck* 8H **9**
Coulthurst St. *Ram* 8G **180**
Coulton Rd. *Brier* 3F **104**
Counsell Ct. *T Clev* 1H **63**
Countess Clo. *Wesh* 2M **111**
Countess Cres. *Blac* 8C **62**
Countess Rd. *Lwr D* 9N **139**
Countess St. *Acc* 2M **141**
Countess Way. *Bam B* 7A **136**
Countess Way. *Eux* 4N **173**
Country Clo. *Ley* 3K **153**
Count St. *Roch* 8D **204**
County Av. *Lanc* 7M **29**
County Brook La. *Foul* 9N **77**
County Rd. *Kirkby* 6K **223**
County Rd. *Orm* 8J **209**
County St. *Lanc* 8J **23**
Coupe Green. 4G **136**
Coupe Grn. *Hogh* 4G **136**
Couplands, The. *Cop* 5A **194**
Coupland St. *Todm* 2L **165**
Coupland St. *Whitw* 6N **183**
Courage Low La. *Wrigh* 9G **192**
Courier Pl. *Wig* 2N **221**
Course La. *Lath* 3G **211**
Courtfield. *Orm* 5J **209**
Courtfield Av. *Blac* 2D **88**

Courtfields—Croxteth Dri.

Courtfields. *Blac* 6C **88**
Court Grn. *Orm* 5J **209**
Court Gro. *Clay D* 3M **119**
Court Hey. *Mag* 1D **222**
Court Rd. *South* 6J **167**
Court, The. *Ful* 2F **114**
Court, The. *Pen* 4F **134**
Courtyard, The. *Bacup* 4L **163**
Cousin Fields. *Brom X* 6J **199**
Cousin's La. *Ruf* 2E **190**
Cove Dri. *Silv* 7G **4**
Covell Ho. Lanc *8J* ***23***
(off Castle Pk. M.)
Coventry St. *Chor* 8E **174**
Coventry St. *Roch* 7C **204**
Coverdale Dri. *B'brn* 9E **138**
Coverdale Rd. *Lanc* 8H **23**
Coverdale Way. *Burn* 2B **124**
Cove Rd. *Silv* 6E **4**
Covert, The. *T Clev* 8F **54**
Cove, The. *More* 1E **22**
Cove, The. *T Clev* 8C **54**
Coveway Av. *Blac* 4E **88**
Cowan Brae. *B'brn* 2L **139**
Cowan Bridge. 8H **9**
Cow Ark. 3M **71**
Cow Clough La. *Whitw* 4M **183**
Cowdrey M. *Lanc* 7H **23**
Cowell Way. *B'brn* 3L **139**
Cower Gro. *Walm B* 2L **151**
Cowes Av. *Has* 5H **161**
Cowfold St. *Todm* 1L **165**
Cowgarth La. *Earby* 2F **78**
Cow Gate La. *Hell* 4D **52**
Cow Gill La. *Saw* 2K **75**
Cowgill St. *Bacup* 4L **163**
Cowgill St. *Earby* 3E **78**
Cow Hill. 1C **116**
Cowhill La. *Rish* 1F **140**
Cowhurst Av. *Todm* 9J **147**
Cow La. *Burn* 3D **124**
Cow La. *Ley* 7J **153**
Cowley Cres. *Pad* 2K **123**
Cowley Rd. *Blac* 1F **108**
Cowley Rd. *Ram* 8F **198**
Cowley Rd. *Rib* 6A **116**
Cowling. 8G **175**
Cowling Brow. *Chor* 7G **175**
Cowling Brow Ind. Est. *Chor* 8G **175**
Cowling Cotts. *Char R* 2N **193**
Cowling Hill La. *Loth* 8N **79**
Cowling La. *Ley* 6G **152**
Cowling Rd. *Chor* 8H **175**
Cowm Pk. Way N. *Whitw* 4N **183**
Cowm Pk. Way S. *Whitw* 6N **183**
Cowm St. *Whitw* 1B **184**
Cowper Av. *Clith* 2L **81**
Cowpe Rd. *Ross & Waterf* 7C **162**
Cowper Pl. *Saw* 3E **74**
Cowper St. *B'brn* 1N **139**
Cowper St. *Burn* 4A **124**
Cowslip Way. *Chor* 4F **174**
Cowtoot La. *Bacup* 4K **163**
Cow Well La. *Whit W* 7D **154**
Coxfield. *App B* 5G **213**
Cox Green. 4F **198**
Cox Grn. Clo. *Eger* 2D **198**
Cox Grn. Rd. *Eger* 1D **198**
Coyford Dri. *South* 2N **167**
Crabtree Av. *Bacup* 6L **163**
Crabtree Av. *Pen* 5D **134**
Crabtree Av. *Ross* 5D **162**
Crabtree Clo. *Burs* 9B **190**
Crabtree La. *Burs* 8N **189**
Crabtree La. *N'bgn* 3A **8**
Crab Tree La. *St M* 3A **66**
Crabtree Orchard. *T Clev* 9H **55**
Crabtree Rd. *T Clev* 9H **55**
Crabtree Rd. *Wig* 4N **221**
Crabtree St. *B'brn* 3B **140**
Crabtree St. *Brier* 5F **104**
Crabtree St. *Col* 7N **85**
Crabtree St. *Ross* 2D **162**
Cracoe Gill. *Barfd* 8G **85**
Craddock Rd. *Col* 6B **86**
Crag Av. *Bury* 3J **201**
Crag Bank. 1N **15**
Crag Bank Cres. *Carn* 1N **15**
Crag Bank La. *Carn* 8M **11**
Crag Bank Rd. *Carn* 9M **11**
Cragdale. Set *3N* ***35***
(off Victoria St.)
Crag Fold. *Bury* 3J **201**
Crag Foot. 2K **11**
Cragg Pl. *L'boro* 9L **185**
Cragg Row. *Salt* 4A **78**
Craggs La. *Lowg* 2L **33**
Cragg's Row. *Pres* 8J **115**
Cragg St. *Blac* 7B **88**
Cragg St. *Col* 6N **85**
Crag La. *Bury* 3J **201**
Crag La. *Hut R* 6A **8**
Crag Rd. *Lanc* 7M **23**
Crag Rd. *War* 2K **11**
Craigflower Ct. *Bam B* 9E **136**
Craighall Rd. *Bolt* 7E **198**
Craiglands Av. *Hey* 6L **21**
Craiglands Ct. *Ald* 2G **29**
Craig St. *Hey* 5L **21**
Crake Av. *Fltwd* 2C **54**
Crake Bank. *Lanc* 6G **22**
Cramond Clo. *Wig* 7N **221**
Cranberry Av. *Todm* 8L **165**
Cranberry Chase. *Dar* 8C **158**
Cranberry Clo. *Dar* 9D **158**
Cranberry La. *Dar* 8C **158**
Cranberry Ri. *Love* 6M **143**
Cranborne Clo. *Stand* 3M **213**
Cranborne St. *Pres* 9M **115**
Cranborne Ter. *B'brn* 2K **139**
Cranbourne Dri. *Chor* 7G **174**
Cranbourne Dri. *Chu* 9N **121**
Cranbourne Gro. *T Clev* 4L **63**
Cranbourne Rd. *Roch* 7J **203**
Cranbourne St. *Bam B* 8A **136**
Cranbourne St. *Chor* 7F **174**
Cranbourne St. *Col* 5B **86**
Cranbrook Av. *Blac* 6D **62**
Cranbrook Av. *Osw* 4J **141**
Cranbrook St. *B'brn* 6L **139**
Cranes La. *Lath* 5B **210**
Crane St. *Cop* 7N **193**
Cranfield Vw. *Dar* 9C **158**
Crangle Way. *Clith* 1N **81**
Crank Rd. *Bil* 9G **220**
Crankshaw St. *Ross* 4M **161**
Cranleigh Av. *Blac* 8C **62**
Cranmer St. *Burn* 3C **124**
Cranshaw Dri. *B'brn* 9M **119**
Cranshaw St. *Acc* 2A **142**
Cranston Rd. *Know I* 8A **224**
Cranwell Av. *Lanc* 2M **29**
Cranwell Clo. *B'brn* 4N **139**
Cranwell Clo. *Liv* 8B **222**
Cranwell Ct. *K'ham* 4L **111**
Crask Wlk. *Liv* 6L **223**
Craven Bank La. *Gigg* 2L **35**
Craven Clo. *Ful* 2J **115**
Craven Corner. *T Clev* 4F **62**
Craven Cotts. Set *3N* ***35***
(off Kirkgate)
Cravendale Av. *Nels* 8J **85**
Craven Gdns. *Roch* 8B **204**
Craven Ho. *Todm* 7K **165**
Craven's Av. *B'brn* 9M **139**
Craven's Brow. *B'brn* 9M **139**
Cravens Heath. *B'brn* 1M **157**
Cravens Hollow. *B'brn* 1L **157**
Craven St. *Acc* 3N **141**
Craven St. *Barn* 2N **77**
Craven St. *Brier* 5F **104**
Craven St. *Burn* 4E **124**
Craven St. *Clith* 4L **81**
Craven St. *Col* 6D **86**
Craven St. *Nels* 2G **105**
Craven St. *Ross* 5L **161**
Craven Ter. Set *3N* ***35***
(off Kirkgate)
Crawford. 9A **220**
Crawford Av. *Adl* 8G **195**
Crawford Av. *Blac* 6D **62**
Crawford Av. *Chor* 7D **174**
Crawford Av. *Ley* 7K **153**
Crawford Av. *Mag* 8A **216**
Crawford Av. *Pres* 8B **116**
Crawford Rd. *Uph* 1N **225**
Crawford St. *Nels* 1J **105**
Crawford St. *Roch* 8D **204**
Crawford St. *Todm* 7L **165**
Crawshawbooth. 9N **143**
Crawshaw Dri. *Ross* 1M **161**
Crawshaw Grange. *Craw* 1M **161**
Crawshaw La. *S'fld* 4N **105**
Cray Ho. Farm, The. *Miln* 7H **205**
Cray, The. *Miln* 7H **205**
(in two parts)
Crediton Av. *South* 1A **168**
Crediton Clo. *B'brn* 8K **139**
Crescent Av. *T Clev* 1D **62**
Crescent Ct. *Blac* 4A **108**
Crescent E. *T Clev* 1D **62**
Crescent Grn. *Augh* 2G **217**
Crescent Rd. *Poul F* 7L **63**
Crescent Rd. *Roch* 9M **203**
Crescent Rd. *South* 2F **186**
Crescent St. *Pres* 8M **115**
Crescent St. *Todm* 2L **165**
Crescent, The. *Ash R* 7D **114**
Crescent, The. *Bam B* 6B **136**
Crescent, The. *B'brn* 7F **138**
Crescent, The. *Blac* 2B **108**
Crescent, The. *Bolt* 9M **199**
Crescent, The. *Brom X* 6G **199**
Crescent, The. *Burn* 6F **104**
Crescent, The. *Chor* 4E **174**
Crescent, The. *Clith* 3K **81**
Crescent, The. *Col* 5A **86**
Crescent, The. *Dun B* 7K **49**
Crescent, The. *Fltwd* 4E **54**
Crescent, The. *Has* 6G **161**
Crescent, The. *Hest B* 8H **15**
Crescent, The. *Holme* 1F **6**
Crescent, The. *Lea* 8A **114**
Crescent, The. *Los H* 8M **135**
Crescent, The. *Lyth A* 2E **128**
Crescent, The. *Mag* 3B **222**
Crescent, The. More *3A* ***22***
(off Queen St.)
Crescent, The. *Poul F* 7J **63**
Crescent, The. *Pre* 9A **42**
Crescent, The. *South* 3B **168**
Crescent, The. *W'ton* 4H **131**
Crescent, The. *Whal* 4G **101**
Crescent, The. *Whitw* 6N **183**
Crescent, The. *Wig* 5N **221**
Crescent, The. *Wors* 4L **125**
Crescent W. *T Clev* 1D **62**
Cressell Pk. *Stand* 2K **213**
Cresswood Av. *T Clev* 2D **62**
Crestway. *Blac* 4F **88**
Crestway. *Tar* 8E **150**
Creswell Av. *Ing* 6C **114**
Creswick Av. *Burn* 7D **124**
Creswick Clo. *Burn* 6D **124**
Crewdson St. *Dar* 5N **157**
Crewgarth Rd. *More* 6B **22**
Cribden End La. *Has* 3G **161**
Cribden La. *Raw* 3K **161**
Cribden Side. 2H **161**
Cribden St. *Ross* 3L **161**
Criccieth Clo. *Has* 6G **161**
Criccieth Pl. *T Clev* 1K **63**
Crichton Pl. *Blac* 4B **108**
Cricketers Grn. *E'ston* 7E **172**
Cricket Path. *Liv* 7A **206**
Cricket Path. *South* 2F **186**
Cricket Vw. *Miln* 8J **205**
Crimble. 9J **203**
Crimble La. *Roch & Heyw* 8J **203**
Crimbles La. *C'ham* 2E **44**
Crimble St. *Roch* 6A **204**
Crimea St. *Bacup* 5L **163**
Crime Well La. *Hey* 9K **21**
Cringle Fold. *Clith* 1N **81**
Cripplegate. *Shev* 2J **213**
Cripple Ga. La. *Hogh* 4K **137**
Crisp Delf. 9C **212**
Critchley Clo. *Much H* 4K **151**
Critchley Way. *Liv* 6L **223**
Croasdale. *Lanc* 6G **22**
Croasdale Av. *Burn* 8H **105**
Croasdale Av. *Rib* 5A **116**
Croasdale Clo. *Carn* 9N **11**
Croasdale Dri. *Clith* 4M **81**
Croasdale Dri. *Parb* 1N **211**
Croasdale Dri. *T Clev* 8F **54**
Croasdale Sq. *B'brn* 5A **140**
Croasdale Wlk. *Blac* 2G **89**
Crockleford Av. *South* 2L **187**
Crocus Clo. *Has* 7E **160**
Crocus Fld. *Ley* 8K **153**
Crocus St. *Bolt* 9F **198**
Croft. 2L **77**
Croftacres. *Ram* 4J **181**
Croft Av. *Burs* 1D **210**
Croft Av. *Orr* 6G **220**
Croft Av. *Slyne* 9J **15**
Croft Bank. *Pen* 5F **134**
Croft Bank. *Whitw* 4A **184**
Cft. Butts La. *Frec* 2A **132**
Croft Clo. *Ross* 2M **161**
Croft Ct. Fltwd *2E* ***54***
(off Croft, The)
Croft Ct. *Frec* 2N **131**
Croft Dri. *Tot* 7D **200**
Crofters Fold. *Gal* 2L **37**
Crofters Fold. *Hey* 7M **21**
Crofters Grn. *Eux* 3M **173**
Crofters Grn. *Pres* 7H **115**
Crofters La. *Liv* 5M **223**
Crofters Mdw. *Far M* 4H **153**
Crofters M. *Blac* 3C **88**
Crofters Wlk. *Bolt* 7J **199**
Crofters Wlk. *Pen* 6G **135**
Crofters Way. *Lyth A* 1L **129**
Croftfield. *Liv* 1D **222**
Croft Ga. *Bolt* 9L **199**
Croftgate. *Ful* 4J **115**
Crofthead. *L'boro* 7L **185**
Cft. Head Dri. *Miln* 6J **205**
Cft. Head Rd. *Whi I* 8B **120**
Croft Hey. *Ruf* 1F **190**
Croft Heys. *Augh* 2G **216**
Crofthill Ct. *Roch* 1G **204**
Croftland Gdns. *Bolt S* 3L **15**
Croftlands. *Orr* 7G **220**
Croftlands. *Ram* 2F **200**
Croftlands. *War* 4B **12**
Croft La. *High* 4L **103**
Croft Manor. *Frec* 2A **132**
Croft Mdw. *Bam B* 1E **154**
Crofton Av. *Blac* 6D **62**
Croft Pk. *Ley* 6M **153**
Croft Rd. *Chor* 7G **175**
Croft Rd. *I'ton* 3N **19**
Crofts St. *Earby* 2F **78**
Crofts Clo. *K'ham* 4A **112**
Crofts Dri. *Grims* 9F **96**
Croftson Av. *Orm* 6L **209**
Croft Sq. *Roch* 2F **204**
Croft St. *Bacup* 4K **163**
Croft St. *Burn* 4E **124**
Croft St. *Clith* 4L **81**
Croft St. *Dar* 6A **158**
Croft St. *Gt Har* 5J **121**
Croft St. *More* 3C **22**
Croft St. *Pres* 9G **115**
(in two parts)
Croft St. *Roch* 2F **204**
Croft, The. *Bil* 7G **221**
Croft, The. *B'brn* 1L **139**
Croft, The. *Burt L* 3K **19**
Croft, The. *Cat* 2G **25**
Croft, The. *Col* 4B **86**
Croft, The. *E'ston* 7F **172**
Croft, The. *Eux* 3L **173**
Croft, The. *Fltwd* 2F **54**
Croft, The. *Gars* 3M **59**
Croft, The. *Goos* 5N **95**
Croft, The. *Gt Plu* 2D **110**
Croft, The. Hogh *6K* ***137***
(off Station Rd.)
Croft, The. *Longt* 7L **133**
Croft, The. *Lyth A* 8H **109**
Croft, The. *Mag* 6A **216**
Croft, The. *Poul F* 9K **63**
Croft, The. *T Clev* 1D **62**
Croftway. *T Clev* 3J **63**
Croftwood Sq. *Wig* 1M **221**
Croft Wood Ter. *B'brn* 7H **139**
Croich Bank. *Hawk* 3A **200**
Crombleholme Rd. *Pres* 8A **116**
Crombleholm Rd. *W'chpl* 2N **69**
Cromer Av. *Burn* 9G **105**
Cromer Gro. *Burn* 9G **104**
Cromer Pl. *B'brn* 1M **139**
Cromer Pl. *Ing* 5D **114**
Cromer Rd. *Blac* 7E **62**
Cromer Rd. *Bury* 8H **201**
(in two parts)
Cromer Rd. *Lyth A* 8G **108**
Cromer Rd. *South* 3E **186**
Cromer St. *Roch* 5B **204**
Cromfield. *Augh* 1H **217**
Cromford Dri. *Wig* 6L **221**
Cromford Wlk. *Pres* 9M **115**
Crompton Av. *Blac* 2E **108**
Crompton Clo. *Bolt* 9G **199**
Crompton Pl. *B'brn* 3J **139**
Crompton St. *Pres* 8M **115**
Crompton Way. *Bolt* 9F **198**
Cromwell Av. *Acc* 9A **122**
Cromwell Av. *Pen* 5F **134**
Cromwell Clo. *Augh* 1H **217**
Cromwell Rd. *Blac* 2C **88**
Cromwell Rd. *Lanc* 9J **23**
Cromwell Rd. *Pen* 5E **134**
Cromwell Rd. *Rib* 5N **115**
Cromwell St. *B'brn* 4A **140**
Cromwell St. *Burn* 2D **124**
Cromwell St. *Foul* 2A **86**
Cromwell St. *Pres* 8K **115**
Cromwell Ter. *Barfd* 8H **85**
Cromwell Way. *Pen* 7J **135**
Cronkeyshaw Rd. *Roch* 4B **204**
Cronkshaw St. *Burn* 2E **124**
Cronshaw Dri. *Lang* 9C **100**
Crookall Clo. *Fltwd* 2E **54**
Crook Dale La. *Stalm* 5C **56**
Crooke. 9M **213**
Crooked La. *Pres* 9K **115**
Crooked Shore. *Bacup* 4K **163**
Crooke Rd. *Wig* 9M **213**
Crookfield Rd. *Adl* 3H **177**
Crook Ga. La. *Out R* 2H **65**
Crookhalgh Av. *Burn* 3K **125**
Crookhey Gdns. *C'ham* 2J **45**
Crookings La. *Pen* 2D **134**
Crooklands Dri. *Gars* 4N **59**
Crookleigh Pl. *Hey* 6L **21**
Crook O' Lune Cvn. Pk. *Crook L* 3E **24**
Crook St. *Adl* 6H **195**
Crook St. *Chor* 9D **174**
Crook St. *Pres* 9L **115**
Crook St. *Roch* 5D **204**
Cropper Gdns. *Hesk B* 4B **150**
Cropper Rd. *Blac* 2H **109**
Cropper's La. *Bic* 2L **217**
Cropton Rd. *Liv* 9A **206**
Crosby Clo. *Dar* 9B **158**
Crosby Gro. *Blac* 7E **88**
Crosby Pl. *Ing* 5D **114**
Crosby Rd. *B'brn* 7M **139**
Crosby Rd. *Lyth A* 8F **108**
Crosby Rd. *South* 2F **186**
Crosby St. *Roch* 3C **204**
Crosfield Av. *S'seat* 3H **201**
Crosier Wlk. *Cot* 4B **114**
Crosland Rd. *Liv* 9M **223**
Crosland Rd. N. *Lyth A* 8F **108**
Crosland Rd. S. *Lyth A* 9G **109**
Crosley Clo. *Acc* 5A **142**
Cross Bank. Pad *1J* ***123***
(off Hambledon St.)
Cross Barn Gro. *Dar* 7B **158**
Cross Barn La. *Liv* 9E **214**
Cross Barn Wlk. *Dar* 7B **158**
Cross Ct. *Bacup* 4L **163**
Crossdale Av. *Hey* 6L **21**
Crossdale Sq. Lanc *8L* ***23***
(off Woodville St.)
Cross Edge. 7N **141**
Cross Edge. *Osw* 7N **141**
Crosse Hall La. *Chor* 7G **175**
Crosse Hall St. *Chor* 7H **175**
Crossens. 2C **168**
Crossens Cricket Club Ground. 3C **168**
Crossens Way. *South* 9B **148**
Cross Fld. *Hut* 7N **133**
Crossfield Clo. *Ward* 7F **184**
Crossfield Ct. *Arns* 2E **4**
Crossfield Pl. *Roch* 8D **204**
Crossfield Rd. *Skel* 3N **219**
Crossfield Rd. *Ward* 8F **184**
Crossfields. *Brom X* 5J **199**
Crossfield St. *B'brn* 5N **139**
Cross Flatts Cres. *Salt* 4B **78**
Cross Fold. *Grin* 4A **74**
Crossford Clo. *Wig* 7N **221**
Cross Gates. *Gt Har* 4J **121**
Crossgates Rd. *Miln* 6J **205**
Crossgill. 7N **25**
Crossgill Pl. Lanc *6H* ***23***
(off Austwick Rd.)
Cross Grn. *Liv* 1A **214**
Cross Grn. Clo. *Liv* 1A **214**
Cross Grn. Rd. *Ful* 3H **115**
Cross Hagg St. *Col* 7A **86**
Crosshall Brow. *Orm & W'head* 8N **209**
Cross Halls. *Pen* 5E **134**
Cross Helliwell St. *Col* 7A **86**
Cross Hey. *Liv* 3D **222**
Cross Hill Ct. *Bolt S* 5L **15**
Cross Hill La. *Rim* 3B **76**
Crosshill Rd. *B'brn* 3J **139**
Crosshills. Pad *9H* ***103***
(off East St.)
Crossing, The. *Hogh* 6K **137**
Cross Keys Dri. *Whit W* 7E **154**
Crossland Rd. *Blac* 9E **88**
Crossland St. *Acc* 3N **141**
Cross La. *B'ley* 7A **84**
Cross La. *Bil* 8G **220**
Cross La. *Hals* 2A **208**
Cross La. *Holc* 9F **180**
Cross La. *L Bent* 6J **19**
Cross La. *Salt* 4A **78**
Cross La. *Trea* 9B **92**
Cross La. *Wadd* 7C **72**
Cross La. Cotts. Salt *4A* ***78***
(off Chapel Hill)
Cross Lee. *Todm* 9J **147**
Cross Lee Ga. *Todm* 9J **147**
Cross Lee Rd. *Todm* 9J **147**
Cross Lees. *Roch* 2D **204**
Crossley Fold. *Burn* 5B **124**
Crossley St. *Miln* 7H **205**
Crossley St. *Todm* 2L **165**
Cross Meanygate. *H'wd* 9N **169**
Crossmoor. 1C **92**
Cross Pit La. *St H* 4K **225**
Cross Rd. *L Bent* 7J **19**
Cross School St. *Col* 7A **86**
Cross Skelton St. *Col* 6B **86**
Cross Stone. 1N **165**
Cross Stone Rd. *Todm* 1M **165**
Cross St. *Acc* 3B **142**
Cross St. *Blac* 3B **88**
Cross St. *Brclf* 8K **105**
Cross St. *Brier* 5F **104**
Cross St. *Brom X* 6F **198**
Cross St. *Chor* 5E **174**
Cross St. *Clay M* 6L **121**
Cross St. *Clith* 3K **81**
Cross St. *Dar* 8B **158**
Cross St. *Earby* 3D **78**
Cross St. *Firg* 6G **205**
Cross St. *Fltwd* 8H **41**
Cross St. *High* 5L **103**
Cross St. *Ley* 5L **153**
Cross St. *L'rdge* 4H **97**
Cross St. *Lwr D* 9N **139**
Cross St. *Lyth A* 9D **108**
Cross St. *More* 3C **22**
Cross St. *Nels* 2H **105**
Cross St. *Orr* 5L **221**
Cross St. *Osw* 4K **141**
Cross St. *Pem* 5L **221**
Cross St. *Pres* 1J **135**
Cross St. *Ram* 8H **181**
Cross St. *Ross* 9M **143**
Cross St. *South* 8H **167**
Cross St. *Wors* 3M **125**
Cross St. N. *Has* 3G **160**
Cross St. S. *Has* 3G **160**
Cross St. W. *Col* 7M **85**
Cross Swords Clo. *Chor* 9D **174**
Cross, The. *Liv* 8E **214**
Cross Way. *T Clev* 8D **54**
Crossways. *W Brad* 5K **73**
Croston. 4M **171**
Croston Av. *Adl* 5J **195**
Croston Barn Rd. *Nate* 4L **59**
Croston Clo. *B'brn* 3B **140**
Croston Clo. Rd. *Bury & Ram* 4A **202**
Croston Dri. *Ruf* 8F **170**
Croston La. *Char R* 3L **193**
Croston Rd. *Far M & Los H* 4H **153**
Croston Rd. *Gars* 3M **59**
Croston Rd. *Ruf* 7F **170**
Croston's Brow. *South* 3M **167**
Crostons Rd. *Bury* 9J **201**
Croston St. *B'brn* 3C **140**
Crowder Av. *T Clev* 1H **63**
Crowell Way. *Walt D* 5A **136**
Crowfoot Row. Barn *3M* ***77***
(off Castle Vw.)
Crow Hills Rd. *Pen* 2D **134**
Crowland Clo. *South* 8N **167**
Crowland St. *South* 8N **167**
(in two parts)
Crowland Way. *Liv* 1B **214**
Crow La. *Dal* 9C **212**
Crow La. *Out R* 3K **65**
Crow La. *Ram* 8H **181**
Crowle St. *Pres* 9N **115**
Crown Clo. *Liv* 1A **214**
Crowndale. *Tur* 7K **179**
Crowneast St. *Roch* 6N **203**
Crownest Cotts. Barn *1N* ***77***
(off Bankfield Ter.)
Crownest Ind. Est. *Barn* 1N **77**
Crownest Rd. *Barn* 1M **77**
Crown Gdns. *Roch* 8D **204**
Crown Gdns. *Tur* 8K **179**
Crown Ho. *Dar* 3N **157**
Crown La. *Btle* 8L **93**
Crown La. *Fltwd* 9H **41**
Crown La. *Hor* 9B **196**
Crownlee. *Pen* 5D **134**
Crown M. *K'ham* 4M **111**
Crown Point. *Tur* 8L **179**
Crown Point Rd. *Burn* 8C **124**
Crown St. *Acc* 3N **141**
Crown St. *Chor* 6E **174**
Crown St. *Dar* 7A **158**
Crown St. *Far* 4L **153**
Crown St. *Pres* 9J **115**
Crown St. *Roch* 8D **204**
Crown Way. *Col* 6N **85**
Crow Orchard Rd. *Wrigh* 2J **213**
(in two parts)
Crow Pk. La. *Gis* 8B **52**
Crowshaw Dri. *Roch* 2B **204**
Crowther Ct. *L'boro* 1H **205**
Crowther Ct. Wors *3M* ***125***
(off Showfield)
Crowther St. *Burn* 5F **124**
Crowther St. *Clay M* 6L **121**
Crowther St. *L'boro* 9H **185**
Crowther St. *Roch* 9E **204**
Crowthorn Rd. *Tur* 5M **179**
Crow Tree Av. *Bacup* 7F **162**
Crow Tree Gdns. *Chat* 7C **74**
Crow Trees. 6D **84**
Crowtrees. *L Bent* 6J **19**
Crow Trees Brow. *Chat* 8C **74**
Crowtrees Gro. *R'lee* 6D **84**
Crow Trees La. *Tur* 7J **179**
Crow Trees Rd. *Sab* 2E **102**
Crow Wood Av. *Burn* 2B **124**
Crow Wood Ct. *Burn* 2C **124**
Crow Wood Rd. *Ross* 9J **161**
Crow Woods. *Ram* 1J **181**
Croxteth Clo. *Liv* 8D **216**
Croxteth Dri. *Rainf* 3K **225**

Croxton Av.—Denby Clo.

Croxton Av. Roch 5E 204
Croxton Wlk. Hor 9C 196 (off Beatrice M.)
Croyde Clo. South 1A 168
Croyde Rd. Lyth A 3G 128
Croydon Rd. Blac 3E 88
Croydon St. B'brn 3K 139
Crummock Pl. Blac 9J 89
Crummock Rd. Pres 8C 116
Crumpax Av. L'rdge 2J 97
Crumpax Cft. L'rdge 2J 97
Crundale Rd. Bolt 7G 198
Crystal Gro. Lyth A 9E 108
Crystal Rd. Blac 9B 88
Crystal Rd. T Clev 7H 55
Cuba St. Nels 2H 105
Cub St. Ley 3K 153 (off Country Clo.)
Cuckoo Brow. B'brn 9L 119
Cuckoo La. Out R 9N 57
Cuckstool La. Fence 3B 104
Cuckstool Rd. Fence 4C 104
Cuddy Hill. 3N 93
Cudworth Rd. Lyth A 8F 108
Cuerdale La. Walt D & Sam 3A 136
Cuerdale St. Burn 7J 105
Cuerden Av. Ley 8G 153
Cuerden Clo. Bam B 3A 154
Cuerden Green. 1M 153
Cuerden Residential Pk. Ley 4A 154
Cuerden Ri. Los H 9M 135
Cuerden St. Chor 7G 174
Cuerden St. Col 8M 85
Cuerden Valley Pk. 4B 154
Cuerden Way. Bam B 8N 135
Culbeck La. Eux 4J 173
Culcross Av. Wig 7M 221
Culshaw St. B'brn 3A 140
Culshaw St. Burn 4G 125
Culshaw Way. Scar 6E 188
Culvert La. Newb 2L 211
Cumberland Av. Blac 7D 88
Cumberland Av. Burn 2M 123
Cumberland Av. Clay M 6N 121
Cumberland Av. Ley 8H 153
Cumberland Av. T Clev 8D 54
Cumberland Ga. Boot 6A 222
Cumberland Ho. Pres 9J 115 (off Warwick St.)
Cumberland Rd. South 9K 167
Cumberland St. B'brn 4A 140
Cumberland St. Col 6B 86
Cumberland St. Nels 1J 105
Cumberland Vw. Lanc 1L 29
Cumberland Vw. Clo. Hey 5L 21
Cumberland Vw. Rd. Hey 5L 21
Cumbrian Av. Blac 3E 88
Cumbrian Way. Burn 1N 123
Cumeragh La. W'ham 4B 96
Cumeragh Village. 5B 96
Cumpstey St. B'brn 5M 139
Cuncliffe Ct. Clay M 7M 121
Cunliffe Av. Ram 1F 200
Cunliffe Clo. B'brn 8B 120
Cunliffe Ho. Ross 6B 162 (off Bacup Rd.)
Cunliffe La. Wis 2M 101
Cunliffe Rd. B'brn 8B 120
Cunliffe Rd. Blac 8D 88
Cunliffe St. Chor 7E 174
Cunliffe St. Pres 9K 115
Cunliffe St. Ram 7H 181
Cunnery Mdw. Ley 6A 154
Cunningham Av. Chor 8C 174
Cunningham Gro. Burn 3N 123
Cunscough La. Liv 9J 217
Curate St. Chor 5G 174
Curate St. Gt Har 4J 121
Curlew Clo. B'brn 9M 119
Curlew Clo. Ley 8F 152
Curlew Clo. Osw 5K 141
Curlew Clo. Roch 6K 203
Curlew Clo. T Clev 8F 54
Curlew Gdns. Burn 4N 123
Curlew Gro. Hey 2L 27
Curlew La. Burs 5B 190
Curteis St. Hor 9C 196
Curtis Dri. Fltwd 1D 54
Curtis St. Ross 4M 161
Curtis St. Wig 5N 221
Curven Edge. Ross 8F 160
Curve St. Bacup 6K 163
Curwen Av. Hey 1K 27
Curwen La. Goos 8M 69
Curwen St. Pres 8M 115 (in two parts)
Curzon Pl. B'brn 5K 139
Curzon Rd. Lyth A 1F 128
Curzon Rd. Poul F 8L 63
Curzon Rd. South 9K 167
Curzon St. Burn 3D 124 (in two parts)
Curzon St. Clith 3K 81
Curzon St. Col 7B 86
Cusson Rd. Know I 9A 224 (in two parts)
Custom Ho. La. Fltwd 8H 41
Customs Way. Ash R 9F 114
Cutgate. 5L 203
Cutgate Rd. Roch 4M 203
Cutgate Shop. Precinct. Roch 5M 203
Cuthbert Mayne Ct. Roch 7B 204
Cuthbert St. Wig 5N 221
Cutland Way. L'boro 1K 205
Cut La. Hals 4E 208
Cut La. Rish 8F 120 (in two parts)
Cut La. Roch 4K 203
Cutler Clo. B'brn 3L 139
Cutler Cres. Bacup 8H 163
Cutler La. Bacup 8H 163
Cutler La. Chip 7F 70
Cutt Clo. Ley 9C 152
Cuttle St. Pres 9N 115
Cutts La. Hamb & Out R 1D 64
Cyclamen Clo. Ley 5A 154
Cygnet Clo. Augh 1H 217
Cygnet Ct. Liv 8M 223
Cyon Clo. Pen 3H 135
Cypress Av. T Clev 1E 62
Cypress Clo. Ley 5A 154
Cypress Clo. Liv 7F 222
Cypress Clo. Rib 5C 116
Cypress Gdns. Firg 6G 204
Cypress Gro. Blac 3D 88
Cypress Gro. Los H 8L 135
Cypress Ridge. B'brn 8G 138
Cypress Rd. South 8L 167
Cypress St. Bacup 7G 163
Cyprus Av. Lyth A 4H 129
Cyprus Rd. Hey 1K 27
Cyprus St. Dar 9B 158

D

Dacca St. Chor 5F 174
Dacre Rd. Roch 9C 204
Dacre Way. Cot 4A 114
Daffodil Clo. Has 7F 160
Daffodil Clo. Roch 2B 204
Daffodil St. Ram 8F 198
Dagger Rd. Trea 8G 92
Daggers Hall La. Blac 1E 108
Daggers La. Pre 1A 56
Dagnall Rd. Liv 9H 223
Dahlia Clo. Ley 5A 154
Dahlia Clo. Lwr D 9A 140
Dahlia Clo. Roch 2A 204
Dailton Rd. Uph 4D 220
Dairy Farm Rd. Rainf 4F 224
Daisy Bank. 8D 162
Daisy Bank. Bacup 4K 163
Daisy Bank. Lanc 9A 24
Daisy Bank. T Clev 1D 62
Daisy Bank Clo. Ley 6G 153
Daisy Bank Cres. Burn 4K 125
Daisy Bank St. Todm 7E 146
Daisy Cft. Lea 9A 114
Daisyfield. 2A 140
Daisyfields. High B 2C 114
Daisyfield St. Dar 2M 157
Daisy Fold. Chor 4G 175
Daisy Hill. 5N 173
Daisy Hill. Ross 4M 161
Daisy Hill Dri. Adl 4J 195
Daisy Hill Fold. Eux 5N 173
Daisy La. B'brn 2N 139
Daisy La. Lath 9F 190
Daisy La. Pres 6M 115
Daisy Mdw. Bam B 1C 154
Daisy Mt. Liv 2D 222
Daisy Row. L'boro 2J 205
Daisy St. B'brn 2N 139
Daisy St. Col 7A 86
Daisy St. Lanc 5K 23
Daisy St. Roch 5B 204
Daisy Wlk. South 7L 167 (off Beacham Rd.)
Dakin St. Chor 7F 174
Dakin Wlk. Liv 8L 223
Dalby Clo. Pres 6N 115
Dalby Clo. T Clev 4F 62
Dalby Cres. B'brn 7H 139
Dalby Lea. B'brn 7H 139
Dale Av. Eux 5N 173
Dale Av. Longt 9J 133
Dale Av. Slyne 9J 15
Dale Av. Todm 2N 165
Dale Clo. Burn 3J 124 (off Tunnel St.)
Dale Clo. Liv 9B 216
Dale Clo. Parb 2M 211
Dale Cres. B'brn 8F 138
Dale Dyke Wlk. Poul F 8H 63
Dalegarth Clo. Blac 9J 89
Dalehead Rd. Ley 8K 153
Dale La. Liv 5M 223
Dales Brow. Bolt 7F 198
Dales Ct. Blac 3D 108
Dalesford. Has 6G 161
Dalesford Clo. T Clev 3J 63
Daleside Rd. Liv 7L 223
Daleside Wlk. Liv 7L 223
Dales, The. Lang 1A 120
Dale St. Acc 2N 141
Dale St. Bacup 4K 163
Dale St. B'brn 4L 139
Dale St. Blac 7B 88
Dale St. Brier 5E 104
Dale St. Burn 3B 124
Dale St. Bury 9H 201
Dale St. Col 6N 85
Dale St. Earby 2E 78
Dale St. Has 4G 160
Dale St. Lanc 9L 23
Dale St. Nels 2G 105
Dale St. Osw 4L 141
Dale St. Pres 9L 115
Dale St. Ram 6H 181
Dale St. Stac 7G 163
Dale St. Todm 2L 165
Dale St. M. Blac 7B 88 (off Yorkshire St.)
Dalesview Cres. Hey 9L 21
Dales Vw. Pk. Salt 1M 77 (off Powell St.)
Dales Wlk. Liv 6A 206
Dalesway. Barfd 8G 85
Dale Ter. Chat 7C 74
Dale Vw. B'brn 1M 157
Daleview. Chor 1E 194
Dale Vw. Earby 3E 78
Dale Vw. L'boro 3J 205
Dale Vw. Ross 6M 161
Daleview Pk. Salt 5M 77
Dalewood Av. Blac 9E 88
Dalkeith Av. Blac 8G 89
Dalkeith Rd. Nels 2G 105
Dallam Av. More 2C 22
Dallas Ct. More 4F 22
Dallas Rd. Lanc 9J 23
Dallas Rd. More 4F 22
Dallas St. Pres 6H 115
Dallicar La. Gigg 3M 35
Dall St. Burn 5E 124
Dalmeny Ter. Roch 9C 204
Dalmore Rd. Ing 6D 114
Dalston Gro. Wig 8N 221
Dalton. 5K 7 (Carnforth)
Dalton. 7A 212 (Wigan)
Dalton Av. Blac 4D 108
Dalton Av. Roch 6G 205
Dalton Clo. B'brn 3A 140
Dalton Clo. Orr 4L 221
Dalton Clo. Ram 1F 200
Dalton Clo. Roch 6G 205
Dalton Dri. Wig 8N 221
Dalton La. Burt 6H 7
Dalton Rd. Hey 5L 21
Dalton Rd. Lanc 8L 23
Dalton Sq. Lanc 8K 23
Dalton St. Burn 6B 124
Dalton St. Lyth A 9D 108
Dalton St. Nels 1J 105
Dalton St. Todm 2L 165
Dalweb Ind. Est. South 3H 169
Dame Fold. High 4L 103
Dame Fold. Pad 1H 123
Damfield La. Liv 1C 222
Dam Head Rd. Barn 2M 77
Dam La. Scar 7G 188
Dampier St. Todm 6K 165
Dam Side. 7J 43
Dam Side. Barn 1M 77 (off Gisburn St.)
Dam Side. Col 7A 86
Damside. Ellel 1M 37
Damside Cotts. Ellel 1M 37
Damside St. Lanc 7K 23
Dam Wood La. Scar 8H 189
Danbers. Uph 5C 220
Dancer La. Rim 3A 76
Dandy Row. Dar 4C 158
Dandy's Meanygate. Tar 8N 149
Dandy Wlk. B'brn 4M 139
Dane Hall La. Eux 4G 173
Dane M. Poul F 2L 89
Danesbury Pl. Blac 5C 88
Danesbury Rd. Bolt 9H 199
Danes Clo. K'ham 4A 112
Danes Ct. South 6K 167
Danes Dri. Walt D 7N 135
Danes Ho. Rd. Burn 1E 124
Danes La. Whitw 5L 183
Danesmoor Dri. Bury 9M 201
Dane St. Burn 2E 124
Dane St. Roch 6B 204
Daneway. Hth C 4H 195
Danesway. Pen 4D 134
Danesway. Walt D 6N 135 (in two parts)
Daneswood Av. Whitw 6N 183
Daneswood Clo. Whitw 6M 183
Daneway. South 7B 186
Danewerk St. Pres 9K 115
Dangerous Corner. 2F 212
Daniel Fold. Roch 3M 203
Daniel Fold La. Catt 1N 67
Daniell St. Rish 7G 121
Daniels La. Skel 4N 219
Daniel St. Clay M 6L 121
Daniel St. Whitw 4A 184
Danson Gdns. Blac 2D 88
Danvers St. Rish 7H 121
Darbishire Rd. Fltwd 8F 40
Daresbury Av. South 8A 186
Daresbury Clo. Liv 8H 223
Darfield. Uph 4C 220
Darkinson La. Cot 5N 113
Darkinson La. Lea T 6K 113
Dark La. B'rod 9K 195
Dark La. Earby 2G 79
Dark La. Lath 6N 209
Dark La. Liv 1C 222
Dark La. Ross 7B 162 (in two parts)
Dark La. Thorn C 8J 53
Dark La. Whit W 1G 174
Darkwood Cres. Chat 7B 74
Dark Wood La. Sam 2K 137
Darley Av. Blac 2E 108
Darley Ct. Lyth A 1D 128
Darley Rd. Roch 9C 204
Darley St. Hor 8C 196
Darlington Clo. Bury 8G 200
Darlington Rd. Roch 9C 204
Darlington St. Cop 4N 193
Darmond Rd. Liv 7M 223
Darnbrook Rd. Barn 2L 77
Darnley St. Burn 4G 125
Dartford Clo. B'brn 4N 139
Dartmouth Av. Liv 8B 222
Dartmouth Clo. K'ham 4L 111
Dart St. Ash R 9F 114
Darwen. 6A 158
Darwen Clo. L'rdge 3K 97
Darwen Enterprise Cen. Dar 5A 158
Darwen Golf Course. 4K 157
Darwen Rd. Eger & Brom X 4E 198
Darwen St. B'brn 4M 139
Darwen St. High W 4D 136
Darwen St. Pad 1H 123
Darwen St. Pres 1M 135
Darwen Vw. Walt D 3A 136
Darwin St. Burn 8E 104
Datchet Ter. Roch 9C 204
Daub Hall La. Hogh 7F 136
Daub La. Bis 5K 191
Dauntesey Av. Blac 4G 89
Davenham Rd. Dar 4M 157
Davenham Rd. Liv 8A 206
Davenhill Pk. Liv 8B 222
Davenport Av. Blac 6C 62
Davenport Fold. Bolt 9N 199
Davenport Fold Rd. Bolt 9N 199
Davenport Gro. Liv 6K 223
Daventry Av. Blac 7B 62
Daventry Rd. Roch 9C 204
David Lewis Clo. Roch 7F 204
Davidson St. Lanc 8L 23
David St. Bacup 7H 163
David St. Barfd 7H 85
David St. Burn 5D 124
David St. Bury 9H 201 (in two parts)
David St. Roch 4C 204
David St. N. Roch 4C 204
Davies Rd. B'brn 2D 140
Davis St. L'rdge 2J 97
Davitt Clo. Has 4G 160
Davy Fld. Rd. B'brn 1A 158
Davyhulme St. Roch 4E 204
Dawber's La. Eux 4G 172
Dawlish Av. Blac 2F 88
Dawlish Clo. B'brn 8K 139
Dawlish Dri. South 1N 167
Dawlish Lodge. Lyth A 1D 128
Dawlish Pl. Ing 6D 114
Dawnay Rd. Rib 6A 116
Dawnwood Sq. Wig 1M 221
Dawson Av. S'stne 8D 102
Dawson Av. South 1B 168
Dawson Gdns. Liv 9B 216
Dawson La. Ley & Whit W 8N 153
Dawson Pl. Bam B 9C 136
Dawson Rd. Lyth A 8F 108
Dawson Rd. Orm 5L 209
Dawson Sq. Burn 2E 124
Dawson St. Bury 9M 201 (in two parts)
Dawson St. Roch 5C 204
Dawson Wlk. Pres 8J 115
Daybrook. Uph 4C 220
Dayfield. Uph 4D 220
Day St. Nels 3J 105
Dayton Pl. Blac 3C 108
Deacons Cres. Tot 8F 200
Deacon St. Roch 3E 204
Deakins Bus. Pk. Eger 4D 198
Deakin's Ter. Bel 9K 177
Deal Pl. Lyth A 8F 108
Deal St. B'brn 1N 139
Dean Brow. K Grn 2F 98
Dean Clo. Ram 3J 181
Dean Clo. Uph 4F 220
Dean Ct. Fltwd 4D 54
Deancourt. Roch 9C 204
Dean Cres. Orr 3L 221
Deancroft Av. Hey 6M 21
Dean Fold. Ross 8E 144
Dean Head. L'boro 3N 185
Dean Head La. Hor 1A 196
Dean La. Gt Har & Whal 2H 121 (in three parts)
Dean La. Ross 8E 144
Dean La. Sam 7J 117
Dean La. Toc 6H 157
Dean Mdw. Clith 4K 81
Deanpoint. More 5C 22
Dean Rd. Has 6F 160
Dean Rd. Helm 7G 160
Deanroyd Rd. Todm 8L 165
Deansgate. Blac 5B 88
Deansgate. More 3B 22
Deansgate La. Liv 7B 206
Deansgate La. N. Liv 6A 206
Deansgrave. Has 5F 160
Deansgreave Rd. Bacup 7M 163
Deans La. Lath 9J 191
Deans La. Newb 2K 211
Deans La. Sam 6H 117
Dean St. Bam B 7A 136
Dean St. B'brn 4M 139
Dean St. Blac 1B 108
Dean St. Burn 3C 124
Dean St. Dar 4N 157
Dean St. Pad 9J 103
Dean St. Roch 4E 204
Dean St. Traw 9E 86
Dean Ter. K'ham 4M 111
Dean Vs. Todm 8L 165
Dean Wood Av. Orr 3H 221
Dean Wood Clo. Chor 8C 174
Dean Wood Golf Course. 2G 221
Dearbought La. Bncr 3D 46
Dearden Cft. Has 4G 160 (off Ratcliffe St.)
Dearden Fold. Ram 4K 181
Dearden Ga. Has 4G 160
Deardengate Cft. Has 4G 160
Dearden Nook. Ross 6M 161
Dearden St. L'boro 8L 185
Deardon Ct. Uph 4D 220
Dearncamme Clo. Bolt 8H 199
Dearnley. 1H 205
Dearnley Clo. L'boro 1H 205
Dearnley Pas. L'boro 1H 205
Deben Clo. Stand 3N 213
Deborah Av. Ful 2K 115
Debra Clo. Liv 6G 222
Dee Clo. Liv 4L 223
Deepdale. 8K 115
Deepdale Av. Poul F 6H 63
Deepdale Av. Roch 7F 204
Deepdale Clo. Sla H 1N 5
Deepdale Ct. Barfd 8G 85
Deepdale Dri. Burn 7G 104
Deepdale Grn. Barfd 8G 85
Deepdale La. Lea T 6H 113
Deepdale Mill St. Pres 8L 115
Deepdale Retail Pk. Pres 6M 115
Deepdale Rd. Blac 1J 109
Deepdale Rd. Fltwd 1G 54
Deepdale Rd. Pres & Ful 9L 115
Deepdale St. Pres 9L 115
Deep La. L'boro 4M 205
Deep La. Miln 6L 205
Deeplish Cotts. Roch 8C 204
Deeplish Rd. Roch 8C 204
Deeplish St. Roch 8C 204
Deeply Va. La. Bury 3A 202
Deerbarn Dri. Boot 6A 222
Deerbolt Clo. Liv 7H 223
Deerbolt Cres. Liv 7H 223
Deerbolt Way. Liv 7H 223
Deer Chace. Fence 2B 104
Deerfold. Chor 4D 174
Deerhurst Rd. T Clev 4E 62
Dee Rd. Lanc 6H 23
Deer Pk. Acc 9D 122
Deer Pk. La. Horn 7C 18
Deer Pk. Rd. Burn 4J 125 (in two parts)
Deerplay Clo. Burn 8J 105
Deerstone Av. Burn 3G 125
Deerstone Rd. Nels 2M 105
Deer St. Bacup 9K 145
Deerside. Blac 4D 108
Dee St. Lyth A 2F 128
Deganwy Av. B'brn 1M 139
Deighton Av. Ley 7K 153
Deighton Rd. Chor 8D 174
De Lacy St. Ash R 7G 114
De Lacy St. Clith 3K 81
Delamere Av. Hey 1N 27
Delamere Clo. B'brn 6J 139
Delamere Pl. Chor 6F 174
Delamere Rd. Brclf 7K 105
Delamere Rd. Roch 9F 204
Delamere Rd. Skel 1K 219
Delamere Rd. South 8B 186
Delamere St. Bury 8M 201
Delamere Way. Uph 4D 220
Delaney Ct. Set 3N 35
Delaney Gdns. Set 3N 35 (off Duke St.)
Delany Dri. Frec 3M 131
Delaware Cres. Liv 7H 223
Delaware Rd. Blac 1E 88
Delaware St. Pres 8M 115
Delfby Cres. Liv 9M 223
Delf Ho. Uph 2N 219
Delf La. Down 7N 207
Delf La. Todm 5F 146
Delius Clo. B'brn 7A 140
Dellar St. Roch 5N 203
Dellfield La. Liv 1D 222
Dell Gdns. Roch 3M 203
Dell La. Hap 5H 123
Dell Mdw. Whitw 9N 183
Dell Rd. Roch 2M 203
Dell Side Way. Roch 3N 203
Dell St. Bolt 8J 199
Dell, The. App B 5G 213
Dell, The. B'brn 1L 157
Dell, The. Bolt 8J 199
Dell, The. Ful 2G 114
Dell, The. H'pey 3J 175
Dell, The. Uph 4E 220
Dell, The. W Grn 6G 111
Dellway, The. Hut 5A 134
Delma Rd. Burn 4J 125
Delph App. B'brn 4C 140
Delph Av. Eger 2D 198
Delph Brook Way. Eger 3D 198
Delph Clo. Augh 2H 217
Delph Clo. B'brn 4C 140
Delph Comn. Rd. Augh 2G 217
Delph Ct. Gt Har 4J 121
Delphene Av. T Clev 5D 62 (in two parts)
Delph La. Augh 2H 217
Delph La. Bncr 4C 60
Delph La. B'brn 4C 140
Delph La. Blea 3L 61
Delph La. Char R 8M 173 (in two parts)
Delph Mt. Gt Har 3H 121
Delph Mt. Nels 3H 105
Delph Pk. Av. Augh 2G 216
Delph Rd. Gt Har 4H 121
Delphside Clo. Orr 6G 220
Delphside Rd. Orr 6G 220
Delph Sq. Burn 8H 105 (off Marsden Rd.)
Delph St. B'brn 6N 139
Delph St. Dar 4B 158
Delph St. Has 3G 160
Delph St. Miln 7J 205
Delph, The. Parb 1N 211
Delph Top. Orm 6M 209
Delph Way. Whit W 8E 154
Delta La. Fltwd 9G 41
Delta Pk. Av. Hesk B 3C 150
Delta Pk. Dri. Hesk B 3C 150
Deltic Way. Kirkby 9N 223
Delves La. S'fld 3N 105
Demming Clo. Lea 9N 113
Denbigh Av. South 3M 167
Denbigh Av. T Clev 2E 62
Denbigh Clo. Ley 6L 153
Denbigh Dri. Clith 1M 81
Denbigh Gro. Burn 2M 123
Denbigh Way. Pres 1K 135
Denby Clo. Los H 5M 135

Duke of Sussex St.—Egerton Ct.

Duke of Sussex St. B'brn 8J 139
Dukes Brow. B'brn 2J 139
Dukes Ct. B'brn 2J 139
Dukes Cut. Blkhd 5K 147
Dukes Dri. Hodd 6E 158
Dukes Mdw. Ing 4D 114
Dukes Playhouse & Theatre. 8K 23
Duke St. Bam B 9A 136
Duke St. Ben 6L 19
Duke St. B'brn 3L 139
Duke St. Blac 9B 88
Duke St. Brclf 7K 105
Duke St. Burn 5F 124
Duke St. Burt L 3K 19
Duke St. Chor 8E 174
Duke St. Clay M 7M 121
Duke St. Col 7A 86
Duke St. Form 1A 214
Duke St. Gt Har 4H 121
Duke St. Hey 9K 21
Duke St. Holme 1F 6
Duke St. Lanc 7J 23
Duke St. L'boro 9K 185
Duke St. Osw 5K 141
Duke St. Pres 1L 135
Duke St. Ram 1F 200
Duke St. Ross 7C 162
Duke St. Set 3N 35
Duke St. South 8G 166
(in two parts)
Duke St. Traw 7E 86
Duke's Wood La. Uph 8A 220
Dulas Grn. Liv 9M 223
Dulas Rd. Kirkby 9M 223
Dumbarton Clo. Blac 3G 108
Dumbarton Rd. Lanc 9L 23
Dumb Tom's La. I'ton 4L 19
Dumfries Clo. Blac 6F 62
Dumfries Way. Liv 4J 223
Dunald Mill La. Neth K 5D 16
Dunbar Clo. Blac 3G 108
Dunbar Cres. South 5F 186
Dunbar Dri. Ful 5G 115
Dunbar Dri. Hey 9K 21
Dunbar Rd. Ing 6C 114
Dunbar Rd. South 3E 186
(in two parts)
Duncan Av. Blac 5C 62
Duncan Clo. Burn 4K 125
Duncan Clo. Lyth A 8D 108
Duncan Pl. Fltwd 9E 40
Duncan Pl. Wig 4N 221
Duncan St. Burn 4M 123
Duncan St. Hor 9D 196
Duncombe. 7D 68
Dun Cft. Clo. Clith 1L 81
Dundas St. Col 7N 85
(off John St.)
Dundee Dri. B'brn 4A 140
Dundee La. Ram 8G 180
Dundee Rd. Todm 8G 146
Dundee St. Lanc 9L 23
Dunderdale Av. Nels 3G 105
Dunderdale St. L'rdge 3K 97
Dundonald St. Pres 9N 115
Dundonnell Rd. Nels 1L 105
Dunedin Rd. G'mnt 3E 200
Dunelt Rd. Blac 8C 88
Dunes Av. Blac 4B 108
Dunfold Clo. Liv 9L 223
Dungeon La. Dal 5N 211
Dunham Dri. Whit W 1E 174
Dunkeld St. Lanc 9L 23
Dunkenhalgh Way. Acc 8L 121
Dunkenshaw Cres. Lanc 5M 29
Dunkirk Av. Carn 1B 16
Dunkirk Av. Ful 5F 114
Dunkirk La. Ley 6C 152
Dunkirk Ri. Roch 6B 204
Dunkirk Rd. South 3F 186
Dunlin Clo. Roch 6K 203
Dunlin Clo. T Clev 7G 54
Dunlin Dri. Lyth A 1L 129
Dunlop Av. Roch 9B 204
Dunlop Av. South 2C 206
Dunlop Dri. Liv 6G 222
Dunmail Av. Blac 8F 88
Dunmore St. Pres 9L 115
Dunnings Bri. Rd. Boot 7A 222
Dunnings Wlk. Boot 6A 222
Dunnockshaw. 4N 143
Dunnocks La. Cot 5B 114
Dunnyshop. 4M 141
Dunny Shop Av. Acc 4N 141
Dunoon Clo. Ing 5C 114
Dunoon Dri. B'brn 5D 140
Dunoon Dri. Bolt 8C 198
Dunoon St. Burn 4B 124
Dunrobin Dri. Eux 5N 173
Dunscar. 5E 198
Dunscar Dri. Chor 5G 175
Dunscar Fold. Eger 5E 198
Dunscar Golf Course. 4C 198
Dunscar Ind. Est. Eger 6E 198
Dunscar Sq. Eger 5E 198
Dunscore Rd. Wig 8N 221
Dunsop Bridge. 7K 49
Dunsop Clo. Bam B 8B 136
Dunsop Clo. Blac 9D 88
Dunsop Ct. Blac 9D 88
Dunsop Gdns. More 6F 22
Dunsop Rd. Rib 5N 115
Dunsop St. B'brn 2N 139
Dunstable. Roch 5B 204
(off Spotland Rd.)
Dunster Av. Osw 3J 141
Dunster Av. Roch 8B 204
Dunster Gro. Clith 5J 81
Dunster Rd. South 5E 186
Dunsters Av. Bury 8H 201
Dunsterville Ter. Roch 8B 204
(off New Barn La.)
Dunvegan Clo. Blac 3G 108
Durants Cotts. Liv 3D 222
Durban Gro. Burn 5C 124
Durban Rd. Ram 8E 198
Durham Av. Burn 2N 123
Durham Av. Lanc 2L 29
Durham Av. Lyth A 1E 128
Durham Av. T Clev 9E 54
Durham Clo. B'brn 4N 139
Durham Clo. Heat O 6B 22
Durham Clo. Ley 9H 153
Durham Dri. B'brn 3N 119
Durham Dri. Osw 5M 141
Durham Dri. Ram 2G 200
Durham Gro. Gars 5M 59
Durham Ho. Pres 2K 135
(off Guildford Ho.)
Durham Rd. Blac 5D 88
Durham Rd. Dar 5M 157
Durham Rd. Wilp 3N 119
Durhams Pas. L'boro 9K 185
Durham St. Acc 1C 142
Durham St. Roch 7C 204
Durham St. Skel 1H 219
Durham St. Bri. Roch 8D 204
Durley Rd. Blac 8D 88
Durn. 8M 185
Durnford Clo. Roch 3H 203
Durn St. L'boro 8M 185
Durn St. Todm 7D 146
Durton La. Brough 9G 95
(in two parts)
Dutch Barn Clo. Chor 4D 174
Duttonfield Cl. Far M 4H 153
Dutton Rd. Blac 4D 88
Dutton St. Acc 2B 142
Duxbury Av. Bolt 8L 199
Duxbury Clo. Liv 8D 216
Duxbury Clo. Rainf 3L 225
Duxbury Hall Rd. Chor 2G 194
Duxbury Pk. Bus. Cen. Chor 2F 194
Duxbury Pk. Golf Course. 2F 194
Duxbury St. Dar 9B 158
Duxbury St. Earby 2F 78
Duxon Hill. Brin 8K 137
Dye Ho. La. Lanc 8K 23
Dye Ho. La. Roch 2F 204
Dyers Ct. L'boro 8K 185
Dyers La. Orm 8K 209
Dyer St. K'ham 4L 111
Dyke Nook. Clith 4M 81
Dykes La. Yeal C 9B 6
Dymock Rd. Pres 8N 115
Dyneley Av. Burn 5K 125
Dyneley La. Cliv 1H 145
Dyneley Rd. B'brn 1C 140
Dyson St. B'brn 6L 139

E

Eachill Gdns. Rish 9H 121
Eachill Rd. Rish 8H 121
Eafield Av. Miln 6J 205
Eafield Clo. Miln 6J 205
Eafield Rd. L'boro 2H 205
Eafield Rd. Roch 4F 204
Eagle La. Liv 3A 216
Eagland Hill. 5N 57
Eagle Cres. Rainf 4L 225
Eagles Ct. Liv 8K 223
Eagles, The. Poul F 6L 63
Eagle St. Acc 3A 142
Eagle St. B'brn 4C 140
Eagle St. Nels 1K 105
Eagle St. Osw 6J 141
Eagle St. Roch 7D 204
Eagle St. Todm 1L 165
Eagle Technology Pk. Roch 9D 204
Eagletown Way. Pen 6K 135
Eagle Way. Roch 9D 204
Eagley. 6F 198
Eagley Bank. Bolt 7F 198
Eagley Bank. Shawf 9B 164
Eagley Brow. Ram 7F 198
Eagley Ct. Brom X 6G 198
Eagley Ind. Est. Brom X 6F 198
Eagley Rd. Brier 6G 104
Eagley Way. Bolt 7F 198
Ealees. 9M 185
Ealees. L'boro 9M 185
Ealees Rd. L'boro 9M 185
Ealing Gro. Chor 2H 175
Eamont Av. South 1A 168
Eamont Pl. Fltwd 2D 54
Eanam. B'brn 3N 139
Eanam Old Rd. B'brn 3N 139
Eanam Wharf. B'brn 3N 139
Eanam Wharf Vis. Cen. 3N 139
(off Eanam Wharf)
Earby. 2E 78
Earby Rd. Salt 4B 78
Earcroft. 1L 157
Eardley Rd. Hey 8K 21
Earlesdon Av. Earby 3C 78
Earlham St. Earby 2F 78
Earl Rd. Ram 8G 181
Earls Av. Bam B 8A 136
Earls Dri. Hodd 6E 158
Earl St. Barn 2N 77
Earl St. B'brn 1M 139
Earl St. Burn 1F 124
Earl St. Clay M 7M 121
Earl St. Col 7A 86
Earl St. Gt Har 4H 121
Earl St. Lanc 7K 23
Earl St. Nels 1K 105
Earl St. Pres 9J 115
Earl St. Ram 8J 181
Earlsway. Blac 5K 89
Earls Way. Eux 4N 173
Earlswood. Skel 2B 220
Earnsdale Av. Dar 5L 157
Earnsdale Clo. Dar 5M 157
Earnsdale Rd. Dar 4M 157
Earnshaw Av. Roch 2B 204
Earnshaw Bridge. 5H 153
Earnshaw Dri. Ley 6G 153
Earnshaw Rd. Bacup 4K 163
Easby Clo. Liv 1A 214
Easdale Av. More 3E 22
Easedale Clo. Bolt S 7K 15
Easedale Clo. Burn 1N 123
Easedale Dri. South 9B 186
Easedale Wlk. Liv 6J 223
Easington. 7B 50
Easington. Lanc 6G 22
Easington Cres. Blac 2H 89
Easington Wlk. B'brn 5N 139
East Av. Barn 2M 77
East Bank. Barfd 7H 85
Eastbank Av. Blac 2G 109
E. Bank Av. Has 5G 160
Eastbank Ho. South 8H 167
E. Bank Rd. Lyth A 3E 128
E. Bank Rd. Ram 2F 200
(in two parts)
Eastbank St. South 7H 167
Eastbank St. Sq. South 7H 167
East Beach. Lyth A 5B 130
E. Boothroyden. Blac 2B 88
Eastbourne Clo. Ing 4C 114
Eastbourne Rd. Blac 3B 108
Eastbourne Rd. South 2G 187
Eastbourne St. Roch 8C 204
E. Cecil St. Lyth A 5N 129
E. Chorley Bus. Cen. Chor 6F 174
Eastcliff. Clau 9A 18
East Cliff. Pres 2J 135
East Cliffe. Lyth A 5B 130
East Cliff Rd. Pres 2J 135
Eastcott Clo. B'brn 8A 140
East Ct. T Clev 7D 54
East Cres. Acc 9A 122
East Cft. Nels 1M 105
Eastdene. Parb 2M 211
East Dri. Eux 2N 173
Eastern Av. Burn 1G 124
Eastfield Dri. Longt 7L 133
Eastfield Dri. W Brad 6M 73
Eastfield Wlk. Liv 9G 223
Eastgate. Acc 2A 142
Eastgate. Ful 4H 115
East Ga. Has 4G 161
Eastgate. Ribch 6F 98
Eastgate. Whi L 6E 22
Eastgate. Whitw 7M 183
E. Gate St. Roch 5C 204
East Gillibrands. 3L 219
Eastgrove Av. Bolt 7E 198
Eastham Av. Bury 7K 201
Eastham Hall Cvn. Site. Lyth A 2C 130
Eastham Pl. Burn 3F 124
Eastham St. Burn 4F 124
Eastham St. Clith 2L 81
Eastham St. Lanc 9L 23
Eastham St. Pres 8H 115
E. Hills St. Barn 2M 77
East Holme. Lyth A 4B 130
East Lancashire Railway. 6L 161
E. Lancashire Rd. B'brn 6N 119
Eastlands. Hey 9M 21
Eastlands. Ley 8F 152
East La. Liv 9H 215
Eastleigh. Skel 2A 220
E. Lodge Pl. Cliv 8J 125
East Marton. 6J 53
East Mead. Augh 2G 216
East Mead. Blac 7E 88
East Meade. Liv 9B 216
Eastmoor Dri. Clith 4M 81
East Mt. Orr 5J 221
Easton Clo. Ful 3N 115
East Pde. Barn 2M 77
East Pde. Ross 4M 161
East Pk. Av. B'brn 1L 139
East Pk. Av. Dar 7N 157
East Pk. Dri. Blac 7F 88
East Pk. Rd. B'brn 2L 139
East Pimbo. 7C 220
Eastpines Dri. T Clev 3E 62
East Rd. Ful 6K 115
East Rd. Lanc 8L 23
East Rd. Liv 1E 222
Eastside. Blac 1F 108
East Sq. Longt 8L 133
East St. Bam B 9A 136
East St. B'brn 5K 139
East St. Brier 5G 104
East St. Far 5L 153
East St. Fen 8E 138
East St. Firg 6G 204
East St. Garg 3M 53
East St. Hap 5H 123
East St. Helm 8F 160
East St. Ley 6L 153
East St. L'boro 9M 185
East St. More 4M 21
East St. Nels 1H 105
East St. Pad 9H 103
East St. Pres 9K 115
East St. Ram 2J 181
East St. Raw 2L 161
East St. Roch 5D 204
East St. South 7K 167
East St. Ward 8F 184
E. Topping St. Blac 5B 88
East Vw. Acc 8F 142
(off Hoyle St.)
East Vw. Bacup 5K 163
East Vw. Barn 2M 77
(off Leonard St.)
East Vw. Frec 2A 132
East Vw. Ful 4B 116
East Vw. Gal 2L 37
(off Chapel St.)
East Vw. Grin 5A 74
East Vw. Los H 9K 135
East Vw. Pres 9K 115
East Vw. Ram 5H 181
East Vw. Read 8C 102
East Vw. Ross 6D 162
East Vw. Traw 9F 86
East Vw. Walt D 2M 135
East Vw. Winm 7K 45
E. View Ct. Lanc 5H 23
E. View Ter. Withn 5C 156
East Wlk. Eger 3D 198
East Way. Bolt 9H 199
Eastway. Frec 2M 131
Eastway. Ful 1F 114
Eastway. Liv 9C 216
(in three parts)
Eastway Bus. Village. Ful 1L 115
E. Way La. Chor 6F 174
Eastwood Av. Blac 2E 88
Eastwood Av. Fltwd 1F 54
Eastwood Cres. Ross 5A 162
Eastwood Rd. Ley 6J 153
Eastwood Rd. Todm 5K 147
Eastwood St. Barn 1N 77
Eastwood St. B'brn 1A 140
Eastwood St. L'boro 9L 185
Eastwood St. Ross 5A 162
Eastwood Ter. Barn 1N 77
(off Eastwood St.)
Eaton Av. Blac 9C 88
Eaton Ct. Lyth A 2F 128
Eaton Pl. K'ham 4L 111
Eaton Rd. Mag 4C 222
Eaton Way. Poul F 2L 89
Eaves Av. Burn 7B 124
Eaves Clo. Hun 8E 122
Eavesdale. Skel 3B 220
Eaves Grn. La. Goos 1B 96
Eaves Grn. Rd. Chor 9D 174
Eaves Hall La. W Brad 4J 73
Eavesham Clo. Pen 7K 135
Eaves La. Chor 5G 174
Eaves La. Ful 6H 115
Eaves La. Wood 3M 93
Eaveslea. K Lon 6E 8
(off New Rd.)
Eaves Rd. Lyth A 8G 108
Eaves St. Blac 3B 88
Eaveswood Clo. Bam B 7A 136
Ebony St. B'brn 1A 140
Ebony Way. Kirkby & Liv 5K 223
Ebor St. Burn 8F 104
Ebor St. L'boro 9L 185
Ecclesgate Rd. Blac 4F 108
(in two parts)
Eccleshill Cotts. E'hill 3C 158
Eccleshill Gdns. E'hill 3D 158
Eccleshill St. Pad 1H 123
Eccles Rd. Orr 2L 221
Eccles's La. Bis 7M 191
Eccles St. Acc 1A 142
Eccles St. B'brn 5M 139
Eccles St. Pres 8M 115
Eccles St. Ram 8G 180
Eccleston. 7E 172
Eccleston Rd. Blac 9D 88
Eclipse Clo. Roch 6F 204
Eclipse Rd. B'brn 8E 138
Ecroyd Rd. Ash R 7F 114
Ecroyd St. Ley 6K 153
Ecroyd St. Nels 2G 104
Edale Av. Has 5H 161
Edale Clo. Ley 8K 153
Edale Ct. Pres 8J 115
Eddington Rd. Lyth A 4H 129
Eddleston Clo. Stain 5K 89
Edelston Rd. Blac 4C 88
Eden Av. Bolt 9E 198
Eden Av. Fltwd 2D 54
Eden Av. Lyth A 5L 129
Eden Av. More 3F 22
Eden Av. Rainf 3J 225
Eden Av. Ram 3J 181
Eden Av. South 3M 167
Edenbreck Dales. Lanc 9H 23
Eden Clo. Barfd 7H 85
Eden Clo. Liv 4L 223
Eden Ct. Ram 4J 181
(off N. Bury Rd.)
Edenfield. 4J 181
Edenfield Av. Poul F 9M 63
Edenfield Clo. South 2L 187
Edenfield Rd. Roch 3G 203
Edenfield St. Roch 4N 203
Eden Gdns. L'rdge 2K 97
Eden Gro. Bolt 9E 198
Eden Gro. Bolt S 3M 15
Eden Hall. Pres 8H 115
(off Ashmoor St.)
Eden La. Ram 4J 181
Eden Lodge. Bolt 9E 198
Eden Mt. Way. Carn 8C 12
Eden Pk. Lanc 3K 29
Edensor Ter. Dar 5N 157
Eden St. Acc 3N 141
Eden St. B'brn 3A 140
Eden St. Blac 4C 88
Eden St. Bolt 9E 198
Eden St. Ley 7K 153
Eden St. Ram 4J 181
Edenvale Av. Blac 7B 62
Edenvale Cres. Lanc 5J 23
Edenvale Rd. Lanc 5J 23
Edenway. Ful 2G 115
Edgar St. Acc 2A 142
Edgar St. Hun 7D 122
Edgar St. Nels 9K 85
Edgar St. Ram 9G 181
Edgar St. Roch 3F 204
Edgar St. W. Ram 9G 181
Edgecott Clo. Hey 9M 21
Edge End. 4H 121
Edge End. Gt Har 4H 121
Edge End Av. Brier 4H 105
Edge End La. Gt Har 4H 121
(in two parts)
Edge End La. Nels 4G 105
Edge End La. Ross 1M 161
Edge End Rd. Gt Har 4H 121
Edge End Ter. Withn 3C 156
Edgefield. Chor 4D 174
Edgefield Ct. Blac 2H 89
Edge Fold. 5G 178
Edgefold Rd. Liv 9L 223
Edge Ga. La. Brins 9A 156
Edge Hall Rd. Orr 7H 221
(in two parts)
Edgehill Clo. Ful 5H 115
Edgehill Cres. Ley 5H 153
Edgehill Dri. Ful 5G 115
Edge La. Barn 3J 77
Edge La. Bolt 8K 197
Edge La. Brit 7N 163
Edge La. Hept 9N 127
Edge La. Ross 5A 162
Edge La. Tur 4D 178
Edgeley Ct. Burn 2B 124
Edgemoor Clo. Shawf 1B 184
Edgemoor Dri. Roch 8K 203
Edge Nook Rd. B'brn 7D 140
Edgeside. 5E 162
Edgeside. Gt Har 4H 121
Edgeside La. Ross 4D 162
Edgeware Gro. Wig 8N 221
Edgeware Rd. B'brn 2K 139
Edgeway Pl. T Clev 2J 63
Edgeway Rd. Blac 3E 108
Edgewood. Shev 7K 213
Edge Yate La. Ross 2N 161
Edgley Dri. Orm 7M 209
Edgworth. 8K 179
Edgworth Gro. Burn 3G 125
Edinburgh Clo. Ley 6M 153
Edinburgh Dri. Osw 5M 141
Edinburgh Dri. Wig 6N 221
Edinburgh Rd. Has 7E 160
Edinburgh Way. Roch 9A 204
Edington. Roch 5B 204
(off Spotland Rd.)
Edisford Rd. Clith 4H 81
Edisford Rd. Wadd 8H 73
Edison St. Dar 6N 157
Edith St. Barn 1M 77
Edith St. B'brn 4A 140
Edith St. Nels 2K 105
Edith St. Ram 6K 181
Edleston Lodge. Rib 5B 116
(off Grange Av.)
Edleston St. Acc 3M 141
Edlingham. Roch 7B 204
Edmondsen Pl. Fltwd 2F 54
Edmondson's La. Brou 7L 53
Edmondson St. Barn 1M 77
Edmonton Dri. B'brn 9H 119
Edmonton Pl. Blac 8F 62
Edmund Gennings Ct. Chat 7C 74
Edmunds Fold. L'boro 8J 185
Edmundson St. B'brn 3K 139
Edmundson St. Chu 2L 141
Edmunds Pas. L'boro 7K 185
Edmund St. Acc 3B 142
Edmund St. B'brn 9L 139
Edmund St. Burn 9F 104
Edmund St. Dar 6B 158
Edmund St. Pres 9L 115
Edmund St. Roch 5A 204
Edmund St. Todm 7K 165
Edward Av. L'boro 2J 205
Edward Clo. Tar 1E 170
Edward Ct. Chu 2L 141
Edward VIII Quay. Ash R 9E 114
Edward Sq. Pres 8K 115
Edward St. Bacup 4L 163
Edward St. Bam B 8A 136
Edward St. Barn 1N 77
Edward St. Bax 7D 142
Edward St. Blac 5B 88
Edward St. Burn 3E 124
Edward St. Carn 8A 12
Edward St. Chor 7F 174
Edward St. Chu 2L 141
Edward St. Craw 8M 143
Edward St. Dar 5A 158
Edward St. Earby 2E 78
Edward St. Gt Har 4J 121
Edward St. Has 1G 160
Edward St. Hor 9B 196
Edward St. Lanc 8L 23
Edward St. Ley 7K 153
Edward St. Lyth A 1F 128
Edward St. More 3A 22
Edward St. Nels 8K 85
(in two parts)
Edward St. Pres 9H 115
Edward St. Rish 8H 121
Edward St. Roch 5D 204
Edward St. T Clev 8H 55
Edward St. Walt D 3M 135
Edward St. Ward 1G 205
Edward St. Whitw 4A 184
Edwell Av. Blac 1D 108
Edwinstowe Rd. Lyth A 2J 129
Edwin Waugh Gdns. Roch 3A 204
Egan St. Pres 9K 115
Egbert St. Pres 8K 115
Egerton. 3D 198
Egerton. Skel 3A 220
Egerton Barn Cottage. Eger 3E 198
Egerton Ct. Ash R 8E 114

244 A-Z Lancashire

F

Fairclough Rd.—Fleet St.

Fairclough Rd. *T Clev* 9G **55**
Fairfax Av. *Blac* 5E **62**
Fairfax Clo. *Gars* 6A **60**
Fairfax Dri. *L'boro* 2J **205**
Fairfax Pl. *Walt D* 6N **135**
Fairfax Rd. *Rib* 5A **116**
Fairfield. 9B 202
Fairfield. *Gars* 4N **59**
Fairfield Av. *Blac* 3H **89**
Fairfield Av. *Poul F* 8K **63**
Fairfield Av. *Ross* 5D **162**
Fairfield Av. *Wig* 6M **221**
Fairfield Clo. *Carn* 9B **12**
Fairfield Clo. *Clith* 4J **81**
Fairfield Clo. *Lanc* 8J **23**
Fairfield Clo. *Orm* 5K **209**
Fairfield Ct. *Fltwd* 2F **54**
Fairfield Dri. *Ash R* 7E **114**
Fairfield Dri. *Burn* 7F **104**
Fairfield Dri. *Bury* 9B **202**
Fairfield Dri. *Clith* 4J **81**
Fairfield Dri. *Orm* 5K **209**
Fairfield Gro. *Hey* 6M **21**
Fairfield Rd. *Blac* 2C **88**
Fairfield Rd. *Ful* 5K **115**
Fairfield Rd. *Hey* 5L **21**
Fairfield Rd. *Lanc* 8J **23**
Fairfield Rd. *Ley* 7J **153**
Fairfield Rd. *Nels* 2M **105**
Fairfield Rd. *Poul F* 3L **89**
Fairfield Rd. *Sing* 3A **90**
Fairfield Rd. *South* 8C **186**
Fairfields. *Eger* 5F **198**
Fairfields Dri. *Lwr D* 1N **157**
Fairfield St. *Acc* 4M **141**
Fairfield St. *Los H* 9L **135**
Fairfield St. *Pem* 6M **221**
Fairgarth Dri. *K Lon* 5E **8**
Fairham Av. *Pen* 6G **134**
Fairhaven. 4G 129
Fairhaven. *Liv* 5K **223**
Fairhaven. *Skel* 9M **211**
Fairhaven Av. *Fltwd* 5D **54**
Fairhaven Clo. *T Clev* 3K **63**
Fairhaven Ct. *Lyth A* 2E **128**
Fairhaven Golf Course. 2M 129
Fairhaven La. *Lyth A* 3E **128**
Fairhaven Rd. *B'brn* 7N **139**
Fairhaven Rd. *Ley* 6G **152**
Fairhaven Rd. *Lyth A* 3E **128**
Fairhaven Rd. *Pen* 3H **135**
Fairhaven Rd. *South* 2A **168**
Fairhaven Way. *More* 3D **22**
Fairheath Rd. *Halt* 9J **19**
Fair Hill. *Ross* 8F **160**
Fairhill Ter. *Ross* 8F **160**
Fairholme Rd. *Burn* 6F **124**
Fairholmes Clo. *T Clev* 9H **55**
Fairholmes Way. *T Clev* 9G **55**
Fairhope Av. *Lanc* 5J **23**
Fairhope Av. *More* 2F **22**
Fairhope Ct. *B'brn* 2K **139**
Fairhurst Av. *Stand* 1N **213**
Fairhurst Ct. T Clev 9D ***54***
(off Beach Rd.)
Fairhurst La. *Ingle* 5K **69**
Fairhurst's Dri. *Parb* 2M **211**
Fairhurst St. *Blac* 4C **88**
Fairlands Rd. *Bury* 6L **201**
Fairlawne Clo. *Liv* 5K **223**
Fairlawn Rd. *Lyth A* 6L **129**
Fairlea Av. *More* 2F **22**
Fairlie. *Skel* 9N **211**
Fairmont Dri. *Hamb* 1C **64**
Fair Mt. *Todm* 6K **165**
Fair Oak Clo. *Rib* 6B **116**
Fairsnape Av. *L'rdge* 3K **97**
Fairsnape Dri. *Gars* 6M **59**
Fairsnape Rd. *Lyth A* 4C **130**
Fairstead. *Skel* 9N **211**
Fairthorn Wlk. *Liv* 7M **223**
Fairview. 5J 195
Fair Vw. *Bacup* 7N **163**
Fairview. K Lon 5E ***8***
(off Fairgarth Dri.)
Fair Vw. *L'boro* 7M **185**
Fairview. *Ross* 2L **161**
Fairview Av. *Lyth A* 1G **129**
Fairview Clo. *Roch* 3G **203**
Fairview Clo. *Walm B* 2K **151**
Fair Vw. Cres. *Bacup* 5M **163**
Fairview Dri. *Hth C* 5H **195**
Fair Vw. Rd. *Burn* 4F **124**
Fairway. *Chor* 4E **174**
Fairway. *Fltwd* 2C **54**
Fairway. *Miln* 7K **205**
Fairway. *Pen* 2E **134**
Fairway. *Poul F* 9G **63**
Fairway. *South* 4J **167**
Fair Way. *Stalm* 5B **56**
Fairway. *Whitw* 7N **183**
Fairway Av. *Bolt* 9N **199**
Fairway Gdns. *Kno S* 8K **41**
Fairway Rd. *Blac* 1E **108**
Fairways. *Ful* 3K **115**
Fairways. *St A* 2G **129**
Fairways Av. *Brough* 7F **94**
Fairways Ct. *Wilp* 4N **119**
Fairways Dri. *Burn* 7C **124**
Fairways, The. *Skel* 9A **212**
Fairweather Ct. *Pad* 9J **103**
Fairwinds Av. *Hesk B* 3B **150**
Falcon Av. *Dar* 4M **157**
Falcon Clo. *B'brn* 9L **119**
Falcon Clo. *Bury* 9M **201**
Falcon Clo. Set 3N ***35***
(off Longdale Av.)
Falcon Ct. *Clay M* 7M **121**
Falcon Dri. *Poul F* 9H **63**
Falcon Gdns. *Set* 3N **35**
Falcon St. *Pres* 7L **115**
Falge M. *Roch* 5B **204**
Falinge Fold. *Roch* 4A **204**
Falinge Rd. *Roch* 4A **204**
Falkirk Av. *Blac* 5C **62**
Falkirk Gro. *Wig* 3M **221**
Falkland. *Skel* 9N **211**
Falkland Av. *Blac* 8F **88**
Falkland Av. *Roch* 5N **203**
Falkland Rd. *South* 1K **187**
Falkland St. *Pres* 1H **135**
Fallbarn Cres. *Ross* 6L **161**
Fallbarn Rd. *Ross* 5N **161**
(in two parts)
Fall Kirk. *A'ton* 6A **18**
Fallowfield. *Liv* 6K **223**
Fallowfield Clo. *Wesh* 3K **111**
Fallowfield Dri. *Burn* 1B **124**
Fallowfield Dri. *Roch* 3N **203**
Fallowfield Rd. *Lyth A* 2J **129**
Falmer Clo. *Bury* 6H **201**
Falmouth Av. *Fltwd* 4C **54**
Falmouth Av. *Has* 5H **161**
Falmouth Rd. *Blac* 8C **88**
Falmouth St. *Roch* 8D **204**
Falshaw Dri. *Bury* 4K **201**
Falstone Av. *Ram* 1H **201**
Falstone Clo. *Wig* 9N **221**
Faraday Av. *Clith* 3K **81**
Faraday Dri. *Ful* 2M **115**
Faraday St. *Burn* 2A **124**
Faraday Way. *Blac* 6F **62**
Far Bank. 7H 149
Far Clo. Dri. *Arns* 3D **4**
Far Cft. *Los H* 7K **135**
Far E. Vw. *Barn* 2M **77**
Fareham Clo. *Ful* 5K **115**
Fareham Clo. *Walt D* 5B **136**
Fareham Dri. *Banks* 1F **168**
Far Fld. *Pen* 4G **134**
Farholme La. *Bacup* 7H **163**
Faringdon. *Roch* 7B **204**
Faringdon Av. *Blac* 4D **108**
Faringdon Park. 8B 116
Farington. 1J 153
Farington Av. *Ley* 8G **153**
Farington Bus. Pk. *Ley* 3K **153**
Farington Ga. *Ley* 5L **153**
Farington Lodges Nature Reserve. 9H 135
Farington Moss. 2G 153
Farington Rd. *Far M & Los H* 1J **153**
Far La. *Pen* 6F **134**
Farleton. 8B 18
Farleton Clo. *War* 6N **11**
Farleton Ct. *Lanc* 4K **23**
Farleton Crossing. *Farl* 8A **18**
Farleton Old Rd. *Clau* 9A **18**
Farleton Vw. *Holme* 2G **6**
Farley La. *Roby M* 9D **212**
Farm Av. *Adl* 5J **195**
Farm Av. *Bacup* 3K **163**
Farm Clo. *Chtwn* 6N **167**
Farm Clo. *T Clev* 1H **63**
Farm Clo. *Tot* 7E **200**
Farmdale Dri. *Liv* 1D **222**
Farmdale Rd. *Lanc* 2M **29**
Farmend Clo. *Longt* 8M **133**
Farmer's Row. *B'brn* 9J **139**
Farm Ho. Clo. *B'brn* 4C **140**
Farmhouse Clo. *Whit W* 9E **154**
Farm Mdw. Rd. *Orr* 6H **221**
Far Moor. 7G 220
Farmoor La. *Lanc* 8N **23**
Farm Wlk. *L'boro* 9J **185**
Farm Wlk. *Roch* 4F **204**
Farnborough St. *Todm* 5K **165**
Farnborough Rd. *Bolt* 7E **198**
Farnborough Rd. *South* 5F **186**
Farndean Way. *Col* 7B **86**
Farnell Pl. *Blac* 3D **108**
Farnham Way. *Poul F* 6J **63**
Farnlea Dri. *More* 3E **22**
Farnley Clo. *Roch* 3K **203**
Far Nook. *Whit W* 8D **154**
Farnworth Gro. *Liv* 5K **223**
Farnworth Rd. *T Clev* 2K **63**
Faroes Clo. *B'brn* 7N **139**
Farrell Clo. *Liv* 6G **222**
Farrell St. *Wig* 6M **221**
Farrer St. *Nels* 2G **105**
Farrier Rd. *Liv* 8M **223**
Farriers Fold. *Hey* 9L **21**
Farriers La. *Roch* 9M **203**
Farriers Yd. *Cat* 2H **25**
Farringdon Clo. *Pres* 8B **116**
Farringdon Cres. *Pres* 8B **116**
Farringdon La. *Rib* 6B **116**
Farringdon Pl. *Pres* 8B **116**
Farrington Clo. *Burn* 6A **124**
Farrington Ct. *Burn* 6A **124**
Farrington Dri. *Orm* 6K **209**
Farrington Pl. *Burn* 6A **124**
Farrington Rd. *Burn* 6N **123**
Farrington St. *Chor* 6E **174**
Farthings, The. *Chor* 5B **174**
Faulkner Clo. *South* 7C **186**
Faulkner Gdns. *South* 7C **186**
Faulkner's La. *Fort* 4M **45**
Faulkner St. *Roch* 6C **204**
Favordale Rd. *Col* 5D **86**
Fawcett. *Skel* 9M **211**
Fawcett Clo. *B'brn* 5L **139**
Fawcett Rd. *Liv* 8C **216**
Fayles Gro. *Blac* 9G **88**
Fazackerley St. *Ash R* 8F **114**
Fazakerley St. *Chor* 6E **174**
Fearnhead Av. *Hor* 8C **196**
Fearns Moss. *Bacup* 6E **162**
Featherstall Rd. *L'boro* 9J **185**
Featherstall Sq. *L'boro* 9K **185**
Fecit La. *Ram* 6N **181**
Fecitt Brow. *B'brn* 4C **140**
Fecitt Rd. *B'brn* 2J **139**
Federation St. *Barn* 1L **77**
Feilden Pl. *B'brn* 8E **138**
Feilden St. *B'brn* 4L **139**
Felgate Brow. *Blac* 5E **88**
Felix St. *Burn* 2F **124**
Fell Brow. *L'rdge* 4K **97**
Fell Clo. *Bam B* 8B **136**
Fell End Cvn. Pk. *Hale* 3B **6**
Fellery St. *Chor* 6E **174**
Fellfoot Rd. *Cast* 5H **9**
Fellgate. *More & Whi L* 6E **22**
Fell La. *Cast* 5J **9**
Fell La. *Man* 1E **8**
Fell Rd. *More* 4F **22**
Fell Rd. *Wadd* 10C **50**
Fellside. *Bolt* 9N **199**
Fellside Clo. *G'mnt* 4E **200**
Fellside Vw. *Hey* 9L **21**
Fellstone Va. *Withn* 6B **156**
Fellstone Vw. *Withn* 7B **156**
Fell Vw. *Burn* 7H **105**
Fell Vw. *Cat* 3H **25**
Fell Vw. *Chor* 8G **175**
Fell Vw. *Gars* 4N **59**
Fell Vw. *Grims* 8E **96**
Fell Vw. *South* 9C **148**
Fell Vw. *W Brad* 5K **73**
Fell Vw. Clo. *Gars* 4N **59**
Fell Vw. Ho. *Whal* 3G **100**
Fell Way. *Stalm* 5C **56**
Fellway Clo. *Los H* 8M **135**
Felstead. *Skel* 1M **219**
Felstead St. *Pres* 9N **115**
Felsted Dri. *Liv* 9D **222**
Feltons. *Skel* 1M **219**
Felton Way. *Much H* 4K **151**
Fenber Av. *Blac* 2C **108**
Fence. 3B 104
Fence Ga. *Fence* 3B **104**
Fengrove. *Longt* 8L **133**
Feniscliffe. 6H 139
Feniscliffe Dri. *B'brn* 6G **139**
Feniscowles. 8E 138
Fenney Ct. *Skel* 2N **219**
Fennyfold Ter. *Pad* 3H **123**
Fensway. *Hut* 6A **134**
Fenton Av. *Barn* 1A **78**
Fenton Clo. *Boot* 9A **222**
Fenton M. *Roch* 8B **204**
Fenton Rd. *Blac* 4C **88**
Fenton Rd. *Ful* 5M **115**
Fenton St. *Bury* 9H **201**
Fenton St. *Lanc* 8J **23**
Fenton St. *Roch* 8B **204**
Fenwick St. *Burn* 6B **124**
Fenwick St. *Roch* 6B **204**
Ferguson Gdns. *Roch* 2C **204**
Ferguson Ri. *Wig* 3N **221**
Ferguson Rd. *Blac* 8E **88**
Ferguson St. *B'brn* 9L **139**
Fermor Rd. *Pres* 8A **116**
Fermor Rd. *Tar* 6C **150**
Fern Av. *Osw* 5M **141**
Fern Bank. Carn 9A ***12***
(off Albert St.)
Fernbank. *Chor* 3F **174**
Fern Bank. *Lanc* 2L **29**
Fern Bank. *Liv* 1C **222**
Fern Bank. *Rainf* 3J **225**
Fern Bank Av. *Barn* 1L **77**
Fernbank Ct. *Nels* 3J **105**
Ferncliffe Dri. *Hey* 6L **21**
Fern Clo. *Los H* 8L **135**
Fern Clo. *Shev* 6K **213**
Fern Clo. *Skel* 2J **219**
Fern Ct. *Fltwd* 3C **54**
Fern Cft. *Cast* 5G **8**
Ferndale. *B'brn* 2A **140**
Ferndale. *Skel* 1M **219**
Ferndale Av. *Blac* 2D **108**
Ferndale Clo. *Frec* 1B **132**
Ferndale Clo. *Ley* 8L **153**
Ferndale Clo. *T Clev* 1J **63**
Ferndale St. *Burn* 1G **124**
Fern Dene. *Roch* 3M **203**
Ferney Lee Rd. *Todm* 1K **165**
Ferney St. Todm 1K ***165***
(off Buckley Vw.)
Fern Gore. 5N 141
Fern Gore Av. *Acc* 5N **141**
Fern Grove. 9A 202
Fern Gro. *Blac* 7C **88**
Ferngrove. *Bury* 8N **201**
Ferngrove W. *Bury* 9N **201**
Fernhill. 9L 201
Fernhill Av. *Bacup* 7J **163**
Fernhill Cvn. Pk. *Bury* 9K **201**
Fernhill Clo. *Bacup* 7J **163**
Fernhill Cres. *Bacup* 7J **163**
Fernhill Dri. *Bacup* 7H **163**
Fernhill Gro. *Bacup* 6J **163**
Fern Hill La. *Roch* 2L **203**
Fernhill Pk. *Bacup* 7J **163**
Fernhills. *Eger* 3E **198**
Fernhill St. *Bury* 9L **201**
Fernhill Way. *Bacup* 7J **163**
Fernhurst Av. *Blac* 9D **88**
Fernhurst Ga. *Augh* 1G **217**
Fernhurst Rd. *Liv* 9H **223**
Fernhurst St. *B'brn* 8L **139**
Fern Isle Clo. *Whitw* 8M **183**
Fernlea Av. *Barn* 2M **77**
Fernlea Av. *Osw* 5M **141**
Fernlea Clo. *B'brn* 8J **139**
Fernlea Clo. *Roch* 3M **203**
Fernlea Dri. *Clay M* 5L **121**
Fern Lea St. *Ross* 7B **162**
Fernleigh. *Ley* 7D **152**
Fernleigh Clo. *Blac* 7D **62**
Fernley Rd. *South* 9G **167**
Fern Mdw. *Whit W* 4E **154**
Fern Rd. *Burn* 5C **124**
Fernside Gro. *Wins* 9N **221**
Fernside Way. *Roch* 4L **203**
Ferns, The. *Ash R* 7F **114**
Ferns, The. *Bacup* 6L **163**
Ferns, The. *Walt D* 5L **135**
Fern St. *Bacup* 4K **163**
Fern St. *Bury* 9L **201**
Fern St. *Col* 5C **86**
Fern St. *Ram* 8J **181**
(in two parts)
Fern St. *Ross* 6D **162**
Fern St. *Ward* 8F **184**
Fern Ter. *Has* 4F **160**
Fernview Dri. *Ram* 4G **200**
Fernville Ter. *Bacup* 7H **163**
Fernwood Av. *T Clev* 3H **63**
Fernwood Clo. *Lyth A* 4L **129**
Fernyhalgh Ct. *Ful* 3N **115**
Fernyhalgh Gdns. *Ful* 3N **115**
Fernyhalgh Gro. *Ful* 3N **115**
Fernyhalgh La. *Ful* 9M **95**
(in two parts)
Fernyhalgh Pl. *Ful* 3N **115**
Ferny Knoll Rd. *Rainf* 8J **219**
Ferrand Lodge. *L'boro* 7M **185**
Ferrand Rd. *L'boro* 8L **185**
Ferrier Bank. *W'ton* 3J **131**
Ferrier Clo. *B'brn* 3C **140**
Ferrier Ct. *B'brn* 3C **140**
Ferry Rd. *Ash R* 9C **114**
Ferry Side La. *South* 1B **168**
Festival Rd. *Rainf* 5L **225**
Fewstone Clo. *Bolt* 8E **198**
Fiddler's Ferry. 9C 148
Fiddler's La. *Chip* 5D **70**
Fiddlers La. *Clay W* 5D **154**
Fidler La. *Far M* 2J **153**
Field Clo. *Burs* 1D **210**
Fieldcroft. *Roch* 6M **203**
Fieldens Farm La. *Mel B* 6C **118**
Fielden Sq. *Todm* 3L **165**
Fielden St. *Burn* 4A **124**
Fielden St. *Chor* 6G **174**
Fielden St. *Ley* 6G **152**
Fielden St. *L'boro* 3H **205**
Fieldfare Clo. *T Clev* 7G **54**
Fieldfare Ct. *Chor* 9B **174**
Fieldhead Av. *Roch* 6M **203**
Fieldhouse Av. *T Clev* 1K **63**
Fieldhouse Ind. Est. *Roch* 3C **204**
Fieldhouse Rd. *Roch* 3C **204**
Fielding Cres. *B'brn* 7H **139**
Fielding La. *Gt Har* 4H **121**
Fielding La. *Osw* 5L **141**
Fielding Pl. *Adl* 5K **195**
Fielding Rd. *Blac* 2D **88**
Fieldings, The. *Liv* 7A **216**
Fielding St. *Rish* 8J **121**
Fieldlands. *South* 3N **187**
Field Maple Dri. *Rib* 6B **116**
Field Rd. *Hey* 1J **27**
Field Rd. *Roch* 6G **205**
Field Rose Ct. *Hth C* 5H **195**
Fieldsend. *Hey* 9M **21**
Fields End. *Lang* 1C **120**
Fieldside Av. *Eux* 5M **173**
Fieldside Clo. *Los H* 5M **135**
Fields Rd. *Has* 6H **161**
Fields, The. *E'ston* 7E **172**
Field St. *B'brn* 6J **139**
Field St. *Blac* 8C **88**
Field St. *Pad* 2H **123**
Field St. *Skel* 1H **219**
Field Top. *Bacup* 9L **145**
Field Wlk. *Orm* 7N **209**
Field Way. *Lyth A* 7E **108**
Fieldway. *Mag* 3C **222**
Fieldway. *Roch* 9E **204**
Fife Clo. *Chor* 8G **174**
Fife St. *Acc* 3N **141**
Fife St. *Barfd* 1G **104**
Fifth Av. *Blac* 2C **108**
Fifth Av. *Burn* 8F **104**
Fifth Av. *Bury* 9B **202**
Fifth St. *Bolt* 9N **197**
Filbert Clo. *Liv* 4L **223**
Filberts Clo. *Ful* 6F **114**
Filberts, The. *Ful* 6F **114**
File St. *Chor* 7E **174**
Filey Pl. *Blac* 4B **88**
Filey Pl. *Ing* 5D **114**
Filey Rd. *Lyth A* 8G **108**
Filey St. *Roch* 2F **204**
Filton Gro. *More* 5E **22**
Finance St. *L'boro* 9H **185**
Finch Av. *Rainf* 5L **225**
Finch Clo. *B'brn* 2N **139**
Finches, The. *Poul F* 9H **63**
Finch La. *App B* 3E **212**
Finch La. *Cot* 5B **114**
Finchley Rd. *Blac* 2B **88**
Finch Mill Av. *App B* 5G **213**
Finch's Cotts. *Pen* 4H **135**
Finch St. *Dar* 5N **157**
Findon. *Skel* 1N **219**
Findon Rd. *Liv* 9L **223**
Fine Jane's Way. *South* 6A **168**
Finney La. *Crost* 6H **171**
Finnington La. *Fen* 1B **156**
Finsbury Av. *Blac* 8D **88**
Finsbury Av. *Lyth A* 4H **129**
Finsbury Pl. *B'brn* 9L **139**
Finsbury St. *Roch* 8A **204**
Finsley Ga. *Burn* 4D **124**
Finsley St. *Brclf* 7J **105**
Finsley Vw. *Brclf* 7K **105**
Firbank. *Eux* 4M **173**
Firbank Av. *Tar* 8E **150**
Firbank Rd. *Lanc* 7L **23**
Firbarn Clo. *Firg* 6G **204**
Firbeck. *Skel* 2M **219**
Fir Clo. *Fltwd* 2C **54**
Fir Cotes. *Liv* 1D **222**
Fir Ct. *Acc* 9D **122**
Fir Cft. *Stand* 2K **213**
Fire Sta. Yd. *Roch* 7C **204**
Firewood La. *Sam* 3J **137**
Firfield Clo. *K'ham* 4K **111**
Firgrove. 6G 205
Fir Gro. *Blac* 8E **88**
Fir Gro. *W'ton* 2J **131**
Firgrove Av. *Roch* 5G **204**
Firgrove Gdns. *Roch* 5G **204**
Fir Gro. Rd. *Burn* 5F **124**
Fir Mt. *Bacup* 6L **163**
Firshill Clo. *T Clev* 3H **63**
Firs La. *Augh* 9D **208**
(in two parts)
First Av. *Ash R* 7D **114**
First Av. *Blac* 2C **108**
First Av. *Chu* 8N **121**
First Av. *Clift* 8G **113**
First Av. *Poul F* 8L **63**
First Av. *Tot* 7E **200**
First Av. *W Grn* 5G **110**
Firstone Gro. *Liv* 9K **223**
Fir St. *Burn* 4F **124**
Fir St. *Has* 5H **161**
Fir St. *Nels* 2K **105**
Fir St. *Ram* 7J **181**
Fir St. *South* 8L **167**
Fir St. *Todm* 7K **165**
First St. *Bolt* 9N **197**
Firswood Clo. *Lyth A* 4L **129**
Firswood Rd. *Skel* 1F **218**
Fir Tree Av. *Ful* 5E **114**
Fir Tree Clo. *Bolt S* 7K **15**
Fir Tree Clo. *Chor* 2E **194**
Fir Tree Clo. *Much H* 4J **151**
Fir Tree Clo. *Skel* 4A **220**
Fir Tree La. *Augh* 8E **208**
Fir Tree Pl. *T Clev* 3F **62**
Fir Trees Av. *Los H* 7K **135**
Fir Trees Av. *Rib* 5B **116**
Fir Trees Cres. *Los H* 8K **135**
Firtrees Dri. *B'brn* 8G **138**
Fir Trees Gro. *High* 5K **103**
Fir Trees La. *High* 5K **103**
Fir Trees Pl. *Rib* 5B **116**
Fir Trees Rd. *Los H* 7K **135**
Firwood. *Skel* 9A **212**
Firwood Clo. *L'rdge* 2J **97**
Firwood Clo. *Todm* 6K **165**
Fisher Dri. *Orr* 4H **221**
Fisher Dri. *South* 7M **167**
Fisherfield. *Roch* 4K **203**
Fishergate. *Pres* 1H **135**
Fishergate Cen. *Pres* 1J **135**
Fishergate Ct. *Pres* 1H **135**
Fishergate Hill. *Pres* 2G **135**
Fishergate Wlk. *Pres* 1J **135**
Fishermans Wlk. *Fltwd* 9G **41**
Fishermans Wharf. Fltwd 9G ***40***
(off Lofthouse Way)
Fisher's La. *Blac* 4F **108**
Fisher's Row. 7K 43
Fisher's Slack La. *Poul F* 9G **64**
Fisher St. *Blac* 4C **88**
Fish Ho. La. *Chip* 5E **70**
Fish La. *Burs & H'wd* 1N **189**
Fishmoor Dri. *B'brn* 8N **139**
Fish Rake La. *Ross* 1J **181**
Fish St. *Pres* 8J **115**
Fishwick. 9M 115
Fishwick Bottoms. *Pres* 2M **135**
Fishwick Hall Golf Course. 9B 116
Fishwick La. *Wheel* 6K **155**
Fishwick Pde. *Pres* 9M **115**
Fishwick Rd. *Pres* 9M **115**
Fishwick St. *Roch* 7D **204**
Fishwick Vw. *Pres* 9M **115**
Fitchfield. *Pen* 6J **135**
Fitton St. *Roch* 5D **204**
Fitzgerald St. *Pres* 8M **115**
Fitzhugh St. *Bolt* 8G **198**
Fitzroy Rd. *Blac* 8D **62**
Fitzroy St. *Pres* 1G **135**
Five Acres. *Far M* 3H **153**
Five Ashes La. *Lanc* 8K **29**
Five La. Ends. *Bay H* 6A **38**
Flag La. *Breth* 1L **171**
Flag La. *Hth C* 9H **175**
Flag La. *Ley & Eux* 2G **172**
Flag La. *Pen* 7J **135**
Flag St. *Bacup* 7J **163**
Flag St. *Fltwd* 9H **41**
Flakefleet Av. *Fltwd* 3E **54**
Flamstead. *Skel* 2N **219**
Flannel St. *Roch* 5D **204**
Flare Rd. *Hey* 1J **27**
Flasby. 1N 53
Flash La. *Ruf* 1G **190**
Flatfield Way. *Liv* 1D **222**
Flat La. *Yeal C* 8B **6**
Flatman's La. *Down* 2L **215**
Flats Retail Pk., The. *Walt D* 3M **135**
Flats, The. *Chor* 8D **174**
Flax Clo. *Has* 7F **160**
Flaxfield Rd. *Liv* 9A **206**
Flaxfield Way. *K'ham* 4M **111**
Flax La. *Burs* 1D **210**
Flax Moss. 7F 160
Flaxmoss Clo. *Helm* 7F **160**
Flax St. *Ram* 1F **200**
Flaxton. *Skel* 2N **219**
Fleece St. *Roch* 6C **204**
Fleet Grn. *Lanc* 5J **23**
Fleet La. *Horn* 6B **18**
Fleet's La. *Cast* 6G **8**
Fleet Sq. Lanc 8K ***23***
(off Cable St.)
Fleet St. *Blac* 6C **88**
Fleet St. *Chor* 7E **174**
Fleet St. *Hor* 9E **196**

Fleet St.—Garden St.

Fleet St. L'rdge 3J 97
Fleet St. Lyth A 1D 128
Fleet St. Nels 1J 105
Fleet St. Orr & Wig 5L 221
Fleet St. Pres 1J 135
Fleet St. La. Hoth 4A 98
Fleet Wlk. Burn 3E 124
Fleetwood. 9H 41
Fleetwood Clo. B'brn 7N 139
Fleetwood Clo. South 3M 167
Fleetwood Cres. South 9F 148
Fleetwood Docks. Fltwd 2G 54
Fleetwood Dri. South 9F 148
Fleetwood Gdns. Liv 5L 223
(in two parts)
Fleetwood Golf Course. 9C 40
Fleetwood Mus. 8J 41
Fleetwood Old Rd. K'ham 7K 91
Fleetwood Rd. Burn 8G 104
Fleetwood Rd. Esp 3H 91
Fleetwood Rd. Fltwd 2E 54
Fleetwood Rd. Pad 1J 123
Fleetwood Rd. Poul F 5H 63
Fleetwood Rd. South 5J 167
(in two parts)
Fleetwood Rd. T Clev 1C 62
Fleetwood Rd. Wesh 1L 111
Fleetwood Rd. N. Fltwd & T Clev 5F 54
Fleetwood Rd. S. T Clev 2H 63
Fleetwood St. Ash R 8G 114
Fleetwood St. Ley 5L 153
Fleming Sq. B'brn 4M 139
Fleming Sq. L'rdge 3K 97
Flensburg Way. Ley 4G 152
Fletcher Av. Tar 9E 150
Fletcher Bank. 8J 181
Fletcher Dri. Burs 9C 190
Fletcher Rd. Pres 9L 115
Fletcher Rd. Rish 9G 121
Fletchers Pas. L'boro 8K 185
Fletcher's Rd. Clith 2H 205
Fletchers Sq. L'boro 8L 185
(off Sutcliffe St.)
Fletcher St. B'brn 5L 139
Fletcher St. L'boro 8K 185
Fletcher St. Nels 3K 105
Fletcher St. Roch 8D 204
Flett St. Ash R 8F 114
Flimby. Skel 2A 220
Flimby Clo. B'brn 8N 139
Flintoff Way. Pres 6L 115
Flinton Brow. Abb 2A 48
Flip Rd. Has 4F 160
Flockton Av. Stand L 8N 213
Floral Hall & Theatre. 6H 167
Floral Hall Gardens. 6H 167
Flordon. Skel 2A 220
Florence Av. Bolt 9F 198
Florence Av. Burn 4A 124
Florence Av. W'ton 3J 131
Florence Pl. B'brn 2A 140
Florence St. B'brn 2A 140
Florence St. Blac 3G 109
Florence St. Burn 4A 124
Florence St. Chu 2L 141
Florence St. Roch 7E 204
Flowerfield. Cot 3B 114
Flower Fields. Catt 1A 68
Flower Hill La. Ward 8D 184
Flower Scar Rd. Todm 1A 164
Floyd Rd. Rib 6A 116
Floyer St. Pres 1L 135
Fluke Hall La. Pil 4E 42
Flush Brow. Cast 4G 9
Fold Gdns. Roch 2M 203
Fold Head. 6M 183
Fold Ho. Cvn. Pk. Pil 9J 43
Foldside. Frec 1A 132
Folds St. Burn 1D 124
Fold, The. Barfd 6J 85
Fold Vw. Eger 4E 198
Folkestone Clo. T Clev 8F 54
Folkestone Clo. W'ton 1K 131
Folkestone Rd. Lyth A 9F 108
Folkestone Rd. South 2L 187
Folly Bank. Ross 8M 143
Folly Cotts. Barn 3L 77
Folly La. Barn 6K 77
Folly La. Slyne 4H 23
Folly Ter. Ross 8M 143
Folly Wlk. Roch 4C 204
(in two parts)
Fooden La. Bolt B 8L 51
Footeran La. Yeal C 8B 6
Foot Mill Cres. Roch 3A 204
Foot Wood Cres. Roch 3A 204
Forbes Ct. Burn 6M 123
Ford Gdns. Roch 7M 203
Ford Green. 2K 59
Fordham Clo. South 2L 187
Ford La. Goos 1B 96
Ford La. Silv 6J 5
Fordoe La. Roch 1G 202
Fordside Av. Clay M 5L 121
Fordstone Av. Pre 9N 41
Ford St. Barfd 7J 85
Ford St. Burn 9F 104
Ford St. Lanc 7H 23
Ford St. Roch 6D 204
Fordway Av. Blac 4E 88
Foregate. Ful 5H 115
Foreside. Barfd 6J 85
Forest Av. Fence 2C 104
Forest Bank. Ross 9M 143
Forest Bank Rd. Ross 9M 143
Forest Becks. 6K 51
Forest Becks Brow. Bolt B 6K 51
Forest Brook Ho. Ful 6J 115
Forest Clo. Los H 5M 135
Forest Dri. Lyth A 4L 129
Forest Dri. Skel 9N 211
Forest Dri. Stand 2K 213
Forester Dri. Fence 2B 104
Forester's Bldgs. Barn 2M 77
Forest Ga. Blac 5D 88
Forest Ga. Whi L 6E 22
Forest Gro. Brtn 2E 94
Forest Hills Golf Course. 9N 29
Forest Holme. 9D 144
Forest Holme Clo. Water 9D 144
Forest La. Barfd 9F 84
Forest of Mewith. 8M 19
Forest Pk. Lanc 9G 23
Fore St. Lwr D 9N 139
Forest Rd. South 8K 167
Forestry Houses. Dun B 7K 49
Forestside. B'brn 9L 139
Forest St. Bacup 5K 163
Forest St. Burn 3E 124
Forest St. Nels 1H 105
(in two parts)
Forest St. Ross 9E 144
Forest Vw. Barfd 8H 85
Forest Vw. Brier 5E 104
Forest Vw. Roch 3A 204
Forest Way. Brom X 7J 199
Forest Way. Ful 4J 115
Forest Way. Ley 7J 153
Forfar Gro. Burn 6B 124
Forfar St. Bolt 8E 198
Forfar St. Burn 6B 124
Forge Clo. W'head 8C 210
Forge La. Bncr 4B 60
Forge St. Bacup 5K 163
Forge St. Ley 6K 153
Forgewood Clo. Halt 2D 24
Forgewood Dri. Halt 2C 24
Formby Av. Fltwd 5D 54
Formby Bus. Pk. Form 1C 214
Formby By-Pass. Liv 5B 206
Formby Clo. B'brn 8N 139
Formby Cres. Longt 8K 133
Formby Fields. Liv 1A 214
Formby Gdns. Liv 8A 206
Formby Hall Golf Course. 4C 206
Formby La. Augh 1C 216
Formby La. Liv 1B 214
Formby M. Liv 8A 206
Formby Pl. Ash R 7B 114
(in two parts)
Formby Rd. Lyth A 8F 108
Forrest Ct. Blac 2E 88
Forrester Clo. Ley 6H 153
Forrest St. B'brn 3A 140
Forshaw Av. Blac 2F 88
Forshaw Av. Lyth A 9D 108
Forshaw Clo. Fltwd 2E 54
Forshaw Rd. Pen 6G 134
Forsters Green. 9A 212
Forsters Grn. Rd. Uph 9A 212
Forsythia Dri. Clay W 3D 154
Forsyth St. Roch 3J 203
Fort Av. Ribch 7E 98
Forton. 2M 45
Forton Rd. Ash R 9B 114
Forts Bldgs. Kel 6D 78
Fort St. Acc 2A 142
Fort St. B'brn 3A 140
Fort St. Clay M 6M 121
Fort St. Clith 4K 81
Fort St. Read 8C 102
Fort St. Ind. Est. B'brn 2A 140
Forty Acre La. L'rdge 1L 97
Forum Ct. South 7G 167
Forward Ind. Est. Ley 5H 153
(off Talbot Rd.)
Foscote Rd. Liv 6M 223
Fossdale Moss. Ley 6F 152
Fosse Clo. B'brn 8A 140
Fossgill Av. Bolt 8J 199
Foster Ct. Bury 9B 202
Foster Cft. Pen 2F 134
Fosterfield Pl. Chor 5G 174
Foster Rd. Barn 1L 77
Fosters Clo. South 6A 168
Foster St. Acc 1B 142
Foster St. Chor 5G 174
Fothergill St. Col 6N 85
Foul Clough Rd. Todm 7G 164
Fould Clo. Col 8N 85
Fouldrey Av. Poul F 6L 63
Foulds Rd. Traw 8E 86
Foulds Ter. Traw 9F 86
Foul La. South 9N 167
Foulridge. 2A 86
Foulridge Wharf. 1A 86
Foundary St. Chor 6E 174
Foundry La. Halt 1N 23
Foundry La. Wig 7N 221
Foundry St. Bacup 5K 163
Foundry St. B'brn 4K 139
Foundry St. Burn 3D 124
Foundry St. Dar 6A 158
Foundry St. Has 5G 161
Foundry St. Ross 6L 161
Foundry St. Todm 3K 165
Fountain Pl. Acc 3A 142
Fountain Retail Pk. Acc 2N 141
Fountains Av. B'brn 9B 120
Fountains Av. S'stne 9C 102
Fountains Clo. Chor 9F 174
Fountains Sq. Barfd 7H 85
Fountains Reach. Walt D 7N 135
Fountain St. Acc 4N 141
Fountain St. Barn 2N 77
Fountain St. Col 7A 86
Fountain St. Dar 7A 158
Fountain St. Nels 1J 105
Fountains Way. Liv 1A 214
Fountains Way. Osw 3H 141
Fouracre. Mel 7F 118
Four Acre La. Thorn 9F 70
(in two parts)
Fouracres. Liv 3A 222
Fourfields. Bam B 6A 136
Four Lane Ends. 9L 119
(Blackburn)
Four Lane Ends. 8C 200
(Bury)
Four Lane Ends. 4E 218
(Skelmersdale)
Four La. Ends. Blac 4G 88
Four La. Ends. Doph 6E 38
Four La. Ends. Hey 7L 21
Four La. Ends. S'stne 6E 102
Four La. Ends Rd. Bacup 7F 162
Four Lanes Way. Roch 4G 203
Four Oaks Rd. Bam B 1C 154
Fourth Av. Blac 2C 108
Fourth Av. Bury 9B 202
Fourth St. Bolt 9N 197
Fowler Av. Far M 1L 153
Fowler Clo. Hogh 6L 137
(in two parts)
Fowler Height Clo. B'brn 9J 139
Fowler Hill La. Cabus 8L 45
Fowler La. Far & Far M 1J 153
Fowler St. Ful 6G 115
Foxcote. Chor 4D 174
Foxcroft. Burn 1B 124
Foxcroft St. L'boro 9J 185
Foxdale Av. Blac 3D 88
Foxdale Clo. Bacup 6L 163
Foxdale Clo. South 2L 187
Foxdale Clo. Tur 7L 179
Foxdale Gro. Pres 6N 115
Foxdale Pl. Lanc 6J 23
Foxen Dole La. High 5M 103
Foxfield Av. More 5C 22
Foxfield Clo. Bury 8G 201
Foxfield Gro. Shev 6L 213
Foxfold. Skel 9A 212
Foxglove Clo. Hesk B 3C 150
Foxglove Clo. Stand 2N 213
Foxglove Ct. Roch 2A 204
Foxglove Dri. Bury 9B 202
Foxglove Dri. Whit W 1D 174
Foxglove Way. Frec 1B 132
Fox Gro. Hey 5M 21
Foxhall Rd. Blac 7B 88
Foxhall Sq. Blac 7B 88
Foxhill Bank. 3L 141
Foxhill Bank. Chu 3K 141
Foxhill Bank Brow. Chu 3L 141
Foxhill Dri. Ross 3D 162
Foxhill Ter. Acc 4L 141
Foxhill W. Osw 4L 141
Foxhole Rd. Chor 5B 174
Foxholes Clo. Roch 4D 204
Foxholes M. Bay H 8A 38
Foxholes Rd. Hor 9E 196
Foxholes Rd. More 2D 22
Foxhouse La. Liv 2D 222
Fox Ho. St. B'brn 3K 139
Fox Ind. Est. Blac 1F 88
Fox La. Hogh 5G 137
Fox La. Ley 7G 153
Fox Lane Ends. 4F 110
Fox La. Ends. W Grn 3F 110
Foxstones Cres. B'brn 8H 139
Foxstones La. Cliv 6L 125
Fox St. Acc 2A 142
Fox St. Burn 3L 123
Fox St. Clith 2L 81
Fox St. Miln 5E 204
Fox St. Pres 1J 135
Foxwell Clo. Has 5H 161
Foxwood Chase. Acc 9D 122
Foxwood Clo. Orr 6H 221
Foxwood Dri. K'ham 3K 111
Foxwood, The. Char R 4M 193
Frailey Clo. South 9C 186
Frances Ho. K'ham 4M 111
Frances Pas. Lanc 8K 23
(off Penny St.)
Frances St. Dar 5N 157
Frances St. Roch 1G 205
France St. B'brn 4L 139
France St. Chu 2L 141
Francis Av. Barfd 6J 85
Francis St. Ash R 8F 114
Francis St. B'brn 7J 139
Francis St. Blac 4B 88
Francis St. Burn 9E 104
Francis St. Clay M 6M 121
Francis St. Col 8M 85
Frankel Clo. New L 8C 134
Franklands. Longt 7L 133
Franklands Dri. Rib 4B 116
Franklands Fold. Longt 8L 133
(off Franklands)
Franklin Gro. Liv 4K 223
Franklin Rd. B'brn 5H 139
Franklin St. Burn 3A 124
Franklin St. Clith 4K 81
Franklin St. Dar 6A 158
Franklin St. Lanc 2K 29
Franklin St. Roch 8E 204
Franklin Ter. L'boro 9K 185
(off William St.)
Frank St. Barn 2M 77
Frank St. Clay M 8N 121
Frank St. Pres 8J 115
Franton Wlk. Liv 8H 223
Fraser Av. Pen 3H 135
Fraser St. Acc 4N 141
Fraser St. Burn 9F 104
Fraser St. Roch 9E 204
Frazer Gro. Blac 9B 88
Freckleton. 2M 131
Freckleton By-Pass. Frec 2M 131
Freckleton Ct. Lyth A 5B 130
(off Freckleton St.)
Freckleton Dri. Liv 5L 223
Freckleton Rd. K'ham 5N 111
Freckleton Rd. South 2M 167
Freckleton St. B'brn 4L 139
(in two parts)
Freckleton St. Blac 7C 88
Freckleton St. K'ham 4N 111
Freckleton St. Lyth A 5B 130
Frederick Row. B'brn 3B 140
Frederick St. Acc 2N 141
Frederick St. Barn 1L 77
Frederick St. B'brn 5M 139
Frederick St. Blac 1D 108
Frederick St. Chor 7G 175
Frederick St. Dar 5A 158
Frederick St. L'boro 8K 185
Frederick St. Osw 4L 141
Frederick St. Ram 9G 180
Fredora Av. Blac 8G 89
Freehold. 7L 23
Freeholds La. Wadd 5F 72
(in two parts)
Freeholds Rd. Shawf 9B 164
Freeholds Ter. Shawf 9B 164
Freehold St. Roch 8B 204
Free La. Ross 9F 160
Freeman's La. Char R 2A 194
Freeman's Wood. Lanc 8E 22
Freemantle Av. Blac 5B 108
Freeport. Fltwd 1G 55
Freeport Village Retail Pk. Fltwd 1H 55
Freestone Clo. Bury 9J 201
Freetown. 9M 201
Free Trade St. Burn 3D 124
Freetrade St. Roch 8B 204
French Clo. B'brn 4J 139
French Rd. B'brn 4J 139
Frenchwood. 2L 135
Frenchwood Av. Lyth A 4M 129
Frenchwood Av. Pres 2L 135
Frenchwood Knoll. Pres 2L 135
Frenchwood St. Pres 2K 135
Freshfield Av. Clay M 6L 121
Freshfields. Lea 6A 114
Friar Ct. Acc 2B 142
Friargate. Pres 9J 115
Friargate Wlk. Pres 1J 135
Friar's Moss Rd. Brook 8E 24
Friars Pas. Lanc 8K 23
Friars, The. Ful 5H 115
Friar St. Lanc 8K 23
Friars Wlk. Liv 1B 214
Friary Clo. K'ham 5A 112
Friday St. Chor 6F 174
Frieldhurst Rd. Todm 7F 146
Frieston. Roch 5B 204
(off Spotland Rd.)
Frinton Gro. Blac 5E 62
Friths Av. Hogh 7G 137
Frobisher Dri. Lyth A 8D 108
Frobisher Rd. L'boro 5M 185
Frodsham Clo. Stand L 9N 213
Frog La. Lath 2H 211
Frome St. Pres 8N 115
Frontierland. 4N 21
Froom St. Chor 6G 174
(in two parts)
Fryer Clo. Pen 7F 134
Fry St. Nels 2K 105
Fulford Av. Lea 8N 113
Fulham St. Nels 9K 85
Fulledge. 5G 124
Fullers Ter. Bacup 6K 163
(off Park Rd.)
Full Pot La. Roch 5J 203
Full Vw. B'brn 8J 139
Fulmar Cres. Hey 2L 27
Fulmar Gdns. Roch 6K 203
Fulmars, The. Poul F 9H 63
Fulshaw Rd. Ash R 7E 114
Fulwood. 6H 115
Fulwood Av. Blac 2F 88
Fulwood Av. South 1K 187
Fulwood Av. Tar 6D 150
Fulwood Dri. More 3F 22
Fulwood Hall La. Ful 5L 115
Fulwood Heights. Ful 4M 115
Fulwood Pk. Ful 2L 115
Fulwood Row. 4A 116
Fulwood Row. Ful & Rib 2A 116
(in two parts)
Furbarn La. Roch 5H 203
Furbarn Rd. Roch 6H 203
(in two parts)
Furlong Cres. Blac 1G 88
Furlong La. Poul F 6K 63
Furnesford Rd. L Bent 9H 19
Furness Av. B'brn 9B 120
Furness Av. Blac 2G 88
Furness Av. Fltwd 3D 54
Furness Av. Form 9A 206
Furness Av. Heyw 9G 202
Furness Av. Lanc 8M 29
Furness Av. L'boro 8K 185
Furness Av. Orm 8K 209
Furness Av. S'stne 9C 102
Furness Clo. Chor 9F 174
Furness Clo. Miln 7H 205
Furness Clo. South 1B 206
Furness Ct. Blac 2G 88
Furness Dri. Ben 6L 19
Furness Dri. Poul I 8M 63
Furness Rd. Hey 6L 21
Furness St. Burn 9F 104
Furness St. Lanc 7H 23
Furnival Dri. Burs 9B 190
Further Ends Rd. Frec 2N 131
Further Fld. Roch 4H 203
Further Ga. B'brn 3B 140
Furthergate Ind. Est. B'brn 3B 140
Further Heights Rd. Roch 3C 204
Further La. Sam & Mel 1N 137
Further Pits. Roch 6N 203
Further Wilworth. B'brn 7M 119
Furze Ga. Roch 9E 204
Fushetts La. Ben 6K 19
Fylde Av. Far M 3H 153
Fylde Av. Lanc 8M 29
Fylde Country Life Mus. 5D 58
Fylde Ct. Kno S 8K 41
Fylde Cres. Weet 4D 90
Fylde Rd. Ash R & Pres 8G 114
Fylde Rd. Lyth A 3K 129
Fylde Rd. Poul F 7L 63
Fylde Rd. South 2M 167
Fylde Rd. Ind. Est. Pres 8G 115
Fylde Rd. Ind. Est. South 2N 167
Fylde St. K'ham 5M 111
Fylde St. Pres 9H 115
Fylde Vw. Clo. Poul F 9K 63

G

Gabbot St. Adl 6J 195
Gable M. Liv 2A 214
Gables Pl. More 3D 22
Gables, The. Cot 5B 114
Gables, The. Dar 3M 157
Gables, The. Mag 3D 222
Gable St. Bolt 8K 199
Gadfield St. Dar 7B 158
Gadsby St. Blac 8B 88
Gage St. Lanc 8K 23
Gaghills Rd. Ross 6D 162
Gaghills Ter. Ross 6D 162
(off Gaghills Rd.)
Gainsborough Av. B'brn 2K 139
Gainsborough Av. Burn 6C 124
Gainsborough Av. Liv 2A 222
Gainsborough Av. Los H 9K 135
Gainsborough Av. More 2D 22
Gainsborough Clo. Wig 8N 221
Gainsborough Rd. Blac 6D 88
Gainsborough Rd. Ram 4G 200
Gainsborough Rd. South 2E 186
Gaisgill Av. More 5B 22
Gait Barrows Nature Reserve. 4L 5
Galbraith Way. Roch 5J 203
Gale. 7M 185
Gale Rd. Know I 9A 224
Gales La. Maw 2L 191
Gales Ter. Roch 8B 204
(off High Barn Clo.)
Gale St. Roch 2C 204
Galgate. 2L 37
Galgate Silk Mills Ind. Est. Gal 2M 37
Galindo St. Bolt 9J 199
Galligreaves St. B'brn 5L 139
Galligreaves Way. B'brn 5K 139
Gall La. Todm 6F 146
Galloway Cres. Blac 6F 62
Galloway Rd. Fltwd 8F 40
Gallowber La. Hut R 6B 8
Gallows La. Ribch 6G 99
Galston Clo. Liv 4J 223
Galway Av. Blac 8D 62
Gamble Rd. T Clev 8G 55
Gambleside Clo. Ross 7M 143
Game St. Gt Har 4J 121
Gamston Wood. Liv 9H 223
Gamull La. Rib 4B 116
Gandy La. Roch 1N 203
Gannet Way. Frec 7N 111
Gannow La. Burn 3N 123
Gantley Av. Bil 7G 220
Gantley Cres. Bil 8G 220
Gantley Rd. Bil 7G 220
Ganton Clo. South 2L 187
Ganton Ct. Pen 2D 134
Gants La. Stalm 8B 56
Garbett St. Acc 4N 141
Garden Av. W Grn 5G 111
Garden City. Ram 3F 200
Garden Clo. L'boro 2J 205
Garden Cotts. Orm 7J 209
Gardeners M. Barfd 3C 88
Gardeners Row. Sab 3E 102
Gardeners Vw. Liv 4L 223
Garden Holme. Garg 3M 53
(off West St.)
Garden Holme. I'ton 2N 19
(off Bank Top)
Gardenia Clo. Clay W 3D 154
Garden M. L'boro 9L 185
(off Industry St.)
Garden Pl. Burt 6H 7
Garden Row. Heyw 9F 202
Gardens Gro. More 4A 22
Gardens La. E'tn 1M 53
Garden Sq. Traw 9E 86
Gardens, The. Bolt 7F 198
Gardens, The. Tur 1K 199
Garden St. Abb V 5D 156
Garden St. Acc 1A 142
Garden St. Barn 2M 77
Garden St. B'brn 4K 139
Garden St. Brier 5F 104
Garden St. Col 7A 86
Garden St. Gt Har 5J 121
Garden St. High 5L 103
Garden St. K'ham 5M 111
Garden St. Los H 9L 135
Garden St. Lyth A 2E 128
Garden St. Miln 9L 205
Garden St. Nels 2J 105
Garden St. Osw 4K 141
Garden St. Pad 9H 103
Garden St. Pres 1J 135
Garden St. Ram 8H 181
Garden St. S'seat 2H 201
Garden St. Todm 1L 165

Garden St.—Gorsefield

Garden St. Tot 6E 200
Garden Ter. Blac 9B 88
Garden Ter. Chor 5E 174
Garden Ter. M'ton 5M 27
Garden Va. Bus. Pk. Col 7M 85
Garden Wlk. Ash R 8E 114
Garden Wlk. T Clev 7D 54
Garden Way. L'boro 3J 205
Gardiners Pl. Skel 3J 219
Gardner Rd. Form 9A 206
Gardner Rd. Hey 5M 21
Gardner Rd. Lanc 6K 23
Gardner Rd. War 5A 12
Gardner's La. Clau B 9G 60
Gardner St. Pres 9J 115
Garfield Av. Lanc 9H 23
Garfield Clo. Roch 5J 203
Garfield Ct. Blac 8J 89
Garfield Dri. More 4F 22
Garfield St. Acc 3C 142
Garfield St. Fltwd 8H 41
Garfield St. Todm 7F 146
Garfield Ter. Chor 4F 174
Gargrave. 3M 53
Gargrave Ho. Gdns. Garg 3L 53
Gargrave Rd. Brou 6M 53
Garland Gro. Fltwd 1D 54
Garlick's Cotts. Lyth A 5B 130
(off N. Warton St.)
Garnet Clo. T Clev 4F 62
Garnet St. Lanc 8L 23
Garnett Grn. Orm 8J 209
Garnett Pl. Skel 4L 219
Garnett Rd. Clith 4J 81
Garnett St. Barfd 9H 85
Garnett St. Bolt 9E 198
Garnett St. Dar 6B 158
Garnett St. More 2B 22
(off Morecombe St. E.)
Garnett St. Ram 8G 180
Garrick Gro. Blac 3E 88
Garrick Pde. South 7G 166
Garrick St. Nels 9K 85
Garrison Rd. Ful 6L 115
Garsdale Av. Burn 6F 104
Garsdale Clo. Walt D 3A 136
Garsdale Rd. Rib 5A 116
Garsden Av. B'brn 6E 140
Gars End. Wray 8E 18
Garside Hey Rd. Bury 7G 201
Garstang. 5N 59
Garstang Clo. Poul F 8J 63
Garstang Country Hotel Golf Course. 8N 59
Garstang New Rd. Sing 8C 64
Garstang Rd. Brtn 9D 68
Garstang Rd. Bils 7D 68
Garstang Rd. Brough & Ful 7F 94
(in two parts)
Garstang Rd. Chip 6E 70
Garstang Rd. Chur 1L 67
Garstang Rd. C'ham & Fort 1H 45
Garstang Rd. Ful & Pres 6H 115
Garstang Rd. Gars & Catt 6A 60
Garstang Rd. Pil 9K 43
Garstang Rd. St M 4G 66
Garstang Rd. Sing 7F 64
Garstang Rd. South 2M 167
Garstang Rd. E.
Poul F & Sing 8K 63
Garstang Rd. N. Wesh 2L 111
Garstang Rd. S. Wesh 3L 111
Garstang Rd. W.
Blac & Poul F 1G 89
Garstang St. Dar 5A 158
Garstangs Yd. Gigg 2N 35
(off Church St.)
Gars, The. Wray 8E 18
Garstone Cft. Ful 3F 114
Garston St. Bury 9M 201
Garswood Av. Rainf 3L 225
Garswood Clo. Burs 8D 104
Garswood Clo. Liv 8D 216
Garswood Dri. Bury 7G 201
Garth Edge. Whitw 1B 184
Garton Av. Blac 3C 108
Gas Fld. Rd. Hey 5K 27
Gas Ho. La. Ben 6L 19
(off Main St.)
Gaskell Clo. L'boro 8K 185
Gaskell Clo. Silv 8G 4
Gaskell Cres. T Clev 1G 63
Gaskell Rd. Pen 3H 135
Gaskell St. Chor 6G 174
Gas St. Adl 7H 195
Gas St. Bacup 5K 163
Gas St. Burn 3D 124
Gas St. Has 6E 160
Gas St. Roch 6B 204
Gas Ter. Ley 5K 153
Gatefield Ct. Burn 5E 124
(off Hollingreave Rd.)
Gate Flats. K Lon 6F 8
(off Lunefield Dri.)
Gate Fold. 8K 199
Gategill Gro. Bil 8G 220
Gateheads Brow. Cast 5G 9
Gateland. Salt 4A 78
Gatelands Cvn. Pk. Tew 2F 12
Gatesgarth Av. Ful 2J 115
Gateside Ct. Blac 2G 88
Gateside Dri. Blac 2F 88
Gates La. Liv 9J 215
Gate St. B'brn 3A 140
Gate St. Roch 8C 204
Gateway Clo. T Clev 4K 63
Gathurst. 9K 213
Gathurst Golf Course. 8H 213
Gathurst La. Shev 9K 213
Gathurst Rd. Ash R 7F 114
Gathurst Rd. Orr 4H 221
Gatley Dri. Liv 3D 222
Gatwick Clo. Bury 6H 201
Gaulter's La. Pre 9B 42
Gauxholme. 4J 165
Gauxholme Fold. Todm 4J 165
Gaw Hill La. Augh 9F 208
Gawthorpe Edge Pk. Pad 2L 123
Gawthorpe Hall. 9L 103
Gawthorpe Rd. Burn 2B 124
Gawthorpe St. Pad 9H 103
Gawthorpe Vw. High 5L 103
Gaydon Way. T Clev 4E 62
Gaylands La. Earby 2F 78
Gayle Way. Acc 4M 141
(off Lynton Rd.)
Gaythorne Av. Pres 8B 116
Gayton Clo. Wig 8N 221
Geddes St. B'brn 6G 139
Geldard Cotts. Wigg 10M 35
Gelder Clough Cvn. Pk.
Heyw 8G 203
Geldof Dri. Blac 2C 88
Gendre St. Eger 5E 198
General St. Blac 4B 88
Generation Cen., The. Roch 6B 204
Geneva Rd. Ful 5M 115
Geneva Ter. Roch 5N 203
Genoa St. Burn 5A 124
Geoffrey St. Bury 9M 201
Geoffrey St. Chor 5F 174
Geoffrey St. Pres 8M 115
Geoffrey St. Ram 1F 200
George Av. Blac 9F 88
George Av. Gt Har 5H 121
George Dri. South 8E 186
George Fox Clo. Lanc 8M 29
George La. Read 8B 102
George Rd. Ram 9G 180
George's La. Banks 7E 148
Georges La. Hor 6E 196
Georges Rd. Pres 1J 135
George's Row. Ross 7D 162
George's Ter. Orr 6E 220
George St. Acc 4M 141
George St. Bacup 5L 163
George St. Barn 10G 52
George St. B'brn 4M 139
George St. Blac 4C 88
(in two parts)
George St. Burn 4D 124
George St. Chor 7E 174
George St. Clay M 6M 121
George St. Clith 5K 81
George St. Dar 5A 158
George St. Earby 2E 78
George St. Firg 6H 205
George St. Gt Har 4J 121
George St. Has 4G 160
George St. Hor 9D 196
George St. Lanc 9K 23
George St. Ley 5L 153
George St. L'rdge 2J 97
George St. Lyth A 5A 130
George St. More 3C 22
George St. Nels 1H 105
George St. Osw 3L 141
George St. Pres 1L 135
George St. Rish 8H 121
George St. Roch 5D 204
George St. Smal 2G 204
George St. Stac 7G 163
George St. Todm 2L 165
(off Union St.)
George St. Whal 5J 101
George St. Whitw 7N 183
George St. W. B'brn 4K 139
Georgia Av. Liv 4J 223
Gerald Ct. Burn 5F 124
(off Kirkgate)
Gerald's Fold. Abb V 5C 156
German La. Char R 6N 173
German La. Cop 4A 194
German's La. Burs 6E 190
Gerona Ct. T Clev 2J 63
Gerrard Pl. Skel 4K 219
Gerrard's Ter. Poul F 7J 63
Gerrard St. Lanc 9G 23
Gerrard St. Pres 1G 135
Gertrude St. Nels 9K 85
Gertrude St. Shawf 9B 164
Ghants La. Hamb 9D 56
Ghyll Fields. 10H 53
Ghyll Golf Course. 10H 53
Ghyll La. Barn 10G 53
Ghyll M. Barn 10G 53
Giants Hall Rd. Stand L 9N 213
Gib Fld. Rd. Col 8L 85
Gib Hey La. Chip 7D 70
Gib Hill La. Ross 7N 143
Gib Hill Rd. Nels 1M 105
Gib La. B'brn 8H 139
Gib La. Hogh 4L 137
Gibraltar St. B'brn 2J 139
Gibralter Rd. Weet 4D 90
Gibson St. Nels 9K 85
Gibson St. Roch 5F 204
Gibson St. Todm 2M 165
Giddygate La. Liv 1G 223
Gidlow Av. Adl 6J 195
Giggleswick. 3M 35
Gilbert Pl. Burs I 9N 189
Gilbertson Rd. Hth C 3G 195
Gilbert St. Burn 8J 105
Gilbert St. Chor 8E 174
Gilbert St. Ram 5H 181
Gilbert St. Ross 6B 162
Gildabrook Rd. Blac 4D 108
Gilderdale Ct. Lyth A 4B 130
Gildow St. Pres 9H 115
Gilescroft Av. Liv 6M 223
Gilescroft Wlk. Liv 6M 223
Giles St. Clith 4L 81
Giles St. Nels 1J 105
Gilhouse Av. Lea 8N 113
Gill Av. Shev 6L 213
Gill Ct. Blac 4B 108
Gillcroft. E'ston 7E 172
Giller Clo. Pen 6H 135
Giller Dri. Pen 6H 135
Giller Fold. Pen 6J 135
Gillett Farm Cvn. Pk. Blac 4L 109
Gillett St. Pres 8M 115
(in two parts)
Gillhead Brow. Ben 5L 19
Gillians La. Barn 3L 77
Gillibrand Clo. Pen 7F 134
Gillibrand Ho. Chor 4E 174
(off Lancaster Ct.)
Gillibrands Rd. Skel 3K 219
(in two parts)
Gillibrand St. Chor 7E 174
Gillibrand St. Dar 4N 157
Gillibrand St. Walt D 3N 135
Gillibrand Walks. Chor 8D 174
Gillies St. Acc 2B 142
Gillies St. B'brn 5N 139
Gillison Clo. Mllng 4D 18
Gill La. Longt 2L 151
Gill Nook. Walm B 2L 151
Gillow Av. Lanc 8L 29
Gillow Pk. L Ecc 5L 65
Gillow Rd. K'ham 3L 111
Gills Cft. Clith 5M 81
Gill St. Burn 3C 124
Gill St. Col 8M 85
Gill St. Nels 1G 105
Gilow Ct. Lanc 2K 29
Gilpin Av. Liv 9D 216
Gilpin Clo. Lanc 6G 22
Gilstead Av. Hey 8M 21
Gin Bow. Chor 8F 174
Gin Cft. La. Ram 3K 181
Gingham Brow. Hor 9E 196
Ginnel, The. Ley 7K 153
Gipsy La. Roch 9N 203
Girvan Gro. Burn 4B 124
Gisburn. 9A 52
Gisburn Av. Lyth A 2H 129
Gisburn Gro. Blac 3E 88
Gisburn Gro. Burn 4H 125
Gisburn Old Rd. Black 5F 76
(in two parts)
Gisburn Rd. Barn 10F 52
Gisburn Rd. Barfd 9H 85
Gisburn Rd. Black 3G 85
Gisburn Rd. Bolt B 8K 51
Gisburn Rd. Hell 1D 52
Gisburn Rd. Rib 5A 116
Gisburn St. Barn 1M 77
Gisburn St. B'brn 4K 139
Gladden Pl. Skel 3J 219
Glades, The. Lyth A 4B 130
Gladeswood Rd. Know N 8N 223
Glade, The. B'brn 1M 157
Glade, The. More 3E 22
Glade, The. Shev 6L 213
Glade Way. T Clev 4K 63
Gladstone Cres. Bacup 5L 163
Gladstone Ho. Roch 8B 204
Gladstone Rd. South 8M 167
Gladstone St. Bacup 5L 163
Gladstone St. B'brn 2B 140
Gladstone St. Blac 9C 88
Gladstone St. Gt Har 4J 121
Gladstone St. Todm 7E 146
Gladstone Ter. Barfd 8H 85
Gladstone Ter. B'brn 7G 139
Gladstone Ter. Lanc 7L 23
(off Bulk Rd.)
Gladstone Ter. Traw 7E 86
Gladstone Ter. Withn 6D 156
Gladstone Vw. Barn 1L 77
Gladstone Way. T Clev 2F 62
Glaisdale Dri. South 2M 187
Glamis Dri. Chor 6C 174
Glamis Dri. South 3A 168
Glamis Rd. Ley 7M 153
Glamorgan Gro. Burn 2M 123
Glasson. 1D 36
Glasson Clo. B'brn 7N 139
Glastonbury. Roch 5B 204
(off Spotland Rd.)
Glastonbury Av. Blac 8E 88
Glasven Rd. Liv 7L 223
Gleaves Av. Bolt 9N 199
Glebe Clo. Acc 3A 142
Glebe Clo. Burt 5H 7
Glebe Clo. Ful 5J 115
Glebe Clo. Liv 1A 222
Glebe Ct. K Lon 5E 8
(off Fairbank)
Glebe Ct. Lanc 8L 23
(off East Rd.)
Glebelands. Tar 1E 170
Glebe La. K'ham 5A 112
Glebe La. South 8F 148
Glebe Pl. South 7H 167
Glebe Rd. Skel 4L 219
Glebe St. Burn 5E 124
Glebe St. Gt Har 4J 121
Glebe, The. Ley 7G 152
Gledhill St. Todm 1L 165
Gledhill Way. Brom X 4G 198
Gledstone Rd. W Mar 6G 53
Glegside Rd. Liv 8M 223
Glenapp Av. Blac 3F 108
Glenarden Av. T Clev 3E 62
Glen Av. Todm 9J 147
Glenavon Dri. Roch 2A 204
Glenborough Av. Bacup 7G 162
Glenbrook Clo. B'brn 8J 139
Glenburn Rd. Skel 8J 211
Glencarron Clo. Hodd 7F 158
Glencoe Av. Blac 1G 89
Glencoe Av. Hodd 6E 158
Glencoe Pl. Roch 6A 204
Glen Cotts. Earby 2F 78
Glencourse Dri. Ful 4M 115
Glencoyne Dri. Bolt 7D 198
Glencoyne Dri. South 9A 148
Glen Cres. Bacup 7E 162
Glencroft. Eux 3L 173
Glencross Pl. Blac 2E 108
Glendale Av. Los H 7M 135
Glendale Clo. Blac 6F 62
Glendale Clo. Burn 6E 124
Glendale Clo. Ley 8L 153
Glendale Clo. Poul F 8J 63
Glendale Cres. Los H 7M 135
Glendale Dri. Mel 7F 118
Glendale Gro. Liv 5M 223
(off Dorchester Dri.)
Glendale Gro. Rib 7N 115
Glendene Pk. Clay D 4M 119
Glenden Foot. Roch 3A 204
Glendor Rd. Burn 4J 125
Glen Dri. App B 4H 213
Gleneagles Av. Hodd 6E 158
Gleneagles Clo. Liv 4J 223
Gleneagles Ct. B'brn 5C 140
Gleneagles Ct. K'ham 5N 111
Gleneagles Dri. Eux 1N 173
Gleneagles Dri. Ful 2E 114
Gleneagles Dri. More 2D 22
Gleneagles Dri. Old L 4C 100
Gleneagles Dri. Pen 2D 134
Gleneagles Dri. South 1B 206
Gleneagles Way. Ram 9G 180
Glen Eldon Rd. Lyth A 1E 128
Glenfield Av. Blac 5E 62
Glenfield Clo. B'brn 1B 140
Glenfield Pk. Bus. Cen.
B'brn 1B 140
Glenfield Pk. Ind. Est. B'brn 9B 120
Glenfield Pk. Ind. Est. Nels 1L 105
Glenfield Rd. Nels 1K 105
Glen Gdns. Roch 3C 204
Glengarry. Lyth A 5B 130
Glen Gth. Barn 1A 78
Glengreave Av. Rams 6M 119
Glen Gro. Rib 4B 116
Glenholme Gdns. Poul F 9H 63
Glenholm Rd. Liv 3B 222
Glenluce Cres. B'brn 5D 140
Glenluce Dri. Pres 9B 116
Glenmarsh Way. Liv 9B 206
Glenmere Cres. T Clev 4C 62
Glenmore. Clay W 4C 154
Glenmore Av. T Clev 1H 63
Glenmore Clo. Acc 6D 142
Glenmore Clo. Roch 8J 203
Glenmore Rd. Ram 3E 200
Glen Pk. Dri. Hesk B 3B 150
Glenpark Dri. South 2A 168
Glen Rd. Ross 7D 162
Glenrose Ter. South 9G 167
Glenroy Av. Col 5A 86
Glen Royd. Roch 4N 203
Glenroyd Clo. Blac 7E 88
Glenroyd Dri. Burs 9C 190
Glenshiels Av. Hodd 6E 158
Glenside. App B 2E 212
Glen Sq. Burn 7D 124
Glen St. Bacup 7J 163
Glen St. Blac 6E 88
Glen St. Burn 3C 124
Glen St. Col 5A 86
Glen Ter. Ross 7D 162
Glen Ter. Todm 8H 147
Glen, The. B'brn 1L 157
Glen, The. Cat 3H 25
Glen, The. Kno S 9L 41
Glen, The. Rib 7B 116
Glen, The. Todm 9J 147
Glen Top. 7E 162
Glentworth Clo. Liv 2C 222
Glentworth Rd. E. More 5D 22
Glentworth Rd. W. More 5C 22
Glen Vw. L'boro 7M 185
Glen Vw. Whitw 4N 183
Glen Vw. Av. Hey 1K 27
Glenview Clo. Rib 6C 116
Glenview Ct. Rib 6C 116
(in two parts)
Glen Vw. Cres. Hey 1K 27
Glen Vw. Dri. Hey 1K 27
Glen Vw. Rd. Burn 7C 124
Glen Vw. St. Todm 7F 146
Glen Way. Brier 5E 104
Glen Way. Liv 4L 223
Glenway. Pen 4F 134
Glenwood St. Blac 5D 88
Global Way. Dar 2A 158
Globe La. Eger 2D 198
Globe, The. Burt 6G 7
Glossop Clo. Blac 5C 62
Gloucester Av. Acc 1N 141
Gloucester Av. Blac 6D 88
Gloucester Av. Clay M 6M 121
Gloucester Av. Far 4M 153
Gloucester Av. Lanc 3L 29
Gloucester Av. Roch 1G 205
Gloucester Av. T Clev 8D 54
Gloucester Ct. Blac 6D 88
Gloucester Dri. Hey 5M 21
Gloucester Rd.
Bkdle & South 9F 166
Gloucester Rd. B'brn 3C 140
Gloucester Rd. Chor 9E 174
Gloucester Rd. Lyth A 4K 129
Gloucester Rd. Rish 8F 120
Gloucester Rd. Wig 5M 221
Glover Clo. Ley 9C 152
Glover Rd. Cop 6N 193
Glovers Bridge. 1E 210
Glover's Brow. Liv 6H 223
Glovers Ct. Pres 1J 135
Glover St. Hor 9C 196
Glover St. Pres 1K 135
Glynn St. Chu 1M 141
Gnat Bank Fold. Roch 8K 203
Godiva St. Burn 9E 104
Godley St. Burn 3F 124
Godwin Av. Blac 7E 88
Goe La. Frec 1N 131
Goffa Mill. Garg 4M 53
(off Church La.)
Goit Pl. Roch 6C 204
Goitside. Nels 1J 105
Goit St. B'brn 6K 139
Golbourne St. Pres 8L 115
Goldacre La. Gt Har 1G 121
Goldburn Clo. Ing 3C 114
Golden Hill. 5K 153
Golden Hill. Ley 5L 153
Golden Hill La. Ley 5H 153
Golden Way. Pen 6E 134
Goldfield Av. Burn 3K 125
Goldfinch Ct. Chor 9B 174
Goldfinch Dri. Bury 9A 202
Goldfinch Grn. Burn 4A 124
Goldfinch St. Pres 7L 115
Goldhey St. B'brn 1A 140
Goldsboro Av. Blac 7F 88
Goldshaw Ct. Newc P 8A 84
Goldstone Dri. T Clev 4F 62
Golf Vw. Ing 3D 114
Golgotha. 1M 29
Golgotha Rd. Lanc 1L 29
Gonder La. Clau B 8H 61
Goodenber Cres. Ben 6L 19
(off Lakeber Dri.)
Goodenber Rd. Ben 6L 19
Goodhall Clo. Earby 2E 78
Goodier St. Pres 9M 115
Good Intent. Miln 8K 205
Goodlad St. Bury 9G 201
Goodmickle La. Man 2C 8
Goodrich. Roch 7B 204
Goodshaw. 8L 143
Goodshaw Av. B'brn 9M 119
Goodshaw Av. Ross 7M 143
Goodshaw Av. N. Ross 6M 143
Goodshaw Chapel. 7N 143
Goodshaw Clo. B'brn 9M 119
Goodshaw Fold. 6L 143
Goodshaw Fold Clo. Raw 6M 143
Goodshaw Fold Rd. Ross 6L 143
Goodshaw La. Ross 8M 143
Goodshaw La. Stone 7G 143
Good St. Pres 1H 135
Goodwood Av. Blac 1D 88
Goodwood Av. Ful 2J 115
Goodwood Av. Slyne 9K 15
Goodwood Ct. Lanc 3M 29
Goodwood Rd. Lanc 3M 29
Goosebutts La. Clith 4M 81
Goosecote Hill. Eger 3E 198
Goosefoot Clo. Sam 1M 137
Goose Foot La. Sam 2L 137
Goose Green. 4J 151
Goose Grn. Av. Cop 4B 194
Goose Hill St. Bacup 4K 163
Goose Ho. La. Dar 3A 158
Gooselands. Rath 7M 35
Goose La. Chip 6G 70
Goose La. Roch 5C 204
Goose La. Traw 9E 86
Goose La. Cotts. Chip 6G 70
Gooseleach La. S'stne 1D 122
Goosnargh. 4N 95
Goosnargh La. Goos 3K 95
Gordale Clo. Barn 2L 77
Gordale Clo. Blac 1G 108
Gordon Av. Acc 4N 141
Gordon Av. Mag 8B 216
Gordon Av. South 5J 167
Gordon Av. T Clev 1H 63
Gordon M. South 5J 167
Gordon Rd. Fltwd 1F 54
Gordon Rd. Lyth A 4K 129
Gordon Rd. Nels 1G 105
Gordonstoun Cres. Orr 4J 221
Gordonstoun Pl. B'brn 5K 139
Gordonstoun Pl. T Clev 1G 63
Gordon St. Bacup 3K 163
Gordon St. Blac 9B 88
Gordon St. Burn 2D 124
Gordon St. Bury 9K 201
Gordon St. Chor 7F 174
Gordon St. Chu 3L 141
Gordon St. Clay M 7N 121
Gordon St. Col 6B 86
Gordon St. Dar 4A 158
Gordon St. Miln 9L 205
Gordon St. Pres 8H 115
(in two parts)
Gordon St. Roch 8D 204
Gordon St. Ross 5L 161
Gordon St. South 6H 167
Gordon St. Todm 2M 165
Gordon St. Wors 3M 125
Gordon Ter. Lanc 2L 29
Gordon Way. South 6J 167
(off Gordon St.)
Gore Dri. Augh 9K 209
Gores Rd. Know I 9N 223
Gore St. Wig 5L 221
Goring St. Chor 7F 174
Gorple Grn. Wors 4M 125
Gorple Rd. Wors 4M 125
Gorple St. Burn 7J 105
Gorrell Clo. Newc P 9B 84
Gorrells Clo. Roch 9A 204
Gorrell St. Roch 8D 204
Gorse Av. T Clev 9F 54
Gorse Clo. Tar 9E 150
Gorse Clo. Whit W 1G 175
Gorsefield. Liv 6A 206

Green St.—Hammond Rd.

Green St. Ram 3K 181
Green St. Ross 4N 161
Green St. Wals 9E 200
Green St. E. Dar 6A 158
Greensward Clo. Stand 3L 213
Greensway. Brough 7F 94
Green Ter. Wors 4M 125
(off Wallstreams La.)
Green, The. Bolt S 4L 15
Green, The. Col 5C 86
Green, The. Dar 6A 158
Green, The. E'ston 7E 172
Green, The. G'mnt 4E 200
Green, The. Hth C 3H 195
Green, The. Hell 1D 52
Green, The. Hesk B 4C 150
Green, The. Nels 9M 85
Green, The. Over K 1E 16
(off Kellet Rd.)
Green, The. Parb 2M 211
Green, The. Rib 7B 116
Green, The. Roch 9N 203
Green, The. Set 3N 35
Green, The. Silv 9H 5
Green, The. Weet 8E 90
Green, The. Wig 4L 221
(in two parts)
Greenthorn Cres. Rib 7C 116
Greenthorne Clo. Tur 7L 179
Greenthorne Ter. Dar 7A 158
(off Ashworth Ter.)
Greenthorne Ter. Dar 5M 157
(off Avondale Rd.)
Greenvale. Roch 5J 203
Greenvale. Shev 8J 213
Greenvale Cotts. L'boro 6N 185
Greenville Dri. Liv 1B 222
Green Wlk. Earby 4D 78
Green Wlk. South 8D 186
Green Way. Blac 2F 108
Green Way. Bolt 9G 199
Green Way. Catt 9A 60
Greenway. E'ston 7E 172
Greenway. Ful 2G 115
Greenway. Hor 9G 197
Greenway. Pen 4E 134
Greenway Av. Skel 4M 219
Greenway Clo. Bolt 9G 199
Greenway Clo. Skel 1J 219
Greenway M. Ram 1H 201
Greenways. Bil 8G 221
Greenways. Lyth A 2H 129
Greenways. Over K 1F 16
Greenways. Tar 6D 150
Greenway St. Dar 4N 157
Greenwich Clo. Roch 7K 203
Greenwich Dri. Lyth A 3K 129
Greenwood. Bam B 2D 154
Greenwood. Catt 1N 67
Greenwood Av. Blac 8D 88
Greenwood Av. Bolt S 7K 15
Greenwood Av. Wig 4N 221
Greenwood Clo. Augh 2H 217
Greenwood Clo. Lyth A 4L 129
Greenwood Ct. Bolt S 7K 15
Greenwood Ct. Ley 5K 153
Greenwood Cres. Bolt S 7K 15
Greenwood Dri. Bolt S 7K 15
Greenwood Gdns. South 9G 166
Greenwood Pl. L'boro 9L 185
(off Hare Hill Rd.)
Greenwood Rd. Stand 2N 213
Greenwoods La. Bolt 9M 199
Greenwood St. Bam B 7A 136
Greenwood St. L'boro 9L 185
Greenwood St. Pres 1L 135
Greenwood St. Roch 6C 204
Greenwood Va. Bolt 9E 198
Greetby Hill. Orm 7M 209
Greetby Pl. Skel 3L 219
Gregareth Clo. Lanc 6G 22
Gregory Av. Blac 6C 62
Gregory Fold. Ross 8F 160
Gregory La. Hals 9N 187
Gregory Mdw. Gars 5M 59
Gregory Pl. Lyth A 5N 129
Gregory's Ct. Lanc 3L 29
Gregson Clo. Blac 3F 108
Gregson Dri. Fltwd 2F 54
Gregson Lane. 6G 137
Gregson La. Hogh 5D 136
Gregson Rd. Lanc 9L 23
Gregson St. B'brn 3L 139
Gregson St. Dar 7A 158
Gregson St. Lyth A 5N 129
Gregson Way. Ful 4L 115
Grenada Clo. Lwr D 1N 157
Grenfell Av. Blac 3E 88
Grenville Av. Lyth A 8E 108
Grenville Av. Walt D 6N 135
Grenville Wlk. L'boro 5M 185
Gresham Rd. T Clev 2D 62
Gresham St. Ross 6D 162
Gresley Ct. Lanc 1K 29
Gresley Pl. Blac 9E 62
Gressingham. 5A 18
Gressingham Ct. Lanc 4L 29
(off Gressingham Dri.)
Gressingham Dri. Lanc 4L 29
Gressingham Ho. Lanc 4L 29
(off Gressingham Dri.)
Gressingham Wlk. Lanc 4M 29
Greta Heath. Burt L 4K 19
Greta Pl. Fltwd 2D 54
Greta Pl. Lanc 6J 23
Gretdale Av. Lyth A 9E 108
Gretna Cres. T Clev 3D 62
Gretna Rd. B'brn 8N 119
Gretna Wlk. B'brn 8N 119
Greyfriars Av. Ful 4G 114
Greyfriars Cres. Ful 4G 114
Greyfriars Dri. Pen 3F 134
Greyfriars Rd. South 7B 186
Grey Heights Vw. Chor 6G 175
(in three parts)
Greyhound Bri. Rd. Lanc 7K 23
Greymont Rd. Bury 7L 201
Greystock Av. Ful 3H 115
Greystock Clo. Bam B 8D 136
Greystock Pl. Ful 3H 115
Greystoke Av. B'brn 8F 138
Greystoke Ct. Blac 4B 108
Greystoke Dri. Bolt 7D 198
Greystoke Pl. Blac 4B 108
Greystokes. Augh 1J 217
Greystonegill. 6N 19
Greystonegill La. Ben 7N 19
Greystones. Ley 6E 152
Greystones Dri. Fence 2B 104
Grey St. Barfd 8H 85
Grey St. Burn 9E 104
Greythwaite Ct. Lanc 1H 29
Griffin. 5K 139
Griffin Clo. Acc 8E 122
Griffin Clo. Burn 5N 123
Griffin Clo. Bury 9N 201
Griffin Ct. B'brn 6K 139
Griffin St. B'brn 5J 139
Griffiths Dri. South 6M 167
Grimeford La. B'rod & And 9K 195
Grimeford Village. 7M 195
Grimes Cotts. Roch 4K 203
Grimeshaw La. Lanc 5A 24
Grimes St. Roch 4K 203
Grime St. Chor 8F 174
Grime St. Dar 5N 157
Grime St. Ram 1F 200
Grimrod Pl. Skel 4L 219
Grimsargh. 9F 96
Grimsargh St. Pres 8N 115
Grimshaw Green. 8N 191
Grimshaw Grn. La. Parb 8N 191
Grimshaw La. Orm 6K 209
Grimshaw Park. 5N 139
Grimshaw Pk. B'brn 5N 139
Grimshaw Retail Pk. B'brn 5M 139
Grimshaw Rd. Skel 3L 219
Grimshaw St. Acc 2N 141
Grimshaw St. Barfd 7H 85
Grimshaw St. Burn 4E 124
Grimshaw St. Chu 2L 141
Grimshaw St. Clay M 7M 121
Grimshaw St. Dar 8B 158
Grimshaw St. Gt Har 4J 121
Grimshaw St. Pres 1K 135
Grindlestone Hurst. Col 8N 85
Grindleton. 4A 74
Grindleton Brow. Grin 5A 74
Grindleton Clo. Blac 2H 89
Grindleton Gro. Burn 5H 125
Grindleton Rd. B'brn 4K 139
Grindleton Rd. W Brad 6L 73
Grindlow Wlk. Wig 9M 221
Grindrod La. Roch 3D 184
Grindrod St. Roch 4B 204
Gringley Rd. More 5C 22
Grinstead Clo. South 4F 186
Grisedale Av. B'brn 6C 140
Grisedale Dri. Burn 1N 123
Grisedale Pl. Chor 9D 174
Grisedale Rd. Roch 9M 203
Grizedale Av. Gars 6M 59
Grizedale Av. Lanc 8M 29
Grizedale Av. Poul F 8J 63
Grizedale Clo. Clay M 7L 121
Grizedale Clo. Rib 7B 116
Grizedale Ct. Blac 5E 88
(off Felgate Brow)
Grizedale Cres. Rib 7B 116
Grizedale Pl. Hey 8M 21
Grizedale Pl. Rib 7B 116
Grizedale Rd. Blac 9J 89
Grizedale Rd. Lanc 6L 23
Grosvenor Clo. South 2E 186
Grosvenor Ct. Carn 9N 11
Grosvenor Ct. Lyth A 8G 109
Grosvenor Ct. T Clev 1C 62
Grosvenor Gdns. South 2F 186
Grosvenor Pl. Ash R 7E 114
Grosvenor Pl. Carn 9N 11
Grosvenor Pl. South 2F 186
Grosvenor Rd.
Bkdle & South 1D 186
Grosvenor Rd. Carn 9A 12
Grosvenor Rd. Chor 8D 174
Grosvenor Rd. Hey 5L 21
Grosvenor Rd. Mag 4B 222
Grosvenor Rd. Poul F 7K 63
Grosvenor St. Blac 5C 88
Grosvenor St. Burn 2D 124
Grosvenor St. Col 6C 86
Grosvenor St. Lyth A 5B 130
Grosvenor St. Pres 1L 135
Grosvenor Way. B'brn 3M 139
Groundwork Countryside Cen. 6K 161
Grouse St. Roch 4C 204
Grove Av. Adl 6J 195
Grove Av. Longt 8K 133
Grove Ct. Osw 5J 141
Grove Cres. Adl 6J 195
Grove La. Pad 9J 103
Grove Mead. Liv 1E 222
Grove Mill Development Cen.
E'ston 9F 172
Grove Pk. Orm 5L 209
Grove Pk. South 6M 167
Grove Pk. Gdns. Set 3N 35
(off High Hill Gro. St.)
Grove Rd. Uph 3F 220
Grove Rd. Walt D 2M 135
Grove St. Acc 2N 141
Grove St. Bacup 4L 163
Grove St. Bam B 8B 136
Grove St. Barfd 8H 85
Grove St. B'brn 6M 139
Grove St. Burn 4B 124
Grove St. Earby 2E 78
Grove St. Ley 7G 152
Grove St. Lyth A 1F 128
Grove St. More 4N 21
Grove St. Nels 2J 105
Grove St. Osw 5J 141
Grove St. Roch 8B 204
Grove St. South 1G 187
Grove Ter. South 9G 167
Grove, The. App B 2F 212
Grove, The. Ash R 8E 114
Grove, The. Augh & Orm 4H 217
Grove, The. Barn 1N 77
(off Eastwood St.)
Grove, The. Bils 6D 68
Grove, The. Burn 3N 123
Grove, The. Carn 9M 11
Grove, The. Chor 4E 174
Grove, The. Clith 2M 81
Grove, The. Lanc 1L 29
Grove, The. Pen 4E 134
Grove, The. Ruf 2E 190
Grove, The. T Clev 9E 54
Grove, The. Whal 5J 101
Grovewood. South 9E 166
Grovewood Dri. App B 4H 213
Grundy Art Gallery. 4B 88
Grundy Clo. South 9L 167
Grundy Homes. South 9L 167
Grundy M. Blac 2C 108
Grundy's La. Chor 4E 194
Grundy St. Ley 5K 153
Grunsagill. 3K 51
Guardian Clo. Ful 5K 115
Gubberford La. Gars & Scor 1N 59
Guernsey Av. B'brn 7N 139
Guide. 8D 140
Guide La. High 3M 103
Guide Rd. Hesk B 9B 132
Guildford Av. Blac 5C 62
Guildford Av. Chor 2G 175
Guildford Rd. Pres 1K 135
Guildford Rd. South 5G 187
Guildford St. Roch 6D 204
(in two parts)
Guildford Way. Poul F 5J 63
Guild Hall. 1K 135
Guild Hall Arc. Pres 1K 135
(off Lancaster Rd.)
Guildhall St. Pres 1J 135
Guild Row. Pres 1K 135
Guild St. Brom X 7G 199
Guild Trad. Est. Pres 8L 115
Guild Way. Pres 1G 134
Guilford St. Brier 5F 104
Guinea Hall La. South 9F 148
Guiness Ho. Roch 7E 204
Guiseley Clo. Bury 5K 201
Gulf La. Pil 5N 43
Gummers Howe Wlk. Carn 1B 16
Gunsmith Pl. Burn 3E 124
Gurney St. B'brn 5J 139
Gutter La. Ram 7G 181
Guy St. Pad 9H 103
Guysyke. Col 7N 85
Gynn Av. Blac 2B 88
Gynn Sq. Blac 2B 88

H

Habergham. 2L 123
Habergham Dri. Burn 1L 123
Habergham St. Pad 9H 103
Hackensall Rd. Kno S 9L 41
Hackford Clo. Bury 8J 201
Hacking Clo. Lang 9C 100
Hacking Dri. L'rdge 5H 97
Hacking St. Dar 6A 158
Hacking St. Nels 9K 85
Hacklands Av. Lea 8M 113
Haddings La. Newc P 1M 103
Haddon Ct. Blac 6C 62
Haddon Pl. Ful 6G 114
Haddon Rd. Blac 6C 62
Haddon St. Roch 9B 204
Hadlee Ter. Lanc 7H 23
Hadleigh Clo. Bolt 7G 198
Hadleigh Rd. Liv 9L 223
Hadleigh Rd. Poul F 5J 63
Hadrian Rd. More 5E 22
Hagg La. St M 3A 66
Hagg St. Col 7N 85
Haig Av. Ash R 7G 114
Haig Av. Lanc 8H 23
Haig Av. Ley 6J 153
Haig Av. South 9L 167
(in three parts)
Haig Av. Tar 8E 150
Haigh Clo. Chor 7C 174
Haigh Ct. South 8M 167
Haigh Cres. Chor 7C 174
Haigh Cres. Liv 7B 216
Haigh Hall Clo. Ram 1G 201
Haigh St. Roch 8D 204
Haighton Ct. Ful 2K 115
Haighton Dri. Ful 4A 116
Haighton Green. 8B 96
Haighton Grn. La. Haig 9M 95
Haighton Top. 9M 95
Haig Rd. Blac 9B 88
Haileybury Av. Liv 8C 222
Hailsham Clo. Bury 6H 201
Hail St. Ram 1F 200
Hailwood St. Roch 9B 204
Hala Cres. Lanc 4L 29
Hala Gro. Lanc 4L 29
Hala Hill. Lanc 4M 29
Hala Rd. Lanc 4L 29
Hala Sq. Scot 4L 29
Halcyon Clo. Roch 3M 203
Haldane Rd. Dar 3M 157
Haldane St. Burn 8F 104
Halden Rd. Hey 5M 21
Hale. 1B 6
Halecarr Gro. Hey 7M 21
Hale Carr La. Hey 7M 21
Hale Nook. 7F 56
Hales Rushes Rd. Pil 7H 57
Hale St. Burn 5E 124
Half Acre. Los H 8K 135
Half Acre Dri. Roch 7N 203
Half Acre La. Roch 7M 203
Half Acre M. Roch 7M 203
Half Acre Rd. Roch 7M 203
Halford Pl. T Clev 4E 62
Halfpenny Bri. Ind. Est.
Roch 7D 204
Halfpenny La. Hesk 2D 192
Halfpenny La. L'rdge 3G 97
Halfpenny La. Uph 2E 218
Halifax Rd. Brclf 7L 105
Halifax Rd. Brier 5F 104
Halifax Rd. Nels 4H 105
Halifax Rd. Roch 4E 204
Halifax Rd. South 8C 186
Halifax Rd. Todm 2L 165
Halifax St. Blac 7F 88
Hallam Cres. Nels 2L 105
Hallam La. M'ton 5M 27
Hallam Rd. Nels 1K 105
Hallam St. Acc 8N 121
Hallam Way. Blac 2L 109
Hall Av. Blac 9C 88
Hallbridge Gdns. Uph 3E 220
Hall Brow Clo. Orm 8N 209
Hall Carr. 6M 161
Hall Carr La.
Longt & Walm B 8G 133
Hall Carr Rd. Ross 6M 161
Hall Clo. Cat 2G 25
Hall Clo. Ross 1M 161
Hall Clo. Shev 6K 213
Hall Coppice, The. Eger 3D 198
Hall Cft. Hut 6A 134
Hallcroft. Skel 1N 219
Hallcroft Gdns. Miln 7H 205
Hall Cft. Head. Hut 6A 134
Hall Cross. 8M 111
Hall Dri. Cat 2G 25
Hall Dri. Liv 7K 223
Hall Dri. M'ton 5M 27
Hall Dri. More 4E 22
Halley Rd. Dar 4M 157
Halley St. Bacup 9L 145
Hallfield La. Neth K 4A 16
Hallfield Rd. Gt Har 3K 121
Hallfold. 6N 183
Hall Fold. Whitw 6M 183
Hall Gdns. Roch 3N 203
Hall Gth. Gdns. Over K 9F 12
Hall Ga. Chor 5C 174
Hallgate Hill. Newt B 7B 50
Hall Ga. La. Pre & Stalm 3B 56
Hall Greaves Clo. Over 7B 28
Hall Green. 4E 220
Hall Grn. Uph 4E 220
Hall Grn. Clo. Uph 4E 220
(in two parts)
Hall Grn. La. Hesk 2C 192
Hall Gro. M'ton 5M 27
Hall Hill. White 2L 71
Hall Hill St. Pad 9H 103
(off St Giles St.)
Halliday Ct. L'boro 1H 205
Halling Pl. Todm 3K 165
Hall I' Th' Wood. 9H 199
Hall i' th' Wood. Bolt 9G 199
Hall i' th Wood Mus. 9G 199
Halliwell Ct. Chor 7E 174
(off Halliwell St.)
Halliwell Cres. Hut 6B 134
Halliwell Ho. Walt D 5B 136
Halliwell La. Chor 2E 174
Halliwell Pl. Chor 7E 174
Halliwell St. Acc 6C 142
Halliwell St. Chor 7E 174
Halliwell St. Firg & Miln 6H 205
Halliwell St. L'boro 9M 185
Halliwell St. Roch 5B 204
(in two parts)
Hall La. App B 2E 212
Hall La. Bic 8C 218
Hall La. Gt Ecc 7N 65
Hall La. Hor 3B 196
Hall La. Ince B 7F 214
Hall La. Kirkby 8J 223
Hall La. Lath 7E 210
Hall La. Ley 4J 153
Hall La. Liv & Mag 2B 222
Hall La. Longt 9H 133
Hall La. Lyd 4A 216
Hall La. Maw 2A 192
Hall La. Pem 7J 221
Hall La. St M 5G 66
Hall La. Sim 3L 223
Hall Meadows. Traw 8E 86
Hallmoor Clo. Augh 1H 217
Hall More Cvn. Pk. Hale 4B 6
Hallows Clo. St M 5G 66
Hallows St. Burn 8E 104
Hall Pk. Lanc 3K 29
Hall Pk. Av. Burn 5K 125
Hall Pk. Dri. Lyth A 2K 129
Hall Rd. Ful 4H 115
Hall Rd. Pen 5H 135
Hall Rd. Scar 6F 188
Hall Rd. Traw 8E 86
Hallroyd Cres. Todm 2M 165
Hallroyd Pl. Todm 2M 165
Hallroyd Rd. Todm 1M 165
Hall St. Ash R 8F 114
Hall St. Bacup 4K 163
Hall St. B'brn 6M 139
Hall St. Burn 3E 124
Hall St. Bury 3H 201
(Railway St. W.)
Hall St. Bury 9H 201
(Tottington Rd.)
Hall St. Clith 4L 81
Hall St. Col 7A 86
Hall St. Has 5G 161
Hall St. More 2B 22
Hall St. Raw 4M 161
Hall St. South 7J 167
Hall St. Todm 2L 165
Hall St. Wals 9E 200
Hall St. Whitw 6N 183
Hall St. Wors 4L 125
Hallwell St. Burn 1E 124
Hallwood Clo. Burn 6F 104
Hallwood Rd. Chor 9C 174
Halmote Av. High 5L 103
Halsall. 3B 208
Halsall Bldgs. South 7K 167
Halsall Clo. Bury 7L 201
Halsall Ct. Orm 6J 209
Halsall Dri. More 2F 22
Halsall Hall Dri. Hals 3A 208
Halsall La. Form & Liv 9A 206
Halsall La. Hals 7C 208
Halsall La. Orm 6J 209
Halsall Rd. Hals 3B 208
Halsall Rd. South 5F 186
Halsall Sq. Gt Ecc 6N 65
Halsbury St. Pres 2K 135
Halstead Clo. Barfd 7H 85
Halstead La. Barfd 7H 85
Halstead Rd. Rib 4N 115
Halsteads Cotts. Set 3N 35
(off Birchwood Clo.)
Halstead St. Burn 4D 124
Halstead St. Bury 8M 201
Halstead St. Wors 3L 125
Halstead Wlk. Bury 8M 201
Halstead Wlk. Liv 9H 223
Halton. 1B 24
Halton Av. Ley 5N 153
Halton Av. T Clev 8E 54
Halton Chase. W'head 8C 210
Halton Ct. More 5B 22
Halton Gdns. Blac 1F 108
Halton Gdns. T Clev 8F 54
Halton Green. 1E 24
Halton Pk. Halt 9G 16
Halton Pl. L'rdge 2K 97
Halton Pl. Rib 5B 116
Halton Rd. Lanc 5L 23
Halton Rd. Liv 8C 216
Halton Rd. Neth K 4B 16
Halton St. Weet 4D 90
Halton West. 3C 52
Halton Wood. Liv 7G 222
Halvard Av. Bury 7L 201
Halvard Ct. Bury 7L 201
Hambledon St. Pad 1J 123
Hambledon Ter. Burn 2L 123
Hambledon Vw. Burn 2L 123
Hambledon Vw. S'stne 9C 102
Hambleton. 2B 64
Hambleton Clo. Longt 7K 133
Hambleton Country Pk. Hamb 8C 56
Hambleton Dri. Pen 6H 135
Hambleton Moss Side. 2D 64
Hambleton Ter. High 4L 103
Hameldon App. Burn 4B 124
Hameldon Av. Acc 6D 142
Hameldon Clo. Hap 6H 123
Hameldon Rd. Hap 7H 123
Hameldon Rd. Ross 6M 143
Hameldon Vw. Gt Har 4K 121
Hamer Av. B'brn 3D 140
Hamer Av. Ross 7M 143
Hamer Ct. Roch 4E 204
Hamer Hall Cres. Roch 3E 204
Hamer La. Roch 4E 204
Hamer Rd. Ash R 6G 114
Hamer St. Ram 3G 200
Hamer St. Ross 5M 161
Hamers Wood Dri. Catt 1A 68
Hamer Ter. Bury 2H 201
(off Ruby St.)
Hamilton Clo. Lytham 4C 130
Hamilton Ct. Blac 6C 88
Hamilton Dri. Lanc 5G 22
Hamilton Gro. Rib 6A 116
Hamilton Rd. Barfd 1G 104
Hamilton Rd. Chor 7D 174
Hamilton Rd. Col 9L 85
Hamilton Rd. More 2G 22
Hamilton Rd. Rib 5N 115
Hamilton St. B'brn 6L 139
Hamilton St. Bolt 8E 198
Hamilton St. Bury 9L 201
Hamlet Clo. B'brn 5K 139
Hamlet Gro. Whar 6D 92
Hamlet Rd. Fltwd 9F 40
Hamlet, The. Hth C 4H 195
Hamlet, The. Lyth A 7F 108
Hammerton Dri. Hell 1D 52
Hammerton Grn. Bacup 4K 163
Hammerton Hall Clo. Lanc 4J 23
Hammerton Hall La. Lanc 4H 23
Hammerton Mere. 3E 50
Hammerton Pl. Blac 2G 89
Hammerton St. Bacup 3K 163
Hammerton St. Burn 4D 124
Hammerton Ter. Todm 1L 165
Hammond Av. Bacup 7H 163
Hammond Ct. Pres 8H 115
Hammond Dri. Read 8B 102
Hammond Rd. Know I 7A 224

Hammond's Row—Hawthorns, The

Hammond's Row. Pres 1K 135
Hammond St. Nels 3K 105
Hammond St. Pres 8G 115
(Bold St., in three parts)
Hammond St. Pres 7J 115
(Garstang Rd.)
Hamnet Clo. Bolt 8G 199
Hampden Av. Dar 8B 158
Hampden Pl. Wig 2N 221
Hampden Rd. Ley 5K 153
Hampden St. Burn 5F 124
Hampden St. Hap 5H 123
Hampden St. Roch 7C 204
Hampden Wlk. Wig 2N 221
Hampsfell Dri. More 5B 22
Hampshire Clo. Wilp 2A 120
Hampshire Pl. Blac 3F 108
Hampshire Rd. Rish 8G 121
Hampshire Rd. Walt D 5N 135
Hampson Av. Ley 6N 153
Hampson Cotts. Hamp 6M 37
Hampson Green. 5M 37
Hampson Gro. Pre 9N 41
Hampson La. Hamp 5M 37
Hampson Ter. Gt Ecc 6A 66
Hampstead Clo. Lyth A 2L 129
Hampstead M. Blac 3C 88
Hampstead Rd. Rib 7N 115
Hampstead Rd. Stand 3N 213
Hampton Clo. Chor 6D 174
Hampton Ct. Lyth A 9J 109
Hampton Gro. Bury 7L 201
Hampton Pl. T Clev 9E 54
Hampton Rd. Blac 1C 108
Hampton Rd. Hey 5M 21
Hampton Rd. South 1H 187
Hampton St. Ash R 7F 114
Hampton St. Hor 9C 196
Hanbury St. Ash R 8F 114
Hancock St. B'brn 5K 139
(in two parts)
Handbridge, The. Ful 4H 115
Handel St. Whitw 6M 183
Hand La. Maw 9C 172
Handley Rd. Blac 4C 88
Handley St. Roch 5A 204
Handshaw Dri. Pen 6K 135
Hands La. Roch 6L 203
Handsworth Ct. Blac 3C 88
Handsworth Rd. Blac 3C 88
Handsworth Wlk. South 2M 187
Hanging Grn. La. Hest B 8J 15
Hanging Lees Clo. Miln 9M 205
Hanley Clo. Stalm 5B 56
Hanmer Pl. Lanc 1L 29
(off Avondale Rd.)
Hanmer Rd. Liv 8G 222
Hannah St. Acc 3A 142
Hannah St. Bacup 4L 163
Hannah St. Dar 6B 158
Hanover Ct. Burn 6B 124
Hanover Ct. Ing 3C 114
Hanover Cres. Blac 5C 62
Hanover St. Col 5A 86
Hanover St. L'boro 9K 185
Hanover St. More 3B 22
Hanover St. Pres 8J 115
Hanson St. Adl 7H 195
Hanson St. Bury 9L 201
Hanson St. Gt Har 5J 121
Hanson St. Rish 8J 121
Hanstock Clo. Orr 6H 221
Hants La. Orm 6K 209
Happy Mt. Ct. More 1F 22
Happy Mt. Dri. More 1E 22
Hapton. 5H 123
Hapton Rd. Pad 2H 123
Hapton St. Pad 1J 123
Hapton St. T Clev 8H 55
Hapton Way. Ross 6M 143
Harborne Wlk. G'mnt 4E 200
Harbour Av. W'ton 2K 131
Harbour La. Miln 8J 205
Harbour La. Tur 9K 179
Harbour La. W'ton 1K 131
Harbour La. Wheel 8L 155
Harbour La. N. Miln 7J 205
Harbour M. Ct. Brom X 5H 199
Harbour Trad. Est. Fltwd 2F 54
Harbour Way. Fltwd 1H 55
Harbury Av. South 9A 186
Harcles Dri. Ram 3G 200
Harcourt M. Hor 9C 196
Harcourt Rd. Acc 5C 142
Harcourt Rd. B'brn 2K 139
Harcourt Rd. Blac 1D 108
Harcourt Rd. Lanc 5J 23
Harcourt St. Bacup 4K 163
Harcourt St. Burn 4B 124
Harcourt St. Pres 8H 115
Hardacre. Nels 3J 105
Hardacre La. Rim 2B 76
Hardacre La. Whit W 1D 174
Hardacre St. Orm 6L 209
Hardaker Ct. Lyth A 2E 128
Hardcastle Clo. Bolt 7J 199
Hardcastle Gdns. Bolt 7J 199
Hardcastle Rd. Ful 6H 115
Harden Rd. Kel 6D 78
Hardhorn. 2K 89
Hardhorn Ct. Poul F 8K 63
Hardhorn Rd. Poul F 8K 63
Hardhorn Village. 2L 89
Hardhorn Way. Poul F 9K 63
Harding Rd. Burs 9B 190
Harding St. Adl 5K 195
Hard Knott Ri. Carn 1B 16
Hardlands Av. More 4F 22
Hardman Av. Ross 6M 161
Hardman Clo. B'brn 4F 140
Hardman Clo. Ross 8D 162
Hardman Dri. Ross 8D 162
Hardmans. Brom X 6F 198
Hardman's La. Brom X 5F 198
Hardman St. B'brn 5K 139
Hardman St. Blac 4C 88
Hardman St. Bury 9L 201
(in two parts)
Hardman St. Miln 8K 205
Hardman's Yd. Pres 1J 135
Hardman Ter. Bacup 7H 163
Hardman Way. Dar 6A 158
Hardsough La. Ram 1H 181
Hardwen Av. Lea 8N 113
Hardwicke St. Roch 9B 204
Hardwick St. Pres 9K 115
Hardy Av. Barn 1L 77
Hardy Av. Brier 4F 104
Hardy Clo. Roch 9C 204
Hardy Ct. Nels 2J 105
Hardy Dri. Chor 7C 174
Hardy Mill Rd. Bolt 9M 199
Hardy St. B'brn 8N 119
Hardy St. Brier 4F 104
Harebell Clo. B'brn 8E 138
Harebell Clo. Liv 2A 214
Harebell Clo. Roch 2A 204
Hare Clough Clo. B'brn 5N 139
Hareden Brook Clo. B'brn 5N 139
Hareden Rd. Rib 7B 116
Haredon Clo. Bam B 8B 136
Harefield Av. Roch 8D 204
Harefield Ri. Burn 1B 124
(in two parts)
Harehill Av. Todm 1K 165
Hare Hill Ct. L'boro 8L 185
Hare Hill Rd. L'boro 8K 185
Harehill St. Todm 1K 165
Hareholme. 6B 162
Hareholme La. Ross 6B 162
Hare Runs. 4J 23
Hares La. South 4B 188
(in two parts)
Harestone Av. Chor 9C 174
Hare St. Roch 8C 204
Harewood. Chor 4D 174
Harewood Av. Blac 1G 88
Harewood Av. Hey 6M 21
Harewood Av. Lanc 4L 29
Harewood Av. Roch 3H 203
Harewood Av. S'stne 8D 102
Harewood Av. South 7C 186
Harewood Clo. Poul F 6J 63
Harewood Clo. Roch 4G 203
Harewood Dri. Roch 4G 203
Hare Wood Rd. Pres 7L 115
Harewood Rd. Roch 3G 203
Harewood Way. Roch 4G 203
Hargate Av. Roch 3L 203
Hargate Clo. Bury 3H 201
Hargate Rd. Liv 8L 223
Hargate Rd. T Clev 1J 63
Hargate Wlk. Liv 8L 223
Hargher St. Burn 4B 124
Hargreaves Av. Ley 7L 153
Hargreaves Ct. Clith 4J 81
Hargreaves Ct. Ing 5C 114
Hargreaves Ct. Ross 1D 162
Hargreaves Dri. Ross 5L 161
Hargreaves Fold La. Ross 9D 144
Hargreaves La. B'brn 5M 139
Hargreaves Rd. Osw 4H 141
Hargreaves St. Acc 3B 142
Hargreaves St. Brclf 7K 105
Hargreaves St. Burn 3D 124
Hargreaves St. Col 7M 85
Hargreaves St. Has 4G 160
Hargreaves St. Hodd 6F 158
Hargreaves St. Nels 2G 105
Hargreaves St. Roch 9N 203
Hargreaves St. Ross 2C 162
Hargreaves St. South 8J 167
Hargreaves St. T Clev 9H 55
Hargrove Av. Burn 9H 103
Hargrove Av. Pad 2B 124
Harland St. Ful 6G 115
Harland Way. Roch 3L 203
Harlech Av. Blac 9D 88
Harlech Clo. Has 6G 161
Harlech Dri. Ley 6M 153
Harlech Dri. Osw 4J 141
Harlech Gro. T Clev 1K 63
Harleston Rd. Liv 7M 223
Harleston Wlk. Liv 7M 223
Harle Syke. 7J 105
Harley Clo. L Bent 6K 19
Harley Rd. Blac 6E 88
Harley St. Burn 3A 124
Harley St. Todm 1L 165
Harley Wood. 9J 147
Harley Wood. Todm 8H 147
Harley Wood Vw. Todm 8H 147
(off Church St.)
Harling Bank. K Lon 6E 8
Harling Rd. Pres 8N 115
Harling St. Burn 3N 123
Harmuir Clo. Stand L 8N 213
Harold Av. Blac 3G 108
Harold Av. Burn 5A 124
Harold St. Burn 5B 124
Harold St. Col 7N 85
Harold St. Roch 3F 204
Harold Ter. Los H 8K 135
Harperley. Chor 4D 174
Harpers La. Chor 5F 174
Harpers La. Fence 2B 104
Harpers St. Chor 4F 174
Harper St. Barn 2L 77
Harper St. Roch 8B 204
Harridge Av. Roch 2N 203
(in two parts)
Harridge Bank. Roch 3N 203
Harridge La. Scar 4E 208
Harridge St. Roch 2N 203
Harridge, The. Roch 2N 203
Harrier Dri. B'brn 9L 119
Harriet St. Burn 5C 124
Harriet St. Roch 6D 204
Harrington Av. Blac 4B 108
Harrington Rd. Chor 6D 174
Harrington Rd. Hey 5M 21
Harrington St. Clay M 8N 121
Harrington St. Pres 9J 115
Harris Av. Blac 9D 88
Harris Ct. Clith 3L 81
Harris Mus. & Art Gallery. 1K 135
Harrison Av. T Clev 1H 63
Harrison Clo. Roch 4K 203
Harrison Cres. Hey 7L 21
Harrison Dri. Col 5N 85
Harrison Dri. Rainf 2K 225
Harrison La. Hut 6E 134
Harrison Rd. Adl 7H 195
Harrison Rd. Chor 8E 174
Harrison Rd. Ful 4H 115
Harrison St. Bacup 7M 163
Harrison St. Barn 2N 77
Harrison St. B'brn 4L 139
Harrison St. Blac 7C 88
Harrison St. Brclf 8K 105
Harrison St. Hor 9C 196
Harrison St. Ram 7H 181
Harrison St. Todm 7E 146
Harrison Trad. Est. Pres 8M 115
Harris Rd. Stand 1L 213
Harris St. Fltwd 9G 40
Harris St. Pres 1K 135
Harrock La. App B 8C 192
Harrock Rd. Ley 6N 153
Harrod Dri. South 2E 186
Harrogate Cres. Burn 8G 105
Harrogate Rd. Lyth A 1J 129
Harrogate Way. South 9B 148
Harrop Pl. Rib 5A 116
Harrow Av. Acc 1B 142
Harrow Av. Fltwd 1F 54
Harrow Av. Roch 7L 203
Harrow Clo. Orr 3J 221
Harrow Clo. Pad 3K 123
Harrowdale Pk. Halt 1C 24
Harrow Dri. B'brn 5B 140
Harrow Dri. Liv 8C 222
Harrow Gro. More 4F 22
Harrow Pl. Blac 4A 108
Harrow Pl. Lyth A 3K 129
Harrow Rd. Wig 2N 221
Harrowside. Blac 4B 108
Harrowside W. Blac 4A 108
Harrow Stiles La. Bacup 7J 145
Harry St. Osw 4L 141
Harry St. Barfd 8H 85
Harry St. Salt 5A 78
Harsnips. Skel 1N 219
Hartford Av. Blac 8D 88
Hartington Rd. Brins 7A 156
Hartington Rd. Dar 3M 157
Hartington Rd. Pres 1G 135
Hartington St. Brier 5F 104
Hartington St. Lanc 8M 23
Hartington St. Rish 8G 121
Hartington St. Traw 7E 86
Hartland. Skel 1N 219
Hartland Av. South 1A 168
Hartland Ct. Bolt 9E 198
(off Blackburn Rd.)
Hartlands Clo. Burn 7H 105
Hartlebury. Roch 7B 204
Hartley Av. Acc 5N 141
Hartley Cres. South 3F 186
Hartley Gro. Liv 5L 223
Hartley Gro. Orr 4L 221
Hartley Homes, The. Lane 5F 86
Hartley La. Roch 9B 204
Hartley Pl. Firg 6G 204
Hartley Rd. South 3F 186
Hartleys Ter. Col 7B 86
Hartley St. B'brn 2M 139
Hartley St. Burn 4A 124
Hartley St. Col 6A 86
Hartley St. Earby 3E 78
Hartley St. Firg 6G 205
Hartley St. Gt Har 3K 121
Hartley St. Has 4G 160
Hartley St. L'boro 9K 185
Hartley St. Nels 3J 105
Hartley St. Osw 4L 141
Hartley St. Ward 8F 184
Hartley St. Wig 5L 221
Hartley Ter. L'boro 9K 185
(off William St.)
Hartley Ter. Roch 9B 204
Hartmann St. Acc 2N 141
Hartshead. Skel 1N 219
Hart's La. Uph 3C 220
(in two parts)
Hart St. B'brn 4N 139
Hart St. Burn 3E 124
Hart St. South 8K 167
Hartwood. 4F 174
Hartwood Grn. Chor 3F 174
Hartwood Rd. South 7K 167
Harvard St. Roch 9D 204
Harvest Dri. Whit W 9E 154
Harvester Way. Boot 6A 222
Harvey Ct. L'boro 8M 185
Harvey Longworth Ct. Ross 7M 143
Harvey St. Bury 9H 201
Harvey St. Nels 1J 105
Harvey St. Osw 4J 141
Harvey St. Roch 3E 204
Harvington Dri. South 8A 186
Harwich Rd. Lyth A 8G 108
Harwin Clo. Roch 2A 204
Harwood. 9M 199
Harwood Av. Lyth A 9E 108
Harwood Bar. 4L 121
Harwood Clo. Stalm 5B 56
Harwood Cres. Tot 6D 200
Harwood Ga. B'brn 2A 140
Harwood Golf Course. 9A 200
Harwood La. Gt Har 3K 121
Harwood Lee. 8L 199
Harwood Mdw. Bolt 9M 199
Harwood New Rd. Gt Har 3L 121
Harwood Rd. B'brn 5D 120
Harwood Rd. Rish 7G 120
Harwood Rd. Tot 9B 200
Harwood's La. Hodd 6D 158
Harwood St. B'brn 1A 140
(in two parts)
Harwood St. Dar 5M 157
Harwood St. L'boro 9J 185
Harwood Va. Bolt 9L 199
Harwood Va. Ct. Bolt 9L 199
Harwood Wlk. Tot 6D 200
Hasgill Ct. Lanc 7J 23
Haskayne. 7M 207
Haslam Dri. Orm 5J 209
Haslam St. Bury 9M 201
Haslemere Av. Blac 7E 88
Haslemere Ind. Est. Ley 4J 153
Haslingden Old Rd. Ross 5J 161
Haslingden Rd. B'brn 5N 139
(in two parts)
Haslingden Rd.
B'brn & Guide 4D 140
Haslingden Rd. Ross 6H 161
Haslow Pl. Blac 3F 88
Hassall Dri. Elsw 1M 91
Hassam Heights. Hey 2L 27
Hassett Clo. Pres 2H 135
Hastings Av. Blac 6E 62
Hastings Av. W'ton 1K 131
Hastings Clo. B'brn 4C 140
Hastings Clo. T Clev 2J 63
Hastings Pl. Lyth A 5N 129
Hastings Rd. Ash R 8E 114
Hastings Rd. Frec 7N 111
Hastings Rd. Lanc 2K 29
Hastings Rd. Ley 5L 153
Hastings Rd. South 3E 186
Hastings Rd. T Clev 2J 63
Hastings St. Roch 8C 204
Hastings, The. Lanc 2K 29
(off Cheltenham Rd.)
Haston Lee Av. B'brn 6N 119
Hasty Brow Rd.
Hest B & Slyne 2H 23
Hatfield Av. Fltwd 2E 54
Hatfield Av. More 2F 22
Hatfield Clo. T Clev 1J 63
Hatfield Ct. More 2G 22
(off Hatfield Av.)
Hatfield Gdns. Fltwd 2E 54
Hatfield M. Fltwd 2E 54
Hatfield Rd. Acc 9C 122
Hatfield Rd. Rib 6A 116
Hatfield Rd. South 7C 186
Hatfield Wlk. Fltwd 2E 54
Hathaway. Blac 1E 108
Hathaway. Liv 3A 222
Hathaway Dri. Bolt 8G 199
Hathaway Fold. Pad 2J 123
Hathaway Rd. Fltwd 9E 40
Hathaway Rd. Lanc 5J 23
Hatlex Dri. Hest B 7J 15
Hatlex Hill. Hest B 7J 15
Hatlex La. Hest B 7J 15
Hattersley St. Burn 3C 124
Hatton Gro. Bolt 8G 198
Haugh. 9M 205
Haugh Av. S'stne 9D 102
Haugh Fold. Miln 9M 205
Haugh La. Miln 9M 205
Haugh Sq. Miln 9M 205
Haughs St. Burn 8F 104
Haunders La. Much H 5F 150
Havelock Clo. B'brn 5L 139
Havelock Rd. Bam B 9A 136
Havelock Rd. Pen 3H 135
Havelock St. B'brn 6K 139
Havelock St. Blac 6B 88
Havelock St. Burn 3N 123
Havelock St. Lanc 1L 29
Havelock St. Osw 5K 141
Havelock St. Pad 9H 103
Havelock St. Pres 7G 115
(in four parts)
Havenbrook Gro. Ram 2F 200
Haven Brow. Augh 3H 217
Haven Rd. Lyth A 5B 130
Haven St. Burn 4G 124
Haven St. Todm 2M 165
Haven Wlk. Liv 7B 216
Haverbreaks. 1J 29
Haverbreaks Pl. Lanc 1J 29
Haverbreaks Rd. Lanc 1J 29
Havercroft Clo. Wig 8N 221
Haverholt Clo. Col 6N 85
Haverholt Rd. Col 6N 85
Haverthwaite Av. Hey 9L 21
Havre Pk. Barn 2N 77
Hawarden Av. More 3C 22
Hawarden Rd. Pres 8A 116
Hawarden St. Bolt 8E 198
Hawarden St. Nels 3J 105
Hawer St. Dar 7B 158
Hawes Clo. Bury 8G 200
Hawes Dri. Col 5C 86
Hawes Side. 9E 88
Hawes Side La. Blac 9E 88
Hawesside St. South 7J 167
Hawes Ter. Burn 8G 104
Haweswater Av. Chor 8D 174
Haweswater Clo. Liv 5J 223
Haweswater Gro. Liv 9E 216
Haweswater Pl. More 4D 22
Haweswater Rd. Acc 8C 122
Hawgreen Rd. Liv 9G 223
Haw Gro. Hell 1D 52
Hawick Clo. Liv 4J 223
Hawk Clo. Bury 9N 201
Hawkhurst Av. Ful 3G 115
Hawkhurst Cres. Ful 3G 115
Hawkhurst Rd. Pen 4H 135
Hawkhurst Rd. Pres 7L 115
Hawking Pl. Blac 6F 62
Hawkins Clo. Pres 8H 115
Hawkins St. B'brn 6J 139
Hawkins St. Pres 8H 115
(in two parts)
Hawkins Way. L'boro 5M 185
Hawksbury Dri. Pen 6G 134
Hawksclough. Skel 1N 219
Hawks Gro. Ross 6M 161
Hawkshaw. 2A 200
(Bury)
Hawkshaw. 4M 157
(Darwen)
Hawkshaw Av. Dar 4M 157
Hawkshaw Bank Rd. B'brn 9L 119
Hawkshaw La. Hawk 2A 200
Hawkshead. Pen 5H 135
Hawkshead Av. Eux 5N 173
Hawkshead Clo. B'brn 4J 139
Hawkshead Clo. Liv 9D 216
Hawkshead Dri. More 5C 22
Hawkshead Rd. Kno S 7M 41
Hawkshead Rd. Rib 4A 116
Hawkshead St. B'brn 4J 139
Hawkshead St. South 6J 167
Hawkshead Ter. Blac 1K 109
Hawksheath Clo. Eger 4F 198
Hawkstone Clo. Acc 8E 122
Hawkstone Clo. T Clev 3K 63
Hawkstone Ct. More 2F 22
Hawk St. Burn 3E 124
Hawk St. Carn 8B 12
Hawkswood. E'ston 8E 172
Hawkswood Gdns. Brier 6E 104
Hawksworth Av. Hey 6M 21
Hawksworth Clo. Liv 6A 206
Hawksworth Dri. Liv 6A 206
Hawksworth Gro. Hey 7L 21
Hawksworth Rd. Acc 9A 122
Haw La. Hell 1D 52
Hawley Grn. Roch 3A 204
Hawley St. Col 7N 85
Hawley St. Traw 6E 86
Haworth Art Gallery. 5C 142
(Tiffany Glass)
Haworth Av. Acc 5C 142
Haworth Av. Ram 3F 200
Haworth Av. Ross 5L 161
Haworth Cres. Poul F 8L 63
Haworth Dri. Bacup 6G 163
Haworth St. Acc 8A 122
Haworth St. Osw 4K 141
Haworth St. Rish 8H 121
Haworth St. Tur 9K 179
Haworth St. Wals 9D 200
Haws Av. Carn 9A 12
Hawshaw Rd. Loth 8K 79
Haws Hill. Carn 9A 12
Hawthorn Av. Brook 3J 25
Hawthorn Av. Bury 9H 201
Hawthorn Av. Dar 5C 158
Hawthorn Av. Orr 5J 221
Hawthorn Av. Osw 4L 141
Hawthorn Av. Ram 3F 200
Hawthorn Av. Wig 5N 221
Hawthorn Bank. Alt 7N 121
Hawthorn Bank. Bolt 9L 199
Hawthorn Clo. Brook 3J 25
Hawthorn Clo. Ley 5G 153
Hawthorn Clo. Nels 2M 105
Hawthorn Clo. New L 9D 134
Hawthorn Clo. Wesh 2K 111
Hawthorn Cres. Lea 9N 113
Hawthorn Cres. Skel 2J 219
Hawthorn Cres. Tot 6E 200
Hawthorn Dri. Rish 9H 121
Hawthorne Av. Burn 5F 104
Hawthorne Av. Fltwd 4E 54
Hawthorne Av. Gars 4M 59
Hawthorne Av. High W 5E 136
Hawthorne Av. Newt 6D 112
Hawthorne Clo. Barfd 1F 104
Hawthorne Clo. Clay W 4D 154
Hawthorne Clo. Lang 1D 120
Hawthorne Cres. Form 1A 214
Hawthorne Dri. Barn 1N 77
Hawthorne Gro. Barfd 8H 85
Hawthorne Gro. Poul F 6G 63
Hawthorne Gro. South 7M 167
Hawthorne Ind. Est. Clith 2N 81
Hawthorne Lea. T Clev 3J 63
Hawthorne Meadows. Craw 8M 143
Hawthorne Pl. Clith 2L 81
Hawthorne Rd. Burn 5C 124
Hawthorne Rd. T Clev 3H 63
Hawthornes, The. Ruf 2F 190
Hawthorne St. B'brn 9N 119
Hawthorne Ter. Foul 2B 86
(off Skipton Old Rd.)
Hawthorn Gdns. Clay M 6N 121
Hawthorn La. Miln 9K 205
Hawthorn Pl. Todm 1L 165
Hawthorn Rd. Bacup 5L 163
Hawthorn Rd. Blac 3C 88
Hawthorn Rd. Bolt S 3L 15
Hawthorn Rd. More 4F 22
Hawthorn Rd. Rib 7A 116
(in two parts)
Hawthorn Rd. Roch 7J 203
Hawthorns, The. B'brn 3N 119
Hawthorns, The. E'ston 7E 172
Hawthorns, The. Ful 3J 115
Hawthorns, The. Lanc 5L 29
Hawthorns, The. Lyth A 7F 108

Higher Bank St.—Holland St.

Higher Bank St. Withn 6B 156
Higher Barn. Hor 9G 196
Higher Barn St. B'brn 3A 140
Higher Bartle. 2B 114
Higher Baxenden. 6D 142
Higher Blackthorn. Bacup 3K 163
Higher Booths La. Craw 7M 143
Higher Calderbrook. L'boro 5M 185
Higher Calderbrook Rd. L'boro 5M 185
Higher Causeway. Barfd 8H 85
Higher Change Vs. Bacup 3M 163
Higher Chapel La. Grin 4A 74
Higher Chu. St. Dar 6B 158
Higher Cleggswood Av. L'boro 2K 205
Higher Cloughfold. 4A 162
Higher Cockcroft. B'brn 3M 139
Higher Commons La. Mel B 6D 118
Higher Constablelee. 2M 161
Higher Copthurst. 8H 155
Higher Crimble. Roch 9K 203
Higher Croft. 7N 139
Higher Cft. Pen 6F 134 (in two parts)
Higher Cft. Rd. Lwr D 8N 139
Higher Cft. St. Set 3N 35 (off Commercial St.)
Higher Cross Row. Bacup 4K 163
Higher Dri. Clay M 6N 121
Higher Dunscar. Eger 4E 198
Higher Eanam. B'brn 3A 140
Higher End. 8G 220
Higher Feniscowles La. Pleas 8C 138
Higherfield. Lang 1C 120
Higher Fold La. Ram 7K 181
Higherford. 6J 85
Higher Furlong. Longt 1K 151
Higher Ga. Acc 8E 122
Highergate Clo. Hun 7E 122
Higher Ga. Rd. Acc 8E 122
Higher Grn. Poul F 8K 63
Higher Greenfield. Ing 4E 114
Higher Heys. Osw 5L 141
Higher Heysham. 1K 27
Higherhouse Clo. B'brn 9H 139
Higher Ho. La. Chor & H'pey 3J 175
Higherlands Clo. Garg 3M 53 (off West St.)
Higher La. Dal 3M 211
Higher La. Has 3G 161
Higher La. Rainf & Crank 2L 225
Higher La. Salt 5M 77
Higher La. Scor 7D 46
Higher La. Tar 4A 170
Higher La. Uph 4F 220
Higher Lawrence St. Dar 5N 157
Higher Lodge. Roch 3H 203
Higher Lomax La. Heyw 9E 202
Higher London Ter. Dar 5B 158
Higher Mdw. Ley 6A 154
Higher Mill St. Ross 4M 161
Higher Moor Fld. Catt 1N 67
Higher Moor Rd. Blac 9F 62
Higher Moss La. Form 9G 206
Higher Mouldings. Bury 8C 202
Higher Pk. Rd. Barn 4N 77
Higher Peel St. Osw 5K 141
Higher Penwortham. 3E 134
Higher Perry St. Dar 5B 158
Higher Ramsgreave Rd. Rams 6J 119
Higher Reedley Rd. Brier 6G 105
Higher Ridings. Brom X 5F 198 (in two parts)
Higher Rd. L'rdge 3K 97
Higher Row. Bury 9N 201
Higher Saxifield. Burn 7J 105
Higher Shady La. Brom X 6H 199
Higher Shore Rd. L'boro 7H 185
Higher S. St. Dar 6B 158
Higher Stanhill. 4H 141
Higher Summerseat. 4G 201
Higher Summerseat. Ram 3G 201
Higher Syke. Abb 2C 48
Higher Tentre. Burn 4F 124
Higher Walton. 4D 136
Higher Walton Rd. Walt D & High W 3N 135
Higher Watermill. 7E 160
Higher Wheat La. Roch 5F 204
Higher Wheelton. 6L 155
Higher Witton Rd. B'brn 4J 139
Higher Woodhill. 8J 201
High Farm La. Bic 3A 218
High Fell Clo. Set 4N 35
Highfield. 7M 221
Highfield. Bacup 5K 163
Highfield. Brins 7A 156
Highfield. Gt Har 4H 121
Highfield. Liv 4L 223
Highfield. Miln 7K 205
Highfield. Pen 6G 134
Highfield. Ross 9M 143
Highfield. Wig 7N 221
Highfield Av. Bolt 9N 199
Highfield Av. Burn 7F 104
Highfield Av. Far 4M 153
Highfield Av. Foul 2B 86
Highfield Av. Ful 5M 115
Highfield Av. Ins 2G 93
Highfield Av. Los H 7M 135
Highfield Av. Shev 6K 213
Highfield Clo. Adl 6J 195
Highfield Clo. Clift 8G 113
Highfield Clo. Osw 5M 141
Highfield Clo. Tar 1E 170
Highfield Cres. Barfd 8H 85
Highfield Cres. More 4N 21
Highfield Cres. Nels 8J 85
Highfield Dri. Ful 1H 115
Highfield Dri. Hest B 8H 15
Highfield Dri. L'rdge 4K 97
Highfield Dri. Longt 1K 151
Highfield Dri. Pen 6G 135
Highfield Gdns. B'brn 6M 139
Highfield Golf Course. 7L 155
Highfield Grange Av. Wig 9N 221
Highfield Gro. Los H 6M 135
Highfield Ind. Est. Chor 4F 174
Highfield La. Bolt S 3N 15
Highfield La. Scar 6H 189
Highfield M. Dar 7B 158
Highfield Pk. Has 5F 160
Highfield Pk. Liv 1E 222
Highfield Rd. Adl 6J 195
Highfield Rd. B'brn 5M 139
Highfield Rd. Blac 3C 108
Highfield Rd. Carn 9B 12
Highfield Rd. Clith 4L 81
Highfield Rd. Crost 4N 171
Highfield Rd. Dar 6B 158
Highfield Rd. Earby 2E 78
Highfield Rd. Orm 5K 209
Highfield Rd. Ram 4J 181
Highfield Rd. Rish 8G 121
Highfield Rd. Ross 6B 162
Highfield Rd. South 3A 168
Highfield Rd. N. Adl 5J 195
Highfield Rd. N. Chor 4E 174
Highfield Rd. S. Chor 5E 174
Highfield St. Dar 7B 158
Highfield St. Has 5F 160
Highfield Ter. L Bent 6K 19 (off Doctor's Hill)
High Fold. Kel 6D 78
Highgale Gdns. Los H 9M 135
Highgate. Blac 4D 108
High Ga. Fltwd 1D 54
Highgate. Goos 4N 95
Highgate. Nels 4H 105
Highgate. Pen 3E 134
Highgate Av. Ful 5H 115
Highgate Clo. Ful 5J 115
Highgate Clo. Newt 6D 112
Highgate Cres. App B 5H 213
High Ga. La. Stalm & Hamb 5M 55
Highgate La. W'ton 2K 131
Highgate La. Whitw & Roch 8N 183
Highgate Pl. Lyth A 2K 129
Highgate Rd. Liv 8C 216
Highgate Rd. Uph 4E 220
High Grn. Ley 6J 153
Highgrove Av. Char R 1H 193
Highgrove Clo. Bolt 9F 198
Highgrove Clo. More 4A 22
Highgrove Ct. Ley 6C 152
Highgrove Ho. Chor 4E 174
High Hill Gro. St. Set 3N 35
High Houses. Bolt 7D 198
High Knott Rd. Arns 2F 4
Highland Av. Pen 4E 134
Highland Brow. Gal 1L 37
Highland Rd. Brom X 5H 199
Highlands. L'boro 2K 205
Highlands Av. Ruf 2E 190
Highlands Rd. Roch 8J 203
High La. Bic 4N 217
High La. Burs 5M 209
High La. Crost 7J 171
High La. Salt 6N 77
High Level Rd. Roch 7C 204
High Mdw. Brom X 5H 199
High Mill. Garg 3L 53
High Moor. 9C 192
Highmoor. Nels 4K 105
High Moor La. Wrigh 9C 192
Highmoor Pk. Clith 3M 81
High Moss. Orm 9J 209
High Park. 6N 167
High Pk. Shev 6M 213
High Pk. Pl. South 6N 167
High Pk. Rd. South 6N 167
High Peak Rd. Whitw 8N 183
Highrigg Dri. Brough 9J 95
High Rd. Barb 1G 9
High Rd. Halt 2B 24
High Rd. L Bent 9J 19
Highsted Gro. Liv 5L 223
High St. Acc 5M 141
High St. Bel 9K 177
High St. B'brn 3M 139
High St. Blac 4B 88
High St. Brier 5F 104
High St. Burt L 3K 19
High St. Chor 6E 174
High St. Clith 3H 81
High St. Col 6B 86
High St. Dar 6A 158
High St. Elsw 1L 91
High St. Fltwd 9H 41
High St. Garg 3M 53
High St. Gars 5N 59
High St. Gt Ecc 6N 65
High St. Has 3G 160
High St. Hor 9C 196
High St. Lanc 9J 23
High St. L'boro 9J 185
High St. Maw 4M 191
High St. Nels 3H 105
High St. Osw 4A 142
High St. Pad 9J 103
High St. Pres 9K 115
High St. Rish 8H 121
High St. Roch 5C 204
High St. Set 3N 35
High St. Skel 3H 219
High St. Stand 3N 213
High St. Todm 4K 165 (off Cannon St.)
High St. Tur 1J 199
Hightown. 7A 214
Hightown. Ross 3C 162
Hightown Rd. Ross 3C 162
Highview St. Bolt 7E 198
High Wardle La. Fac 5D 184
Highway. L'clif 2N 35
Highways Av. Eux 5N 173
Highwood. Roch 4J 203
Highwood Ct. Liv 6L 223
Higson St. B'brn 3L 139
Hilary Av. Blac 6C 62
Hilary St. Burn 9E 104
Hilbre Clo. South 5M 167
Hilbre Dri. South 5M 167
Hilda Av. Tot 7E 200
Hilderstone. 5E 6
Hilderstone La. Yeal R 7E 6
Hilgay Clo. Wig 8N 221
Hillam La. C'ham 8D 36
Hillary Av. Wig 6N 221
Hillary Cres. Liv 1C 222
Hillbrook Grn. Ley 5J 153
Hillbrook Rd. Ley 5J 153
Hill Brow. Hals 5N 207
Hill Clo. App B 4H 213
Hill Cot Rd. Bolt 8F 198
Hill Cres. Newt 7D 112
Hill Crest. Bacup 6H 163
Hillcrest. Liv 2E 222
Hillcrest. Skel 4M 219
Hillcrest Av. Bolt S 4L 15
Hill Crest Av. Burn 5K 125
Hillcrest Av. Ful 1H 115
Hillcrest Av. Ing 5D 114
Hillcrest Av. L'rdge 3J 97
Hillcrest Clo. Tar 7E 150
Hillcrest Dri. L'rdge 3J 97
Hillcrest Dri. Scar 5E 188
Hillcrest Dri. Sla H 1N 5
Hillcrest Dri. Tar 8E 150
Hillcrest Rd. B'brn 6G 139
Hillcrest Rd. Blac 5B 108
Hillcrest Rd. Lang 1C 120
Hillcrest Rd. Orm 6K 209
Hillcroft. Ben 7L 19 (off Wenning Av.)
Hillcroft. Ful 2F 114
Hill Cft. K'ham 4N 111
Hill Dale. 8A 192
Hilldean. Uph 3F 220
Hill End. Traw 9F 86
Hill End La. Ross 6A 162
Hill Ho. Fold La. Wrigh 8F 192
Hill Ho. La. Brin 8J 137
Hill Ho. La. Wrigh 6E 192
Hillhouses. Dar 8A 158
Hillingdon Rd. Burn 7H 105
Hillingdon Rd. N. Burn 6G 105
Hillkirk Dri. Roch 2N 203
Hill La. Col 4E 86
Hill La. Neth K 5C 16
Hillmore Rd. More 3A 22
Hillmount Av. Hey 8L 21
Hillock Clo. Scar 6F 188
Hillock La. Dal 6N 211
Hillock La. Scar 6F 188
Hillock La. W'ton 1J 131
Hillocks, The. Crost 5M 171
Hillock, The. Bolt 8K 199
Hillock Vale. 9D 122
Hillpark Av. Ful 5G 114
Hillpark Av. Hogh 7F 136
Hill Pl. Nels 4H 105
Hill Pl. Todm 4K 165
Hill Ri. Has 6H 161
Hill Ri. Ram 1F 200
Hill Rise Vw. Augh 2F 216
Hill Rd. Lanc 5K 23
Hill Rd. Ley 6M 153
Hill Rd. Pen 3F 134
Hill Rd. S. Pen 5F 134
Hillsborough Av. Brier 5H 105
Hills Ct. Bury 9G 201
Hills Ct. Lanc 6K 23
Hillsea Av. Hey 8L 21
Hillside. 4E 186
Hillside. Burn 6B 124
Hillside. Holme 1G 6
Hillside. Lanc 8J 23
Hillside. Whit W 7E 154
Hillside Av. Acc 5M 141
Hillside Av. B'brn 4C 140
Hillside Av. Brom X 4H 199
Hillside Av. Burn 6G 104
Hillside Av. Dar 7A 158
Hillside Av. Far M 9J 135
Hillside Av. Ful 5G 114
Hillside Av. Hor 9D 196
Hillside Av. K'ham 4A 112
Hillside Av. Orm 8J 209
Hillside Av. Parb 8N 191
Hillside Av. Pre 9A 42
Hillside Clo. B'brn 4C 140
Hillside Clo. Blac 4E 88
Hillside Clo. Brad 8L 199
Hillside Clo. Brier 5G 105
Hillside Clo. Burn 6B 124
Hillside Clo. Clith 5L 81
Hillside Clo. Eux 5M 173
Hillside Clo. Gt Har 3J 121
Hillside Clo. T Clev 3K 63
Hillside Clo. Wig 8N 221
Hillside Cres. Bacup 9K 145
Hillside Cres. Bury 7L 201
Hillside Cres. Hor 9D 196
Hillside Cres. Whit W 6E 154
Hillside Dri. Ross 5C 162
Hillside Dri. Stalm 5B 56
Hillside Dri. W Brad 6L 73
Hillside Gdns. Bury 3H 201
Hillside Gdns. Dar 8A 158
Hillside Golf Links. 5C 186
Hillside Rd. Has 5G 161
Hillside Rd. L Bent 6J 19
Hillside Rd. Pres 2M 135
Hillside Rd. Ram 9F 180
Hillside Rd. South 4E 186
Hillside Vw. Brier 5G 105
Hillside Vw. Miln 7K 205
Hillside Wlk. B'brn 4C 140
Hillside Wlk. Roch 1A 204
Hillside Way. Whitw 5N 183
Hills, The. Pres 2D 116
Hillstone Av. Roch 1N 203
Hillstone Clo. G'mnt 3E 200
Hill St. Acc 3B 142 (Hollins La.)
Hill St. Acc 6C 142 (Wellington St.)
Hill St. Barn 2N 77
Hill St. B'brn 2B 140
Hill St. Blac 9B 88
Hill St. Brier 4D 104 (Burnley Rd.)
Hill St. Brier 5F 104 (Montford Rd.)
Hill St. Carn 9A 12
Hill St. Clay M 8N 121
Hill St. Col 7A 86
Hill St. Osw 3K 141
Hill St. Pad 1H 123
Hill St. Pres 9J 115
Hill St. Roch 6D 204
Hill St. Ross 9M 143
Hill St. South 6H 167
Hill St. S'seat 2H 201
Hill St. Tot 9E 200
Hillsview Rd. South 9C 186
Hill Top. 9E 86
Hill Top. Barfd 7H 85
Hill Top. New L 1D 152
Hilltop. Whitw 9N 183
Hill Top Clo. Frec 1B 132
Hilltop Dri. Has 8H 161
Hilltop Dri. Tot 7D 200
Hill Top La. Earby 2D 78
Hill Top La. Whit W 7E 154
Hilltop Rd. Nels 1K 105
Hill Top Rd. Rainf 8M 225
Hilltop Wlk. Orm 9H 209
Hill Vw. B'brn 8M 119
Hill Vw. L'boro 5N 185
Hill Vw. Ross 6L 161
Hillview Ct. Bolt 9E 198
Hill Vw. Dri. Cop 5N 193
Hillview Rd. Bolt 9E 198
Hill Vw. Rd. Gars 3N 59
Hillview Rd. Wesh 3M 111
Hill Wlk. Ley 5K 153
Hilly Cft. Brom X 5F 198
Hillylaid Rd. T Clev 1J 63
Hilmarton Clo. Brad 8L 199
Hilstone La. Blac 1D 88
Hilton Av. Blac 9B 88
Hilton Av. Hor 9B 196
Hilton Av. Lyth A 2J 129
Hilton Ct. Lyth A 3E 128
Hilton Rd. Dar 7B 158
Hilton's Brow. Brin 3K 155
Hilton St. Bury 9L 201
Hilton St. Dar 7A 158
Hinchcliffe St. Roch 5A 204
Hinchley Grn. Liv 1A 222
Hindburn Av. Liv 9E 216
Hindburn Clo. Carn 8C 12
Hindburn Pl. Lanc 6J 23
Hinde St. Lanc 7L 23
Hindle Ct. Dar 5A 158
Hindle Fold La. Gt Har 2J 121
Hindle St. Acc 2A 142
Hindle St. Bacup 7H 163
Hindle St. Dar 5M 157
Hindle St. Has 4G 160
Hindley Beech. Liv 3B 216
Hindley Clo. Ful 2M 115
Hindley Ct. Barfd 1G 104
Hindley Ho. La. Ful 3M 115
Hindley St. Chor 8D 174
Hind Rd. Wig 3N 221
Hind's Head Av. Wrigh 7J 193
Hind St. Burn 8F 104
Hind St. Pres 2H 135
Hinton. Roch 5B 204 (off Spotland Rd.)
Hinton Clo. Roch 7J 203
Hinton St. Burn 4F 124
Hippings La. Ross 6D 162
Hippings Av. Osw 4K 141 (off Holly St.)
Hippings Way. Clith 1L 81
Hirst St. Burn 5F 124 (in two parts)
Hirst St. Pad 9H 103
Hirst St. Todm 7E 146
Hoarstones Av. Fence 3B 104
Hobart Dri. Liv 4K 223
Hobart Pl. T Clev 3F 62
Hobart St. Burn 3F 124
Hobbs La. Clau B 7J 61
Hobcross La. Lath 3E 210
Hob Grn. Mel 7G 118
Hob La. Tur 7J 179
Hob La. Wlk. Liv 8G 222
Hobsons La. Cap 6J 13
Hobson St. Ross 4L 161
Hockley Pl. Blac 3F 88
Hodder Av. Blac 9D 88
Hodder Av. Chor 9D 174
Hodder Av. Fltwd 2C 54
Hodder Av. L'boro 8J 185
Hodder Av. Liv 9E 216
Hodder Av. More 5F 22
Hodder Brook. Rib 6C 116
Hodder Clo. Bam B 8B 136
Hodder Clo. Fltwd 2C 54
Hodder Clo. Wig 4N 221
Hodder Ct. Stony 7C 80
Hodder Dri. Lyth A 1J 129
Hodder Dri. W Brad 5K 73
Hodder Gro. Clith 4J 81
Hodder Gro. Dar 3M 157
Hodder Pl. B'brn 2N 139 (in two parts)
Hodder Pl. Lanc 2M 29
Hodder St. Acc 2C 142
Hodder St. B'brn 2N 139
Hodder St. Burn 7G 104
Hodder St. L'rdge 3K 97
Hodder Way. Poul F 9K 63
Hoddlesden. 6F 158
Hoddlesden Fold. Hodd 6F 158
Hoddlesden Rd. Hodd 6E 158
Hodge Bank Pk. Nels 9H 85
Hodge Brow. Hor 1A 196
Hodge La. Barn 4M 77
Hodge St. South 7H 167
Hodgson Av. Frec 3M 131
Hodgson Pl. Poul F 9K 63
Hodgson Rd. Blac 1C 88
Hodgson St. Dar 6B 158
Hodgson St. Osw 4L 141
Hodson St. Bam B 7A 136
Hodson St. South 8J 167
Hogarth Av. Burn 6C 124
Hogath Cres. Whar 6D 92
Hogg's La. Chor 9G 174
Hoghton. 6K 137
Hoghton Av. Bacup 6L 163
Hoghton Bottoms. 6A 138
Hoghton Clo. Lanc 1H 29
Hoghton Clo. Lyth A 7F 108
Hoghton Gro. South 6J 167
Hoghton La. High W & Hogh 5E 136
Hoghton Pl. South 7H 167
Hoghton Rd. Ley 6G 152
Hoghton Rd. L'rdge 3K 97
Hoghton St. South 7H 167
Hoghton Tower. 7N 137
Hoghton Vw. Pres 2M 135
Holbeach Clo. Bury 8J 201
Holbeck Av. Blac 1F 108
Holbeck Av. More 4F 22
Holbeck Av. Roch 1A 204
Holbeck St. Burn 9E 104
Holborn Dri. Orm 9H 209
Holborn Gdns. Roch 8A 204
Holborn Hill. Orm 9H 209
Holborn Sq. Roch 8A 204
Holborn St. Roch 8A 204
Holcombe. 8F 180
Holcombe Brook. 3F 200
Holcombe Ct. Ram 3F 200
Holcombe Dri. Burn 3F 124
Holcombe Gro. Chor 5G 175
Holcombe Lee. Ram 1F 200
Holcombe M. Ram 2E 200
Holcombe Old Rd. Holc 9F 180
Holcombe Rd. Blac 1E 88
Holcombe Rd. Ross 6D 160
Holcombe Rd. Tot & G'mnt 8E 200
Holcombe Village. Bury 8F 180 (off Helmshore Rd.)
Holcroft Pl. Lyth A 4M 129
Holden. 8J 51
Holden Av. Bolt 7E 198
Holden Av. Bury 9C 202
Holden Av. Ram 9F 180
Holden Clo. Barfd 1G 105
Holden Fold. Dar 4B 158
Holden La. Bolt B 5G 51
Holden Rd. Brier 5E 104
Holden Rd. Burn 7F 104
Holden St. Acc 3A 142
Holden St. Adl 6H 195
Holden St. Belt 1F 158
Holden St. B'brn 4K 139
Holden St. Burn 3D 124
Holden St. Clith 3M 81
Holden St. Roch 3D 204
Holden Vale. 3F 160
Holden Way. Lanc 2K 29
Holden Wood. 6E 160
Holden Wood Dri. Has 6F 160
Holderness St. Todm 2N 165
Hole Bottom. 9L 147
Hole Bottom Rd. Todm 1L 165
Hole House. 2C 140
Hole Ho. La. Slai 1E 50
Hole Ho. St. B'brn 3C 140
Holford Wlk. Firg 6G 204
Holgate. Blac 3F 108
Holgate Dri. Orr 5H 221
Holgates Cvn. Pk. Silv 6F 4
Holgate St. Brclf 7K 105
Holgate St. Gt Har 4J 121
Holhouse La. G'mnt 3E 200
Holiday Moss. 3M 225
Holker Bus. Cen. Col 7M 85
Holker Clo. Hogh 5G 136
Holker Clo. Lanc 1H 29
Holker La. Ley 2C 172
Holker St. Col 7M 85
Holker St. Dar 7B 158
Holland Av. Ross 3L 161
Holland Av. Walt D 6A 136
Holland Ho. Rd. Walt D 5N 135
Holland Lees. 7F 212
Holland Lodge. Rib 5B 116 (off Grange Av.)
Holland Moor. 4B 220
Holland Moss. Skel 6L 219
Holland Ri. Roch 5B 204
Holland Rd. Ash R 8F 114
Holland Slack. 5A 136
Holland's La. Skel 1E 218
Holland St. Acc 3M 141
Holland St. B'brn 2L 139
Holland St. Bolt 9F 198
Holland St. Hur 1G 205
Holland St. Pad 1G 123

Holland St.—Huntley La.

Holland St. *Roch* 6B **204**
Holliers Clo. *Liv* 1C **222**
Hollies Clo. *B'brn* 8G **138**
Hollies Clo. *Catt* 1A **68**
Hollies Rd. *Wilp* 2A **120**
Hollies, The. South 8F **166**
(off Beechfield Gdns.)
Hollin Bank. 6L **139**
Hollin Bank St. *Brier* 4F **104**
Hollin Bri. St. *B'brn* 6K **139**
(in two parts)
Hollin Clo. Ross 3D **162**
(off Foxhill Dri.)
Hollinghurst Rd. *Liv* 5L **223**
Hollingreave Rd. *Burn* 5E **124**
Hollin Gro. Ross 3M **161**
(off Hollin La.)
Hollings. *New L* 9C **134**
Hollington St. *Col* 6E **86**
Hollington Way. *Wig* 9M **221**
Hollingworth. 2K **205**
Hollingworth Lake Cvn. Site.
L'boro 4M **205**
Hollingworth Lake Country Pk. & Vis. Cen. 2L **205**
Hollingworth La. *Todm* 7L **165**
Hollingworth Rd. *L'boro* 2L **205**
Hollin Hall. 1F **106**
Hollinhead Cres. *Ing* 5E **114**
Hollinhey Clo. *Boot* 5A **222**
Hollin Hill. *Burn* 6F **124**
Hollinhurst Av. *Pen* 2F **134**
Hollinhurst Brow. *Wray* 3J **33**
Hollinhurst Vw. High 5L **103**
(off Anderton Rd.)
Hollin La. *H'pey* 4L **175**
Hollin La. *Roch* 7J **203**
Hollin La. *Ross* 3M **161**
Hollin Mill St. *Brier* 4F **104**
Hollins. 3N **157**
Hollins Av. *Burn* 5K **125**
Hollins Clo. *Acc* 4B **142**
Hollins Clo. *Hogh* 5L **137**
Hollins Ct. Barn 1M **77**
(off Hollins Rd)
Hollins Grn. *Todm* 3F **164**
Hollins Grove. 4N **157**
Hollins Gro. *Ful* 6E **114**
Hollins Gro. St. *Dar* 4N **157**
Hollinshead St. *Chor* 6E **174**
Hollinshead Ter. *Toc* 8J **157**
Hollins Hill. *Fort* 3N **45**
Hollins Lane. 2A **46**
Hollins La. *Acc* 4B **142**
Hollins La. *Arns & Silv* 2G **4**
Hollins La. *Fort* 4N **45**
Hollins La. *Ley* 1F **172**
Hollin's La. *Ram* 5K **181**
Hollins La. *Saw* 1H **75**
Hollins La. *Silv & Silv* 1G **11**
Hollins Mdw. *Todm* 6K **165**
Hollins Pl. *Todm* 6K **165**
Hollins Rd. *Barn* 2L **77**
Hollins Rd. *Dar* 3M **157**
Hollins Rd. *Nels* 9L **85**
Hollins Rd. *Pres* 6L **115**
Hollins Rd. *Todm* 5K **165**
Hollins St. *Todm* 7L **165**
Hollins, The. *Todm* 1L **165**
Hollin St. *B'brn* 6K **139**
Hollin Way. *Raw* 3M **161**
Hollin Way. *Ross* 1M **161**
Hollinwood Dri. *Raw* 2M **161**
Hollowbrook Way. *Roch* 3A **204**
Hollow Fld. *Roch* 4H **203**
Hollowford La. *Lath* 1G **210**
Hollowforth La. *Wood* 6B **94**
Hollowhead Av. *Wilp* 4N **119**
Hollowhead Clo. *Wilp* 4A **120**
Hollowhead La.
B'brn & Wilp 4N **119**
Hollowrayne. *Burt* 5H **7**
Hollows Farm Av. *Roch* 3A **204**
Hollowspell. *Roch* 2F **204**
Hollsworth Ct. *Blac* 8D **88**
Holly Av. *Has* 6H **161**
Holly Bank. *Acc* 4B **142**
Holly Bank. *War* 5A **12**
Hollybank Clo. *Ing* 4C **114**
Hollybrook Rd. *South* 9G **166**
Holly Clo. *Clay W* 5D **154**
Holly Clo. *Skel* 2J **219**
Holly Clo. *T Clev* 9J **55**
Holly Clo. *W'head* 8C **210**
Holly Cres. *Cop* 2A **194**
Holly Cres. *Rainf* 5L **225**
Holly Fold La. *Bic* 8J **219**
Holly Gro. *L'rdge* 2J **97**
Holly Gro. *Tar* 8E **150**
Holly La. *Augh* 8G **208**
Holly La. *Bic* 7H **219**
Holly La. *Ruf* 2G **190**
Holly M. *Lyth A* 7F **108**
Holly Mill Cres. *Bolt* 9F **198**
Holly Mt. *Ross* 8F **160**
Holly Mt. La. *G'mnt* 4C **200**
Holly Pl. *Bam B* 9D **136**
Holly Rd. *Blac* 1C **88**
Holly Rd. *T Clev* 9H **55**
Holly Rd. *Wig* 4N **221**
Holly St. *B'brn* 1N **139**
Holly St. *Bolt* 9F **198**
Holly St. *Burn* 4F **124**
Holly St. *Nels* 2K **105**
Holly St. *Osw* 4K **141**
Holly St. *S'seat* 2H **201**
Holly St. *Tot* 7E **200**
Holly St. *Ward* 8F **184**
Holly Ter. *B'brn* 9N **119**
Holly Tree Clo. *Dar* 1A **178**
Holly Tree Clo. *Ross* 2L **161**
Holly Tree Way. *B'brn* 8G **138**
Holly Wlk. Lanc 8H **23**
(off Sycamore Gro.)
Hollywood Av. *Blac* 5E **88**
Hollywood Av. *Pen* 5F **134**
Hollywood Gro. *Fltwd* 9F **40**
Holman St. *Pres* 8M **115**
Holmbrook Clo. *B'brn* 8N **139**
Holmby St. *Burn* 8F **104**
Holmdale Av. *South* 2A **168**
Holme. 1F **6**
Holme Av. *Bury* 8H **201**
Holme Av. *Fltwd* 4D **54**
Holme Bank. *Ross* 6L **161**
Holme Chapel. 2L **145**
Holme Clo. *Sough* 4D **78**
Holme Cres. *Traw* 8E **86**
Holme End. *Burn* 6D **104**
Holmefield. *Holme* 2G **6**
Holmefield Av. *T Clev* 9E **54**
Holmefield Clo. *T Clev* 1E **62**
Holmefield Ct. *Barfd* 8H **85**
Holmefield Rd. *Lyth A* 1F **128**
Holme Head. *L'clif* 1N **35**
Holme Hill. *Clith* 1L **81**
Holme Ho. *L'boro* 5N **185**
Holme Ho. Rd. *Todm* 7F **146**
Holme Ho. St. *L'boro* 5N **185**
Holme La. *Brook* 1J **25**
(in two parts)
Holme La. *Has & Ross* 7J **161**
(in two parts)
Holme Lea. *Clay M* 5M **121**
Holme Mills. 2F **6**
Holme Mills Ind. Est. *Holme* 3F **6**
Holme Pk. Ben 7L **19**
(off Wenning Av.)
Holme Rd. *Bam B* 8N **135**
Holme Rd. *Burn* 2C **124**
Holme Rd. *Clay M* 5L **121**
Holme Rd. *Pen* 1F **134**
Holmes. 3N **169**
Holmes Cotts. *Bolt* 9C **198**
Holmes Ct. *Pres* 6H **115**
Holmes Dri. *Bacup* 3K **163**
Holmes Ho. Av. *Wig & Wins* 8M **221**
Holme Slack. 6M **115**
Holme Slack La. *Pres* 6L **115**
Holmes La. *Bacup* 4K **163**
Holmes Mdw. *Ley* 6E **152**
Holmes Moss. 2L **169**
Holmes Rd. *Roch* 6A **204**
Holmes Rd. *T Clev* 9G **55**
Holmes Sq. *Burn* 4F **124**
Holmes St. *Burn* 4F **124**
Holmes St. *Pad* 1J **123**
Holmes St. *Roch* 2F **204**
Holmes St. *Ross* 9E **144**
(Burnley Rd. E.)
Holmes St. *Ross* 4N **161**
(Newchurch Rd.)
Holmes Ter. *Reed* 2L **161**
Holmes, The. *Reed* 2L **161**
Holmestrand Av. *Burn* 5M **123**
Holme St. *Acc* 2A **142**
Holme St. *Bacup* 7H **163**
Holme St. *Barfd* 9H **85**
Holme St. *Col* 6E **86**
Holme St. *Dar* 7A **158**
Holme St. *Nels* 2J **105**
Holme St. *Todm* 9H **147**
Holmeswood. 8A **170**
Holmeswood. *K'ham* 4M **111**
Holmeswood Cres. *Brtn* 2E **94**
Holmeswood Pk. *Ross* 7K **161**
Holmeswood Rd. *Ruf* 7N **169**
Holme Ter. *L'boro* 5N **185**
Holme Ter. *Nels* 2G **104**
Holme Ter. *Tow F* 7K **161**
Holme, The. *Cald V* 4H **61**
Holmfield Cres. *Lea* 8A **114**
Holmfield Rd. *Blac* 1B **88**
Holmfield Rd. *Ful* 5K **115**
Holmfield Rd. *Kno S* 8L **41**
Holm Nook. 4D **64**
Holmrook Rd. *Pres* 8L **115**
Holmsley St. *Burn* 4F **124**
Holroyd St. *Roch* 6D **204**
Holsands Clo. *Ful* 3A **116**
Holstein Av. *Roch* 1A **204**
Holstein St. *Pres* 9K **115**
Holt Av. *Cop* 3B **194**
Holt Brow. *Ley* 9K **153**
Holt Coppice. *Augh* 4F **216**
Holt Green. 4G **216**
Holthouse Rd. *Tot* 8D **200**
Holt La. *Brin* 4F **154**
Holt Mill Rd. *Ross* 7B **162**
Holts La. *Poul F* 8M **63**
Holts Pas. *L'boro* 9K **185**
Holt Sq. *Barfd* 6J **85**
Holts Ter. *Roch* 3B **204**
Holt St. *L'boro* 4N **185**
Holt St. *Miln* 8K **205**
Holt St. *Orr* 6G **221**
Holt St. *Ram* 8J **181**
Holt St. *Rish* 7J **121**
Holt St. *Ross* 7C **162**
Holt St. *Whitw* 5N **183**
Holt St. W. *Ram* 9G **180**
Holt Way. *Liv* 8J **223**
Holyoake Av. *Blac* 1E **88**
Holyoake St. *Burn* 3L **123**
Holyoake St. *Todm* 7D **146**
Homeacre Av. *Sab* 2E **102**
Homechase Ho. *South* 1F **186**
Home Fld. *Gars* 4N **59**
Homefield Gro. *Liv* 1B **222**
Homelinks Ho. *Lyth A* 5K **129**
Homeport Ho. South 6J **167**
(off Hoghton St.)
Homer Av. *Tar* 8D **150**
Homer Green. 9J **215**
Homer St. *Burn* 4A **124**
Homesands Ho. *South* 6K **167**
Homestead. *Bam B* 2D **154**
Homestead Av. *Boot* 7A **222**
Homestead Clo. *Ley* 6G **152**
Homestead Dri. *Fltwd* 3E **54**
Homestead Farm. *Wstke* 9G **135**
Homestead Gdns. *Roch* 1G **204**
Homestead, The. Lyth A 5N **129**
(off Henry St.)
Homestead Way. *Fltwd* 3E **54**
Homewood Av. *More* 2F **22**
Homfray Av. *More* 5E **22**
Homfray Gro. *More* 5E **22**
Hondwith Clo. *Bolt* 8J **199**
Honey Hole. *B'brn* 6M **139**
Honey Hole Clo. *Todm* 3L **165**
Honey Hole Rd. *Todm* 3L **165**
Honey Holme La. *Cliv* 1K **145**
Honey Holme Ter. *Cliv* 1L **145**
Honey Pot La. *Sing* 7C **64**
Honeysuckle Clo. *Whit W* 1D **174**
Honeysuckle Pl. *Blac* 5F **62**
Honeysuckle Row. *Rib* 7A **116**
Honeysuckle Way. *Roch* 2A **204**
Honeywood Clo. *Ram* 2F **200**
Honister Av. *Blac* 8E **88**
Honister Clo. *Fltwd* 2D **54**
Honister Rd. *Burn* 7F **104**
Honister Rd. *Lanc* 6M **23**
Honister Rd. *Wig* 5L **221**
Honister Sq. *Lyth A* 7F **108**
Honister Way. *Roch* 9M **203**
Honiton Av. *B'brn* 8K **139**
Honiton Way. *Cot* 3C **114**
Hood Ho. St. *Burn* 5C **124**
Hood St. *Acc* 1B **142**
Hoohill. 3E **88**
Hoo Hill Ind. Est. *Blac* 2E **88**
Hoole La. *Banks* 9F **148**
Hoole La. *Nate* 8E **58**
Hooles La. *Pil* 8F **42**
Hooley Bridge. 9G **203**
Hooley Bri. Ind. Est. *Heyw* 9G **203**
Hooley Clough. *Heyw* 9H **203**
Hope Av. *Brad* 8L **199**
Hope Bldgs. Todm 2M **165**
(off Derdale St.)
Hope Ct. Roch 5C **204**
(off Wilson St.)
Hope Cres. *Shev* 6L **213**
Hope La. *Thorn* 8F **70**
Hope Sq. *South* 7J **167**
Hope St. *Acc* 3A **142**
Hope St. *Adl* 5K **195**
Hope St. *Bacup* 3K **163**
Hope St. *B'brn* 3L **139**
Hope St. *Brier* 5F **104**
Hope St. *Chor* 5E **174**
Hope St. *Dar* 6N **157**
Hope St. *Gt Har* 5J **121**
Hope St. *Has* 5G **161**
Hope St. *Hor* 9C **196**
Hope St. *Lanc* 9L **23**
Hope St. *Lyth A* 1G **128**
Hope St. *More* 4C **22**
Hope St. *Nels* 3H **105**
Hope St. *Pad* 1J **123**
Hope St. *Pres* 9J **115**
Hope St. *Ram* 9G **180**
Hope St. *Raw & Ross* 6A **162**
Hope St. *Roch* 5C **204**
Hope St. *South* 7J **167**
Hope St. *Todm* 2M **165**
Hope St. *Wors* 3M **125**
Hope St. N. *Hor* 8C **196**
Hope Ter. *B'brn* 8K **139**
Hope Ter. *Los H* 8K **135**
Hophouse La. *K Lon* 5D **8**
Hopkinson St. *Traw* 8E **86**
Hopkinson Ter. Traw 8E **86**
(off Skipton Rd.)
Hopton Rd. *Blac* 8B **88**
Hopwood Av. *Hor* 9D **196**
Hopwood Cres. *Rainf* 5L **225**
Hopwood St. *Acc* 4A **142**
Hopwood St. *Bam B* 8A **136**
Hopwood St. *B'brn* 5M **139**
Hopwood St. *Burn* 3C **124**
Hopwood St. *Pres* 9K **115**
Horace St. *Burn* 3B **124**
Horby St. *Pres* 9L **115**
Horden Rake. *B'brn* 9E **138**
Horden Vw. *B'brn* 9F **138**
Hordley St. *Burn* 3M **123**
Horeb Clo. Pad 2J **123**
(off Victoria Rd.)
Horley Clo. *Bury* 6H **201**
Hornbeam Clo. *Pen* 5E **134**
Hornby. 7C **18**
Hornby Av. *Fltwd* 4D **54**
Hornby Av. *Rib* 5A **116**
Hornby Bank. *Horn* 6C **18**
Hornby Bank. *Neth K* 4C **16**
Hornby Castle. 7C **18**
Hornby Chase. *Liv* 3C **222**
Hornby Ct. B'brn 4K **139**
(off Garden St.)
Hornby Ct. *K'ham* 5N **111**
Hornby Ct. *Lanc* 4J **23**
Hornby Cft. *Ley* 7E **152**
Hornby Dri. *Lanc* 3L **29**
Hornby Dri. *Newt* 6D **112**
Hornby Hall Clo. *Horn* 7C **18**
Hornby La. *Ins* 1D **92**
Hornby Pk. Ct. *Blac* 6D **88**
Hornby Rd. *Blac* 6B **88**
Hornby Rd. *Cat* 2H **25**
Hornby Rd. *Chor* 8G **175**
Hornby Rd. *L'rdge* 2K **97**
Hornby Rd. *Lyth A* 3E **128**
Hornby Rd. *South* 1N **167**
Hornby Rd. *Wray* 8D **18**
Hornby's La. *Pil* 6J **57**
Hornby's La. *Raw* 7F **56**
(in two parts)
Hornby St. *Burn* 4E **124**
Hornby St. *Bury* 8L **201**
Hornby St. *Osw* 5L **141**
Hornby Ter. *More* 2C **22**
Horncastle Clo. *Bury* 8J **201**
Hornchurch Dri. *Chor* 6C **174**
Horncliffe Clo. *Ross* 7K **161**
Horncliffe Heights. *Brier* 5J **105**
Horncliffe Rd. *Blac* 3B **108**
Horncliffe Vw. *Has* 7G **161**
Horne St. *Acc* 1B **142**
Horning Cres. *Burn* 8H **105**
Hornsea Clo. *Ing* 5D **114**
Hornsea Clo. *T Clev* 1K **63**
Hornsey Av. *Lyth A* 5B **108**
Hornsey Gro. *Wig* 8N **221**
Horns La. *Goos* 1B **96**
Horridge Fold. *Eger* 2E **198**
Horridge St. *Bury* 9G **200**
Horrobin La. *And & Hor* 4L **195**
Horrobin La. *Tur* 3J **199**
Horrocks Fold. 6D **198**
Horrocks Fold Av. *Bolt* 7D **198**
Horrocksford. 8L **73**
Horrocksford Way. *Lanc* 1H **29**
Horrocks Rd. *Tur* 7K **179**
Horsebridge Rd. *Blac* 2H **89**
Horsfall Av. *Whitw* 8N **183**
Horse Mkt. K Lon 6F **8**
(off Mill Brow)
Horse Pk. La. *Pil* 6L **43**
Horseshoe La. *Brom X* 5G **198**
Horsfall Av. *Lyth A* 5N **129**
Horsfall Clo. *Acc* 1A **142**
Horsfield Clo. *Col* 6C **86**
Horsham Clo. *Bury* 6H **201**
Horton. 7D **52**
Horton Av. *Bolt* 7E **198**
Horton Av. *Burn* 7F **104**
Horton St. *Wig* 9N **213**
Horwich. 9C **196**
Hoscar. 9H **191**
Hoscar Moss Rd. *Lath* 1G **210**
Hospital Cotts. *Hoth* 4A **98**
Hospital Rd. *Brom X* 5F **198**
Hosta Clo. *Liv* 5J **223**
Hosticle La. *Whit* 8D **8**
Hothersall La. *Hoth* 6M **97**
Houghclough La. *Chip* 6D **70**
Hough Fold Way. *Bolt* 8K **199**
Hough La. *Brom X* 6F **198**
Hough La. *Ley* 6K **153**
Houghton Av. *Blac* 1D **108**
Houghton Av. *Wig* 1N **221**
Houghton Clo. *Pen* 5G **134**
Houghton Clo. *Roch* 7F **204**
Houghton Ct. *Halt* 1B **24**
Houghton Ct. T Clev 9H **55**
(off Holmes Rd.)
Houghton La. *Shev* 6J **213**
Houghton Rd. *Pen* 5F **134**
Houghtons Ct. K'ham 4M **111**
(off Marsden St.)
Houghton's La. *Uph* 2N **219**
(in two parts)
Houghtons Rd. *Uph* 9L **211**
Houghton St. *Chor* 6F **174**
Houghton St. *Los H* 8K **135**
Houldsworth Rd. *Ful* 6H **115**
Houlston Rd. *Liv* 8G **222**
Houlston Wlk. *Liv* 8G **222**
Hounds Hill Cen. *Blac* 5B **88**
Houseman Pl. *Blac* 2E **108**
Hove Av. *Fltwd* 4C **54**
Hove Clo. *G'mnt* 4D **200**
Hove Rd. *Lyth A* 2F **128**
Hovingham St. *Roch* 5E **204**
Howard Clo. *Acc* 3M **141**
Howard Clo. *Lyth A* 8E **108**
Howard Clo. *Mag* 1E **222**
Howard Ct. *South* 5K **167**
Howard Dri. *Tar* 8D **150**
Howard M. *Carn* 9N **11**
Howard Pl. *Roch* 5C **204**
Howard Rd. *Chor* 9D **174**
Howard's La. *Orr* 4J **221**
Howard St. *Blac* 4C **88**
Howard St. *Burn* 4B **124**
Howard St. *Nels* 2G **105**
Howard St. *Rish* 8G **121**
Howard St. *Roch* 5B **204**
Howard St. *Wig* 6M **221**
Howard Way. *L'boro* 5M **185**
Howarth Av. *Chu* 1M **141**
Howarth Cross. 3E **204**
Howarth Cross St. *Roch* 3E **204**
Howarth Farm Way. *Roch* 2F **204**
Howarth Grn. *Roch* 2F **204**
Howarth Knoll. *Roch* 9F **184**
Howarth Pl. *Roch* 9A **204**
Howarth Rd. *Ash R* 6G **114**
Howarth Sq. *Roch* 5D **204**
Howarth St. *L'boro* 8L **185**
Howarth St. *Ross* 8D **144**
Howden Heights. *Poul F* 8H **63**
Howe Av. *Blac* 1E **108**
Howe Cft. *Clith* 3M **81**
Howe Dri. *Ram* 3G **200**
Howe Gro. *Chor* 7C **174**
Howells Clo. *Liv* 9C **216**
Howe Wlk. *Burn* 3E **124**
Howgill. 3A **76**
Howgill Av. *Lanc* 4K **23**
Howgill Clo. *Nels* 4K **105**
Howgill La. *Rim* 3B **76**
(in two parts)
Howgills, The. *Ful* 2K **115**
Howgill Way. *Lyth A* 3C **130**
Howick Cross. 4C **134**
Howick Cross La. *Pen* 3A **134**
Howick Moor La. *Pen* 5C **134**
Howick Pk. Av. *Pen* 4C **134**
Howick Pk. Clo. *Pen* 4C **134**
Howick Pk. Dri. *Pen* 4C **134**
Howick Row. *Pen* 3A **134**
How La. *Bury* 7K **201**
How Lea Dri. *Bury* 7L **201**
Howorth Clo. *Burn* 6E **124**
Howorth Rd. *Burn* 6E **124**
Howorth St. *Todm* 8H **147**
Howsin Av. *Bolt* 9H **199**
Howsin St. *Burn* 9E **104**
Howsons La. *L'clif* 1N **35**
Howsons Yd. Set 3N **35**
(off Market Pl.)
Hoylake Clo. *Ful* 3E **114**
Hoyle Av. *Lyth A* 7F **108**
Hoyle Botton. 7L **141**
Hoyles La. *Cot* 4M **113**
Hoyle's Ter. *Miln* 7H **205**
Hoyle St. *Acc* 8F **142**
Hoyle St. *Bacup* 7J **163**
Hoyle St. *Bolt* 9E **198**
Hoyle St. *Whitw* 3A **184**
Hozier St. *B'brn* 3C **140**
Hubert Pl. *Lanc* 8H **23**
Hubie St. *Burn* 2D **124**
Huck La. *Lyth A* 1D **130**
Hudcar La. *Bury* 9M **201**
Huddersfield Rd. *Miln* 9L **205**
Hud Hey. 2F **160**
Hud Hey Ind. Est. *Ross* 1G **160**
Hud Hey Rd. *Has* 1F **160**
Hud Rake. *Has* 2G **160**
Hudson Clo. *B'brn* 9K **119**
Hudson Ct. *Bam B* 9E **136**
Hudson Pl. *B'brn* 9J **119**
Hudson Rd. *Blac* 8D **88**
Hudson Rd. *Liv* 3C **222**
Hudsons Pas. *L'boro* 7M **185**
Hudson St. *Acc* 4B **142**
Hudson St. *Brier* 5F **104**
Hudson St. *Burn* 4B **124**
Hudson St. *Pres* 1K **135**
Hudson St. *Todm* 7F **146**
Hudson Wlk. *Roch* 6M **203**
Hudswell Clo. *Boot* 9A **222**
Hufling Ct. Burn 5F **124**
(off Hufling La.)
Hufling La. *Burn* 6F **124**
Hugh Barn La. *New L* 9B **134**
Hugh Bus. Pk. *Ross* 7D **162**
Hughendon Ct. *Tot* 6E **200**
Hughes Av. *Hor* 9B **196**
Hughes Gro. *Blac* 1E **88**
Hughes St. *Burn* 4E **124**
Hugh La. *Ley* 4F **152**
Hugh Lupus St. *Bolt* 8G **198**
Hugh Mill. 7D **162**
Hugh Rake. *Ross* 1L **161**
Hugh St. *Roch* 5D **204**
Hughtrede St. *Roch* 9E **204**
Hullet Clo. *App B* 4H **213**
Hull Rd. *Blac* 6B **88**
Hull St. *Ash R* 9F **114**
Hull St. *Burn* 4F **124**
(in two parts)
Hulme Av. *T Clev* 1J **63**
Hulme Rd. *Bolt* 7L **199**
Hulme St. *South* 7G **167**
Hulton Dri. *Nels* 4J **105**
Humber Av. *Blac* 2E **88**
Humber Dri. *Bury* 5L **201**
Humber Pl. *Wig* 4M **221**
Humber Rd. *Miln* 7K **205**
Humber Sq. *Burn* 7G **105**
Humber St. *L'rdge* 3J **97**
Humblescough La. *Nate* 6G **59**
Hume St. *Roch* 7D **204**
Humphrey St. *Brier* 4F **104**
Huncoat. 7D **122**
Huncoat Ind. Est. *Acc* 8B **122**
Hundred End. 6L **149**
Hundred End La. *H End* 5L **149**
Hungar Hill. 1J **213**
Hungerford Rd. *Lyth A* 3F **128**
Hunger Hill. *Roch* 8G **185**
Hunger Hill La. *Roch* 2K **203**
Hunniball Ct. *Ash R* 7F **114**
Hunslet St. *Burn* 3F **124**
Hunslet St. *Nels* 3K **105**
Hunstanton Clo. *Eux* 1N **173**
Hunstanton Dri. *Bury* 8J **201**
Hunter Av. *Tar* 9E **150**
Hunter Rd. *Frec* 7N **111**
Hunter Rd. *Wig* 2N **221**
Hunters Dri. *Burn* 1B **124**
Hunters Fold. *Walm B* 2L **151**
Hunters Ga. *Lanc* 2J **29**
Hunters Grn. *Ram* 2E **200**
Hunter's La. *Mere B* 3M **169**
Hunters La. *Roch* 5C **204**
Hunter's La. *Tar* 6B **170**
Hunters La. *Todm* 9J **147**
Hunters Lodge. *B'brn* 7G **138**
Hunters Lodge. *Walt D* 5N **135**
Hunters Rd. *Ley* 6N **153**
Hunter St. *Brier* 6F **104**
Hunter St. *Carn* 8A **12**
Hunters Wood Ct. *Chor* 8B **174**
Hunt Fold Dri. *G'mnt* 3E **200**
Huntingdon Gro. *Liv* 7B **216**
Huntingdon Hall Rd. *K Grn* 9K **71**
Huntingdon Rd. *T Clev* 1C **62**
Hunting Hill Cvn. Pk. *Carn* 9M **11**
Hunting Hill Rd. *Carn* 9M **11**
Huntington Dri. *Dar* 8A **158**
Huntley Av. *Blac* 3E **88**
Huntley Clo. *More* 3E **22**
Huntley La. *Sam* 7M **117**

Junction St.—Kirkby Sports Cen.

Junction St. *Col* 8K 85
Junction St. *Dar* 8B 158
Junction Ter. *Eux* 1M 173
June Av. *Blac* 9G 88
June St. *B'brn* 4A 140
June's Wlk. *Walm B* 2K 151
Juniper Clo. *Pre* 8N 41
Juniper Ct. *Hun* 9D 122
Juniper Cft. *Clay W* 6C 154
Juniper Dri. *Firg* 6G 204
Juniper St. *B'brn* 1A 140
Juno St. *Nels* 9K 85
Jutland Av. *Roch* 5N 203
Jutland St. *Pres* 9K 115

K

Kairnryan Clo. *Blac* 6F 62
Kale Gro. *Liv* 5M 223
Kaley La. *Chat* 7D 74
Kane St. *Ash R* 8F 114
Karan Way. *Liv* 7F 222
Kateholme. *Bacup* 9L 145
Kate St. *Ram* 8G 180
Kathan Clo. *Roch* 6E 204
Kathleen St. *Roch* 6A 204
Katie Cotts. *Fltwd* 1G 54
Kay Brow. *Ram* 8H 181
Kayfields. *Bolt* 9L 199
Kay Fold Lodge. *B'brn* 7L 119
Kay Gdns. *Burn* 4F 124
Kay La. *Con C* 3H 53
Kaymar Ind. Est. *Pres* 1M 135
Kay St. *B'brn* 5M 139
Kay St. *Blac* 6B 88
Kay St. *Brier* 5F 104
Kay St. *Bury* 9M 201
Kay St. *Clith* 4K 81
Kay St. *Dar* 6B 158
Kay St. *Eden* 4J 181
Kay St. *Osw* 5K 141
Kay St. *Pad* 9J 103
Kay St. *Pres* 1H 135
Kay St. *Ross* 5M 161
Kay St. *S'seat* 2H 201
Kay St. *Tur* 1J 199
Kayswell Rd. *More* 3F 22
Kearsley Av. *Tar* 9E 150
Kearstwick. 4E 8
Keasden Av. *Blac* 2D 108
Keating Ct. *Fltwd* 1F 54
Keats Av. *Bil* 9G 220
Keats Av. *Bolt S* 4L 15
Keats Av. *Roch* 4L 203
Keats Av. *Stand L* 9N 213
Keats Av. *Todm* 1N 165
Keats Av. *W'ton* 1K 131
Keats Clo. *Acc* 6D 142
Keats Clo. *Col* 5A 86
Keats Clo. *E'ston* 9G 172
Keats Clo. *T Clev* 1G 62
Keats Fold. *Burn* 2K 123
Keats Rd. *G'mnt* 3E 200
Keats Ter. *South* 8M 167
Keats Way. *Cot* 5A 114
Keble Dri. *Liv* 7B 222
Kebs Rd. *Todm* 4G 146
Keele Clo. *T Clev* 1G 62
Keele Wlk. *B'brn* 4N 139
Keelham La. *Todm* 7N 147
Keepers Dri. *Roch* 3J 203
Keepers Ga. *Lyth A* 1K 129
Keeper's Hey. *T Clev* 8G 54
Keeper's La. *Bncr* 3C 60
Keepers Wood Clo. *Chor* 8B 174
Keer Bank. *Lanc* 6G 22
Keer Holme La. *Cap* 4J 13
Keer Vs. *Carn* 7A 12
Keighley Av. *Col* 5A 86
Keighley Rd. *Col* 6B 86
Keighley Rd. *Lane* 7F 86
Keighley Rd. *Traw* 9F 86
Keirby Wlk. *Burn* 3E 124
Keith Gro. *T Clev* 2D 62
Keith St. *Burn* 3A 124
Kelbrook. 6D 78
Kelbrook Dri. *Burn* 6C 124
Kelbrook Rd. *Barn & Salt* 3N 77
Kelday Clo. *Liv* 8K 223
Keld Clo. *Bury* 8G 200
Kelkbeck Clo. *Liv* 9E 216
Kellamergh. 1H 131
Kellet Acre. *Los H* 9K 135
Kellet Av. *Ley* 6N 153
Kellet Ct. *Lanc* 8J 23
Kellet La. *Bam B* 1D 154
Kellet La. *Slyne & Bolt S* 3M 23
Kellet La. *Tew* 2F 12
Kellet Rd. *Carn* 9B 12
Kellet Rd. Ind. Est. *Carn* 9C 12
Kellett Clo. *Wig* 2N 221
Kellett St. *Bolt* 7F 198
Kellett St. *Chor* 6E 174
Kellett St. *Roch* 5E 204
Kelmarsh Clo. *Blac* 8H 89
Kelne Ho. Lanc 8J 23
(off Castle Pk. M.)
Kelsall Av. *B'brn* 9B 120
Kelsall St. *Roch* 5D 204
Kelsey St. *Lanc* 8J 23
Kelso Av. *T Clev* 1D 62
Kelso Clo. *Liv* 4J 223
Kelsons Av. *T Clev* 1J 63
Kelswick Dri. *Nels* 4J 105
Kelverdale Rd. *T Clev* 3F 62
Kelvin Rd. *T Clev* 5D 62
Kelvin St. *Dar* 6N 157
Kelwood Av. *Bury* 8B 202
Kemble Clo. *Hor* 8C 196
Kem Mill La. *Whit W* 7D 154
Kemp Av. *Roch* 8A 204
Kemp Ct. *B'brn* 6N 119
Kemple Vw. *Clith* 5J 81
Kemp St. *Fltwd* 8H 41
Kempton Av. *Blac* 7E 88
Kempton Pk. Fold. *South* 2M 187
Kempton Pk. Rd. *Liv* 7D 222
Kempton Ri. *B'brn* 5N 139
Kempton Rd. *Lanc* 3M 29
Kenbury Clo. *Liv* 6M 223
Kenbury Rd. *Liv* 6M 223
Kendal Av. *Barfd* 7H 85
Kendal Av. *Blac* 1F 88
Kendal Av. *Roch* 3J 203
Kendal Av. *T Clev* 8D 54
Kendal Clo. *Hell* 1D 52
Kendal Clo. *Rainf* 9K 219
Kendal Dri. *Liv* 9C 216
Kendal Dri. *More* 4F 22
Kendal Dri. *Rainf* 9J 219
Kendal Ho. *Pres* 1K 135
Kendalmans. Garg 3M 53
(off West St.)
Kendalmans. *Gigg* 3N 35
Kendal Rd. *Hell* 1D 52
Kendal Rd. *K Lon* 6E 8
Kendal Rd. *Lyth A* 8D 108
Kendal Rd. *Ram* 3F 200
Kendal Rd. W. *Ram* 3E 200
Kendal Row. *Belt* 1F 158
Kendal St. *B'brn* 2M 139
Kendal St. *Clith* 2M 81
Kendal St. *Nels* 1H 105
Kendal St. *Pres* 9H 115
(in two parts)
Kendal Way. *South* 1B 206
Kenford Dri. *Wins* 9N 221
Kenilworth. *Roch* 7B 204
Kenilworth Av. *Fltwd* 1E 54
Kenilworth Clo. *Pad* 1J 123
Kenilworth Ct. *Fltwd* 1D 54
Kenilworth Ct. *Lyth A* 2F 128
Kenilworth Dri. *Clith* 5J 81
Kenilworth Dri. *Earby* 4D 78
Kenilworth Gdns. *Blac* 2B 108
Kenilworth Pl. *Fltwd* 1D 54
Kenilworth Pl. *Lanc* 2L 29
Kenilworth Rd. *Lyth A* 2F 128
Kenilworth Rd. *More* 5B 22
Kenilworth Rd. *South* 8B 186
Kenion Rd. *Roch* 7M 203
Kenion St. *Roch* 6C 204
Kenlis Rd. *Bncr* 8C 60
Kenmay Wlk. *Liv* 7M 223
Kenmure Pl. *Pres* 7J 115
Kennedy Clo. *Lanc* 1H 29
Kennelwood Av. *Liv* 7L 223
Kennessee Clo. *Liv* 2D 222
Kennessee Green. 2C 222
Kennet Dri. *Ful* 1J 115
Kennett Dri. *Ley* 5L 153
Kennington Rd. *Ful* 5K 115
Kensington Av. *Pen* 2E 134
Kensington Clo. *G'mnt* 4E 200
Kensington Clo. *Miln* 7K 205
Kensington Ct. *More* 2E 22
Kensington Ho. Lanc 2K 29
(off Kensington Rd.)
Kensington Ind. Est. *South* 8J 167
Kensington Pl. *Burn* 5B 124
Kensington Rd. *Blac* 6D 88
Kensington Rd. *Chor* 7D 174
Kensington Rd. *Lanc* 2K 29
Kensington Rd. *Lyth A* 4K 129
Kensington Rd. *More* 3B 22
Kensington Rd. *South* 7J 167
Kensington Rd. *T Clev* 9C 54
Kensington Rd. *Wig* 6N 221
Kensington St. *Nels* 3G 104
Kensington St. *Roch* 9B 204
Kent Av. *Form* 2A 214
Kent Av. *T Clev* 8E 54
Kent Av. *Walt D* 5N 135
Kent Ct. *Barfd* 7H 85
Kent Dri. *B'brn* 4E 140
Kent Dri. *Ley* 5N 153
Kentmere Av. *Far* 4K 153
Kentmere Av. *Roch* 2E 204
Kentmere Av. *Walt D* 6N 135
Kentmere Clo. *Burn* 1N 123
Kentmere Clo. *Fltwd* 1D 54
Kentmere Dri. *B'brn* 8F 138
Kentmere Dri. *Blac* 9J 89
Kentmere Dri. *Longt* 8M 133
Kentmere Gro. *More* 4D 22
Kentmere Rd. *Lanc* 4L 29
Kenton Clo. *Form* 6A 206
Kent Rd. *Blac* 6B 88
Kent Rd. *Form* 2A 214
Kent Rd. *South* 1G 187
Kent's Clo. *Wesh* 2K 111
Kent St. *B'brn* 4N 139
Kent St. *Burn* 2D 124
Kent St. *Fltwd* 8H 41
Kent St. *Lanc* 6K 23
Kent St. *Pres* 7J 115
Kent St. *Roch* 7C 204
Kent Wlk. *Has* 7F 160
Kent Way. *More* 5F 22
Kenway. *Rainf* 4L 225
Kenwood Av. *More* 4A 22
Kenworthy's Flats. *South* 6H 167
Kenworthy St. *B'brn* 2N 139
Kenworthy St. *Roch* 6F 204
Kenworthy Ter. *Roch* 6F 204
Kenwyn Av. *Blac* 7E 88
Kenyon Clo. *Liv* 4L 223
Kenyon Clough. *Ross* 1G 180
Kenyon Fold. 8J 203
Kenyon Fold. *Roch* 8J 203
Kenyon La. *Dink* 5N 99
Kenyon La. *H'pey* 8H 155
Kenyon Rd. *Brier* 3E 104
Kenyon Rd. *More* 3F 22
Kenyon Rd. *Stand* 2N 213
Kenyons La. *Form* 9A 206
Kenyons La. *Lyd & Mag* 7C 216
Kenyon's Lodge. *Liv* 8D 216
Kenyon St. *Acc* 2B 142
Kenyon St. *Bacup* 7M 163
Kenyon St. *B'brn* 3C 140
Kenyon St. *Bury* 9M 201
Kenyon St. *Ram* 7H 181
Kenyon St. *Ross* 4M 161
Kenyon Way. *Tot* 8E 200
Keppel Pl. *Burn* 4C 124
Kepple La. *Gars* 6L 59
Kerenhappuch St. Ram 9G 181
(off Buchanan St.)
Kerfoots La. *Skel* 3G 218
Kermoor Av. *Bolt* 7E 198
Kerr Pl. *Pres* 9G 114
Kersey Rd. *Liv* 9L 223
Kersey Wlk. *Liv* 9L 223
Kershaw Clo. Ross 9M 143
(off Burnley Rd.)
Kershaw Pas. *L'boro* 1H 205
Kershaw Rd. *Todm* 6K 165
Kershaw St. Bacup 5K 163
(off Union St.)
Kershaw St. *Bolt* 8J 199
Kershaw St. *Chor* 5G 174
Kershaw St. *Chu* 1L 141
Kershaw St. *Orr* 5L 221
Kerslake Way. *Liv* 7A 214
Kerslea Av. *Blac* 2K 89
Kerton Row. *South* 1F 186
Keston Gro. *Blac* 4C 108
Kestor La. *L'rdge* 3J 97
Kestrel Clo. *B'brn* 9L 119
Kestrel Clo. *H'pey* 3J 175
Kestrel Clo. *T Clev* 7F 54
Kestrel Ct. *South* 7K 167
Kestrel Dri. *Bury* 9N 201
Kestrel Dri. *Dar* 4L 157
Kestrel M. *Roch* 6K 203
Kestrel M. *Skel* 8N 211
Kestrel Pk. *Skel* 8N 211
Keswick Clo. *Acc* 8C 122
Keswick Clo. *Liv* 9D 216
Keswick Clo. *South* 1C 206
Keswick Clo. *Todm* 9J 147
Keswick Ct. Lanc 7M 23
(off Keswick Wlk.)
Keswick Dri. *B'brn* 8F 138
Keswick Gro. *Hey* 2K 27
Keswick Gro. *Kno S* 8M 41
Keswick Rd. *Blac* 7C 88
Keswick Rd. *Burn* 8E 104
Keswick Rd. *Lanc* 7L 23
Keswick Rd. *Lyth A* 9E 108
Keswick Wlk. *Lanc* 7M 23
Keswick Way. *Rainf* 9K 219
Kettering Rd. *South* 8B 186
Kevin Av. *Poul F* 6M 63
Kevin Gro. *Over* 6B 28
Kew Gdns. *Far* 4L 153
Kew Gdns. *Pen* 3E 134
Kew Gro. *T Clev* 2D 62
Kew Rd. *Nels* 9K 85
Kew Rd. *South* 2G 187
Keynsham Gro. *Burn* 2B 124
Key Sike La. *Todm* 2M 165
Key Vw. *Dar* 1C 178
Khyber St. *Col* 7N 85
Kibble Cres. *Burn* 7G 105
Kibble Gro. *Brier* 6H 105
Kibbles Brow. *Brom X* 5H 199
Kibboth Crew. *Ram* 7G 180
Kidbrooke Av. *Blac* 5B 108
Kidder St. *B'brn* 8L 139
Kiddrow La. *Burn* 2L 123
Kidlington Clo. *Los H* 8M 135
Kidsgrove. *Ing* 4C 114
Kielder Ct. *Lyth A* 4B 130
Kielder Dri. *Burn* 2C 124
Kilbane St. *Fltwd* 3F 54
Kilburn Dri. *Shev* 5K 213
Kilburn Gro. *Wig* 8N 221
Kilburn Rd. *Orr* 6F 220
Kilcrash La. *Nate* 5G 58
Kildale Clo. *Liv* 9B 216
Kildare Av. *T Clev* 8G 55
Kildare Rd. *Blac* 8D 62
Kildonan Av. *Blac* 3F 108
Kilgrimol Gdns. *Lyth A* 8C 108
Kilkerran Clo. *Chor* 6F 174
Killer St. *Ram* 7H 181
Killiard La. *B'brn* 3F 138
Killingbeck Clo. *Burs* 9B 190
Killington St. *Burn* 8G 105
Kilmory Pl. *Blac* 6F 62
Kilmuir Clo. *Ful* 4M 115
Kiln Bank. Whitw 4N 183
(off Tong End)
Kilnbank Av. *More* 3A 22
Kiln Bank La. *Whitw* 4N 183
Kiln Brow. *Brom X* 5J 199
Kiln Clo. *Clith* 1N 81
Kilncroft. *Clay W* 4D 154
Kilnerdeyne Ter. *Roch* 7B 204
Kilnfield. *Brom X* 5F 198
Kilngate. *Los H* 5M 135
Kiln Hill. *High* 4L 103
Kilnhouse La. *Lyth A* 8F 108
Kiln Ho. Way. *Osw* 5N 141
Kilnhurst. 3M 165
Kilnhurst Av. *Todm* 2M 165
Kilnhurst La. *Todm* 3M 165
Kilnhurst Mt. *Todm* 2N 165
Kilnhurst Rd. *Todm* 2M 165
Kiln La. *Gis* 1K 75
Kiln La. *Hamb* 1A 64
Kiln La. *Miln* 7J 205
Kiln La. *Pay* 6A 52
Kiln La. *Skel* 1J 219
Kiln La. *Wray* 7D 18
Kiln Mt. *Miln* 7J 205
Kilns, The. *Burn* 6F 124
Kiln St. *Nels* 2H 105
Kiln St. *Ram* 9G 180
Kiln Ter. Bacup 7H 163
(off Holme St.)
Kiln Wlk. *Roch* 3B 204
Kilruddery Rd. *Pres* 3H 135
Kilsby Clo. *Walt D* 5A 136
Kilshaw St. *Pem & Wig* 6M 221
Kilshaw St. *Pres* 9J 115
Kilworth Height. *Ful* 4F 114
Kilworth St. *Roch* 9A 204
Kimberley Av. *Blac* 4D 108
Kimberley Clo. *Brclf* 7K 105
Kimberley Rd. *Ash R* 7F 114
Kimberley Rd. *Bolt* 8E 198
Kimberley St. *Bacup* 8E 162
Kimberley St. *Brclf* 7K 105
Kimberley St. *Cop* 4A 194
Kimberly Clo. *Frec* 2N 131
Kimble Bank. *Brier* 6H 105
Kimble Clo. *G'mnt* 3E 200
Kimble Gro. *Brier* 6H 105
Kime St. *Burn* 3A 124
Kincardine Av. *Blac* 3G 108
Kincraig Ct. *Blac* 7F 62
Kincraig Pl. *Blac* 5F 62
Kincraig Rd. *Blac* 5F 62
Kinder Corner. *Poul F* 8H 63
Kinders Fold. *L'boro* 7J 185
Kineton Av. *Todm* 1M 165
King Edward Av. *Blac* 1B 88
King Edward Av. *Lyth A* 4G 128
King Edward St. *Osw* 5J 141
King Edward Ter. *Barfd* 9H 85
Kingfisher Bank. *Burn* 5N 123
Kingfisher Clo. *B'brn* 9M 119
Kingfisher Clo. *Chor* 9B 174
Kingfisher Clo. *Kirkby* 3K 223
Kingfisher Ct. *Cat* 3H 25
Kingfisher Ct. *Osw* 5L 141
Kingfisher Ct. *Roch* 1F 204
Kingfisher Ct. *South* 6K 167
Kingfisher Dri. *Bury* 9N 201
Kingfisher Dri. *Poul F* 9H 63
Kingfisher M. *Poul F* 9H 63
Kingfisher Pk. *Skel* 8N 211
Kingfisher St. *Pres* 7L 115
King George Av. *Blac* 1B 88
King Henry M. *Bolt B* 9K 51
King La. *Clith* 3L 81
Kings Arc. Lanc 8K 23
(off King St.)
Kings Arms Clo. *Lanc* 8J 23
Kings Av. *Ross* 6M 161
Kingsbarn Clo. *Ful* 3N 115
King's Bri. Clo. *B'brn* 7J 139
Kingsbridge Clo. *Pen* 7H 135
King's Bri. St. *B'brn* 7J 139
Kingsbridge Wharf. *B'brn* 7J 139
Kingsbury Clo. *South* 9B 186
Kingsbury Ct. *Skel* 8N 211
Kingsbury Pl. *Burn* 7H 105
King's Causeway. *Brier* 5H 105
Kings Clo. *Arns* 2F 4
King's Clo. *Poul F* 8L 63
King's Clo. *Stain* 5L 89
Kingscote Dri. *Blac* 3E 88
(in two parts)
Kings Ct. K Lon 6F 8
(off Market St.)
Kings Ct. *Ley* 6K 153
King's Cres. *Hey* 5M 21
Kings Cres. *Ley* 6K 153
King's Croft. *Walt D* 3N 135
King's Cft. M. *Walt D* 3N 135
Kingsdale Av. *Burn* 7F 104
Kingsdale Av. *Hey* 7L 21
Kingsdale Av. *Rib* 4N 115
Kingsdale Clo. *Ley* 9L 153
Kingsdale Clo. *Walt D* 3B 136
Kingsdale Rd. *Lanc* 9H 23
King's Dri. *Carn* 9B 12
Kings Dri. *Ful* 4G 115
Kings Dri. *Hodd* 6F 158
Kings Dri. *Pad* 3J 123
Kingsfield Rd. *Liv* 3B 222
Kingsfold. 6H 135
Kingsfold Dri. *Pen* 6F 134
King's Gardens. 7G 167
Kings Gro. *Roch* 1F 204
Kingshaven Dri. *Pen* 6H 135
Kings Hey Dri. *South* 5M 167
King's Highway. *Acc* 8E 122
(in two parts)
King's Highway. *Stone & Has* 5G 142
Kingshotte Gdns. *Barfd* 8G 84
Kingsland Gro. *Blac* 7D 88
Kingsland Gro. *Burn* 5F 124
Kingsland Rd. *Burn* 6F 124
Kingsland Rd. *Roch* 9M 203
Kingslea. *Adl* 5H 195
Kingsley Av. *Pad* 2K 123
Kingsley Clo. *Chu* 1M 141
Kingsley Clo. *Liv* 6B 216
Kingsley Clo. *T Clev* 9G 54
Kingsley Dri. *Chor* 9C 174
Kingsley Rd. *Blac* 7E 88
Kingsley Rd. *Cot* 3B 114
Kingsley Rd. *Lane* 5G 87
Kingsley St. *Nels* 9K 85
Kingsmead. *B'brn* 4D 140
Kingsmead. *Chor* 9E 174
Kings Mdw. *Ains* 1D 206
Kingsmede. *Blac* 3E 108
Kingsmere Av. *Lyth A* 8F 108
Kingsmill Av. *Whal* 2G 101
Kings Mill La. *Set* 3N 35
Kingsmuir Av. *Ful* 5N 115
Kingsmuir Clo. *Hey* 9K 21
King's Rd. *Acc* 9A 122
King's Rd. *B'brn* 8J 139
King's Rd. *Lyth A* 3E 128
Kings Rd. *Roch* 8E 204
Kings Rd. *T Clev* 1C 62
King's Sq. *Blac* 5C 88
Kingston Av. *Acc* 4N 141
Kingston Av. *Blac* 4C 108
Kingston Clo. *Kno S* 7M 41
Kingston Cres. *Ross* 8E 160
Kingston Cres. *South* 1B 168
Kingston Dri. *Lyth A* 2K 129
Kingston M. T Clev 9H 55
(off Crabtree Orchard)
Kingston Pl. *Lwr D* 9M 139
King St. *Acc* 2A 142
King St. *Bacup* 5K 163
King St. *Barn* 2M 77
King St. Ben 6L 19
(off Main St.)
King St. *B'brn* 4L 139
King St. *Blac* 5C 88
King St. *Brad* 8K 199
King St. *Brclf* 7K 105
King St. *Brier* 5E 104
King St. *Brom X* 5F 198
King St. *Carn* 9A 12
King St. *Chor* 8F 174
King St. *Chu* 2L 141
King St. *Clay M* 7M 121
King St. *Clith* 3L 81
King St. *Col* 6B 86
King St. *Fltwd* 9G 41
King St. *Gt Har* 4J 121
King St. *Has* 3G 160
King St. *Hor* 9B 196
King St. *Lanc* 8K 23
King St. *Ley* 6K 153
King St. *L'rdge* 3K 97
King St. *Los H* 9L 135
King St. *More* 3B 22
King St. *Pad* 1H 123
King St. *Ram* 8H 181
King St. *South* 8G 167
King St. *Todm* 1N 165
King St. *Waterf* 7C 162
King St. *Whal* 6J 101
King St. *Whitw* 3A 184
King St. E. *Roch* 8C 204
King St. S. *Roch* 8B 204
(in two parts)
King St. Ter. *Brier* 5E 104
King's Wlk. *T Clev* 7D 54
Kingsway. *Acc* 8E 122
Kingsway. *Ash R* 7C 114
Kingsway. *Bam B* 8A 136
Kingsway. *Blac* 2C 108
Kingsway. *Burn* 3E 124
Kingsway. *Chu* 9N 121
Kingsway. *Eux* 4A 174
Kingsway. *Gt Har* 3M 121
Kingsway. *Hap* 6H 123
Kingsway. *Hey* 9L 21
Kingsway. *Lanc* 7L 23
Kingsway. *Ley* 8H 153
Kingsway. *Lwr D* 9A 140
Kingsway. *Lyth A* 4J 129
Kingsway. *Pen* 2E 134
Kingsway. *Roch* 8E 204
Kingsway. *South* 7G 166
Kingsway. *T Clev* 1C 62
Kingsway Av. *Brough* 7F 94
Kingsway Ct. *Hey* 7M 21
Kingsway Retail Pk. *Roch* 6G 204
Kingsway W. *Pen* 2D 134
Kingswood Clo. *Lyth A* 4L 129
Kingswood Ct. *Liv* 6L 223
Kingswood Rd. *Ley* 6K 153
Kingswood St. *Pres* 1H 135
King William St. *B'brn* 3M 139
Kingwood Cres. *Wig* 5N 221
Kinlet Rd. *Wig* 7M 221
Kinloch Way. *Orm* 7J 209
Kinnerton Pl. *T Clev* 3F 62
Kinnical La. *Hale* 1C 6
Kinross Clo. *B'brn* 4A 140
Kinross Clo. *Ram* 3F 200
Kinross Cres. *Blac* 9G 88
Kinross St. *Burn* 4B 124
Kinross Wlk. B'brn 4A 140
(off William Hopwood St.)
Kinsway W. Ind. Est. *Roch* 8E 204
Kintbury Rd. *Lyth A* 4F 128
Kintour Rd. *Lyth A* 2L 129
Kintyre Clo. *Blac* 2F 108
Kintyre Way. *Hey* 9K 21
Kipling Ct. *Blac* 8H 89
Kipling Dri. *Blac* 8H 89
Kipling Mnr. *Blac* 8H 89
Kipling Pl. *Gt Har* 5H 121
Kirby Dri. *Frec* 2N 131
Kirby Rd. *B'brn* 7L 139
Kirby Rd. *Blac* 8B 88
Kirby Rd. *Nels* 2F 104
Kirk Av. *Clith* 3J 81
Kirkbeck Clo. *Brook* 2K 25
Kirkburn Vw. *Bury* 8H 201
Kirkby. 7H 223
Kirkby Av. *Ley* 6A 154
Kirkby Av. *T Clev* 9F 54
Kirkby Bank Rd. *Know I* 8N 223
Kirkby Lonsdale. 6E 8
Kirkby Lonsdale Golf Course. 3F 8
Kirkby Lonsdale Rd. *Halt* 1C 24
Kirkby Lonsdale Rd. *Over K* 9F 12
Kirkby Park. 7H 223
Kirkby Pool. 8K 223
Kirkby Rank La. *Know I* 9C 224
Kirkby Row. *Liv* 7H 223
Kirkby Sports Cen. 9H 223

Kirkby Stadium—Larchwood

Kirkby Stadium. 9H 223
Kirkdale Av. Lyth A 1F 128
Kirkdale Av. Ross 6C 162
Kirkdale Clo. Dar 9C 158
Kirkdale Gdns. Skel 4D 220
Kirkdale Rd. Lang 1C 120
Kirkdene Av. Foul 2A 86
Kirkdene M. Foul 2A 86
(off Dene Av.)
Kirkes Rd. Lanc 9L 23
Kirkfell Dri. Burn 1A 124
Kirkfield. Chip 5F 70
Kirkgate. Burn 5E 124
Kirkgate. K'ham 4N 111
Kirkgate. Set 3N 35
Kirkgate Cen. K'ham 4N 111
Kirkgate La. Tew 3F 12
Kirkham. 4N 111
Kirkham & Wesham By-Pass.
K'ham 4K 111
Kirkham Av. Blac 8E 88
Kirkham By-Pass. K'ham 5L 111
Kirkham Clo. Ley 6G 152
Kirkham Rd. Frec 7M 111
Kirkham Rd. South 2N 167
Kirkham Rd. Trea 3B 112
Kirkham Rd. Weet 8E 90
Kirkham St. Pres 9H 115
Kirkham St. Weet 4D 90
Kirkham Trad. Pk. K'ham 5N 111
Kirk Head. Much H 5J 151
Kirkhill Av. Has 5H 161
Kirk Hill Rd. Has 4H 161
Kirk Ho. Chu 2L 141
Kirkland Pl. Ash R 9B 114
Kirklands. Chip 5G 70
Kirklands. Hest B 8J 15
Kirklands Rd. Over K 1F 16
Kirklees Clo. Tot 6F 200
Kirklees Ind. Est. Tot 7F 200
Kirklees Rd. South 4F 186
Kirklees St. Tot 6E 200
Kirkmoor Clo. Clith 2K 81
Kirkmoor Rd. Clith 2K 81
Kirk Rd. Chu 1L 141
Kirkstall. Roch 5B 204
(off Spotland Rd.)
Kirkstall Av. Blac 8E 88
Kirkstall Av. Heyw 9G 202
Kirkstall Av. L'boro 8K 185
Kirkstall Av. S'stne 9C 102
Kirkstall Clo. Chor 9F 174
Kirkstall Dri. Barn 1N 77
Kirkstall Dri. Chor 9F 174
Kirkstall Dri. Liv 1B 214
Kirkstall Rd. Chor 9F 174
Kirkstall Rd. South 3F 186
Kirkstile Cres. Wig 9N 221
Kirkstone. Wig 4M 221
Kirkstone Av. B'brn 8F 138
Kirkstone Av. Fltwd 3D 54
Kirkstone Dri. More 3D 22
Kirkstone Dri. T Clev 4C 62
Kirkstone Rd. Lyth A 8D 108
Kirk Vw. Ross 6E 162
Kirstead Wlk. Liv 7G 223
Kirton Cres. Lyth A 2J 129
Kirton Pl. T Clev 2E 62
Kit Brow La. Ellel 1N 37
Kitchen St. Roch 5D 204
Kitson Wood Rd. Todm 8H 147
Kitter St. Roch 2E 204
Kitt Green. 3L 221
Kitt Grn. Rd. Wig 2L 221
Kittiwake Clo. T Clev 2F 62
Kittiwake Rd. H'pey 3J 175
Kittlingbourne Brow.
High W 5C 136
Kittygill La. K Lon 6E 8
Kitty La. Blac 5G 109
Knacks La. Roch 9L 183
Knaresboro Av. Blac 7F 88
Knaresborough Clo. Poul F 6J 63
Knebworth Clo. Clay W 5E 154
Kneps Farm Holiday Home &
Touring Pk. T Clev 9L 55
Knightbridge Wlk. Liv 3J 223
Knight Cres. Lwr D 1A 158
Knighton Av. B'brn 9K 119
Knightsbridge Av. Blac 3D 108
Knightsbridge Av. Col 6M 85
Knightsbridge Clo. Lyth A 2K 129
Knightsbridge Clo. Wesh 3K 111
Knightscliffe Cres. Shev 6G 213
Knights Clo. T Clev 2F 62
Knitting Row. 9F 56
Knitting Row. Out R 8F 56
Knob Hall Gdns. South 3M 167
Knob Hall La. South 3M 167
Knoll La. L Hoo 3K 151
Knoll, The. Slyne 9J 15
Knot Acre. New L 8D 134
Knot La. News 6C 52
Knot La. Walt D 3A 136
Knott End Golf Course. 9K 41
Knott End-on-Sea. 8L 41
Knott Hill. Shawf 9A 164
Knott Hill St. Shawf 9B 164
Knott La. Arns 2E 4
Knott Mt. Col 8N 85
Knotts. 4H 51
Knotts Dri. Col 8N 85
Knotts La. Bolt B 3H 51
Knotts La. Burn 3K 123
Knotts La. Col 7N 85
Knotts Rd. Todm 8G 146
Knott St. Dar 6A 158
Knowe Hill Cres. Lanc 4M 29
Knowl Clo. Ram 2H 201
Knowle Av. Blac 1B 88
Knowle Av. South 7C 186
Knowle Av. T Clev 2E 62
Knowle Green. 1C 98
Knowle Grn. Rd. Ribch 3N 97
Knowle La. Dar 4A 158
Knowles Brow. Stony 8A 80
Knowlesly Meadows. Dar 9C 158
Knowlesly Rd. Dar 9B 158
Knowles Rd. Lyth A 1E 128
Knowles St. Chor 8E 174
Knowles St. Pres 9N 115
Knowles St. Rish 8H 121
Knowles Wood Dri. Chor 8C 174
Knowle, The. Blac 9C 62
Knowley. 4H 175
Knowley Brow. Chor 4G 175
Knowl Gap Av. Has 6F 160
Knowl Hill Dri. Roch 3J 203
Knowl La. Roch 9F 182
Knowl Mdw. Ross 8F 160
Knowlmere St. Acc 1A 142
Knowl Rd. Roch 6G 205
Knowl Syke St. Ward 7F 184
Knowl Vw. L'boro 3J 205
Knowl Vw. Tot 7F 200
Knowl Wood. 5K 165
Knowlwood Bottom. Todm 5J 165
Knowlwood Rd. Todm 5K 165
Knowlys Av. Hey 8L 21
Knowlys Cres. Hey 8L 21
Knowlys Dri. Hey 8L 21
Knowlys Gro. Hey 8L 21
Knowlys Rd. Hey 8K 21
Knowsley Av. Blac 7E 88
Knowsley Av. Far 3M 153
Knowsley Av. Todm 6K 165
(off Rochdale Rd.)
Knowsley Clo. Hogh 6H 137
Knowsley Clo. Lanc 1H 29
Knowsley Cres. Shawf 9B 164
Knowsley Cres. T Clev 1J 63
Knowsley Cres. Weet 9D 90
Knowsley Dri. Hogh 6H 137
Knowsley Ga. Fltwd 9D 40
Knowsley Ind. Pk. Know I 8N 223
Knowsley La. Hth C 1N 195
Knowsley La. Tur 2L 179
Knowsley Pk. Way. Has 7G 160
Knowsley Rd. B'brn & Wilp 4N 119
Knowsley Rd. Has 6G 160
Knowsley Rd. Ley 7M 153
Knowsley Rd. Orm 8L 209
Knowsley Rd. South 5H 167
Knowsley Rd. Ind. Est. Has 6G 160
Knowsley Rd. W. Clay D 3M 119
Knowsley Sports Club. 9G 223
Knowsley St. Col 7A 86
Knowsley St. Pres 1K 135
(in two parts)
Knowsley St. Roch 5B 204
Knowsley Vw. Rainf 2J 225
Knox Gro. Blac 7D 88
Knunck Knowles Dri. Clith 2L 81
Knutsford Rd. Blac 8H 89
Knutsford Wlk. Liv 7C 216
Korea Rd. Ful 4L 115
Kramar Wlk. Liv 8L 223
Kumara Cres. Blac 9H 89
Kyan St. Burn 8F 104
Kylemore Av. Blac 9D 62
Kytson Clo. Blac 3C 88

L

Laburnham Cotts. Good 7M 143
Laburnum Av. Los H 8L 135
Laburnum Av. Lyth A 3A 130
Laburnum Av. Tot 6E 200
Laburnum Clo. Burn 5B 124
Laburnum Clo. Pres 6M 115
Laburnum Cotts. Burn 1M 123
Laburnum Ct. Tot 6E 200
Laburnum Cres. Liv 7J 223
Laburnum Dri. Ful 1G 115
Laburnum Dri. Osw 5M 141
Laburnum Dri. Skel 2H 219
Laburnum Gro. Burs 7C 190
Laburnum Gro. Lanc 8H 23
Laburnum Gro. Mag 1D 222
Laburnum Gro. South 7M 167
Laburnum La. Miln 9K 205
Laburnum Pk. Bolt 8H 199
Laburnum Pk. Carn 1N 15
Laburnum Rd. B'brn 9A 120
Laburnum Rd. Chor 3F 174
Laburnum Rd. Lanc 6K 23
Laburnum Rd. Ross 8F 160
Laburnum St. Blac 3D 88
Laburnum St. Has 4F 160
Laburnum Ter. Roch 9B 204
Laburnum Way. L'boro 9J 185
Lacey Ct. Has 4G 161
Lachman Rd. Traw 8E 86
Lacy Av. Pen 6H 135
Lacy Av. Todm 6K 165
Ladbrooke Gro. Burn 7C 124
Lade End. Hey 8K 21
Ladies Row. Whar 6D 92
Ladies Wlk. Lanc 6L 23
Ladies Wlk. Trad. Est. Lanc 6L 23
Lady Alice's Dri. Lath 4B 210
Lady Anne Clo. Scar 6F 188
Lady Av. Lwr D 1A 158
Lady Bank Av. Ful 2N 115
Ladybower La. Poul F 8H 63
Lady Crosse Dri. Whit W 8E 154
Lady Green. 7D 214
Lady Grn. Ct. Ince B 8E 214
Lady Grn. La. Liv 7D 214
Lady Hey Cres. Lea 8N 113
Lady House. 9H 205
Ladyhouse Clo. Miln 8K 205
Lady Ho. Fold. Miln 9J 205
(off Ashfield La.)
Ladyhouse La. Miln 8J 205
(in two parts)
Ladyman St. Pres 1H 135
Lady Pl. Walt D 4A 136
Ladysmith Av. Bury 8M 201
Ladysmith Rd. Ash R 7F 114
Lady St. Pres 9J 115
Lady's Wlk. W'head 7N 209
Ladyway Dri. Ful 2M 115
Ladywell St. Pres 9H 115
Lafford La. Roby M & Uph 9F 212
Lagonda Dri. Blac 3M 109
Laidley's Wlk. Fltwd 8E 40
Lairgill. Ben 6L 19
Laitha La. K Lon 6F 8
Laithbutts La. Neth K 4C 16
Laithe St. Burn 5D 124
Laithe St. Col 7N 85
Laithwaite Rd. Wig 4N 221
Lake Av. More 5N 21
Lake Bank. L'boro 3K 205
Lakeber Av. Ben 6L 19
Lakeber Clo. Ben 6L 19
(off Lakeber Av.)
Lakeber Dri. Ben 6L 19
Lake Gro. More 4N 21
Lakeland Clo. Bill 7G 100
Lakeland Clo. Fort 2M 45
Lakeland Gdns. Chor 9C 174
Lakeland Way. Burn 1N 123
Lakeland Wildlife Oasis. 2B 6
Lakenheath Dri. Bolt 7F 198
Lake Point. Lyth A 5K 129
Lake Rd. Lyth A 5J 129
Lake Rd. More 5N 21
Lake Rd. N. Lyth A 4J 129
Lakes Dri. Orr 5H 221
Lake Side. L'boro 3K 205
Lakeside Av. Bil 8H 221
Lakeside Ct. Rainf 4L 225
Lakeside Gdns. Rainf 4L 225
Lakeside Miniature Railway. 7G 166
Lake St. Roch 7C 204
Lake Vw. Bel 9K 177
Lake Vw. L'boro 7J 185
Lake Vw. Rd. Col 4A 86
Lake Wlk. Wig 4L 221
Lakeway. Blac 4F 88
Lakewood Av. T Clev 2D 62
Lamaleach Dri. Frec 2M 131
Lamaleach Pk. Frec 3L 131
Lamberhead Green. 5L 221
Lamberhead Ho. Wig 5L 221
Lamberhead Ind. Est. Wig 6L 221
Lamberhead Rd. Wig 5L 221
Lambert Clo. Rib 6A 116
Lambert Rd. Lanc 5J 23
Lambert Rd. Rib 6N 115
Lambert St. Traw 9F 86
Lambeth Clo. B'brn 4A 140
Lambeth St. B'brn 3A 140
Lambeth St. Col 6E 86
Lambeth Ter. Roch 8A 204
Lambing Clough La. Hur G 2M 99
Lambourne. Skel 8M 211
Lambourne Gro. Miln 8J 205
Lambridge Clo. More 5B 22
Lamb Roe. 2J 101
Lambshear La. Liv 7B 216
Lambs Hill Clo. T Clev 2K 63
Lamb's La. Pil 1F 56
Lambs Rd. T Clev 2K 63
Lambton Gates. Ross 5A 162
Lambton St. Wig 6M 221
Lamlash Rd. B'brn 4D 140
Lammack. 8K 119
Lammack Rd. B'brn 8K 119
Lamour Pl. Fltwd 1D 54
Lanark Av. Blac 5C 62
Lanark St. Burn 5B 124
Lancambe Ct. Lanc 6G 22
Lancashire Dri. Ley 3K 153
Lancashire Enterprise Bus. Pk. Ley 3K 153
Lancashire Lynx R.L.F.C. 8F 174
(off Duke St., Victory Pk.)
Lancashire St. More 4M 21
Lancaster. 9J 23
Lancaster Av. Acc 1N 141
Lancaster Av. Gt Ecc 6A 66
Lancaster Av. Has 7F 160
Lancaster Av. Ley 6A 154
Lancaster Av. Lyth A 4F 128
Lancaster Av. Ram 1F 200
Lancaster Av. T Clev 1J 63
Lancaster Castle. 7J 23
Lancaster Cathedral. 8L 23
Lancaster City F.C. 8J 23
(Giant Axe)
Lancaster City Mus. 8K 23
Lancaster Clo. Adl 6K 195
Lancaster Clo. Gt Ecc 6A 66
Lancaster Clo. Kno S 8M 41
Lancaster Clo. Mag 1E 222
Lancaster Clo. South 1E 186
Lancaster Ct. Chor 8E 174
Lancaster Cres. Skel 2J 219
Lancaster Dri. Brins 7N 155
Lancaster Dri. Bury 5L 201
Lancaster Dri. Clay M 6M 121
Lancaster Dri. Clith 4J 81
Lancaster Dri. Pad 3J 123
Lancaster Dri. South 1D 168
Lancaster Gdns. South 1E 186
Lancaster Ga. Banks 1E 168
Lancaster Ga. Fltwd 1D 54
Lancaster Ga. Lanc 8K 23
(off Penny St.)
Lancastergate. Ley 7J 153
Lancaster Ga. Nels 3G 105
Lancaster Ho. Ley 4K 153
Lancaster Ho. Pres 1K 135
Lancaster La. Ley 6N 153
Lancaster La. Parb 1N 211
Lancaster Maritime Mus. 7J 23
Lancaster Morecambe By-Pass.
Hey & Heat O 2L 27
Lancaster Pl. Adl 5J 195
Lancaster Pl. B'brn 3J 139
Lancaster Rd. Blac 8G 89
Lancaster Rd. Cabus 2N 59
Lancaster Rd. Carn 2M 15
Lancaster Rd. Cat 2G 24
Lancaster Rd. C'ham 7G 37
Lancaster Rd. Heat O 1C 28
Lancaster Rd. Horn 7C 18
Lancaster Rd. Kno S 8L 41
Lancaster Rd. More 3C 22
Lancaster Rd. Out R 4M 65
Lancaster Rd. Over 6B 28
Lancaster Rd. Pil 9K 43
(in two parts)
Lancaster Rd. Pre 1B 56
Lancaster Rd. Pres 9J 115
Lancaster Rd. South 2D 186
Lancaster Rd. Wig 2M 221
Lancaster Rd. N. Pres 8J 115
Lancaster St. B'brn 4K 139
Lancaster St. Col 6A 86
Lancaster St. Cop 4B 194
Lancaster St. Osw 5J 141
Lancaster Ter. Roch 3H 203
Lancaster Wlk. Wig 2N 221
Lancaster Way. Pres 9K 115
(off St John's Shop. Cen.)
Lancaster W. Bus. Pk. Hey 4N 27
Lancewood Pl. Wig 5N 221
Lancia Cres. Blac 3N 109
(off Bentley Dri.)
Lancing Dri. Liv 8C 222
Lancing Pl. B'brn 5K 139
Landcrest Clo. Frec 7N 111
Land Ga. Shawf 1B 184
Landing La. Bolt B 8F 50
Land La. Longt 1A 152
Land La. South 2C 168
Landless St. Brier 5E 104
Landseer Av. Blac 7C 62
Landseer Clo. Burn 6C 124
Landseer St. Pres 8M 115
Landsmoor Dri. Longt 7L 133
Lane Bottom. 9N 205
Lanedale. Longt 7L 133
Lane End. 10F 52
Lane End La. Bacup 6L 163
Lane End Rd. Bacup 7L 163
Lane Ends. 7H 123
(Burnley)
Lane Ends. 7F 50
(Clitheroe)
Lane Ends. Nels 4H 105
Lane Ends Trad. Est. Ash R 6F 114
Lanefield Dri. T Clev 8C 54
Lane Foot Brow. Ben 1L 33
Lane Head. 4L 163
(Bacup)
Lane Head. 4G 86
(Colne)
Lane Head La. Bacup 4K 163
Lane Heads. 7B 66
Lane Ho. Traw 9F 86
Lane Ho. Clo. B'brn 8J 139
Laneshaw Bridge. 5H 87
Laneshaw Clo. Dar 3M 157
Laneside. 9B 122
Lane Side. 5G 160
Laneside. Alt 3C 122
Laneside Av. Acc 9A 122
Laneside Av. High 5K 161
Laneside Clo. Has 6H 161
Laneside Clo. L'boro 8K 185
Laneside Ct. Ross 5N 161
Laneside Rd. Has 5H 161
Laneside St. Todm 3K 165
Laneside Wlk. Miln 6J 205
Lane, The. Sun P 6C 26
Lane Top. Traw 7F 86
Langber End La. I'ton 5N 19
Langcliffe. 2N 35
Langcliffe Rd. Rib 5A 116
Langcliffe Rd. Set 2N 35
Langdale. Cat 3H 25
Langdale Av. Clith 4J 81
Langdale Av. Crost 3M 171
Langdale Av. Hesk B 3B 150
Langdale Av. Ross 5K 161
Langdale Clo. Acc 8C 122
Langdale Clo. B'brn 8F 138
Langdale Clo. Frec 2M 131
Langdale Clo. Kirkby 9L 223
Langdale Clo. T Clev 1H 63
Langdale Clo. Walt D 7N 135
Langdale Ct. Fltwd 2E 54
Langdale Ct. Gars 5M 59
Langdale Ct. Pen 4F 134
Langdale Cres. Orr 3L 221
Langdale Cres. Rib 6A 116
Langdale Dri. Burs 9C 190
Langdale Dri. Liv 9D 216
Langdale Gdns. South 4F 186
Langdale Gro. Whit W 8D 154
Langdale Pl. Blac 9J 89
Langdale Pl. Lanc 6L 23
Langdale Ri. Col 5C 86
Langdale Rd. B'brn 9E 138
Langdale Rd. Blac 9H 89
Langdale Rd. Carn 1B 16
Langdale Rd. Lanc 6L 23
Langdale Rd. Ley 9K 153
Langdale Rd. L'rdge 5H 97
Langdale Rd. Lyth A 8D 108
Langdale Rd. More 3C 22
Langdale Rd. Orr 4L 221
Langdale Rd. Pad 8H 103
Langdale Rd. Rib 6A 116
Langden Brook M. More 6F 22
Langden Brook Sq. B'brn 5A 140
Langden Cres. Bam B 9B 136
Langden Dri. Rib 6C 116
Langden Fold. Grims 9F 96
Langdon Way. Blac 9E 62
Langfield. Wors 3M 125
Langfield Av. Blac 4C 108
Langfield Clo. Ful 1J 115
Langford St. Acc 7D 142
Langham Av. Acc 9A 122
Langham Clo. Bolt 8G 198
Langham Rd. B'brn 1L 139
Langham Rd. Stand 3N 213
Langham St. Burn 3N 123
Langho. 9C 100
Langholm Clo. Wins 8N 221
Langholme Clo. Barfd 1G 104
Langholme Clo. Ley 7G 152
Langholme Rd. Pen 4D 134
Langholme St. Nels 3J 105
Langho St. B'brn 7K 139
Langho Woods. Old L 5C 100
Langley Brook Rd. Burs I 9N 189
Langley Clo. Form 9A 214
Langley Clo. Stand 2N 213
Langley Ct. Burs I 8N 189
Langley La. Goos 6J 95
Langley Pl. Burs I 9N 189
Langley Rd. Burs I 8N 189
Langley Rd. Lanc 9L 23
Langley St. Wig 5N 221
Langport Clo. Ful 1J 115
Langridge Way. More 5B 22
Langroyd M. Col 4B 86
(off Croft, The)
Langroyd Rd. Col 5B 86
Langsford Clo. Barn 2N 77
Langshaw Dri. Clith 5L 81
Langshaw La. Ellel 2M 37
Lang St. Acc 2N 141
Lang St. Blac 4C 88
Langthwaite Rd. Quer 1A 30
Langton Av. Stand 3N 213
Langton Brow. E'ston 9F 172
Langton Brow. L'rdge 3K 97
Langton Clo. E'ston 9G 172
Langton Clo. Lanc 4L 23
Langton Clo. Ley 7F 152
Langton Pl. Stand 3N 213
Langton Rd. Kirkby 5L 223
Langton Rd. K'ham 4M 111
Langton St. Pres 1G 135
Langton Ter. Roch 9B 204
Langtree. 1N 213
Langtree. Skel 9M 211
Langtree La. Elsw 9L 65
Langtree La. Stand 1N 213
Langwood. Fltwd 2E 54
Langwood La. Uph 1N 225
Langwyth Rd. Burn 4J 125
Lansborough Clo. Ley 7D 152
Lansbury Pl. Nels 9K 85
Lansbury St. Orr 5K 221
Lansdowne Clo. Burn 5C 124
Lansdowne Gro. More 1E 22
Lansdowne Pl. Blac 4B 88
Lansdowne Rd. Lyth A 3J 129
Lansdowne Rd. More 1E 22
Lansdowne Rd. South 8L 167
Lansdowne St. B'brn 5J 139
Lansdowne St. Roch 6N 203
Lansdown Hill. Ful 1F 114
Lansdown Rd. Wesh 2M 111
Lansil Golf Course. 5M 23
Lansil Ind. Est. Lanc 4L 23
Lansil Wlk. Lan I 5L 23
Lansil Way. Lan I 5L 23
Lanterns, The. Poul F 7K 63
Lapford Cres. Liv 6M 223
Lapford Wlk. Liv 6M 223
Lappet Gro. Cot 4B 114
Lapwing Clo. Roch 6J 203
Lapwing Row. Lyth A 1L 129
Lapwings, The. Poul F 9H 63
Larbreck. 5J 65
Larbreck Av. Blac 3E 88
Larbreck Av. Elsw 1L 91
Larbreck Rd. Poul F 1G 90
Larbreck Rd. Sing 7F 64
(in two parts)
Larch Av. Chor 4G 174
Larch Av. Wig 5N 221
Larch Clo. B'brn 8G 139
Larch Clo. Frec 3L 131
Larch Clo. Pre 8N 41
Larch Clo. Ross 7L 161
Larch Clo. Skel 2J 219
Larch Dri. Brins 8A 156
Larch Dri. Frec 3L 131
Larches. 9A 114
Larches Av. Ash R 8C 114
Larches La. Ash R 8B 114
Larches, The. B'brn 1N 139
Larch Ga. Ful 2M 115
Larch Ga. Hogh 6G 136
Larch Gro. Bam B 7B 136
Larch Gro. Gars 4N 59
Larch Gro. Lanc 8H 23
Larch Rd. Osw 5M 141
Larch St. B'brn 1A 140
Larch St. Burn 2A 124
Larch St. Nels 2K 105
Larch St. South 9L 167
Larch Towers. Liv 7L 223
Larchway. Firg 6G 205
Larch Way. L'rdge 2J 97
Larchwood. Ash R 8B 114

A-Z Lancashire 257

Larchwood—Lincoln St.

Larchwood. *Lanc* 3L 29
Larchwood. *Pen* 4E 134
Larchwood Av. *Liv* 3B 222
Larchwood Clo. *Lyth A* 4L 129
Larchwood Cres. *Ley* 6H 153
Largs Rd. *B'brn* 6C 140
Lark Av. *Pen* 4H 135
Lark Ct. *Fltwd* 3D 54
Larkfield. *E'ston* 8E 172
Larkfield Clo. *G'mnt* 3E 200
Larkfield Ct. *South* 3N 167
Larkfield La. *South* 3N 167
Larkhill. *B'brn* 3N 139
Lark Hill. *High W* 5D 136
Larkhill. *Old L* 5C 100
Lark Hill. *Ross* 4M 161
Larkhill. *Skel* 8M 211
Larkhill Av. *Burn* 5G 104
Larkhill Gro. *Liv* 8A 214
Larkhill Pl. *Roch* 4B 204
Larkhill Rd. *Pres* 1L 135
Lark Hill St. *Blac* 4C 88
Larkhill St. *Pres* 1L 135
Larkholme Av. *Fltwd* 3E 54
Larkholme La. *Fltwd* 3E 54
Larkholme Lodge. *Fltwd* 3F 54
Larkholme Pde. *Fltwd* 3C 54
(in two parts)
Larkspur Clo. *B'brn* 8E 138
Larkspur Clo. *South* 8K 167
Lark St. *Burn* 2A 124
Lark St. *Col* 5B 86
Lark St. *Dar* 1B 178
Last Drop Village. 4G 199
Latham Av. *Blac* 7E 88
Latham Av. *Orm* 7M 209
Latham Cres. *Tar* 9E 150
Latham La. *Orr* 2K 221
Latham St. *Burn* 9F 104
Latham St. *Pres* 2K 135
Lathom. 2F 210
Lathom Av. *More* 4D 22
Lathom Av. *Parb* 1M 211
Lathom Clo. *Burs* 9C 190
Lathom Dri. *Liv* 8D 216
Lathom Dri. *Rainf* 3K 225
Lathom Gro. *More* 4D 22
Lathom Ho. *Burs* 9C 190
Lathom La. *Lath* 5A 210
Lathom Pk. & Gardens. 5G 210
Lathom Rd. *Bic* 4C 218
Lathom Rd. *South* 5H 167
Lathom St. *Bury* 9M 201
Lathom Way. *Gars* 6A 60
Latimer Clo. *Orr* 4J 221
Latimer Dri. *New L* 8C 134
Latin St. *Roch* 7B 204
Lauder Clo. *Liv* 4J 223
Lauderdale Av. *T Clev* 2D 62
Lauderdale Cres. *Rib* 5B 116
Lauderdale Rd. *Rib* 5B 116
Lauderdale St. *Pres* 2H 135
Laund. 3L 161
Laund Clough Nature Reserve. 5D 142
Laund Ga. *Fence* 2B 104
Laund Gro. *Acc* 5D 142
Laund Hey Vw. *Has* 6G 161
Laund La. *Has* 4H 161
Laund La. *Withn* 2N 155
Laund Rd. *Acc* 5C 142
Laundry La. *I'ton* 3N 19
Laundry Rd. *Blac* 4G 109
Laundry Rd. N. *Blac* 3G 108
Laund St. *Ross* 3L 161
Laund, The. *Ley* 6D 152
Laura St. *Bury* 3H 201
Laurel Av. *Blac* 8E 88
Laurel Av. *Burs* 7C 190
Laurel Av. *Dar* 5B 158
Laurel Av. *Eux* 3L 173
Laurel Av. *Fltwd* 4F 54
Laurel Av. *Lyth A* 3A 130
Laurel Bank. *Lanc* 9H 23
Laurel Bank Av. *Ful* 6F 114
Laurel Ct. *Roch* 7E 204
Laurel Dri. *Skel* 1J 219
Laurel Dri. *T Clev* 3H 63
Laurel Gro. *South* 7L 167
Laurels Dri. *L'boro* 2J 205
Laurels, The. *Cop* 3B 194
Laurel St. *Bacup* 4K 163
Laurel St. *Burn* 5F 124
Laurel St. *Pres* 1K 135
Laurel St. *Tot* 7E 200
Laureston Av. *Hey* 1L 27
Laurie Pl. *Roch* 4C 204
Laurier Av. *Blac* 3C 108
Laurier Rd. *Burn* 8F 104
(in two parts)
Lauriston Clo. *Blac* 3G 108
Lavender Clo. *Ful* 3M 115
Lavender Gro. *Chor* 9E 174
Lavender Hill. *Ross* 6L 161
Laverick Rd. *Halt* 7C 16
Laverton Rd. *Lyth A* 3G 128
Lawflat. *Ward* 8F 184
Lawley Rd. *B'brn* 3H 139
Lawn Ct. *Blac* 6D 88
Lawns Av. *Orr* 6F 220
Lawnsdale Cvn. Pk. *Lyth A* 8D 110
Lawns, The. *South* 4M 167
Lawn St. *Burn* 1E 124
Lawnswood. *Roch* 9N 203
Lawnswood Av. *Lanc* 4L 29
Lawnswood Av. *Poul F* 9H 63
Lawnswood Cres. *Blac* 8J 89
Lawnswood Dri. *More* 6B 22
Lawn Tennis Ct. *Blac* 4D 108
Lawnwood Av. *Chor* 9C 174
Lawrence Av. *Burn* 5A 124
(in two parts)
Lawrence Av. *Lyth A* 2G 129
Lawrence Av. *Pres* 3L 135
Lawrence Av. *S'stne* 8D 102
Lawrence Av. *Walt D* 6N 135
Lawrence Clo. *Roch* 4L 203
Lawrence Ct. *Lanc* 2K 29
Lawrence Dri. *Arns* 2E 4
Lawrence La. *E'ston* 7F 172
Lawrence Rd. *Chor* 7D 174
Lawrence Rd. *Pen* 3E 134
Lawrence Row. *Fltwd* 9G 40
Lawrence St. *B'brn* 4K 139
(in two parts)
Lawrence St. *Blac* 9B 88
Lawrence St. *Ful* 6G 115
Lawrence St. *Pad* 9J 103
Lawrence St. *Ross* 3D 162
Lawrie Av. *Ram* 9G 180
Lawson Av. *Hor* 9D 196
Lawson Clo. *Lanc* 4K 29
Lawson Gdns. *Slyne* 9J 15
Lawson Pl. *Slyne* 9J 15
Lawson Rd. *Blac* 7F 88
Lawson Rd. *Lyth A* 7G 108
Lawsons Ct. *T Clev* 2J 63
Lawsons Rd. *T Clev* 1J 63
Lawson St. *Bolt* 9E 198
Lawson St. *Chor* 6G 174
Lawson St. *Pres* 9J 115
Lawson St. *Ross* 8M 143
Lawson St. *South* 7N 167
Laws Ter. *L'boro* 9J 185
Law St. *Roch* 9N 203
Law St. *Ross* 6D 162
Law St. *Todm* 7E 146
Law St. *W'den* 8L 165
Lawswood. *T Clev* 2J 63
Lawton Clo. *Wheel* 6K 155
Lawton St. *Roch* 4D 204
Lawton St. *South* 6J 167
Laxey Gro. *Pres* 6N 115
Laxey Rd. *B'brn* 7M 139
Laycock Ga. *Blac* 4D 88
Laycock St. *Roch* 2F 204
Layfield Clo. *Tot* 6C 200
Laythe Barn Clo. *Miln* 7H 205
Layton. 4E 88
Layton Rd. *Ash R* 8B 114
Layton Rd. *Blac* 3E 88
Lazenby Av. *Fltwd* 2C 54
Lea. 7A 114
Lea Bank. *Ross* 5B 162
Leach Clo. *Roch* 3F 204
Leach Ct. *Roch* 8C 204
Leach Cres. *Lyth A* 7F 108
Leaches Rd. *Ram* 5J 181
Leachfield Clo. *Gal* 2L 37
Leachfield Ind. Est. *Gars* 3M 59
Leachfield Rd. *Gal* 2K 37
Leach La. *Lyth A* 7E 108
Leach Pl. *Bam B* 8D 136
Leach's Pas. *L'boro* 1J 205
Leach St. *B'brn* 6M 139
Leach St. *Col* 7N 85
Leach St. *Miln* 8J 205
Leach St. *Roch* 7E 204
Lea Cres. *Orm* 5K 209
Leacroft. *Lwr D* 1A 158
Leadale. *Lea* 7A 114
Leadale Clo. *Stand* 3N 213
Leadale Grn. *Ley* 6G 153
Leadale Rd. *Ley* 6G 153
Leader St. *Pem* 5M 221
Lea Dri. *B'brn* 1L 157
Leaford Av. *Blac* 2E 88
Leaf Ter. *Roch* 1A 204
Leafy Clo. *Ley* 8L 153
Lea Ga. Clo. *Bolt* 8K 199
Leagram Cres. *Rib* 6B 116
League St. *Roch* 8D 204
Leah St. *L'boro* 9L 185
Lea La. *A'ton* 6A 18
Lea La. *Hey* 1K 27
Lea La. *Lea T* 6K 113
Leamington Av. *Burn* 9G 105
Leamington Av. *Bury* 5K 201
Leamington Av. *South* 8D 186
Leamington Rd. *B'brn* 2J 139
Leamington Rd. *Blac* 5C 88
Leamington Rd. *Lyth A* 2F 128
Leamington Rd. *More* 5D 22
Leamington Rd. *South* 8C 186
Leamington St. *Nels* 3J 105
Leamington St. *Roch* 5B 204
Lea Mt. Dri. *Bury* 9B 202
Leander Gdns. *Poul F* 9K 63
Leapers Vw. *Over K* 1F 16
Lea Rd. *Cot & Lea T* 5N 113
Lea Rd. *Whit W* 1E 174
Leaside Clo. *Roch* 3A 204
Leatherbarrows La. *Liv* 3E 222
Leathercote. *Gars* 6N 59
Leathwood. *Liv* 1D 222
Lea Town. 6K 113
Leavengreave Ct. *Whitw* 2A 184
Leaverholme Clo. *Cliv* 1L 145
Leaver St. *Burn* 4M 123
Leavesley Rd. *Blac* 2C 88
Lea Way Clo. *T Clev* 4K 63
Lebanon St. *Burn* 4G 124
Leck. 8J 9
Leckhampton Rd. *Blac* 2B 88
Leckonby St. *Gt Ecc* 6N 65
Leckwith Rd. *Boot* 8A 222
Ledburn. *Skel* 9M 211
Ledbury Av. *Lyth A* 3H 129
Ledbury Rd. *Blac* 3G 89
Ledsham Rd. *Liv* 8H 223
Ledsham Wlk. *Liv* 8H 223
Ledson Gro. *Augh* 4G 217
Ledson Pk. *Liv* 4L 223
Lee. 2A 48
Lee Brook Clo. *Ross* 3M 161
Leebrook Rd. *Ross* 3L 161
Lee Ct. *Dar* 3M 157
Leeds Clo. *B'brn* 4A 140
Leeds Rd. *Blac* 5D 88
Leeds Rd. *Nels* 2J 105
(in two parts)
Lee Ga. *Bolt* 8K 199
Lee Grn. St. Burn 1E 124
(off North St.)
Lee Gro. *Burn* 5K 125
Leek St. *Pres* 9A 116
Lee La. *Bis* 6N 191
Lee La. *Hor* 9B 196
Lee La. *Rish* 6G 120
Leemans Hill St. *Tot* 8F 200
Leeming La. *Burt L* 3K 19
Lee Rd. *Bacup* 7J 163
Lee Rd. *Blac* 1H 109
Lee Rd. *Nels* 9K 85
Lees. 4L 71
Leesands Clo. *Ful* 4N 115
Lees Ct. *Hey* 9K 21
Leeside Av. *Liv* 9K 223
Leeside Clo. *Liv* 9L 223
Lees La. *Dal & Roby M* 4N 211
Leeson Av. *Char R* 1N 193
(in two parts)
Lees Rd. *And* 5K 195
Lees Rd. *Know I* 9N 223
Lee's St. *Bacup* 7N 163
Lees, The. *Cliv* 1L 145
Lee St. *Acc* 2B 142
Lee St. *Bacup* 5K 163
Lee St. *Barfd* 8H 85
Lee St. *Burn* 1E 124
Lee St. *Bury* 5L 201
Lee St. *L'boro* 8L 185
Lee St. *L'rdge* 3H 97
Lee St. *Ross* 3M 161
Leeswood. *Skel* 9M 211
Leet Rd. *High* 5L 103
Leeward Clo. *Lwr D* 1N 157
Leeward Rd. *Ash R* 9C 114
Legh La. *Tar* 3M 169
Leicester Av. *Gars* 5M 59
Leicester Av. *Hor* 9B 196
Leicester Av. *T Clev* 9D 54
Leicester Ga. *T Clev* 9E 54
Leicester Lodge. Rib 5B 116
(off Grange Av.)
Leicester Rd. *B'brn* 3C 140
Leicester Rd. *Blac* 5D 88
Leicester Rd. *Pres* 8K 115
Leicester St. *Roch* 8D 204
Leicester St. *South* 5H 167
Leicester Wlk. *Has* 7G 160
Leigh Brow. *Bam B* 6L 135
Leigh Clo. *Tot* 6D 200
Leigh Pk. *Hap* 6H 123
Leigh Row. *Chor* 7E 174
Leighs Hey Cres. *Liv* 9L 223
Leigh St. *Chor* 7E 174
Leigh St. *Firg* 6G 205
Leigh St. *Wals* 9E 200
Leighton Av. *Fltwd* 1D 54
Leighton Av. *L'boro* 3J 205
Leighton Av. *Liv* 9C 216
Leighton Beck Rd. *Beet* 3M 5
Leighton Clo. *Sla H* 1M 5
Leighton Ct. *More* 5A 22
Leighton Dri. *Lanc* 1H 29
Leighton Dri. *Sla H* 1M 5
Leighton Hall. 1N 11
Leighton Moss Nature Reserve & Vis. Cen. 9K 5
Leighton St. *Pres* 9H 115
Leinster Ct. Lanc 2L 29
(off Leinster Rd.)
Leinster Rd. *Lanc* 2L 29
Leith Av. *T Clev* 1D 62
Lemonius St. *Acc* 4B 142
Lemon Tree Ct. *Lyth A* 5B 108
Lenches. 7A 86
Lenches Fold. *Col* 8A 86
Lenches Rd. *Col* 8A 86
Lench Rd. *Ross* 7B 162
Lench St. *Ross* 7D 162
Lennon St. *Chor* 7E 174
Lennox Ct. *Blac* 3D 108
Lennox Ga. *Blac* 2D 108
Lennox Rd. *Todm* 7C 146
(in two parts)
Lennox St. *Pres* 1K 135
Lennox St. *Wors* 3L 125
Lentworth Av. *Blac* 6D 62
Lentworth Dri. *Lanc* 3L 29
Lentworth Ho. Lanc 4L 29
(off Lentworth Dri.)
Leo Case Ct. *Pres* 9N 115
Leonard St. Bacup 7G 163
(off Booth Rd.)
Leonard St. Bacup 7F 162
(off West Vw.)
Leonard St. *Barn* 2M 77
Leonard St. *Nels* 3J 105
Leonard Ter. *Waters* 4E 158
Leopold Gro. *Blac* 5B 88
Leopold Rd. *B'brn* 2J 139
Leopold St. *Col* 7M 85
Leopold St. *Roch* 6A 204
Leopold St. *Wig & Pem* 6L 221
Leopold Way. *B'brn* 8A 140
Lepp Cres. *Bury* 7H 201
Lesley Rd. *South* 7L 167
Leslie Av. *Cat* 3H 25
Leslie Av. *T Clev* 1J 63
Letchworth Av. *Roch* 8D 204
Letchworth Dri. *Chor* 8D 174
Letchworth Pl. *Chor* 8D 174
Lethbridge Rd. *South* 9K 167
Levant St. *Pad* 2H 123
Leven Av. *Fltwd* 2D 54
Leven Gro. *Dar* 3M 157
Levens Clo. *Banks* 1F 168
Levens Clo. *B'brn* 8N 139
Levens Clo. *Lanc* 9H 23
Levens Clo. *Poul F* 2K 89
Levens Ct. *Blac* 8C 88
Levens Ct. *Hey* 6M 21
Levens Dri. *Hey* 6M 21
Levens Dri. *Ley* 5N 153
Levens Dri. *Poul F* 1K 89
Levensgarth Av. *Ful* 1J 115
Levens Gro. *Blac* 8C 88
Levens Pl. *Wig* 4M 221
Levens St. *Pres* 8N 115
Leven St. *Burn* 5F 124
Levens Wlk. *Wig* 4M 221
Levens Way. *Silv* 8G 5
Lever Ct. *Lyth A* 1G 129
Lever Ho. La. *Ley* 5M 153
Lever Pk. 5B 196
Lever Pk. Av. *Hor* 8B 196
Lever St. *Blac* 6E 88
Lever St. *Heyw* 9H 203
Lever St. *Ram* 8H 181
Lever St. *Ross* 5N 161
Lever St. *Todm* 2L 165
Levine Av. *Blac* 9G 88
Lewis Clo. *Adl* 7G 195
Lewis St. *Gt Har* 4K 121
Lewtas St. *Blac* 4B 88
Lewth. 4L 93
Lewth La. *Wood* 4J 93
Lexington Way. *Liv* 4K 223
Lex St. *Pres* 9M 115
Lexton Dri. *South* 3A 168
Leybourne Av. *South* 6F 186
Leyburn Av. *Blac* 6C 62
Leyburn Av. *Fltwd* 2E 54
Leyburn Clo. *Acc* 3D 142
Leyburn Clo. *Rib* 4A 116
Leyburn Rd. *B'brn* 9J 139
Leyburn Rd. *Lanc* 5K 23
Leycester Dri. *Lanc* 5G 22
Ley Ct. *Lanc* 8H 23
Leyfield. *Pen* 6G 135
Leyfield Clo. *Blac* 1G 88
Leyfield Ct. *K Lon* 6F 8
Leyfield Rd. *Ley* 6J 153
Leyfield Rd. *Miln* 7G 205
Leyland. 7K 153
Leyland Clo. *South* 1D 168
Leyland Clo. *Traw* 8E 86
Leyland Golf Course. 7N 153
Leyland La. *Ley* 4F 172
Leyland Mans. *South* 6K 167
Leyland Rd. *Burn* 3F 124
Leyland Rd. *Pen & Los H* 3G 135
Leyland Rd. *Rainf* 4K 225
Leyland Rd. *South* 5J 167
Leylands, The. *Lyth A* 5M 129
Leyland St. *Acc* 3M 141
Leyland Way. *Ley* 6L 153
Leyland Way. *Orm* 7L 209
Leys Clo. *Elsw* 1M 91
Leys Clo. *Wis* 2M 101
Leys Rd. *Blac* 1D 88
Leyster St. *More* 3C 22
Ley St. *Acc* 6D 142
Leyton Av. *Ley* 8G 153
Leyton Clo. *Wig* 6N 221
Leyton Grn. *Ley* 8H 153
Leyton St. *Roch* 3C 204
Libby La. *Pil* 7H 43
Library Av. *Lanc* 8L 29
Library M. *Blac* 2E 108
Library Rd. *Clay W* 3D 154
Library St. *Chor* 7E 174
Library St. *Chu* 2L 141
Library St. *Pres* 1K 135
Lichen Clo. *Char R* 1N 193
Lichfield Av. *More* 2D 22
Lichfield Dri. *Bury* 9J 201
Lichfield Rd. *Ash R* 7C 114
Lichfield Rd. *Blac* 2C 88
Lichfield Rd. *Chor* 8D 174
Lichfield St. *Wig* 6M 221
Lichfield Ter. *Roch* 9F 204
Liddell Av. *Liv* 6F 222
Liddesdale Rd. *Nels* 9M 85
Liddington Clo. *B'brn* 8A 140
Liddington Hall Dri. *Ram* 1G 201
Lidgate Clo. *Liv* 5L 223
Lidgate Clo. *Wig* 8N 221
Lidget Av. *Lea* 8N 113
Lidgett. *Col* 6D 86
Lidun Pk. Ind. Est. *Lyth A* 3D 130
Liege Rd. *Ley* 7K 153
Lifton Rd. *Liv* 8L 223
Liggard Ct. *Lyth A* 4B 130
Lightbown Av. *Blac* 7E 88
Lightbown Cotts. Dar 5L 157
(off Sunnyhurst La.)
Lightbown St. *Dar* 4A 158
Lightburn Av. *L'boro* 1H 205
Lightburne Av. *Lyth A* 4F 128
Lightfoot Clo. *Ful* 1G 115
Lightfoot Grn. La. *L Grn* 1E 114
Lightfoot La. *High B & Ful* 2C 114
(in three parts)
Lighthorne Dri. *South* 9A 186
Lighthouse. *L'boro* 5M 185
Lighthouse Clo. Fltwd 8H 41
(off Kent St.)
Lighthurst Av. *Chor* 8E 174
Lighthurst La. *Chor* 9F 174
Lightowlers La. *L'boro* 7N 185
Lightwood Av. *Blac* 1C 108
Lightwood Av. *Lyth A* 5K 129
Lilac Av. *Blac* 8D 88
Lilac Av. *Has* 4G 161
Lilac Av. *Lyth A* 3A 130
Lilac Av. *Miln* 9K 205
Lilac Av. *Pen* 6J 135
Lilac Av. *South* 2D 206
Lilac Clo. *W'ton* 3J 131
Lilac Cres. *Whar* 6D 92
Lilac Gro. *Abb V* 5C 156
Lilac Gro. *Clith* 4J 81
Lilac Gro. *Dar* 4B 158
Lilac Gro. *Pres* 6M 115
Lilac Gro. *Skel* 2J 219
Lilac Rd. *B'brn* 9A 120
Lilac St. *Col* 5C 86
Lilac Ter. *Bacup* 7H 163
Lilburn Clo. *Ram* 1H 201
Liley St. *Roch* 6D 204
Lilford Clo. *Tar* 1E 170
Lilford Rd. *B'brn* 2L 139
Lily Gro. *Lanc* 2L 29
Lily Gro. *Pres* 6M 115
Lily St. *Bacup* 5K 163
Lily St. *Blac* 5C 88
Lily St. *Dar* 6B 158
Lily St. *Miln* 7J 205
Lily St. *Nels* 4K 105
Lily St. *Todm* 8H 147
Lima Rd. *Lyth A* 2G 129
Lima St. *Bury* 9N 201
Limbrick. 9H 175
Limbrick. *B'brn* 2M 139
Limbrick Rd. *Chor* 7G 175
Lime Av. *Gal* 2L 37
Lime Av. *K'ham* 5N 111
Lime Av. *Osw* 6K 141
Lime Av. *Todm* 1K 165
Limebrest Av. *T Clev* 3K 63
Lime Chase. *Ful* 1F 114
Limechase Clo. *Blac* 3G 109
Lime Clo. *Pen* 4D 134
Lime Ct. *Liv* 5K 223
Lime Ct. *Lyth A* 9D 108
Lime Ct. *Skel* 2J 219
Limefield. 7L 201
Limefield. *Roch* 2H 205
Limefield Av. *Brier* 4G 104
Limefield Av. *Whal* 5J 101
(in two parts)
Limefield Brow. *Bury* 6L 201
Limefield Clo. *Bolt* 9B 198
Limefield Ct. *B'brn* 3J 139
Limefield Dri. *Skel* 4B 220
Limefield Rd. *Bolt* 9A 198
Limefield St. *Acc* 3C 142
Lime Gro. *Ash R* 7C 114
Lime Gro. *Blac* 9E 62
Lime Gro. *Bury* 6L 201
Lime Gro. *Chor* 9E 174
Lime Gro. *Gars* 4M 59
Lime Gro. *Heyw* 9G 202
Lime Gro. *Lanc* 8H 23
Lime Gro. *L'boro* 8J 185
Lime Gro. *L'rdge* 2J 97
Lime Gro. *Lyth A* 9C 108
Lime Gro. *Poul F* 9L 63
Lime Gro. *Rainf* 4K 225
Lime Gro. *Ram* 7J 181
Lime Gro. *Skel* 2H 219
Lime Gro. *T Clev* 2J 63
Limerick Rd. *Blac* 8D 62
Lime Rd. *Acc* 1A 142
Lime Rd. *Has* 4H 161
Limers Ga. *Shawf* 7D 164
Limers Ga. *Todm* 2B 164
Limers Ga. *Whitw* 9C 184
Limers La. *Gt Har* 4G 121
Limes Av. *Dar* 7N 157
Limes Av. *Eux* 2M 173
Limes Av. *Hey* 5M 21
Limes, The. *Pres* 8L 115
Lime St. *B'brn* 2M 139
Lime St. *Bury* 7L 201
Lime St. *Clith* 2M 81
Lime St. *Col* 5B 86
Lime St. *Gt Har* 3J 121
Lime St. *Nels* 2G 105
Lime St. *South* 8L 167
Lime St. *Todm* 1K 165
Lime Tree Gro. *Ross* 3M 161
Limewood Clo. *Acc* 2C 142
Limey La. *Dunn* 2C 144
Limont Rd. *South* 8D 186
Linacre La. *Liv* 3G 215
Linaker Dri. *Hals* 4A 208
Linaker St. *South* 9H 167
Lina St. *Acc* 2M 141
Linby St. *Burn* 4F 124
Lincoln Av. *Fltwd* 1E 54
Lincoln Av. *T Clev* 9E 54
Lincoln Chase. *Lea* 8N 113
Lincoln Clo. *B'brn* 4B 140
Lincoln Clo. *More* 5D 22
Lincoln Clo. *Roch* 7D 204
Lincoln Clo. Ind. Est. *Roch* 7D 204
Lincoln Ct. *Blac* 6C 88
Lincoln Ct. *Chu* 1N 141
Lincoln Dri. *L'boro* 2K 205
Lincoln Dri. *Liv* 7C 222
Lincoln Grn. *Liv* 2A 222
Lincoln Gro. *Bolt* 9M 199
Lincoln Ho. Pres 1L 135
(off Arundel Pl.)
Lincoln Leach Ct. *Roch* 8C 204
Lincoln Pl. *Has* 4F 160
Lincoln Pl. *Wig* 2M 221
Lincoln Rd. *B'brn* 4B 140
Lincoln Rd. *Blac* 5C 88
Lincoln Rd. *Earby* 2E 78
Lincoln Rd. *Lanc* 8J 23
Lincoln Rd. *South* 4G 186
Lincoln St. *Burn* 5E 124
Lincoln St. *Has* 4F 160
Lincoln St. *Pres* 8L 115
Lincoln St. *Roch* 7D 204

Lincoln St.—Lord St.

Lincoln St. Todm . . . 7E 146
Lincoln Wlk. Pres . . . 8L 115
Lincoln Way. Clith . . . 1N 81
Lincoln Way. Gars . . . 5M 59
Lindadale Av. Acc . . . 5N 141
Lindadale Av. T Clev . . . 1H 63
Lindadale Clo. Acc . . . 5N 141
Lindale Av. Grims . . . 9G 96
Lindale Clo. Arns . . . 1F 4
Lindale Cres. Burn . . . 8E 104
Lindale Gdns. Blac . . . 3E 108
Lindale Rd. Ful . . . 5K 115
Lindale Rd. L'rdge . . . 5H 97
Lindbeck Ct. Blac . . . 1J 109
Lindbeck Rd. Blac . . . 9J 89
Lindby Rd. Liv . . . 9M 223
Lindel La. Pre . . . 2N 55
Lindel Rd. Fltwd . . . 2E 54
Linden Av. B'brn . . . 2L 139
Linden Av. Orr . . . 5H 221
Linden Av. Ram . . . 8J 181
Linden Av. T Clev . . . 9F 54
Linden Av. Todm . . . 1K 165
Linden Clo. Barfd . . . 1F 104
Linden Clo. Los H . . . 7L 135
Linden Clo. Ram . . . 4J 181
Linden Clo. T Clev . . . 1F 62
Linden Ct. Earby . . . 3D 78
(off Linden Rd.)
Linden Ct. Orr . . . 5H 221
(off Linden Gro.)
Linden Cres. Dar . . . 5B 158
Linden Dri. Clith . . . 4M 81
Linden Dri. Los H . . . 8L 135
Linden Fold. Elsw . . . 1M 91
Linden Grn. T Clev . . . 9F 54
Linden Gro. Chor . . . 3F 174
Linden Gro. Gars . . . 4N 59
Linden Gro. Orr . . . 5H 221
(in two parts)
Linden Gro. Rib . . . 6A 116
Linden Lea. B'brn . . . 8G 138
Linden Lea. Raw . . . 7L 161
Linden M. Lyth A . . . 7F 108
Linden Pl. Blac . . . 8E 62
Linden Rd. Col . . . 6A 86
Linden Rd. Earby . . . 3D 78
Lindens. Skel . . . 9M 211
Lindens, The. Liv . . . 3B 222
Linden St. Burn . . . 4F 124
Linden St. Wig . . . 6M 221
Linden Wlk. Bolt . . . 8H 199
Linden Wlk. Orr . . . 5H 221
Lindenwood. Liv . . . 9L 223
Lindeth Clo. Neth K . . . 3C 16
Lindeth Clo. Silv . . . 9G 4
Lindeth Gdns. Lanc . . . 5K 23
Lindeth Rd. Silv . . . 9G 4
Lindholme. Skel . . . 9N 211
Lindisfarne. Roch . . . 5B 204
(off Spotland Rd.)
Lindisfarne Av. B'brn . . . 7N 139
Lindisfarne Clo. Burn . . . 2C 124
Lindle Av. Hut . . . 6B 134
Lindle Clo. Hut . . . 6B 134
Lindle Cres. Hut . . . 6B 134
Lindle La. Hut . . . 5B 134
Lindley Av. Orr . . . 6F 220
Lindley Cft. T Clev . . . 1L 63
Lindley Dri. Parb . . . 1N 211
Lindley St. B'brn . . . 6J 139
Lindley St. Los H . . . 8K 135
Lindon Pk. Rd. Has . . . 8H 161
Lindow Clo. Bury . . . 7G 201
Lindow Clo. Lanc . . . 9K 23
(off Lindow St.)
Lindow Sq. Lanc . . . 9J 23
Lindow St. Lanc . . . 9K 23
Lindred Rd. Brier . . . 3E 104
Lindsay Av. Blac . . . 7E 88
Lindsay Av. Ley . . . 6L 153
Lindsay Av. Lyth A . . . 2H 129
Lindsay Av. Poul F . . . 9K 63
Lindsay Ct. Lyth A . . . 5B 108
Lindsay Ct. More . . . 6C 22
Lindsay Dri. Chor . . . 7C 174
Lindsay Pk. Burn . . . 4K 125
Lindsay St. Burn . . . 3E 124
Lindsey Ho. Chu . . . 1N 141
Linedred La. Brier . . . 3F 104
Lineholme Av. Todm . . . 8H 147
Lines St. More . . . 3B 22
Line St. Bacup . . . 7J 163
Linfield Clo. Bolt . . . 9K 199
Linfield Ter. Blac . . . 3E 108
Lingart La. Bncr . . . 3A 60
Lingdales. Liv . . . 6B 206
Lingfield Av. Clith . . . 5L 81
Lingfield Clo. Bury . . . 6H 201
Lingfield Clo. Lanc . . . 4M 29
Lingfield Ct. Fen . . . 8D 138
Lingfield Rd. Fltwd . . . 2E 54
Lingfield Way. B'brn . . . 8E 138
Linghaw La. Ben . . . 7N 19
Lingmoor Dri. Burn . . . 1M 123
Lingmoor Rd. Lanc . . . 7M 23
Lingtree Rd. Liv . . . 8G 223
Lingwell Clo. Whit W . . . 1E 174
Links Av. South . . . 4L 167
Links Dri. Ben . . . 6L 19
Linksfield. Ful . . . 6F 114
Links Ga. Ful . . . 6F 114
Links Ga. Lyth A . . . 2F 128
Links Ga. T Clev . . . 4K 63
Linkside Av. Nels . . . 2M 105
Links La. Pleas . . . 8D 138
Links Lodge. Lyth A . . . 2G 128
Links Rd. Blac . . . 1C 88
Links Rd. Bolt . . . 9N 199
Links Rd. Kirkby . . . 9M 223
Links Rd. Kno S . . . 8K 41
Links Rd. Lyth A . . . 3E 128
Links Rd. Pen . . . 2E 134
Links, The. T Clev . . . 8C 54
Links Vw. Lyth A . . . 3J 129
Links Vw. Roch . . . 7M 203
Linley Clo. Stand L . . . 8M 213
Linley Gro. Ram . . . 3F 200
Linley Rd. Wig . . . 6N 221
Linnell Dri. Roch . . . 5J 203
Linnet Clo. Blac . . . 4H 89
Linnet Dri. Bury . . . 9N 201
Linnet Hill. Roch . . . 7N 203
Linnet La. Lyth A . . . 1L 129
Linnet St. Pres . . . 7L 115
Linnet Way. Liv . . . 3K 223
Linslade Clo. Liv . . . 6L 223
Linslade Cres. Liv . . . 6L 223
Linton Av. Bury . . . 8L 201
Linton Av. Hey . . . 7L 21
Linton Dri. Burn . . . 6B 124
Linton Gdns. Barfd . . . 8G 85
Linton Gro. Pen . . . 3D 134
Linton St. Ful . . . 6G 115
Lion Ct. Chu . . . 2L 141
Lionel St. Burn . . . 2A 124
Lion St. Chu . . . 1L 141
Lion St. Todm . . . 4K 165
Liptrott Rd. Chor . . . 9C 174
Lisbon Dri. Burn . . . 4C 124
Lisbon Dri. Dar . . . 6C 158
Lisbon St. Roch . . . 5N 203
Liskeard Clo. Roch . . . 4F 204
Lisle St. Roch . . . 5D 204
Lister Cft. Thorn C . . . 9J 53
Lister Gro. Hey . . . 8L 21
Lister St. Acc . . . 2N 141
Lister St. B'brn . . . 5M 139
Lister Well Rd. Barn . . . 8K 77
Lit. Acre. Liv . . . 2D 222
Lit. Acre. Longt . . . 8L 133
Lit. Acre. T Clev . . . 3K 63
Little Altcar. . . . 2A 214
Lit. Banks Clo. Bam B . . . 1D 154
Little Bispham. . . . 3C 62
Littleborough. . . . 9L 185
Littleborough Ind. Est. L'boro . . . 9K 185
Littlebourne Wlk. Bolt . . . 7G 198
Lit. Brewery La. Liv . . . 6A 206
Lit. Brook La. Liv . . . 9J 223
Lit. Brow. Brom X . . . 6G 198
Little Carleton. . . . 1F 88
Lit. Carr La. Chor . . . 9F 174
Lit. Church St. Wig . . . 5L 221
Little Clegg. . . . 3J 205
Lit. Clegg Rd. L'boro . . . 3H 205
Little Clo. Far M . . . 4H 153
Little Clo. Pen . . . 5F 134
Littledale. . . . 8M 25
Littledale Av. Hey . . . 8M 21
Littledale M. Slyne . . . 2M 23
Littledale Rd. Brook . . . 3K 25
Littledale Rd. Quer . . . 1C 30
Littledale St. Roch . . . 5B 204
(in two parts)
Little Eccleston. . . . 7K 65
Lit. Fell La. Lanc & Quer . . . 6A 30
Lit. Fell Rd. Brook . . . 9C 24
Lit. Flatt. Roch . . . 4M 203
Little Harwood. . . . 1A 140
Lit. Hey La. Liv . . . 8B 206
Littleholme St. Todm . . . 4K 165
Little Hoole Moss Houses. . . 3M 151
Little Hoole Much. . . . 3A 152
Little Howarth Way. Roch . . . 1F 204
Little Knowley. . . . 3H 175
Little La. Banks . . . 8G 149
Little La. L'rdge . . . 3J 97
Little La. South . . . 4A 168
Little La. Wig . . . 6N 221
Little Layton. . . . 2F 88
Little Marsden. . . . 3G 105
Little Marton. . . . 9K 89
Lit. Meadow. Eger . . . 6F 198
Lit. Meadow La. Maw . . . 1H 191
Little Moor. . . . 5L 81
Littlemoor. Clith . . . 5L 81
Littlemoor Clo. Sab . . . 2F 102
Lit. Moor Clough. Eger . . . 3E 198
Little Moor End. . . . 5J 141
Littlemoor Houses. Sab . . . 3F 102
Littlemoor Rd. Clith . . . 5L 81
Lit. Moor Vw. Clith . . . 5L 81
Lit. Peel St. B'brn . . . 3L 139
Little Plumpton. . . . 3C 110
Little Poulton. . . . 7M 63
Lit. Poulton La. Poul F . . . 8M 63
Lit. Queen St. Col . . . 7N 85
Little Singleton. . . . 7C 64
Lit. Stones Rd. Eger . . . 3E 198
Lit. St. Acc . . . 2N 141
Little Thornton. . . . 4L 63
Lit. Toms La. Burn . . . 7H 105
Lit. Tongues La. Pre . . . 9A 42
Little Town. . . . 6G 99
Lit. Twining. Longt . . . 9L 133
Littlewood. . . . 8K 201
Littlewood. Fltwd . . . 1E 54
Littlewood Av. Bury . . . 8L 201
Lit. Wood Clo. Chor . . . 8B 174
Littondale Gdns. B'brn . . . 9E 138
Liverpool Av. South . . . 8D 186
Liverpool Castle. . . . 6A 196
Liverpool Municipal Golf Course. . . . 9F 222
Liverpool New Rd.
L Hoo & Much H . . . 3K 151
Liverpool Old Rd.
Much H & Tar . . . 7G 150
Liverpool Old Rd. Tar . . . 4E 170
Liverpool Old Rd. Walm B . . . 1K 151
Liverpool Rd. Ains . . . 1G 186
Liverpool Rd. Augh . . . 1G 216
Liverpool Rd. Bic . . . 7L 217
Liverpool Rd. Blac . . . 5D 88
Liverpool Rd.
Breth & Much H . . . 1G 170
Liverpool Rd. Burn . . . 3M 123
Liverpool Rd. Form . . . 1A 214
Liverpool Rd. Hut & Pen . . . 7M 133
Liverpool Rd. Longt . . . 1K 151
Liverpool Rd. Lyd . . . 8B 216
Liverpool Rd. Ruf . . . 6E 170
Liverpool Rd. Skel . . . 3G 218
(in two parts)
Liverpool Rd. South . . . 2C 206
Liverpool Rd. Tar & Much H . . . 2E 170
Liverpool Rd. N. Burs . . . 9C 190
Liverpool Rd. N. Liv . . . 8B 216
Liverpool Rd. S. Burs . . . 3N 209
Liverpool Rd. S. Liv . . . 1B 222
Liverpool Way, The. Liv . . . 9M 223
Livesey Branch Rd.
B'brn & Fen . . . 8E 138
Livesey Ct. B'brn . . . 6K 139
Livesey Fold. . . . 5N 157
Livesey Fold. Dar . . . 5N 157
Livesey Fold. Withn . . . 6B 156
Livesey Hall Clo. B'brn . . . 7F 138
Livesey St. Lyth A . . . 5N 129
Livesey St. Pad . . . 1H 123
Livesey St. Pres . . . 1L 135
Livesey St. Rish . . . 7G 121
(in two parts)
Livesleys La. Form . . . 1F 214
Livet Av. Blac . . . 2D 108
Livingstone Rd. Acc . . . 9A 122
Livingstone Rd. B'brn . . . 4J 139
Livingstone Rd. Blac . . . 6C 88
Livingstone St. Brier . . . 5F 104
Livingstone Wlk. Brier . . . 4F 104
Livsey St. Roch . . . 6D 204
Lloyd Clo. Lanc . . . 7H 23
Lloyd Clo. Nels . . . 2J 105
Lloyd's Av. More . . . 4A 22
Lloyd St. Bacup . . . 7G 162
Lloyd St. Dar . . . 4N 157
Lloyd St. Roch . . . 9A 204
Lloyd St. Todm . . . 1L 165
Lloyd St. Whitw . . . 5N 183
Lloyd Wlk. Nels . . . 3J 105
Lobden Cres. Whitw . . . 7N 183
Lobden Golf Course. . . . 7B 184
Lobley Clo. Roch . . . 3E 204
Lochinch Clo. Blac . . . 3G 108
Loch St. Orr . . . 5L 221
Locka La. Ark . . . 4N 13
Locka La. Lanc . . . 4J 23
Lockerbie Av. T Clev . . . 2D 62
Lockerbie Pl. Wig . . . 9N 221
Lockfield Dri. Barn . . . 10G 52
Lock Ga. Ross . . . 6H 161
Lockhart Rd. Pres . . . 7J 115
Lockhart St. Roch . . . 8E 204
Lockhurst Av. T Clev . . . 3F 62
Lock La. Tar . . . 4F 170
Lockside. B'brn . . . 6L 139
Lockside Rd. Ash R . . . 1C 134
Lock St. Osw . . . 4L 141
Lock St. Todm . . . 4K 165
Lockwood Av. Poul F . . . 7K 63
Lockyer Av. Burn . . . 3N 123
Lodge Bank. Brins . . . 8N 155
Lodge Bank Rd. L'boro . . . 2J 205
Lodge Clo. Bam B . . . 7B 136
Lodge Clo. Frec . . . 1N 131
Lodge Clo. Holme . . . 1F 6
Lodge Clo. T Clev . . . 4C 62
Lodge Ct. Stain . . . 6K 89
Lodge Ct. T Clev . . . 4C 62
Lodge La. Bacup . . . 6K 163
Lodge La. Bic . . . 1G 225
Lodge La. Elsw . . . 1M 91
Lodge La. Far M . . . 9G 135
Lodge La. Lyth A & W'ton . . . 3E 130
Lodge La. Mllng . . . 4E 18
Lodge La. Sing . . . 8C 64
Lodge Mill La. Ram . . . 5M 181
Lodge Pk. Catt . . . 9A 60
Lodge Rd. Clau B . . . 3D 68
Lodge Rd. Orr . . . 7H 221
Lodge Rd. Set . . . 4N 35
Lodges Gro. More . . . 2E 22
Lodgeside. Clay M . . . 6M 121
Lodge St. Acc . . . 2B 142
Lodge St. Bury . . . 9M 201
Lodge St. Lanc . . . 8K 23
Lodge St. L'boro . . . 8L 185
Lodge St. Pres . . . 9G 115
(in two parts)
Lodge St. Ram . . . 6K 181
(Bye Rd.)
Lodge St. Ram . . . 8H 181
(Kay Brow)
Lodge St. Ward . . . 8F 184
Lodge Ter. Acc . . . 3L 141
Lodge Vw. Far M . . . 9H 135
Lodge Vw. L'rdge . . . 4J 97
Lodge Vw. Pen . . . 5J 135
Lodge Wood Clo. Chor . . . 8C 174
Lodgings, The. Ful . . . 3M 115
Lodore Rd. Blac . . . 3C 108
Loen Cres. Bolt . . . 9C 198
Lofthouse Way. Fltwd . . . 9G 40
Loftos Av. Blac . . . 1D 108
Logan St. Bolt . . . 8E 198
Lognor Rd. Liv . . . 8H 223
Lognor Wlk. Liv . . . 8H 223
Logwood Av. Bury . . . 9J 201
Logwood Av. Wig . . . 4N 221
Logwood St. B'brn . . . 1N 139
Loisine Clo. Roch . . . 9M 203
Lois Pl. B'brn . . . 3K 139
Lomas La. Ross . . . 6L 161
Lomax Sq. Gt Har . . . 4K 121
Lomax St. Dar . . . 5A 158
Lomax St. Gt Har . . . 4J 121
Lomax St. G'mnt . . . 4E 200
Lombard St. Roch . . . 5A 204
Lomeshaye. . . . 2F 104
Lomeshaye Bus. Village.
Nels . . . 2G 104
Lomeshaye Ind. Est. Nels . . . 1F 104
(Churchill Way)
Lomeshaye Ind. Est. Nels . . . 2E 104
(Lindred Rd.)
Lomeshaye Pl. Nels . . . 2G 104
Lomeshaye Rd. Nels . . . 2G 105
Lomeshaye Way. Nels . . . 2G 104
Lomond Av. Blac . . . 7F 88
Lomond Av. Lyth A . . . 2H 129
Lomond Clo. Eux . . . 1N 173
Lomond Dri. Bury . . . 9G 200
Lomond Gdns. B'brn . . . 7G 139
Lomond Ter. Roch . . . 9F 204
London Clo. Wig . . . 3N 221
Londonderry Rd. Hey . . . 2K 27
London La. South . . . 6J 187
London Rd. B'brn . . . 2M 139
London Rd. Blac . . . 4D 88
London Rd. Pres . . . 9L 115
London Sq. South . . . 7H 167
London St. Fltwd . . . 8G 41
London St. South . . . 7H 167
London Ter. Dar . . . 5B 158
London Wlk. B'brn . . . 2M 139
London Way. Walt D . . . 4M 135
Long Acre. Bam B . . . 2E 154
Longacre. Longt . . . 8K 133
Longacre. South . . . 3M 167
Long Acre Clo. Carn . . . 1N 15
Longacre Pl. Lyth A . . . 4N 129
Longacres Dri. Whitw . . . 4A 184
Longacres La. Whitw . . . 4A 184
Long Bank La. Halt W . . . 3A 52
Long Barn Brow. Hogh . . . 6N 137
Longber La. Burt L . . . 2H 19
Longbrook. Shev . . . 5L 213
Longbrook Av. Bam B . . . 6A 136
Long Building. Saw . . . 3E 74
Long Butts. Pen . . . 6G 134
Long Causeway. Gis . . . 9A 52
Long Causeway, The. Blkhd . . . 4M 147
Long Causeway, The. Cliv . . . 7L 125
Longcliffe Dri. South . . . 9B 186
Long Clo. Clith . . . 1M 81
Long Clo. Ley . . . 7D 152
Long Copse. Chor . . . 5B 174
Longcroft. Brtn . . . 2E 94
Long Cft. Longt . . . 7L 133
Long Cft. Mdw. Chor . . . 3D 174
Longdale Av. Set . . . 3N 35
Long Dales La. Neth K . . . 6C 16
Long Dike. Ross & Acc . . . 7H 143
Longendale Rd. Stand . . . 4N 213
Longfield. Bury . . . 8M 201
Longfield. Ful . . . 1H 115
Longfield. Liv . . . 7B 206
Longfield. Pen . . . 3E 134
Longfield Av. Cop . . . 3A 194
Longfield Av. Poul F . . . 7K 63
Longfield Clo. Todm . . . 3L 165
Longfield Ct. Barn . . . 3M 77
Longfield Dri. Carn . . . 1N 15
Longfield Gro. Todm . . . 3L 165
Longfield La. Barn . . . 3M 77
Longfield La. Todm . . . 4L 165
Longfield Mnr. Chor . . . 9C 174
Longfield Pl. Poul F . . . 7K 63
Longfield Ri. Todm . . . 3L 165
Longfield Rd. Roch . . . 5N 203
Longfield Rd. Todm . . . 3L 165
Longfield Ter. Cliv . . . 9J 125
Longfield Ter. Todm . . . 3L 165
Longfield Way. Todm . . . 3L 165
Longfold. Liv . . . 1D 222
Longford Av. Blac . . . 6E 62
Longford Rd. South . . . 3G 187
Long Grn. Earby . . . 2F 78
Longhey. Skel . . . 8N 211
Long Hey La. Pick B . . . 6F 158
Long Hey La. Todm . . . 4M 165
Long Heys La. Dal . . . 8B 212
Long Hill. Roch . . . 9A 204
Longhirst Clo. Bolt . . . 9B 198
Longholme Rd. Raw . . . 5M 161
Longhouse La. Poul F . . . 2K 89
Long Ing. . . . 2N 77
Long Ing La. Barn . . . 2N 77
Longlands Av. Hey . . . 8K 21
Longlands Cres. Hey . . . 8L 21
Longlands La. Hey . . . 9K 21
Longlands Rd. Lanc . . . 5J 23
Long La. Abb . . . 3A 48
Long La. Augh & Bic . . . 9H 209
Long La. Bncr . . . 4D 46
Long La. Bury . . . 6K 201
Long La. Ellel & Quer . . . 8C 30
Long La. Hth C . . . 9J 175
Long La. Lane . . . 3G 86
Long La. L Bent . . . 7H 19
Long La. Pleas . . . 6B 138
Long La. Scor . . . 4D 60
Long La. South . . . 9G 148
Long La. Thor . . . 9H 215
Long La. Toc . . . 4G 157
Long La. Todm . . . 1N 165
Long La. Uph . . . 8B 220
Long La. End. Ellel . . . 8B 30
Long Level. Cast . . . 6G 9
Longley Clo. Ful . . . 1J 115
Long Lover La. Rim . . . 4A 76
Long Marsh La. Lanc . . . 7H 23
Long Mdw. Brom X . . . 6J 199
Long Mdw. Chor . . . 9C 174
Long Mdw. Col . . . 6D 86
Long Mdw. K'ham . . . 4K 111
Long Mdw. L Hoo . . . 3K 151
Long Mdw. Mel B . . . 7C 118
Longmeadow La. Hey . . . 9M 21
Longmeadow La. Red M . . . 9J 55
Longmeanygate.
Midg H & Ley . . . 5D 152
Long Meanygate. South . . . 6E 168
Longmere Cres. Carn . . . 1N 15
Longmire Way. More . . . 3A 22
Longmoor La. Nate . . . 7F 58
Long Moss. Ley . . . 7D 152
Long Moss La.
New L & Wstke . . . 1B 152
Longridge. . . . 3J 97
Longridge. Brom X . . . 5J 199
Longridge Av. Blac . . . 4E 108
Longridge Golf Course. . . . 9G 71
Longridge Heath. Brier . . . 6H 105
Longridge Rd. Chip . . . 7G 70
Longridge Rd. Hur G . . . 2H 99
Longridge Rd. L'rdge . . . 1J 97
Longridge Rd. Rib & Grims . . . 5B 116
Long Row. Blkhd . . . 5N 147
Long Row. Cald V . . . 4H 61
Long Row. Mel . . . 7J 119
Longroyd Rd. Earby . . . 3E 78
Longsands La. Ful . . . 4M 115
Longshaw. . . . 7M 139
Longshaw Clo. Ruf . . . 9E 170
Longshaw Ford Rd. Bolt . . . 8M 197
Longshaw La. B'brn . . . 6L 139
Longshaw St. B'brn . . . 7L 139
Longshoot. . . . 4H 161
Longsight. Bolt . . . 8L 199
Longsight Av. Acc . . . 9D 122
Longsight Av. Clith . . . 2M 81
Longsight Golf Course. . . . 9K 199
Longsight Rd. Lang . . . 8D 100
Longsight Rd.
Mel B & Clay D . . . 6C 118
Longsight Rd. Ram & G'mnt . . . 2F 200
Longton. . . . 8K 133
Longton Av. T Clev . . . 1H 63
Longton By-Pass.
L Hoo & Longt . . . 3K 151
Longton Clo. B'brn . . . 3C 140
Longton Ct. South . . . 6K 167
Longton Dri. Liv . . . 6A 206
Longton Dri. More . . . 4E 22
Longton Rd. Blac . . . 5C 88
Longton Rd. Burn . . . 1C 124
Longtons La. Toss . . . 1H 51
Longton St. B'brn . . . 3B 140
Longton St. Chor . . . 6G 174
Longway. Blac . . . 1F 108
Long Wham La. Much H . . . 6N 151
Longwood Clo. Lyth A . . . 5L 129
Longwood Clo. Rainf . . . 9M 225
Longworth Av. Burn . . . 3H 125
Longworth Av. Cop . . . 3B 194
(in two parts)
Longworth Clough. Eger . . . 3D 198
Longworth La. Eger . . . 4D 198
Longworth Rd. Bill . . . 6H 101
Longworth Rd. Hor . . . 9D 196
Longworth Rd. N. Bel . . . 9K 177
Longworth St. Bam B . . . 6A 136
Longworth St. Chor . . . 8D 174
Longworth St. Pres . . . 8M 115
Lonmore. Walt D . . . 5N 135
Lonmore Clo. Banks . . . 1F 168
Lonsdale Av. Fltwd . . . 1E 54
Lonsdale Av. Lanc . . . 8L 29
Lonsdale Av. More . . . 4E 22
Lonsdale Av. Orm . . . 5L 209
Lonsdale Av. Roch . . . 8E 204
Lonsdale Chase. Los H . . . 8K 135
Lonsdale Clo. Ley . . . 9K 153
Lonsdale Cres. Fltwd . . . 1E 54
Lonsdale Dri. Crost . . . 3M 171
Lonsdale Gdns. Barfd . . . 8H 85
Lonsdale Gro. More . . . 4E 22
Lonsdale Pl. Lanc . . . 1L 29
Lonsdale Ri. K Lon . . . 6F 8
(off Lunefield Dri.)
Lonsdale Rd. Blac . . . 8B 88
Lonsdale Rd. Hest B . . . 8H 15
Lonsdale Rd. More . . . 4E 22
Lonsdale Rd. Pres . . . 8M 115
Lonsdale Rd. South . . . 1K 187
Lonsdale St. Acc . . . 3M 141
Lonsdale St. Burn . . . 2A 124
Lonsdale St. Nels . . . 2K 105
Lonsdale Wlk. Orr . . . 3L 221
Lonworth Clough Nature Reserve. . . . 1A 198
Lord Av. Bacup . . . 7G 162
Lord Nelson Wharf. Ash R . . . 9E 114
Lord's Av. Los H . . . 9L 135
Lord's Clo. Rd. Lowg . . . 2M 33
Lord's Cres. Lwr D . . . 1A 158
Lords Cft. Clay W . . . 5C 154
Lord Sefton Way. Liv . . . 1D 214
Lords Fold. Rainf . . . 3J 225
Lordsgate Dri. Burs . . . 1C 210
Lordsgate La. Burs . . . 2A 210
Lord's La. Chip . . . 10E 70
Lord's La. Pen . . . 7H 135
Lord's Lot Rd. Over K . . . 1H 17
Lordsome Rd. Hey . . . 6M 21
Lord Sq. B'brn . . . 3M 139
Lord's Stile La. Brom X . . . 6H 199
Lord St. Acc . . . 2A 142
Lord St. Bacup . . . 5K 163
Lord St. B'brn . . . 3M 139
Lord St. Blac . . . 4B 88
Lord St. Brier . . . 5F 104
Lord St. Burs . . . 8C 190
Lord St. Chor . . . 7F 174
Lord St. Col . . . 6N 85
Lord St. Craw . . . 9L 143
Lord St. Dar . . . 5A 158
Lord St. E'ston . . . 9F 172

Lord St.—Mainway

Lord St. *Fltwd* 9G **41**
Lord St. *Gt Har* 5J **121**
Lord St. *Hor* 9C **196**
Lord St. *Lanc* 7K **23**
Lord St. *L'boro* 9M **185**
Lord St. *Lyth A* 1E **128**
Lord St. *More* 2B **22**
Lord St. *Osw* 4L **141**
Lord St. *Pres* 9K **115**
Lord St. *Raw* 5M **161**
Lord St. *Rish* 8H **121**
Lord St. *South* 8G **166**
(in two parts)
Lord St. *Todm* 6K **165**
Lord St. *Whit W* 6E **154**
Lord St. Mall. B'brn *3M* ***139***
(off Lord Sq.)
Lord St. W. *B'brn* 3M **139**
Lord St. W. *South* 8G **166**
Lord's Wlk. *Pres* 9K **115**
Lorne Rd. *Blac* 9D **62**
Lorne St. *Chor* 7E **174**
Lorne St. *Dar* 5N **157**
Lorne St. *Lyth A* 4C **130**
Lorne St. *Roch* 2E **204**
Lorraine Av. *Ful* 6H **115**
Lorton Clo. *Burn* 1N **123**
Lorton Clo. *Ful* 3J **115**
Lostock Ct. *Los H* 9L **135**
Lostock Dri. *Bury* 7L **201**
Lostock Gdns. *Blac* 3D **108**
Lostock Hall. 9K **135**
Lostock La. *Los H & Bam B* 9M **135**
Lostock Mdw. *Clay W* 6C **154**
Lostock Rd. *Crost* 3N **171**
Lostock Sq. *Los H* 9L **135**
Lostock Vw. *Los H* 9K **135**
Lothersdale Clo. *Burn* 7H **105**
Lothian Av. *Fltwd* 1D **54**
Lothian Pl. *Blac* 6E **62**
Lottice La. *B'brn & Osw* 7F **140**
Lotus Dri. *Blac* 3N **109**
Lotus St. Bacup *4K* ***163***
(off Burnley Rd.)
Loud Bri. Back La. *Goos* 7C **70**
Loudbridge Rd. *Goos* 8C **70**
Loughlin Dri. *Liv* 5L **223**
Loughrigg Clo. *Burn* 2N **123**
Loughrigg Ter. *Blac* 9J **89**
Louis Av. *Bury* 9L **201**
Louise Clo. *Roch* 2E **204**
Louise Gdns. *Roch* 2E **204**
Louise St. *Blac* 7B **88**
Louise St. *Roch* 2E **204**
(in three parts)
Louis St. *Ram* 1J **181**
Louis Tussaud's Waxworks. 6B **88**
Louis William St. *Guide* 8D **140**
Loupsfell Dri. *More* 4C **22**
Lourdes Av. *Los H* 7K **135**
Louvaine Av. *Bolt* 9N **197**
Louvain St. *Barn* 1L **77**
Lovat Rd. *Pres* 7J **115**
Love Clough. 5M **143**
Loveclough Rd. *Ross* 6L **143**
Love La. *Ram* 5K **181**
Lovely Hall La. *Sale* 1K **119**
Lovers La. *Has* 3G **160**
Lover's Wlk. *Acc* 5M **141**
Lovers Wlk. *Todm* 2K **165**
Loves Cotts. *Orm* 6J **209**
Low Bank. *Burn* 3K **123**
Low Bank. *Roch* 2F **204**
Low Bentham. 6J **19**
Low Bentham Rd.
Ben & L Bent 6K **19**
Low Biggins. 6E **8**
Lwr. Burgh Way. *Chor* 2D **194**
Lowcroft. *Skel* 9N **211**
Low Cft. *Wood* 7E **94**
Lowcross Rd. *Poul F* 9L **63**
Lwr. Abbotsgate. K Lon *6E* ***8***
(off Abbotsgate)
Lwr. Alt Rd. *Liv* 7A **214**
Lwr. Antley St. *Acc* 3M **141**
Lwr. Ashworth Clo. *B'brn* 4K **139**
Lwr. Aspen La. *Osw* 3J **141**
Lower Audley. 4N **139**
Lwr. Audley Ind. Est. *B'brn* 4M **139**
Lwr. Audley St. *B'brn* 4M **139**
Lower Ballam. 6A **110**
Lwr. Bank Rd. *Ful* 6J **115**
Lwr. Bank St. *Withn* 6B **156**
Lwr. Barnes St. *Clay M* 5L **121**
Lwr. Barn St. *Dar* 8C **158**
Lower Bartle. 2N **113**
Lower Baxenden. 7E **142**
Lwr. Beacon La. *Dal* 7L **211**
Lwr. Beechwood. *Roch* 8A **204**
Lwr. Burgh Way. *Chor* 1C **194**
Lwr. Calderbrook. *L'boro* 5M **185**
Lwr. Carr La. *Liv* 4H **215**
(in two parts)
Lwr. Chapel La. *Grin* 4A **74**
Lwr. Chesham. *Bury* 9N **201**
Lower Cloughfold. 5A **162**
Lwr. Clough St. *Barfd* 9G **85**
Lwr. Clowes. *Ross* 7L **161**
Lwr. Clowes Rd. *Ross* 7K **161**
Lwr. Cockcroft. *B'brn* 3M **139**
Lower Copthurst. 7G **155**
Lwr. Copthurst La. *Whit W* 8G **155**
Lwr. Cribden Av. *Ross* 5J **161**
Lwr. Crimble. *Roch* 9J **203**
Lwr. Croft. *Pen* 6G **134**
Lowercroft Dri. *Bury* 9E **200**
Lwr. Croft St. *Earby* 2E **78**
Lwr. Croft St. Set *3N* ***35***
(off Albert Hill)
Lwr. Cross St. *Dar* 6A **158**
Lower Darwen. 9N **139**
Lwr. East Av. *Barn* 1M **77**
Lwr. Eccleshill Rd. *Dar* 2A **158**
Lwr. Falinge. *Roch* 5B **204**
Lwr. Ferney Lee. *Todm* 1K **165**
Lwr. Field. *Far M* 1J **153**
Lowerfield. *Lang* 1C **120**
Lowerfields. *Burn* 3L **123**
Lower Fold. 2A **142**
(Accrington)
Lower Fold. 3J **121**
(Blackburn)
Lower Fold. 2N **203**
(Rochdale)
Lwr. Fold. *Bolt* 9M **199**
Lowerfold. *Gt Har* 3J **121**
Lowerfold Clo. *Roch* 1N **203**
Lowerfold Cres. *Roch* 1N **203**
Lowerfold Dri. *Roch* 1N **203**
Lowerfold Rd. *Gt Har* 3J **121**
Lowerfold Way. *Roch* 1N **203**
Lowerford. 8J **85**
Lower Gate. 7E **122**
Lowergate. *Clith* 3L **81**
Lwr. Gate Rd. *Acc* 7E **122**
Lwr. George St. *Todm* 2L **165**
Lwr. Green. *Poul F* 8L **63**
Lwr. Green. *Roch* 4N **203**
Lower Green Bank. 5G **38**
Lwr. Greenfield. *Ing* 5E **114**
Lwr. Greenfoot. *Set* 3N **35**
Lwr. Hazel Clo. *B'brn* 4K **139**
Lower Healey. 2B **204**
Lwr. Healey La. *Roch* 3B **204**
Lwr. Hey. *Longt* 7L **133**
Lower Heysham. 8K **21**
Lwr. Hill Dri. *Hth C* 4J **195**
Lwr. Hollin Bank St. *B'brn* 5L **139**
Lower House. 7G **153**
Lowerhouse. 3L **123**
Lowerhouse Cres. *Burn* 3M **123**
Lowerhouse Fold. *Burn* 3L **123**
Lwr. House Grn. *Lumb* 8D **144**
Lowerhouse La. *Burn* 3L **123**
Lwr. House La. *Ward* 7E **184**
Lwr. House Rd. *Ley* 7H **153**
Lwr. House Wlk. *Brom X* 5G **199**
Lwr. Jowkin La. *Roch* 6H **203**
Lwr. Knotts. *Bolt* 7M **199**
Lwr. Knowl La. *Whitw* 9G **183**
Lwr. Laith Av. *Todm* 2M **165**
Lwr. Laithe Dri. *Barfd* 9G **85**
Lower La. *Blkhd* 5N **147**
Lower La. *Frec* 7N **111**
Lower La. *Has* 3G **160**
Lower La. *L'rdge* 4K **97**
Lower La. *Roch & Miln* 9F **204**
Lower Lea. 2A **48**
Lwr. Lune St. *Fltwd* 8H **41**
Lwr. Lyndon Av. *Shev* 6K **213**
Lwr. Manor La. *Burn* 8D **104**
Lwr. Marlands. *Brom X* 5F **198**
Lwr. Mead. *Eger* 4F **198**
Lwr. Mead Dri. *Burn* 8D **104**
Lwr. Meadow. *Tur* 8K **179**
Lwr. North Av. *Barn* 2M **77**
Lwr. Nuttall Rd. *Ram* 1J **201**
Lwr. Park St. *Barn* 2N **77**
Lwr. Parrock Rd. *Barfd* 1G **104**
Lower Penwortham. 4H **135**
Lwr. Philips Rd. *Whi I* 9C **120**
Lower Place. 9E **204**
Lwr. Promenade. *South* 7G **166**
(in two parts)
Lwr. Ridge Clo. *Burn* 3F **124**
Lower Rd. *Ram* 6J **181**
Lwr. Rook St. *Barn* 2N **77**
Lwr. Rosegrove La. *Burn* 4L **123**
Lwr. School St. Col *7A* ***86***
(off School St.)
Lwr. Sheriff St. *Roch* 5B **204**
Lwr. Standrings. *Roch* 5L **203**
Lower St. *Roch* 9D **204**
Lower Summerseat. 4H **201**
Lwr. Tenterfield. *Roch* 3H **203**
Lwr. Tentre. *Burn* 4F **124**
Lower Thurnham. 4G **36**
Lwr. Timber Hill La. *Burn* 6E **124**
Lwr. Tong. *Brom X* 6F **198**
Lwr. Tweedale St. *Roch* 7C **204**
Lower Wlk. *Blac* 4B **88**
Lwr. West Av. *Barn* 2M **77**
Lower Westhouse. 2L **19**
Lwr. Wheat End. *Roch* 5E **204**
Lwr. Wilworth. *B'brn* 8M **119**
Lwr. Wood Bank. Dar *5M* ***157***
(off Higher Avondale Rd.)
Lwr. Woodhill Rd. *Bury* 9J **201**
(in two parts)
Lowesby Clo. *Walt D* 5A **136**
Lowes Ct. Blac *9B* ***88***
(off Shaw Rd.)
Lowes Ct. *T Clev* 9H **55**
Lowes Grn. *Liv* 9B **206**
Lowe's La. *Uph* 4J **211**
Lowes Pk. Golf Course. 6M **201**
Lowes Rd. *Bury* 7L **201**
Loweswater Cres. *Burn* 1N **123**
Loweswater Dri. *More* 4D **22**
Loweswater Way. *Liv* 6J **223**
Lowesway. *Blac* 1F **108**
Lowesway. *T Clev* 9H **55**
Lowe Vw. *Ross* 6D **162**
Lowfield Clo. *Newt* 7D **112**
Lowfield Rd. *Blac* 2F **108**
Lowfields La. *Barb* 3F **8**
Low Fold. *Kel* 6D **78**
Lowgill. 2K **33**
Lowgill La. *Lowg* 1K **33**
Low Grn. *Ley* 6J **153**
Low Hill. *Dar* 9A **158**
Low Hill. *Roch* 2F **204**
Lowhouse Clo. *Miln* 6K **205**
Lowick Clo. *Hogh* 4G **136**
Lowick Dri. *Poul F* 2K **89**
Lowlands Rd. *Bolt S* 3L **15**
Lowlands Rd. *More* 4C **22**
Lowland Way. *Blac* 5F **62**
Low La. *Leck* 8J **9**
Low La. *More* 2F **22**
Low La. *Wigg* 10N **35**
Low Ling La. *C'den* 2M **147**
Low Moor. 3J **81**
Low Moor La. *Barn* 3M **77**
Low Moor Rd. *Blac* 8E **62**
Lowndes St. *Pres* 7H **115**
(in two parts)
Lowood Clo. *Miln* 7J **205**
Lowood Gro. *Lea* 8A **114**
Lowood Lodge. *Lyth A* 5N **129**
Lowood Pl. *B'brn* 2H **139**
Lowrey Ter. *Blac* 8B **88**
Low Rd. *Halt* 2B **24**
Low Rd. *M'ton* 5M **27**
Lowry Clo. *Los H* 9K **135**
Lowry Hill La. *Lath* 2F **210**
Lowside La. *Yeal R* 7C **6**
Low's Pl. *Roch* 3D **204**
Lowstead Pl. *Blac* 3E **108**
Lowstern Clo. *Eger* 4E **198**
Low St. *Burt L* 3K **19**
Low St. *Ram* 8H **181**
Lowther Av. *Ain* 8C **222**
Lowther Av. *Blac* 9B **62**
Lowther Av. *Mag* 9D **216**
Lowther Av. *More* 5E **22**
Lowther Ct. *Blac* 9B **62**
Lowther Ct. *Lytham* 5N **129**
Lowther Cres. *Ley* 4G **153**
Lowther Dri. *Ley* 5G **153**
Lowther Gardens. 5M **129**
Lowther La. *Foul* 2A **86**
Lowther Pl. *B'brn* 9A **120**
Lowther Rd. *Fltwd* 9F **40**
Lowther Rd. *Lanc* 7M **23**
Lowther Rd. *Roch* 9B **204**
Lowther St. *Ash R* 8F **114**
Lowther St. *Col* 5B **86**
Lowther St. *Nels* 2G **105**
Lowther Ter. *App B* 4F **212**
Lowther Ter. *Lyth A* 5N **129**
Lowthian Ho. Pres *9J* ***115***
(off Lowthian St.)
Lowthian St. *Pres* 9J **115**
Lowthorpe Cres. *Pres* 7L **115**
Lowthorpe Pl. *Pres* 7L **115**
Lowthorpe Rd. *Pres* 6L **115**
Lowthwaite Dri. *Nels* 4J **105**
Lowton Rd. *Lyth A* 9G **108**
Loxham Gdns. *Blac* 3D **108**
Loxley Grn. *Ful* 3M **115**
Loxley Pl. *T Clev* 4E **62**
Loxley Pl. E. *T Clev* 4E **62**
Loxley Rd. *South* 1K **187**
Loxwood Clo. *Walt D* 5K **135**
Loynd St. *Gt Har* 4J **121**
Loynd St. *Ram* 8J **181**
Loyne Pk. *Whit* 8E **8**
Lubbock St. *Burn* 3A **124**
Lucas Av. *Char R* 7N **173**
Lucas Dri. *Whit W* 9E **154**
Lucas Green. 1E **174**
Lucas La. *Whit W* 1E **174**
Lucas La. E. *Whit W* 1E **174**
Lucas St. *Bury* 9M **201**
Lucerne Clo. *Ful* 5M **115**
Lucerne Rd. *Ful* 5M **115**
Lucknow St. *Roch* 8C **204**
Lucy St. *Barfd* 8H **85**
Lucy St. *Lanc* 8K **23**
Lucy St. *More* 2B **22**
Ludlow. *Skel* 8N **211**
Ludlow Dri. *Orm* 5J **209**
Ludlow Gro. *Blac* 9F **62**
Ludlow St. *Stand* 1M **213**
Luke St. *Bacup* 7G **162**
Lulworth. *Skel* 8M **211**
Lulworth Av. *Ash R* 7G **114**
Lulworth Av. *Blac* 8G **88**
Lulworth Clo. *Bury* 7H **201**
Lulworth Pl. *Walt D* 6N **135**
Lulworth Rd. *Ful* 5K **115**
Lulworth Rd. *South* 1F **186**
Lulworth Vw. *South* 1E **186**
Lumb. 1D **162**
Lumb Carr Av. *Ram* 1F **200**
Lumb Carr Rd. *Holc* 2F **200**
Lumb Holes La. *Ross* 8C **162**
Lumb La. *Ross* 2D **162**
Lumb Scarr. *Bacup* 5K **163**
Lumbutts Rd. *Todm* 5K **165**
Lumn St. *Bury* 5L **201**
Lumwood. *Bolt* 9B **198**
Lunds La. *Much H* 6H **151**
Lund St. *B'brn* 4K **139**
Lund St. *Pres* 9J **115**
Lune Av. *Liv* 9D **216**
Lune Clo. *K Lon* 6F **8**
Lune Clo. *K'ham* 4N **111**
Lunedale Av. *Blac* 9C **88**
Lune Dri. *Ley* 5A **154**
Lune Dri. *More* 5F **22**
Lunefield Dri. *K Lon* 6F **8**
Lunefield Gdns. K Lon *6F* ***8***
(off Ruskin Dri.)
Lune Gro. *Blac* 7C **88**
Lune Ind. Est. *Lanc* 8G **22**
Lune Rd. *Fltwd* 9F **40**
Lune Rd. *Lanc* 7H **23**
Lunesdale Clo. *Lyth A* 1J **129**
Lunesdale Ct. *Horn* 8C **18**
Lunesdale Ct. *Lanc* 7M **23**
(Derwent Rd.)
Lunesdale Ct. *Lanc* 5H **23**
(Watery La.)
Lunesdale Dri. *Fort* 2M **45**
Lunesdale Rd. *K'ham* 4M **111**
Lunesdale Ter. *Clau* 9M **17**
Lunesdale Vw. *Halt* 1C **24**
Luneside. *Lanc* 8G **22**
Lune St. *Col* 7B **86**
Lune St. *Lanc* 7K **23**
Lune St. *L'rdge* 2K **97**
Lune St. *Pad* 1J **123**
Lune St. *Pres* 1J **135**
Lune Ter. *Lanc* 7K **23**
Lune Valley. *Lanc* 4M **23**
Lune Vw. *Kno S* 8L **41**
Lunt Rd. *Liv* 9J **215**
Lunt's La. *Liv* 2A **214**
Lupin Clo. *Acc* 1N **141**
Lupin Clo. *Whit W* 1D **174**
Lupin Rd. *Acc* 1A **142**
Lupton Dri. *Barfd* 7H **85**
Lupton Pl. *Lanc* 5H **23**
Lupton St. *Chor* 7E **174**
Lutner St. *Burn* 4E **124**
Luton Rd. *Ash R* 7B **114**
Luton Rd. *T Clev* 2D **62**
Lutwidge Av. *Pres* 8M **115**
Lutwidge St. *Pres* 9L **115**
Lower Lea. 2A **48**
Lyceum Av. *Blac* 6D **88**
Lyceum Pas. *Roch* 6C **204**
Lychfield Dri. *Bam B* 9A **136**
Lychgate. *Pres* 9K **115**
Lych Ga. *Wadd* 8H **73**
Lychgate. *Wig* 6N **221**
Lydbury Cres. *Liv* 9L **223**
Lyddesdale Av. *T Clev* 2D **62**
Lydd Gro. *Chor* 7C **174**
Lydford. *Roch* 7B **204**
Lydgate. 9H **147**
Lydgate. *Burn* 8J **105**
Lydgate. *Chor* 9C **174**
Lydia St. *Acc* 4A **142**
Lydiate. 6A **216**
Lydiate La. *Clau B* 4E **68**
Lydiate La. *E'ston* 6E **172**
Lydiate La. *Ley* 3M **153**
Lydiate Sta. Rd. *Lyd* 7J **215**
(in two parts)
Lydric Av. *Hogh* 6G **136**
Lyefield Wlk. *Roch* 7E **204**
Lyelake Clo. *Liv* 9L **223**
Lyelake La. *W'head* 2D **218**
Lyelake Rd. *Liv* 9L **223**
Lyme Gro. *Kno S* 8L **41**
Lymm Av. *Lanc* 5G **22**
Lynbridge Clo. *Orr* 6H **221**
Lyncroft Cres. *Blac* 3E **88**
Lyndale. *Skel* 8M **211**
Lyndale Av. *Has* 5G **160**
Lyndale Av. *Los H* 6M **135**
Lyndale Av. *Wilp* 2A **120**
Lyndale Cvn. Pk. *Blac* 3M **109**
Lyndale Clo. *Ley* 9L **153**
Lyndale Clo. *Ross* 9M **143**
Lyndale Clo. *Wilp* 2A **120**
Lyndale Ct. Fltwd *8H* ***41***
(off Bold St.)
Lyndale Dri. *L'boro* 8K **185**
Lyndale Gro. *Los H* 6M **135**
Lyndale Rd. *Hap* 6H **123**
Lynden Av. *More* 4E **22**
Lyndeth Clo. *Ful* 3A **116**
Lyndhurst. *Liv* 1C **222**
Lyndhurst. *Skel* 8M **211**
Lyndhurst Av. *B'brn* 3E **140**
Lyndhurst Av. *Blac* 9D **88**
Lyndhurst Dri. *Ash R* 7B **114**
Lyndhurst Gro. *Gt Har* 3L **121**
Lyndhurst Rd. *B'brn* 6M **139**
Lyndhurst Rd. *Burn* 4F **124**
Lyndhurst Rd. *Dar* 4M **157**
(in two parts)
Lyndhurst Rd. *South* 3G **187**
Lyndon Av. *Gt Har* 3L **121**
Lyndon Av. *Shev* 6K **213**
Lyndon Clo. *Tot* 7E **200**
Lyndon Ct. *Gt Har* 3L **121**
Lyndon Ho. *Gt Har* 3L **121**
Lynfield Rd. *Gt Har* 3L **121**
Lynn Gro. *Blac* 3B **88**
Lynn Pl. *Rib* 7N **115**
Lynnwood Dri. *Roch* 5L **203**
Lynroyle Way. *Roch* 9A **204**
Lynslack Ter. *Arns* 3F **4**
Lynthorpe Rd. *B'brn* 6M **139**
Lynthorpe Rd. *Nels* 1L **105**
Lynton Av. *Blac* 1D **108**
Lynton Av. *Ley* 7M **153**
Lynton Av. *Roch* 9M **203**
Lynton Ct. *Fltwd* 4C **54**
Lynton Dri. *South* 4E **186**
Lynton Rd. *Acc* 4M **141**
Lynton Rd. *South* 5E **186**
Lynwood Av. *Augh* 9H **209**
Lynwood Av. *Blac* 2E **88**
Lynwood Av. *Clay M* 6M **121**
Lynwood Av. *Dar* 4M **157**
Lynwood Av. *Grims* 8E **96**
Lynwood Clo. *Clay M* 5M **121**
Lynwood Clo. *Col* 4A **86**
Lynwood Clo. *Dar* 4M **157**
Lynwood Clo. *Skel* 4A **220**
Lynwood Dri. *Stalm* 5B **56**
Lynwood End. *Augh* 9H **209**
Lynwood Gro. *Bolt* 9K **199**
Lynwood Pk. *W'ton* 2L **131**
Lynwood Rd. *Acc* 7D **122**
Lynwood Rd. *B'brn* 2J **139**
Lyons La. *Chor* 7F **174**
Lyons Rd. *South* 9G **167**
Lythall Av. *Lyth A* 4C **130**
Lytham. 5A **130**
Lytham Clo. *Ful* 6G **114**
Lytham Clo. *Liv* 9E **222**
Lytham Ct. *Liv* 6H **223**
Lytham Golf Course. 3B **130**
(Green Dri.)
Lytham Hall. 4M **129**
Lytham Lifeboat Mus. 6B **130**
Lytham Rd. *Ash R* 6F **114**
Lytham Rd. *B'brn* 8N **139**
Lytham Rd. *Blac* 8B **88**
Lytham Rd. *Burn* 8G **105**
Lytham Rd. *Lyth A & W'ton* 3D **130**
Lytham Rd. *Mos S* 8C **110**
Lytham Rd. *South* 2N **167**
(in two parts)
Lytham St Anne's. 3J **129**
Lytham St Anne's Nature Reserve & Vis. Cen. 7C **108**
Lytham St. *Chor* 7G **174**
Lytham St. *Lyth A* 1K **129**
Lytham St. *Roch* 2B **204**
Lythcoe Av. *Ful* 5F **114**
Lythe Fell Av. *Halt* 1C **24**
Lythe Fell La. *Lowg* 3M **33**
Lythe La. *Lowg* 3L **33**
Lythra Ct. *Lyth A* 3F **128**
Lyth Rd. *Lanc* 7M **23**
Lytles Clo. *Liv* 1A **214**
Lytton St. *Burn* 2L **123**

M

Maaruig Cvn Pk. *Pre* 7N **41**
Mabel St. *Col* 6C **86**
Mabel St. *Roch* 3A **204**
Maberry Clo. *Shev* 5G **213**
McCall Clo. *W Grn* 6F **110**
Macauley Av. *Blac* 1E **108**
McAuley Mt. *Burn* 1M **123**
Macauley St. *Burn* 4A **124**
Macbeth Rd. *Fltwd* 9E **40**
Maccles Ct. *L'boro* 8K **185**
McDonald Rd. *Hey* 2J **27**
Macdonald St. *Orr* 5L **221**
Mackay Cft. *Chor* 6F **174**
McKenna M. *Pen* 3E **134**
Mackenzie Clo. *Chor* 6F **174**
Mackenzie Gro. *Bolt* 9D **198**
McKenzie St. *Bam B* 8B **136**
Mackenzie St. *Bolt* 8D **198**
Maclaren Clo. *Blac* 5K **89**
Macleod St. *Nels* 2H **105**
Maclure Rd. *Roch* 7C **204**
McNaught St. *Roch* 7E **204**
McOwen Pl. *Roch* 6D **204**
McOwen St. *Roch* 6D **204**
Maddy St. *Pres* 9G **114**
Madeley Gdns. *Roch* 4A **204**
Maden Clo. *Bacup* 5K **163**
Maden Rd. *Bacup* 5H **163**
Madens Sq. *L'boro* 9L **185**
Maden St. *Chu* 2L **141**
Madingley Ct. *South* 4M **167**
Madison Av. *Blac* 6B **62**
Madison Av. *Bolt S* 7J **15**
Madryn Av. *Liv* 8M **223**
Maesbrook Clo. *Banks* 1G **168**
Mafeking Av. *Bury* 8M **201**
Mafeking Rd. *Ash R* 7F **114**
Magdalen Rd. *T Clev* 2D **62**
Maggotts Nook Rd. *Rainf* 1L **225**
Maghull. 9C **216**
Maghull Hey Cop. *Liv* 6G **215**
Maghull La. *Liv* 1G **222**
(in two parts)
Maghull Smallholdings Est.
Liv 8F **216**
Magnolia Clo. *Ful* 3M **115**
Magnolia Dri. *Ley* 5A **154**
Magnolia Rd. *Pen* 5E **134**
Magpie Clo. *Burn* 4A **124**
Maida Va. *T Clev* 3D **62**
Maiden St. *Ross* 1G **160**
Main Av. *Hey* 5L **27**
Main Clo. *Over* 7B **28**
Main Dri. *Poul F* 9L **63**
Main Rd. *Bolt S* 6L **15**
Main Rd. *Gal* 2L **37**
Main Rd. *Hell* 1D **52**
Main Rd. *Neth K* 4B **16**
Main Rd. *Slyne* 9K **15**
Main Rd. *Thur* 3F **36**
Mains Dri., The. *Gigg* 2N **35**
Mainsfield Clo. Gigg *2N* ***35***
(off Stackhouse La.)
Mainsfield Ri. Gigg *2N* ***35***
(off Stackhouse La.)
Mainside Rd. *Liv* 9L **223**
Mains La. *Lath* 7K **191**
Mains La. *Poul F* 5M **63**
Main Sprit Weind. *Pres* 1K **135**
Mainstones. 9E **30**
Main St. *Ben* 6L **19**
Main St. *Bolt B* 8K **51**
Main St. *Burt* 6G **7**
Main St. *C'ham* 9H **37**
Main St. *D'ham* 7G **74**
Main St. *Gis* 9A **52**
Main St. *Grin* 3A **74**
Main St. *Hey & Over* 8K **21**
Main St. *I'ton* 3N **19**
Main St. *Kel* 6D **78**
Main St. *K Lon* 6F **8**
Main St. *Lanc* 6K **23**
Main St. *L'clif & Stainf* 2N **35**
Main St. *L Bent* 6J **19**
Main St. *Over* 7A **28**
Main St. *Rath* 7M **35**
Main St. *War* 5N **11**
Main St. *Whit* 8E **8**
Main St. *Wray* 8E **18**
Mainway. *Lanc* 7K **23**

Mainway Ct.—Marybank Clo.

Mainway Ct. Bam B 8A 136
Mairscough La. Down & Liv 3N 215
Maitland Av. T Clev 2D 62
Maitland Clo. Pres 9M 115
Maitland Clo. Roch 2F 204
Maitland Clo. Todm 7K 165
Maitland Pl. Ross 6M 161
Maitland St. Bacup 5K 163
Maitland St. Pres 9M 115 (in two parts)
Maitland St. Todm 7K 165
Majestic, The. Lyth A 2D 128
Major Ind. Pk., The. Hey 4L 27
Major St. Acc 4A 142
Major St. Miln 7J 205
Major St. Ram 8G 181
Major St. Ross 9M 143
Major St. Todm 2M 165
Major St. Wig 5M 221
Makinson La. Hor 9G 197
Makinsons Row. Gal 2L 37 (off Chapel St.)
Malcolm Pl. Fltwd 9E 40
Malcolm St. Pres 8N 115
Malden St. Ley 6K 153
Maldern Av. Poul F 6J 63
Maldon Pl. Rib 7N 115
Maldon St. Roch 8C 204
Malham Av. Acc 4M 141
Malham Av. Blac 1D 108
Malham Clo. Lanc 5H 23
Malham Clo. South 2L 187
Malham Pl. Rib 5A 116
Malham Rd. Burn 7H 105
Malham Rd. Hell 1E 52
Malham Wend. Barfd 8G 85
Maliff Rd. Brclf 8E 106
Malkin Clo. Black 3J 85
Malkin La. Clith 8F 80
Mallard Clo. Augh 1H 217
Mallard Clo. Ley 7G 152
Mallard Clo. T Clev 7G 54
Mallard Ct. Blac 4H 89
Mallard Ct. Lanc 8J 23
Mallard Ho. Liv 7A 216
Mallard Pl. Osw 5K 141
Mallards Wlk. Bam B 2C 154
Mallee Av. South 3N 167
Mallee Cres. South 3N 167
Malley La. Wood 2N 93
Mallison St. Bolt 9F 198
Mallom Av. Eux 5A 174
Mallory Av. Liv 7A 216
Mallow Cft. Roch 9F 204
Mallowdale. Ful 3E 114
Mallowdale Av. Hey 8M 21
Mallowdale Rd. Lanc 6H 23
Mallow Wlk. More 6B 22
Mall, The. Burn 3E 124
Mall, The. Lyth A 1J 129
Mall, The. Orm 7L 209
Mall, The. Rib 7A 116
Malta St. Dar 7B 158
Maltby Pl. Blac 8F 88
Malt Dubs Clo. I'ton 3N 19 (off Laundry La.)
Malthouse Ct. Ash R 8G 115
Malthouse, The. Ash R 8G 115
Malthouse Way. Pen 5G 134
Maltings, The. Longt 8K 133
Maltings, The. Pen 4G 134
Maltings, The. T Clev 8G 55
Maltings, The. Whit 8E 8
Malt Kiln Brow. Chip 5G 70
Malt Kiln Gro. L Ecc 6M 65
Maltkiln La. Augh 2J 217
Maltkiln La. Bis 4M 191 (in two parts)
Malton Dri. Los H 9K 135
Malt St. Acc 1A 142
Malvern Av. B'brn 7L 139
Malvern Av. Blac 9D 88
Malvern Av. Bury 8L 201
Malvern Av. Lanc 1L 29
Malvern Av. Osw 5L 141
Malvern Av. Pad 3J 123
Malvern Av. Pres 3L 135
Malvern Av. Stalm 5B 56
Malvern Clo. Acc 1N 141
Malvern Clo. Hor 8D 196
Malvern Clo. Liv 6H 223
Malvern Clo. Los H 8M 135
Malvern Clo. Miln 6K 205
Malvern Clo. Wig 8M 221
Malvern Ct. South 8G 167
Malvern Gdns. South 8G 167
Malvern Gro. Liv 8B 222
Malvern Ho. Pen 6H 135
Malvern Rd. Lyth A 3K 129
Malvern Rd. Nels 1K 105
Malvern Rd. Pres 2L 135
Malvern St. Stand 1M 213
Malvern St. E. Roch 6N 203
Malvern St. W. Roch 6N 203
Malvern Way. Ross 8F 160
Manby Clo. Hogh 5H 137
Manchester Mill Ind. Est. Pres 9M 115
Manchester Rd. Acc 3B 142
Manchester Rd. Barn 3M 77
Manchester Rd. Blac 4D 88
Manchester Rd. Dunn 4N 143
Manchester Rd. Hap & Pad 5H 123
Manchester Rd. Has 4G 160
Manchester Rd. Nels 3G 104
Manchester Rd. Pres 1K 135
Manchester Rd. Ram 8K 181
Manchester Rd. South 6J 167
Mancknols St. Nels 3K 105
Mancknols Walton Cottage Homes, The. Nels 2M 105
Mandela Ct. B'brn 1M 139 (off Wimberley St.)
Manderville Clo. Wig 9N 221
Mandeville Rd. South 8B 186 (in two parts)
Mandeville Ter. Hawk 3A 200
Manfield. Skel 9L 211
Manhattan Sq. Liv 9A 222
Manion Av. Liv 6A 216
Manion Clo. Liv 6A 216
Manitoba Clo. B'brn 9J 119
Manley Clo. Bury 3H 201
Manley Rd. Roch 9N 203 (in two parts)
Manley Ter. Bolt 9E 198
Manner Sutton St. B'brn 3N 139
Manning Rd. Pres 8A 116 (in two parts)
Manning Rd. South 8L 167
Manor Av. Burs 2B 210
Manor Av. Ful 5L 115
Manor Av. Pen 4E 134
Manor Av. Ribch 7E 98
Manor Av. Slyne 9J 15
Manor Brook. Acc 2B 142
Manor Clo. Burt L & I'ton 3K 19
Manor Clo. Hogh 5H 137
Manor Clo. Slyne 9J 15
Manor Ct. Blac (FY1) 3C 88
Manor Ct. Blac (FY4) 1E 108
Manor Ct. Bolt 9K 199
Manor Ct. Ful 2E 114
Manor Ct. South 4N 167
Manor Ct. T Clev 9C 54
Manor Courtyard. Hey 8K 21
Manor Cres. Burs 2B 210
Manor Cres. Slyne 9K 15
Manorcroft. Longt 8L 133
Manor Dri. Boot 7A 222
Manor Dri. Burs 2B 210
Manor Dri. K'ham 5A 112
Manor Dri. Poul F 7L 63
Manor Dri. Slyne 9J 15
Manor Dri. T Clev 9D 54
Manor Farm. Whit 8D 8
Manor Fields. Whal 5J 101
Manor Gdns. Burs 2B 210
Manor Gro. Hey 6N 21
Manor Gro. Liv 8G 222
Manor Gro. Orr 3L 221
Manor Gro. Pen 4D 134
Manor Gro. Skel 2K 219
Mnr. Ho. Clo. Ley 7E 152
Mnr. Ho. Clo. Liv 1B 222
Mnr. Ho. Cres. Pres 6L 115
Mnr. Ho. Dri. Skel 8B 220
Mnr. Ho. La. Pres 6L 115
Mnr. Ho. Pk. T Clev 9C 54
Manor La. Pen 4D 134
Manor La. Slyne 8J 15
Manor Pk. Ful 6M 115
Manor Pl. Chu 1M 141
Manor Ri. Thorn C 9J 53
Manor Rd. B'brn 3J 139
Manor Rd. Blac 6D 88
Manor Rd. Burn 2N 123
Manor Rd. Burs 2B 210
Manor Rd. Clay W 4D 154
Manor Rd. Clith 4K 81
Manor Rd. Col 4B 86
Manor Rd. Dar 7N 157
Manor Rd. Fltwd 8E 40
Manor Rd. Gars 3N 59
Manor Rd. Hor 9E 196
Manor Rd. Ins 2G 92
Manor Rd. Shev 6J 213
Manor Rd. Slyne 9J 15
Manor Rd. South 4N 167
Manor Rd. Whal 5J 101
Manor Rd. W Grn 5G 111
Manor St. Acc 1B 142
Manor St. Bacup 6K 163
Manor St. Nels 3K 105
Manor St. Ram 7G 180 (in two parts)
Manor Way. W Grn 6G 111
Manorwood. Fltwd 9E 40
Manor Wood. Wesh 2N 111
Manse Av. Wrigh 8J 193
Mansergh. 2E 8
Mansergh High La. Man 1E 8
Mansergh St. Burn 8G 105
Mansfield Av. Ram 3G 200
Mansfield Cres. Brier 4G 104
Mansfield Dri. Hogh 5G 137
Mansfield Grange. Roch 7N 203
Mansfield Gro. Brier 4G 104
Mansfield Rd. Blac 3D 88
Mansfield Rd. Roch 6J 203
Mansion St. S. Acc 2C 142
Manston Gro. Chor 7C 174
Manx Jane's La. South 2N 167
Manxman Rd. B'brn 7M 139
Maple Av. Blac 5D 88
Maple Av. Brins 8A 156
Maple Av. Burs 9C 190
Maple Av. Clith 4K 81
Maple Av. Fltwd 4F 54
Maple Av. Has 4H 161
Maple Av. Hey 5M 21
Maple Av. T Clev 3J 63
Maple Bank. Burn 2G 124
Maplebank. Lea 8N 113
Maple Clo. Clay D 3M 119
Maple Clo. Newt 7D 112
Maple Clo. Whal 4K 101
Maple Ct. Gars 3N 59
Maple Cres. Pres 1H 135
Maple Cres. Rish 9H 121
Maple Dri. Bam B 7B 136
Maple Dri. Osw 5M 141
Maple Dri. Poul F 9L 63
Maple Gro. Chor 3F 174
Maple Gro. Grims 9G 96
Maple Gro. Lanc 8H 23 (off Sycamore Gro.)
Maple Gro. Pen 4E 134
Maple Gro. Ram 9J 181
Maple Gro. Rib 5C 116
Maple Gro. Tot 8F 200
Maple Gro. W'ton 2J 131
Maple Ho. Chor 8B 174
Maple Rd. Gars 4N 59
Maples, The. Ley 9C 152
Maple St. B'brn 1A 140
Maple St. Bolt 8J 199
Maple St. Clay M 7M 121
Maple St. Gt Har 3K 121
Maple St. Rish 8H 121
Maple St. South 8L 167
Maple St. Todm 8K 165
Maple Towers. Liv 7L 223
Maplewood. Skel 8L 211
Maplewood. South 4M 167
Maplewood Av. Pre 8N 41
Maplewood Clo. Chor 8G 174
Maplewood Clo. Ley 7H 153
Maplewood Clo. Lyth A 4M 129
Maplewood Dri. T Clev 3C 62
Maplewood Gdns. Lanc 5L 29
Marabou Dri. Dar 4L 157
Marathon Pl. Ley 4F 152
Marble Av. T Clev 4F 62
Marble Pl. Shop. Cen. South 7H 167
Marble St. Osw 4L 141
Marbury Gro. Stand 4N 213
Marbury Rd. Liv 8H 223
Marc Av. Liv 6G 223
Marchbank Rd. Skel 2H 219
March Dri. Bury 8J 201
March St. Burn 1D 124
March St. Roch 6D 204
Marchwood Rd. Blac 2H 89
Marcliffe Dri. Roch 7M 203
Marcroft Av. Blac 2E 108
Marcroft Pl. Roch 9D 204
Mardale Av. Blac 9J 89
Mardale Av. More 3D 22
Mardale Clo. South 9B 186
Mardale Cres. Ley 8L 153
Mardale Rd. Lanc 7L 23
Mardale Rd. L'rdge 5H 97
Mardale Rd. Pres 8C 116
Mardyke. Roch 5B 204
Maresfield Rd. Pres 3G 135
Margaret Av. Roch 6F 204
Margaret Av. Stand L 8M 213
Margaret Rd. Pen 4H 135
Margaret St. B'brn 4D 140
Margaret St. Osw 6J 141
Margaret St. Pres 9K 115
Margaret St. Ross 3L 161
Margaret Ward Ct. Roch 8D 204
Margate Av. Blac 3E 108
Margate Rd. Ing 5D 114
Margate Rd. Lyth A 9F 108
Margroy Clo. Roch 3D 204
Maria Ct. Burn 5E 124 (off Glebe St.)
Marians Dri. Orm 4K 209
Maria Sq. Bel 1L 197
Maria St. Dar 9B 158
Maricourt Av. B'brn 3D 140
Marigold St. Roch 8C 204 (in two parts)
Marigold St. Wig 4N 221
Marilyn Av. Los H 8L 135
Marina Av. Blac 8D 88
Marina Av. Stain 2K 89
Marina Clo. Los H 7K 135
Marina Cres. Boot 9A 222
Marina Dri. Ful 2H 115
Marina Dri. Los H 7K 135
Marina Dri. Wig 6N 221
Marina Gro. Los H & Pen 7K 135
Marina M. Fltwd 1H 55
Marina Rd. Liv 2A 214
Marine Av. Burn 5A 124
Marine Dri. Hest B 9G 14
Marine Dri. Lyth A 5K 129
Marine Dri. South 7F 166
Marine Ga. Mans. South 6H 167
Marine Pde. Fltwd 3C 54
Marine Pde. South 6G 166
Marine Rd. Central. More 3N 21
Marine Rd. E. More 2B 22
Marine Rd. W. More 4M 21
Mariners Clo. Fltwd 3E 54
Mariners Way. Ash R 9D 114
Marino Clo. T Clev 3K 63
Maritime Ct. South 7H 167
Maritime St. Fltwd 2F 54
Maritime Way. Ash R 1C 134
Mark Clo. Pen 7J 135
Market Av. B'brn 3M 139
Market Ga. Lanc 8K 23
Market Hall. Lanc 8K 23 (off King St.)
Market Pl. Adl 6J 195
Market Pl. Chor 6E 174
Market Pl. Clith 3L 81
Market Pl. Col 6B 86
Market Pl. Fltwd 9J 41
Market Pl. Gars 5N 59
Market Pl. L'rdge 3K 97
Market Pl. Poul F 8K 63
Market Pl. Pres 1J 135
Market Pl. Ram 7G 181
Market Pl. Roch 6C 204
Market Pl. Set 3N 35
Mkt. Promenade. Burn 3E 124
Market Sq. Burn 3E 124
Market Sq. Kirkby 8K 223 (off St Chads Pde.)
Market Sq. K Lon 6F 8 (off Main St.)
Market Sq. K'ham 4N 111
Market Sq. Lyth A 5N 129
Market Sq. Nels 2H 105
Market Sq. Pres 9J 115
Market St. Adl 7J 195
Market St. Bacup 6K 163
Market St. Barn 2M 77 (off Brook St.)
Market St. Blac 5B 88
Market St. Brit & Shawf 8A 164
Market St. Carn 8A 12
Market St. Chor 6E 174
Market St. Chu 3L 141
Market St. Col 6B 86
Market St. Dar 6A 158
Market St. Hamb 1B 64
Market St. K Lon 6F 8
Market St. Lanc 8J 23
Market St. More 3A 22
Market St. Nels 2H 105
Market St. Ram 2J 181
Market St. Ross 7C 162
Market St. South 7G 167
Market St. Stand 3N 213
Market St. Todm 4K 165 (off Rochdale Rd.)
Market St. Wesh 3K 111
Market St. La. B'brn 4M 139
Market St. W. Pres 9J 115
Market Wlk. Chor 6E 174
Market Way. B'brn 3M 139 (off Blackburn Shop. Cen.)
Market Way. Orm 7K 209
Market Way. Roch 6C 204
Markham Dri. South 3L 187
Markham Rd. B'brn 5J 139
Markham St. Ash R 8F 114
Mark Ho. La. Garg 2L 53
Markland St. Pres 1H 135
Markland St. Ram 8G 181
Mark La. Todm 9J 147
Markross St. Ross 5M 161
Mark's Av. Far M 2H 153
Marksbury Shop. Cen. Fltwd 3C 54
Mark Sq. Tar 9E 150
Mark St. Bacup 7G 162
Mark St. Burn 9F 104
Mark St. Roch 4E 204
Marland. 9M 203
Marland. Skel 8L 211
Marland Av. Roch 9M 203
Marland Clo. Roch 8M 203
Marland Fold. Roch 9M 203
Marland Grn. Roch 9M 203
Marland Hill Rd. Roch 8N 203
Marland Old Rd. Roch 9M 203
Marland Tops. Roch 9M 203
Marl Av. Pen 4E 134
Marlborough. Skel 8L 211
Marlborough Av. Liv 8C 216
Marlborough Av. T Clev 7C 54
Marlborough Av. W'ton 2J 131
Marlborough Clo. Ram 2H 201
Marlborough Clo. Whitw 7N 183
Marlborough Ct. Skel 8L 211
Marlborough Ct. South 7J 167
Marlborough Dri. Ful 2G 115
Marlborough Dri. Walt D 4N 135
Marlborough Gdns. Skel 8L 211
Marlborough Gdns. South 6J 167
Marlborough Rd. Acc 9A 122
Marlborough Rd. Blac 6D 88
Marlborough Rd. Hey 5M 21
Marlborough Rd. Lyth A 8E 108
Marlborough Rd. South 7J 167
Marlborough St. Burn 4D 124
Marlborough St. Chor 5G 174
Marlborough St. Roch 4N 203
Marlborough Ter. South 7J 167 (off Marlborough Rd.)
Marl Cop. Breth 9L 151
Marl Cft. Pen 6G 134
Marles Ct. Burn 1F 124 (off Pheasantford Grn.)
Marley Hey. Tur 9K 179
Marlfield. L Hoo 3K 151
Marlfield Clo. Ing 4C 114
Marl Gro. Orr 7G 220
Marl Hill Cres. Rib 7C 116
Marl Hill La. Loth 5L 79
Marlhill Rd. Blac 2G 89
Marlin St. Nels 9K 85
Marlow Ct. Adl 7H 195
Marlowe Av. Acc 6D 142
Marlowe Av. Pad 2K 123
Marlowe Cres. Gt Har 5H 121
Marl Pits. Ross 4N 161
Marl Rd. Boot 7A 222
Marl Rd. Know I 7A 224
Marlton Rd. B'brn 6L 139
Marlton Way. Lanc 1J 29
Marne Cres. Roch 6N 203
Marnwood Rd. Liv 9H 223
Marnwood Wlk. Liv 9H 223
Marple Av. Bolt 9G 198
Marple Clo. Stand 2L 213
Marquis Av. Bury 9K 201
Marquis Clo. Lwr D 9N 139
Marquis Dri. Frec 1A 132
Marquis St. K'ham 4L 111
Marron Clo. Ley 7H 153
Marsden Clo. E'ston 7E 172
Marsden Ct. Burn 7G 104
Marsden Cres. Nels 2L 105
Marsden Dri. Brier 4H 105
Marsden Gro. Brier 5G 105
Marsden Hall Rd. Nels 2L 105
Marsden Hall Rd. N. Nels 1L 105
Marsden Hall Rd. S. Nels 2L 105
Marsden Height. 5J 105
Marsden Height Clo. Brier 5J 105
Marsden Pk. Golf Course. 2N 105
Marsden Pl. Nels 2L 105
Marsden Rd. Blac 1D 108
Marsden Rd. Burn 7G 105
Marsden Rd. South 7L 167
Marsden Sq. Has 3G 161
Marsden's Sq. L'boro 8L 185 (off Sutcliffe St.)
Marsden St. Acc 4A 142
Marsden St. B'brn 6J 139
Marsden St. Has 4F 160
Marsden St. K'ham 4M 111
Marsett Clo. Roch 4L 203
Marsett Pl. Rib 4A 116
Marsh. 8H 23
Marshall Av. Acc 7E 122
Marshall Clo. Kirkby 5L 223
Marshall Gro. Ing 5D 114
Marshall Ho. Pres 9J 115 (off Ring Way)
Marshallsay. Liv 1A 214
Marshall's Brow. Pen 5H 135
Marshall's Clo. Lyd 7B 216
Marshall's Clo. Pen 4H 135
Marshall St. Roch 6F 204
Marsham Clo. Gars 6A 60
Marsham Gro. Dar 6C 158
Marshaw Pl. Gars 6L 59
Marshaw Rd. Lanc 6H 23
Marsh Clo. C'ham 1F 44
Marsh Ct. T Clev 1G 63
Marsh Cres. More 4F 22
Marshdale Rd. Blac 2F 108
Marsh Dri. Frec 1B 132
Marshes La., The. Mere B 4L 169
Marsh Farm Cvn. Pk. Carn 9L 11
Marshfield Rd. Set 3N 35
Marsh Gates. Frec 1B 132
Marsh Green. 2N 221
Marsh Grn. Wig 2N 221
Marsh House. 6C 158
Marsh Ho. La. Dar 6B 158
Marsh Houses. 1F 44
Marsh Houses. C'ham 1F 44
Marsh La. Brin 4J 155
Marsh La. C'ham 2E 44
Marsh La. Glas D 3A 36
Marsh La. Hamb 2B 64
Marsh La. Liv 5C 214
Marsh La. Longt 9F 132
Marsh La. Pres 1G 134
Marsh La. Scar 4J 209
Marsh La. Withn 2K 155
Marsh Mill Village. T Clev 1G 63
Marsh Moss La. Burs 6N 189
Marsh Rd. Banks 7G 148
Marsh Rd. Hesk B 3D 150
Marsh Rd. T Clev 1G 63
Marshside. 3N 167
Marshside Rd. South 1L 167
Marsh St. B'brn 2M 139
Marsh St. Hor 9B 196
Marsh St. Lanc 8H 23
Marsh Ter. Dar 5A 158
Marsh Vw. Newt 7D 112
Marsh Way. Pen 6F 134
Mars St. Tur 8L 179
Marston Clo. Ful 2F 114
Marston Cres. Liv 9A 214
Marston Moor. Ful 2F 114
Martha's Ter. Roch 2F 204
Martholme. 1N 121
Martholme Av. Clay M 6N 121
Martholme La. Gt Har 1M 121
Martin Av. Lyth A 5C 108
Martin Cft. Rd. Has 2F 160
Martindale Av. Fltwd 2C 54
Martindale Clo. B'brn 6C 140
Martindales, The. Clay W 4C 154
Martin Dri. Dar 9C 158
Martine Clo. Liv 6G 223
Martinfield. Ful 1J 115
Martinfield Rd. Pen 6G 135
Martinfields. Burn 6G 104
Martinique Dri. Lwr D 1N 157
Martin La. Burs 5K 189 (in two parts)
Martin La. Roch 4M 203
Martins Av. Hth C 3G 195
Martins Fields. Roch 4K 203
Martins La. Skel 4A 220
Martin St. Burn 9F 104
Martin St. Bury 9B 202
Martin St. Tur 1K 199
Martin Top La. Rim 4A 76
Martland Av. Liv 7D 222
Martland Av. Shev 7J 213
Martland Bus. Pk. Wig 1N 221
Martland Cres. Wig 9N 213
Martland Mill. 1N 221
Martland Mill Ind. Est. Wig 1M 221
Martland Mill La. Wig 1N 221 (in two parts)
Mart La. Burs 8C 190
Martlett Av. Roch 6J 203
Marton Clo. Garg 3L 53
Marton Dri. Blac 1D 108
Marton Dri. Burn 6C 124
Marton Dri. More 2F 22
Marton Fold. 5F 108
Marton Moss Side. 1G 109
Marton Pl. More 2F 22
Marton Rd. Ash R 9C 114
Marton Rd. Garg 4L 53
Marton St. Lanc 9K 23
Marton Vw. Blac 6E 88
Marton Wlk. Dar 9B 158
Marwick Clo. Stand 2N 213
Mary Av. South 7E 186
Marybank Clo. Ful 3M 115

Middleham Clo.—Moorland Rd.

Middleham Clo. Liv 9H 223
Middle Healey. 1A 204
Middle Hey. Much H 4J 151
Middle Hill. Roch 1C 204
Middle Holly. Fort 9K 37
Middle Holly Rd. Fort 5N 45
Middle Meanygate. Tar 9M 149
Middle Moss La. Form 9F 206
Middlesex Av. Burn 2M 123
Middle St. Blac 7B 88
Middle St. Col 7N 85
Middle St. Lanc 8K 23
Middle St. Whitw 5N 183
Middleton. 5M 27
Middleton Av. Fltwd 3D 54
Middleton Dri. Barfd 5J 85
Middleton Rd. Hey 2K 27
Middleton Way. Hey 1K 27
Middle Wlk. Blac 3B 88
Middle Withins La. Liv 4F 214
Middlewood. Skel 8L 211
Middlewood Clo. Augh 4H 217
Middlewood Clo. E'ston 8F 172
Middlewood Dri. Augh 4H 217
Middle Wood La. Roch 8H 185
Middlewood Rd. Augh 3H 217
Midfield. Lang 1C 120
Midford Dri. Bolt 6E 198
Midge Hall. 4E 152
Midge Hall Dri. Roch 7L 203
Midge Hall La. Midg H 2B 152
Midge Hall La. South 1G 189
Midgeland Rd. Blac 2G 108
Midgeland Ter. Blac 4J 109
Midgery La. Brough & Ful 9K 95
(in two parts)
Midgley St. Col 7B 86
Midhurst Dri. South 9B 186
Midhurst St. Roch 8C 204
Midland St. Acc 3B 142
Midland St. Nels 1J 105
Midland Ter. Carn 7A 12
Midland Ter. Hell 1D 52
(off Station Rd.)
Midsummer St. B'brn 3K 139
Midville Pl. Dar 6A 158
Milbanke Av. K'ham 3M 111
Milbeck Clo. L'rdge 5H 97
Milbourne Rd. Bury 7L 201
Milbourne St. Blac 5C 88
Milbrook Clo. Burn 4N 123
Milbrook Cres. Liv 7K 223
Milbrook Dri. Liv 7K 223
Milbrook Wlk. Liv 7K 223
Milburn Av. T Clev 7F 54
Milbury Dri. L'boro 3K 205
Mildred Clo. T Clev 9G 55
Mile End Clo. Foul 2A 86
Mile End Row. B'brn 2J 139
Mile Rd. Sing 1E 90
Miles Av. Bacup 7H 163
Miles La. App B & Shev 4G 213
(in two parts)
Miles St. Pres 7J 115
Milestone Ho. K Lon 6F 8
(off Main St.)
Mile Stone Mdw. Eux 2N 173
Milestone Pl. Cat 3H 25
Miles Wlk. Pres 7H 115
Miletas Pl. Lyth A 5J 129
Milford Av. Blac 1D 88
Milford Clo. Catt 1A 68
Milford Cres. L'boro 8L 185
Milford Rd. Harw 9M 199
Milford St. Col 6N 85
Milford St. Roch 4C 204
Milking La. Lwr D 1N 157
(in two parts)
Milking Stile La. Lanc 8H 23
Milkstone Pl. Roch 7C 204
Milkstone Rd. Roch 7C 204
(in two parts)
Milk St. Ram 9G 181
Milk St. Roch 7C 204
Mill Acre Ct. Cat 2G 24
Millar Barn La. Ross 7C 162
Millar Ct. Lanc 2J 29
Millard Clo. Hey 2L 27
Millar's Pacc. South 1A 168
Millbank. App B 5G 212
Millbank. Ful 6F 114
Millbank. Pres 9L 115
Millbank Brow. Burs 1D 210
Millbank Cotts. Liv 8D 216
Millbank La. Liv 8E 216
Millbeck Cres. Pem 6M 221
Mill Brook. Catt 9A 60
Millbrook. Fence 2C 104
Millbrook Bank. Roch 4H 203
Millbrook Bus. Pk. Rainf 7N 225
Millbrook Clo. Skel 1J 219
Millbrook Clo. Wheel 8J 155
Millbrook Ct. W Brad 7L 73
Millbrook M. Lyth A 4B 130
Mill Brook Pl. Barr 1K 101
Millbrook Row. Hth C 4K 195
Millbrook St. Lwr D 9N 139
Millbrook Way. Pen 6E 134
Mill Brow. K Lon 6F 8
Mill Brow. Wray 3J 33
Mill Brow Rd. Earby 2F 78
Mill Clo. Ins 2G 93
Mill Clo. Set 3N 35
Millcombe Way. Walt D 5A 136
Mill Cotts. Salt 5B 78
(off Moor Vw.)
Mill Ct. L'rdge 2K 97
Millcroft. Chor 4C 174
Mill Cft. Ful 5F 114
Millcroft Av. Orr 6G 220
Mill Cft. Clo. Roch 3G 203
Mill Dam. 8N 19
Mill Dam Clo. Burs 2A 210
Mill Dam La. Burs 2A 210
Mill Dyke Clo. Blac 3F 108
Mill Entrance. Clay M 7M 121
Miller Arc. Pres 1K 135
Miller Av. Abb V 5C 156
Miller Clo. Osw 3J 141
Miller Cres. Sing 1D 90
Miller Fld. Lea 6B 114
Miller Fold Av. Acc 5A 142
Millergate. Cot 5B 114
Miller La. Catf 6H 93
Miller La. Cot 3B 114
Miller Rd. Pres & Rib 8N 115
Miller's Brow. Fort 3A 46
Millers Clo. Lyth A 1K 129
Millers Ct. Orm 7L 209
Millers Ct., The. Ben 6L 19
(off Main St.)
Millerscroft. Liv 7H 223
Millersdale Clo. T Clev 3K 63
Miller's La. Ley 4E 152
Miller St. Blac 9B 88
Miller St. Bolt 9E 198
Miller St. Bury 3H 201
Miller St. Pres 9M 115
Millet St. Ram 7J 181
Millett Ter. Bury 6C 202
Mill Fld. Clay M 5M 121
Millfield. Parb 3N 211
Millfield Clo. W'ton 2L 131
Millfield Gro. Roch 7E 204
Millfield Rd. Blac 3F 108
Millfield Rd. Chor 5D 174
Mill Fold. Pres 8J 115
Millfold. Whitw 4A 184
Mill Gap St. Dar 7A 158
Mill Gdns. Orm 7L 209
Millgate. Eger 3D 198
Millgate. Eux 6N 173
Mill Ga. Ful 6G 114
Mill Ga. Roch 3E 204
Mill Ga. Ross 4M 161
Millgate Rd. Ross 4M 161
Millgate Ter. Whitw 1B 184
Mill Grn. Col 7A 86
Millham St. B'brn 2M 139
Millhaven. Ful 5G 114
Millhead. 7A 12
Mill Hey Av. Poul F 1L 89
Mill Hey La. Ruf 2G 190
Mill Hill. 7J 139
(Blackburn)
Mill Hill. 7F 150
(Preston)
Mill Hill. Osw 4K 141
Mill Hill. Pres 9H 115
Mill Hill Bri. St. B'brn 6J 139
Mill Hill Gro. M'ton 5M 27
Mill Hill La. Garg 4M 53
Mill Hill La. Gigg 2M 35
Mill Hill La. Hap 7F 122
Mill Hill St. B'brn 6J 139
Millholme Dri. Ben 7L 19
(off Wenning Av.)
Mill Ho. Clo. Roch 1G 204
Mill Ho. La. Brin 8G 137
Mill Ho. La. L'rdge 2B 98
Mill House Lodge. South 8D 186
Mill Ho. M. Moor 8L 23
(off Moor Clo.)
Millhouse St. Ram 6K 181
Mill Ho. Vw. Uph 4F 220
Millington Av. Blac 1E 108
Mill La. App B 5F 212
Mill La. Augh 2E 216
Mill La. B'brn 4M 139
Mill La. Bolt S 3K 15
Mill La. Burr 9F 8
Mill La. Burs 9C 190
(Junction La.)
Mill La. Burs 8C 190
(Liverpool Rd. N.)
Mill La. Bury 9G 201
Mill La. Cat 2G 24
Mill La. Char R 3K 193
Mill La. Chip & Goos 7E 70
Mill La. Clay W & Whit W 6E 154
Mill La. Cop 4A 194
Mill La. Earby 3F 78
Mill La. E'ston 9F 172
Mill La. Elsw 1M 91
Mill La. Eux 5K 173
(in two parts)
Mill La. Far M 4H 153
Mill La. Fltwd 9H 41
Mill La. Ful 5F 114
Mill La. Garg 3M 53
Mill La. Gis 8A 52
Mill La. Goos 1N 95
Mill La. Gt Har 3M 121
Mill La. Halt 2B 24
Mill La. Hamb 3C 64
Mill La. Hell 3D 52
Mill La. Hesk B 5D 150
Mill La. Hor 9E 196
Mill La. Hut R 6B 8
Mill La. Kirkby 7H 223
Mill La. K Lon 6F 8
Mill La. Ley 7G 153
Mill La. L Bent 6J 19
Mill La. Parb 3N 211
Mill La. Rainf 7M 225
Mill La. Rath 6K 35
Mill La. Set 3N 35
Mill La. South 5N 167
(in three parts)
Mill La. Stain 4K 89
Mill La. Stalm 5C 56
Mill La. Uph 2D 220
Mill La. Walt D 3N 135
Mill La. W'ton 2L 131
Mill La. War 6N 11
Mill La. W Grn 6E 110
Mill La. Cres. Chtwn & South 5N 167
Mill Leat Clo. Parb 2N 211
Mill Leat M. Parb 2N 211
Millom Av. Blac 7D 62
Millom Clo. Fltwd 4C 54
Millom Clo. Roch 4F 204
Millom Ct. Arns 2F 4
Millrace Ct. Lanc 6K 23
Mill Rd. Orr 6G 220
Mill Rd. South 8D 186
Mill Rd. Walm & Bury 5L 201
Millrose Clo. Skel 1K 219
Mill Row. Pen 5J 135
Mill Row. Ross 2L 161
Mills Fold. Ross 6C 162
Mill Sq. Liv 8D 222
Mills St. Whitw 5A 184
Millstone Clo. Cop 4B 194
Mill St. Acc 2M 141
Mill St. Adl 5J 195
Mill St. Bacup 4K 163
Mill St. Barn 2L 77
Mill St. Barfd 7H 85
Mill St. Brom X 5F 198
Mill St. Chu 7D 142
Mill St. Clay M 7M 121
Mill St. Cop 4A 194
Mill St. Dar 8B 158
Mill St. Far 4L 153
Mill St. Gt Har 4J 121
Mill St. Has 3G 160
Mill St. K'ham 4M 111
Mill St. Lanc 8L 23
Mill St. Ley 7G 152
Mill St. L'boro 2J 205
Mill St. Nels 1J 105
Mill St. Orm 8L 209
Mill St. Osw 5K 141
Mill St. Pad 1H 123
Mill St. Pre 1A 56
Mill St. Pres 9G 115
Mill St. Ram 1F 200
Mill St. South 8J 167
Mill St. Tot 6E 200
Mill St. W Brad 7L 73
Mill St. Wheel 8J 155
Millthorne Av. Clith 4K 81
Mill Vw. Frec 1N 131
Mill Vw. Kirkby 6H 223
Mill Vw. Ct. Bic 5B 218
Mill Vw. Ct. Ley 5G 152
Millwood. 2M 165
Millwood Clo. B'brn 7H 139
Mill Wood Clo. Withn 4L 155
Millwood Glade. Chor 5D 174
Millwood La. Todm 2N 165
Millwood Rd. Los H 5L 135
Milman Clo. Orm 9J 209
Milner Av. Bury 8L 201
Milner Rd. Dar 3M 157
Milner Rd. Lyth A 4L 129
Milner St. Burn 1E 124
Milner St. Pres 7J 115
Milner St. Whitw 6N 183
Milne St. Ram 1H 181
Milnrow. 7H 205
Milnrow Rd. L'boro 3J 205
Milnshaw. 1A 142
Milnshaw Gdns. Acc 1N 141
Milnshaw La. Acc 2A 142
Milnthorpe Av. T Clev 7D 54
Milnthorpe Rd. Holme 1F 6
Milton Av. Blac 5E 88
Milton Av. Clith 2L 81
Milton Av. T Clev 9G 54
Milton Clo. Dar 6C 158
Milton Clo. Gt Har 5H 121
Milton Clo. Ross 8F 160
Milton Clo. Walt D 6N 135
Milton Ct. Cop 4A 194
Milton Cres. Poul F 2K 89
Milton Dri. Orm 8M 209
Milton Gro. Barn 1L 77
Milton Gro. Orr 5K 221
Milton Rd. Col 6A 86
Milton Rd. Cop 5A 194
Milton St. Acc 2A 142
Milton St. Barfd 7H 85
Milton St. B'brn 3A 140
Milton St. Brclf 7J 105
Milton St. Brier 5F 104
Milton St. Clay M 6M 121
Milton St. Fltwd 8G 40
Milton St. Nels 1H 105
Milton St. Osw 4L 141
Milton St. Pad 2J 123
Milton St. Ram 8G 180
Milton St. Roch 5C 204
Milton St. South 7M 167
Milton Ter. Chor 4F 174
Milton Way. Liv 9A 216
Mimosa Clo. Chor 3C 174
Mimosa Rd. Rib 7A 116
Mincing La. B'brn 4M 139
Minden Rd. Weet 5D 90
Minehead Av. Burn 8H 105
Minerva Ter. L'boro 9K 185
(off William St.)
Mine St. Heyw 9G 203
Miniature Railway. 7G 166
Minnie St. Whitw 4A 184
Minnie Ter. B'brn 2K 139
Minorca Clo. Roch 5J 203
Minor St. Ross 9M 143
Minstead Av. Liv 8L 223
Minster Cres. Dar 7C 158
Minster Dri. Heat O 6B 22
Minster Pk. Cot 4B 114
Minstrel Wlk. Poul F 7K 63
Mint Av. Barfd 7H 85
Mintholme Av. Hogh 6G 137
Mintor Rd. Liv 8M 223
Mint St. Ram 4H 181
Minverva Rd. Lanc 8G 22
Mire Ash Brow. Mel 8E 118
Mire Ridge. Col 7D 86
Mirfield Gro. Blac 9D 88
Miry La. Parb 2A 212
Mitcham Rd. Blac 1H 109
Mitchelgate. K Lon 6E 8
Mitchell Hey. 6B 204
Mitchell Hey. Roch 6B 204
Mitchell St. Burn 3A 124
Mitchell St. Bury 9H 201
Mitchell St. Clith 4K 81
Mitchell St. Col 6A 86
Mitchell St. Roch 2F 204
Mitchell St. Todm 9H 147
Mitella St. Burn 4G 124
Mitre St. Bolt 9E 198
Mitre St. Burn 3C 124
Mitten's La. Liv 8A 206
(in two parts)
Mitton Av. Barfd 5K 85
Mitton Av. Ross 3M 161
Mitton Cres. K'ham 4M 111
Mitton Dri. Rib 6C 116
Mitton Gro. Burn 4H 125
Mitton La. Loth 3L 79
Mitton Rd. Whal 9F 80
Mitton St. B'brn 1N 139
Mizpah St. Burn 4G 124
Mizzy Rd. Roch 4B 204
Moira Cres. Rib 5A 116
Moleside Clo. Acc 2C 142
Molesworth St. Roch 6D 204
Mollington Rd. B'brn 1J 139
Mollington Rd. Liv 8H 223
Molly Wood La. Burn 4L 123
Molyneux Ct. Pres 9K 115
Molyneux Dri. Blac 2D 108
Molyneux Pl. Lyth A 4N 129
Molyneux Rd. Augh 4H 217
Molyneux Rd. Mag 3E 222
Molyneux St. Roch 5A 204
Molyneux Way. Liv 7B 222
Mona Pl. Pres 9H 115
Monarch Cres. Lyth A 9J 109
Monarch St. Osw 4L 141
Mona Rd. B'brn 7M 139
Monash Clo. Liv 4K 223
Mona's Ter. Todm 5J 165
Money Clo. Gro. Hey 2J 27
Money Clo. La. Hey 4J 27
(in two parts)
Monk Hall St. Burn 2E 124
Monkroyd. 4K 87
Monkroyd Av. Barn 2L 77
Monks Carr La. Liv 5G 214
Monks Clo. Liv 2A 214
Monks Clo. Miln 7H 205
Monks Cotts. Barn 2M 77
(off Walmsgate)
Monks Dri. Liv 2A 214
Monks Dri. L'rdge 4J 97
Monks Dri. Withn 6B 156
Monks Ga. Lyth A 1K 129
Monk's La. Burs 7B 190
Monk's La. Pre 3M 55
Monk St. Acc 2N 141
Monk St. Clith 4K 81
Monks Wlk. Pen 2F 134
Monkswell Av. Bolt S 4L 15
Monkswell Dri. Bolt S 4L 15
Monkswood Av. More 3E 22
Monmouth Av. Bury 8L 201
Monmouth Dri. Liv 9E 222
Monmouth Rd. B'brn 3C 140
Monmouth St. Burn 3B 124
(off Shale St.)
Monmouth St. Col 6D 86
Monmouth St. Roch 7C 204
Monroe Dri. Fltwd 1D 54
Mons Av. Roch 5N 203
Mons Rd. Todm 9J 147
Montague Clo. B'brn 4L 139
Montague Rd. Burn 4C 124
Montague St. B'brn 3L 139
Montague St. Blac 1B 108
Montague St. Brier 5F 104
Montague St. Clith 3K 81
Montague St. Col 5B 86
Montbegon. Horn 7C 18
Montcliffe. 8F 196
Montcliffe Rd. Chor 5G 175
Monteagle Dri. Horn 7C 18
Monteagle Sq. Horn 7C 18
(off Monteagle Dri.)
Montfieldhey. Brier 5E 104
Montford Rd. Brier 4D 104
Montford Rd. Rdly 3B 104
Montgomery. Roch 7B 204
Montgomery Av. South 8N 167
Montgomery Clo. Bax 6D 142
Montgomery Gro. Burn 2A 124
Montgomery St. Bam B 8B 136
Montgomery St. Roch 9N 203
(off Manchester Rd.)
Monthall Ri. Lanc 7M 23
(off Patterdale Rd.)
Montjoly St. Pres 1M 135
Monton Rd. Dar 3M 157
Montpelier Av. Blac 6C 62
Montreal Av. Blac 6D 88
Montreal Rd. B'brn 9K 119
Montreal St. Todm 6K 165
Montrose Av. Blac 7C 88
Montrose Av. Ram 3F 200
Montrose Av. Wig 3L 221
Montrose Clo. Chor 8G 174
Montrose Cres. Hey 9K 21
Montrose Dri. Brom X 6H 199
Montrose Dri. South 5M 167
Montrose St. B'brn 5K 139
Montrose St. Brier 5F 104
Montrose St. Burn 5D 124
Montrose Ter. Barn 2M 77
(off Leonard St.)
Moody La. Maw 4B 192
Moon Av. Blac 8B 88
Moon St. Bam B 8A 136
Moor Av. App B 4H 213
Moor Av. Pen 5C 134
Moor Bank La. Miln 9G 204
Moorber La. Con C 4H 53
Moorbottom Rd. Holc 7C 180
Moorbrook St. Pres 8H 115
Moor Clo. Dar 7D 158
Moor Clo. Lanc 8L 23
Moor Clo. South 2C 206
Moor Clo. La. Over K 9F 12
Moorcock Rd. Blkhd 2M 147
Moorcroft. Brough 8E 94
Moorcroft. Lwr D 1A 158
Moorcroft. Ram 4J 181
Moorcroft. Roch 9C 204
Moorcroft Cres. Rib 6N 115
Moor Dri. Skel 4A 220
Moor Edge. Whal 4H 101
Moore Dri. High 5L 103
Moor End. 6C 56
Moor End. Clith 4M 81
Moores La. Stand 2N 213
Moore St. Blac 9B 88
Moore St. Burn 2L 123
(in two parts)
Moore St. Col 6N 85
Moore St. Nels 3K 105
Moore St. Pres 1M 135
Moore St. Roch 6C 204
Moore Tree Dri. Blac 1G 108
Mooreview Ct. Blac 2F 108
Moorfield. Liv 5L 223
Moor Fld. New L 9D 134
Moorfield. Tur 8K 179
Moor Fld. Whal 4H 101
Moorfield Av. Acc 9E 122
Moorfield Av. Blac 4E 88
Moorfield Av. L'boro 7K 185
Moorfield Av. Poul F 6H 63
Moorfield Av. Rams 6M 119
Moorfield Clo. Acc 6A 122
Moorfield Clo. Ful 1H 115
Moorfield Clo. Pen 5D 134
Moorfield Dri. Acc 6A 122
Moorfield Dri. Lyth A 4N 129
Moorfield Dri. Rib 6A 116
Moorfield Ind. Est. Alt 6A 122
Moorfield La. Scar 1G 209
Moorfield Pl. Roch 4B 204
Moorfield Rd. Ley 7F 152
Moorfields. Blac 7F 62
Moorfields. Chor 5G 175
Moorfields Av. Ful 1H 115
Moorfield Shop. Cen. Liv 4L 223
Moorfield Vw. L'boro 8K 185
Moorfield Way. Acc 6A 122
Moorfoot Way. Liv 4J 223
Moorgate. 7K 139
Moorgate. Acc 6A 142
Moorgate. Blac 3F 108
Moorgate. Bolt 8K 199
Moorgate. Ful 4J 115
Moor Ga. Lanc 8L 23
Moorgate. Orm 8K 209
Moor Ga. Todm 4M 165
Moorgate Av. Roch 6L 203
Moorgate Gdns. B'brn 7K 139
Moor Ga. La. L'boro 7H 185
Moorgate Rd. Know I 9M 223
Moorgate St. B'brn 7K 139
Moor Hall La. Newt 5D 112
Moor Hall St. Pres 7H 115
Moorhead Gdns. W'ton 1K 131
Moorhead St. Col 6N 85
Moorhen Pl. T Clev 2F 62
Moorhey Cres. Bam B 8C 136
Moorhey Cres. Pen 3E 134
Moorhey Dri. Pen 3E 134
Moorhey Rd. Liv 4B 222
Moor Hill. Roch 4K 203
Moorhouse Av. Acc 4N 141
Moorhouse Clo. Acc 4N 141
Moorhouse Fold. Miln 7H 205
Moorhouse St. Acc 4N 141
Moor Ho. St. Blac 3B 88
Moorhouse St. Burn 4A 124
Moorings, The. Burn 2C 124
Moorings, The. Chor 6G 175
Moorings, The. Hest B 8H 15
(off Hest Bank La.)
Moorings, The. Liv 7A 216
Moorland Av. B'brn 9E 138
Moorland Av. Clith 1M 81
Moorland Av. Dar 5L 157
Moorland Av. Earby 3F 78
Moorland Av. Miln 7K 205
Moorland Av. Poul F 7L 63
Moorland Av. Rib 4N 115
Moorland Av. Roch 5K 203
Moorland Av. Whitw 7N 183
Moorland Clo. Barfd 5K 85
Moorland Ct. Poul F 7L 63
Moorland Cres. Clith 1M 81
Moorland Cres. Rib 4N 115
Moorland Cres. Whitw 7N 183
Moorland Dri. Brier 6H 105
Moorland Gdns. Poul F 7L 63
Moorland Ga. Chor 8H 175
Moorland Ri. Has 5H 161
Moorland Rd. B'brn 9K 139
Moorland Rd. Burn 6C 124
Moorland Rd. Clith 1M 81
Moorland Rd. Lang 9C 100

North Rd.—Orchard, The

North Rd. B'brn 4B 140
North Rd. Breth 9H 151
North Rd. Carn 9A 12
North Rd. Holme 1F 6
North Rd. Lanc 8K 23
North Rd. Pres 8J 115
North Rd. Ross 5A 162
North Rd. South 2A 168
North Shore. 2B 88
North Shore Golf Course. 8C 62
Northside. Eux 3M 173
North Sq. Blac 4D 88
North Sq. T Clev 7C 54
North St. Barn 3M 77
North St. Brclf 7K 105
North St. Burn 9E 104
North St. Chor 4E 174
North St. Clith 2M 81
North St. Col 5B 86
North St. Fltwd 8H 41
North St. Garg 3M 53
North St. Hap 4H 123
North St. Has 6H 161
North St. More 3B 22
North St. Nels 1H 105
North St. Pad 9H 103
North St. Pres 9J 115
North St. Ram 4H 181
North St. Raw 5M 161
North St. Roch 5D 204
North St. Ross 6C 162
North St. South 6J 167
North St. Water 8E 144
North St. Whitw 5N 183
N. Syke Av. Lea 8M 113
Northumberland Av. Blac 1B 88
Northumberland Av. T Clev 8E 54
Northumberland Ho. Pres 9J 115
Northumberland St. Chor 7F 174
Northumberland St. More 3A 22
North Va. Hth C 4H 195
N. Valley Rd. Col 6N 85
North Vw. Bury 3G 201
North Vw. K'ham 4L 111
North Vw. Ram 4H 181
North Vw. Ross 8M 143
North Vw. Traw 9E 86
North Vw. Whitw 5A 184
N. View Clo. Gt Ecc 6A 66
N. Warton St. Lyth A 5B 130
North Way. Bolt 9H 199
Northway. Brough 7F 94
Northway. Fltwd 3D 54
Northway. Ful 3G 115
Northway. Mag & Augh 3B 222
(in three parts)
Northway. Skel 9M 211
Northways. Stand 2N 213
Northwold Clo. Wig 8N 221
Northwood. 7L 223
Northwood. Bolt 9K 199
Northwood Clo. Burn 1B 124
Northwood Clo. Lyth A 4L 129
Northwood Way. Poul F 9K 63
Norton Av. Hey 5L 21
Norton Ct. Lyth A 4F 128
Norton Dri. Hey 6M 21
Norton Gro. Hey 6L 21
Norton Gro. Liv 4C 222
Norton Pl. Hey 6L 21
Norton Rd. Cabus 2N 59
Norton Rd. Hey 6L 21
Norton Rd. Roch 2C 204
Norton St. Hap 5H 123
Norwich Av. Roch 6L 203
Norwich Dri. Bury 9J 201
Norwich Pl. Blac 6D 62
Norwich Pl. Pres 1K 135
Norwich St. B'brn 1N 139
Norwich St. Roch 8D 204
Norwich Way. Kirkby 8K 223
Norwood Av. B'brn 6M 139
Norwood Av. Blac 2E 88
Norwood Av. Hesk B 5D 150
Norwood Av. Nels 9K 85
Norwood Av. South 6L 167
Norwood Clo. Adl 5J 195
Norwood Cres. South 7L 167
Norwood Dri. More 4E 22
Norwood Gdns. South 7M 167
Norwood Gro. Rainf 4L 225
Norwood Rd. Lyth A 9C 108
Norwood Rd. South 7M 167
Notre Dame Gdns. B'brn 2N 139
Nottingham Rd. Pres 8K 115
Nottingham St. B'brn 4A 140
Novak Pl. More 4F 22
Nova Scotia. 5M 139
Nowell Gro. Read 8C 102
Nowell St. Gt Har 4J 121
Noyna Av. Foul 2B 86
Noyna Rd. Foul 2B 86
Noyna St. Col 5B 86
Noyna Vw. Col 4B 86
Nun Hills. 7G 162
Nun St. Lanc 8L 23
Nurseries, The. Form 1A 214
Nursery Av. Orm 6M 209
Nursery Clo. Char R 1A 194
Nursery Clo. Ley 7J 153
Nursery Dri. Tar 6D 150
Nursery Gdns. Roch 5F 204
Nursery La. New L 8B 134
Nursery Nook. E'hill 2D 158
Nursery Rd. Liv 7B 216
Nutfield St. Todm 1L 165
Nutgill La. Ben 6N 19
Nuthall Rd. South 2M 187
Nuttall. 1H 201
Nuttall Av. Gt Har 5J 121
Nuttall Clo. Ram 9H 181
Nuttall Hall Cotts. Ram 9J 181
Nuttall Hall Rd. Ram 1J 201
Nuttall Lane. 9H 181
Nuttall La. Ram 9G 181
Nuttall Rd. Blac 9D 88
Nuttall St. Acc 9C 122
(Burnley Rd.)
Nuttall St. Acc 3B 142
(Mount St.)
Nuttall St. Bacup 4M 163
Nuttall St. B'brn 7L 139
Nuttall St. Burn 5F 124
Nuttall St. For H 9E 144
Nuttall St. Ross 4N 161
Nuttall St. M. Acc 3B 142
(off Nuttall St.)
Nutter Cres. High 5L 103
Nutter Rd. Acc 1B 142
Nutter Rd. Pres 1H 135
Nutter Rd. T Clev 1D 62
Nutter's Platt. 7F 134
Nye Bevan Pool. 2M 219

O

Oak Av. Acc 8F 142
Oak Av. Blac 1D 108
Oak Av. Eux 3N 173
Oak Av. Gal 2K 37
Oak Av. K'ham 5N 111
Oak Av. L'rdge 3J 97
Oak Av. More 2E 22
Oak Av. Newt 7D 112
Oak Av. Orm 8J 209
Oak Av. Pen 5E 134
Oak Av. Ram 3F 200
Oak Av. T Clev 3J 63
Oak Av. Todm 9K 147
Oak Bank. Acc 7C 122
Oakbank Dri. Bolt 7D 198
Oak Bank Ter. Barfd 8G 84
Oakcliffe Rd. Roch 1F 204
Oak Clo. Barr 1K 101
Oak Clo. Rish 9H 121
Oak Clo. Whitw 2A 184
Oak Cres. Skel 2H 219
Oak Cft. Clay W 5D 154
Oakdale. Bolt 9K 199
Oakdene Av. Acc 8D 122
Oak Dri. Chor 3E 174
Oak Dri. Frec 3M 131
Oak Dri. Halt 1C 24
Oaken Bank. Burn 7J 105
Oaken Clo. Bacup 4M 163
Oakenclough. 9H 47
Oakenclough Rd. Bacup 4M 163
Oakenclough Rd. Goos 5A 70
Oakenclough Rd. Scor 2F 46
Oakeneaves Av. Burn 7B 124
Oakengate. Ful 2M 115
Oakenhead Clo. W'chpl 4N 69
Oakenhead St. Pres 8A 116
Oakenhead Wood. 4K 161
Oakenhead Wood Old Rd.
Ross 4J 161
Oakenhurst Rd. B'brn 4L 139
Oakenrod Hill. Roch 7A 204
Oakenshaw. 6L 121
Oakenshaw Av. Whitw 8N 183
Oakenshaw Vw. Whitw 8N 183
Oakfield. Ash R 8E 114
Oakfield. Ful 2J 115
Oakfield Av. Acc 8D 122
Oakfield Av. Barn 1L 77
Oakfield Av. Clay M 6L 121
Oakfield Cres. Osw 4M 141
Oakfield Dri. Ley 7E 152
Oakfield Rd. B'brn 9L 139
Oakfield Rd. Form 9A 214
Oakfields. Orm 7M 209
Oakfields Ter. Roch 5N 203
Oakford Clo. Banks 1G 168
Oakgate Clo. Tar 1D 170
Oak Gates. Eger 4E 198
Oak Grn. Orm 7L 209
Oakgrove. Blac 3D 108
Oak Gro. Dar 5B 158
Oak Gro. New L 1D 152
Oakham Clo. Bury 8J 201
Oakham Ct. Pres 1K 135
Oakham Ct. South 6J 167
Oakham Dri. Liv 9E 222
Oak Hill. L'boro 9J 185
Oak Hill Clo. Acc 4B 142
Oakhill Clo. Mag 9C 216
Oakhill Cottage La. Liv 7C 216
Oakhill Dri. Liv 7C 216
Oakhill Rd. Mag 9C 216
Oak Ho. Chor 8B 174
Oakhurst Av. Acc 8D 122
Oakland Av. T Clev 5D 62
Oakland Glen. Walt D 5K 135
Oaklands Av. Barfd 8H 85
Oaklands Av. Tar 8E 150
Oaklands Ct. Ald 2G 29
Oaklands Dri. Pen 4D 134
Oaklands Dri. Ross 5K 161
Oaklands Gro. Ash R 8B 114
Oaklands Rd. Ram 4J 181
Oakland St. Bam B 7A 136
Oakland St. Nels 2J 105
Oak La. Acc 3C 142
Oak La. Newt 7D 112
Oaklea. Stand 2K 213
Oakleaf Clo. Goos 4M 95
Oakleaf Ct. T Clev 8D 54
Oakleaf Way. Blac 9K 89
Oaklee Gro. Liv 6M 223
Oakleigh. Skel 9A 220
Oakleigh Ter. Todm 7E 146
Oakley Rd. Hey 6L 21
Oakley Rd. Ross 5L 161
Oakley St. L'boro 1H 205
Oakley St. Ross 6K 161
Oakmere. Brin 4E 154
Oakmere Av. Withn 5M 155
Oakmere Clo. B'brn 1L 157
Oakmoor Av. Blac 7E 62
Oak Mt. Todm 1L 165
Oak Ridge. W Brad 5K 73
Oakridge Clo. Ful 2J 115
Oak Rd. Gars 4M 59
Oakroyd Clo. Arns 1F 4
Oaks Av. Bolt 8J 199
Oaks Brow. Clay D 2K 119
Oaksfield. Dar 2M 157
Oakshaw Dri. Roch 4L 203
Oakshott Pl. Bam B 9D 136
Oaks La. Bolt 8H 199
Oaks, The. Chor 1D 194
Oaks, The. Poul F 6K 63
Oaks, The. St M 4G 67
Oaks, The. Walt D 5L 135
Oak St. Acc 3B 142
Oak St. Bacup 4L 163
Oak St. B'brn 9N 119
Oak St. Brier 4F 104
Oak St. Burn 3A 124
Oak St. Clay M 7M 121
Oak St. Col 5B 86
Oak St. Dunn 4N 143
Oak St. Fltwd 9G 40
Oak St. Gt Har 3J 121
Oak St. Heyw 9F 202
Oak St. L'boro 9M 185
Oak St. Miln 9K 205
Oak St. Nels 1J 105
Oak St. Osw 5K 141
Oak St. Pres 1K 135
Oak St. Ram 9G 181
Oak St. S'bri 2J 205
Oak St. South 8L 167
Oak St. Todm 3K 165
Oak St. Whitw & Shawf 2A 184
Oak Ter. Barn 1N 77
Oak Ter. L'boro 4N 185
Oak Towers. Liv 7L 223
Oaktree Av. Ing 5D 114
Oak Tree Av. Ley 3N 153
Oaktree Clo. Ing 5D 114
Oak Tree Ct. Skel 9A 212
Oak Vw. Ley 5H 153
Oak Vw. Whitw 2A 184
Oakville Rd. Hey 2K 27
Oak Way. L'rdge 2J 97
Oakwood. Skel 9A 212
Oakwood Av. B'brn 8A 120
Oakwood Av. Lyth A 4L 129
Oakwood Av. Shev 7J 213
Oakwood Av. South 7D 186
Oakwood Av. Walt D 4M 135
Oakwood Clo. Blac 5F 108
Oakwood Clo. Burn 7H 105
Oakwood Clo. Dar 2M 157
Oakwood Clo. T Clev 1K 63
Oakwood Dri. Ful 1G 114
Oakwood Dri. South 8E 186
Oakwood Gdns. Lanc 5L 29
Oakwood Gro. Bolt S 7K 15
Oakwood Rd. Acc 5C 142
Oakwood Rd. Chor 8D 174
Oakwood Rd. Cop 3B 194
Oakwood Vw. Chor 1D 194
Oakworth Av. Rib 4B 116
Oakworth Clo. Liv 6K 223
Oakworth Dri. Bolt 8D 198
Oasis Clo. Ruf 2F 190
Oatlands Rd. Liv 8H 223
Oat St. Pad 2J 123
Oban Ct. Grims 9F 96
Oban Cres. Pres 6N 115
Oban Dri. B'brn 5C 140
Oban Gro. Bolt 8E 198
Oban Pl. Blac 5E 62
Oban St. Burn 1G 124
Oberlin St. Roch 8A 204
Observatory Rd. B'brn 6A 140
Occupation La. Poul F 7C 64
Occupation Rd. T Clev 1H 63
Occupation Rd. War 3L 11
Ocean Boulevd. Blac 2A 108
Ocean Ct. Kno S 8K 41
Ocean Edge Cvn. Pk. Hey 5J 27
Ocean Way. T Clev 9C 54
Oddies Yd. Roch 3D 204
Odell Way. Walt D 5A 136
O'er the Bridge. Hodd 6F 158
(off Hoddlesden Rd.)
Off Botanic Rd. South 5N 167
Offerton St. Hor 9B 196
Office Rd. Bacup 8L 145
Off Mt. Pleasant St. Osw 4L 141
(off Chapel St.)
Ogden Clo. Helm 8F 160
Ogden Dri. Helm 8F 160
Ogden La. Miln 9N 205
O'Hagan Ct. Brier 4F 104
Old Acre. Liv 8A 214
Old Back La. Wis 3L 101
Old Bank La. B'brn 6A 140
(in two parts)
Old Bank St. B'brn 4M 139
Old Barn Pl. Brom X 5G 199
Old Bent La. Ward 7D 184
Old Birtle. 6C 202
Old Boundary Way. Orm 6L 209
Old Bri. La. Hamb 4A 64
Old Bri. Way. Chor 5F 174
Old Brow La. Roch 2F 204
Old Brown La. Bam B 5C 136
Old Buckley La. K Grn 3E 98
Oldbury Pl. T Clev 3F 62
Old Carr Mill St. Ross 2G 160
Old Clay Dri. Roch 1G 204
Old Clay La. Chip 1H 97
Old Clitheroe Rd. Dutt 1L 97
Oldcock Yd. Pres 1K 135
Old Cft. Ful 1G 115
Old Cross Stone Rd. Todm 2M 165
Old Dawber's La. Eux 5L 173
Old Delph Rd. Roch 4J 203
Old Doctors St. Tot 6E 200
Old Eagley M. Bolt 7F 198
Old Engine La. Ram 8J 181
Old Engine La. Skel 1G 218
Olde Stoneheath Ct. Hth C 1K 195
Old Farmside. B'brn 9L 139
Oldfield. L Hoo 3K 151
Oldfield. Pen 6G 134
Oldfield Av. Blac 7C 62
Oldfield Av. Dar 4M 157
Old Fld. Carr La. Poul F 1K 89
Oldfield Clo. Poul F 1L 89
Oldfield Cres. Poul F 8L 63
Oldfield Rd. Bam B 9C 136
Old Fold. Wig 5L 221
Old Gates Dri. B'brn 7G 138
Old Greaves Town La. Lea 8A 114
Old Grn. Bolt 7L 199
Old Green. G'mnt 4E 200
Old Ground St. Ram 8H 181
Old Hall Clo. Bam B 8A 136
Old Hall Clo. Bury 6G 201
Old Hall Clo. Liv 3C 222
Old Hall Clo. More 4F 22
Old Hall Clo. R'lee 6E 84
Old Hall Cft. Garg 3M 53
Old Hall Dri. Bam B 8A 136
Old Hall Dri. Hun 8E 122
Old Hall Gdns. Rainf 3L 225
Old Hall La. Char R 8L 173
Old Hall La. Liv 8J 223
Old Hall La. Pleas 6D 138
Old Hall Pk. Cvn. Pk. Cap 8H 13
Old Hall Rd. Liv 3C 222
Old Hall Sq. Wors 4L 125
Old Hall St. Burn 1E 124
Oldham Rd. Roch 6C 204
(in two parts)
Oldhams La. Bolt 8D 198
Oldham St. Burn 5D 124
Oldham St. More 2B 22
Oldham Ter. Bolt 8D 198
(in three parts)
Old Hey Cft. Pen 6G 135
Old Hive. Chip 5F 70
Old Ho. La. Blac 2J 109
Old Kiln. Bacup 7H 163
Old Lancaster La. Pres 8G 114
Old Lancaster Rd. Catt 1M 67
Old La. Bis 6N 191
Old La. Brou 6M 53
Old La. Bury 5L 201
Old La. Earby 2E 78
(in two parts)
Old La. Hask 8K 207
Old La. Kel 8C 78
Old La. Liv 6A 206
(Lit. Brewery La.)
Old La. Liv 7D 216
(Moss La.)
Old La. Rainf 3K 225
Old La. Salt 5L 77
(in two parts)
Old La. Shawf 8A 164
Old La. Shev 6L 213
Old La. Thorn C 9J 53
Old La. Todm 4K 165
Old Langho. 6C 100
Old Langho Rd. Old L 7B 100
Old Laund St. Fence 2C 104
Old Links Clo. South 6A 168
Old Links Golf Course. 9M 197
Old Lodge La. Clau B 3C 68
Old Lord's Cres. Hor 8C 196
Old Mains La. Poul F 5M 63
Old Mkt. Ct. More 2B 22
(off Green St.)
Old Meadow Ct. Blac 7E 88
Old Meadows La. Blac 7E 88
Old Meadows Rd. Bacup 2K 163
Old Mill Ct. Walm B 2K 151
Old Mill Dri. Col 7C 86
Old Mill Hill. Orm 9J 209
Old Mill La. Bis 7C 192
Old Millstones. Pres 1G 135
Old Mill St. B'brn 2N 139
Oldmill St. Roch 5C 204
Old Mill Ter. Chor 5G 174
Old Moor Rd. Wenn 6F 18
Old Moss La. Augh 7G 206
Old Nab Rd. Lang & Whal 1E 120
Old Nursery Fold. Bolt 9L 199
Old Oak Gdns. Walt D 5L 135
Old Pk. La. South 7N 167
Old Parsonage La. Pad 1G 123
Old Pepper La. Stand 2L 213
Old Pope La. Wstke 8E 134
Old Prescot Clo. Liv 9H 217
Old Quarry La. Eger 4F 198
Old Racecourse Rd. Liv 2A 222
Old Rake. Hor 8E 196
Old Rectory Grn. Augh 4F 216
Old Riggs Yd. Burt 6H 7
Old Rd. Bolt 9E 198
Old Roman Rd. Whal & Read 6N 101
Old Rough La. Liv 7K 223
Old Row. Barr 9K 81
Old Row. K'ham 5N 111
Old Row. Ross 6K 161
Oldroyd. 2N 165
Oldroyd Rd. Todm 2N 165
Old Sawmill, The. Rath 6L 35
Old School Clo. Ley 7D 152
Old School Ho., The. L'boro 8J 185
(off Shore Rd.)
Old School La. Adl 8G 195
Old School La. Eux 3N 173
(in two parts)
Old School La. Los H 1M 153
Old School La. Toc 5G 157
Old School M. Stac 7G 163
Old Scotch Rd. Man 1D 8
Old Sta. Clo. Grims 9F 96
Old Sta. Ct. Clith 3L 81
(off Station Rd.)
Old Stone Brow. Kel 8D 78
Old Stone Trough. 7D 78
Old Stone Trough La. Kel 7D 78
Old St. Ross 6C 162
Old Swan Clo. Eger 3E 198
Old Swan Cotts. Eger 3E 198
Old Tom's La. Stalm 5C 56
Old Town. 2D 8
Old Towns Clo. Tot 6E 200
Old Tram Rd. Bam B 8A 136
(in two parts)
Old Tram Rd. Pen & Walt D 4K 135
(in three parts)
Old Vicarage. Pres 9K 115
Old Will's La. Hor 7C 196
Olivant St. Burn 2A 124
Olive Bank. Bury 9G 201
Olive Clo. Liv 8F 222
Olive Clo. Whit W 1E 174
Olive Gro. Blac 5E 88
Olive Gro. Boot 9A 222
Olive Gro. Skel 2J 219
Olive Gro. South 7L 167
Olive Gro. W'ton 2J 131
Olive La. Dar 5A 158
Oliver Clo. L'boro 9J 185
Olive Rd. Lanc 6K 23
Oliver Pl. Carn 8B 12
Olivers Pl. Ful 1K 115
Oliver St. Bacup 7G 163
Olive St. Bacup 7J 163
Olive Ter. Ross 2L 161
Ollerton. Roch 5B 204
(off Spotland Rd.)
Ollerton Fold. 3M 155
Ollerton La. Withn 3M 155
Ollerton Rd. Lyth A 3K 129
Ollerton St. Adl 4J 195
Ollerton St. Bolt 7F 198
Ollerton Ter. Bolt 7F 198
(off Ollerton St.)
Ollerton Ter. Withn 4N 155
Ollery Grn. Boot 6A 222
Olney. Roch 7B 204
Olympia St. Burn 4G 124
Onchan Dri. Bacup 6M 163
Onchan Rd. B'brn 7M 139
One Ash Clo. Roch 3C 204
Onslow Cres. South 3G 186
Onslow Rd. Blac 3E 88
Onslow St. Roch 9N 203
Ontario Clo. B'brn 9H 119
Oozebooth Ter. B'brn 1M 139
Oozehead La. B'brn 3J 139
Opal Clo. T Clev 4F 62
Opal St. B'brn 7M 119
Openshaw Dri. B'brn 8M 119
Oporto Clo. Burn 4C 124
Oram Rd. Brin 8H 137
Oram St. Bury 9M 201
(in two parts)
Orange St. Acc 9A 122
Orchan Rd. Todm 9J 147
Orchard Av. Blac 3C 108
Orchard Av. Bolt 9F 198
Orchard Av. Bolt S 3L 15
Orchard Av. New L 9D 134
Orchard Av. Poul F 1L 89
Orchard Bri. Burn 3D 124
(off Active Way)
Orchard Clo. B'brn 1L 157
Orchard Clo. Burt 5H 7
Orchard Clo. Eux 2N 173
Orchard Clo. Frec 2M 131
Orchard Clo. Grin 4A 74
Orchard Clo. Hesk B 4D 150
Orchard Clo. Ing 4D 114
Orchard Clo. Shev 5K 213
Orchard Clo. Silv 9F 4
Orchard Clo. Slyne 9K 15
Orchard Clo. T Clev 8H 55
Orchard Clo. W Grn 6G 111
Orchard Ct. Liv 1D 222
Orchard Cres. Arns 1F 4
Orchard Cft. Los H 8K 135
Orchard Dri. Fltwd 3E 54
Orchard Dri. Osw 3M 141
Orchard Dri. Whit W 1E 174
Orchard End. Gt Ecc 6A 66
(off N. View Clo.)
Orchard Hey. Boot 6A 222
Orchard Hey. Liv 2D 222
Orchard La.
Ains & South 9D 186
Orchard La. Lanc 9H 23
Orchard La. Longt 8K 133
Orchard Mill St. Dar 5N 157
Orchard Rd. Arns 1F 4
Orchard Rd. Lyth A 2E 128
Orchards, The. Barn 1N 77
(off Skipton Rd.)
Orchards, The.
Poul F 6H 63
Orchard St. Barn 2M 77
Orchard St. Gt Har 5J 121
Orchard St. Ley 6L 153
Orchard St. Pres 9J 115
Orchard Ter. Traw 9E 86
Orchard, The. Burn 5A 124
(off Heather Bank)

Orchard, The—Park St.

Orchard, The. Crost 3N 171
Orchard, The. L Ecc 6M 65
Orchard, The. Orm 7J 209
Orchard, The. W'ton 2K 131
Orchard, The. Wood 9B 94
Orchard Vw. Augh 2J 217
Orchard Wlk. G'mnt 4E 200
(off Lomax St.)
Orchard Wlk. Grims 8E 96
Orchid Way. Roch 2A 204
Ord Av. Blac 8F 88
Orders La. K'ham 5M 111
Ordnance St. B'brn 3A 140
Ord Rd. Ash R 7F 114
Oregon Av. Blac 2E 88
Oriel Clo. Old R 7C 222
Oriel Dri. Liv 7B 222
Oriel St. Roch 8C 204
Oriole Clo. B'brn 2N 139
Orkney Clo. B'brn 5C 140
Orkney Rd. Blac 8C 88
Orme Ho. Orm 7M 209
Ormerod Rd. Burn 3E 124
Ormerod St. Acc 4N 141
Ormerod St. Burn 4D 124
Ormerod St. Col 7N 85
Ormerod St. Has 9G 142
Ormerod St. Nels 2K 105
Ormerod St. Raw 5M 161
Ormerod St. T Clev 8H 55
Ormerod St. Water 8E 144
Ormerod St. Wors 5L 125
Ormerod Ter. Barr 2K 101
(off Whiteacre La.)
Ormerod Ter. Foul 2B 86
Ormerod Vw. Wors 4M 125
(off Ormerod St.)
Orme St. Blac 7C 88
Ormond Av. Blac 2B 88
Ormond Av. W'head 8C 210
Ormonde Av. Liv 3B 222
Ormonde Cres. Liv 8M 223
Ormonde Dri. Liv 2B 222
Ormont Av. T Clev 1E 62
Ormrod Pl. Blac 8B 88
Ormrods, The. Bury 8D 202
Ormrod St. Brad 9J 199
Ormskirk. 7K 209
Ormskirk Bus. Pk. Orm 6L 209
Ormskirk Cricket Club Ground. 8L 209
Ormskirk Golf Course. 6C 210
Ormskirk Old Rd. Bic 4D 218
Ormskirk Rd. Bic 9H 219
(Rainford Rd.)
Ormskirk Rd. Bic 2N 217
(St Helens Rd.)
Ormskirk Rd. Liv 9A 222
Ormskirk Rd. Pres 9K 115
Ormskirk Rd. Rainf 1H 225
Ormskirk Rd. Skel 2G 218
(Blaguegate La.)
Ormskirk Rd. Skel 3M 219
(Spencers La.)
Ormskirk Rd. Uph 4C 220
Ormskirk Rd. Wig 5L 221
Ormskirk Swimming Pool. 7K 209
Ormston Av. Hor 8C 196
Ormstons La. Hor 7E 196
Ornatus St. Bolt 8F 198
Orpen Av. Burn 6D 124
Orpington Sq. Burn 7G 105
Orpington St. Wig 5M 221
Orrell. 6G 221
Orrell Clo. Ley 6G 153
Orrell Gdns. Orr 5J 221
Orrell Hall Clo. Orr 3L 221
Orrell Hill La. Liv 7C 214
Orrell La. Burs 8B 190
Orrell M. Burs 8C 190
Orrell Rd. Orr 4G 220
Orrell R.U.F.C. 2J 221
(Edge Hall Rd.)
Orrell Water Pk. 7H 221
Orrel Post. 5H 221
Orrest Rd. Pres 8C 116
Orron St. L'boro 9K 185
Ortner. 5H 39
Orton Ct. Barfd 7H 85
Orwell Clo. Bury 9J 201
Osbaldeston. 5E 118
Osbaldeston Green. 3E 118
Osbaldeston La. Osb 2E 118
Osbert Cft. Longt 7L 133
Osborne Cres. More 5N 21
Osborne Dri. Clay W 5E 154
Osborne Gro. More 5A 22
Osborne Gro. T Clev 7D 54
Osborne Pl. Todm 2M 165
(off Halifax Rd.)
Osborne Rd. B'brn 2J 139
Osborne Rd. Blac 1B 108
Osborne Rd. Hey & More 5N 21
Osborne Rd. Lyth A 3F 128
Osborne Rd. South 7B 186
Osborne Rd. T Clev 7D 54
Osborne Rd. Walt D 5N 135
Osborne St. Pres 1H 135
Osborne St. Roch 8B 204
Osborne Ter. Bacup 7H 163
Osborne Ter. Dar 5M 157
Osborne Ter. Newc P 9B 84
Osborne Ter. Raw 5K 161
Osborne Ter. Waterf 3D 162
Osborne Way. Has 6F 160
Osbourne Av. T Clev 1F 62
Oscar St. Blac 8F 88
Oslo Rd. Burn 4N 123
Osprey Clo. B'brn 9L 119
Osprey Clo. H'pey 3J 175
Osprey Pl. Ley 5F 152
Osprey's, The. Wig 7M 221
Oswald Clo. Liv 4K 223
Oswald Rd. Ash R 8F 114
Oswald Rd. Lyth A 4C 130
Oswald St. Acc 2B 142
Oswald St. B'brn 2M 139
Oswald St. Burn 1D 124
Oswald St. Osw 5J 141
Oswald St. Rish 7D 121
Oswald St. Roch 5D 204
Oswaldtwistle. 5K 141
Oswestry Clo. G'mnt 5D 200
Otley Rd. Lyth A 1H 129
Ottawa Clo. B'brn 9J 119
Otterburn Clo. Blac 1H 89
Otterburn Gro. Burn 3H 125
Otterburn Rd. B'brn 9K 139
Otters Clo. Rib 7B 116
Ottershaw Gdns. B'brn 9M 119
Otterwood Sq. Wig 1M 221
Ottery Clo. South 1N 167
Otway St. Pres 7H 115
Oulder Hill. Roch 6L 203
Oulder Hill Dri. Roch 6M 203
Ouldfield Clo. Roch 7E 204
Oulton Clo. Liv 7A 216
Oulton St. Bolt 8G 198
Oundle Dri. Liv 7B 222
Ousby Av. More 6B 22
Ousby Rd. More 6B 22
Ouseburn Rd. B'brn 8K 139
Outer Promenade. Fltwd 8D 40
Outer Promenade. Lyth A 5H 129
(in two parts)
Outgate. Cot 5A 114
Out La. Crost 4M 171
Outlet La. Liv & Bic 1K 223
Out Moss La. More 4B 22
Outram La. B'brn 8M 119
Outram Way. Bam B 8A 136
Out Rawcliffe. 3H 65
Outterside St. Adl 7J 195
Outwood Gro. Bolt 8E 198
Outwood Rd. Burn 5F 124
Oval, The. Frec 9D 112
Oval, The. Shev 7J 213
Ovangle Rd. Heat O & Lanc 7E 22
Over Burrow. 9F 8
Overdale Gro. Blac 1G 89
Overdell Dri. Roch 2N 203
Overdene Wlk. Liv 9L 223
Overfield Way. Roch 3C 204
Overhill Way. Wig 8N 221
Overhouses. Tur 8H 179
Over Kellet. 1F 16
Overshores Rd. Tur 7G 179
Overton. 7B 28
Overton Clo. Liv 9J 223
Overton Grn. Liv 9J 223
Overton Rd. Ash R 9B 114
Overtown. 8G 9
Over Town. 8L 125
Over Town La. Roch 2E 202
Overt St. Roch 8C 204
Ovington Dri. South 2L 187
Owen Av. Orm 6L 209
Owen Ct. Clay M 6M 121
Owen Rd. Lanc 6K 23
Owen's La. Down 1K 215
Owens Row. Hor 9D 196
(off Bk. Chapel St.)
Owens St. Chor 7G 175
Owen St. Acc 1A 142
Owen St. Burn 4M 123
Owen St. Dar 4A 158
Owen St. Pres 9L 115
Owlerbarrow Rd. Bury 9F 200
Owlers Wlk. Todm 8J 147
Owlet Hall Rd. Dar 5M 157
Owtram St. Pres 9M 115
Oxcliffe Av. Hey 7L 21
Oxcliffe Gro. Hey 7L 21
Oxcliffe Rd. Hey & Heat O 7L 21
Ox Clo. La. Pil 9H 43
Oxendale Rd. T Clev 1K 63
Oxenholme Av. T Clev 8D 54
Oxenhurst Rd. Blac 2G 89
Oxford Av. Clay M 6N 121
Oxford Av. Roch 7L 203
Oxford Clo. B'brn 4N 139
Oxford Clo. Pad 3J 123
Oxford Ct. Lyth A 4K 129
Oxford Ct. South 1F 186
Oxford Dri. B'brn 4E 140
Oxford Dri. K'ham 5A 112
Oxford Gdns. South 1E 186
Oxford Pl. Burn 4F 124
Oxford Pl. Lanc 5J 23
Oxford Pl. Roch 8D 204
Oxford Rd. Ans 4K 129
Oxford Rd. Bam B 8B 136
Oxford Rd. Blac 5D 88
Oxford Rd. Burn 4F 124
Oxford Rd. Fltwd 1E 54
Oxford Rd. Ful 5G 115
Oxford Rd. Lyth A 9E 108
Oxford Rd. Nels 9L 85
Oxford Rd. Orr 4J 221
Oxford Rd. Skel 2J 219
Oxford Rd. South 9E 166
Oxford Rd. T Clev 9C 54
Oxford Sq. Blac 8E 88
Oxford St. Acc 2A 142
Oxford St. Adl 7J 195
Oxford St. Brier 5F 104
Oxford St. Carn 9A 12
Oxford St. Chor 7E 174
Oxford St. Col 6B 86
Oxford St. Dar 3N 157
Oxford St. Lanc 5J 23
Oxford St. More 2B 22
Oxford St. Pres 1K 135
Oxford St. Todm 3L 165
Oxford Way. Fltwd 1E 54
Ox Ga. Bolt 8K 199
Ox Hey. Clay M 5M 121
Ox Hey Av. Lea 7N 113
Oxhey Clo. Burn 3K 125
Oxhey Clo. Ram 7H 181
Oxheys Ind. Est. Pres 7G 115
Oxheys St. Pres 7G 115
Oxhill Pl. T Clev 4E 62
Oxhouse Rd. Orr 7G 220
Oxlands. Holme 1F 6
Oxley Clo. K'ham 4L 111
Oxley Rd. Pres 8N 115
(in two parts)
Ox St. Ram 9G 181
Oystercatcher Ga. Lyth A 1L 129

P

Paa La. Pay 5B 52
Packer St. Roch 6C 204
Packet La. Bolt S 5L 15
Paddington Av. St M 4G 66
Paddock Av. Ley 7D 152
Paddock Dri. Blac 8J 89
Paddock Head. L'boro 1H 205
Paddock La. B'brn 4D 140
Paddock Rd. Skel 6N 219
Paddock St. Osw 4L 141
Paddock, The. Augh 9H 209
Paddock, The. B'brn 9H 119
Paddock, The. Burn 7F 104
Paddock, The. Form 7A 206
Paddock, The. Ful 3K 115
Paddock, The. Osw 4L 141
Paddock, The. Over 7B 28
(off Main St.)
Paddock, The. Pen 6H 135
Paddock, The. Poul F 6J 63
Paddock, The. Ram 7G 181
Paddock, The. Ruf 1G 190
Paddock, The. Saw 3E 74
Paddock, The. South 9B 186
Paddock, The. T Clev 3H 63
Padgate Pl. Burn 5N 123
Padiham. 1K 123
Padiham Rd. Burn 2L 123
(in two parts)
Padiham Rd. Sab 3E 102
Padstow Clo. South 1N 167
Padway. Pen 6G 135
Pagefield Cres. Clith 4N 81
Pagen St. Roch 5C 204
Pages Ct. Los H 9L 135
Paignton Rd. B'brn 1L 139
Painley Clo. Lyth A 4N 129
Painter Wood. Bill 6H 101
Paisley St. Burn 4B 124
Palace Gdns. Burn 2N 123
Palace Rd. South 9E 166
Palace St. Burn 2A 124
Palais Bldgs. Burs 8C 190
Palatine Av. Lanc 2L 29
Palatine Av. Roch 5L 203
Palatine Clo. Stain 4J 89
Palatine Dri. Bury 5L 201
Palatine Rd. B'brn 3K 139
Palatine Rd. Blac 6C 88
Palatine Rd. Roch 5L 203
Palatine Rd. South 9F 166
Palatine Rd. T Clev 8D 54
Palatine Sq. Burn 4C 124
Palatine St. Ram 8H 181
Palatine St. Roch 6F 204
Palatine Ter. Roch 5L 203
Pale Ditch La. Burs 6D 170
Pale Ditch La. Tar 5B 170
Paley Grn. La. Gigg 4L 35
Paley Rd. Pres 1G 135
Palfrey Clo. Poul F 5H 63
Palladium Arc. More 3A 22
(off Marine Rd. Central)
Pall Mall. B'brn 3F 138
Pall Mall. Chor 8E 174
Pallotine Wlk. Roch 8A 204
Palmaston Clo. Lanc 1J 29
Palma St. Todm 7E 146
Palm Ct. Skel 1J 219
Palm Dri. Poul F 5H 63
Palmer Av. Blac 8C 88
Palmer Gro. More 2F 22
Palmerston Clo. Ram 1G 201
Palmerston Rd. South 8M 167
Palmerston St. Pad 2J 123
Palmer St. B'brn 2L 139
Palm Gro. South 8L 167
Palm Gro. Wig 5N 221
Palm St. B'brn 1A 140
Palm St. Bolt 9E 198
Palm St. Burn 4B 124
(off Burdett St.)
Pansy St. N. Acc 1A 142
Pansy St. S. Acc 1A 142
Paper Mill Rd. Brom X 6G 198
Parade, The. Carn 9M 11
Parade, The. Has 7F 160
Paradise Clo. Whit W 7D 154
Paradise La. B'brn 4M 139
Paradise La. Ley 6E 152
Paradise La. Liv 6A 206
Paradise St. Acc 3A 142
Paradise St. Barfd 6J 85
Paradise St. B'brn 4L 139
Paradise St. Burn 3D 124
Paradise St. Chor 3H 175
Paradise St. Ram 7H 181
Paradise St. Ross 5D 162
Paradise Ter. B'brn 4M 139
Paragon Way. Lanc 8G 23
Parbold. 2N 211
Parbold Clo. Blac 1F 88
Parbold Clo. Burs 1C 210
Parbold Hill. Parb 2A 212
Parbrook La. Shev 5L 213
Pardoe Clo. Hesk B 4C 150
Pardoe Ct. Burs 1D 210
Pares Land Wlk. Roch 7E 204
Paris. Rams 5N 119
Paris Av. Wins 8M 221
Parish St. Pad 9H 103
Park Av. Barn 3M 77
Park Av. Barfd 1G 104
Park Av. B'brn 2L 139
Park Av. Bolt 9E 198
Park Av. Burn 5C 124
Park Av. Chat 7C 74
Park Av. Clith 2L 81
Park Av. Eux 4N 173
Park Av. Fltwd 1F 54
Park Av. Gt Har 3K 121
Park Av. Has 6G 160
Park Av. Hell 1D 52
Park Av. Lanc 9M 23
Park Av. Lyd 8C 216
Park Av. Lyth A 5L 129
Park Av. Much H 5J 151
Park Av. New L 7B 134
Park Av. Orm 7K 209
Park Av. Pres 7L 115
Park Av. Ram 8J 181
Park Av. Salt 4B 78
Park Av. Shev 5L 213
Park Av. South 5L 167
Parkbourn. Liv 9F 216
Parkbourn Dri. Liv 9F 216
Parkbourn N. Liv 9F 216
Parkbourn Sq. Liv 9F 216
Pk. Bridge Rd. Burn 6H 125
Pk. Brow Dri. Liv 9L 223
Park Clo. Kirkby 6G 223
Park Clo. Parb 1N 211
Park Clo. Pen 3G 135
Park Clo. Rib 6N 115
Park Cotts. Bolt 9C 198
Park Cotts. Traw 3G 107
Park Ct. Kirkby 7H 223
Park Ct. Lanc 4K 29
Park Ct. Roch 7B 204
(Castle Av.)
Park Ct. Roch 7C 204
(Suffolk St.)
Park Ct. South 6K 167
Park Ct. Todm 9J 147
Park Cres. Acc 4N 141
Park Cres. Bacup 7K 163
Park Cres. B'brn 2K 139
Park Cres. Has 6G 161
(Park Av.)
Park Cres. Has 8M 207
(Riding La.)
Park Cres. Hell 1D 52
Park Cres. More 1E 22
Park Cres. South 5K 167
Park Cres. Ct. South 5L 167
Parkdale Gdns. B'brn 1L 157
Parkdene Clo. Bolt 9K 199
Park Dri. Brier 5G 104
Park Dri. Lea 8A 114
Park Dri. Nels 3K 105
Parke M. Withn 4L 155
Parker Av. Clith 5L 81
Parker Clo. Boot 9A 222
Parker Cres. Orm 5K 209
Parker La. Burn 4E 124
Parker La. Wstke 1F 152
(in two parts)
Parke Rd. Brins 7N 155
Parkers Fold. Catt 1N 67
Parker St. Acc 6D 142
(Hollins La.)
Parker St. Acc 9D 122
(South St.)
Parker St. Ash R 7G 114
Parker St. Barn 1L 77
Parker St. Blac 5C 88
Parker St. Brclf 7K 105
Parker St. Burn 3E 124
(off Barnes St.)
Parker St. Burn 3E 124
(Kingsway, in two parts)
Parker St. Chor 5E 174
Parker St. Col 6N 85
Parker St. Lanc 8L 23
Parker St. Nels 9K 85
Parker St. Rish 7H 121
Parkers Wood Clo. Chor 8C 174
Parkers Yd. Gigg 2N 35
(off Church St.)
Pk. Farm Clo. Longt 8K 133
Pk. Farm Rd. B'brn 9E 138
Parkfield. Shev 5L 213
Parkfield Av. Ash R 7E 114
Parkfield Av. Boot 9A 222
Parkfield Clo. Lea 8N 113
Parkfield Clo. Ley 7F 152
Parkfield Clo. Orm 9H 209
Parkfield Cres. Lea 9N 113
Parkfield Dri. Lanc 1L 29
Parkfield Dri. Lea 9N 113
Parkfield Gro. Liv 1B 222
Parkfield Vw. Lea 9N 113
Park Gate. 7J 123
Parkgate. Goos 4N 95
Parkgate. Wals 8D 200
Parkgate Dri. Bolt 8F 198
Parkgate Dri. Lanc 8N 23
Parkgate Dri. Ley 8H 153
Park Ga. Rd. Sale 9L 99
Pk. Hall Rd. Char R & Hesk 1H 193
Park Head. Whal 8M 101
Parkhead La. Bncr 4C 60
Pk. Hey Dri. App B 5H 213
Park Hill. 9H 219
Pk. Hill. Barn 3N 77
Park Hill. Roch 4C 204
Parkhill Gro. Todm 7E 146
(off Parkside Rd.)
Park Hill Rd. Gars 5N 59
Park Ho. La. L Bent 9H 19
Parkin La. Todm 1G 165
Parkinson Av. Blac 9C 88
Parkinson Fold. Has 9H 161
Parkinson La. Chip 7E 70
Parkinson St. B'brn 6J 139
Parkinson St. Burn 5E 124
Parkinson St. Bury 8L 201
Parkinson St. Foul 2A 86
Parkinson St. Has 4F 160
Parkinson Ter. Traw 9E 86
Parkinson Way. Blac 9C 88
Parkland Clo. T Clev 2C 62
Parklands. Has 6G 161
Parklands. Rainf 3K 225
Parklands. Skel 1A 220
Parklands. South 6L 167
Parklands Av. Pen 4D 134
Parklands Clo. Pen 4D 134
Parklands Dri. Ful 1H 115
Parklands Gro. Ful 1H 115
Parklands Gro. Hey 6M 21
Parklands, The. Catt 1A 68
Parklands Way. B'brn 8J 139
Parkland Vw. Burn 6C 124
Park La. Brier 5G 104
Park La. Fort & Winm 4K 45
Park La. Gis 9B 52
Park La. Gt Har 3J 121
Park La. Halt 1E 24
Park La. Hor 9E 196
Park La. Mag 8E 216
Park La. Osw 5L 141
Park La. Pen 5H 135
Park La. Pre 9N 41
Park La. Roch 5C 204
Park La. Tar 4N 169
Park La. Wenn 6F 18
Park La. Wesh 2M 111
Park La. Dri. Liv 9F 216
Pk. Lee Rd. B'brn 7M 139
Park Link. Augh 2G 216
Park M. Gis 9A 52
(off Park Rd.)
Pk. Mill Pl. Pres 8K 115
Park Place. 5N 139
Park Pl. B'brn 5J 139
(off Spring La.)
Park Pl. Fen 9E 138
Park Pl. Hell 1D 52
Park Pl. Pres 1J 135
(off Glovers Ct.)
Park Pl. Walt D 4A 136
Park Rd. Acc 2N 141
Park Rd. Adl 7H 195
Park Rd. Bacup 6K 163
Park Rd. Barn 2M 77
Park Rd. B'brn 5M 139
Park Rd. Blac 5C 88
Park Rd. Bury 9K 201
Park Rd. Chor 5E 174
Park Rd. Cliv 8J 125
Park Rd. Cop 4A 194
Park Rd. Dar 9B 158
Park Rd. Ful 5K 115
Park Rd. Gis 9A 52
Park Rd. Gt Har 3K 121
Park Rd. Helm 7D 160
Park Rd. Kirkby 7G 223
Park Rd. K'ham 5L 111
Park Rd. Lanc 8L 23
Park Rd. Ley 8K 153
Park Rd. L'boro 8L 185
Park Rd. Lyth A 2E 128
Park Rd. Mel B 8N 117
Park Rd. Orm 7K 209
Park Rd. Orr 5K 221
Park Rd. Pad 2H 123
Park Rd. Poul F 7L 63
Park Rd. Pres 4G 135
(in two parts)
Park Rd. Ram 2E 200
Park Rd. Rish 8J 121
Park Rd. Silv 7H 5
Park Rd. South 5K 167
Park Rd. T Clev 3H 63
Park Rd. Todm 1L 165
Park Rd. Tur 9L 179
Park Rd. Waterf 6D 162
Park Rd. Ind. Est. Bacup 6K 163
Park Rd. W. South 5J 167
Park Row. Bolt 7F 198
Parkside. Lea 7A 114
Parkside. More 5C 22
Parkside. Pres 6L 115
Pk. Side. Sough 4D 78
Parkside. Whitw 4A 184
Parkside Av. Chor 6E 174
Parkside Clo. Todm 7E 146
Parkside Ct. More 5C 22
(off Parkside)
Parkside Cres. Orr 5J 221
Parkside Dri. Arns 2E 4
Parkside Dri. Whit W 9D 154
Parkside Dri. S. Whit W 9D 154
Parkside La. Nate 5L 59
Parkside Rd. Lyth A 1G 129
Pk. Side Rd. Nels 2M 105
Parkside Rd. Todm 7E 146
Parkside Vw. T Clev 8G 54
Park Sq. Lanc 8L 23
Parkstone Av. Poul F 6H 63
Parkstone Av. T Clev 3K 63
Park Stone Rd. Brough 7F 94
Park St. Acc 2B 142
Park St. Barn 3M 77

Primrose Ter.—Ranger St.

Primrose Ter. *Dar* 7B **158**
Primrose Ter. Lang 9C **100** (off Whalley New Rd.)
Primrose Way. *Chu* 1L **141**
Primrose Way. *Poul F* 5H **63**
Primula Dri. *Lwr D* 9A **140**
Primula St. *Bolt* 9F **198**
Prince Av. *Carn* 9B **12**
Prince Charles Gdns. *South* 9F **166**
Prince Lee Meadows. *Dar* 7B **158**
Princes Ct. *Lyth A* 1D **128**
Princes Ct. *Pen* 2E **134**
Princes Cres. *More* 1E **22**
Princes Dri. *Ful* 3H **115**
Princes Pk. 6F 166
Prince's Pk. *Shev* 8J **213**
Princes Reach. *Ash R* 9D **114**
Princes Rd. *Lyth A* 4K **129**
Princes Rd. *Pen* 2E **134**
Prince's Rd. *Walt D* 3A **136**
Princess Alexandra Way. *Hey* 2J **27**
Princess Av. *Clith* 2M **81**
Princess Av. *Lanc* 2K **29**
Princess Av. *Poul F* 8K **63**
Princess Av. *Roch* 1F **204**
Princess Av. *Wesh* 3L **111**
Princess Ct. *Blac* 7B **88**
Princess Gdns. *B'brn* 9E **138**
Princess Pde. *Blac* 4B **88**
Princess Rd. *And* 5K **195**
Princess Rd. *Roch* 6G **205**
Princess Rd. *Stand L* 8M **213**
Princess Rd. *T Clev* 1C **62**
Princess St. *Acc* 2M **141**
Princess St. *Bacup* 5K **163**
Princess St. *Bam B* 8B **136**
Princess St. *B'brn* 6K **139**
Princess St. *Blac* 7B **88**
Princess St. *Chor* 8F **174**
Princess St. *Chu* 2L **141**
Princess St. *Col* 6N **85**
Princess St. *Gt Har* 4K **121**
Princess St. *Has* 5G **161**
Princess St. *Ley* 6L **153**
Princess St. *Los H* 9L **135**
Princess St. *Nels* 3H **105**
Princess St. *Pad* 1G **122**
Princess St. *Pres* 1L **135**
Princess St. *Roch* 5C **204** (in two parts)
Princess St. *Whal* 5J **101**
Prince's St. *B'brn* 4L **139**
Princes St. *Rish* 8H **121**
Princes St. *South* 8G **167**
Princess Way. *Burn* 2D **124**
Princess Way. *Eux* 4N **173**
Prince St. *Bacup* 8A **164**
Prince St. *Burn* 4C **124**
Prince St. *Dar* 6N **157**
Prince St. *Ram* 8H **181**
Prince St. *Roch* 8D **204**
Princes Way. *Fltwd* 2C **54**
Princes Way. *T Clev* 3C **62**
Princeway. *Blac* 2C **108**
Pringle Bank. *War* 4A **12**
Pringle St. *B'brn* 5N **139**
Pringle Wood. *Brough* 8F **94**
Prinny Hill Rd. *Has* 4F **160**
Printers Ct. *Tur* 1K **199**
Printers Fold. *Burn* 3K **123**
Printers La. *Bolt* 7J **199**
Printshop La. *Dar* 9A **158**
Prior's Clo. *B'brn* 2H **139**
Priorsgate. *Heat O* 6C **22**
Prior's Oak Cotts. *Pen* 3F **134**
Priors Wlk. *Saw* 3D **74**
Priorswood Pl. *Skel* 7C **220**
Priory Clo. *B'brn* 4E **140**
Priory Clo. *Burs* 8B **190**
Priory Clo. *Form* 1B **214**
Priory Clo. *Heat O* 6C **22**
Priory Clo. Lanc 8J **23** (off Church St.)
Priory Clo. *Ley* 5M **153**
Priory Clo. *Pen* 2F **134**
Priory Clo. *Ross* 5C **162**
Priory Clo. *Tar* 9E **150**
Priory Clo. *Wig* 6L **221**
Priory Ct. *Blac* 5C **88**
Priory Ct. *Burn* 7F **124**
Priory Ct. *Lyth A* 1E **128**
Priory Ct. *Pleas* 6D **138**
Priory Ct. *South* 8F **166**
Priory Cres. *Pen* 2F **134**
Priory Dri. *Dar* 6C **158**
Priory Gdns. *South* 1F **186**
Priory Ga. *Blac* 4C **108**
Priory Grange. *Dar* 7C **158**
Priory Grange. *South* 1G **186**
Priory Gro. *Orm* 8J **209**
Priory La. *Horn* 7B **18**
Priory La. *Pen* 3E **134**
Priory M. *Lyth A* 1K **129**
Priory M. *South* 8F **166**
Priory Nook. *Uph* 4F **220**
Priory Pl. *Dar* 7C **158**
Priory Rd. *Uph* 4F **220**
Priory St. *Ash R* 9G **115**
Priory St. *Nels* 1K **105**
Priory Vw. Todm 1L **165** (off Nutfield St.)
Priory Wlk. Lanc 8L **23** (off Wolseley St.)
Priory Way. *Barn* 2L **77**
Pritchard St. *B'brn* 6L **139**
Pritchard St. *Burn* 5C **124**
Private La. *Has* 7H **161**
Private Rd. *Hogh* 7J **137**
Procter Moss Rd. *Abb* 6A **30**
Procter St. *B'brn* 5N **139**
Proctor Clo. *Brier* 5K **105**
Proctor Clo. *Wig* 2N **221**
Proctor Cft. *Traw* 9E **86**
Proctor Moss Rd. *Ellel* 9D **30**
Proctor's Brow. *Halt* 9J **19**
Proctors Row. Set 3N **35** (off Mill Clo.)
Progress Av. *B'brn* 1A **140**
Progress Bus. Pk. *K'ham* 5M **111**
Progress Ct. *Blac* 2G **89**
Progress Rd. *Whit I* 8K **85**
Progress St. *Chor* 6G **174**
Progress St. *Dar* 6B **158**
Progress Way. *Blac* 4F **108**
Promenade. *Ains* 7A **186**
Promenade. *Blac* 2A **108**
Promenade. *Kno S* 7L **41**
Promenade. *South* 7G **167**
Promenade. *T Clev* 4C **62**
Promenade N. *T Clev* 8C **54**
Promenade Rd. *Fltwd* 8G **40**
Promenade S. *T Clev* 1C **62**
Promenade, The. *Arns* 1E **4**
Prospect Av. *Bolt* 9M **199**
Prospect Av. *Dar* 5M **157**
Prospect Av. *Hest B* 8J **15**
Prospect Av. *Los H* 8L **135**
Prospect Ct. *L'rdge* 4K **97**
Prospect Ct. *Tot* 6E **200**
Prospect Dri. *Hest B* 8J **15**
Prospect Gro. *More* 4C **22**
Prospect Hill. *Has* 5F **160**
Prospect Hill. Raw 4M **161** (off Prospect Rd.)
Prospect Ho. Dri. *Wheel* 7J **155**
Prospect Pl. *Ash R* 8E **114**
Prospect Pl. *Pen* 4H **135**
Prospect Pl. *Skel* 6C **220**
Prospect Rd. *Ross* 4M **161**
Prospect St. *Gt Har* 4K **121**
Prospect St. *Lanc* 9L **23**
Prospect St. *Roch* 9B **204**
Prospect St. *Ross* 6D **162**
Prospect Ter. *Bacup* 8J **163**
Prospect Ter. *Barfd* 7H **85**
Prospect Ter. *Bury* 9J **201**
Prospect Ter. *Dunn* 4N **143**
Prospect Ter. Hun 7D **122** (off Enfield Rd.)
Prospect Ter. Ross 6D **162** (off Prospect St.)
Prospect Ter. Ross 2L **161** (off East St.)
Prospect Ter. *Withn* 7B **156**
Prospect Vw. *Los H* 9L **135**
Prospect Way. *Boot* 7A **222**
Providence St. *B'brn* 9A **120**
Providence St. *Todm* 8K **165**
Prudy Hill. *Poul F* 7K **63**
Prunella Dri. *Lwr D* 9A **140**
Pudding La. *Todm* 6F **146**
Pudding Pie Nook La. *Goos* 6J **95**
Puddle Ho. La. *Sing* 2M **89**
Pudsey. 7E 146
Pudsey Rd. *Todm* 7E **146**
Pulborough Clo. *Bury* 6G **201**
Pullman St. *Roch* 8C **204**
Pump Ho. La. *Ley* 9C **152**
Pump St. *B'brn* 4K **139**
Pump St. *Burn* 3C **124**
Pump St. *Clith* 3K **81**
Pump St. *Pres* 9K **115**
Punnell's La. *Liv* 6M **215**
Punstock La. *Dar* 7N **157**
Punstock Rd. *Dar* 6N **157**
Purbeck Dri. *Bury* 7H **201**
Purdon St. *Bury* 7L **201**
Pye Busk. *Ben* 6M **19**
Pye Busk Clo. *Ben* 6M **19**
Pyes Bri. La. *Hale* 1C **6**
Pygon's Hill La. *Liv* 4C **216**

Q

Quaile Holme Rd. *Kno S* 8K **41**
Quakerfields. *Dar* 5A **158**
Quaker La. *Dar* 5A **158**
Quaker's Brook La. *Hogh* 5J **137**
Quakers Fld. *Tot* 5E **200**
Quakers Pl. *Stand* 3N **213**
Quakers Ter. *Stand* 1M **213**
Quantock Clo. *Wig* 9M **221**
Quarlton Dri. *Hawk* 2A **200**
Quarry Bank. *Gars* 6N **59**
Quarry Bank. *Has* 6E **160**
Quarry Bank. *Liv* 7L **223**
Quarry Bank. *T Clev* 3F **62**
Quarry Bank St. *Burn* 2A **124**
Quarry Clo. *Kirkby* 7L **223**
Quarry Dale. *Liv* 7L **223**
Quarry Dri. *Augh* 3H **217**
Quarry Farm Ct. *Chat* 7C **74**
Quarry Grn. *Liv* 7L **223**
Quarry Grn. Flats. *Liv* 7L **223**
Quarry Hey. *Liv* 7L **223**
Quarry Hill. *Roch* 1B **204**
Quarry Hill Nature Reserve. **4K 105**
Quarry Mt. *Orm* 6M **209**
Quarry Mt. M. *Lanc* 9L **23**
Quarry Rd. *Brook* 3L **25**
Quarry Rd. *Chor* 8G **175**
Quarry Rd. *Lanc* 9K **23**
Quarryside Dri. *Liv* 7M **223**
Quarry St. *Acc* 3B **142**
Quarry St. *Bacup* 5L **163**
Quarry St. *B'brn* 3N **139**
Quarry St. *Hap* 7H **123**
Quarry St. *Pad* 9J **103**
Quarry St. *Ram* 8J **181** (in three parts)
Quarry St. *Shawf* 9B **164**
Quarry Vw. *Roch* 2B **204**
Quayle Av. *Blac* 1E **108**
Quayside. *Fltwd* 1H **55**
Quay West. *Lyth A* 3E **128**
Quebec Av. *Blac* 8D **62**
Quebec Rd. *B'brn* 9J **119**
Quebec St. *Todm* 6K **165**
Queen Anne St. *Has* 4F **160**
Queen Anne St. South 7H **167** (off Market St.)
Queenby Clo. *Bolt* 8D **198**
Queen Elizabeth Ct. *More* 3A **22**
Queen Elizabeth Cres. *Acc* 3B **142**
Queen Mary Av. *Lyth A* 3G **129**
Queen Mary Ter. *Whal* 3H **101**
Queen's Av. *Brom X* 6G **198**
Queens Av. *Roch* 1F **204**
Queensberry Rd. *Burn* 4C **124**
Queensborough Rd. *Acc* 1A **142**
Queensbury Rd. *T Clev* 1C **62**
Queens Clo. *Clith* 4L **81**
Queen's Clo. *Poul F* 8L **63**
Queens Ct. *Blac* 9B **62**
Queens Ct. Ful 6H **115** (off Queens Rd.)
Queenscourt Av. *Pen* 6H **135**
Queens Cres. *K'ham* 5N **111**
Queensdale Clo. *Walt D* 4A **136**
Queens Dri. *Arns* 2F **4**
Queen's Dri. *Carn* 9B **12**
Queen's Dri. *Ful* 3G **115**
Queens Dri. *L'rdge* 3J **97**
Queens Dri. *More* 2E **22**
Queen's Dri. *Osw* 5M **141**
Queens Dri. *Roch* 9B **204**
Queens Dri. *Stain* 5L **89**
Queensgate. *Thorn C* 3J **53**
Queensgate. *Chor* 7D **174**
Queensgate. *Nels* 3G **105**
Queens Grn. *Hask* 7M **207**
Queen's Gro. *Chor* 6E **174**
Queen's Lancashire Regiment Mus. ***5L 115*** (off Watling St. Rd.)
Queen's Lancashire Way. *Burn* 3D **124**
Queen's Park. 5B 140
Queen's Pk. Rd. *B'brn* 4A **140**
Queen's Pk. Rd. *Burn* 1F **124**
Queen's Pk. Rd. *Heyw* 9H **203**
Queens Pl. *Bury* 3H **201**
Queens Pl. *Wesh* 2L **111**
Queen's Promenade. *Blac & T Clev* 1B **88**
Queen Sq. *Blac* 5B **88**
Queen Sq. *Lanc* 9K **23**
Queens Retail Pk. *Pres* 1L **135**
Queen's Rd. *Acc* 1A **142**
Queen's Rd. *B'brn* 5B **140**
Queen's Rd. *Burn* 8F **104**
Queen's Rd. *Chor* 6D **174**
Queens Rd. *Clith* 4L **81**
Queen's Rd. *Dar* 1B **178**
Queens Rd. *Ful* 6G **115**
Queen's Rd. *L'boro* 9L **185**
Queen's Rd. *Lyth A* 3F **128**
Queens Rd. *Orr* 6F **220**
Queen's Rd. *South* 6J **167**
Queen's Rd. *Walt D* 3A **136**
Queen's Rd. Ter. L'boro 9L **185** (off Queen's Rd.)
Queens Rd. W. *Chu* 9M **121**
Queen's Sq. *Hodd* 6F **158**
Queen's Sq. *K Lon* 6F **8**
Queens Sq. *Poul F* 8K **63**
Queen's Sq. *Ross* 5M **161**
Queen's St. *L'rdge* 4J **97**
Queen's Ter. *Bacup* 7J **163**
Queen's Ter. *B'brn* 7J **139**
Queen's Ter. *Fltwd* 8H **41**
Queen's Ter. *Pad* 1H **123**
Queen's Ter. Ross 5M **161** (off Queen St.)
Queenstown. 3D 88
Queen St. *Acc* 2B **142**
Queen St. *Bacup* 5K **163**
Queen St. *Barn* 3L **77**
Queen St. *Barfd* 7H **85**
Queen St. *Blac* 5B **88**
Queen St. *Brclf* 7K **105**
Queen St. *Burn* 4D **124**
Queen St. *Carn* 9N **11**
Queen St. *Clay M* 6M **121**
Queen St. *Clith* 3J **81**
Queen St. *Col* 7N **85**
Queen St. *Dar* 5N **157**
Queen St. *Fltwd* 9G **41**
Queen St. *Gt Har* 4J **121**
Queen St. *Hodd* 6F **158**
Queen St. *Hor* 9B **196**
Queen St. *Lanc* 9K **23**
Queen St. *L'boro* 9L **185**
Queen St. *Los H* 9L **135**
Queen St. *Lyth A* 5N **129**
Queen St. *More* 3B **22**
Queen St. *Nels* 1J **105**
Queen St. *Orm* 8K **209**
Queen St. *Orr* 5K **221**
Queen St. *Osw* 4L **141**
Queen St. *Pad* 1H **123**
Queen St. *Pres* 1L **135**
Queen St. *Ram* 8G **180**
Queen St. *Roch* 5C **204**
Queen St. *Ross* 5M **161**
Queen St. *Stac* 7G **163**
Queen St. *Todm* 2L **165**
Queen St. *Tot* 8F **200**
Queen St. *Whal* 6J **101**
Queen St. *Wig* 6N **221**
Queen St. E. *Chor* 8F **174**
Queens Vw. *L'boro* 2K **205**
Queens Wlk. *Gt Har* 4K **121**
Queen's Wlk. *T Clev* 8D **54**
Queensway. *Ash R* 7C **114**
Queensway. *Bam B* 7A **136**
Queensway. *B'brn* 9H **139**
Queensway. *Blac* 2C **108**
Queensway. *Brins* 8A **156**
Queensway. *Chu* 1M **141**
Queensway. *Clith* 4L **81**
Queensway. *Eux* 4A **174**
Queensway. *Ley* 8H **153**
Queensway. *Lyth A* 6G **109**
Queensway. *Pen* 2E **134**
Queens Way. *Poul F* 8K **63**
Queensway. *Rainf* 5L **225**
Queensway. *Ross* 6C **162**
Queensway. *Shev* 8J **213**
Queensway. *Wadd* 8H **73**
Queensway. *W'ton* 1K **131**
Queensway Clo. *Pen* 2E **134**
Queensway Ct. *Lyth A* 8G **109**
Queensway Lodge. *Poul F* 8K **63**
Queen Vera Rd. *Blac* 5B **88**
Queen Victoria Rd. *Blac* 7C **88**
Queen Victoria Rd. *Burn* 9F **104** (Briercliffe Rd.)
Queen Victoria Rd. *Burn* 2F **124** (Ormerod Rd.)
Queen Victoria St. *B'brn* 6J **139**
Queen Victoria St. *Roch* 9D **204**
Quenby Corner. *Poul F* 8H **63**
Quernmore. 4F 30
Quernmore Av. *Blac* 7G **89**
Quernmore Brow. *Quer* 4F **30**
Quernmore Dri. *Glas D* 2C **36**
Quernmore Dri. *Kel* 7D **78**
Quernmore Ind. Est. *Frec* 2A **132**
Quernmore Rd. Cat 2G **25** (off Caton)
Quernmore Rd. Lanc 8M **23** (off Moorlands)
Quernmore Rd. *Liv* 7M **223**
Quernmore Wlk. *Liv* 7M **223**
Quin St. *Ley* 6K **153**
Quinton. Roch 5B **204** (off Spotland Rd.)
Quinton Clo. *South* 9A **186**

R

Rabbit La. *Bas E* 4N **71**
Rabbit La. *Burs* 1L **209**
Rabbit Wlk. *Burn* 6F **124**
Raby St. *More* 3B **22**
Raby St. *Ross* 5M **161**
Radburn Brow. *Clay W* 4D **154**
Radburn Clo. *Clay W* 4D **154**
Radcliffe Rd. *Fltwd* 3F **54**
Radeclyffe St. *Clith* 2L **81**
Radfield Av. *Dar* 7A **158**
Radfield Head. *Dar* 7N **157**
Radfield Rd. *Dar* 7N **157**
Radford. 7A 158
Radford Bank Gdns. *Dar* 7A **158**
Radford Gdns. *Dar* 8A **158**
Radford St. *Dar* 7A **158**
Radley Av. *Blac* 2E **88**
Radley Dri. *Liv* 7B **222**
Radnor Av. *Burn* 2M **123**
Radnor Av. *T Clev* 2F **62**
Radnor Clo. *Osw* 4J **141**
Radnor Dri. *South* 3L **167**
Radnor St. *Acc* 1A **142**
Radnor St. *Pres* 9H **115**
Radshaw Ct. *Liv* 5L **223**
Radstock Clo. *Bolt* 6E **198**
Radway Clo. *T Clev* 4F **62**
Radworth Cres. *Blac* 9H **89**
Raeburn Av. *Burn* 6C **124**
Raedale Av. *Burn* 6F **104**
Raglan Rd. Ash R 7G **115** (off Raglan St.)
Raglan Rd. *Burn* 4C **124**
Raglan Rd. *Hey* 5M **21**
Raglan St. *Ash R* 7G **114**
Raglan St. *Col* 7A **86**
Raglan St. *Nels* 1H **105**
Raglan St. *Todm* 2L **165**
Raikes Hill. *Blac* 5C **88**
Raikeshill Dri. *Hest B* 9H **15**
Raikes M. *Blac* 5C **88**
Raikes Pde. *Blac* 5C **88**
Raikes Rd. *Gt Ecc* 6N **65**
Raikes Rd. *Pres* 8M **115**
Raikes Rd. *T Clev* 2L **63**
Rail Clo. *Rainf* 9K **219**
Railgate. *Bacup* 7N **163**
Railton Av. *B'brn* 8H **139**
Railway App. *Orm* 7L **209**
Railway Av. *South* 1E **168**
Railway Cotts. *Hesk B* 5G **112**
Railway Crossing La. *Lanc* 2F **28**
Railway Gro. *B'brn* 1A **140**
Railway Path. *Orm* 9K **209**
Railway Pl. *Glas D* 1D **36**
Railway Rd. *Adl* 6J **195**
Railway Rd. *B'brn* 3M **139**
Railway Rd. *Brins & Withn* 8A **156**
Railway Rd. *Chor* 5F **174**
Railway Rd. *Dar* 6A **158**
Railway Rd. *Has* 3G **160**
Railway Rd. *Orm* 7L **209**
Railway Rd. *Skel* 2G **219**
Railway St. *Bacup* 7F **162**
Railway St. *Barn* 2M **77**
Railway St. *Brier* 5F **104**
Railway St. *Burn* 2D **124**
Railway St. *Bury* 3H **201**
Railway St. *Chor* 7F **174**
Railway St. *Foul* 2A **86**
Railway St. *Lanc* 1K **29**
Railway St. *Ley* 5L **153**
Railway St. *L'boro* 9L **185**
Railway St. *Miln* 9L **205**
Railway St. *Nels* 2J **105**
Railway St. *Ram* 8H **181**
Railway St. *Roch* 6D **204**
Railway St. *South* 9G **167**
Railway St. *Todm* 1L **165**
Railway St. W. *Bury* 3G **201**
Railway Ter. *Brier* 5E **104**
Railway Ter. *Cop* 4B **194**
Railway Ter. *Gt Har* 5J **121**
Railway Ter. *Ross* 6L **161**
Railway Ter. *S'stne* 1E **122**
Railway Ter. *South* 9G **167**
Railway Ter. S'seat 3H **201** (off Miller St.)
Railway Ter. *Wesh* 3L **111**
Railway Vw. *Acc* 2A **142**
Railway Vw. *Adl* 6J **195**
Railway Vw. *Bill* 6H **101**
Railway Vw. *B'brn* 6J **139**
Railway Vw. Brier 4F **104** (off Wesley St.)
Railway Vw. *Crost* 4L **171**
Railway Vw. *Liv* 7H **223**
Railway Vw. *Todm* 6K **165**
Railway Vw. Av. *Clith* 2L **81**
Railway Vw. Rd. *Clith* 2L **81**
Rainbow Dri. *Mell* 6G **222**
Raines Crest. *Miln* 7K **205**
Raines Rd. *Gigg* 3N **35**
Rainford. 4K 225
Rainford By-Pass. *Rainf* 1H **225**
Rainford Ind. Est. *Rainf* 6N **225**
Rainford Junction. 9K 219
Rainford Rd. *Bic* 5E **218**
Rainford St. *Bolt* 7J **199**
Rainhall. 1A 78
Rainhall Cres. *Barn* 2A **78**
Rainhall Rd. *Barn* 2M **77**
Rainshaw St. *Bolt* 9F **198**
Rain Shore. 1G 202
Rake. *Roch* 6H **203**
Rake Foot. 9M 143
Rake Foot. *Has* 3G **161**
Rake Head. 8E 162
Rake Head Barn La. *Todm* 7J **165**
Rakehead La. *Bacup* 7F **162**
Rakehouse Brow. *Abb* 2A **48**
Rake La. *W'ton* 3J **131**
Rakes Bri. *Lwr D* 9A **140**
Rakes Head La. *Slyne* 1G **23**
Rakes Ho. Rd. *Nels* 9J **85**
Rakes La. *Hort* 7D **52**
Rakes La. *Rim* 3A **76**
Rakes Rd. *Brook* 1M **25**
Rake St. *Bury* 9L **201**
Rake Ter. *L'boro* 8M **185**
Rake, The. *Abb* 5N **39**
Rake, The. *Ram* 8G **180**
Rake Top. *Roch* 4M **203**
Rake Top Av. *High* 4L **103**
Rakewood. 4M 205
Rakewood Rd. *L'boro* 2L **205**
Raleigh Av. *Blac* 4B **108**
Raleigh Clo. *Lyth A* 8D **108**
Raleigh Gdns. *L'boro* 5M **185**
Raleigh Rd. *Ful* 3H **115**
Raleigh St. *Pad* 2J **123**
Ralph Sherwin Ct. *Roch* 1G **204**
Ralph St. *Acc* 9B **122**
Ralph St. *Roch* 4D **204**
Ralph's Wife's La. *South* 9D **148**
Ramparts, The. *Lanc* 6L **23**
Ramper Ga. *T Clev* 1D **62**
Ramsay Ct. *Kno S* 8K **41**
Ramsay Pl. *Roch* 5D **204**
Ramsay St. *Bolt* 9E **198**
Ramsay St. *Roch* 5D **204**
Ramsay Ter. *Roch* 5D **204**
Ramsbottom. 9G 180
Ramsbottom La. *Ram* 7H **181**
Ramsbottom Rd. *Tur & Hawk* 3M **199**
Ramsbottom St. *Acc* 1A **142**
Ramsbottom St. *Ross* 7C **162**
Rams Clough La. *Osw* 9N **141**
Ramsden La. *Todm* 8H **165**
Ramsden Rd. *Ward* 7F **184** (in two parts)
Ramsden St. *Carn* 8A **12**
Ramsden St. *Todm* 8K **165**
Ramsden Wood Rd. *Todm* 8J **165**
Ramsey Av. *Bacup* 6L **163**
Ramsey Av. *Blac* 3D **88**
Ramsey Av. *Pres* 6N **115**
Ramsey Clo. *Lyth A* 8D **108**
Ramsey Gro. *Burn* 8G **105**
Ramsey Rd. *B'brn* 7L **139**
Ramsgate Clo. *W'ton* 1K **131**
Ramsgate Rd. *Lyth A* 9F **108**
Ramsgreave. 6M 119
Ramsgreave Av. *B'brn* 7L **119**
Ramsgreave Dri. *B'brn* 8K **119**
Ramsgreave Rd. *Rams* 6L **119**
Ramshill Av. *Poul F* 6H **63**
Ramson Ct. More 6B **22** (off Yarrow Wlk.)
Ramwells Brow. *Brom X* 5F **198**
Ramwells Ct. *Brom X* 5H **199**
Ramwells M. *Brom X* 5H **199**
Ranaldsway. *Ley* 7G **152**
Randall Av. *Shev* 7K **213**
Randall St. *Burn* 9F **104**
Randal St. *B'brn* 2M **139**
Randle Av. *Rainf* 2J **225**
Randle Brook Ct. *Rainf* 2J **225**
Randolph St. *B'brn* 4A **140**
Random Row. *Bacup* 7G **162**
Ranelagh Dri. *South* 6F **186**
Ranger St. *Acc* 3N **141**

270 A-Z Lancashire

Rangeway Av.—Riley Ct.

Rangeway Av. Blac 2C 108
Ranglet Rd. Bam B 9D 136
Rangletts Av. Chor 8E 174
Ranglit Av. Lea 8N 113
Rankin Av. Hesk B 5D 150
Rankin Clo. Barn 2N 77
Rankin Dri. Hodd 7E 158
Ranlea Av. More 2G 22
Ranleigh Dri. Newb 3L 211
Rann. 1E 158
Rannoch Dri. B'brn 7G 139
Ranslett Ct. Liv 9A 206
Ransom Ct. More 3F 22
(off Buseph Barrow)
Rantree Rd. Halt 9K 19
Ranworth Clo. Bolt 7G 198
Rapley La. Wood 1K 93
Ratcliffe Fold. Has 4G 160
Ratcliffe St. Dar 6B 158
Ratcliffe St. Has 4G 160
Ratcliffe Wharf La. Fort 4K 45
Rathbone Rd. H'twn 7A 214
Rathbone St. Roch 6F 204
Rathlyn Av. Blac 3E 88
Rathmell. 7M 35
Rathmell Clo. Blac 1H 89
Rathmill Sike. Grin 3C 74
Rathmore Cres. South 3A 168
Ratten La. Hut 5M 133
Ratten Row. 3A 66
Raveden Clo. Bolt 9C 198
Raven Av. Ross 8G 160
Raven Clo. Chor 9B 174
Raven Cft. Has 7G 160
Ravendale Clo. Roch 4L 203
Ravenglass Av. Liv 9C 216
Ravenglass Clo. B'brn 7A 140
Ravenglass Clo. Blac 2E 108
Ravenglass Clo. Wesh 2M 111
Ravenhead Dri. Uph 4D 220
Ravenhead Way. Uph 5C 220
Ravenhill Dri. Chor 5E 174
Raven Meols La. Liv 1A 214
Ravenoak La. Wors 4M 125
Raven Pk. Has 7G 160
Raven Rd. B'brn 3J 139
Ravens Clo. Blac 3H 89
Ravens Clo. Lanc 5J 23
Ravens Clo. Brow. Wenn 5G 18
Ravenscroft Av. Orm 8K 209
Ravenscroft Clo. B'brn 8A 120
Ravenscroft Way. Barn 1N 77
Ravens Gro. Burn 6G 104
Ravens, The. Liv 2A 214
Ravensthorpe. Chor 5C 174
Raven St. Bury 9L 201
Raven St. Nels 1K 105
Raven St. Pres 7M 115
Ravenswing Av. B'brn 1J 139
Ravens Wood. B'brn 3J 139
Ravenswood. Gt Har 3H 121
Ravenswood. Rib 7A 116
Ravenswood Av. Blac 3H 89
Ravenswood Av. Wig 8N 221
Ravenwood Av. Blac 4D 108
Rawcliffe Dri. Ash R 9B 114
Rawcliffe Rd. Chor 7E 174
Rawcliffe Rd. Out R & St M 4M 65
Rawcliffe St. Blac 1B 108
Rawcliffe St. Burn 3E 124
Rawlinson Ct. South 6K 167
(off Rawlinson Rd.)
Rawlinson Gro. South 5L 167
Rawlinson La. Hth C 3G 195
Rawlinson Rd. South 6K 167
Rawlinson St. Dar 9B 158
Rawlinson St. Hor 9C 196
Rawlinson St. Wesh 3L 111
Raws Ct. Burn 3E 124
(off Bank Pde.)
Rawson Av. Acc 4N 141
Rawsons Rake. Ram 8F 180
Rawson St. Burn 9F 104
Rawsthorne Av. Has 5G 160
Rawsthorne Av. Ram 4J 181
Rawstorne Clo. Frec 2M 131
Rawstorne Rd. Pen 3E 134
Rawstorne St. B'brn 4K 139
Raw St. Burn 3E 124
(off Bank Pde.)
Rawstron St. Whitw 5N 183
Rawtenstall. 6L 161
Rawtenstall Rd. Has 6H 161
Rawthey Rd. Lanc 6H 23
Raybourne Av. Poul F 8J 63
Ray Bridge La. Garg 2M 53
Raygarth. K Lon 5E 8
Raygarth La. K Lon 5E 8
Raygill Av. Burn 6B 124
Raygill La. Loth 4M 79
Raygill Pl. Lanc 6H 23
Ray La. Bncr 8C 60
Raylees. Ram 1H 201
Raymond Av. Blac 2D 88
Raymond Av. Boot 9A 222
Raymond Av. Bury 8L 201
Raynor St. B'brn 3L 139
Rays Dri. Lanc 4K 29
Ray St. Brier 5E 104
Read. 8C 102
Reading Clo. B'brn 4A 140
Read's Av. Blac 6C 88
Reads Ct. Blac 6C 88
Read St. Clay M 8N 121
Reaney Av. Blac 2E 108
Reapers Way. Boot 6A 222
Record St. Barn 3M 77
Recreation St. Brad 8L 199
Rectory Clo. Chor 6E 174
Rectory Clo. Crost 4M 171
Rectory Clo. Dar 7C 158
Rectory Clo. Ross 6C 162
Rectory Gdns. C'ham 9G 37
Rectory Gdns. Tar 1E 170
Rectory Hill. Bury 9B 202
Rectory La. Bury 9B 202
Rectory Paddock. Halt 2B 24
Rectory Rd. Blac 9E 88
Rectory Rd. Burn 2D 124
Rectory Rd. South 5M 167
Red Bank. 9F 174
Redbank. Bury 7C 202
Red Bank. Chor 9F 174
Red Bank Rd. Blac 7B 62
Red Bri. La. Silv 7J 5
Red Brook St. Roch 6A 204
Redbrow Way. Liv 6K 223
Redcar Av. Ing 5C 114
Redcar Av. T Clev 7E 54
Redcar Clo. South 2M 187
Redcar Rd. Blac 2B 88
Redcar Rd. Bolt 9B 198
Redcar Rd. Lanc 4M 29
Redcar St. Roch 5B 204
Red Cat La. Burs 5C 190
Redcliffe Gdns. Augh 9K 209
Red Cross St. Pres 1H 135
Redcross St. Roch 5C 204
Redcross St. N. Roch 4B 204
Red Cut La. Liv 9C 224
Red Delph La. Rainf 1H 225
Reddish Clo. Bolt 7L 199
Reddyshore Brow. L'boro 6M 185
Reddyshore Scout Ga.
Todm 1L 185
Redearth Rd. Dar 6A 158
Redearth St. Dar 7A 158
Rede Av. Fltwd 2C 54
Redeswood Av. T Clev 3E 62
Redfearn Wood. Roch 3M 203
Redfern Cotts. Roch 4H 203
Redfern Way. Roch 4H 203
Red Fold. Augh 9H 209
Redford St. Bury 9H 201
(in two parts)
Redgate. Liv 1A 214
Redgate. Orm 7J 209
Redgate Clo. Burn 6F 124
Redgate Dri. Liv 1B 214
Redgrave Ri. Wig 8N 221
Redhill. Hut 7N 133
Redhill Dri. South 2M 187
Redhill Gro. Chor 3G 175
Red Hills Rd. Arns 2E 4
Red Ho. La. E'ston 8E 172
Redisher Clo. Ram 2E 200
Redisher Cft. Holc 2E 200
Redisher La. Hawk 1D 200
Redlam. B'brn 5J 139
Redlam Brow. B'brn 5K 139
Redland Clo. L'boro 8L 185
Red La. Col 5K 85
Red La. E'ston 7G 173
Red La. Roch 3E 204
Red Lees Av. Burn 5K 125
Red Lees Rd. Burn 4J 125
Red Lion Clo. Liv 1B 222
Red Lion St. Burn 4E 124
Red Lion St. Earby 2F 78
Red Lumb. 1E 202
Red Lumb St. Roch 1E 202
Redman Rd. Burn 6F 104
Red Marsh Dri. Red M 9J 55
Red Marsh Ind. Est. T Clev 9J 55
Redmayne Dri. Carn 8B 12
Redmayne St. Pres 9N 115
Redmoor Cres. Liv 5K 223
Redness Clo. Nels 4J 105
Red Rake. B'brn 1K 139
Red Rose Ct. Clay M 8L 121
Red Rose Dri. Ley 3J 153
Red Ruth Dri. Carn 1N 15
Redruth St. Burn 3B 124
Red Sands. Augh 9J 209
Redsands Dri. Ful 4N 115
Red Scar. 4D 116
Red Scar Ind. Est. Rib 4C 116
(in two parts)
Redscar St. Col 8M 85
Redshaw Av. Bolt 7H 199
Red Shell La. Osw 8H 141
(in two parts)
Red Spar Rd. Burn 8H 105
Redstart Pl. T Clev 2F 62
Redvers Rd. Dar 2M 157
Redvers St. Burn 9F 104
Redvers St. Lanc 9H 23
Redvers Ter. Blac 2B 88
Redwald Clo. Liv 4L 223
Redwing Av. T Clev 8F 54
Redwing Dri. Chor 9B 174
Redwing Rd. G'mnt 3E 200
Redwood. 5K 221
Redwood. Shev 6L 213
Redwood Av. Ley 6H 153
Redwood Av. Liv 8B 216
Redwood Av. Orr 5K 221
Redwood Clo. Blac 5C 108
Redwood Clo. Roch 2M 203
Redwood Dri. Chor 8F 174
Redwood Dri. L'rdge 2J 97
Redwood Dri. More 3E 22
Redwood Dri. Orm 8J 209
Redwood Dri. Ross 7L 161
Redwood Gdns. T Clev 1L 63
Redwood Heights. Lanc 9N 23
Redwood Pk. Gro. Firg 6G 205
Redwood Way. Liv 4K 223
Reedfield. Bam B 3E 154
Reedfield. Burn 6G 105
Reedfield Pl. Bam B 1B 154
Reed Hill. Roch 5C 204
Reedley. 6F 104
Reedley Av. Nels 3K 105
Reedley Dri. Burn 6F 104
(in two parts)
Reedley Gro. Burn 7F 104
Reedley Mt. Burn 6G 104
Reedley Rd. Brier & Burn 6F 104
Reedmace Wlk. More 6B 22
Reeds Brow. Rainf 2M 225
Reeds Clo. Ross 1M 161
Reeds Holme. 2M 161
Reedsholme Clo. Ross 1M 161
Reed's La. Rainf 7J 225
Reeds La. Ross 1M 161
(in two parts)
Reeds, The. Orm 6J 209
Reed St. Bacup 4L 163
Reed St. Burn 5E 124
Reedy Acre Pl. Lyth A 4M 129
Reedyford Rd. Nels 9H 85
Reedymoor La. Foul 3M 85
Reeford Gro. Clith 4K 81
Reepham Clo. Wig 8N 221
Rees Pk. Burs 9D 190
Reeth Way. Acc 4M 141
(off Lynton Rd.)
Reeval Clo. Earby 2F 78
Reeveswood. E'ston 8E 172
Reform St. Roch 5C 204
Regal Av. Blac 3E 108
Regency Av. Los H 9N 135
Regency Ct. Roch 6K 203
Regency Cres. K'ham 4K 111
Regency Gdns. Bkdle 1E 186
Regent Av. Col 5B 86
Regent Av. Lyth A 2K 129
Regent Cvn. Pk., The.
More 5A 22
Regent Clo. Pad 2H 123
Regent Clo. South 1F 186
Regent Ct. Blac 4B 88
Regent Ct. Ful 4H 115
Regent Ct. Lyth A 9D 108
Regent Ct. South 6J 167
Regent Dri. Ful 5G 114
Regent Gro. Ful 4H 115
Regent Pk. Ful 3H 115
Regent Pk. Av. More 5N 21
Regent Pk. Gro. More 4N 21
Regent Pl. Nels 9J 85
Regent Rd. Blac 5C 88
Regent Rd. Chor 7D 174
Regent Rd. Chu 1M 141
Regent Rd. Ley 6J 153
Regent Rd. More 4M 21
Regent Rd. South 1E 186
Regent Rd. Walt D 4N 135
Regent Rd. E. Blac 5C 88
Regents Clo. Pleas 6D 138
Regent St. Bacup 5L 163
Regent St. B'brn 3M 139
Regent St. Brier 5F 104
Regent St. Bury 9L 201
Regent St. Cop 4A 194
Regent St. Has 4F 160
Regent St. Lanc 9J 23
Regent St. L'boro 9L 185
Regent St. L'rdge 3J 97
Regent St. Nels & Col 1J 105
Regent St. Pres 2J 135
Regent St. Ram 9F 180
Regent St. Todm 6K 165
Regent St. Wadd 8H 73
Regents Vw. B'brn 8M 119
Regentsway. Bam B 7A 136
Regents Way. Eux 4N 173
Regent Ter. Poul F 8L 63
Reginald St. Col 6M 85
Reigate. Chor 3H 175
Reiver Rd. Ley 4F 152
Renacres La. Hals 8L 187
Rendel St. Burn 2A 124
Rendsburg Way. Lanc 8K 23
(off St Nicholas Arch)
Renfrey Clo. Orm 4K 209
Rennell St. Roch 6D 204
Rennie Clo. Gars 6A 60
Rennie Ct. Lanc 2J 29
Rennie St. Burn 4G 125
Renshaw Dri. Bury 9A 202
Renshaw Dri. Walt D 6A 136
Renshaw St. Burn 9F 104
Renwick Av. Blac 1D 108
Repton Av. Blac 1C 88
Repton Av. More 4F 22
Repton Gro. Liv 8B 222
Reservoir Rd. Bncr 1G 60
Reservoir St. Burn 5D 124
Reservoir St. Dar 6N 157
Reservoir St. Roch 5F 204
Reta Dri. T Clev 9G 55
Retford Av. Roch 9E 204
Retford Clo. Bury 8J 201
Retford Rd. Liv 8L 223
Retford Wlk. Liv 8L 223
Revidge. 2K 139
Revidge Rd. B'brn 2J 139
Revoe. 8C 88
Rewe Clo. B'brn 8K 139
Rexington Bldgs. Burn 4A 124
Reynolds St. Burn 6C 124
Reynolds St. Lanc 7J 23
Rhine Clo. Tot 6E 200
Rhoda St. Nels 2K 105
Rhoden Rd. Ley 6F 152
Rhoden Rd. Osw 6K 141
Rhodes Av. B'brn 9L 119
Rhodes Av. Ross 8F 160
Rhodes Cres. Roch 9C 204
Rhodes St. Roch 2E 204
Rhode St. Tot 7E 200
Rhodesway. Hogh 6G 136
Rhosleigh Av. Bolt 9D 198
Rhuddlan Clo. Has 6G 160
Rhuddlan Gdns. T Clev 1K 63
Rhyddings St. Osw 4L 141
Rhyl Av. B'brn 1M 139
Rhyl St. Fltwd 8H 41
Ribbesford Rd. Wig 7M 221
Ribble Av. Burn 8G 104
Ribble Av. Dar 3M 157
Ribble Av. Frec 2M 131
Ribble Av. Gt Har 3L 121
Ribble Av. L'boro 8J 185
Ribble Av. Liv 9D 216
Ribble Av. South 2B 168
(in two parts)
Ribble Av. Whal 3G 100
Ribble Bank. Pen 2E 134
Ribble Bank St. Pres 1H 135
Ribble Brook Ho. Pres 8H 115
Ribble Bus. Pk. B'brn 9B 120
Ribble Clo. Frec 2M 131
Ribble Clo. Pen 4H 135
Ribble Clo. Pres 2H 135
Ribble Clo. Withn 6B 156
Ribble Ct. Ash R 8F 114
Ribble Ct. Pres 2G 135
Ribble Cres. K'ham 4N 111
Ribble Cres. Walt D 2M 135
Ribble Dri. Bury 5L 201
Ribble Dri. Hesk B 3C 150
Ribble Dri. W Brad 5K 73
Ribble Dri. Wig 4M 221
Ribble Gro. Heyw 9E 202
Ribble Hall. Pres 8J 115
(off Ashmoor St.)
Ribble Ho. B'brn 3N 139
(off Primrose Bank)
Ribble Ho. Pres 9N 115
(off Cliffe Ct.)
Ribble La. Chat 5A 74
Ribble Lodge. Lyth A 5N 129
(off West Beach)
Ribble Marshes Nature Reserve.
2G 149
Ribble Rd. Blac 6C 88
Ribble Rd. Fltwd 9F 40
Ribble Rd. Ley 7G 153
Ribble Rd. Stand 2L 213
Ribblesdale Av. Acc 9A 122
Ribblesdale Av. Clith 2L 81
Ribblesdale Av. Wilp 2A 120
Ribblesdale Clo. Blac 1G 108
Ribblesdale Clo. K'ham 3L 111
Ribblesdale Ct. More 3B 22
Ribblesdale Dri. Fort 2M 45
Ribblesdale Dri. Grims 1E 116
Ribblesdale Pl. Barfd 6J 85
Ribblesdale Pl. B'brn 3K 139
Ribblesdale Pl. Chor 7D 174
Ribblesdale Pl. Pres 2J 135
Ribblesdale Rd. Ribch 7F 98
Ribblesdale St. Burn 1F 124
Ribblesdale Vw. Chat 7D 74
Ribble St. Bacup 7L 163
Ribble St. B'brn 2M 139
Ribble St. Lyth A 2D 128
Ribble St. Pad 1J 123
Ribble St. Pres 1H 135
Ribble St. Roch 9B 204
Ribble Ter. Set 2N 35
(off Church St.)
Ribbleton. 8A 116
Ribbleton Av. Pres & Rib 8N 115
Ribbleton Dri. Acc 9A 122
Ribbleton Hall. 6B 116
Ribbleton Hall Cres. Rib 6B 116
Ribbleton Hall Dri. Rib 6B 116
Ribbleton La. Pres 9L 115
Ribbleton Pl. Pres 9L 115
Ribbleton St. Pres 9L 115
Ribble Vw. Clith 5A 74
Ribble Vw. Frec 2B 132
Ribble Vw. W Brad 5K 73
Ribble Vw. Clo. W'ton 2L 131
Ribble Way. Clith 3J 81
Ribby. 5J 111
Ribby Av. K'ham 4L 111
Ribby Av. W Grn 5G 111
Ribby Hall Holiday Village.
K'ham 5J 111
Ribby Pl. Ash R 8C 114
Ribby Pl. Blac 9H 89
Ribby Rd. K'ham 5L 111
Ribby Rd. W Grn 5G 111
Ribchester. 7E 98
Ribchester Av. Blac 9H 89
Ribchester Av. Burn 4H 125
Ribchester Rd. Clay D 8H 99
(in two parts)
Ribchester Rd. Hoth & Ribch 4N 97
Ribchester Rd. Lyth A 4C 130
Ribchester Roman Mus. 7F 98
Ribchester Way. Brier 6H 105
Rib, The. Augh 7F 206
(in two parts)
Rice Gro. Blac 2D 88
Richard Burch St. Bury 9L 201
Richard Hesketh Dri. Liv 8H 223
Richardson Clo. Frec 2A 132
Richardson St. Blac 6B 88
Richards Rd. Stand 1L 213
Richard's St. K'ham 3L 111
Richard St. Bacup 9K 145
Richard St. B'brn 4L 139
Richard St. Brier 5F 104
Richard St. Burn 4F 124
Richard St. Ram 7K 181
Richards Wlk. Lanc 7H 23
Richards Way. Lyth A 7E 108
Richards Way. T Clev 2F 62
Richmond Av. Acc 3A 142
Richmond Av. Barn 1L 77
Richmond Av. Burn 5K 125
Richmond Av. Burs 1C 210
Richmond Av. Has 6H 161
Richmond Av. Lanc 4K 23
Richmond Av. More 3D 22
Richmond Av. T Clev 1E 62
Richmond Av. W Grn 6G 111
Richmond Clo. Brins 7N 155
Richmond Clo. Roch 9F 204
Richmond Clo. Tot 7E 200
Richmond Ct. Blac 3B 88
Richmond Ct. Burs 1C 210
Richmond Ct. Ley 6E 152
Richmond Cres. B'brn 3E 140
Richmond Gro. Liv 8D 216
Richmond Hill. B'brn 3M 139
Richmond Hill. Wig 5M 221
Richmond Hill La. Fort 2A 46
Richmond Hill St. Acc 3N 141
Richmond Ho. Pres 1K 135
(off Pembroke Pl.)
Richmond Ind. Est. Acc 3A 142
Richmond M. Burs 1D 210
Richmond Pk. 9C 190
Richmond Pk. Dar 5A 158
Richmond Rd. Acc 4M 141
Richmond Rd. Barn 1L 77
Richmond Rd. Blac 3B 88
Richmond Rd. Chor 8G 174
Richmond Rd. E'ston 7F 172
Richmond Rd. Lyth A 2E 128
Richmond Rd. Nels 1G 104
Richmond Rd. South 3F 186
Richmonds Ct. Col 6B 86
(off New Ho. St.)
Richmond St. Acc 3N 141
Richmond St. Burn 4C 124
Richmond St. Hor 9C 196
Richmond St. Pres 1L 135
Richmond St. Todm 2M 165
Richmond Ter. B'brn 3M 139
Richmond Ter. Clith 4K 81
Richmond Ter. Dar 5A 158
Rickard Rd. Nels 4J 105
Rickerby Ct. South 6J 167
Ridd Cotts. Roch 5G 202
Ridding La. Whal 5G 101
(in two parts)
Riddings Av. Burn 3K 125
Riddings La. Whal 4J 101
Ridehalgh La. Brclf 7C 106
Ridehalgh St. Col 8M 85
Riders Ga. Bury 9D 202
Ridge. 7M 23
Ridge Av. Burn 2G 125
Ridge Bank. Todm 2L 165
Ridge Clo. South 1B 168
Ridge Ct. Burn 3G 125
Ridge Ct. L'rdge 2L 97
Ridgeford Gdns. Ful 4G 114
Ridge Gro. Hey 8L 21
Ridge La. Barfd 7D 84
Ridge La. Lanc 7L 23
(Bulk Rd.)
Ridge La. Lanc 7N 23
(Crag Rd.)
Ridgemont. Ful 3F 114
Ridge Rd. Burn 3F 124
Ridge Rd. Chor 7G 175
Ridge Rd. Todm 2L 165
Ridge Row. Burn 3H 125
Ridge Sq. Lanc 7M 23
Ridge St. Barn 2M 77
Ridge St. Lanc 7L 23
Ridge, The. Nels 4J 105
Ridgeway. Barfd 8G 85
Ridgeway. Gt Har 3H 121
Ridgeway. Pen 4H 135
Ridgeway Av. B'brn 8A 140
Ridgeway Ct. Lyth A 1G 129
Ridgeway Dri. Liv 7C 216
Ridgeway Dri. T Clev 3K 63
Ridgeways. Has 5H 161
Ridgeway, The. Fltwd 1D 54
Ridgeway, The. Nels 3K 105
Ridgmont Clo. Hor 9G 196
Ridgwood Av. Blac 5E 88
Riding Barn St. Chu 2M 141
Riding Ga. Bolt 7L 199
Riding Ga. M. Bolt 7L 199
Riding Head La. Ram 6L 181
Riding La. Hask 8K 207
Ridings Clo. Barn 2N 77
Ridings, The. Burn 1B 124
Ridings, The. South 3N 167
Ridings, The. Whit W 9E 154
Riding St. Adl 6J 195
Riding St. Burn 4C 124
Riding St. Pres 8J 115
Riding St. South 8H 167
Ridley La. Crost 2A 172
Ridley La. Liv 1C 222
Ridley La. Maw 3B 192
Ridley Rd. Ash R 7F 114
Ridley St. Blac 5D 88
Ridyard St. Wig 4N 221
Riesling Dri. Liv 5J 223
Rifle St. Has 5G 161
Rigby Clo. Frec 2A 132
Rigby Ct. Roch 4J 203
Rigby La. Bolt 7J 199
(in two parts)
Rigby Rd. Blac 7B 88
Rigby Rd. Liv 8A 216
Rigby St. Col 7N 85
Rigby St. Nels 2H 105
Rigby St. Pres 8M 115
Rigby's Yd. Wig 5L 221
Rigg La. Goos 6B 70
Rigg La. Quer 4F 30
Rigg St. Nels 2J 105
Riley Av. Lyth A 4F 128
Riley Clo. Ley 7K 153
Riley Ct. Lyth A 4F 128

Riley Green—Rothwell Clo.

Riley Green. 9N 137
Riley Grn. Switch Rd. Hogh 9N 137
Riley St. Acc 4A 142
Riley St. Bacup 2K 163
Riley St. Brier 5F 104
Riley St. Burn 5F 124
Riley St. Earby 2E 78
Rilldene Wlk. Roch 5H 203
Rimington. 4L 75
Rimington Av. Acc 5N 141
Rimington Av. Burn 4H 125
Rimington Av. Col 5N 85
Rimington Cvn. Pk. Rim 2A 76
Rimington Clo. B'brn 6N 139
Rimington La. D'ham & Rim 5H 75
Rimington Pl. Nels 1M 105
Rimmer Grn. South 4C 188
Rimmer's Av. South 8H 167
Rimmington Pl. Lyth A 2H 129
Ring Dyke Way. Lyth A 4N 129
Ringley Gro. Bolt 8E 198
Ring Lows La. Roch 1C 204
Ring O' Bells. 2F 210
Ring O'Bells La. Lath 2F 210
Rings St. Love 6M 143
Ringstone Cres. Nels 2M 105
Ringstones La. Lowg 1L 33
Ringtail Ct. Burs I 9N 189
Ringtail Pl. Burs I 9N 189
Ringtail Rd. Burs I 9M 189
Rington Av. Poul F 5H 63
Ringway. Chor 7C 174
Ring Way. Pres 1H 135
Ringway. T Clev 8E 54
Ringwood Av. Ram 1F 200
Ringwood Clo. Acc 8A 122
Ringwood Clo. Lyth A 5M 129
Ringwood Rd. Pres 7M 115
Rinkton. 5H 63
Ripley Clo. Liv 1D 222
Ripley Ct. Lanc 1K 29
(off Princess Av.)
Ripley Dri. Lyth A 2H 129
Ripley Dri. Wig 7M 221
Ripley St. Bolt 9H 199
Ripon Av. Lanc 4K 23
Ripon Clo. Gt Ecc 6A 66
Ripon Clo. South 2M 187
Ripon Clo. T Clev 7E 54
Ripon Hall Av. Ram 1G 200
Ripon Pl. Hey 1K 27
Ripon Rd. Blac 6D 88
Ripon Rd. Lyth A 3K 129
Ripon Rd. Osw 3J 141
Ripon St. B'brn 4A 140
Ripon St. Nels 3H 105
Ripon St. Pres 7G 115
Ripon Ter. Pres 8B 116
Risedale Dri. L'rdge 3K 97
Risedale Gro. B'brn 9H 139
Rise La. Todm 2K 165
(in two parts)
Rise, The. Bolt S 3M 15
Rise, The. Lanc 2J 29
Rise, The. Stand L 9M 213
Rishton. 8H 121
Rishton Golf Course. 1H 141
Rishton Rd. Clay M 6L 121
Rishton Rd. Rish 4B 120
Rishton St. Blac 6C 88
Rising Bridge. 9F 142
Rising Bri. Rd. Acc & Has 9F 142
Ritherham Av. T Clev 9D 54
Riverbank Dri. Bury 9J 201
River Clo. Liv 2B 214
Riverdale Clo. Stand L 8N 213
River Dri. Pad 1J 123
River Heights. Los H 8M 135
River Lea Gdns. Clith 3M 81
Rivermead. Miln 9L 204
Rivermead Ct. Gars 3N 59
Rivermead Dri. Gars 4N 59
Rivermeade. South 1K 187
River Pde. Pres 2G 135
River Pl. Garg 3M 53
(off South St.)
River Pl. Miln 7J 205
River Rd. T Clev 1L 63
Riversdale. Gigg 3N 35
Riversdale Clo. Liv 6K 223
Riversedge Rd. Ley 7F 152
Riversgate. Fltwd 9F 40
Riverside. Bam B 9A 136
Riverside. Clith 3H 81
Riverside. Garg 3M 53
(off Church St.)
Riverside. Gars 5N 59
Riverside. Pres 3H 135
(in two parts)
Riverside Av. Far M 3H 153
Riverside Cvn. Site. South 3J 169
Riverside Chalet Pk. Poul F 7C 64
Riverside Clo. Far M 3H 153
Riverside Clo. Halt 2B 24
Riverside Ct. Whitw 2A 184
Riverside Cres. Crost 4L 171
Riverside Dri. Hamb 1A 64
Riverside Dri. Roch 3E 204
Riverside Dri. S'seat 3G 201
Riverside Ind. Pk. Catt 9N 59
Riverside Leisure Cen. 1F 168
Riverside Mill. Col 7M 85
Riverside Pk. Ind. Est. Lan I 4M 23
Riverside Ter. Earby 3E 78
(off Cowgill St.)
Riverside Ter. Far M 3H 153
Riverside Wlk. Helm 8F 160
Riversleigh Av. Blac 1C 88
Riversleigh Av. Lyth A 5L 129
Riversleigh Clo. Bolt 9N 197
Riversmeade. Brom X 6J 199
Rivers St. Orr 5H 221
Riverstone Bri. L'boro 9K 185
River St. Bacup 6K 163
River St. B'brn 4N 139
River St. Col 7A 86
River St. Dar 5N 157
River St. Heyw 9H 203
River St. Lanc 7J 23
River St. Pres 1H 135
River St. Ram 8H 181
River St. Todm 2M 165
River St. Traw 8F 86
Riversway. Ash R 9N 113
Riversway. Blac 4F 88
Riversway. Garg 3L 53
Riversway. Lanc 6K 23
Riversway. Poul F 6M 63
Riversway Bus. Village.
Ash R 9D 114
Riversway Docklands. 9E 114
Riversway Dri. Lwr D 1N 157
Riversway Enterprise Workshops.
Ash R 9B 114
Riversway Managed Workshops.
Ash R 9C 114
Riversway Motor Pk. Ash R 9B 114
River Vw. Barfd 8H 85
(off River Way)
River Vw. Glas D 1C 36
River Vw. Tar 7E 150
Riverview Ct. More 5B 22
Riverview Fold. Low D 7E 38
River Way. Barfd 8H 85
River Way Clo. Los H 8N 135
River Wyre Cvn. Pk. Poul F 7B 64
Riviera Ct. Roch 3G 202
Rivington. 4A 196
Rivington Av. Adl 6K 195
Rivington Av. Blac 6C 62
Rivington Clo. Poul F 8K 63
Rivington Clo. South 2G 186
Rivington Clo. Tar 7D 150
Rivington Country Pk. 4B 196
Rivington Dri. Burs 1C 210
Rivington Dri. Uph 4F 220
Rivington Hall Clo. Ram 1H 201
Rivington Ho. Hor 9C 196
Rivington La. And 7M 195
Rivington La. Hor 4A 196
Rivington Pl. Cop 7N 193
Rivington Rd. Bel 1F 196
Rivington Rd. Chor 5G 174
Rivington St. B'brn 4B 140
Rivington St. Roch 4C 204
Roach Pl. Roch 5D 204
Roach Rd. Sam 1G 137
Roach Va. Roch 3F 204
Roading Brook Rd. Bolt 9A 200
Road La. Roch 1A 204
Roads Ford Av. Miln 6J 205
Robert Saville Ct. Roch 7M 203
(off Half Acre M.)
Roberts Ct. Ley 7H 153
Roberts Ct. War 4A 12
Roberts Pas. L'boro 4N 185
Roberts Pl. L'boro 2J 205
Roberts St. Chor 7E 174
Roberts St. Nels 2K 105
Roberts St. Raw 4M 161
Robert St. Acc 1B 142
Robert St. Barn 2M 77
Robert St. B'brn 5M 139
Robert St. Bolt 8L 199
Robert St. Col 6B 86
Robert St. Dar 5N 157
Robert St. Gt Har 3K 121
Robert St. Lanc 8K 23
Robert St. Osw 5K 141
Robert St. Ram 5H 181
Robert St. Roch 5D 204
Robert St. Waterf 5D 162
Robin Bank Rd. Dar 5A 158
Robin Clo. Char R 2N 193
Robin Cft. Horn 5B 18
Robin Hey. Ley 6E 152
Robin Hill Dri. Stand 2L 213
Robin Hill La. Stand 1L 213
Robin Hood. 9F 192
Robin Hood La. Wrigh 1E 212
Robin Ho. Pres 9H 115
(off Rodney St.)
Robin Ho. La. Brclf 7N 105
Robin La. Ben 6L 19
Robin La. Parb 8N 191
Robin La. Rim 3A 76
Robin Rd. Bury 2G 201
Robins Clo. Poul F 7G 62
Robins La. Poul F 6F 62
Robinson La. Brier 6D 104
Robinson St. B'brn 1A 140
Robinson St. Burn 9E 104
Robinson St. Chat 7D 74
Robinson St. Col 6N 85
Robinson St. Foul 2A 86
Robinson St. Ful 6G 115
Robinson St. Hor 9C 196
Robinson St. Roch 6D 204
Robin St. Pres 8N 115
Robinwood Ter. Todm 8H 147
Robraine. K Lon 6F 8
Robson St. Brier 4F 104
Robson Way. Blac 9G 62
Roby Mill. 9E 212
Roby Mill. Roby M 9E 212
Rochbury Clo. Roch 7K 203
Rochdale. 6D 204
Rochdale F.C. 5N 203
(Spotland)
Rochdale Golf Course. 5L 203
Rochdale Hornets R.L.F.C. 5N 203
(Spotland)
Rochdale Ind. Cen. Roch 7A 204
Rochdale Old Rd. Bury 9A 202
Rochdale Pioneers Mus. 5C 204
Rochdale Rd. Bacup 6L 163
Rochdale Rd. Ram 3K 181
Rochdale Rd. Todm & W'den 4K 165
Rochester Av. More 5C 22
Rochester Av. T Clev 8F 54
Rochester Clo. Bacup 9L 145
Rochester Dri. Burn 7G 105
Rochford Av. T Clev 2E 62
Roch Mills Cres. Roch 8N 203
Roch Mills Gdns. Roch 8N 203
Roch St. Roch 4E 204
Roch Valley Way. Roch 7N 203
Rock Bri. Fold. Ross 2C 162
Rock Brow. Thorn 7H 71
Rockburgh Cres. Walm B 2L 151
Rockcliffe. 6K 163
Rockcliffe Av. Bacup 6J 163
Rockcliffe Dri. Bacup 6J 163
Rockcliffe Rd. Bacup 6K 163
Rockcliffe St. B'brn 6M 139
Rockfield Gdns. Liv 9B 216
Rockfield Rd. Acc 2C 142
Rockfield St. B'brn 5M 139
Rock Fold. Eger 4F 198
Rock Hall Rd. Has 3G 161
Rockhaven Av. Hor 9D 196
Rockingham Ct. Liv 6L 223
Rockingham Rd. Blac 8D 62
Rock La. Burn 6F 124
Rock La. Liv 4E 222
Rock La. Toc 4H 157
Rock La. Traw 9F 86
(Church St.)
Rock La. Traw 8F 86
(Keighley Rd.)
Rockliffe. Ross 4M 161
Rockliffe La. Bacup 6L 163
Rockm' Jock. Cat 3G 25
(off Copy La.)
Rock Nook. L'boro 5N 185
Rock St. Clith 3L 81
Rock St. Has 4G 161
Rock St. Hor 9C 196
Rock St. Ram 7K 181
Rock St. T Clev 8H 55
Rock Ter. Arns 1F 4
Rock Ter. Eger 4F 198
Rock Ter. Ross 9M 143
Rock Ter. Todm 5K 165
Rock Ter. Wig 6J 193
Rock Vw. Mag 6F 222
Rock Vw. Ross 7C 162
Rock Villa Rd. Whit W 7E 154
Rockville. Barfd 6J 85
Rockville Av. T Clev 3F 62
Rockwater Bird Conservation Cen. 6N 125
Rockwood Clo. Burn 7J 105
Roddlesworth. 7F 156
Roddlesworth La. Withn 7E 156
Rodhill La. Bolt B 9G 51
Rodmell Clo. Brom X 6F 198
Rodney Av. Lyth A 8E 108
Rodney St. B'brn 5K 139
Rodney St. Pres 9H 115
Rodwell Wlk. Blac 2F 88
Roebuck Clo. B'brn 5L 139
Roebuck St. Ash R 7F 114
Roeburndale Cres. Hey 8M 21
Roeburndale Rd. Brook 5M 25
Roeburn Dri. More 6F 22
Roeburn Hall. Pres 9H 115
Roeburn Pl. Lanc 6J 23
Roedean Av. More 4F 22
Roedean Clo. Mag 9C 216
Roedean Clo. T Clev 1G 62
Roefield. Roch 5N 203
Roefield Ter. Roch 5N 203
Roe Greave Rd. Osw 5K 141
Roehampton Clo. T Clev 1G 62
Roe Hey Dri. Cop 3B 194
Roe La. South 6K 167
Roe Lee. 8N 119
Roe Lee Pk. B'brn 7N 119
Roe Pk. M. South 6K 167
Roe St. Roch 4N 203
Rogerley Clo. Lyth A 4N 129
Rogersfield. Lang 9B 100
Roleton Clo. Boot 6A 222
Rollesby Clo. Bury 8J 201
Rolleston Rd. B'brn 4J 139
Roman Cres. Cat 3H 25
Roman Rd. B'brn 6A 140
Roman Rd. Hodd 8E 158
Roman Rd. Pres 1L 135
Roman Rd. W. Ind. Est.
B'brn 1B 158
Roman Way. Clith 3M 81
Roman Way. K'ham 5A 112
Roman Way. Rib 3E 116
Roman Way. T Clev 2F 62
Roman Way Ind. Est. Rib 3E 116
Rome Av. Burn 5A 124
Romford Rd. Pres 7M 115
Romford St. Burn 2A 124
Romiley Dri. Skel 1K 219
Romney Av. Barfd 8H 85
Romney Av. Blac 9D 88
Romney Av. Burn 6C 124
Romney Av. Fltwd 1E 54
Romney St. Nels 3H 105
Romney Wlk. B'brn 4C 140
Romsey. Roch 5B 204
(off Spotland Rd.)
Romsey Av. Liv 1B 214
Romsey Gro. Wig 9N 221
Ronald St. B'brn 3C 140
Ronald St. Burn 4M 123
Ronaldsway. Ley 7G 152
Ronaldsway. Nels 9M 85
Ronaldsway. Pres 6M 115
Ronaldsway Clo. Bacup 6L 163
Ronaldway. Blac 1E 108
Ronbury Clo. Barfd 1G 105
Roney St. B'brn 3K 139
Ronwood Clo. Elsw 1L 91
Ronwood Ct. Ash R 9E 114
Roods La. Roch 4G 202
Roods, The. War 4B 12
Rookery Av. App B 4H 213
Rookery Clo. Chor 8C 174
Rookery Clo. Pen 6J 135
Rookery Dri. Pen 6J 135
Rookery Dri. Rainf 4L 225
Rookery La. Rainf 5L 225
Rookery Rd. Barn 2N 77
Rookery Rd. South 5L 167
Rook Hill Rd. Bacup 7F 162
Rook St. Barn 2M 77
Rook St. Col 6A 86
Rook St. Nels 1H 105
Rook St. Pres 7L 115
Rook St. Ram 8H 181
Rookswood Dri. Roch 9M 203
Rookwood. E'ston 8E 172
Rookwood Av. Chor 4E 174
Rookwood Av. T Clev 3D 62
Rooley Moor Rd. Bacup 8F 162
Rooley Moor Rd. Roch 5H 183
(in two parts)
Rooley St. Roch 4N 203
Rooley Ter. Roch 5N 203
Rooley Vw. Bacup 6J 163
Roomfield Ct. Todm 2L 165
(off Halifax Rd.)
Roomfield St. Todm 2L 165
Roosevelt Av. Lanc 9H 23
Roots La. Catf 7J 93
Ropefield Way. Roch 2B 204
Rope St. Roch 5C 204
Rope Wlk. Gars 5N 59
Rosary Av. Blac 9E 88
Roscoe Lowe Brow. Grim V 6M 195
Roseacre. Blac 4C 108
Roseacre Clo. Ross 3D 162
(off Foxhill Dri.)
Roseacre Clo. Ross 6B 162
(off Bacup Rd.)
Roseacre Dri. Elsw 1M 91
Rose Acre La. Yeal C 9B 6
Roseacre Pl. Ash R 8B 114
Roseacre Pl. Lyth A 9H 109
Roseacre Rd. Elsw 1M 91
Rose Av. Ash R 6F 114
Rose Av. Blac 8D 88
Rose Av. Burn 5C 124
Rose Av. L'boro 2J 205
Rose Av. Roch 3H 203
Rosebank. Clay M 6N 121
Rosebank. Lea 8N 113
Rosebank. Ram 5J 181
Rose Bank. Ross 4M 161
Rosebank Av. Blac 4C 108
Rose Bank Rd. Todm 2K 165
Rose Bank St. Bacup 4K 163
Rosebay Av. B'brn 8E 138
Rosebay Clo. Liv 9A 206
Roseberry Av. Cot 4B 114
Roseberry Clo. Ram 2H 201
Roseberry St. Burn 8F 104
Roseberry St. Todm 7F 146
Rosebery Av. Blac 3B 108
Rosebery Av. Lanc 2L 29
Rosebery Av. Lyth A 4H 129
Rosebery Av. More 4C 22
Rosebery St. South 8N 167
Rose Clo. Ley 5A 154
Rose Cotts. Brclf 8L 105
Rose Cotts. Whit W 1F 174
Rose Cres. Skel 2J 219
Rose Cres. South 2C 206
Rosecroft Clo. Orm 6K 209
Rosedale Av. Blac 8G 88
Rosedale Av. Bolt 8E 198
Rosedale Av. Hey 8M 21
Rosedale St. Ross 2L 161
(off Holmes, The)
Rosedene Clo. Cot 4B 114
Rose Dri. Rainf 5L 225
Rosefield Cres. Roch 6F 204
Rose Fold. Pen 4G 135
Rose Gdns. Hesk B 3C 150
Rosegarth. Slyne 1K 23
Rose Gro. Blac 2D 108
Rose Gro. Gal 2K 37
Rosegrove Cvn. Pk. Pre 7N 41
Rosegrove La. Burn 4M 123
Rose Hill. 5C 124
(Burnley)
Rosehill. 8C 158
(Darwen)
Rose Hill. 5M 221
(Wigan)
Rose Hill. B'brn 3A 140
Rose Hill. Eux 2M 173
Rose Hill. Ram 8G 181
Rose Hill. South 8K 167
Rose Hill Av. B'brn 4A 140
Rosehill Av. Burn 6C 124
Rosehill Av. Nels 1K 105
Rose Hill Av. Wig 5M 221
Rose Hill Clo. Brom X 6G 199
Rosehill Dri. Augh 1H 217
Rose Hill Dri. Brom X 6G 199
Rosehill Mt. Burn 5C 124
Rosehill Rd. Burn 5C 124
Rosehill Rd. Col 9L 85
Rose Hill Rd. Pleas 7D 138
Rose Hill St. Bacup 5K 163
Rose Hill St. Dar 7B 158
Rose Hill St. Ross 7M 143
Roseland Av. Brier 4G 104
Roseland Clo. Liv 7A 216
Rose La. Pres 6M 115
Rose Lea. Bolt 9L 199
Rose Lea. Ful 3N 115
Roselea Dri. South 2B 168
Roselyn Av. Blac 4C 108
Rosemary Av. Blac 4C 108
Rosemary Av. T Clev 9F 54
Rosemary Ct. Pen 6F 134
Rosemary Dri. L'boro 8J 185
Rosemary La. Btle 8L 93
Rosemary La. Down 7N 207
Rosemary La. Lanc 8K 23
Rosemeade Av. Los H 8L 135
Rosemede Av. Blac 8F 88
Rosemount. Bacup 3L 163
Rose Mt. Blac 5G 108
Rosemount. Ross 6D 162
Rosemount Av. Barn 1L 77
Rosemount Av. Burn 5C 124
Rosemount Av. Pre 8N 41
Rosendale Clo. Bacup 4M 163
Rosendale Cres. Bacup 4L 163
Rose Pl. Acc 4A 142
Rose Pl. Augh 1J 217
Rose Pl. Rainf 5L 225
Rose St. Acc 4A 142
Rose St. Bacup 5K 163
Rose St. B'brn 5M 139
Rose St. Dar 6B 158
Rose St. Far 4L 153
Rose St. More 2B 22
Rose St. Pres 1K 135
Rose St. Ross 5C 162
Rose St. Todm 2L 165
Rose Ter. Ash R 8E 114
Rose Va. St. Ross 5N 161
Roseway. Ash R 8D 114
Roseway. Blac 4C 108
Roseway. Brier 3E 104
Roseway. Lyth A 2H 129
Roseway. Poul F 8J 63
Rosewood. Cot 4B 114
Rosewood. Roch 4J 203
Rosewood Av. B'brn 8M 119
Rosewood Av. Burn 6C 124
Rosewood Av. Has 4H 161
Rosewood Av. High W 5E 136
Rosewood Av. Tot 8F 200
Rosewood Bus. Pk. B'brn 9M 119
Rosewood Clo. Chor 8F 174
Rosewood Clo. Lyth A 4L 129
Rosewood Clo. T Clev 2K 63
Rosewood Ct. Burn 4M 123
(off Owen St.)
Rosewood Dri. High W 5D 136
Rosewood Flats. South 4M 167
Roshaw. Grims 9F 96
Rosklyn Rd. Chor 7G 174
Rosley St. Traw 6E 86
Rossall Av. Liv 7C 222
Rossall Beach. 7D 54
Rossall Clo. Fltwd 4D 54
Rossall Clo. Hogh 4G 136
Rossall Clo. Pad 3J 123
Rossall Ct. Fltwd 1E 54
Rossall Ct. T Clev 7C 54
Rossall Dri. Ful 5F 114
Rossall Gdns. T Clev 8D 54
Rossall Ga. Fltwd 4C 54
Rossall Grange La. Fltwd 1D 54
Rossall La. Fltwd 5D 54
Rossall Promenade. T Clev 7C 54
Rossall Rd. Blac 3D 88
Rossall Rd. Chor 5G 174
Rossall Rd. Ful 5F 114
Rossall Rd. Lanc 6G 23
Rossall Rd. Lyth A 4J 129
Rossall Rd. Roch 3D 204
Rossall Rd. T Clev 1D 62
Rossall St. Ash R 8F 114
Rossall Ter. B'brn 7M 139
Rossendale Av. Burn 7B 124
Rossendale Av. Lanc 7M 29
Rossendale Av. More 2C 22
Rossendale Av. N. T Clev 1H 63
Rossendale Av. S. T Clev 2H 63
Rossendale Golf Course. 8G 161
Rossendale Mus. 5K 161
Rossendale Rd. Burn 4N 123
Rossendale Rd. Lyth A 1G 128
Rossendale Rd. Ind. Est.
Burn 5N 123
Rossendale Valley. 6J 163
Rosser Ct. Nels 2J 105
Rosset Clo. Wig 9N 221
Rossett Av. Blac 9J 89
Rossetti Av. Burn 7D 124
Rossington Av. Blac 6E 62
Rosslyn Av. Liv 2A 222
Rosslyn Av. Pre 7N 41
Rosslyn Cres. Pre 8N 41
Rosslyn Cres. E. Pre 8A 42
Rossmere Av. Roch 7N 203
Rossmoyne Rd. Lanc 3K 29
Ross St. Brier 5F 104
Ross St. Dar 9A 158
Rostle Top Rd. Earby 3D 78
Rostrevor Clo. Ley 6E 152
Rostron Rd. Ram 8G 181
Rostron's Bldgs. Ross 6B 162
(off Bacup Rd.)
Rothay Av. Fltwd 2D 54
Rothbury Pl. Lyth A 4B 130
Rotherwick Av. Chor 7D 174
Rothesay Cres. Hey 2J 27
Rothesay Rd. B'brn 6C 140
Rothesay Rd. Brier 4G 104
Rothesay Rd. Hey 2J 27
Rothesay Ter. Roch 9F 204
Rothley Av. South 9A 186
Rothwell Av. Acc 4B 142
Rothwell Clo. Orm 7J 209

Rothwell Ct.—St Hubert's St.

Rothwell Ct. Ley 5K 153
Rothwell Cres. Rib 5B 116
Rothwell Dri. Augh 1G 217
Rothwell Dri. Fltwd 1D 54
Rothwell Dri. South 8A 186
Rothwell Lodge. Rib 5B 116
(off Grange Av.)
Rothwell Rd. And 6K 195
Rothwell St. Ram 8G 181
Rotten Row. Brook 2K 25
Rotten Row. South 9E 166
Rough Bank. Whitw 9N 183
Rough Hey. Acc 6M 141
Rough Hey La. C'den 9M 127
Rough Hey La. Todm 6J 165
Rough Hey Pl. Ful 2D 116
Rough Hey Rd. Grims 2D 116
Rough Heys La. Blac 2E 108
Rough Hey Wlk. Roch 7E 204
Rough Hill La. Bury 9B 202
Rough La. Form 3D 206
Rough Lea Rd. T Clev 1C 62
Roughlee. 6F 84
Roughlee Gro. Burn 4H 125
Rough Lee Rd. Acc 4B 142
Roughlee St. Barfd 9H 85
Roughlee Ter. Dunn 4N 143
Rough Side La. Todm 3M 165
Roughwood Dri. Liv 7L 223
Round Acre. Pen 7K 135
Round Acre. Sam 1N 137
Roundell Rd. Barn 1N 77
Roundell Ter. Barn 1N 77
(off Roundell Rd.)
Roundel St. Burn 8F 104
Roundhay. Blac 1G 108
Roundhill. 1E 160
Roundhill La. Has 1E 160
Roundhill Pl. Cliv 8J 125
Roundhill Rd. Acc & Has 9C 142
Roundhill Vw. Acc 8F 142
Round Meade, The. Liv 9A 216
Round Mdw. Ley 6F 152
Roundway. Fltwd 4C 54
Roundway Down. Ful 1F 114
Round Wood. Pen 1E 134
Roundwood Av. Burn 6E 104
Rouse St. Roch 9N 203
Rowan Av. Osw 6K 141
Rowan Av. Rib 5C 116
Rowan Bank. Halt 1B 24
Rowan Clo. B'brn 8A 120
Rowan Clo. Gars 6A 60
Rowan Clo. Pen 5E 134
Rowan Clo. Roch 2L 203
Rowan Cft. Clay W 6C 154
Rowan Dri. Liv 7H 223
Rowangate. Ful 2M 115
Rowan Gro. Burn 3G 124
Rowan Gro. Chor 3E 174
Rowan La. Skel 8M 211
Rowan Pl. Lanc 8H 23
Rowans St. Bury 9H 201
Rowans, The. Augh 4F 216
Rowans, The. Poul F 9H 63
Rowan Tree Clo. Acc 1D 142
Rowberrow Clo. Ful 3N 115
Rowen Pk. B'brn 9J 119
Rowland Av. Nels 2L 105
Rowland Clo. T Clev 1F 62
Rowland Ct. Roch 7E 204
Rowland La. T Clev 1F 62
Rowlands. 3J 201
Rowlands Rd. Bury 3H 201
Rowland St. Acc 3N 141
Rowland St. Roch 7E 204
Rowntree Av. Fltwd 1F 54
Roworth Clo. Walt D 5A 136
Rowsley Rd. Lyth A 1D 128
Row, The. 7J 5
Row, The. H'pey 3M 175
Row, The. Silv 7J 5
Rowton Heath. Ful 2F 114
Rowton St. Bolt 9H 199
Roxburgh Rd. Blac 3G 108
Roxton Clo. Hor 8C 196
Royal Av. Blac 7E 88
Royal Av. Bury 8L 201
Royal Av. Ful 3H 115
Royal Av. K'ham 5N 111
Royal Av. Ley 8H 153
Royal Bank Rd. Blac 7E 88
Royal Beach Ct. Lyth A 1D 128
Royal Birkdale Golf Course.
4D 186
Royal Clo. Liv 2A 214
Royal Ct. Brclf 7K 105
Royal Cres. Liv 2A 214
Royal Fold. Hey 9K 21
Royal Lytham St Anne's Golf Course.
3G 129
Royal Oak. 7L 217
Royal Oak Av. B'brn 8M 119
Royal Oak Mdw. Horn 6C 18
Royal Pennine Trad. Est.
Roch 9A 204
Royal Pl. Lyth A 9J 109
Royal Rd. More 2C 22
Royal St. Roch 2F 204
Royal Ter. South 7G 167
Royal Troon Ct. K'ham 5M 111
Royalty Av. New L 8D 134
Royalty Gdns. New L 8C 134
Royalty La. New L 8C 134
Royal Umpire Touring Pk.
Crost 3B 172
Royd La. Todm 9L 147
Royd Mills Ind. Pk. Hey 2L 27
Royd Rd. Todm 9K 147
Royds Av. Acc 4B 142
Royds Av. Hey 6L 21
Royds Clo. Tot 8F 200
Royds Gro. Hey 7L 21
Royds Pl. Roch 8D 204
Royds Rd. Bacup 8E 162
Royds St. Acc 3B 142
Royds St. L'boro 9M 185
Royds St. Lyth A 3E 128
Royds St. Tot 6E 200
Royds St. W. Roch 8D 204
Royd St. Bury 9B 202
Royd St. Todm 1K 165
Roylelands Bungalows. Roch 9N 203
Roylen Av. Poul F 6H 63
Royle Rd. Burn 2D 124
(in three parts)
Royle Rd. Chor 6D 174
Royles Brook Clo. T Clev 9H 55
Royles Ct. T Clev 1H 63
Royle St. Blac 9B 88
Roynton Rd. Hor 7C 196
Royshaw Av. B'brn 9M 119
Royshaw Clo. B'brn 9M 119
Royston Clo. G'mnt 4E 200
Royston Rd. Poul F 6M 63
Roy St. Todm 7D 146
Royton Dri. Whit W 1E 174
Ruby St. B'brn 7N 119
Ruby St. Bury 2H 201
Ruby St. Pas. Roch 7B 204
Ruddington Rd. South 2L 187
Rudd St. Has 4F 160
Rudgwick Dri. Bury 6H 201
Rudman St. Roch 3B 204
Rudyard Dri. Dar 7D 158
Rudyard Pl. Blac 3F 88
Rudyard Pl. Lyth A 9E 108
Ruff La. Orm & W'head 8L 209
Rufford. 1G 191
Rufford Av. Liv 8D 216
Rufford Av. Roch 9A 204
Rufford Clo. Chor 2D 194
Rufford Clo. Liv 9E 222
Rufford Dri. South 1E 168
Rufford Old Hall. 9G 171
Rufford Pk. La. Ruf 9E 170
Rufford Rd. Bis 3J 191
Rufford Rd. Lyth A 3J 129
Rufford Rd. Rainf 3K 225
Rufford Rd. South 3B 168
Rufus St. Pres 7M 115
Rugby Av. Acc 9B 122
Rugby Dri. Liv 9D 222
Rugby Dri. Orr 3J 221
Rugby Rd. Roch 4D 204
Rugby Rd. Ind. Est. Roch 4D 204
Rugby St. Blac 9D 88
Ruins. 9L 199
Ruins La. Bolt 9L 199
Rumley's Fold. Burn 7C 124
Runcorn Av. Blac 9F 62
Rundle Rd. Ful 6G 115
Runley Mill. Set 4N 35
Runnell Vs. Blac 2G 109
Runnel, The. Hals 2A 208
Runnymede Av. T Clev 1D 62
Runshaw Av. App B 4H 213
Runshaw Hall. Eux 1J 173
Runshaw Hall La. Eux 1K 173
Runshaw La. Eux 4G 173
Runshaw Moor. 2J 173
Rupert St. Carn 7A 12
Rupert St. Nels 3G 105
Rupert St. Roch 4N 203
Rush Bed. 1M 161
Rushbed Dri. Ross 1M 161
Rushden Rd. Liv 9M 223
Rushes Farm Clo. Osw 5J 141
Rushey Clo. Raw 1M 161
Rushey Fld. Brom X 5F 198
Rushey Hey Rd. Liv 8K 223
Rushford Gro. Bolt 9F 198
Rushlake Gdns. Roch 5J 203
Rushley Dri. Hest B 8H 15
Rushley Way. Hest B 8H 15
Rushmere Dri. Bury 8H 201
Rushton Av. Earby 3E 78
Rushton Clo. Nels 9M 85
Rushton St. Bacup 7J 163
Rushton St. Barfd 8H 85
Rushton St. Gt Har 5H 121
Rushworth St. Burn 9F 104
Rushworth St. E. Burn 9F 104
Rushy Fld. Clay M 4M 121
Rushy Hey. Los H 8K 135
Rushy Hill Vw. Roch 4N 203
Ruskin Av. Blac 8B 88
Ruskin Av. Col 5A 86
Ruskin Av. Ley 6K 153
Ruskin Av. Osw 3J 141
Ruskin Av. Pad 2K 123
Ruskin Av. T Clev 9G 54
Ruskin Clo. Tar 9D 150
Ruskin Ct. K Lon 6F 8
Ruskin Dri. More 2E 22
Ruskin Gro. Bolt S 4L 15
Ruskin Gro. Hap 5H 123
Ruskin Pl. Nels 9K 85
Ruskin Rd. Frec 2N 131
Ruskin Rd. Lanc 5K 23
Ruskin St. Burn 8E 104
Ruskin St. Pres 2L 135
Rusland Av. Blac 9K 89
Rusland Dri. Hogh 4G 136
Rusland Gdns. More 4B 22
Russell Av. Col 5B 86
Russell Av. Ley 7M 153
Russell Av. Pres 8C 116
Russell Av. South 7N 167
Russell Av. T Clev 3D 62
Russell Ct. Burn 5F 124
Russell Ct. Lyth A 2F 128
Russell Dri. More 4F 22
Russell Pl. Gt Har 4H 121
Russell Rd. Carn 9B 12
Russell Rd. South 7N 167
Russell Sq. Chor 5F 174
Russell Sq. W. Chor 5F 174
Russell St. Acc 3B 142
Russell St. Bacup 3K 163
Russell St. B'brn 5M 139
Russell St. Bury 9L 201
Russell St. Lanc 8K 23
Russell St. Nels 2H 105
Russell St. Todm 2M 165
Russell Ter. Pad 2J 123
Russell Wlk. Bolt 9E 198
Russia St. Acc 2M 141
Rutherford Pl. Blac 5B 108
Rutherford Rd. Mag 3D 222
Ruthin Clo. B'brn 1M 139
Ruthin Dri. T Clev 1K 63
Ruth St. Bury 9L 201
Ruth St. Ram 4J 181
Ruth St. Whitw 5N 183
Rutland. Roch 7B 204
Rutland Av. B'brn 4E 140
Rutland Av. Burn 3M 123
Rutland Av. Fltwd 1F 54
Rutland Av. Frec 1A 132
Rutland Av. Lanc 3L 29
Rutland Av. Poul F 8J 63
Rutland Av. T Clev 9E 54
Rutland Av. Walt D 5N 135
Rutland Clo. Clay M 6M 121
Rutland Clo. Gars 4M 59
Rutland Ct. Ans 3K 129
Rutland Cres. Orm 5J 209
Rutland Ga. Blac 3B 88
Rutland Pl. Pad 2J 123
Rutland Rd. Lyth A 3K 129
Rutland Rd. South 9K 167
Rutland St. Acc 3M 141
Rutland St. B'brn 5J 139
Rutland St. Col 6C 86
Rutland St. Nels 1J 105
Rutland St. Pres 9M 115
Rutland Wlk. Has 7F 160
Ryan Clo. Ley 6H 153
Ryburn Av. B'brn 1H 139
Ryburn Av. Blac 9E 88
Ryburn Rd. Orm 9J 209
Ryburn Sq. Roch 7J 203
Rycliffe St. Pad 9H 103
Rydal Av. Blac 7C 88
Rydal Av. Dar 7A 158
Rydal Av. Fltwd 9E 40
Rydal Av. Frec 2L 131
Rydal Av. Orr 4J 221
Rydal Av. Pen 5F 134
Rydal Av. Poul F 8K 63
Rydal Av. T Clev 2H 63
Rydal Av. Walt D 7N 135
Rydal Clo. Acc 8C 122
Rydal Clo. Ain 8E 222
Rydal Clo. Burn 6G 104
Rydal Clo. Ful 5M 115
Rydal Clo. Kirkby 6J 223
Rydal Clo. Pad 9H 103
Rydal Ct. More 3B 22
Rydal Gro. Hey 6L 21
Rydal Gro. Kno S 7M 41
Rydal Lodge. Blac 8E 88
Rydal Mt. Belt 1F 158
Rydal Pl. Chor 8D 174
Rydal Pl. Col 6D 86
Rydal Rd. B'brn 1A 140
Rydal Rd. Bolt S 5K 15
Rydal Rd. Hamb 1B 64
Rydal Rd. Has 7H 161
Rydal Rd. Hey 6L 21
Rydal Rd. Lanc 8L 23
Rydal Rd. Lyth A 9E 108
Rydal Rd. Pres 7N 115
Rydal St. Burn 8E 104
Rydal Wlk. Wig 4L 221
Ryddingwood. Pen 2E 134
Ryde Clo. Has 6H 161
Ryden Av. Ley 6M 153
Ryden Av. T Clev 9D 54
Ryden Rd. B'brn 3L 119
Ryder Clo. Augh 1H 217
Ryder Cres. Augh 2H 217
Ryder Cres. South 5E 186
Ryding Clo. Far M 4H 153
Rydinge, The. Liv 6A 206
Ryding's La. South 6J 149
Rydings La. Ward 8D 184
Rydings Rd. Roch 1E 204
Rydings, The. Lang 1A 120
Ryeburn Dri. Bolt 8H 199
Ryecroft. H'pey 8J 155
Ryecroft Av. Hamb 2B 64
Ryecroft Av. Tot 7E 200
Ryecroft La. Bel 9K 177
Ryecroft Pl. Hamb 1B 64
Ryefield. H'pey 8H 155
Ryefield Av. Has 5G 160
Ryefield Av. Pen 6G 134
Ryefield Av. W. Has 5F 160
Ryefield Pl. Has 5G 160
Ryefields. Roch 1G 205
Rye Gdns. B'brn 1L 157
Ryeground La. Liv 7A 206
Rye Gro. Pad 2J 123
Rye Hey Rd. Liv 8K 223
Ryeheys Rd. Lyth A 9E 108
Ryelands Clo. Roch 9E 204
Ryelands Cres. Ash R 9B 114
Ryelands Rd. Lanc 6J 23
Rye Moss La. Liv 3G 215
Rye St. Pres 8K 115
Ryknild Way. More 5F 22
Ryland Av. Poul F 8J 63
Rylands Rd. Chor 7D 174
Rylands St. Burn 9F 104
Ryldon Pl. Blac 8G 88
Rylstone Dri. Barn 2L 77
Rylstone Dri. Hey 8L 21
Rysdale Cres. More 4C 22
Ryson Av. Blac 9F 88
Ryton Rd. Liv 9J 223

S

Sabden. 3E 102
Sabden Brook Ct. Sab 3F 102
Sabden Clo. Bury 6L 201
Sabden Pl. Lyth A 1J 129
Sabden Rd. High 4L 103
Sabden Rd. Pad & High 4G 102
Sabden Rd. Whal 6M 101
Sabden Wlk. B'brn 6N 139
Saccary La. Mel 4H 119
Sackville Av. Blac 3C 108
Sackville Gdns. Brier 5E 104
Sackville St. Barn 3M 77
Sackville St. Brier 5F 104
Sackville St. Burn 4D 124
Sackville St. Chor 7G 174
Sackville St. Nels 4K 105
Sackville St. Todm 2L 165
Saddleback Cres. Wig 5L 221
Saddleback Rd. Wig 4L 221
Saddlers M. Clith 3L 81
Saddlers Nook La. H Big 8D 8
Sadler St. Chu 3L 141
Saer Clo. Fltwd 1D 54
Saffron Clo. Barfd 1G 104
Sagar Dri. Frec 2M 131
Sagar Fold. Augh 3J 217
Sagar Holme Ter. Ross 2C 162
Sagar St. E'ston 8F 172
Sagar St. Nels 2J 105
Sage Ct. Pen 6F 134
Sage La. Pres 6L 115
Sahara Fold. B'brn 1A 140
(off Warmden Gdns.)
St Aidans Av. B'brn 7K 139
(in two parts)
St Aidan's Av. Dar 7B 158
St Aidan's Clo. B'brn 7K 139
St Aidan's Clo. Roch 8N 203
St Aidan's Pk. Bam B 6A 136
St Aidan's Rd. Bam B 6A 136
St Alban's Ct. B'brn 2N 139
St Albans Ct. Roch 7B 204
St Albans Ho. Roch 7B 204
(off St Albans St.)
St Albans Pl. Chor 9F 174
St Alban's Rd. Blac 6D 88
St Alban's Rd. Dar 4M 157
St Albans Rd. Lyth A 1F 128
St Albans Rd. More 2F 22
St Albans Rd. Rish 9G 120
St Albans St. Roch 7B 204
St Alban's Ter. Roch 7B 204
St Ambrose Ter. Ley 5L 153
St Andrew's Av. Ash R 7D 114
St Andrew's Av. T Clev 1D 62
St Andrews Clo. Col 8N 85
St Andrews Clo. Eux 2N 173
St Andrew's Clo. Ley 8K 153
St Andrews Clo. Osw 4K 141
St Andrews Clo. Ram 9H 181
St Andrews Ct. Lyth A 1D 128
St Andrews Ct. Osw 5K 141
St Andrew's Ct. South 8H 167
St Andrews Gro. More 2D 22
St Andrew's Pl. B'brn 2L 139
St Andrew's Pl. South 8H 167
St Andrews Rd. Old L 4C 100
St Andrew's Rd. Pres 7K 115
St Andrew's Rd. N. Lyth A 9D 108
St Andrew's Rd. S. Lyth A 2E 128
St Andrew's St. B'brn 2L 139
St Andrew's St. Burn 9F 104
St Andrews Vw. Liv 4K 223
St Andrews Way. Ley 7K 153
St Anne's. 2E 128
St Anne's Av. More 2F 22
St Annes Clo. B'brn 5N 139
St Anne's Clo. Brook 3K 25
St Anne's Clo. Chu 3L 141
(off Blackpool St.)
St Anne's Clo. Liv 6A 206
St Anne's Ct. Blac 9C 88
St Annes Ct. Shev 7J 213
St Anne's Cres. Ross 4D 162
St Anne's Dri. Fence 3B 104
St Anne's Dri. Shev 7K 213
St Annes M. W. Tot 6E 200
St Anne's Old Links Golf Course.
7C 108
St Anne's Path. Liv 6A 206
St Anne's Pl. Lanc 8K 23
(off Moor La.)
St Anne's Rd. Blac 9C 88
St Anne's Rd. Chor 7G 174
St Annes Rd. Gt Ecc 6A 66
St Anne's Rd. Hor 9D 196
St Anne's Rd. Ley 4M 153
St Anne's Rd. Orm 8J 209
St Anne's Rd. South 2M 167
St Anne's Rd. E. Lyth A 1E 128
St Anne's Rd. W. Lyth A 2D 128
St Anne's St. Bury 9L 201
St Anne's St. Pad 2H 123
St Anne's St. Pres 7K 115
St Anne's Way. Burn 3B 104
St Ann's Ct. Clith 3H 81
St Ann's Rd. Roch 5F 204
St Anns Sq. Clith 3J 81
St Ann's St. B'brn 5M 139
St Anthony's Clo. Ful 5F 114
St Anthony's Cres. Ful 5F 114
St Anthony's Dri. Ful 5F 114
St Anthony's Pl. Blac 3C 88
St Anthony's Pl. K'ham 5M 111
St Anthony's Rd. Pres 7K 115
St Austell Dri. G'mnt 3E 200
St Austell Pl. Carn 1N 15
St Austin's Pl. Pres 1K 135
St Austin's Rd. Pres 1K 135
St Barnabas Dri. L'boro 8K 185
St Barnabas Pl. Pres 8K 115
St Barnabas St. B'brn 3K 139
St Barnabas St. Dar 9B 158
St Bede's Av. Blac 9B 88
St Bedes Clo. Orm 9J 209
St Bede's Pk. Dar 2M 157
St Bee's Clo. B'brn 7N 139
St Benet's Clo. Bam B 7N 135
St Bernard Av. Blac 3F 88
St Bernard's Rd. Kno S 8L 41
St Brides Clo. Hor 9B 196
St Catherine Clo. Blac 1H 89
St Catherines Clo. Ley 5M 153
St Catherines Ct. Lanc 8K 23
(off Moor La.)
St Catherine's Dri. Ful 5F 114
St Cecilia St. Gt Har 4K 121
(in two parts)
St Celia's Way. More 2E 22
St Chad's Av. Chat 7C 74
St Chads Clo. Poul F 9K 63
St Chad's Clo. Roch 6C 204
St Chads Ct. Roch 6C 204
St Chad's Dri. Kirkby & Liv 8K 223
St Chad's Dri. Lanc 5H 23
St Chads Pde. Liv 8K 223
St Chad's Rd. Blac 8B 88
St Chad's Rd. Pres 8M 115
St Charles Rd. Rish 8G 121
St Christine's Av. Far 3M 153
St Christopher Ct. Stand L 8M 213
St Christopher's Rd. Pres 7K 115
St Christopher's Way. More 2D 22
St Clair Dri. South 5N 167
St Clair Rd. G'mnt 2E 200
St Clares Av. Ful 3K 115
St Clement's Av. Blac 5E 88
St Clements Av. Far 4M 153
St Clements Clo. B'brn 4B 140
St Clements Ct. Barfd 8H 85
St Clement St. B'brn 3B 140
St Crispin Way. Has 5F 160
St Cuthbert's Clo. Dar 4M 157
St Cuthbert's Clo. Ful 6G 114
St Cuthbert's Clo. Lyth A 5N 129
St Cuthbert's Clo. South 4N 167
St Cuthberts Rd. Los H 7K 135
St Cuthbert's Rd. Pres 7K 115
St Cuthbert's Rd. South 4N 167
St Cuthbert St. Burn 8F 104
St David's Av. B'brn 9F 138
St David's Av. T Clev 1D 62
St David's Gro. Lyth A 9D 108
St David's Rd. Ley 5M 153
St David's Rd. Pres 7K 115
St David's Rd. N. Lyth A 8D 108
St David's Rd. S. Lyth A 2E 128
St David's Wood. Acc 1C 142
St Denys Cft. Clith 2L 81
St Edmund Hall Clo. Ram 1H 201
St Edmund's Rd. Blac 9E 88
St Edmund St. Gt Har 4K 121
St Frances Clo. B'brn 5N 139
St Francis Clo. Ful 2K 115
St Francis Rd. B'brn 6H 139
St Gabriel Clo. Roby M 9E 212
St Gabriel's Av. B'brn 6N 119
St George Ct. Blac 4D 88
St George's Av. B'brn 7J 139
St George's Av. Lyth A 1D 128
St George's Av. T Clev 2D 62
St Georges Clo. Col 8N 85
St Georges Ct. Chor 7F 174
(off Halliwell St.)
St George's La. Lyth A 2D 128
St George's La. T Clev 1D 62
St Georges Pk. K'ham 3K 111
St George's Pl. South 7H 167
St George's Quay. Lanc 7H 23
St George's Rd. Blac 3C 108
St George's Rd. H'twn 6A 214
St George's Rd. Lyth A 2D 128
St George's Rd. Nels 3K 105
St George's Rd. Pres 7J 115
St George's Rd. Roch 5K 203
St George's Shop. Cen. Pres 1J 135
St George's Sq. Lyth A 1D 128
St Georges St. Chor 7E 174
St Georges Ter. Dar 5N 157
(off Harwood St.)
St Georges Ter. Ross 9E 162
St Gerrard's Rd. Los H 7K 135
St Giles St. Pad 9H 103
St Giles Ter. Pad 9H 103
(off East St.)
St Gregory Rd. Pres 7L 115
St Gregory's Pl. Chor 9E 174
St Helen's Clo. Chur 1L 67
St Helens Clo. Osw 5M 141
St Helen's Ct. T Clev 9D 54
St Helens Rd. Orm 7L 209
St Helen's Rd. Over 7B 28
St Helens Rd. Rainf 8M 225
St Helen's Rd. Whit W 6E 154
St Helens Well. Tar 1F 170
St Helier Clo. B'brn 8J 139
St Helier's Pl. Brtn 3D 94
St Heliers Rd. Blac 8C 88
St Hilda's Clo. Chor 1E 194
St Hilda's Rd. Lyth A 9D 108
St Hilda's Way. Chor 1E 194
St Hubert's Rd. Gt Har 5J 121
St Hubert's St. Gt Har 4K 121

St Ignatius Pl.—Satinwood Cres.

St Ignatius Pl. *Pres* 9K **115**
St Ignatius Sq. *Pres* 9K **115**
St Ives Av. *Blac* 7D **88**
St Ives Av. *Frec* 2M **131**
St Ives Cres. *Pres* 5D **114**
St Ives Rd. *B'brn* 4D **140**
St James Av. *Bury* 9G **201**
St James Clo. *Chu* 1L **141**
St James Clo. *Has* 4G **160**
St James Clo. *Los H* 8L **135**
St James Clo. *W'head* 9A **210**
St James Ct. *B'brn* 1M **139**
St James Ct. *Hey* 9K **21**
St James Ct. Lanc 8J 23
(off Wheatfield St.)
St James Ct. *Los H* 8L **135**
St James Ct. *Stand* 2N **213**
St James Cres. *Dar* 5B **158**
St James Gdns. *Ley* 7D **152**
St James Lodge. *Ley* 7E **152**
St James Lodge. *Lyth A* 3G **128**
St James M. *Chu* 1L **141**
St James Pl. *Pad* 1J **123**
St James Rd. Barn 2M 77
(off Bessie St.)
St James Rd. *Blac* 3C **108**
St James' Rd. *Chu* 1L **141**
St James Rd. *Orr* 7G **220**
St James' Rd. *Pres* 7J **115**
St James Row. *Ross* 4M **161**
St James's Dri. *Burt* 5G **7**
St James's La. Burn 3E 124
(off St James Row)
St James's Pl. B'brn 1M 139
(off St James's Rd.)
St James's Pl. *Chor* 7G **175**
St James Sq. *Bacup* 4K **163**
St James' Sq. *Barn* 2M **77**
St James's Rd. *B'brn* 1M **139**
St James's Row. *Burn* 3E **124**
St James's St. *Burn* 3D **124**
(in two parts)
St James's St. *Chor* 7G **175**
St James St. *Acc* 3A **142**
St James St. *Bacup* 5K **163**
St James St. *B'brn* 7K **139**
St James St. *Brier* 5F **104**
St James St. *Clith* 4L **81**
St James St. *Miln* 7J **205**
St James St. *Raw* 4M **161**
St James St. *South* 9H **167**
St James' St. *Waterf* 7C **162**
St James Ter. *Sam* 1N **137**
St John Av. *Fltwd* 2D **54**
St John's. *B'brn* 2L **139**
St John's Av. *Dar* 7B **158**
St John's Av. *Hey* 6M **21**
St John's Av. *K'ham* 5L **111**
St Johns Av. *Pil* 8H **43**
St John's Av. *Poul F* 6L **63**
St John's Av. *Silv* 8G **5**
St Johns Av. *T Clev* 2K **63**
St John's Clo. *Acc* 6D **142**
St John's Clo. *Craw* 9M **143**
St John's Clo. *Read* 8C **102**
St John's Clo. *Whit W* 8D **154**
St John's Ct. *Bacup* 4K **163**
St Johns Ct. *Brough* 9J **95**
St Johns Ct. Burn 3A 124
(off Gannow La.)
St John's Ct. *Roch* 7E **204**
St John's Dri. *Roch* 7E **204**
St John's Grn. *Ley* 6H **153**
St John's Gro. *Hey* 6M **21**
St John's Gro. *Silv* 8G **5**
St Johns M. *Lanc* 7K **23**
St Johns Pl. *Nels* 2L **105**
St John's Pl. *Pres* 1K **135**
St John's Rd. *Burn* 3A **124**
St John's Rd. *Hey* 6L **21**
St John's Rd. *Pad* 3H **123**
St John's Rd. *South* 4F **186**
St John's Rd. *Walt D* 3N **135**
St Johns Row. *L'clif* 2N **35**
St John's Shop. Cen. Pres 9K 115
(off Lancaster Rd.)
St John's St. *Dar* 7B **158**
St John's St. *Gt Har* 5J **121**
St John's St. *Lyth A* 5B **130**
St John's St. *Ross* 7D **162**
St John's Ter. *More* 6C **22**
St John St. *Bacup* 4K **163**
St John St. *Hor* 9C **196**
St John St. *Wig* 5L **221**
St John's Wlk. *Blac* 5B **88**
St Johns Wood. *Lyth A* 5L **129**
St Joseph's Clo. *Blac* 5E **88**
St Joseph's Dri. *Roch* 9E **204**
St Joseph's Pl. *Chor* 5F **174**
St Joseph's Ter. *Pres* 8M **115**
St Jude's Av. *Far* 3M **153**
St Jude's Av. *Walt D* 7N **135**
St Kitts Clo. *Lwr D* 1M **157**
St Laurence Gro. *Liv* 9L **223**
St Lawrence Av. *B'brn* 9J **119**
St Lawrence's Av. *Brtn* 2E **94**
St Lawrence St. *Gt Har* 4J **121**
St Leger Ct. Acc 3B 142
(off Plantation St.)
St Leger Ct. Acc 3B 142
(off Midland St.)
St Leonard's Clo. *Ing* 6D **114**
St Leonard's Ct. *Lyth A* 9D **108**
St Leonard's Ga. *Lanc* 8K **23**
St Leonard's Rd. *Blac* 8F **88**
St Leonard's Rd. E. *Lyth A* 9D **108**
St Leonard's Rd. W. *Lyth A* 1D **128**
St Leonard's St. *Pad* 9H **103**
St Louis Av. *Blac* 3F **88**
St Lucia Clo. *Lwr D* 1N **157**
St Lukes Ct. *Roch* 8C **204**
St Luke's Dri. *Orr* 7G **221**
St Luke's Gro. *South* 7L **167**
St Luke's Pl. *Pres* 8M **115**
St Luke's Rd. *Blac* 3C **108**
St Luke's Rd. *South* 7K **167**
St Luke St. *Roch* 8C **204**
St Margarets Clo. *Ing* 5D **114**
St Margaret's Ct. *B'brn* 3B **140**
St Margarets Ct. Fltwd 9G 41
(off Queen St.)
St Margaret's Gdns. *Hap* 5H **123**
St Margaret's Rd. *Bolt S* 3L **15**
St Margarets Rd. *Ley* 5M **153**
St Margaret's Rd. *More* 2D **22**
St Margaret's Way. *B'brn* 3B **140**
St Mark's Pl. *B'brn* 4J **139**
St Mark's Pl. *Blac* 2E **88**
St Mark's Pl. E. *Pres* 9G **114**
St Mark's Pl. W. *Pres* 9G **114**
St Mark's Rd. *B'brn* 4J **139**
St Mark's Rd. *Pres* 9G **114**
St Marks Sq. *Bury* 9L **201**
St Marlowes Av. *Ley* 4M **153**
St Martins Clo. *Poul F* 6H **63**
St Martin's Ct. *T Clev* 1F **62**
St Martin's Dri. *B'brn* 8E **138**
St Martin's Rd. *Blac* 3C **108**
St Martin's Rd. *Lanc* 1L **29**
St Martin's Rd. *Pres* 7K **115**
St Mary's Av. *Barn* 1A **78**
St Mary's Av. *Walt D* 7N **135**
St Mary's Clo. *B'brn* 3B **140**
St Marys Clo. *Blac* 1H **89**
St Marys Clo. *L'rdge* 2J **97**
St Mary's Clo. *Pres* 9M **115**
St Mary's Clo. *Roch* 9E **204**
St Mary's Clo. *Walt D* 7N **135**
St Mary's Ct. *Clay M* 7M **121**
St Mary's Ct. *Mel* 7F **118**
St Mary's Ct. *Pres* 9L **115**
St Mary's Ct. *Raw* 5L **161**
St Mary's Dri. *Lang* 1C **120**
St Mary's Gdns. *Mel* 7F **118**
St Mary's Gdns. *South* 6F **186**
St Mary's Ga. *Burn* 4F **124**
St Mary's Ga. *Eux* 3M **173**
St Marys Ga. *Lanc* 8J **23**
St Mary's Ga. *Roch* 6B **204**
St Mary's Pde. *Lanc* 8J **23**
St Mary's Pl. *Ross* 5L **161**
St Mary's Rd. *Bam B* 7A **136**
St Mary's Rd. *Gt Ecc* 6N **65**
St Mary's Rd. *Hey* 8K **21**
St Mary's St. *Clith* 2L **81**
St Mary's St. *Nels* 2G **105**
St Mary's St. *Pres* 9L **115**
St Mary's St. N. *Pres* 9L **115**
St Mary's Ter. *Ross* 5M **161**
St Mary's Wlk. *Chor* 6E **174**
St Mary's Way. *Ross* 5M **161**
St Mary's Wharf. *B'brn* 5N **139**
St Matthew's Clo. *Wig* 7M **221**
St Matthew's Ct. Burn 4C 124
(off Harriet St.)
St Matthew's Ct. Burn 4B 124
(off Colin St.)
St Matthew St. *Burn* 4C **124**
St Michael Rd. *Augh* 4E **216**
St Michael's Clo. *B'brn* 9F **138**
(in two parts)
St Michael's Clo. *Bolt S* 4L **15**
St Michael's Clo. *Chor* 5D **174**
St Michael's Clo. *South* 3M **167**
St Michael's Ct. *Barfd* 9G **85**
St Michael's Ct. *B'brn* 2N **139**
St Michael's Cres. *Bolt S* 4L **15**
St Michael's Gro. *Bolt S* 5L **15**
St Michael's Gro. *More* 4D **22**
St Michael's La. *Bolt S* 4K **15**
St Michael's on Wyre. 4G 66
St Michaels Pk. *Augh* 4F **216**
St Michael's Pl. *Brtn* 5E **94**
St Michael's Pl. *Bolt S* 5L **15**
St Michael's Rd. *Blac* 8D **62**
St Michael's Rd. *K'ham* 4A **112**
St Michael's Rd. *Ley* 4M **153**
St Michael's Rd. *Pres* 7K **115**
St Michael's Rd. *S'by & Bils* 6K **67**
St Michael's St. *B'brn* 1N **139**
St Mildred's Way. *Hey* 1K **27**
St Monica's Way. *Blac* 9K **89**
St Nicholas Arcades. *Lanc* 8K **23**
St Nicholas Av. *Sab* 2E **102**
St Nicholas Cres. *Bolt S* 3M **15**
St Nicholas Gro. *W Grn* 5G **110**
St Nicholas La. *Bolt S* 3L **15**
St Nicholas M. Sab 2E 102
(off St Nicholas Av.)
St Nicholas Rd. *Blac* 4G **109**
St Nicholas Rd. *Chu* 1M **141**
St Ogg's Rd. *More* 5C **22**
St Oswald's Clo. *B'brn* 4E **140**
St Oswald's Clo. *Pres* 7M **115**
St Oswald's Rd. *B'brn* 4E **140**
St Oswald St. *Lanc* 1L **29**
St Patrick's Clo. *Liv* 5K **223**
St Patrick's Pl. *Walt D* 4A **136**
St Patrick's Rd. N. *Lyth A* 9E **108**
St Patrick's Rd. S. *Lyth A* 1F **128**
St Patrick's Wlk. *Hey* 9K **21**
St Paul's Av. *B'brn* 3L **139**
St Paul's Av. *Lyth A* 4H **129**
St Paul's Av. *Pres* 8K **115**
St Paul's Clo. *Adl* 5J **195**
St Pauls Clo. *Clith* 3J **81**
St Paul's Clo. *Far M* 9J **135**
St Pauls Clo. *Liv* 5J **223**
St Paul's Clo. *Wheel* 8J **155**
St Pauls Ct. *Burn* 4D **124**
St Pauls Ct. *Bury* 9M **201**
St Paul's Ct. Osw 4L 141
(off Union Rd.)
St Paul's Ct. *Pres* 9K **115**
St Paul's Dri. *Brook* 3K **25**
St Paul's Dri. *Lanc* 2K **29**
St Paul's Pas. *South* 8G **167**
St Paul's Rd. *Blac* 2B **88**
St Paul's Rd. *Lanc* 2K **29**
St Paul's Rd. *Nels* 3H **105**
St Paul's Rd. *Pres* 7K **115**
St Paul's Rd. *Rish* 8G **121**
St Pauls Sq. *Pres* 9K **115**
St Paul's Sq. *South* 8G **166**
St Paul's St. *B'brn* 3L **139**
St Paul's St. *Clith* 3J **81**
St Paul's St. *Osw* 4L **141**
St Paul's St. *Ram* 7H **181**
St Paul's St. *South* 8G **166**
St Pauls Ter. *Clith* 3J **81**
St Paul's Ter. *Hodd* 5E **158**
St Pauls Wlk. *Lyth A* 4J **129**
St Peter's Av. *Has* 5G **160**
St Peter's Clo. *Clay D* 3L **119**
St Peter's Clo. *Dar* 7B **158**
St Peters Clo. *Kirkby* 5J **223**
St Peter's Clo. Pres 9J 115
(off St Peter's St.)
St Peter's Ga. *Todm* 7K **165**
St Peter's M. *Lanc* 8L **23**
St Peter's Pl. *Fltwd* 9H **41**
St Peter's Pl. *Has* 5G **161**
St Peter's Rd. *Lanc* 9L **23**
St Peter's Rd. *Ross* 5C **162**
St Peter's Rd. *South* 2G **186**
St Peters Row. *Liv* 4C **222**
St Peter's Sq. *Pres* 9H **115**
St Peter's St. *Chor* 5G **174**
St Peter's St. *Pres* 9J **115**
St Peter's St. *Roch* 7E **204**
St Peter St. *B'brn* 4L **139**
St Peter St. *Rish* 8G **121**
St Philip's Rd. *Pres* 7K **115**
St Philip's St. *B'brn* 5J **139**
St Philip St. *Burn* 9E **104**
St Phillips St. *Nels* 1J **105**
St Saviour's Clo. *Bam B* 9B **136**
St Saviours Ct. Bacup 6K 163
(off Park Rd.)
St Silas's Rd. *B'brn* 3J **139**
St Stephen's Av. *B'brn* 1A **140**
St Stephen's Av. *Blac* 9B **62**
St Stephen's Rd. *B'brn* 1A **140**
St Stephens Rd. *K'ham* 5L **111**
St Stephen's Rd. *Pres* 7K **115**
St Stephens Rd. *Stand* 3M **213**
St Stephen's St. *Burn* 5F **124**
St Stephen's Way. *Col* 5C **86**
St Teresa's Av. *T Clev* 2D **62**
St Theresa's Dri. *Ful* 5F **114**
St Thomas Clo. *Blac* 1H **89**
St Thomas Clo. *Ross* 8F **160**
St Thomas More Wlk. *Lanc* 8H **23**
St Thomas' Pl. *Pres* 8J **115**
St Thomas Rd. *K'ham* 5M **111**
St Thomas Rd. *Lyth A* 2F **128**
St Thomas Rd. *Pres* 7J **115**
St Thomas's Ct. *Uph* 5F **220**
St Thomas's Rd. *Chor* 6D **174**
St Thomas's Rd. *Ross* 9M **143**
St Thomas St. *B'brn* 4B **140**
St Thomas St. *Pres* 8J **115**
St Vincent Av. *Blac* 7E **88**
St Vincent Clo. *Lwr D* 1N **157**
St Vincents Rd. *Ful* 4H **115**
St Vincent's Way. *South* 1G **186**
St Walburga's Rd. *Blac* 2F **88**
St Walburge Av. *Ash R* 9H **115**
St Walburge's Gdns. *Ash R* 9G **115**
St Wilfred's Dri. *Roch* 2A **204**
St Wilfrid's Pk. *Halt* 1B **24**
St Wilfrid's Ter. *L'rdge* 3J **97**
St Wilfrid St. *Pres* 1J **135**
Salcombe Av. *Blac* 9E **62**
Salcombe Dri. *South* 1N **167**
Salcombe Rd. *Lyth A* 8C **108**
Salem M. *Hey* 8K **21**
Salem St. *Has* 4G **160**
Salesbury. 3L 119
Salesbury Hall Rd. *Ribch* 6H **99**
Salesbury Vw. *Wilp* 5N **119**
Sales's La. *Bury* 4M **201**
Sale St. *L'boro* 8L **185**
Salford. 3K 165
Salford. *B'brn* 3M **139**
Salford. *Todm* 2K **165**
Salford Rd. *Gal* 3L **37**
Salford Rd. *South* 8C **186**
Salford St. *Bury* 9M **201**
Salford Way. *Todm* 2K **165**
Salik Gdns. *Roch* 8C **204**
Salisbury Av. *Kno S* 8L **41**
Salisbury Av. *Grims* 9F **96**
Salisbury Clo. *Heat O* 6B **22**
Salisbury Ct. *Kno S* 8L **41**
Salisbury Rd. *Blac* 6D **88**
Salisbury Rd. *Brins* 7A **156**
Salisbury Rd. *Dar* 4M **157**
Salisbury Rd. *Lanc* 8H **23**
Salisbury Rd. *Pres* 1G **135**
Salisbury St. *Chor* 7F **174**
Salisbury St. *Col* 6B **86**
Salisbury St. *Gt Har* 3K **121**
Salisbury St. *Has* 4G **160**
Salisbury St. *Pres* 8N **115**
Salisbury St. *South* 8N **167**
Salkeld St. *Roch* 8C **204**
Salley St. *L'boro* 4M **185**
Sallowfields. *Wig* 6G **221**
Sally's La. *Chtwn* 4N **167**
Salmesbury Av. *Blac* 9E **62**
Salmesbury Hall Clo.
Ram 1G **201**
Salmon St. *Pres* 1M **135**
Salop Av. *Blac* 7C **62**
Saltash Rd. *T Clev* 7H **55**
Salt Ayre La. *Lanc* 7F **22**
(in two parts)
Saltburn St. *Burn* 3N **123**
Saltcotes. 4C 130
Saltcotes Pl. *Lyth A* 4C **130**
Saltcotes Rd. *Lyth A* 8B **110**
Salter Fell Rd. *Lanc* 6H **23**
Salterford La. *Cliv* 6L **125**
Salterforth. 5A 78
Salterforth La. *Barn* 1A **78**
Salterforth La. *Salt* 6A **78**
Salterforth Rd. *Earby* 3D **78**
Salter Rake Ga. *Todm* 5L **165**
(in two parts)
Salter St. *Pres* 8J **115**
Salthill Ind. Est. *Clith* 1N **81**
Salthill Rd. *Clith* 2M **81**
Salthill Vw. *Clith* 2M **81**
Salthouse Av. *Blac* 7C **88**
Salthouse Clo. *Bury* 7H **201**
Salt Marsh Clo. *Hamb* 2A **64**
Salt Marsh La. *Hamb* 2A **64**
Salt Pie La. *K Lon* 6F **8**
Saltpit La. *Liv* 1D **222**
Salt Pit La. *Maw* 1C **192**
Saltram Rd. *Wig* 7M **221**
Salts Dri. *L'boro* 8K **185**
Salus St. *Burn* 9F **104**
Salvia Way. *Liv* 5J **223**
Salwick. 6H 113
Salwick Av. *Blac* 6D **62**
Salwick Clo. *South* 1M **167**
Salwick Pl. *Ash R* 8B **114**
Salwick Pl. *Lyth A* 9G **109**
Salwick Rd. *Whar* 6E **92**
Sambourn Fold. *South* 9A **186**
Samlesbury. 8F 116
Samlesbury Aerodrome. 6A 118
Samlesbury Bottom. 1M 137
Samlesbury Hall. 7N 117
Samson St. *Roch* 5F **204**
Samuel St. *Bury* 9M **201**
Samuel St. *Pres* 9N **115**
Sandbank Gdns. *Whitw* 4N **183**
Sand Banks. *Bolt* 7F **198**
Sandbeds La. *Horn* 7B **18**
Sand Beds La. *Ross* 2L **181**
Sandbrook Gdns. *Orr* 6G **220**
Sandbrook Pk. *Roch* 9B **204**
Sandbrook Rd. *Orr* 6F **220**
Sandbrook Rd. *South* 1D **206**
(in two parts)
Sandbrook Way. *South* 1C **206**
Sanderling Clo. *Lyth A* 1L **129**
Sanderling Clo. *T Clev* 2F **62**
Sanderling Rd. *Liv* 7M **223**
Sanders Gro. *More* 4A **22**
Sanderson La. *Hesk* 4D **192**
Sanderson M. *Hesk* 4D **192**
Sandersons Way. *Blac* 1F **108**
Sanderson Way. *Cop* 4B **194**
Sandfield. *T Clev* 1G **63**
Sandfield Cotts. *Augh* 1J **217**
Sandfield Ho. Lanc 4L 29
(off Hala Rd.)
Sandfield Rd. *Bacup* 6L **163**
Sandfield Rd. *Roch* 8E **204**
Sandfield St. *Ley* 6L **153**
Sandford Clo. *Bolt* 9L **199**
Sandford Dri. *Liv* 9C **216**
Sandford Rd. *Orr* 6F **220**
Sandgate. *Blac* 4D **108**
Sandgate. *Chor* 9F **174**
Sandgate. *Lyth A* 1C **128**
Sandham's Green. 1K 109
Sandham St. *Chor* 6F **174**
Sandheys Dri. *South* 5M **167**
Sandhills Av. *Blac* 4B **108**
Sandhills Clo. *Salt* 4B **78**
Sandhill St. *Dar* 1B **178**
Sand Hole La. *Roch* 8J **203**
Sandholme Clo. *Gigg* 3N **35**
Sandholme Dri. Gigg 3N 35
(off Station Rd.)
Sandholme La. *Bncr* 7D **60**
Sandholme Vs. *Earby* 3D **78**
Sandhurst Av. *Blac* 6B **62**
Sandhurst Av. *Lyth A* 1E **128**
Sandhurst Clo. *K'ham* 4L **111**
Sandhurst Ct. *Lyth A* 2D **128**
Sandhurst Dri. *Liv* 8C **222**
Sandhurst Grange. *Lyth A* 1E **128**
Sandhurst St. *Burn* 3F **124**
Sandhurst Way. *Liv* 6A **216**
Sandicroft Av. *Hamb* 2B **64**
Sandicroft Pl. *Pre* 9A **42**
Sandicroft Rd. *Blac* 1C **88**
Sandilands Gro. *Liv* 8A **214**
Sandiway Ct. *South* 6L **167**
Sandiway Dri. *Brclf* 7K **105**
Sandiways. *Mag* 1D **222**
Sandiways Clo. *T Clev* 3J **63**
Sand La. *War* 7M **11**
Sandlewood Gro. *Liv* 6L **223**
Sandon Gro. *Rainf* 4L **225**
Sandon Pl. *Blac* 5C **108**
Sandon Rd. *South* 4F **186**
Sandon St. *B'brn* 5K **139**
Sandon St. *Dar* 5B **158**
Sandon Ter. *B'brn* 5K **139**
Sandown Clo. *K'ham* 4K **111**
Sandown Ct. *Pres* 1K **135**
Sandown Ct. *South* 6J **167**
Sandown Pk. Rd. *Liv* 7D **222**
Sandown Rd. *Bolt* 9L **199**
Sandown Rd. *Has* 5H **161**
Sandown Rd. *Lanc* 4M **29**
Sandown Rd. *T Clev* 2H **63**
Sandpiper Clo. *B'brn* 2N **139**
Sandpiper Clo. *Blac* 4H **89**
Sandpiper Clo. *Roch* 6K **203**
Sandpiper Ct. *T Clev* 1C **62**
Sandpiper Pl. *T Clev* 2F **62**
Sandpiper Rd. *Wig* 7L **221**
Sandpiper Sq. *Burn* 4A **124**
Sandridge Av. *Chor* 7D **174**
Sandridge Ct. Kno S 7L 41
(off Arnside Vw.)
Sandridge Pl. *Blac* 5B **108**
Sandringham Av. *Ley* 6M **153**
Sandringham Av. *T Clev* 2H **63**
Sandringham Clo. *Adl* 7G **195**
Sandringham Clo. *Barfd* 1G **104**
Sandringham Clo. *B'brn* 8M **119**
Sandringham Clo. *Liv* 5K **223**
Sandringham Clo. *Tar* 9E **150**
Sandringham Clo. *Wig* 6N **221**
Sandringham Ct. *Lyth A* 4K **129**
Sandringham Ct. *More* 4A **22**
Sandringham Ct. *South* 6J **167**
Sandringham Dri. *Brins* 7A **156**
Sandringham Dri. *G'mnt* 4F **200**
Sandringham Dri. *Miln* 7K **205**
Sandringham Gro. *Has* 6F **160**
Sandringham Lodge. *T Clev* 1C **62**
Sandringham Pk. Dri. *New L* 8D **134**
Sandringham Rd. *Ains* 8C **186**
Sandringham Rd. *Chor* 7D **174**
Sandringham Rd. *Dar* 3M **157**
Sandringham Rd. *E'ston* 7F **172**
Sandringham Rd. *Liv* 2B **222**
Sandringham Rd. *Lyth A* 3G **129**
Sandringham Rd. *More* 4A **22**
Sandringham Rd.
South & Bkdle 2E **186**
Sandringham Rd. *Walt D* 5N **135**
Sandringham Way. *Cot* 3B **114**
Sands Clo. *Rish* 7H **121**
Sandsdale Av. *Ful* 4M **115**
Sand Side. 3B 44
Sandside Cvn. Pk. *Bolt S* 4K **15**
Sandside Dri. *More* 5C **22**
Sandside Rd. *Arns* 1G **4**
Sands La. *Over K* 1F **16**
Sands Rd. *Rish* 7H **121**
Sands, The. *Whal* 5H **101**
Sandstone Rd. *Miln* 6J **205**
Sandstone Rd. *Wig* 9N **221**
Sands Way. *Blac* 7C **88**
Sandwash Clo. *Rainf* 6M **225**
Sandwich Clo. *B'brn* 4C **140**
Sandwick Clo. *Ful* 2J **115**
Sandy Bank Rd. *Tur* 9K **179**
Sandy Bank Ter. *Ross* 6B **162**
Sandy Bay Cvn. Pk. *Pre* 6N **41**
Sandybeds Clo. *Acc* 6C **142**
Sandybrook Clo. *Ful* 4A **116**
Sandybrook Clo. *Tot* 7E **200**
Sandy Brow La. *Liv* 9C **224**
Sandy Clo. *T Clev* 9C **54**
Sandycroft. *Rib* 7B **116**
Sandyfields. *Cot* 3B **114**
Sandyforth Av. *T Clev* 9H **55**
Sandyforth La. *L Grn* 2D **114**
Sandyforth La. *Loth* 1N **87**
Sandygate. *Burn* 3C **124**
Sandygate La. *Brough* 8E **94**
Sandyhall La. *Barfd* 8D **84**
Sandyland Arc. *Hey* 5L **21**
Sandylands. 6N 21
Sandylands Promenade. *Hey* 5L **21**
Sandy La. *Acc* 3B **142**
(in two parts)
Sandy La. *Adl* 6F **194**
(in two parts)
Sandy La. *Augh* 5G **216**
Sandy La. *Barfd* 9H **85**
Sandy La. *Blac* 5G **109**
Sandy La. *Brin* 1K **155**
Sandy La. *Brins* 7N **155**
Sandy La. *Clay W* 4E **154**
Sandy La. *Dar & Lwr D* 1M **157**
Sandy La. *Fltwd* 5D **54**
Sandy La. *Hamb* 2B **64**
Sandy La. *H'twn* 7A **214**
Sandy La. *H'wd* 8A **170**
(in two parts)
Sandy La. *Lath* 5A **210**
Sandy La. *Ley* 7K **153**
Sandy La. *Lwr B & Cot* 1A **114**
Sandy La. *Lyd* 5A **216**
Sandy La. *Maw* 3K **191**
Sandy La. *Mell* 5F **222**
Sandy La. *Newb* 3K **211**
Sandy La. *Orr* 7G **220**
Sandy La. *Out R* 1L **65**
Sandy La. *Pleas* 6C **138**
Sandy La. *Pre* 8N **41**
Sandy La. *Roch* 6N **203**
Sandy La. *Skel* 2H **219**
Sandy La. Cen. *Uph* 2H **219**
Sandy Pl. *Ley* 7K **153**
Sanfield Clo. *Orm* 6K **209**
Sangara Dri. *Lwr D* 1N **157**
Sangness Dri. *South* 2L **187**
Sankey Rd. *Liv* 3C **222**
Sansbury Cres. *Nels* 9L **85**
Santon Clo. *Wesh* 2M **111**
Sanvino Av. *South* 8D **186**
Sanworth St. *Todm* 2M **165**
Sapphire Dri. *Liv* 5K **223**
Sapphire St. *B'brn* 8N **119**
Sarah Butterworth Ct. *Roch* 7E **204**
Sarah Butterworth St. *Roch* 7E **204**
Sarah Jane St. *Miln* 7J **205**
Sarah La. *Breth* 1K **171**
Sarah St. *Bacup* 7N **163**
Sarah St. *Dar* 6B **158**
Sarah St. *Ram* 3K **181**
Sarah St. *Roch* 7D **204**
Sarmatian Fold. *Ribch* 7E **98**
Sarscow La. *Ley* 5B **172**
Saswick Ct. *Elsw* 3N **91**
Satinwood Cres. *Liv* 7F **222**

Shaw St.—Somerset Av.

Shaw St. Pres 8K 115
Shaw St. Roch 3E 204
Shay La. L'rdge 5H 97
Shay La. Slai 5B 50
Shay La. Ind. Est. L'rdge 4H 97
Shays Dri. Clith 4M 81
Shay, The. T Clev 4F 62
Shear Bank Clo. B'brn 2L 139
Shear Bank Gdns. B'brn 2L 139
Shear Bank Rd. B'brn 1L 139
Shear Brow. B'brn 1L 139
Shearing Av. Roch 4K 203
Shearwater Dri. B'brn 2N 139
Sheddon Gro. Burn 4J 125
Shed St. Col 7N 85
Shed St. Osw 5K 141
Shed St. Whitw 5A 184
Sheep Gap. Roch 4M 203
Sheepgate Dri. Tot 8D 200
Sheep Grn. Has 4G 161
Sheep Hey. Ram 5J 181
Sheep Hill La. Clay W 5B 154
(in two parts)
Sheep Hill La. New L 9C 134
Sheep Ho. La. Hor 3A 196
Sheernest. Holme 2G 6
Sheernest La. Holme 2F 6
Shefferland's La. Halt 2N 23
Sheffield Dri. Lea 7A 114
Shefford Cres. Wig 9M 221
Sheldon Av. Stand 2N 213
Sheldon Ct. Pres 8J 115
(off Thorpe Clo.)
Shelfield. Roch 4K 203
Shelfield Clo. Roch 5K 203
Shelfield La. Roch 4J 203
Shelfield La. S'fld 3B 106
Shelfield Rd. Nels 1M 105
Shelley Clo. Bolt S 4L 15
Shelley Clo. Cop 5B 194
Shelley Dri. Acc 6D 142
Shelley Dri. E'ston 9G 172
Shelley Dri. Orm 6J 209
Shelley Dri. Orr 5K 221
Shelley Gdns. Gt Har 5H 121
Shelley Gro. Dar 6C 158
Shelley Gro. South 7M 167
Shelley Gro. T Clev 3D 62
Shelley M. Ash R 8F 114
Shelley Rd. Ash R 7F 114
Shellfield Rd. South 3N 167
Shellingford Clo. Shev 5G 213
Shelton Dri. South 9A 186
Shenley Way. South 1C 168
Shenstone Rd. Blac 3F 88
Shepherd Ct. Roch 7E 204
Shepherd Rd. Lyth A 9G 108
Shepherd Rd. N. Lyth A 9G 108
Shepherd's Av. Bowg 8A 60
Shepherds Clo. G'mnt 4E 200
Shepherds Grn. Ross 8E 144
Shepherd's La. Crost 6H 171
Shepherd's La. Hals 7C 208
Shepherd St. Bacup 4K 163
Shepherd St. Dar 8A 158
Shepherd St. G'mnt 5E 200
Shepherd St. Lyth A 5A 130
Shepherd St. Pres 1K 135
Shepherds Way. Chor 6F 174
Sheppard St. Blac 5B 88
Shepton Clo. Bolt 6D 198
Sheraton Clo. Orr 2L 221
Sheraton Pk. Ing 3D 114
Sherborne Lodge. Rib 5B 116
(off Grange Av.)
Sherborne Rd. Orr 3K 221
Sherbourne Av. K'ham 4L 111
Sherbourne Clo. Poul F 6J 63
Sherbourne Ct. Poul F 6J 63
Sherbourne Cres. Pres 6L 115
Sherbourne Rd. Acc 5D 142
Sherbourne Rd. Blac 2B 88
Sherbourne Rd. Hamb 1B 64
Sherbourne St. Chor 7F 174
Sherburn Rd. Pen 5H 135
Sherdley Rd. Los H 9L 135
Sherfin. 9G 143
Sheridan Rd. Lane 5G 86
Sheridan St. Burn 8J 105
(off Stanbury Dri.)
Sheridan St. Nels 9K 85
Sheriff St. Miln 8K 205
Sheriff St. Roch 5B 204
Sheringham Av. T Clev 4D 62
Sheringham Dri. Bury 8J 201
Sheringham Way. Poul F 8L 63
Sherrat St. Skel 2H 219
Sherringham Rd. South 3E 186
Sherwood Av. Augh 1H 217
Sherwood Av. Blac 2E 88
Sherwood Clo. Tot 6E 200
Sherwood Ct. Blac 2E 88
(off Sherwood Av.)
Sherwood Ct. Burn 4G 125
Sherwood Cres. Wig 4N 221
Sherwood Dri. Skel 9A 212
Sherwood Dri. Wig 5N 221
Sherwood Gro. Wig 4N 221
Sherwood Ho. South 8C 186
Sherwood Pl. Chor 6F 174
Sherwood Pl. T Clev 2F 62
Sherwood Rd. B'brn 4B 140
Sherwood Rd. Lyth A 2J 129
Sherwood's La. Liv 9E 222
Sherwood St. Bolt 9F 198
Sherwood Way. Acc 8N 121
Sherwood Way. Ful 3K 115
Shetland Clo. B'brn 5C 140
Shetland Clo. Wilp 2N 119
Shetland Rd. Blac 8C 88
Shevington. 6K 213
Shevington Causeway. Crost 4L 171
Shevington La. Shev 6K 213
Shevington Moor. 2L 213
Shevington Moor. Stand 2K 213
Shevington's La. Liv 5J 223
Shevington Vale. 5G 213
Shillingstone Clo. Bolt 9M 199
Shilton St. Ram 9G 180
Ship All. Burn 4E 124
(off Parker La.)
Shipley Clo. Blac 1H 89
Shipley Rd. Lyth A 1H 129
Shipper Bottom La. Ram 9J 181
(in two parts)
Shipston Clo. Bury 9G 200
Shirburn. Roch 7B 204
Shirdley Cres. South 1C 206
Shirdley Hill. 7N 187
Shire Bank Cres. Ful 4H 115
Shireburn Av. Clith 4J 81
Shireburn Cotts. Hur G 1M 99
Shire La. Hur G 2L 99
Shireshead. 2B 46
Shireshead Cres. Lanc 5L 29
Shires, The. B'brn 1L 157
Shirewell Rd. Orr 6H 221
Shirley Cres. Blac 5D 62
Shirley Gdns. Toc 5G 157
Shirley Heights. Poul F 6K 63
Shirley La. Longt 7L 133
Shoebroad La. Todm 3L 165
Shop La. Acc 3C 142
Shop La. High W 4D 136
Shop La. Liv 1B 222
Shoppers Wlk. Lyth A 5A 130
(off Clifton St.)
Shore. 8J 185
(Littleborough)
Shore. 6F 146
(Todmorden)
Shore Av. Burn 8K 105
Shore Clo. Silv 9F 4
Shorefield Clo. Miln 6J 205
Shorefield Mt. Eger 5E 198
Shore Fold. L'boro 8J 185
Shore Grn. Silv 9F 4
Shore Grn. T Clev 9F 54
Shore Grn. Todm 6F 146
Shoreham Clo. Bury 6H 201
Shore Hill. L'boro 8M 185
Shore La. Bolt S 6J 15
Shore La. L'boro 9M 185
Shore Lea. L'boro 8J 185
Shore Mt. L'boro 8J 185
Shore New Rd. Todm 7E 146
Shore Rd. Ains & South 7A 186
Shore Rd. Hesk B 5L 149
Shore Rd. Hey 1H 27
Shore Rd. L'boro 8J 185
Shore Rd. Silv 9F 4
Shore Rd. T Clev 3C 62
Shore St. Miln 7J 205
Shoreswood. Bolt 8D 198
Shore, The. Bolt S 4K 15
Shore, The. Hamb 2A 64
Shore, The. Hest B 8G 15
Shorey Bank. 5A 158
Shorey Bank. Burn 2E 124
Shorrock La. B'brn 8J 139
Shorrocks Av. St M 3G 67
Shorrocks St. Bury 9E 200
Shorrock St. Dar 7A 158
Short Clough Clo. Ross 1M 161
Short Clough La. Ross 1M 161
Short Cft. La. Liv 2D 214
Shortenbrook Dri. Alt 3D 122
Shortenbrook Way. Alt 3D 122
Shortlands Dri. Hey 9K 21
Short La. Goos 5J 95
Shortridge Rd. Blac 1F 108
Short St. Bacup 7F 162
Short St. Col 7A 86
Short St. Todm 2L 165
(off Dalton St.)
Short St. Wig 5L 221
Shottwood Fold. L'boro 6M 185
Showfield. Wors 3M 125
Showley Brook Clo. Wilp 5N 119
Showley Ct. Clay D 3M 119
Showley Rd. Clay D 3H 119
Shrewsbury Av. Old R 7B 222
Shrewsbury Clo. K'ham 4A 112
Shrewsbury Dri. Lanc 2M 29
Shrewsbury Dri. T Clev 1G 62
Shropshire Dri. Wilp 3N 119
Shuttle Clo. Acc 2N 141
(off Dale St.)
Shuttle St. Pres 9L 115
Shuttleworth. 6K 181
Shuttleworth Rd. Pres 7J 115
Shuttleworth St. Burn 8F 104
Shuttleworth St. Earby 2E 78
Shuttleworth St. Pad 1H 123
Shuttleworth St. Rish 7H 121
Shuttling Fields La. Bam B 7C 136
(in two parts)
Sibbering Brow. Char R 6M 173
Sibsey St. Lanc 8J 23
Siddow's Av. Clith 4J 81
Sidebeet La. Rish 9E 120
Sidegarth La. A'ton 3J 17
Side La. Rim 5N 75
Side Of The Moor. 7M 199
Sidgreaves La. Lea T 3M 113
Siding La. Liv 4A 224
Siding La. Rainf 1G 225
Siding Rd. Fltwd 1G 54
Sidings Ind. Est., The. Set 3N 35
Sidings Rd. Hey 5L 27
Sidings, The. Bacup 7L 163
Sidings, The. Dar 8B 158
Sidings, The. Set 3N 35
Sidings, The. Whal 4J 101
Siding St. Bacup 7G 162
Sidmouth Av. Has 5H 161
Sidmouth Rd. Lyth A 8C 108
Sidney Av. Blac 9E 62
Sidney Av. Hesk B 4D 150
Sidney Powell Av. Liv 8H 223
Sidney Rd. South 6M 167
Sidney Ter. Lanc 8L 23
(off Denis St.)
Sigget La. Todm 1J 165
Silbury Clo. B'brn 8A 140
Silk Mill La. Ingle 7L 69
Silk St. Roch 9N 203
Silloth Clo. B'brn 7N 139
Silly La. Lowg 2L 33
Silsden Av. Rib 4N 115
Silsden Clo. Blac 1H 89
Silver Birch Way. Liv 6A 216
Silverburn. Lyth A 9G 109
Silverdale. 9G 4
Silverdale. Blac 5E 62
Silverdale. Hesk B 4D 150
Silverdale. South 1E 186
Silverdale Av. Fltwd 3C 54
Silverdale Av. Hey 9L 21
Silverdale Clo. B'brn 8N 139
Silverdale Clo. Burn 7G 104
Silverdale Clo. Clay M 7L 121
Silverdale Clo. Hogh 4G 137
Silverdale Clo. Ley 9L 153
Silverdale Ct. South 1L 187
Silverdale Dri. Rib 4N 115
Silverdale Golf Course. 8J 5
Silverdale Green. 8H 5
Silverdale Moss Rd. Silv 4H 5
Silverdale Rd. Arns 1F 4
Silverdale Rd. Chor 7G 174
Silverdale Rd. Lyth A 1J 129
Silverdale Rd. Orr 4L 221
Silverdale Rd. Silv 6E 4
Silverdale Rd. Yeal R 6N 5
Silver Hill. Miln 6J 205
Silver Ridge Cvn. Pk. Hale 2B 6
Silversmiths Row. Lyth A 1K 129
Silverstone Gro. Liv 6A 216
Silver St. Clift 8G 113
Silver St. Hur G 1M 99
Silver St. Ram 8H 181
Silver St. Todm 8K 165
Silverthorne Dri. South 5M 167
Silverton Gro. Bolt 9F 198
Silverwell St. Hor 9C 196
Silverwood Av. Blac 1C 108
Silverwood Clo. Lyth A 4L 129
Silverwood Ct. Blac 1D 108
Silvester Rd. Chor 8E 174
Silvia Way. Fltwd 9E 40
Simeon St. Miln 7J 205
Simeon St. Todm 7K 165
Simfield Clo. Stand 3N 213
Simmonds Way. Brier 3F 104
Simmons Av. Walt D 5L 135
Simmons St. B'brn 3L 139
Simon Ct. Liv 5K 223
Simon's Ter. Kno S 7L 41
Simonstone. 8D 102
Simonstone La. S'stne 9D 102
Simonstone Rd. Sab 5E 102
Simonswood. 4M 223
Simonswood La. Bic 7L 217
Simonswood La. Liv 9M 223
Simonswood Wlk. Liv 8M 223
Simpson Clo. Barn 1A 78
Simpson Clough. 8G 202
Simpsons Pl. Roch 4C 204
Simpson's Pl. South 8H 167
Simpson St. Blac 1B 108
Simpson St. Hap 5H 123
Simpson St. Osw 5K 141
Simpson St. Pres 9J 115
Sinclair Ct. Lyth A 1H 129
Sinclair Pl. Wig 3N 221
Sineacre La. Liv 2C 224
Singleton. 1D 90
Singleton Av. Hor 8D 196
Singleton Av. Lyth A 1G 129
Singleton Av. Read 8C 102
Singleton Clo. Ful 2J 115
Singleton Rd. Weet 4D 90
Singleton Row. Pres 8J 115
Singleton St. Blac 7B 88
Singleton Way. Ful 2J 115
Sinnott Ho. South 1H 187
Sion Clo. Rib 5B 116
Sion Hill. Rib 5B 116
Sir Frank Whittle Way. Blac 5E 108
Sir Simon's Arc. Lanc 8K 23
Sir Tom Finney Way. Ful & Pres 7L 115
Siss Clough. 6D 162
Six Acre La. Longt 1N 151
Sixfields. T Clev 4F 62
Sixpenny La. Form 4E 206
Sixteen Acre La. Liv 6A 206
Sixth Av. Blac 2C 108
Sixth Av. Bury 9B 202
Size Ho. Rd. Has 5G 161
Sizehouse St. Pres 9J 115
Size Ho. Village. Has 5H 161
Sizergh Ct. Lanc 9H 23
Sizergh Rd. More 3E 22
Sizer St. Pres 8J 115
Size St. Whitw 5A 184
Skaithe, The. Slai 5C 50
Skeffington Rd. Pres 7L 115
Skegness Clo. Bury 8J 201
Skeleron La. Rim 7M 75
Skelmersdale. 2M 219
Skelmersdale Hall Dri. Skel 9K 211
Skelmersdale Hall Rd. Uph 9L 211
Skelmersdale Rd. Bic 4E 218
Skelmersdale United F.C. 3H 219
Skelshaw Clo. B'brn 5A 140
Skelton St. Col 6B 86
Skelwith Rd. Blac 8H 89
Skerryvore Cvn. Pk. Blac 3D 108
Skerton. 5K 23
Skerton Ct. Lanc 6K 23
Skerton Ho. Lanc 6L 23
Skiddaw Clo. Burn 9A 104
Skiddaw Pl. Wig 5M 221
Skiddaw Rd. Blac 1F 108
Skiddaw Rd. Lanc 6L 23
Skiddaw St. B'brn 3A 140
Skip La. Hut 4M 133
Skippool. 6L 63
Skippool Av. Poul F 6L 63
Skippool Rd. T Clev 4L 63
Skipton Av. Poul F 6J 63
Skipton Av. South 9B 148
Skipton Clo. Bam B 6B 136
Skipton Clo. Blac 9F 88
Skipton Cres. Rib 4A 116
Skipton Ga. Burt L 4K 19
Skipton New Rd. Col 3B 86
Skipton Old Rd. Col 5D 86
Skipton Old Rd. Foul 2B 86
Skipton Rd. Barn 1M 77
Skipton Rd. Col 4B 86
Skipton Rd. Garg 3M 53
Skipton Rd. Hell 1D 52
Skipton Rd. Lyth A 2H 129
Skipton Rd. Set 4N 35
Skipton Rd. Thorn C 10J 53
Skipton Rd. Traw 8E 86
Skipton St. More 3A 22
Skipton St. News 5C 52
Skitham. 8N 57
Skitham La. Out R 9M 57
Skull Ho. La. App B 3F 212
Skye Cres. B'brn 5C 140
Slack. High 4L 103
Slack Booth. Traw 1F 106
Slackey's La. South 2B 168
Slack Ga. Whitw 6B 184
Slack Head. 1N 5
Slack La. Bolt 6K 199
Slack La. C'ham 5A 36
Slack Royd. Traw 1F 106
Slack's La. Hth C 3K 195
Slack St. Roch 6C 204
Slackwood La. Silv 9H 5
Slade La. Pad 8H 103
(in two parts)
Sladen St. Roch 4C 204
Sladen Ter. L'boro 6N 185
Slade St. Pres 1H 135
Slaidburn. 5C 50
Slaidburn Av. Burn 5H 125
Slaidburn Av. Ross 3M 161
Slaidburn Clo. Miln 8J 205
Slaidburn Cres. South 1N 167
Slaidburn Dri. Acc 4N 141
Slaidburn Dri. Bury 9E 199
Slaidburn Dri. Lanc 4L 29
Slaidburn Ind. Est. South 1N 167
Slaidburn Pl. Rib 7C 116
Slaidburn Rd. Ben 9M 19
Slaidburn Rd. Rib 7B 116
Slaidburn Wlk. Blac 2G 89
Slant La. Todm 1N 165
Slape La. Burt 5H 7
Slate La. Skel 9G 210
Slater Av. Col 5A 86
Slater Av. Hor 9D 196
Slater La. Ley 7D 152
(in three parts)
Slater Rd. T Clev 1C 62
Slater St. B'brn 7K 139
Slaunt Bank. Roch 3H 203
Sleaford Clo. Bury 8J 201
Sledbrook St. Wig 6M 221
Slinger Rd. T Clev 9C 54
Slip Inn La. Lanc 8K 23
Slipper Hill. 3L 85
Sliven Clod Rd. Ross 5K 143
Sluice La. Lyth A 6H 109
Sluice La. Ruf 3E 190
Slyne. 9K 15
Slyne Cvn. Pk. Slyne 9K 15
Slyne Hall Heights. Slyne 8L 15
Slyne Rd. Lanc 4K 23
(in two parts)
Slyne Rd. Lanc 8K 15
Slyne Rd. More 4F 22
Smalden La. Bolt B 7G 50
Smallbridge. 2F 204
Smalley Cft. Pen 5J 135
Smalley St. Burn 5F 124
(in two parts)
Smalley St. Stand 3N 213
Smalley Thorn Brow. Gt Har 4F 120
Smalley Way. B'brn 6M 139
Small La. Augh 9F 208
Small La. Burs 4K 189
Small La. Orm 8L 209
Small La. N. Hals 2C 208
Small La. S. Hals 7B 208
Smallshaw Ind. Est. Burn 4A 124
Smallshaw La. Burn 3N 123
(in two parts)
Smallshaw Rd. Roch 1L 203
Smallwood Hey. 8H 43
Smallwood Hey Rd. Pil 8F 42
Smethick Wlk. Boot 6A 222
Smethurst Hall Pk. Bil 9F 220
Smethurst Hall Rd. Bury 9C 202
Smethurst La. Wig 6M 221
Smethurst Rd. Bil 9E 220
Smethurst St. Bury 9G 201
Smethurst St. Wig 6M 221
Smirthwaite St. Burn 4B 124
Smith Av. Orr 3L 221
Smith Av. Tar 6D 150
Smith Clo. Grims 9E 96
Smith Cft. Ley 7E 152
Smith Fold. 9J 117
Smith Green. 3N 37
Smith Hill. Miln 7J 205
Smithills. 9B 198
Smithills Clo. Chor 5G 175
Smithills Cft. Rd. Bolt 9A 198
Smithills Dean. 7M 197
Smithills Dean Rd. Bolt 7A 198
Smithills Hall Clo. Ram 9H 181
Smithill's Hall Mus. 9B 198
Smith La. Eger 5F 198
Smith Rd. T Clev 1D 62
Smith's La. Tar 5B 170
Smith St. Adl 7H 195
Smith St. Bam B 8B 136
Smith St. Barn 3L 77
Smith St. Burn 3D 124
Smith St. Bury 9M 201
Smith St. Chor 8F 174
Smith St. Col 7N 85
Smith St. Fltwd 2F 54
Smith St. K'ham 4L 111
Smith St. Nels 2J 105
Smith St. Ram 9G 180
Smith St. Skel 2H 219
Smith St. Whit W 7E 154
Smith St. Wors 4M 125
Smithy. H'wd 8A 170
Smithy Bridge. 2J 205
Smithy Bri. Rd. Roch & L'boro 1H 205
Smithy Bri. St. Osw 5K 141
Smithy Brow. Abb 3A 48
Smithy Brow. Has 3G 160
(off High St.)
Smithy Brow. Newb 3L 211
Smithy Brow. Wrigh 5F 192
Smithy Brow Ct. Has 3G 160
Smithy Cvn. Pk. Cabus 8L 45
Smithy Clo. Brin 2H 155
Smithy Clo. Gars 4N 59
Smithy Clo. Liv 8B 206
Smithy Clo. Stalm 5B 56
Smithy Cft. Brom X 5F 198
Smithy Cft. Garg 3M 53
Smithy Cft. Lyth A 2J 129
Smithy Fld. L'boro 8K 185
Smithyfield Av. Burn 3K 125
Smithy Fold. Roch 4N 203
Smithy Fold. W Grn 6G 111
Smithy Grn. Liv 8B 206
Smithy How. Cast 5G 8
Smithy La. Augh 5E 216
Smithy La. Bar 6N 207
Smithy La. Brin 2H 155
Smithy La. Clau B 1D 68
Smithy La. Col 3M 85
Smithy La. Hey 1J 27
Smithy La. I'ton 2M 19
Smithy La. Lyth A 2J 129
Smithy La. Maw 3M 191
Smithy La. Much H 5J 151
Smithy La. Pre 1A 56
Smithy La. Scar 9F 188
Smithy La. Stain 4K 89
Smithy La. Stalm 5B 56
Smithy Lane Ends. 7J 189
Smithy M. Blac 3C 88
Smithy Nook. L'boro 5M 185
Smithy Row. Hur G 1M 99
Smithy St. Bam B 8A 136
Smithy St. Has 4G 160
(off Ratcliffe St.)
Smithy St. Ram 8H 181
Smithy Wlk. Burs 8C 190
Snaefell Rd. B'brn 7M 139
Snape Green. 4C 188
Snape Grn. South 5C 188
Snape La. Yeal C 1B 12
Snape Rake La. Goos 6M 61
(in two parts)
Snape St. Dar 4N 157
Snapewood La. Cabus 2L 59
Snell Gro. Col 5C 86
Sniddle Hill La. Dar 7M 157
Snipe Av. Roch 6K 203
Snipe Clo. Blac 4H 89
Snipe Clo. T Clev 7F 54
Snipewood. E'ston 8E 172
Snodworth Rd. Lang 1D 120
Snowden Av. B'brn 1M 139
Snowden Av. Hey 5L 21
Snowden St. Burn 3N 123
Snowdon Clo. Blac 7D 88
Snowdon Dri. Hor 8D 196
Snowdon Rd. Lyth A 7G 108
Snowdrop Clo. Has 7E 160
Snowdrop Clo. Ley 5A 154
Snow Hill. Pres 9J 115
Snowhill La. Scor 7B 46
Snowshill Cres. T Clev 4F 62
Snowshill Dri. Wig 7M 221
Snow St. B'brn 2N 139
Sod Hall La. New L & Midg H 2D 152
Sod Hall Rd. New L 1D 152
Sollam's Clo. Bam B 6B 136
Sollom. 4E 170
Sollom La. Tar 4F 170
Solness St. Bury 7L 201
Solway Av. B'brn 7G 139
Solway Clo. Blac 5C 62
Solway Clo. Pen 5H 135
Somerby Rd. More 4C 22
Somerford Clo. Burn 2B 124
Somersby Clo. Walt D 5A 136
Somersby Dri. Brom X 5F 198
Somerset Av. Blac 7D 88
Somerset Av. Chor 5E 174
Somerset Av. Clith 1M 81

Somerset Av.—Standen Pk. Ho.

Somerset Av. *Dar* 4N 157
Somerset Av. *Lanc* 1L 29
Somerset Av. *Wilp* 3N 119
Somerset Clo. *Osw* 5M 141
Somerset Ct. *Blac* 7D 88
Somerset Dri. *South* 2C 206
Somerset Gro. *Chu* 1M 141
Somerset Gro. *Roch* 5L 203
Somerset Pk. *Ful* 2E 114
Somerset Pl. *Nels* 1L 105
Somerset Rd. *Ley* 5L 153
Somerset Rd. *Pres* 8K 115
Somerset Rd. *Rish* 8F 120
Somerset Rd. *Wig* 5M 221
Somerset St. *Burn* 6E 124
Somerset Wlk. *Has* 7G 161
Somerton Clo. *Stand* 3N 213
Sorrel Clo. *T Clev* 7F 54
Sorrel Ct. *Pen* 6F 134
Sorrel Dri. *L'boro* 8J 185
Soudan St. *Burn* 8F 104
Sough. 4D 78 **(Barnoldswick)**
Sough. 8B 158 **(Darwen)**
Sough La. *Earby* 5D 78
Sough La. *Guide* 6F 140
Sough Rd. *Dar* 7B 158
Sourhall Cotts. *Todm* 1G 165
Sourhall Rd. *Todm* 3F 164
South Av. *Barn* 1M 77
South Av. *Chor* 8F 174
South Av. *More* 3C 22
South Av. *New L* 8C 134
South Av. *T Clev* 8C 54
South Bank. *Blac* 4E 108
Southbank Av. *Blac* 2G 108
Southbank Rd. *South* 8H 167
S. Boundary Rd. *Know I* 9N 223
Southbourne Av. *Poul F* 9J 63
Southbourne Rd. *Blac* 8F 88
Southbrook Rd. *Ley* 6J 153
Southcliffe. *Gt Har* 3H 121
Southcliffe Av. *Burn* 2A 124
S. Cliff St. *Pres* 2H 135
S. Clifton St. *Lyth A* 5A 130
South Ct. *Roch* 5D 204
Southdene. *Parb* 2M 211
Southdown Clo. *Roch* 9N 203
Southdown Dri. *T Clev* 3K 63
Southdowns Rd. *Chor* 8F 174
South Dri. *App B* 2F 212
South Dri. *Bolt* 9L 199
South Dri. *Ful* 2H 115
South Dri. *Ins* 2G 93
South Dri. *Pad* 1J 123
South End. *Pres* 3H 135
Southern Av. *Burn* 2A 124
Southern Av. *Pres* 2M 135
Southern Clo. *L'rdge* 4J 97
Southern Pde. *Pres* 2L 135
Southern Rd. *South* 8G 166
Southern's La. *Rainf* 4L 225
Southern St. *Wig* 6N 221
Southery Av. *Wig* 8N 221
Southey Clo. *Ful* 2J 115
Southey Clo. *L'boro* 2J 205
Southey Gro. *Liv* 4C 222
Southey St. *Burn* 3C 124
Southfield. 4M 105
Southfield. *Much H* 4J 151
Southfield Av. *Bury* 7L 201
Southfield Dri. *Blac* 2J 89
Southfield Dri. *New L* 9C 134
Southfield Dri. *W Brad* 7M 73
Southfield Gdns. *Much H* 4K 151
Southfield La. *S'fld & Col* 3N 105
Southfield Rd. *Ram* 3F 200
Southfield Sq. *Nels* 2K 105
Southfield St. *Nels* 2J 105
Southfield Ter. *Col* 5H 87
Southfleet Av. *Fltwd* 3E 54
Southfleet Pl. *Fltwd* 3E 54
Southfold Pl. *Lyth A* 4N 129
Southgate. *Fltwd* 4D 54
Southgate. *Ful* 4G 115
Southgate. *Harw* 9L 199
Southgate. *Pres* 8J 115
Southgate. *Whi L* 6D 22
Southgate. *Whitw* 7M 183
Southgates. *Char R* 2N 193
South Gro. *Brtn* 2E 94
South Gro. *Ful* 1H 115
South Gro. *More* 3C 22
Southgrove Av. *Bolt* 7E 198
South Hey. *Lyth A* 2J 129
South Hill. 9H 155
South Hill. *South* 8G 166
South Holme. *Lyth A* 4B 130
S. King St. *Blac* 5C 88
Southlands. *K'ham* 5M 111
Southlands Av. *Los H* 7M 135
Southlands Av. *Stand* 4N 213
Southlands Dri. *Ley* 8E 152
South Lawn. *Blac* 8E 88
South Marine Gardens. 7G 167
South Meade. *Liv* 1A 222
S. Meadow La. *Pres* 2H 135
S. Meadow St. *Pres* 9K 115
S. Moss Rd. *Lyth A* 1J 129
Southney Clo. *Liv* 8G 222
South Pde. Barn *1M 77* *(off South Av.)*
South Pde. *Kirkby* 8K 223
South Pde. *Roch* 6C 204
South Pde. *T Clev* 2E 62
South Pk. *Lyth A* 4M 129
S. Park Ct. *Liv* 7H 223
S. Park Dri. *Blac* 8F 88
S. Park Rd. *Liv* 7G 223
South Pl. *Roch* 5D 204
Southport. 7H 167
Southport & Ainsdale Golf Course. 6D 186
Southport & Birkdale Cricket Club Ground. 2F 186
Southport Bus. Pk. *South* 2K 187
Southport Enterprise Cen. *South* 8N 167
Southport F.C. 9L 167 **(Haig Av.)**
Southport New Rd. *South* 1D 168
Southport Old Rd. *Form* 4B 206
Southport Railway Cen. 8J 167
Southport R.F.C. Ground. 4E 186
Southport Rd. *Bar & Orm* 6N 207
Southport Rd. *Chor* 5A 174
Southport Rd. *Crost & Ley* 4B 172
Southport Rd. *Form* 7A 206
Southport Rd. *Lyd* 3N 215
Southport Rd. *Scar* 1F 208
Southport Rd. *South & Scar* 1N 187
Southport Ter. *Chor* 7G 174
Southport Zoo. 7F 166
South Promenade. *Lyth A* 2D 128
S. Ribble Ind. Est. *Walt D* 3M 135
South Ribble Mus. & Exhibition Cen. 7K 153
S. Ribble St. *Walt D* 2M 135
South Rd. *Breth* 1J 171
South Rd. *Cop* 4A 194
South Rd. *Lanc* 9K 23
South Rd. *More* 3C 22
S. Royd St. *Tot* 6E 200
South Shore. 2B 108
S. Shore St. *Chu* 3L 141
S. Shore St. *Has* 4F 160
Southside. *Eux* 3M 173
South Sq. *Blac* 4D 88
South Sq. *T Clev* 7C 54
South Strand. *Fltwd* 5D 54
South St. *Acc* 9D 122 (Burnley Rd.)
South St. *Acc* 3B 142 (Nuttall St.)
South St. *Bacup* 7F 162 (Brandwood Rd.)
South St. *Bacup* 5K 163 (St James St.)
South St. *Burn* 3E 124
South St. *Dar* 6A 158
South St. *Garg* 3M 53
South St. *Gt Ecc* 6N 65
South St. *Has* 6H 161
South St. *Lyth A* 4C 130
South St. *Newc* 6C 162
South St. *Ram* 8J 181
South St. *Raw* 4M 161
South Ter. *Orm* 8K 209
South Ter. *Ram* 4H 181
S. Terrace Ct. *Roch* 8D 204
S. Valley Dri. *Col* 8N 85
South Vw. *Bel* 9K 177
South Vw. *Gt Har* 4J 121
South Vw. *Has* 4G 161
South Vw. *K'ham* 5M 111
South Vw. *Los H* 9K 135 (School La.)
South Vw. *Los H* 9L 135 (Watkin La.)
South Vw. *Nels* 3H 105
South Vw. *S'stne* 7D 102
Southview Rd. *Roch* 1H 205
S. View St. *Todm* 7F 146
S. View Ter. *Ley* 7K 153
S. View Ter. *Roch* 1H 205
Southward Bottom. 9L 125
Southwark. Burn *3A 124* *(off Woodbine Rd.)*
S. Warton St. *Lyth A* 5B 130
Southway. *Fltwd* 3D 54
Southway. *Skel* 2M 219
S. Westby St. *Lyth A* 5A 130
Southwood Av. *Fltwd* 1E 54
Southwood Clo. *Lyth A* 4L 129
Southwood Dri. *Acc* 5D 142
Southworth Av. *Blac* 2E 108
Southworth St. *B'brn* 6L 139
Southworth Way. *T Clev* 7E 54
Sovereign Ga. *Blac* 4F 108
Sowarth Fld. *Set* 3N 35
Sowarth Light Ind. Est. *Gigg* 3N 35
Sow Clough Rd. *Bacup* 6H 163
Sowerbutt's Green. 9N 117
Sowerby Av. *Blac* 1D 108
Sowerby Rd. *S'by* 7J 67
Sowerby St. *Pad* 1H 123
Sower Carr. 8C 56
Sower Carr La. *Hamb* 8B 56
Spa Fold. *Lath* 8E 210
Spa Gth. *Clith* 3M 81
Spa La. *Lath* 8E 210
Spark La. *Ruf* 8F 170
Spa Rd. *Pres* 9G 115
Sparrow Hill. *App B* 2C 212
Sparrow Hill. *Roch* 6B 204
Sparth Av. *Clay M* 6M 121
Sparth Bottoms Rd. *Roch* 7A 204
Sparthfield Av. *Roch* 8B 204
Sparth Rd. *Clay M* 6L 121
Spa St. *Burn* 2C 124
Spa St. *Pad* 1J 123
Spa St. *Pres* 9G 114
Spa Well La. *Crost* 7K 171
Speakman Dri. *App B* 6F 212
Speedwell Clo. *T Clev* 7F 54
Speedwell St. *B'brn* 6J 139
Speke St. *B'brn* 6J 139
Spelding Dri. *Stand L* 8N 213
Spen Brook. 9B 84
Spenbrook Rd. *Newc P* 8A 84
Spen Brow Rd. *L Bent* 8H 19
Spencer Ct. *Blac* 3C 88
Spencer Dri. *Tar* 7E 150
Spencer La. *Roch* 8J 203
Spencer La. *Ruf* 1E 190
Spencer's La. *Hals* 1H 207
Spencer's La. *Liv* 8D 222
Spencer's La. *Orr* 4G 221
Spencers La. *Skel* 3M 219
Spencer St. *Acc* 2C 142
Spencer St. *Bacup* 7G 162
Spencer St. *Burn* 9E 104
Spencer St. *L'boro* 8M 185
Spencer St. *Ram* 9G 181
Spencer St. *Ross* 8M 143
Spendmore. *Cop* 3B 194
Spendmore La. *Cop* 5N 193
Spen Fold. *L'boro* 1K 205
Spen La. *Trea* 3C 112
Spenleach La. *Hawk* 1B 200
Spen Pl. *Blac* 1F 108
Spenser Clo. *Wors* 5N 125
Spenser Gro. *Gt Har* 4H 121
Spenser St. *Pad* 2J 123
Spenwood Rd. *L'boro* 9J 185
Spey Clo. *Ley* 7H 153
Spey Clo. *Stand* 3N 213
Speyside. *Blac* 2D 108
Spicer Gro. *Liv* 8K 223
Spindle Berry Ct. *Acc* 4B 142
Spinners Ct. Lanc *9K 23* *(off Queen St.)*
Spinners Gdns. *Ward* 1F 204
Spinners Grn. *Roch* 3C 204
Spinners Sq. *Bam B* 9A 136
Spinney Brow. *Rib* 5N 115
Spinney Clo. *New L* 8C 134
Spinney Clo. *Orm* 9J 209
Spinney Clo. *Whit W* 9D 154
Spinney Dri. *Bury* 7K 201
Spinney La. *Arns* 3G 4
Spinney, The. *Arns* 3G 4
Spinney, The. *B'brn* 9H 119
Spinney, The. *Burn* 1B 124
Spinney, The. *Chor* 3E 174
Spinney, The. *Form* 7A 206
Spinney, The. *Grin* 5A 74
Spinney, The. *Hey* 9M 21
Spinney, The. *Lanc* 2M 29
Spinney, The. *Pen* 5C 134
Spinney, The. *Poul F* 7L 63
Spinney, The. *Rainf* 3K 225
Spinney, The. *Tar* 8E 150
Spinney, The. *T Clev* 4F 62 (in two parts)
Spinney, The. *Tur* 3J 199
Spinnings, The. *S'seat* 2H 201
Spire Clo. *Dar* 7D 158
Spires Gro. *Cot* 4B 114
Spodden Cotts. *Whitw* 4A 184
Spodden Fold. *Whitw* 6N 183
Spodden St. *Roch* 5A 204
Spod Rd. *Roch* 4N 203
Spokeshave Way. *Roch* 3F 204
Spotland Bridge. 5A 204
Spotland Fold. 4N 203
Spotland Rd. *Roch* 5A 204
Spotland Tops. *Roch* 4M 203
Spout Ho. La. *Acc* 8E 122
Spout La. *Wenn* 5F 18
Spread Eagle St. *Osw* 3J 141
Spring Av. *Gt Har* 3J 121
Spring Bank. 5N 221
Spring Bank. *App B* 4F 212
Springbank. *Barfd* 6J 85
Springbank. *Gars* 6N 59
Springbank. *Heal* 1A 204
Spring Bank. *Pres* 1H 135
Spring Bank. *Silv* 8G 5
Spring Bank. *Whit W* 5A 184
Springbank Av. *T Clev* 1J 63
Springbank Gdns. *Good* 6L 143
Spring Bank La. *Roch* 5J 203 (in two parts)
Spring Bank Ter. *B'brn* 6K 139
Spring Bottom. *Todm* 8J 165
Springbrook Av. *T Clev* 3E 62
Spring Brook Ho. Clay M *7M 121* *(off Canal St.)*
Spring Clo. *Liv* 5L 223
Spring Clo. *Ram* 8G 181
Spring Clo. *South* 9G 166
Spring Clo. *Tot* 7D 200
Spring Ct. Col *6A 86* *(off Derby St.)*
Spring Ct. *Roch* 4C 204
Springcroft. *Far* 4M 153
Springdale Rd. *Lang* 1C 120
Springfield. *Arns* 2F 4
Springfield. *Ben* 6M 19
Springfield. *Black* 3G 85
Springfield. *Rainf* 9J 219
Springfield Av. *Acc* 4M 141
Springfield Av. *Bacup* 4L 163
Springfield Av. *B'brn* 7F 138
Springfield Av. *Earby* 3F 78
Springfield Av. *K'ham* 4K 111
Springfield Av. *L'boro* 7K 185
Springfield Bank. *Burn* 4E 124
Springfield Clo. *Burs* 2B 210
Springfield Clo. *Whal* 4K 101
Springfield Ct. Bacup *4L 163* *(off Springfield Av.)*
Springfield Ct. *Blac* 7E 88
Springfield Cres. *Ben* 6M 19
Springfield Dri. *Ross* 6C 162
Springfield Dri. *T Clev* 8H 55
Springfield Flats. *Dar* 7A 158
Springfield Gdns. *Scor* 7B 46
Springfield Ind. Est. Pres *8H 115* *(off Eastham St.)*
Springfield La. *Roch* 2G 204
Springfield Public Golf Course. 8L 203
Springfield Rd. *Adl* 5J 195
Springfield Rd. *Augh* 6E 216
Springfield Rd. *Blac* 4B 88
Springfield Rd. *Bolt* 6E 198
Springfield Rd. *Burn* 5E 124 (in two parts)
Springfield Rd. *Chor* 6E 174
Springfield Rd. *Cop* 5A 194
Springfield Rd. *Gt Har* 5H 121
Springfield Rd. *Ley* 8G 153
Springfield Rd. *Lyth A* 2E 128
Springfield Rd. *Nels* 4J 105
Springfield Rd. *Ram* 3F 200
Springfield Rd. *Ross* 4N 161
Springfield Rd. N. *Cop* 4A 194
Springfield St. *B'brn* 5J 139
Springfield St. *Dar* 7A 158
Springfield St. *Lanc* 9K 23
Springfield St. *More* 4N 21
Springfield St. *Osw* 5K 141
Springfield St. *Pres* 8H 115
Springfield Ter. Ben *6M 19* *(off Springfield)*
Springfield Ter. *B'brn* 7H 139
Springfield Ter. *Fltwd* 6G 54
Springfield Ter. *Hth C* 4K 195
Springfield Vw. *Dunn* 3A 144
Spring Gdns. *Acc* 3B 142
Spring Gdns. *Bacup* 4L 163
Spring Gdns. *Bolt* 9L 199
Spring Gdns. *Dar* 7A 158
Spring Gdns. *Frec* 9N 111
Spring Gdns. *Hor* 9C 196
Spring Gdns. *Ley* 7J 153
Spring Gdns. *Liv* 2D 222
Spring Gdns. *Lyth A* 8F 108
Spring Gdns. *Pen* 6J 135
Spring Gdns. *Roch* 6B 204
Spring Gdns. Ross *9M 143* *(off Lord St.)*
Spring Gdns. *Ross* 9D 162 (Springside)
Spring Gdns. *Wadd* 8H 73
Spring Gdns. Rd. *Col* 7A 86
Spring Gdns. St. *Ross* 7D 162
Spring Gdns. Ter. *Pad* 9H 103
Spring Garden St. *Lanc* 8K 23
Spring Gro. *Col* 5F 86
Spring Hall. *Acc* 4M 121
Spring Hill. 3N 141
Spring Hill. B'brn *3M 139* *(off Lord Sq.)*
Spring Hill. *Frec* 1B 132
Spring Hill. *Roch* 9E 204
Springhill. *Ross* 5A 162
Springhill Av. *Bacup* 7H 163
Spring Hill Rd. *Acc* 4M 141
Spring Hill Rd. *Burn* 4D 124
Springhill Vs. *Bacup* 7G 163
Spring La. *B'brn* 5J 139 (in two parts)
Spring La. *Col* 6A 86
Spring La. *Has* 3G 160
Spring La. *Sam* 8J 117
Spring Mdw. *Ley* 6A 154
Spring Meadows. *Dar* 8D 158
Spring M. *Whit W* 9G 154
Spring Mill Wlk. *Roch* 2F 204
Springmount. *Earby* 3F 78
Springmount Dri. *Parb* 8N 191
Spring Pl. *Col* 6A 86
Spring Pl. *Whitw* 4A 184
Springpool. *Wins* 9L 221
Spring Rd. *Orr* 3J 221
Springs. *Roch* 6J 203
Springsands Clo. *Ful* 4A 116
Springs Brow. *Wrigh* 8N 193
Springs Cres. *Whit W* 1G 174
Springside. 4N 161
Spring Side. *Roch* 2A 184
Springside. *Ross* 9D 162
Spring Side La. *Ward* 8D 184
Springside Rd. *Bury* 5J 201 (in two parts)
Springside Vw. *Bury* 6G 201
Springside Vw. Cotts. *Bury* 6H 201
Springs Rd. *Chor* 4F 174
Springs Rd. *L'rdge* 2K 97
Spring St. *Acc* 4M 141
Spring St. *Bacup* 6K 163
Spring St. *Hor* 9C 196
Spring St. *Ley* 6L 153
Spring St. *Nels* 3G 105
Spring St. *Osw* 4L 141
Spring St. *Ram* 7J 181
Spring St. *Rish* 7H 121
Spring St. *Ross* 8M 143
Spring St. *Todm* 7F 146
Spring St. *Tot* 6D 200
Spring St. *Wals* 9E 200
Spring Ter. *Bacup* 7H 163
Spring Ter. Lang *9D 100* *(off Clayton Row)*
Spring Ter. L'rdge *3H 97* *(off Whittingham Rd.)*
Spring Ter. *Roch* 5L 203
Spring Ter. *Ross* 6L 143
Spring Ter. S. *Ross* 5K 161
Springthorpe St. *Dar* 9B 158
Spring Vale. 8C 158 **(Darwen)**
Spring Vale. 5F 160 **(Haslingden)**
Springvale. *Acc* 4M 141
Spring Va. *Fort* 2M 45
Springvale Bus. Pk. *Dar* 9B 158
Springvale Dri. *Tot* 6D 200
Spring Vale Garden Village. 9C 158
Spring Va. Rd. *Dar* 8B 158
Spring Va. St. *Tot* 7D 200
Spring Va. Ter. L'boro *9L 185* *(off Victoria St.)*
Spring Vw. *B'brn* 3K 139
Spring Vw. *Cliv* 9L 125
Spring Vs. *Corn* 7E 146
Springwater Av. *Ram* 2F 200
Springwood Clo. *Walt D* 5K 135
Springwood Dri. *Chor* 9G 175
Springwood Dri. *Ruf* 8E 170
Spring Wood Nature Trail. 5L 101
Springwood Rd. *Burn* 4J 125
Spring Wood St. *Ram* 7G 181
Spring Yd. *Col* 6A 86
Sprodley Dri. *App B* 2E 212
Spruce Av. *Lanc* 3K 29
Spruce Ct. *Acc* 9D 122
Spruce Cres. *Bury* 6L 201
Spruce St. *Ram* 9F 180
Spruce St. *Roch* 7E 204
Spruce Wlk. *Todm* 7K 165
Sprucewood Clo. *Acc* 2C 142
Spurriers La. *Liv* 2H 223
Spurrier St. *Ley* 3K 153
Spymers Cft. *Liv* 6A 206
Square Ho. La. *Banks* 8G 149
Square La. *Burs* 1C 210
Square La. *Catf* 6K 93
Square Rd. *Todm* 7K 165
Square St. *Ram* 8H 181
Square, The. *Blac* 8G 89
Square, The. *Brins* 8A 156
Square, The. *Burt* 6G 7
Square, The. *Far* 5L 153
Square, The. *T Clev* 7D 54
Square, The. *Wadd* 8H 73
Square, The. *Walt D* 3B 136
Square, The. *W'ham* 5B 96
Square, The. Wors *4M 125* *(off Water St.)*
Square Vw. *Todm* 7L 165
Squire Rd. *Nels* 2K 105
Squires Clo. *Hogh* 6G 136
Squires Ct. *Blac* 4D 108
Squires Ga. Ind. Est. *Blac* 5E 108
Squires Ga. La. *Blac* 5B 108
Squires Ga. Rd. *Ash R* 6F 114
Squires Rd. *Pen* 2F 134
Squires Wood. *Ful* 3N 115
Squirrel Chase. *Lanc* 2J 29
Squirrel Fold. *Rib* 7B 116
Squirrel La. *Hor* 9B 196
Squirrels Chase. *Clift* 8H 113
Squirrel's Chase. *Los H* 9K 135
Squirrels Clo. *Acc* 9D 122
Stable Clo. Gis *9A 52* *(off Park Rd.)*
Stable Clo. *Wesh* 3M 111
Stable La. *Wheel* 8J 155
Stables Clo. *Ross* 1M 161
Stables, The. *Hap* 4H 123
Stackcroft. *Clay W* 5C 154
Stackhills Rd. *Todm* 2M 165
Stackhouse La. *Gigg* 2N 35
Stackhouses, The. Burn *3E 124* *(off Bank Pde.)*
Stack La. *Bacup* 7M 163
Stacksteads. 7F 162
Stadium Av. *Blac* 4D 108
Staffa Cres. *B'brn* 4D 140
Stafford Av. *Poul F* 1K 89
Stafford Ct. *Roch* 1H 205
Stafford Moreton Way. *Liv* 1B 222
Stafford Rd. *Pres* 8K 115
Stafford Rd. *South* 4G 186
Stafford St. *Burn* 2E 124
Stafford St. *Bury* 9J 201
Stafford St. *Dar* 3N 157
Stafford St. *Nels* 2K 105
Stafford St. *Skel* 1H 219
Staghills. 6B 162
Staghills Rd. *Ross* 5B 162
Stag La. *Boot* 8A 222
Stainburn Clo. *Shev* 6G 213
Stainforth Av. *Blac* 6E 62
Stainforth La. *L'clif* 1N 35
Stainforth Rd. *L'clif* 1N 35
Staining. 5K 89
Staining Av. *Ash R* 8C 114
Staining Old Rd. *Blac* 3K 89
Staining Old Rd. W. Blac *5K 89* *(off Nook, The)*
Staining Ri. *Stain* 5K 89
Staining Rd. *Blac* 3H 89
Stainton Dri. *Burn* 1C 124
Stainton Gro. *More* 4E 22
Stainton St. *Carn* 7A 12
Stake Pool. 9K 43
Stakepool Dri. *Pil* 9K 43
Stakes Hall Pl. *B'brn* 6K 139
Stalls Rd. *Hey* 5L 27
Stalmine. 5B 56
Stalmine Moss Side. 5C 56
Stambourne Dri. *Bolt* 9F 198
Stamford Av. *Blac* 2D 108
Stamford Ct. Lyth A *9D 108* *(off St Leonards Rd. W.)*
Stamford Dri. *Whit W* 1E 174
Stamford Pl. *Clith* 2M 81
Stamford Rd. *Skel* 1H 219
Stamford Rd. *South* 2H 187
Stamford St. *Roch* 7E 204
Stanagate. *Clift* 8G 113
Stanah. 1L 63
Stanah Gdns. *T Clev* 1L 63
Stanah Rd. *T Clev* 2K 63
Stanalea La. *Goos* 3K 69
Stanbury Clo. *Burn* 8J 105
Stanbury Dri. *Burn* 8J 105
Stancliffe St. *B'brn* 5J 139
Stancliffe St. Ind. Est. *B'brn* 5K 139
Standedge Clo. *Ram* 2H 201
Standen Hall Clo. *Burn* 7J 105
Standen Hall Dri. *Burn* 8H 105
Standen Pk. Ho. *Lanc* 8N 23

Standen Rd.—Sudren St.

Standen Rd. Clith 4M 81
Standen Rd. Bungalows. Clith 4M 81
Standhouse La. Augh 1H 217
Standing Stone La. Foul 1L 85
Standish Cricket Club Ground. 4N 213
Standish Dri. Rainf 3L 225
Standish Lower Ground. 9N 213
Standish St. Burn 3E 124
Standish St. Chor 7F 174
Standridge Clough La. Earby 2G 79
Standroyd Dri. Col 6D 86
Standroyd Rd. Col 6D 86
Stanfield Ct. Todm 1L 165 (off Stanfield Hall Rd.)
Stanford Gdns. B'brn 7A 140
Stanford Hall Cres. Ram 1G 200
Stangate. Liv 9A 216
Stang Top Rd. R'lee 4D 84
Stanhill. 4H 141
Stanhill La. Osw 4H 141
Stanhill Rd. B'brn & Osw 4E 140
Stanhill St. Osw 5J 141
Stanhope Av. More 5E 22
Stanhope Ct. More 5F 22
Stanhope Rd. Blac 3C 88
Stanhope St. Burn 2D 124
Stanhope St. Dar 5A 158
Stanhope St. Pres 7G 115
Stanhope St. Roch 8C 204
Stanifield Clo. Far 4L 153
Stanifield La. Far & Los H 5L 153
Stankelt Rd. Silv 9G 4
Stanley. 3G 71 (Preston)
Stanley. 9J 211 (Skelmersdale)
Stanley Av. Far 3M 153
Stanley Av. Hut 6A 134
Stanley Av. Pen 3H 135
Stanley Av. Poul F 8J 63
Stanley Av. Rainf 3J 225
Stanley Av. South 2F 186
Stanley Av. T Clev 1D 62
Stanley Clo. L'rdge 3K 97
Stanley Ct. Acc 1C 142
Stanley Ct. Burs 8C 190
Stanley Ct. K'ham 5N 111
Stanley Cft. Wood 7E 94
Stanley Dri. Dar 1B 178
Stanley Dri. Horn 7C 18 (off Monteagle Dri.)
Stanleyfield Clo. Pres 8K 115
Stanleyfield Rd. Pres 8K 115
Stanley Fold. Los H 8J 135
Stanley Gate. 4C 218
Stanley Ga. Fltwd 1D 54
Stanley Ga. Mel 7F 118
Stanley Gro. Pen 4D 134
Stanley Ind. Est. Uph 9J 211
Stanley Mt. Bacup 4K 163
Stanley Pk. Clo. Blac 7F 88
Stanley Pl. Chor 6E 174
Stanley Pl. Lanc 8H 23
Stanley Pl. Pres 1H 135
Stanley Pl. Roch 5B 204
Stanley Range. B'brn 6J 139
Stanley Rd. Blac 6C 88
Stanley Rd. Far 3M 153
Stanley Rd. Fltwd 1F 54
Stanley Rd. Hey 5M 21
Stanley Rd. Lyth A 5K 129
Stanley Rd. Mag 4B 222
Stanley Rd. Uph 4D 220
Stanley Rd. Wesh 2L 111
Stanley St. Acc 2B 142
Stanley St. Bacup 3K 163
Stanley St. B'brn 2A 140
Stanley St. Brier 5F 104
Stanley St. Burn 4D 124
Stanley St. Carn 9A 12
Stanley St. Chor 7G 174
Stanley St. Col 6A 86
Stanley St. K'ham 5N 111
Stanley St. Ley 6L 153
Stanley St. L'rdge 2J 97
Stanley St. More 2B 22 (off Bk. Morcambe St.)
Stanley St. Nels 2H 105
Stanley St. Orm 7L 209
Stanley St. Osw 5K 141
Stanley St. Pres 9L 115
Stanley St. Ram 9G 181
Stanley St. South 7H 167
Stanley Ter. Pres 1H 135
Stanley Way. Skel & Stan I 9J 211
Stanmere Ct. Hawk 2A 200
Stanmore Av. Blac 3E 108
Stanmore Dri. Lanc 2J 29
Stannally St. Todm 8H 147
Stannanought Rd. Skel 9N 211 (in two parts)
Stanneybrook Clo. Roch 5E 204
Stanney Clo. Miln 8H 205
Stanney Rd. Roch 5E 204
Stanning Clo. Ley 7H 153
Stanrose Clo. Eger 4E 198
Stansfeld St. B'brn 5K 139
Stansfield Av. Liv 1E 222
Stansfield Clo. Barfd 7H 85
Stansfield Dri. Roch 4J 203
Stansfield Hall. L'boro 5M 185
Stansfield Hall Rd. Todm 1L 165
Stansfield Rd. Ross 7C 162
Stansfield Rd. Todm 2L 165
Stansfield St. Bacup 7G 163
Stansfield St. Blac 9C 88
Stansfield St. Burn 4N 123
Stansfield St. Dar 7A 158
Stansfield St. Nels 2J 105
Stansfield St. Todm 1L 165
Stansfield Ter. Todm 7E 146
Stansford Ct. Pen 4G 135
Stansted Rd. Chor 7C 174
Stansy Av. Hey 7M 21
Stanthorpe Wlk. Burn 9E 104
Stanton Cres. Liv 8H 223
Stanworth. 3D 156
Stanworth Rd. Nels 2H 105
Stanworth St. Wors 4M 125
Stanworth Ter. Withn 3C 156
Stanzaker Hall Dri. Catt 4M 67
Star Bank. Bacup 8H 163
Starbeck Av. Blac 1D 108
Starfield Av. L'boro 3J 205
Starfield Clo. Lyth A 4N 129
Star Inn Cotts. Rainf 5L 225
Starkie Ind. Est. Ash R 7G 115
Starkie St. B'brn 3N 139
Starkie St. Burn 4C 124
Starkie St. Dar 7B 158
Starkie St. Ley 6L 153
Starkie St. Pad 1H 123
Starkie St. Pres 1J 135
Starr Ga. Blac 5B 108
Starrgate Dri. Ash R 8B 114
Starr Hills Nature Reserve. 6B 108
Starring Gro. L'boro 9J 185 (off Starring Rd.)
Starring La. L'boro 9H 185
Starring Rd. L'boro 9H 185 (in two parts)
Starring Way. L'boro 9J 185
Stars Brow. Wig 8N 193
Star St. Acc 3M 141
Star St. Dar 6B 158
Startifants La. Chip 5D 70
Startley Nook. Wstke 1E 152
State Mill Cen. Roch 8E 204
States Rd. Lyth A 2H 129
Statham Rd. Uph 9H 211
Statham Way. Orm 8K 209
Station App. Burs 8C 190 (in two parts)
Station App. Orm 7L 209
Station App. Todm 2L 165
Station App. Bus. Cen. Roch 7C 204 (off Station Rd.)
Station Av. Orr 6G 221
Station Brow. Ley 5L 153
Station Clo. Horn 7C 18
Station Clo. Rish 9G 121
Station Clo. Wilp 5N 119
Stationers Entry. Roch 6C 204 (off Walk, The)
Station La. Burt 4F 6
Station La. Nate 3F 58
Station La. Scor 6N 45
Station La. Wood 4B 94
Station M. Liv 7H 223
Station Pde. Todm 7C 146
Station Rd. Acc 7D 122
Station Rd. Adl 7H 195
Station Rd. Ains 8C 186
Station Rd. Arns 1F 4
Station Rd. Bam B 9A 136 (in two parts)
Station Rd. Banks 1D 168
Station Rd. Barn 2M 77
Station Rd. Bar 5K 207
Station Rd. Ben 7L 19
Station Rd. Blac 1B 108
Station Rd. Burn 2E 124
Station Rd. Cat 2H 25
Station Rd. Clith 3L 81
Station Rd. Cop 4B 194
Station Rd. Crost 3M 171
Station Rd. Fltwd 9G 41
Station Rd. Foul 2A 86
Station Rd. Gigg 3N 35
Station Rd. Gt Har 4K 121
Station Rd. G'mnt 4E 200
Station Rd. Has 3G 160
Station Rd. Helm 8E 160
Station Rd. Hesk B 3C 150
Station Rd. Hest B 8H 15
Station Rd. Hogh 6K 137
Station Rd. Holme 1F 6
Station Rd. Horn 7C 18
Station Rd. Lanc 8J 23
Station Rd. L'boro 9L 185
Station Rd. L Hoo 2G 150
Station Rd. Lyd 5N 215
Station Rd. Lyth A 5A 130
Station Rd. Mag 2D 222
Station Rd. Mell 7F 222
Station Rd. Midg H 4D 152
Station Rd. More 3B 22
Station Rd. New L 8C 134
Station Rd. Orm 6L 209
Station Rd. Pad 1H 123
Station Rd. Parb 2N 211
Station Rd. Poul F 7L 63
Station Rd. Poul F & Sing 3A 90
Station Rd. Rim 3K 75
Station Rd. Rish 9G 121
Station Rd. Roch 7C 204
Station Rd. Ruf 1H 191
Station Rd. Salw & Hesk B 4G 112
Station Rd. T Clev 2J 63
Station Rd. Todm 7F 146
Station Rd. Tur 1J 199
Station Rd. Wesh & K'ham 3L 111 (in two parts)
Station Rd. Whal 5J 101
Station Rd. Whitw 3A 184
Station Rd. W Grn 5G 110
Station Sq. Lyth A 5N 129
Station Ter. Abb V 5D 156
Station Ter. Blac 1B 108
Station Ter. Burt 4F 6
Station Way. Gars 4N 59
Station Way. Horn 8C 18
Staveley Av. Bolt 7E 198
Staveley Av. Burs 9C 190
Staveley Gro. Fltwd 2D 54
Staveley Pl. Ash R 7B 114
Staveley Rd. South 9D 186
Staveley Rd. Uph 9J 211
Staverton Pk. Liv 9H 223
Stavordale. Roch 5B 204 (off Spotland Rd.)
Staynall. 8M 55
Staynall La. Hamb 8M 55
Stead St. Ram 8H 181
Sted Ter. B'brn 2L 139
Steeley La. Chor 7F 174
Steeple Vw. Ash R 9G 114
Steeple Vw. Liv 5K 223
Steer St. Burn 9F 104
Steeton Rd. Blac 1H 89
Stefano Rd. Pres 9M 115
Steiner's La. Chu 1L 141 (off York St.)
Steiner St. Acc 2N 141
Stephenage Pk. Pen 6J 135
Stephendale Av. Bam B 8D 136
Stephens Gro. Over 7B 28
Stephenson Dri. Burn 2N 123
Stephenson St. Chor 6G 174
Stephenson Way. Form 9B 206
Stephen St. B'brn 6J 139
Stephen St. Lyth A 1E 128
Step Row. Bacup 2K 163
Steps Mdw. Roch 1F 204
Sterndale Av. Stand 2N 213
Stevenson Av. Far 4M 153
Stevenson Sq. Roch 2F 204
Stevenson St. E. Acc 3N 141
Stevenson St. W. Acc 4M 141
Steward Av. Lanc 2M 29
Stewart Clo. Arns 3F 4
Stewart St. B'brn 8L 139
Stewart St. Burn 5F 124
Stewart St. Bury 9G 201 (in two parts)
Stewart St. Miln 9L 205
Stewart St. Pres 9G 115
Stile Moor Ri. Todm 9K 147
Stile Rd. Todm 9K 147
Stiles Av. Hut 7N 133
Stiles Rd. Liv 4L 223
Stiles, The. Orm 7K 209
Stirling Clo. Chor 7G 174
Stirling Clo. Clith 5J 81
Stirling Clo. Ley 6M 153
Stirling Ct. Brclf 6M 105
Stirling Ct. South 4N 167
Stirling Dri. B'brn 4N 139
Stirling Rd. Blac 4D 88
Stirling Rd. Bolt 8E 198
Stirling Rd. Lanc 9L 23
Stirling St. B'brn 7J 139
Stiups La. Roch 9E 204
Stock. 8E 52
Stockbridge Dri. Pad 1K 123
Stockbridge Rd. Pad 1J 123
Stockclough La. Fen 9E 138
Stockdale Cres. Bam B 9B 136
Stockdove Way. T Clev 9D 54
Stockdove Wood. T Clev 9E 54 (in two parts)
Stock Gro. Miln 6J 205
Stockholm St. Burn 4N 123
Stockley Cres. Bic 5C 218
Stockley Dri. App B 4H 213
Stockpit Rd. Know I 8A 224
Stock Rd. Roch 3D 204
Stocks Clo. Wheel 6K 155
Stocks Ct. Poul F 8K 63
Stocks Ga. Roch 3M 203
Stocks La. Hesk 2H 193
Stocks La. Poul F 7G 62
Stocks La. Rim 5E 76
Stocks Rd. Ash R 7F 114
Stocks Rd. Poul F 8F 62
Stocks St. Pres 9H 115
Stock St. Bury 8K 201
Stockton Dri. Bury 8G 201
Stockton St. L'boro 9K 185
Stockwell Clo. Wig 8N 221
Stockwood Clo. B'brn 9H 119
Stockydale Rd. Blac 3G 109
Stodday. 5G 29
Stoke Av. Blac 8D 88
Stokes Hall Av. Ley 7K 153
Stokesley Av. Liv 8H 223
Stoke St. Roch 7E 204
Stoneacre Dri. Adl 4J 195
Stonebarn Dri. Liv 8B 216
Stonebridge Clo. Los H 8M 135
Stone Bri. La. Osw 5K 141
Stonebridge Ter. Col 6B 86
Stonebridge Ter. L'rdge 4J 97
Stonechat Clo. Blac 4H 89
Stone Clo. Ram 1F 200
Stone Cft. Barfd 5J 85
Stone Cft. Pen 6G 134
Stonecroft Rd. Ley 8G 152
Stone Cross Gdns. Catt 1A 68
Stonedross La. Barb 3G 8
Stone Edge Rd. Barfd 5J 85
Stonefield. Longt 8K 133
Stonefield. Pen 4H 135
Stonefield St. Miln 8J 205
Stoneflat Ct. Roch 5A 204
Stone Fold. 7G 143
Stonefold Av. Hut 7N 133
Stonegate. L Bent 6K 19 (off Doctor's Hill)
Stonegate Fold. Hth C 4K 195
Stone Hall La. Uph 8C 212
Stonehaven. Wig 9N 221
Stone Head La. Loth 8N 79
Stonehey Rd. Liv 9K 223
Stone Hey Wlk. Liv 9K 223
Stonehill Cres. Roch 2L 203
Stone Hill Dri. B'brn 8A 120
Stonehill Dri. Roch 2L 203
Stone Hill La. Roch 3L 203
Stonehill Rd. Roch 2L 203
Stoneholme Ind. Est. Ross 8M 143
Stoneholme Rd. Ross 8M 143
Stone Holme Ter. Ross 8M 143
Stonehouse. Brom X 6H 199
Stonehouse Grn. Clay W 4D 154
Stone House Rd. Wig 1N 221
Stoneleigh Clo. South 9C 186
Stoneleigh Ct. Silv 8G 4
Stonely Dri. Todm 8K 165
Stonemoor Bottom. Pad 3H 123
Stone Pits. Ram 3K 181
Stone Row Head. Lanc 8N 23
Stones Bank Rd. Eger 9N 177
Stones La. Catt 1A 68
Stones La. Todm 2H 165
Stones Rd. Todm 3J 165
Stonesteads Dri. Brom X 5G 199
Stonesteads Way. Brom X 5G 198
Stones Ter. Todm 5J 165
Stone St. Bacup 8F 162
Stone St. Miln 8J 205
Stone St. Ross 5E 160 (Hutch Bank Rd.)
Stone St. Ross 7D 162 (Townsend St.)
Stone Trough Brow. Kel 9C 78
Stoneway Rd. T Clev 2E 62
Stonewell. Lanc 8K 23
Stoney Bank Rd. Earby 2F 78
Stoneyboyd. Whitw 5A 184
Stoney Brow. Roby M 9E 212 (in two parts)
Stoneybutts. B'brn 3M 139 (off Lord Sq.)
Stoney Butts. Lea 9A 114
Stoney Ct. Foul 2B 86
Stoneycroft. Wors 4L 125
Stoneycroft Av. Hor 9E 196
Stoneycroft Clo. Hor 8E 196
Stoney Cft. Dri. War 3B 12
Stoneyfield. 9C 204
Stoneygate. Pres 1K 135
Stoneygate. T Clev 2F 62
Stoneygate La. App B 2E 212
Stoneygate La. K Grn & Ribch 2D 98
Stoneyholme. 2C 124
Stoney Holt. Ley 6A 154
Stoneyhurst Av. Liv 7B 222
Stoneyhurst Av. T Clev 3K 63
Stoneyhurst Height. Brier 6H 105
Stoney La. Adl 9G 195
Stoney La. Foul 2B 86
Stoney La. Frec 3N 131
Stoney La. Gal & Ellel 3L 37
Stoney La. Goos 8B 70
Stoney La. Hamb 1B 64
Stoney La. Los H 1M 153
Stoney Royd La. Todm 8J 147
Stoney St. Burn 5F 124
Stoneyvale Ct. Roch 9C 204
Stonie Heys Av. Roch 3E 204
Stonor Rd. Adl 6H 195
Stony Bank. Brin 2J 155
Stonycroft Av. Blac 4C 108
Stonycroft Dri. Arns 2F 4
Stonycroft Pl. Blac 4C 108
Stony Head. L'boro 4M 185 (off Higher Calderbrook Rd.)
Stony Hill. 4B 108
Stony Hill. Todm 6H 147
Stony Hill Av. Blac 4B 108
Stonyhurst. 8B 80
Stonyhurst. Chor 1E 194
Stonyhurst Av. Bolt 8E 198
Stonyhurst Av. Burn 4H 125
Stonyhurst Clo. B'brn 4L 139
Stonyhurst Clo. Pad 3K 123
Stonyhurst College. 8A 80
Stonyhurst Pk. Golf Course. 9N 71
Stonyhurst Rd. B'brn 4L 139
Stony La. Fort 2A 46 (Hollins La.)
Stony La. Fort 4K 45 (Ratcliffe Wharf La.)
Stony La. Parb 9N 191
Stony Rake. Has 5M 159
Stoopes Hill. Earby 2F 78
Stoops Fold. Mel 6F 118
Stoop St. Burn 4A 124
Stopes Brow. Lwr D 9A 140
Stopford Av. Blac 9E 62
Stopford Av. L'boro 1H 205
Stopford Ct. Clay M 6M 121
Stopgate La. Sim 4M 223
Stopper Lane. 4M 75
Stopper La. Rim 4M 75
Store Pas. L'boro 9K 185
Store St. Has 4G 161
Store St. Hor 9D 196
Store St. Lwr D 9A 140
Storey Av. Lanc 8H 23
Stork Clo. T Clev 2F 62
Stork Street. 7D 158
Stormer Hill Fold. Tot 5E 200
Storrs La. Silv 8K 5
Storth Rd. Carr B 2J 5
Stott St. Hur & Roch 2G 205
Stott St. Nels 2H 105
Stott St. Roch 4C 204
Stour Lodge. Ful 3F 114
Stourton Rd. South 9C 186
Stourton St. Rish 7G 121
Stout St. B'brn 4L 139
Stow Clo. Bury 8J 201
Stowe Av. Liv 8D 222
Straight Up La. South 6B 168
Straitgate Cotts. R'lee 6E 84
Strait La. Abb 3A 48
Straits. Osw 4L 141
Straits La. Read 8C 102
Straits, The. Hogh 5J 137
Strand Rd. Pres 1G 134
Strand St. W. Ash R 9F 114
Strand, The. Blac 5B 88
Strand, The. Fltwd 4C 54
Strange St. Burn 5F 124
Strang St. Ram 8H 181
Stranraer Rd. Wig 2M 221
Stransdale Clo. Gars 5M 59
Stratfield Pl. Ley 6L 153
Stratford Av. Bury 5K 201
Stratford Clo. Lanc 5J 23
Stratford Clo. South 7A 186
Stratford Dri. Ful 5G 115
Stratford Pl. Blac 7E 88
Stratford Pl. Fltwd 9E 40
Stratford Rd. Chor 6F 174
Stratford Rd. Lyth A 2H 129
Stratford Way. Acc 1N 141
Stratford Way. Col 6C 86
Strathclyde Rd. B'brn 4A 140
Strathdale. Blac 2F 108
Strathmore Clo. Ram 1H 201
Strathmore Gro. Chor 7D 174
Strathmore Rd. Ful 5H 115
Strathyre Clo. Blac 6F 62
Stratton Gro. Hor 8C 196
Stratton Rd. Liv 9H 223
Stratton Wlk. Liv 9H 223
Strawberry Bank. B'brn 3L 139
Strawberry Fields. Chor 3E 174
Strawberry M. Hey 8L 21
Stray, The. Bolt 9H 199
Streatly Wlk. B'brn 8A 140
Strellas La. Halt 8N 15
Stretford Clo. Liv 5K 223
Stretford Pl. Roch 2B 204
Stretton Av. Blac 1E 108
Stretton Clo. Stand 4N 213
Stretton Dri. South 6M 167
Stretton Rd. Ram & G'mnt 3F 200
Strickens La. Bncr 6D 60
Strickland Dri. More 4E 22
Stricklands La. Pen 4G 135
Strickland's La. Stalm 6B 56
Strike La. Frec 9N 111 (in two parts)
Strines St. Todm 8K 165
Strine, The. Ruf 6E 170
Strongstry. 4H 181
Strongstry Rd. Ram 4H 181
Stronsay Pl. Blac 5F 62
Stroops La. Rim 4L 75
Stroyan St. Burn 4G 125
Strutt St. Pres 8L 115
Stryands. Hut 7N 133
Stuart Av. Bacup 7H 163
Stuart Av. More 2D 22
Stuart Clo. Dar 6A 158
Stuart Clo. Rib 6A 116
Stuart Pl. Blac 1G 89
Stuart Rd. Mell 7G 222
Stuart Rd. Rib 6A 116
Stuart Rd. T Clev 1J 63
Stuart St. Acc 1A 142
Stuart St. Barn 2N 77
Stuart St. Roch 7D 204 (in two parts)
Stubbins. 1B 68 (Preston)
Stubbins. 5G 180 (Ramsbottom)
Stubbins La. Clau B 1B 68
Stubbins La. Ram 7H 181
Stubbins La. Sab 3F 102
Stubbins St. Ram 5H 181
Stubbins Va. Cvn. Pk. Sab 3F 102
Stubbins Va. Rd. Ram 4H 181
Stubbins Va. Ter. Ram 5G 181
Stubbylee La. Bacup 7K 163
Stub La. Burs 2M 209
Stubley. 9K 185
Stubley Gdns. L'boro 9K 185
Stubley Holme. Todm 7D 146
Stubley La. L'boro 9J 185
Stubley La. Todm 7D 146
Stubley Mill Rd. L'boro 1H 205 (in two parts)
Studfold. Chor 4D 174
Studholme Av. Pen 6H 135
Studholme Clo. Pen 6H 135
Studholme Cres. Pen 5H 135
Stump Cross La. Bolt B 7M 51
Stump Hall Rd. High 3K 103
Stump La. Chor 6F 174
Stunstead Rd. Traw 8F 86
Sturgess Clo. Orm 5L 209
Sturminster Clo. Pen 6H 135
Styan St. Fltwd 9G 41 (in two parts)
Stydd. 6F 98
Stydd La. Ribch 6F 98
Sudden. 9N 203
Sudden St. Roch 9N 203
Sudell Av. Liv 9E 216
Sudell Clo. Dar 6C 158
Sudell Cross. B'brn 3M 139 (off Limebrick)
Sudell La. Liv 5C 216
Sudell Nook. Guide 8C 140
Sudell Rd. Dar 6A 158
Sudellside St. Dar 6B 158
Sudley Rd. Roch 8N 203
Sudlow St. Roch 3E 204
Sudren St. Bury 9E 200

Suffolk Av.—Tenby Rd.

Suffolk Av. Burn 3M 123
Suffolk Clo. Ley 9H 153
Suffolk Rd. Blac 8G 89
Suffolk Rd. Pres 8K 115
Suffolk Rd. South 5G 186
Suffolk St. B'brn 6K 139
Suffolk St. Roch 7C 204
Suffton Pk. Liv 9H 223
Sugar Ho. All. Lanc 8K 23
(off Phoenix St.)
Sugar La. Todm 6G 147
Sugar Stubbs La. South 2H 169
Sugham La. Hey 8L 21
Sulby Clo. South 2F 186
Sulby Dri. Lanc 1K 29
Sulby Dri. Rib 4B 116
Sulby Gro. More 2E 22
Sulby Gro. Rib 4C 116
Sulby Rd. B'brn 7M 139
Sullivan Dri. B'brn 7A 140
Sullom Side La. Bncr 7F 60
Sullom Vw. Gars 6N 59
Sulphur Wells. Brou 6M 53
Sultan St. Acc 2B 142
Sulyard St. Lanc 8K 23
Summer Brook. Nels 3G 104
Summer Castle. Roch 6C 204
Summerdale Dri. Ram 3G 200
Summerer Gro. Weet 4D 90
Summerfield. Ley 4J 153
Summerfield. Thorn C 9J 53
Summerfield Clo. Walt D 6L 135
Summerfield Dri. Slyne 1J 23
Summerfield Rd. Todm 2M 165
Summerfield Rd. W. Todm 2M 165
Summerfields. Cop 5B 194
Summerfields. Lyth A 9C 108
Summerhill. Ben 7L 19
Summer Hill Clo. Bolt 7D 198
Summerhill Dri. Liv 3E 222
Summersales Ind. Est. Wig 7L 221
Summers Barn. Ful 3A 116
Summerseat. 3H 201
Summerseat La. Ram 2F 200
(in two parts)
Summerseat Rd. Ram 3G 201
Summersgill Rd. Lanc 6H 23
Summer St. Hor 9C 196
Summer St. Nels 3G 104
Summer St. Roch 6D 204
Summer St. Skel 8K 211
Summerton Wlk. Dar 5A 158
(off Allerton Clo.)
Summer Trees Av. Lea 6A 114
Summerville. Blac 3C 108
Summerville Av. Stain 5K 89
Summerville Wlk. B'brn 3L 139
Summerwood Clo. Blac 1D 88
Summerwood La. Hals 3B 208
Summit. 4N 185
Summit Clo. Bury 9D 202
Summit Dri. Frec 2A 132
Summit Works. Burn 7C 124
Sumner Av. Hask 8M 207
Sumner Gro. Liv 5L 223
Sumner Rd. Liv 9A 206
Sumners La. Crost 7K 171
Sumner St. B'brn 5L 139
(in two parts)
Sumner St. Ley 6K 153
Sumpter Ct. Pen 6J 135
Sumpter Cft. Pen 6H 135
Sunacre Ct. Hey 6M 21
Sunbank Clo. Roch 3A 204
Sunbury Av. Pen 5G 134
Sunbury Dri. South 9B 186
Suncliffe Rd. Brier 6H 105
Sunderland Av. Hamb 1C 64
Sunderland Av. T Clev 8E 54
Sunderland Dri. More 6A 22
Sunderland Pl. Wig 2N 221
Sunderland St. Burn 3N 123
Sunfield Clo. Blac 2G 108
Sun Ga. L'boro 4J 205
Sunnindale Av. Ross 6E 162
Sunningdale. Wood 7E 94
Sunningdale Av. Blac 8G 88
Sunningdale Av. Fltwd 5D 54
Sunningdale Av. Hest B 8H 15
Sunningdale Clo. K'ham 5M 111
Sunningdale Ct. St A 2G 129
Sunningdale Cres. Hest B 9H 15
Sunningdale Dri. T Clev 3K 63
Sunningdale Gdns. Burn 7H 105
Sunningdale Pl. Ins 2G 93
Sunny Av. Bury 8L 201
Sunny Bank. K'ham 4L 111
(in two parts)
Sunnybank. Ross 8M 143
Sunny Bank Av. Blac 7C 62
Sunny Bank Av. Newt 7E 112
Sunnybank Clo. Pen 4H 135
Sunnybank Clo. Ross 9F 160
Sunny Bank Cotts. Ross 1E 180
Sunnybank Dri. Osw 6J 141
Sunny Bank Farm Ind. Est.
Hamb 2C 64
Sunny Bank Rd. B'brn 7L 139
Sunnybank Rd. Bolt S 4L 15
Sunny Bank Rd. Helm 9E 160
Sunnybank St. Dar 6A 158
Sunnybank St. Has 4F 160
Sunny Bank Ter. Todm 7E 146
Sunny Bower. 8B 120
Sunny Bower Clo. B'brn 8B 120
Sunny Bower Rd. B'brn 8B 120
Sunny Bower St. Tot 7D 200
Sunny Brow. Cop 3C 194
Sunnycliff Retail Pk.
Heat O 7D 22
Sunny Dri. Orr 5J 221
Sunnyfield Av. Cliv 9L 125
Sunnyfield Av. More 2E 22
Sunnyfield La. Hodd 6F 158
Sunnyfields. Orm 7M 209
Sunnyfields. Wins 9M 221
Sunnyhill. Ful 4M 115
Sunnyhill Clo. Dar 5L 157
Sunnyhurst. 5M 157
Sunnyhurst Av. Blac 3D 108
Sunnyhurst Clo. Dar 5L 157
Sunnyhurst La. Dar 5L 157
Sunnyhurst Pk. Blac 3D 108
Sunnyhurst Rd. B'brn 4L 139
Sunnyhurst Wood & Vis. Cen. 5L 157
Sunny Lea St. Ross 2L 161
Sunnymead Av. Bolt 9F 198
Sunnymede Dri. Liv 8C 216
Sunnymede Va. Ram 2F 200
Sunnymere Dri. Dar 5M 157
Sunny Rd. South 4N 167
Sunnyside. Augh 4H 217
Sunnyside. South 2F 186
Sunnyside. Todm 2K 165
Sunnyside Av. Bill 6H 101
Sunnyside Av. Cher T 8F 138
Sunnyside Av. Ribch 7E 98
Sunnyside Av. W'ton 2J 131
Sunnyside Av. Wilp 2A 120
Sunnyside Camp Site. More 6A 22
Sunnyside Clo. Frec 1N 131
Sunnyside Clo. Lanc 9J 23
Sunnyside Clo. Ross 1M 161
Sunny Side Cotts. Roch 3F 202
Sunnyside Ct. South 5J 167
Sunnyside La. Lanc 9H 23
Sunnyside Ter. Pre 1B 56
Sunny Vw. Abb V 5D 156
Sunnywood Dri. Tot 7F 200
Sunnywood La. Tot 7F 200
Sunrise Vw. L'boro 5N 185
Sunset Clo. Liv 5L 223
Sunset Holiday Hamlet.
Hamb 8C 56
Sun Set Well La. War 5B 12
Sun St. Col 6B 86
Sun St. Lanc 8K 23
Sun St. Nels 2G 104
Sun St. Osw 4L 141
Sun St. Ram 7G 180
Sun Ter. Todm 7E 146
Sun Vale Av. Todm 8L 165
Super St. Clay M 5L 121
Surgeon's Ct. Pres 1J 135
Surma Clo. Roch 8E 204
Surrey Av. Burn 2N 123
Surrey Av. Dar 4N 157
Surrey Clo. South 1B 168
Surrey Rd. B'brn 3D 140
Surrey Rd. Nels 9H 85
Surrey St. Acc 1C 142
Surrey St. Pres 9M 115
Surrey St. Todm 1L 165
Sussex Clo. Chu 1M 141
Sussex Dri. B'brn 4A 140
Sussex Dri. Gars 4M 59
Sussex Dri. Has 7G 160
Sussex Rd. Blac 4E 88
Sussex Rd. Liv 3C 222
Sussex Rd. Rish 8F 120
Sussex Rd. South 7J 167
Sussex St. Barn 2M 77
Sussex St. Burn 5F 124
Sussex St. Nels 1J 105
Sussex St. Pres 8K 115
Sussex St. Roch 7C 204
Sussex Wlk. B'brn 4A 140
Sutch La. Lath 9F 190
Sutcliffe St. Bacup 7N 163
Sutcliffe St. Brclf 7K 105
Sutcliffe St. Burn 3D 124
Sutcliffe St. Chor 7F 174
Sutcliffe St. L'boro 8L 185
Sutherland Clo. Wilp 2A 120
Sutherland Rd. Blac 3C 88
Sutherland St. Col 7N 85
Sutherland Vw. Blac 3C 88
Sutton Av. Burn 8H 105
Sutton Av. Tar 7E 150
Sutton Clo. Weet 4D 90
Sutton Cres. Hun 8E 122
Sutton Dri. Lea 9A 114
Sutton Gro. Chor 2H 175
Sutton La. Adl 4J 195
(in two parts)
Sutton La. Tar 1D 170
Sutton Pl. Blac 6C 88
Sutton's La. Liv 1E 214
Sutton St. B'brn 8E 138
Swainbank St. Burn 4F 124
Swaine St. Nels 2G 105
Swainson St. Blac 4C 88
Swainson St. Lyth A 5M 129
Swain St. Roch 4B 204
Swaledale. Gal 2M 37
Swaledale Av. Burn 6F 104
Swalegate. Liv 9B 216
Swallow Av. Pen 4H 135
Swallow Bank Dri. Roch 9M 203
Swallow Clo. Kirkby 3K 223
Swallow Clo. T Clev 8G 54
Swallow Ct. Clay W 6E 154
Swallow Dri. B'brn 2M 139
Swallow Dri. Bury 9N 201
Swallow Fld. Much H 4J 151
Swallowfields. B'brn 9L 119
Swallowfold. Grims 9F 96
Swallow Pk. Burn 4A 124
Swanage Av. Blac 3B 108
Swanage Clo. Bury 7H 201
Swanage Rd. Burn 9G 104
Swan All. Orm 7K 209
(off Burscough St.)
Swan Courtyard. Clith 3L 81
Swan Delph. Augh 1H 217
Swan Dri. T Clev 2F 62
Swan Farm Clo. Lwr D 9N 139
Swanfield Ct. Col 6D 86
Swanfield Ter. Col 6D 86
Swanhey. Liv 3D 222
Swan La. Augh 5D 216
Swan Mdw. Clith 2K 81
Swan Pl. Col 6B 86
(off Market St.)
Swanpool La. Augh 2H 217
Swan Rd. G'mnt 3E 200
Swansea St. Ash R 8F 114
Swansey La.
Clay W & Whit W 6E 154
Swan St. B'brn 5M 139
Swan St. Dar 9B 158
Swan St. Pres 9M 115
Swan Wlk. Liv 3D 222
Swan Yd. Lanc 8L 23
Swarbrick Av. Grims 9F 96
Swarbrick Clo. Blac 3D 88
Swarbrick Ct. L'rdge 3K 97
Swarbrick St. K'ham 5M 111
Swarthdale. 3H 17
Sweet Briar Clo. Roch 3B 204
Sweet Briar La. Roch 3B 204
Sweet Clough Dri. Burn 3L 123
Sweetlove's Gro. Bolt 8E 198
Sweetlove's La. Bolt 8E 198
Swift Clo. B'brn 3N 139
Swift Rd. Roch 6K 203
Swifts Fold. Skel 3H 219
Swilkin La. Poul F 6D 56
Swill Bk. La. Pres 2M 135
Swillbrook. 8M 93
Swinburne Clo. Acc 6D 142
Swinden. 3D 52
Swinden Hall Rd. Nels 9J 85
Swinden La. Col 9L 85
Swinderby Dri. Liv 7G 222
Swindon Av. Blac 1D 108
Swindon St. Burn 4B 124
Swineshead La. Todm 4L 165
Swineshead Rd. Todm 4K 165
Swinless St. Burn 9F 104
Swinnate Rd. Arns 2G 4
Swinshaw Clo. Ross 6M 143
Swinside. Cot 5A 114
Swire Cft. Rd. Garg 3M 53
Swiss St. Acc 2M 141
Switch Island. Boot 5A 222
Swithemby St. Hor 9B 196
Sword Meanygate. Tar 1N 169
Sybil St. L'boro 8K 185
Sycamore Av. Blac 4F 108
Sycamore Av. Burn 2M 123
Sycamore Av. Eux 3N 173
Sycamore Av. Gars 4M 59
Sycamore Av. Miln 9K 205
Sycamore Av. Todm 9K 147
Sycamore Clo. B'brn 9N 119
Sycamore Clo. Burn 3A 124
Sycamore Clo. Elsw 1M 91
Sycamore Clo. Ful 3M 115
Sycamore Clo. L'boro 9J 185
Sycamore Clo. Maw 3N 191
Sycamore Clo. Rish 9H 121
Sycamore Ct. Chor 9D 174
Sycamore Cres. Brook 2J 25
Sycamore Cres. Clay M 4N 121
Sycamore Cres. Ross 6L 161
Sycamore Dri. Bury 7L 201
Sycamore Dri. Pen 5H 135
Sycamore Dri. Skel 1J 219
Sycamore Dri. Wins 9L 221
Sycamore Gdns. Foul 2A 86
Sycamore Gdns. Hey 1K 27
Sycamore Gro. Acc 5D 142
Sycamore Gro. Dar 5B 158
Sycamore Gro. Lanc 8H 23
Sycamore Ho. Chor 8B 174
Sycamore Ri. Foul 2A 86
Sycamore Rd. Bils 6D 68
Sycamore Rd. B'brn 9N 119
Sycamore Rd. Brook 2J 25
Sycamore Rd. Chor 4F 174
Sycamore Rd. Rib 7A 116
(in two parts)
Sycamore Rd. Tot 8E 200
Sycamore Trad. Est.
Blac 4F 108
Sycamore Way. Barn 3L 77
Syd Brook La. Maw 6A 172
Sydenham Ter. Roch 2A 204
Sydney Av. Whal 5K 101
Sydney Gdns. L'boro 5M 185
Sydney St. Acc 2B 142
Sydney St. Burn 3D 124
Sydney St. Clay M 8N 121
Sydney St. Dar 8B 158
Sydney St. Hodd 6F 158
Sydney St. Lyth A 2F 128
Sydney Ter. Traw 8F 86
Syke. 1C 204
Sykefield. Brier 5E 104
Syke Hill. Pres 1K 135
Syke Ho La. Goos 9A 70
Sykelands Av. Halt 1C 24
Sykelands Gro. Halt 1C 24
Syke La. Roch 1C 204
Syke Rd. L'boro 3M 205
Syke Rd. Roch 1C 204
Sykes Ct. Roch 7E 204
Sykes Cres. Wins 9M 221
Syke Side Dri. Alt 3D 122
Sykes St. Miln 9K 205
Sykes St. Roch 7E 204
Syke St. Has 6H 161
Syke St. Pres 1K 135
Sylvancroft. Ing 4D 114
Sylvan Gro. Bam B 6C 136
Sylvan Pl. Hey 1K 27
Sylvester St. Lanc 9J 23
Symonds Rd. Ful 6H 115

T

Tabby Nook. Mere B 5L 169
Tabby's Nook. Newb 3L 211
Tabley La. High B 9A 94
Tabor St. Burn 2B 124
Tadema Gro. Burn 7D 124
Tag Cft. Ing 4C 114
Tag Farm Ct. Ing 4C 114
Tag La. High B & Ing 3C 114
Tailor's La. Liv 2D 222
Talaton Clo. South 1N 167
Talbot Av. Clay M 7M 121
Talbot Clo. Clith 4M 81
Talbot Clo. Ross 7K 161
Talbot Ct. Bolt 9F 198
Talbot Ct. Lyth A 9G 109
Talbot Dri. Brclf 8K 105
Talbot Dri. Eux 4N 173
Talbot Dri. South 8H 167
Talbot Gro. Bury 7M 201
Talbot Ho. Chor 4E 174
(off Lancaster Ct.)
Talbot Rd. Acc 9N 121
Talbot Rd. Blac 5B 88
Talbot Rd. Ley 5H 153
Talbot Rd. Lyth A 4B 130
Talbot Rd. Pen 3H 135
Talbot Rd. Pres 1G 135
Talbot Row. Eux 5N 173
Talbot Sq. Blac 5B 88
Talbot St. Brclf 7K 105
Talbot St. Burn 3F 124
Talbot St. Chip 5G 70
Talbot St. Chor 5G 174
Talbot St. Col 5A 86
Talbot St. Ful 6G 114
Talbot St. Rish 8J 121
Talbot St. Roch 7C 204
Talbot St. South 8G 167
Talbot Ter. Lyth A 5A 130
Tallarn Rd. Liv 8G 223
Tamar Clo. Ley 8L 153
Tamar St. Pres 9A 116
Tamar Way. Heyw 9E 202
Tame Barn Clo. Miln 7K 205
Tamneys, The. Skel 2K 219
Tamworth Dri. Bury 8H 201
Tancaster. Skel 2J 219
Tanfield Nook. Parb 2N 211
Tanfields. Skel 2K 219
Tanglewood. Ful 4L 115
Tan Hill Dri. Lanc 5K 23
Tanhouse. 2A 220
Tanhouse. Gal 2L 37
Tan Ho. Clo. Parb 1N 211
Tan Ho. Dri. Wig 9M 221
Tanhouse La. H'pey 9H 155
Tan Ho. La. Parb 2N 211
Tan Ho. La. Wig 9M 221
Tanhouse Rd. Skel 3N 219
Tanners. 8G 180
Tanners Cft. Ram 8G 180
Tannersmith La. Maw 9C 172
Tanners St. Ram 8G 180
Tanner St. Burn 3D 124
Tan Pit Cotts. Heyw 9H 203
Tan Pit La. Wig 9N 221
Tanpits La. Burt 5G 7
Tanpits Rd. Chu 2L 141
Tansley Av. Cop 4N 193
Tansley Sq. Wig 6N 221
Tansy La. Fort 1K 45
Tanterton Hall Rd. Ing 3C 114
Tanyard Clo. Cop 4N 193
Tan Yard La. L'rdge 2L 97
Taper St. Ram 8G 180
Tape St. Ram 8G 180
Tapestry St. B'brn 7L 139
Tarbert Cres. B'brn 4D 140
Tarbet St. Lanc 9L 23
Tardy Gate. 8H 135
Tardy Ga. Trad. Cen. Los H 8K 135
Tarleton. 9E 150
Tarleton Av. Burn 5F 124
Tarleton Moss. 8N 149
Tarleton Rd. South 6N 167
Tarleton St. Burn 5F 124
Tarlscough. 4B 190
Tarlscough La. Burs 4A 190
Tarlswood. Skel 2K 219
Tarnacre La. St M 2H 67
Tarnacre Vw. Gars 6N 59
Tarn Av. Clay M 5M 121
Tarnbeck Dri. Maw 2N 191
Tarnbrick Av. Frec 1A 132
Tarnbrook Clo. Bolt S 7K 15
Tarnbrook Clo. Carn 9N 11
Tarn Brook Clo. Hun 8E 122
Tarnbrook Ct. More 3B 22
Tarnbrook Dri. Blac 3G 89
Tarnbrook Rd. Hey 8L 21
Tarnbrook Rd. Lanc 6H 23
Tarn Brow. Orm 9H 209
Tarn Clo. Pen 4C 134
Tarn Ct. Fltwd 3D 54
Tarnhows Clo. Chor 9D 174
Tarn La. Yeal R 7D 6
Tarnrigg Clo. Wig 8N 221
Tarn Rd. T Clev 4K 63
Tarnside. Blac 9H 89
Tarnside Clo. Roch 2F 204
Tarnside Rd. Orr 5H 221
Tarnsyke Rd. Lanc 6H 23
Tarnwater La. Ash S 7H 29
Tarnway Av. T Clev 3K 63
Tarradale. Longt 7K 133
Tarrant Clo. Wig 9N 221
Tarry Barn La. Pend 8N 81
Tarves Wlk. Liv 8L 223
Tarvin Clo. Brclf 7K 105
Tarvin Clo. South 1C 168
Tarzan's Adventureland. 8C 56
Taskers Cft. Wis 2M 101
Tasker St. Acc 2B 142
Tatham. 6E 18
Tatham Ct. Fltwd 3C 54
Tatham Gro. Wins 9N 221
Tatham St. Roch 6D 204
Tatterhorn Rd. Ben 6M 19
Tattersall Sq. Ross 4D 162
Tattersall St. B'brn 4M 139
Tattersall St. Osw 4K 141
Tattersall St. Pad 1J 123
Tattersall St. Ross 1G 160
Tatton St. Chor 7F 174
Tatton St. Col 8M 85
Taunton Av. Roch 6M 203
Taunton Dri. Liv 8D 222
Taunton Rd. B'brn 3J 139
Taunton St. Blac 9D 88
Taunton St. Pres 8N 115
Tavistock Dri. South 7B 186
Tavistock St. Nels 2K 105
Tawd Bridge. 4N 219
Tawd Brow. Uph 3L 219
Tawd Rd. Skel 3N 219
Tawd Valley Park. 1L 219
Taybank Av. Blac 2D 108
Taylor Av. Orm 7M 209
Taylor Av. Roch 5K 203
Taylor Av. Ross 5D 162
Taylor Clo. B'brn 5L 139
Taylor Gro. More 2F 22
Taylor Holme Ind. Est. Bacup 7F 162
Taylor Ho. Bury 8H 201
Taylor's Bldgs. Lang 9C 100
(off Whalley New Rd.)
Taylors Clo. Poul F 6J 63
Taylors Ind. Est. Pil 8K 43
Taylor's La. Pil 7J 43
Taylor's La. Tar 3B 170
Taylor's Meanygate.
H End & Tar 7L 149
Taylors Pl. Roch 4C 204
Taylor St. Barn 2L 77
Taylor St. B'brn 5L 139
Taylor St. Brier 4F 104
Taylor St. Burn 1E 124
Taylor St. Bury 9L 201
Taylor St. Chor 9D 174
Taylor St. Clith 3M 81
Taylor St. Dar 7A 158
Taylor St. Hor 9C 196
Taylor St. Pres 2G 135
Taylor St. Ross 4M 161
(Greenfield St.)
Taylor St. Ross 1G 160
(Pilling St.)
Taylor St. Skel 2G 219
Taylor St. Whitw 6A 184
Taylor St. W. Acc 2A 142
Taylor Ter. L'boro 9M 185
(off Ealees Rd.)
Taymouth Rd. Blac 3G 108
Tay St. Burn 4B 124
Tay St. Pres 8N 115
Taywood Clo. Poul F 7M 63
Taywood Rd. T Clev 8G 55
Teal Clo. Augh 1H 217
Teal Clo. B'brn 9L 119
Teal Clo. Ley 8G 152
Teal Clo. T Clev 8G 54
Teal Clo. Wig 7L 221
Teal Ct. Blac 4H 89
Teal Ct. Roch 6K 203
Teal La. Lyth A 1L 129
Teanlowe Cen. Poul F 8K 63
Tears La. Newb 4J 211
Teasel Wlk. More 6B 22
Tebay Av. K'ham 4A 112
Tebay Av. T Clev 8D 54
Tebay Clo. Liv 9E 216
Tebay Ct. Lanc 4J 23
Tedder Av. Burn 3N 123
Tedder Av. South 7N 167
Teenadore Av. Blac 2E 108
Tees Ct. Fltwd 2D 54
Teesdale. Gal 2L 37
Teesdale Av. Blac 2D 88
Tees St. Pres 7M 115
Tees St. Roch 7E 204
Teil Grn. Ful 3A 116
Telegraph Way. Liv 8K 223
Telford St. Burn 2A 124
Tell St. Roch 6A 204
Temperance St. Chor 6G 174
Temple Clo. B'brn 4B 140
Templecombe Dri. Bolt 6D 198
Temple Ct. B'brn 3M 139
Temple Ct. Pres 1J 135
(off Cannon St.)
Temple Dri. B'brn 4B 140
Temple La. L'boro 5M 185
Templemartin. Skel 1K 219
Temple St. Blac 5B 88
Temple St. Burn 4F 124
Temple St. Col 5B 86
Temple St. Nels 2K 105
Templeton Clo. Dar 5A 158
Temple Way. Chor 2E 174
Tems Side. Gigg 3N 35
Tems St. Gigg 3N 35
Tenby. Skel 1J 219
Tenby Clo. B'brn 1M 139
Tenby Gro. Roch 4N 203
Tenby Rd. Pres 2K 135

Tenby St.—Tower Ter.

Tenby St. Roch . . . 4N 203
Tennis St. Burn . . . 1E 124
Tennyson Av. Chor . . . 8E 174
Tennyson Av. Lyth A . . . 4C 130
Tennyson Av. Osw . . . 4J 141
Tennyson Av. Pad . . . 2K 123
Tennyson Av. Read . . . 8C 102
Tennyson Av. T Clev . . . 9G 54
Tennyson Av. Todm . . . 1N 165
Tennyson Av. W'ton . . . 2J 131
Tennyson Clo. Bolt S . . . 4L 15
Tennyson Dri. Bil . . . 9G 220
Tennyson Dri. Orm . . . 6J 209
Tennyson Pl. Gt Har . . . 5H 121
Tennyson Pl. Walt D . . . 6N 135
Tennyson Rd. Blac . . . 2F 88
Tennyson Rd. Col . . . 6N 85
Tennyson Rd. Fltwd . . . 9G 40
Tennyson Rd. Pres . . . 8N 115
(in three parts)
Tennyson St. Brclf . . . 7K 105
Tennyson St. Burn . . . 4B 124
Tennyson St. Hap . . . 5H 123
Tennyson St. Roch . . . 8D 204
Ten Row. Glas D . . . 1C 36
Tensing Av. Blac . . . 6D 62
Tensing Rd. Liv . . . 1C 222
Tentercroft. Roch . . . 6B 204
Tenterfield St. Pres . . . 9J 115
Tenterfield St. Ross . . . 7D 162
Tenterfield Ter. Todm . . . 1N 165
Tenterheads. Ross . . . 8D 162
Tenterhill La. Roch . . . 3H 203
Terance Rd. Blac . . . 1E 108
Tern Clo. Liv . . . 3K 223
Tern Clo. Roch . . . 6K 203
Terrace Row. Bill . . . 6J 101
Terrace St. Pres . . . 8M 115
Terry St. Nels . . . 9L 85
Tetbury Clo. B'brn . . . 8F 138
Tetlows Yd. L'boro . . . 4N 185
Teven St. Bam B . . . 7A 136
Teversham. Skel . . . 1K 219
Teviot. Skel . . . 1J 219
Teviot Av. Fltwd . . . 1D 54
Tewitfield. . . . 2E 12
Tewkesbury. Skel . . . 1J 219
Tewkesbury Av. Blac . . . 4D 108
Tewkesbury Clo. Acc . . . 5D 142
Tewkesbury Dri. Lyth A . . . 3C 130
Tewksbury St. B'brn . . . 7J 139
Thames Av. Burn . . . 7G 104
Thames Clo. Bury . . . 5L 201
Thames Dri. Orr . . . 4J 221
Thames Ho. Pres . . . 9N 115
(off Cliffe Ct.)
Thames Rd. Blac . . . 2B 108
Thames Rd. Miln . . . 7L 205
Thames St. Newt . . . 7E 112
Thames St. Roch . . . 7E 204
Thanet. Skel . . . 1K 219
Thanet Lee Clo. Cliv . . . 8J 125
Thealby Clo. Skel . . . 1J 219
Theatre St. Pres . . . 1J 135
Thelma St. Ram . . . 8G 180
Theobald Clo. Gars . . . 5M 59
Thetford. Roch . . . 5B 204
(off Spotland Rd.)
Thetford Clo. Bury . . . 8J 201
Thetis Rd. Lanc . . . 8G 22
Thickrash Brow. Ben . . . 7L 19
Thickwood Moss La. Rainf . . . 5K 225
Thimble Clo. Roch . . . 1G 204
Thimbles, The. Roch . . . 1G 204
Third Av. Blac . . . 2C 108
Third Av. Bury . . . 9B 202
Third St. Bolt . . . 9N 197
Thirlmere Av. Burn . . . 8E 104
Thirlmere Av. Col . . . 5C 86
Thirlmere Av. Fltwd . . . 4C 54
Thirlmere Av. Form . . . 1A 214
Thirlmere Av. Has . . . 7H 161
Thirlmere Av. Orr . . . 3J 221
Thirlmere Av. Pad . . . 8H 103
Thirlmere Av. Poul F . . . 7H 63
Thirlmere Av. Uph . . . 4E 220
Thirlmere Clo. Acc . . . 8C 122
Thirlmere Clo. Adl . . . 5K 195
Thirlmere Clo. B'brn . . . 2N 139
Thirlmere Clo. Kno S . . . 7M 41
Thirlmere Clo. Liv . . . 9D 216
Thirlmere Clo. Longt . . . 8M 133
Thirlmere Ct. Lanc . . . 7M 23
(off Thirlmere Rd.)
Thirlmere Dri. Dar . . . 5C 158
Thirlmere Dri. L'rdge . . . 5H 97
Thirlmere Dri. More . . . 3A 22
Thirlmere Dri. South . . . 1B 206
Thirlmere Dri. Withn . . . 5M 155
Thirlmere Gdns. More . . . 4B 22
Thirlmere Rd. Blac . . . 1C 108
Thirlmere Rd. Burn . . . 4J 125
Thirlmere Rd. Chor . . . 8C 174
Thirlmere Rd. H'twn . . . 7A 214
Thirlmere Rd. Lanc . . . 7M 23
Thirlmere Rd. Pres . . . 8B 116
Thirlmere Rd. Roch . . . 9M 203
Thirlmere Rd. Wig . . . 4L 221
Thirlmere Wlk. Liv . . . 6J 223
Thirlmere Way. Ross . . . 7M 143
Thirlspot Clo. Bolt . . . 7E 198
Thirnby Ct. K Lon . . . 6F 8
(off Lunefield Dri.)
Thirsk. Skel . . . 1K 219
Thirsk Av. Lyth A . . . 1H 129
Thirsk Clo. Bury . . . 8G 201
Thirsk Gro. Blac . . . 8D 88
Thirsk Rd. Lanc . . . 3M 29
Thirty Acre La. Form . . . 7D 206
Thistle Break. Hey . . . 9M 21
Thistle Clo. Chor . . . 6G 175
Thistle Clo. Hesk B . . . 3C 150
Thistle Clo. T Clev . . . 7F 54
Thistlecroft. Ing . . . 4D 114
Thistlemount Av. Ross . . . 6D 162
Thistle St. Bacup . . . 5K 163
Thistleton. . . . 2H 91
Thistleton M. South . . . 6J 167
Thistleton Rd. Ash R . . . 8B 114
Thistleton Rd. This . . . 1H 91
Thistleyfield. Miln . . . 6H 205
Thistley Hey Rd. Liv . . . 8L 223
Thomas Gro. More . . . 3B 22
Thomas Henshaw Ct. Roch . . . 9N 203
Thomason Fold. Tur . . . 8K 179
Thomason Sq. L'boro . . . 9K 185
Thomas St. B'brn . . . 4L 139
Thomas St. Blac . . . 3C 88
Thomas St. Burn . . . 4E 124
Thomas St. Col . . . 7N 85
Thomas St. Has . . . 4F 160
Thomas St. L'boro . . . 1H 205
Thomas St. Nels . . . 5E 104
(Clitheroe Rd.)
Thomas St. Nels . . . 3J 105
(Duerden St.)
Thomas St. Osw . . . 5K 141
Thomas St. Pres . . . 1M 135
Thomas St. Todm . . . 7F 146
Thomas St. Whitw . . . 4A 184
Thomas Weind. Gars . . . 5N 59
Thompson Av. Orm . . . 7M 209
Thompson St. B'brn . . . 4K 139
Thompson St. Dar . . . 8B 158
Thompson St. Hor . . . 9B 196
Thompson St. Pad . . . 1H 123
Thompson St. Pres . . . 7N 115
Thompson St. Wesh . . . 3L 111
Thompson St. Ind. Est. B'brn . . . 4K 139
(off Thompson St.)
Thonock Rd. More . . . 5D 22
Thorburn Dri. Whitw . . . 7M 183
Thorburn Ho. Wig . . . 4M 221
(off Green, The)
Thorburn La. Wig . . . 4N 221
Thorburn Rd. Wig . . . 5M 221
Thorn Bank. Bacup . . . 5L 163
Thornbank. Blac . . . 3H 89
Thornbank Dri. Catt . . . 1A 68
Thornbeck Av. Liv . . . 7A 214
(in two parts)
Thornber Clo. Burn . . . 9G 104
Thornber Gro. Blac . . . 7D 88
Thornber St. B'brn . . . 5K 139
Thornbridge Av. Burs . . . 1C 210
Thornbury. Roch . . . 7B 204
Thornbury. Skel . . . 1K 219
Thornbush Way. Roch . . . 5F 204
Thornby. Skel . . . 1K 219
Thorncliffe Dri. Dar . . . 7D 158
Thorncliffe Rd. Bolt . . . 8E 198
Thorn Clo. Bacup . . . 5L 163
Thorn Clo. Heyw . . . 9F 202
Thorn Cres. Bacup . . . 5L 163
Thorndale. Skel . . . 1K 219
Thorndale St. Hell . . . 1D 52
Thorn Dri. Bacup . . . 5L 163
Thorndyke Av. Bolt . . . 8E 198
Thorne St. Nels . . . 9L 85
Thorneybank Ind. Est. Hap . . . 7H 123
Thorneybank St. Burn . . . 4D 124
Thorneycroft Clo. Poul F . . . 6H 63
Thorney Holme. . . . 6C 84
Thorneyholme Rd. Acc . . . 1B 142
Thorneyholme Sq. Rou . . . 6C 84
Thorneylea. Whitw . . . 5A 184
Thornfield. Much H . . . 4J 151
Thornfield Av. L'rdge . . . 2J 97
Thornfield Av. Rib . . . 6B 116
Thornfield Av. Ross . . . 6C 162
Thornfield Av. T Clev . . . 3K 63
Thornfield Rd. Tot . . . 6D 200
Thornfield Ter. Traw . . . 6E 86
(off Rosley St.)
Thorn Gdns. Bacup . . . 5L 163
Thorngate. Pen . . . 4E 134
Thorngate Clo. Pen . . . 4E 134
Thorn Gro. Blac . . . 8E 88
Thorn Gro. Col . . . 5C 86
Thornham Clo. Bury . . . 7H 201
Thornham Ct. Blac . . . 5E 88
(off Hollywood Av.)
Thornham Dri. Bolt . . . 7F 198
Thornham St. Lanc . . . 9K 23
Thornhill. Augh . . . 2G 217
Thornhill Av. Pre . . . 8N 41
Thornhill Av. Rish . . . 9G 120
Thornhill Clo. Augh . . . 3G 217
Thorn Hill Clo. B'brn . . . 3A 140
Thornhill Clo. Blac . . . 4F 108
Thornhill Rd. Chor . . . 9F 104
Thornhill Rd. Ley . . . 7G 152
Thornhill Rd. Ram . . . 4F 200
Thornhill St. Burn . . . 3M 123
Thorn La. Als . . . 8J 97
Thorn Lea. Bolt . . . 9K 199
Thornlea Dri. Roch . . . 3M 203
Thornleigh Clo. T Clev . . . 1G 62
Thornleigh Dri. Burt . . . 6H 7
Thornley Av. B'brn . . . 2C 140
Thornley Pl. Rib . . . 6C 116
Thornley Rd. Rib . . . 6C 116
Thornpark Dri. Lea . . . 9A 114
Thorn Pl. Todm . . . 2M 165
(off Beaconsfield St.)
Thorns Av. Bolt . . . 9D 198
Thorns Av. Hest B . . . 8H 15
Thorns Clo. Bolt . . . 9D 198
Thorns Rd. Bolt . . . 9D 198
Thorns, The. Liv . . . 9A 216
Thorn St. Bacup . . . 5L 163
Thorn St. Burn . . . 1E 124
Thorn St. Clith . . . 3K 81
Thorn St. Gt Har . . . 3K 121
Thorn St. Pres . . . 7M 115
Thorn St. Ross . . . 2L 161
Thorn St. Sab . . . 3F 102
Thorn St. S'seat . . . 2H 201
Thornthwaite Rd. Cot . . . 5A 114
Thornton. . . . 2J 63
Thornton. Skel . . . 1K 219
Thornton Av. Ful . . . 5E 114
Thornton Av. Lyth A . . . 9H 109
Thornton Av. More . . . 2C 22
Thornton Cen. T Clev . . . 2J 63
Thornton Clo. Acc . . . 9N 121
Thornton Clo. B'brn . . . 8N 139
Thornton Clo. Ruf . . . 1G 190
Thornton Cres. Burn . . . 4J 125
Thornton Cres. More . . . 3C 22
Thornton Dri. Far M . . . 3H 153
Thornton Dri. Hogh . . . 5F 136
Thornton Ga. T Clev . . . 8C 54
Thornton Gro. More . . . 3C 22
Thornton-in-Craven. . . . 9H 53
Thornton in Lonsdale. . . . 2N 19
Thornton La. I'ton . . . 2N 19
Thornton La. More . . . 2C 22
Thornton Mnr. Ct. Thorn C . . . 9J 53
(off Colne & Broughton Rd.)
Thornton Rd. Burn . . . 4J 125
Thornton Rd. More . . . 3C 22
Thornton Rd. South . . . 7M 167
Thornton St. Roch . . . 8C 204
Thorntree Pl. Roch . . . 5B 204
Thorntrees Av. Brtn . . . 5E 94
Thorntrees Av. Lea . . . 8A 114
Thorn Vw. Bury . . . 9A 202
Thornview Rd. Hell . . . 1D 52
Thornway Av. T Clev . . . 3K 63
Thornwood. Skel . . . 1K 219
Thornwood Clo. B'brn . . . 8M 119
Thornwood Clo. Lyth A . . . 4L 129
Thoroughfare, The. War . . . 5A 12
Thoroughgood Clo. Burs . . . 2B 210
Thorough Way. Winm . . . 7H 45
Thorpe. Skel . . . 1K 219
Thorpe Av. More . . . 4F 22
Thorpe Clo. Pres . . . 8J 115
Thorpe Green. . . . 3G 154
Thorpe St. Ram . . . 9G 180
Thorsby Clo. Brom X . . . 5F 198
Thrang Brow La. Yeal R . . . 6N 5
Threagill La. War . . . 4C 12
Threefields. Ing . . . 4D 114
Three Nooks. Bam B . . . 2E 154
Three Oaks Clo. Lath . . . 2F 210
Three Pools. South . . . 3B 168
(in two parts)
Three Rivers Cvn. Site. W Brad . . . 5K 73
Three Tuns La. Liv . . . 9A 206
Threlfall. Chor . . . 4B 174
Threlfall Rd. Blac . . . 8D 88
Threlfalls Clo. South . . . 3M 167
(off Threlfalls La.)
Threlfalls La. South . . . 4M 167
Threlfall St. Ash R . . . 8F 114
Threlkeld Rd. Bolt . . . 7D 198
Threshers Ct. Fort . . . 3N 45
Threshers, The. Boot . . . 6A 222
Threshfield Av. Hey . . . 8L 21
Threshfield Clo. Bury . . . 6L 201
Thrimby Ct. More . . . 4B 22
Thrimby Pl. More . . . 4B 22
Thropps La. Longt . . . 9N 133
Throstle Clo. Burn . . . 2E 124
Throstle Gro. Bury . . . 8H 201
Throstle Gro. Slyne . . . 1J 23
Throstle Nest La. Winm . . . 8G 45
Throstle St. B'brn . . . 4K 139
Throstle St. Nels . . . 1J 105
Throstle Wlk. Slyne . . . 9K 15
Throstle Way. T Clev . . . 2F 62
Throup Pl. Nels . . . 9J 85
Thrum Fold. Roch . . . 2A 204
Thrum Hall La. Roch . . . 2B 204
(in three parts)
Thrush Dri. Bury . . . 9N 201
Thrushgill Dri. Halt . . . 1C 24
Thrush St. Roch . . . 4N 203
Thurcroft Dri. Skel . . . 1J 219
Thurland Castle. . . . 2F 18
Thurland Ct. More . . . 5A 22
Thurnham Moss. . . . 4C 36
Thurnham Rd. Ash R . . . 9B 114
Thurnham St. Lanc . . . 9K 23
Thursby Av. Blac . . . 3D 108
Thursby Clo. Liv . . . 9L 223
Thursby Clo. South . . . 1B 206
Thursby Cres. Liv . . . 9L 223
Thursby Ho. Wig . . . 4M 221
Thursby Pl. Nels . . . 9K 85
Thursby Rd. Burn . . . 9F 104
Thursby Rd. Nels . . . 9K 85
Thursby Sq. Burn . . . 1E 124
Thursby St. Burn . . . 9F 104
Thursby Wlk. Liv . . . 9L 223
Thursden Av. Brclf . . . 7K 105
Thursden Pl. Nels . . . 1M 105
Thursfield Av. Blac . . . 1E 108
Thursfield Rd. Burn . . . 4F 124
Thursgill Av. More . . . 5C 22
Thurston. Skel . . . 1J 219
Thurston Rd. Ley . . . 6K 153
Thurston St. Burn . . . 3F 124
Thwaite Brow La. Bolt S . . . 3M 15
Thwaite La. Halt . . . 9J 19
Thwaites Av. Mel . . . 7F 118
Thwaites Rd. Osw . . . 5J 141
Thwaites St. Osw . . . 5J 141
Tiber Av. Burn . . . 5A 124
Tiber St. Pres . . . 1L 135
Tibicar Dri. E. Hey . . . 7L 21
Tibicar Dri. W. Hey . . . 7L 21
Tib St. Ram . . . 9G 181
Tideswell Av. Orr . . . 2K 221
Tiflis St. Roch . . . 5B 204
Tiger, The. Ley . . . 5G 152
(off Longmeanygate)
Tilbury Gro. Shev . . . 5G 213
Tilcroft. Skel . . . 1J 219
Tile St. Bury . . . 9L 201
Tillman Clo. Set . . . 3N 35
Tilston Rd. Kirkby . . . 8H 223
Timberbottom. Bolt . . . 9J 199
Timber Brook. Chor . . . 4C 174
Timbercliffe. . . . 5N 185
Timbercliffe. L'boro . . . 5N 185
Timber St. Acc . . . 3B 142
Timber St. Bacup . . . 6K 163
Timber St. Brier . . . 4F 104
Timbrills Av. Sab . . . 2E 102
Tim's Ter. Miln . . . 7J 205
Tincklers La. Maw & E'ston . . . 9C 172
Tinedale Vw. Pad . . . 9J 103
Tinkerfield. Ful . . . 2H 115
Tinker's La. Scor . . . 8F 38
Tinklers La. Slai . . . 5E 50
Tinkler's Rd. Chor . . . 8H 175
Tinniswood. Ash R . . . 8E 114
Tinsley Av. South . . . 2L 187
Tinsley's La. Pil . . . 7H 57
Tinsley's La. South . . . 4M 187
Tintagel. Skel . . . 1H 219
Tintagell Clo. Fen . . . 9D 138
Tintern Av. Chor . . . 9F 174
Tintern Av. Heyw . . . 9G 202
Tintern Av. L'boro . . . 7K 185
Tintern Clo. Acc . . . 6D 142
Tintern Clo. S'stne . . . 9C 102
Tintern Cres. B'brn . . . 9B 120
Tintern Dri. Liv . . . 1B 214
Tintern Pl. Heyw . . . 9G 202
Tippet Clo. B'brn . . . 7A 140
Titan Way. Ley . . . 5F 152
Tithe Barn Clo. Roch . . . 1G 204
Tithe Barn Cres. Bolt . . . 9H 199
Tithebarn Ga. Poul F . . . 7K 63
Tithebarn Hill. Glas D . . . 2C 36
Tithe Barn La. H'pey . . . 3J 175
Tithe Barn La. Kirkby . . . 9J 223
Tithe Barn La. Ley & Eux . . . 1J 173
Tithebarn La. Mag . . . 5E 222
Tithe Barn La. Scor . . . 7B 46
Tithebarn Pl. Poul F . . . 7K 63
Tithebarn Rd. South . . . 8K 167
Tithebarn St. Poul F . . . 7J 63
Tithe Barn St. Pres . . . 9K 115
(in three parts)
Tithebarn St. Uph . . . 4E 220
Tiverton Av. Skel . . . 1J 219
Tiverton Clo. Ful . . . 1J 115
Tiverton Dri. B'brn . . . 8K 139
Tiverton Dri. Brclf . . . 7K 105
Toad La. Roch . . . 5C 204
(in two parts)
Tockholes. . . . 5H 157
Tockholes Rd. Dar . . . 5M 157
Tockholes Rd. Toc . . . 5H 157
Todber Cvn. Pk. Rim . . . 2C 76
Todd Carr Rd. Ross . . . 6D 162
Todd Hall Rd. Has . . . 4F 160
Todd La. N. Los H . . . 5M 135
Todd La. S. Los H . . . 8M 135
Todd's La. South . . . 9F 148
Todd St. Bury . . . 9K 201
Todd St. Roch . . . 6D 204
Toddy Fold. B'brn . . . 8M 119
Tod Holes La. Wigg . . . 9L 35
Todmanhaw La. Wigg . . . 1A 52
Todmorden. . . . 2L 165
Todmorden Golf Course. . . . 9M 147
Todmorden Old Rd. Bacup . . . 4L 163
Todmorden Rd. Bacup . . . 4L 163
Todmorden Rd. Brclf . . . 7L 105
Todmorden Rd. Burn . . . 4F 124
Todmorden Rd. L'boro . . . 3N 185
Todmorden Rd. Lyth A . . . 9C 108
Toll Bar Bus. Pk. Bacup . . . 7G 163
Tollbar Cres. Lanc . . . 4K 29
Tollgate. Pen . . . 4H 135
Tollgate Rd. Burs . . . 2N 209
Tollgate Way. Roch . . . 5F 204
Tolsey Dri. Hut . . . 6A 134
Tom Benson Way. Ash R . . . 6C 114
Tom La. Loth . . . 7M 79
Tom La. Ross . . . 5D 162
Tomlinson Rd. Ash R . . . 7F 114
Tomlinson Rd. Hey . . . 1L 27
Tomlinson Rd. Ley . . . 5J 153
Tomlinson St. Hor . . . 9C 196
Tomlinson St. Roch . . . 9N 203
Tonacliffe. . . . 8N 183
Tonacliffe Rd. Whitw . . . 9N 183
Tonacliffe Ter. Whitw . . . 7N 183
Tonacliffe Way. Whitw . . . 8N 183
Tonbridge Clo. Bury . . . 6H 201
Tonbridge Dri. Liv . . . 7C 222
Tongbarn. Skel . . . 1J 219
Tong Clough. Brom X . . . 5F 198
(in two parts)
Tonge Fold Cotts. Bury . . . 2B 200
Tonge Hey. Liv . . . 9L 223
Tonge Moor Rd. Bolt . . . 9L 199
Tong End. Whitw . . . 4N 183
Tonge St. Roch . . . 7D 204
Tong Fields. Eger . . . 5F 198
Tong Head Av. Bolt . . . 9H 199
Tong La. Bacup . . . 4L 163
Tong La. Whitw . . . 5N 183
Tongues La. Pre . . . 7B 42
Tontine. . . . 6F 220
Tontine. Orr . . . 6F 220
Tontine Rd. Uph . . . 5F 220
Tontine St. B'brn . . . 3M 139
Toogood La. Wrigh . . . 6G 192
Toon Cres. Bury . . . 7H 201
Tootell St. Chor . . . 8D 174
Tootle La. Ruf . . . 2D 190
Tootle Rd. L'rdge . . . 2K 97
Top Acre. Hut . . . 7N 133
Top Acre Rd. Skel . . . 4N 219
Topaz St. B'brn . . . 7N 119
Top Barn La. Ross . . . 6B 162
Topham Dri. Ain R . . . 8A 222
Top Of Fawna Rd. K Grn . . . 1E 98
Top of Town. . . . 3A 74
Top of Wallsuches. Hor . . . 9G 196
Top o' th Clo. Rd. Todm . . . 9M 165
Top o' th' Cft. B'brn . . . 8L 139
Top o' the Hill Rd. W'den . . . 6K 165
Top o' th' Lane. . . . 4H 155
Top o' th' La. Brin . . . 4G 155
Top o' th' Wood. . . . 8F 202
Topping Fold Rd. Bury . . . 9A 202
Toppings. . . . 6H 199
Toppings Grn. Brom X . . . 6G 199
Toppings, The. Gars . . . 6N 59
Topping St. Blac . . . 5B 88
Topping St. Bury . . . 9L 201
Top Rd. Pen . . . 5D 134
Top Row. Sab . . . 2E 102
Top St. Todm . . . 8J 165
Tor Av. G'mnt . . . 4E 200
Torcross Clo. South . . . 1N 167
Tor End Rd. Ross . . . 9E 160
Torentum Ct. T Clev . . . 2J 63
Tor Hey M. G'mnt . . . 3E 200
Tormore Clo. H'pey . . . 4J 175
Toronto Av. Blac . . . 8E 62
Toronto Av. Fltwd . . . 2D 54
Toronto Rd. B'brn . . . 9K 119
Torquay Av. Blac . . . 8G 88
Torquay Av. Burn . . . 8G 105
Torra Barn Clo. Eger . . . 2E 198
Torridon Clo. B'brn . . . 7G 139
Torrisholme. . . . 4F 22
Torrisholme Rd. Lanc . . . 5G 22
Torrisholme Sq. More . . . 4F 22
Torside Gro. Poul F . . . 8H 63
Torsway Av. Blac . . . 4F 88
Torver Clo. Burn . . . 1N 123
Tor Vw. Ross . . . 6M 161
Tor Vw. Rd. Has . . . 6H 161
Tosside. . . . 2J 51
Totnes Clo. Poul F . . . 6J 63
Totnes Dri. South . . . 1N 167
Tottenham Rd. Lwr D . . . 9N 139
Tottington. . . . 7D 200
Tottington Fold. Bolt . . . 8L 199
Tottington Rd. Bolt . . . 8L 199
Tottington Rd. Tur . . . 3M 199
Tottleworth. . . . 6J 121
Tottleworth Rd. B'brn . . . 6J 121
Toulmin Clo. Catt . . . 1A 68
Tourist Info. Cen. . . . 2B 142
(Accrington)
Tourist Info. Cen. . . . 2M 77
(off Fernlea Av., Barnoldswick)
Tourist Info. Cen. . . . 3M 139
(Blackburn)
Tourist Info. Cen. . . . 5B 88
(Blackpool)
Tourist Info. Cen. . . . 4D 124
(Burnley)
Tourist Info. Cen. . . . 2K 193
(Charnock Richard Services)
Tourist Info. Cen. . . . 1D 62
(Cleveleys)
Tourist Info. Cen. . . . 2L 165
(Clitheroe)
Tourist Info. Cen. . . . 8J 41
(Fleetwood)
Tourist Info. Cen. . . . 5N 59
(Garstang)
Tourist Info. Cen. . . . 6F 8
(Kirkby Lonsdale)
Tourist Info. Cen. . . . 8J 23
(Lancaster)
Tourist Info. Cen. . . . 2E 128
(Lytham St Anne's)
Tourist Info. Cen. . . . 3N 21
(Morecambe)
Tourist Info. Cen. . . . 2H 105
(Nelson)
Tourist Info. Cen. . . . 1K 135
(Preston)
Tourist Info. Cen. . . . 5M 161
(off Kay St., Rawtenstall)
Tourist Info. Cen. . . . 6C 204
(Rochdale)
Tourist Info. Cen. . . . 3N 35
(off Cheapside, Settle)
Tourist Info. Cen. . . . 7H 167
(Southport)
Tourist Info. Cen. . . . 2L 165
(Todmorden)
Tower Av. Lanc . . . 8M 29
Tower Av. Ram . . . 9F 180
Tower Causeway. Todm . . . 8E 146
Tower Clo. T Clev . . . 8G 55
Tower Ct. G'mnt . . . 5E 200
Tower Ct. Lanc . . . 9K 23
Tower Ct. Tur . . . 1J 199
Tower Dri. Tur . . . 2J 199
Tower Grn. Ful . . . 2J 115
Tower Hill. . . . 5L 223
Tower Hill. Clith . . . 2M 81
Tower Hill. Orm . . . 7M 209
Tower Hill Rd. Uph . . . 6C 220
Tower La. Ful . . . 2J 115
Tower Nook. Uph . . . 6D 220
Tower Rd. B'brn . . . 6E 138
Tower Rd. Dar . . . 7B 158
Towers Av. Liv . . . 9B 216
Tower St. Bacup . . . 5K 163
Tower St. Blac . . . 5B 88
Tower St. Osw . . . 3H 141
Tower St. Todm . . . 7D 146
Tower St. Tur . . . 1J 199
Tower Ter. G'mnt . . . 5E 200

Vaughan St.—Warth Old Rd.

Vaughan St. Nels 3K 105
Vauxhall St. B'brn 5J 139
Vavasour Ct. Roch 7E 204
Vavasour St. Roch 7E 204
(in two parts)
Vaynor. Roch 5B 204
(off Spotland Rd.)
Veevers St. Brier 5E 104
Veevers St. Burn 3D 124
(off Calder St.)
Veevers St. Pad 1J 123
Venables Av. Col 5C 86
Venice Av. Burn 5A 124
Venice St. Burn 4B 124
Ventnor Av. Bolt 9F 198
Ventnor Pl. Ful 5D 114
Ventnor Rd. Blac 3B 108
Ventnor Rd. Chor 8D 174
Ventnor Rd. Has 6H 161
Ventnor St. Roch 8C 204
Venture Ct. Alt 4C 122
Venture Rd. Fltwd 6G 54
Venture St. Bacup 4L 163
Verax St. Bacup 6K 163
Verdun Cres. Roch 5N 203
Vermont Clo. Liv 3J 223
Vermont Gro. T Clev 3E 62
Verna St. Ram 8H 181
Vernon Av. Blac 7E 88
Vernon Av. W'ton 2K 131
Vernon Ct. South 9K 167
Vernon Cres. Gal 2L 37
Vernon Pk. Gal 2K 37
Vernon Rd. G'mnt 4E 200
Vernon Rd. Lane 5G 87
Vernon Rd. Lyth A 8E 108
Vernon Rd. South 6N 167
Vernon St. B'brn 4M 139
Vernon St. Bury 9L 201
Vernon St. Dar 6B 158
Vernon St. Nels 3J 105
Vernon St. Pres 8J 115
Vernon St. Todm 4K 165
Verona Av. Burn 4A 124
(off Florence Av.)
Verona Ct. T Clev 1G 63
Veronica St. Dar 3M 157
Verulam Rd. South 3A 168
Vesta St. Ram 8G 181
Vevey St. Ley 6K 153
Viaduct Rd. Hogh 6A 138
Vicarage Av. Brook 3J 25
Vicarage Av. Pad 1G 123
Vicarage Av. T Clev 9D 54
Vicarage Clo. Adl 5J 195
Vicarage Clo. Burt 5H 7
Vicarage Clo. Bury 5K 201
Vicarage Clo. Eux 3N 173
Vicarage Clo. Ful 5J 115
Vicarage Clo. Heat O 6C 22
Vicarage Clo. Lyth A 9F 108
Vicarage Clo. W'head 9N 209
Vicarage Clo. W Grn 5G 110
Vicarage Dri. Dar 7C 158
Vicarage Dri. Roch 2F 204
Vicarage Fold. Wis 3L 101
Vicarage Gdns. Burs 8B 190
Vicarage Gdns. Orr 7G 220
Vicarage La. Acc 7D 142
Vicarage La. Blac 9E 88
Vicarage La. Burt 5H 7
Vicarage La. Ful 5J 115
Vicarage La. K Lon 6F 8
Vicarage La. Lanc 8J 23
Vicarage La. Mart 9E 88
Vicarage La. Newt 6E 112
Vicarage La. Sam 8G 116
(in two parts)
Vicarage La. Shev 7K 213
Vicarage La. South 8E 148
Vicarage La. W'head 9N 209
Vicarage La. Wilp 3M 119
Vicarage Rd. Barn 1N 77
Vicarage Rd. Kel 6D 78
Vicarage Rd. Nels 3H 105
Vicarage Rd. Orr 7G 221
Vicarage Rd. Poul F 8K 63
Vicarage St. Chor 5F 174
Vicarage Ter. Lanc 7J 23
(off Vicarage La.)
Vicarage Wlk. Orm 7K 209
Vicar La. Mllng 4D 18
Vicars Dri. Roch 7C 204
Vicarsfields Rd. Ley 8K 153
Vicars Ga. Roch 6C 204
Vicar St. B'brn 3N 139
Vicar St. Gt Har 5J 121
Viceroy Ct. South 8G 167
(off Lord St.)
Victor Av. Bury 9K 201
Victor Av. More 3E 22
Victor Clo. Wig 3N 221
Victoria Apartments. Pad 9H 103
(off Habergham St.)
Victoria Av. Bax 6C 142
Victoria Av. B'brn 7F 138
Victoria Av. Brier 4F 104
Victoria Av. Chat 7D 74
Victoria Av. Lanc 2K 29
Victoria Bri. Rd. South 8J 167
Victoria Bldgs. Waters 4E 158
Victoria Bus. & Ind. Cen.
Acc 3A 142
Victoria Ct. Barn 1M 77
(off Bairstow St.)
Victoria Ct. B'brn 3M 139
(off Blackburn Shop. Cen.)
Victoria Ct. Brough 8F 94
Victoria Ct. Chat 7C 74
Victoria Ct. Ful 6H 115
Victoria Ct. Pad 2K 123
Victoria Ct. Skel 2G 219
Victoria Ct. South 1F 186
(in two parts)
Victoria Dri. Has 5F 160
Victoria Gdns. Barfd 9G 85
Victoria Ho. B'brn 5B 140
Victoria Lodge. Read 8C 102
Victoria Mans. Ash R 9D 114
Victoria M. More 2C 22
Victorian Lanterns. Bury 3H 201
Victoria Pde. Ash R 8E 114
Victoria Pde. More 2C 22
Victoria Pde. Ross 7C 162
Victoria Pk. 8C 190
(Burscough)
Victoria Pk. 8F 166
(Southport)
Victoria Pk. Skel 2G 219
Victoria Pk. Av. Lea 8A 114
Victoria Pk. Av. Ley 8G 152
Victoria Pk. Dri. Lea 8A 114
Victoria Pl. Halt 2B 24
Victoria Pl. Lanc 9K 23
Victoria Quay. Ash R 1D 134
Victoria Rd. Augh 9H 209
Victoria Rd. B'brn 7D 138
Victoria Rd. Earby 2E 78
Victoria Rd. Ful 6H 115
Victoria Rd. Hor 9D 196
Victoria Rd. Ince B 8E 214
Victoria Rd. K'ham 4L 111
Victoria Rd. Lyth A 3F 128
Victoria Rd. Pad 1J 123
Victoria Rd. Poul F 7L 63
Victoria Rd. Todm 1L 165
Victoria Rd. Walt D 2M 135
Victoria Rd. E. T Clev 2F 62
Victoria Rd. W. T Clev 1C 62
(in two parts)
Victoria Sq. T Clev 1D 62
Victoria St. Acc 3A 142
Victoria St. Bacup 7H 163
Victoria St. Barfd 8H 85
Victoria St. B'brn 3M 139
Victoria St. Blac 5B 88
Victoria St. Burn 4D 124
Victoria St. Burs 8C 190
Victoria St. Carn 9A 12
Victoria St. Chor 7F 174
Victoria St. Chu 2L 141
Victoria St. Clay M 7M 121
Victoria St. Clith 4K 81
Victoria St. Dar 6A 158
Victoria St. Earby 2E 78
Victoria St. Fltwd 8H 41
Victoria St. Gt Har 4K 121
Victoria St. Has 4F 160
Victoria St. L'boro 9L 185
Victoria St. L'rdge 3J 97
Victoria St. Los H 8L 135
Victoria St. Lyth A 5B 130
Victoria St. More 3A 22
Victoria St. Nels 2G 105
Victoria St. Osw 5K 141
Victoria St. Pres 8H 115
Victoria St. Rainf 3K 225
Victoria St. Ram 8G 181
Victoria St. Raw 4A 162
Victoria St. Rish 8H 121
Victoria St. Ross 7C 162
Victoria St. Set 3N 35
Victoria St. South 6H 167
Victoria St. Todm 7F 146
Victoria St. Tot 6D 200
Victoria St. Wheel 8J 155
Victoria St. Whitw 6N 183
Victoria Ter. Abb V 5C 156
Victoria Ter. Bill 6G 101
(off Whalley New Rd.)
Victoria Ter. Cald V 4H 61
Victoria Ter. Chor 5F 174
Victoria Ter. Glas D 1D 36
Victoria Ter. Heyw 9G 202
Victoria Ter. Ley 7K 153
Victoria Ter. Los H 8K 135
(off Watkin La., in two parts)
Victoria Ter. Miln 8K 205
Victoria Ter. Toc 5G 157
Victoria Way. Raw 5A 162
Victoria Way. South 7F 166
Victor St. Clay M 6M 121
Victory Av. South 7N 167
Victory Cen, The. Nels 2J 105
Victory Clo. Nels 2J 105
Victory Rd. Barn 2N 77
Victory Rd. Blac 4C 88
Victory Wharf. Ash R 9E 114
View Rd. Dar 2M 157
View St. E'ston 7F 172
Vihiers Clo. Whal 4J 101
Viking Pl. Burn 2E 124
Viking St. Roch 5N 203
Viking Way. Hey 2L 27
Village Ct. Whitw 5N 183
(off North St.)
Village Cft. Eux 3N 173
Village Dri. Rib 7B 116
Village Grn. La. Ing 3C 114
Village Nook. Ain 8D 222
Village, The. Sing 1D 90
Village Walks. Poul F 8K 63
Village Way. Blac 6D 62
Village Way. Liv 7A 214
Villas Rd. Liv 1G 222
Villas, The. Cot 4B 114
Villa Way. Gars 6N 59
Villiers Ct. Pres 7G 115
(in two parts)
Villiers St. Burn 4A 124
Villiers St. Bury 9M 201
Villiers St. Pad 2J 123
Villiers St. Pres 7G 115
(in three parts)
Vincent Ct. B'brn 8L 139
Vincent Rd. Nels 2K 105
Vincent St. B'brn 8L 139
Vincent St. Col 5C 86
Vincent St. Lanc 9L 23
Vincent St. L'boro 8K 185
Vincent St. Roch 8D 204
Vincent Way. Wig 3N 221
Vincit St. Burn 1F 124
Vine Cvn. Pk. W'ton 4H 131
Vine Ct. Blac 1C 88
(off Gosforth Rd.)
Vine Ct. Roch 6E 204
Vine Pl. Roch 8C 204
Vinery, The. New L 8C 134
Vine St. Acc 2N 141
Vine St. Brier 5F 104
Vine St. Chor 5F 174
Vine St. Lanc 1K 29
Vine St. Osw 5J 141
Vine St. Pres 9G 115
Vine St. Ram 1F 200
(in two parts)
Vineyard Clo. Ward 7F 184
Vineyard Cotts. Roch 7F 184
Vineyard Ho. Roch 7F 184
(off Knowl Syke St.)
Viola Clo. Liv 5J 223
Viola Clo. Stand 2N 213
Violet St. Burn 9E 104
Virginia Av. Liv 8B 216
Virginia Gro. Liv 8B 216
Virginia St. Roch 9B 204
Virginia St. South 8J 167
Virginia Way. Wig 3M 221
Viscount Av. Lwr D 1A 158
Viscount Rd. Wig 3N 221
Vivary Way. Col 7M 85
Vivian Dri. South 3G 186
Vivian St. Roch 8B 204
Voce's La. Augh 8N 217
Vulcan Ct. South 7J 167
Vulcan Rd. Frec 8N 111
Vulcan Rd. Wig 3N 221
Vulcan St. Burn 3D 124
Vulcan St. Nels 1K 105
Vulcan St. South 7J 167
Vulcan St. Todm 6K 165
Vulcan Ter. L'boro 9J 185

W

Wackersall Rd. Col 8M 85
Waddicar. 6F 222
Waddicar La. Liv 7F 222
Waddington. 8H 73
Waddington Av. Burn 3H 125
Waddington Ct. Lyth A 2J 129
Waddington Hospital. Wadd 7H 73
Waddington Rd. Acc 1C 142
Waddington Rd. Clith 1K 81
Waddington Rd. Lyth A 1H 129
Waddington Rd. Rib 7C 116
Waddington Rd. W Brad 7K 73
Waddington St. Earby 2E 78
Waddington St. Pad 1J 123
Waddow Grn. Clith 3J 81
Waddow Gro. Wadd 8J 73
Waddow Vw. Wadd 8H 73
Wade Brook Rd. Ley 9C 152
Wade Hall. 8G 153
Wades Ct. Blac 1F 88
Wades Cft. Frec 2A 112
Wade St. Pad 9J 103
Wadham Rd. Pres 2L 135
Wadsworth Av. Todm 4K 165
(off Lion St.)
Wagg Fold. L'boro 7J 185
Wagon Rd. Doph & Low D 6E 38
Waidshouse Clo. Nels 4J 105
Waidshouse Rd. Nels 4J 105
Wain Ct. B'brn 4J 139
Wainfleet Clo. Wig 8N 221
Waingap Cres. Whitw 6A 184
Waingap Ri. Roch 1C 204
Waingap Vw. Whitw 7A 184
Waingate. Grims 9E 96
Waingate Clo. Ross 4N 161
Waingate Ct. Grims 9E 96
Waingate La. Ross 4N 161
Waingate Rd. Ross 4N 161
Waithlands Rd. Roch 7E 204
Waitholme La. Yeal R 5D 6
Wakefield Av. More 2D 22
Wakefield Dri. Lanc 3L 29
Wakefield Rd. Blac 7E 62
Wakefield Rd. Boot 8A 222
Walden Rd. B'brn 5N 119
Walden St. Pres 8A 116
Waldorf Clo. Wig 9N 221
Waldron. Skel 3H 219
Walesby Pl. Lyth A 3K 129
Wales Rd. Ross 6D 162
Wales St. Ross 5D 162
Wales Ter. Ross 6D 162
Walgarth Dri. Chor 7C 174
Walkdale. Hut 6A 134
Walkden St. Roch 4C 204
Walker Av. Acc 8L 121
Walker Fold. 8L 197
(Bolton)
Walker Fold. 7M 71
(Clitheroe)
Walker Gro. Hey 8L 21
Walker La. Ful 2D 114
Walker Pk. Guide 9C 140
Walker Pl. Pres 1L 135
Walker Rd. Guide 9C 140
Walker's Hill. 2G 109
Walker's Hill. Blac 2G 108
Walker St. B'brn 4N 139
Walker St. Blac 4B 88
Walker St. Clith 3M 81
Walker St. Pres 9J 115
Walker St. Roch 6D 204
Walker Way. T Clev 8H 55
Walk Mill. 8K 125
Walk Mill Clo. Roch 1G 204
Walk Mill Pl. Cliv 8J 125
Walk, The. Hesk B 3A 150
Walk, The. Roch 6C 204
Walk, The. South 1G 186
Wallace La. Fort 9M 37
Wallbank. 7M 183
Wallbank Dri. Whitw 7M 183
Wall Bank La. Whitw 7M 183
Wallbank St. Tot 6E 200
Wallcroft St. Skel 3J 219
Wallend Rd. Ash R 1A 134
Walleach Fold Cotts. Tur 8L 179
Walled Garden, The. Whit W 9D 154
Waller Av. Blac 6C 62
Waller Clo. South 6J 167
Waller Hill. Foul 2A 86
Walletts Rd. Chor 8D 174
Walletts Wood Ct. Chor 9C 174
Wallgarth Clo. Wig 9N 221
Wall Head Rd. Roch 6F 204
Wallhurst Clo. Wors 4M 125
(in two parts)
Wallings La. Silv 7F 4
Wall La. L Ecc 6K 65
Wallstreams La. Wors 4M 125
Wall St. Blac 3C 88
Wall St. Ross 5C 162
Wallsuches. 9F 196
Wallsuches La. Hor 9F 196
Wallwork Clo. Roch 4J 203
Walmer Bridge. 2K 151
Walmer Ct. South 1F 186
Walmer Grn. Walm B 2K 151
Walmer Rd. Lyth A 9F 108
Walmer Rd. South 2G 186
Walmersley. 5K 201
Walmersley Dri. Rainf 5L 225
Walmersley Golf Course. 5N 201
Walmersley Old Rd. Bury 5L 201
Walmersley Rd. Bury 3K 201
Walmesley Ct. Clay M 8M 121
Walmsgate. Barn 3M 77
Walmsley Av. L'boro 2J 205
Walmsley Av. Rish 9G 121
Walmsley Bri. La. Clau B 2H 69
Walmsley Brow. Bill 6H 101
Walmsley Clo. Chu 2L 141
Walmsley Clo. Gars 5N 59
Walmsley St. Bury 9G 201
Walmsley St. Dar 5B 158
Walmsley St. Fltwd 9G 41
Walmsley St. Gt Har 4J 121
Walmsley St. Rish 8H 121
Walney Gdns. B'brn 7N 139
Walney Pl. Blac 3G 89
Walney Rd. Wig 9N 221
Walnut Av. Has 4H 161
Walnut Clo. Pen 5E 134
Walnut Gro. Liv 7F 222
Walnut St. Bacup 4K 163
Walnut St. B'brn 1N 139
Walnut St. South 1J 187
Walpole Av. Blac 4B 108
Walpole St. B'brn 4N 139
Walpole St. Burn 9F 104
Walpole St. Roch 6D 204
Walro M. South 3N 167
Walsden. 6K 165
Walsden Est. Todm 8L 165
Walsden Gro. Burn 3G 125
Walshaw. 9E 200
Walshaw Brook Clo. Bury 9E 200
Walshaw La. Burn 8H 105
Walshaw La. Bury 9E 200
Walshaw Rd. Bury 9E 200
Walshaw St. Burn 1F 124
Walshaw Wlk. Tot 8E 200
Walshaw Way. Tot 8E 200
Walsh St. B'brn 6M 139
Walsh St. Hor 9C 196
Walter Av. Lyth A 7G 108
Walter Pl. Lyth A 7G 108
Walter Robinson Ct. Blac 4D 88
Walter St. Acc 2N 141
Walter St. B'brn 4A 140
Walter St. Brier 6F 104
Walter St. Dar 1B 178
Walter St. Hun 7D 122
Walter St. Osw 5K 141
Walter St. Wig 5N 221
Waltham Av. Blac 4D 108
Waltham Clo. Acc 5D 142
Waltham Ct. Halt 1B 24
Walthew Green. 9F 212
Walthew Ho. La. Wig 2L 221
(in two parts)
Walthew La. Wig 1M 221
Walthew Pk. 1E 220
Waltho Av. Liv 1D 222
Walton Av. Garg 3L 53
Walton Av. More 3E 22
Walton Av. Pen 5E 134
Walton Clo. Bacup 6L 163
Walton Clo. Garg 4L 53
Walton Cottage Homes. Nels 1L 105
(off Broadway Pl.)
Walton Cres. B'brn 7A 140
Walton Dri. Alt 3D 122
Walton Dri. Bury 5K 201
Walton Fold. Todm 1N 165
(off Millwood La.)
Walton Grn. Walt D 4N 135
Walton Gro. More 3F 22
Walton La. Nels 9K 85
Walton-le-Dale. 4N 135
Walton-le-Dale. Bam B 9N 135
Walton's Pde. Pres 1H 135
Walton St. Acc 8N 121
Walton St. Adl 7J 195
Walton St. Barfd 7J 85
Walton St. Col 6A 86
(in two parts)
Walton St. Nels 1J 105
Walton St. South 6J 167
Walton Summit. 9D 136
Walton Summit Ind. Est.
Bam B 9D 136
Walton Summit Rd.
Bam B 1C 154
Walton Vw. Pres 9N 115
Walverden Av. Blac 1D 108
Walverdon Cres. Nels 2K 105
Walverden Rd. Brclf 6M 105
Walverden Rd. Brier 5H 105
Walverden Ter. Nels 3K 105
Wandales La. Cast 5G 9
Wanes Blades Rd. Lath 9J 191
Wango La. Liv 9D 222
Wanishar La. Down 7N 207
Wansbeck Av. Fltwd 2D 54
Wansbeck Ho. Fltwd 2E 54
Wansfell Rd. Clith 4J 81
Wanstead Cres. Blac 9E 88
Wanstead St. Pres 9A 116
Wapping. 3L 77
Warbreck. 1D 88
Warbreck Ct. Blac 1B 88
Warbreck Dri. Blac 1B 88
Warbreck Hill. Blac 9E 62
Warbreck Hill Rd. Blac 2B 88
Warburton Bldgs. Has 6F 160
Warburton St. Has 6E 160
Warbury St. Pres 8A 116
Warcock La. Bacup 4M 163
Warcock La. Blkhd 4N 147
Ward Av. Osw 5J 141
Ward Av. T Clev 9D 54
Warden Hall. 9J 153
(Arts & Craft Cen.)
Ward Grn. La. L'rdge 2A 98
Wardle. 8F 184
Wardle Clo. Whit W 9E 154
Wardle Dri. T Clev 9F 54
Wardle Edge. Roch 2E 204
Wardle Fold. 7F 184
Wardle Fold. Ward 7F 184
Wardle Gdns. Roch 2F 204
Wardle Rd. Roch 9F 184
Wardle St. Bacup 7H 163
Wardle St. L'boro 8K 185
Wardley's La. Hamb 8N 55
Wardley St. Wig 6L 221
Wardlow Av. Orr 2K 221
Ward's End. Pres 1K 135
Ward's La. Ben 8M 19
Wards New Row. Los H 9K 135
Ward St. Bel 9K 177
Ward St. Blac 9B 88
Ward St. Burn 3C 124
Ward St. Chor 7G 174
Ward St. Gt Har 4J 121
Ward St. K'ham 5M 111
Ward St. Los H 9L 135
Ward St. Nels 2J 105
Wareham Clo. Acc 8A 122
Wareham Rd. Blac 1F 88
Wareham Rd. Ind. Est. Blac 1F 88
Wareham St. B'brn 1A 140
Warehouse La. Foul 2A 86
Wareings Yd. Roch 9D 204
Waring Dri. T Clev 9G 55
Warings, The. Hesk 1G 193
Warings, The. Nels 4J 105
Warkworth Ter. Bacup 4L 163
(off Venture St.)
Warlands End Ga. Todm 1N 185
Warley Av. More 5E 22
Warley Dri. More 4E 22
Warley Rd. Blac 2B 88
Warley St. L'boro 8L 185
Warley Wise La. Lane 9K 79
Warmden Av. Acc 5D 142
Warmden Gdns. B'brn 1A 140
Warminster Gro. Wig 9N 221
Warncliffe St. Wig 6N 221
Warne Pl. Lanc 7H 23
Warner Rd. Pres 8N 115
Warner St. Acc 3B 142
Warner St. Has 4G 160
War Office Rd. Roch 7J 203
Warper's Moss Clo. Burs 8D 190
Warper's Moss La. Burs 8D 190
Warren Av. N. Fltwd 9F 40
Warren Av. S. Fltwd 9F 40
Warren Clo. Slyne 9J 15
Warren Ct. South 9E 166
Warren Dri. Bacup 7N 163
Warren Dri. Barfd 8G 84
Warren Dri. Slyne 9J 15
Warren Dri. T Clev 3D 62
Warren Fold. Hur G 2N 99
Warren Gro. Hey 2K 27
Warren Gro. T Clev 3E 62
Warrenhouse Rd. Kirkby 6M 223
Warrenhurst Rd. Fltwd 9G 40
Warren Rd. Hey 1K 27
Warren Rd. South 6N 167
Warrenside Clo. B'brn 5A 120
Warren St. Fltwd 8H 41
Warren, The. B'brn 1H 139
Warren, The. Pres 3A 116
Warrington St. B'brn 9A 120
Warrington Ter. Barr 2K 101
(off Whiteacre La.)
Warth La. I'ton 3N 19
Warth Old Rd. Ross 7C 162

Warton—Westhead Rd.

Warton. 4A 12 (Carnforth)
Warton. 2K 131 (Preston)
Warton Aerodrome. W'ton 4J 131
Warton Av. Hey 1K 27
Warton Crag Nature Reserve. 4N 11
Warton Old Rectory. 5A 12
Warton Pl. Chor 6C 174
Warton Rd. Carn 7A 12
Warton St. Lyth A 5B 130
Warton St. Pres 2G 135
Wartonwoods Vw. Carn 9A 12
Warwick Av. Acc 1N 141
Warwick Av. Clay M 6M 121 (in two parts)
Warwick Av. Dar 4M 157
Warwick Av. Lanc 2L 29
Warwick Av. More 2F 22
Warwick Av. T Clev 8F 54
Warwick Clo. Bury 9G 200
Warwick Clo. Chu 1M 141
Warwick Clo. Ful 5H 115
Warwick Clo. G'mnt 4F 200
Warwick Clo. South 1H 187
Warwick Dri. Brier 5H 105
Warwick Dri. Clith 1M 81
Warwick Dri. Earby 3C 78
Warwick Dri. Pad 2J 123
Warwick Ho. Pres 2K 135
Warwick Pl. Blac 2H 89
Warwick Pl. Fltwd 8G 41
Warwick Rd. Blac 3D 88
Warwick Rd. E'ston 7F 172
Warwick Rd. Ley 8H 153
Warwick Rd. Lyth A 2F 128
Warwick Rd. Walt D 4N 135
Warwick St. Adl 7H 195
Warwick St. Bolt 9E 198
Warwick St. Chu 1M 141
Warwick St. Has 4G 161
Warwick St. L'rdge 3J 97
Warwick St. Nels 3J 105
Warwick St. Pres 9J 115
Warwick St. South 1H 187
Wasdale Av. B'brn 5C 140
Wasdale Av. Liv 9D 216
Wasdale Clo. Ley 9L 153
Wasdale Clo. Pad 9H 103
Wasdale Gro. L'rdge 5H 97
Wasdale Rd. Blac 1G 108
Washbrook Clo. Barr 1K 101
Washbrook Way. Orm 8K 209
Wash Brow. Bury 8G 200
Washburn Ct. Heat O 6F 22
Wash Fold. Bury 8G 200
Washington Av. Blac 9E 62
Washington Clo. Lanc 9H 23
Washington Ct. Blac 9E 62
Washington Ct. Bury 9L 201
Washington Dri. Liv 4J 223
Washington Dri. War 4B 12
Washington La. Eux 4A 174
Washington St. Acc 2B 142
Wash Ter. Bury 8G 200
Waste La. Doph 8J 39
Wastwater Dri. More 4E 22
Watchwood Dri. Lyth A 3A 130
Watchyard La. Liv 9A 206
Water. 8E 144
Waterbarn. 7E 162
Waterbarn La. Bacup 7F 162
Waterbarn St. Burn 9F 104
Watercroft. Roch 4H 203
Waterdale. Blac 6E 62
Waterfall. 6K 139
Waterfall Ind. Est. B'brn 6K 139 (off Dimmock St.)
Waterfall Ter. Bel 9K 177
Waterfield Av. Dar 9B 158
Waterfield Clo. Bury 6L 201
Water Fold. Ross 8E 144
Waterfoot. 7D 162
Waterfoot Av. Blac 4E 88
Waterfoot Av. South 1B 206
Waterford Clo. Ful 4M 115
Waterford Clo. Hth C 4J 195
Waterford St. Nels 1K 105
Waterfront Marine Bus. Pk. Lyth A 4D 130
Water Head. Ful 6E 114
Waterhead Cres. T Clev 5C 62
Waterhouse Clo. Ward 9F 184
Waterhouse Grn. Whit W 8D 154
Waterhouse St. Roch 5C 204
Watering Pool La. Los H 6L 135
Water La. Ash R 8F 114
Water La. Miln 8K 205
Water La. Ram 4J 181
Water La. South 1C 168
Waterloo. 8J 139
Waterloo. Acc 1A 142
Waterloo Clo. B'brn 8J 139
Waterloo Rd. Ash R 7E 114
Waterloo Rd. Blac 9B 88
Waterloo Rd. Burn 4F 124 (in two parts)
Waterloo Rd. Clith 3M 81
Waterloo Rd. Kel 6D 78
Waterloo Rd. South 3C 106
Waterloo St. Chor 5E 174
Waterloo St. Clay M 8N 121
Waterloo Ter. Ash R 8F 114
Watermans Clo. Hor 9D 196
Waterman Vw. Roch 5F 204
Water Meadows. B'brn 9L 139
Watermede. Bil 8H 221
Watermill Clo. Roch 7G 205
Watermillock Gdns. Bolt 9F 198
Waters Edge. B'brn 5N 139
Water's Edge. Ing 6C 114
Watershed Mill Bus. Cen. Gigg 2N 35
Waterside. 4D 104 (Burnley)
Waterside. 7B 86 (Colne)
Waterside. 4E 158 (Darwen)
Waterside Clo. Gars 5M 59
Waterside Ind. Est. Col 7B 86
Waterside La. Roch 5E 204
Waterside M. Pad 1H 123
Waterside Pl. More 5B 22
Waterside Rd. Bury & S'seat 3G 201
Waterside Rd. Col 7A 86
Waterside Rd. Has 5F 160
Waterside Ter. Bacup 4K 163 (off Myrtle Bank Rd.)
Waterside Ter. Waters 4E 158
Waterslack Rd. Silv 5J 5
Waters Reach. Lyth A 5K 129
Waters Reach. T Clev 9C 54
Water St. Acc 2B 142 (in two parts)
Water St. Adl 7J 195
Water St. Bam B 6A 136
Water St. Barfd 7H 85
Water St. Brin 2H 155
Water St. Chor 6E 174
Water St. Clay M 4M 121
Water St. Col 6B 86
Water St. Craw 8E 144 (Ash Gro)
Water St. Craw 8M 143 (Burnley Rd.)
Water St. Earby 2E 78
Water St. Eger 3D 198
Water St. Garg 3M 53 (off Hellifield Rd.)
Water St. Gt Har 4J 121
Water St. Hap 5H 123
Water St. Hth C 1L 195
Water St. Lanc 7K 23
Water St. Nels 2J 105
Water St. Ram 9G 180
Water St. Ribch 7F 98
Water St. Roch 7J 205
Water St. Todm 2L 165
Water St. Whitw 6N 183
Water St. Wors 4M 125
Waterview Clo. Miln 9L 205
Waterway Av. Boot 7A 222
Waterworks Rd. Orm 6M 209
Watery Ga. La. Gt Ecc 9B 66
Watery La. Ash R 9D 114
Watery La. Barb 2G 9
Watery La. Bncr 3B 60
Watery La. Dar 9B 158
Watery La. Gigg 4M 35
Watery La. Lanc 5H 23
Watery La. Pres 9N 115
Watford St. B'brn 2M 139
Watkin Clo. Boot 9A 222
Watkin La. Los H 8K 135
Watkin Rd. Clay W 7D 154
Watkins Clo. Brier 6G 105
Watkin St. Roch 9D 204
Watling Clo. B'brn 8A 140
Watling Clo. More 5E 22
Watling St. Aff 3M 199
Watling St. Rd. Ful 6H 115
Watling St. Rd. Rib 5M 115 (off Churchill Rd.)
Watson Gdns. Roch 3A 204
Watson Rd. Blac 2B 108
Watson St. B'brn 6J 139
Watson St. Osw 5L 141
Watton Beck Clo. Liv 9E 216
Watts Clo. Liv 6M 223
Watts St. Roch 5D 204
Watt St. Burn 2A 124
Watt St. Sab 3E 102
Watty La. Todm 4J 165
Watty Ter. Todm 4J 165
Wavell Av. South 7A 168
Wavell Clo. Acc 7E 142
Wavell Clo. South 7A 168 (in two parts)
Wavell St. Burn 3A 124
Waverledge. 5H 121
Waverledge Bus. Pk. Gt Har 5H 121
Waverledge Rd. Gt Har 5H 121
Waverledge St. Gt Har 5J 121
Waverley. Roch 5B 204 (off Spotland Rd.)
Waverley. Skel 2H 219
Waverley Av. Blac 2C 88
Waverley Av. Fltwd 1D 54
Waverley Clo. Brier 6H 105
Waverley Clo. S'stne 9C 102
Waverley Ct. Wig 8N 221
Waverley Dri. New L 9C 134
Waverley Dri. Tar 1E 170
Waverley Gdns. Rib 7A 116
Waverley Pl. B'brn 3J 139
Waverley Rd. Acc 5D 142
Waverley Rd. Int 4E 140
Waverley Rd. Pres 8N 115
Waverley Rd. Rams 5M 119
Waverley Rd. South 2L 29
Waverley St. Burn 3C 124
Waverley St. South 7G 167
Waxy La. Frec 1A 132
Wayfarers Arc. South 7H 167
Way Ga. T Clev 7D 54
Wayman Rd. Blac 4D 88
Wayoh Cft. Tur 8K 179
Wayoh Nature Reserve. 8J 179
Wayside. Kno S 8K 41
Way, The. More 5F 22
Weald, The. Cot 4A 114
Weasel La. Hogh 6N 137
Weasel La. Toc 4H 157
Weatherhill Cres. Brier 5J 105
Weaver Av. Burs 8D 190
Weaver Av. Liv 4L 223
Weaver Dri. Bury 5L 201
Weavers Brow. Chor 8H 175
Weavers Cft. Bill 6G 100
Weavers La. Cabus 7N 45
Weavers La. Liv 4E 222
Weavers Row. Lyth A 1K 129
Weavers' Triangle Vis. Cen. 4D 124
Webber Ct. Burn 6M 123
Webber Rd. Know I 9N 223
Weber St. Ross 6B 162
Webster Av. Blac 2E 108
Webster Dri. Liv 8K 223
Webster Gro. More 2G 22
Webster St. Ash R 8F 114
Webster St. Roch 4B 204
Wedgewood Ct. Lyth A 1G 129
Wedgewood Dri. Stand L 9N 213
Wedgewood Rd. Acc 8E 122
Weedon St. Roch 5E 204
Weeton. 8D 90
Weeton Av. Blac 4E 108
Weeton Av. Lyth A 9G 108
Weeton Av. T Clev 9D 54
Weeton Camp. 4E 90
Weeton Pl. Ash R 8B 114
Weeton Rd. Sing 2D 90
Weeton Rd. Weet & Wesh 7E 90
Weets Vw. Barn 1N 77
Weind, The. Gt Ecc 6N 65
Weir. 9L 145
Weirden Clo. Pen 7F 134
Weir La. Bacup 9L 145
Weir Rd. Miln 6H 205
Weir St. B'brn 4M 139
Weir St. Roch 6C 204
Weir St. Todm 4K 165
Welbeck Av. B'brn 9B 120
Welbeck Av. Blac 9E 88
Welbeck Av. Fltwd 9F 40
Welbeck Av. L'boro 8K 185
Welbeck Clo. Miln 7H 205
Welbeck Gdns. Fltwd 1F 54
Welbeck Ho. Fltwd 9F 40
Welbeck Rd. Roch 9E 204
Welbeck Rd. South 1F 186
Welbeck Ter. South 1G 186
Welbourne. Skel 3H 219
Welburn St. Roch 8C 204
Welburn Clo. Earby 2E 78
Weld Av. Chor 9E 174
Weld Bank. 9E 174
Weldbank La. Chor 9E 174
Weldbank St. Chor 9E 174
Weld Blundell Av. Liv 6A 216
Weldon Dri. Orm 8L 209
Weldon St. Burn 4C 124
Weld Pde. South 1F 186
Weld Rd. South 9E 166
Welland Clo. Blac 7E 62
Well Bank. 4F 160
Wellbank St. Tot 7E 200
Wellbank Vw. Roch 4K 203
Wellbrow Dri. L'rdge 2K 97
Well Brow Ter. Roch 3B 204
Well Ct. Clith 2M 81 (off Causeway Cft.)
Wellcross Rd. Uph 5E 220
Wellesley Clo. Wig 3N 221
Wellesley St. Burn 3L 123
Wellfield. Clay M 7N 121
Wellfield. Longt 7K 133
Wellfield. Rainf 6L 225
Wellfield Av. Ley 6J 153
Wellfield Av. Liv 9K 223
Wellfield Bus. Pk. Pres 9G 115
Wellfield Dri. Burn 1A 124
Wellfield La. W'head 9A 210
Wellfield Pl. Roch 8D 204
Wellfield Rd. B'brn 2K 139
Wellfield Rd. Los H 9K 135
Wellfield Rd. Pres 9G 115
Wellfield St. Roch 8D 204
Wellfield Ter. Todm 3L 165
Well Fold. Clith 3M 81
Wellgate. Clith 3L 81
Well Grn. L'boro 9L 185
Well Head Rd. Newc P 9M 83
Wellhouse Rd. Barn 1M 77
Wellhouse Sq. Barn 2M 77 (off Wellhouse Rd.)
Wellhouse St. Barn 2M 77
Wellington Av. Ley 7L 153
Wellington Clo. Liv 7B 222
Wellington Ct. Acc 3B 142
Wellington Ct. Burn 4F 124
Wellington Fold. Dar 6A 158
Wellington Lodge. L'boro 8L 185 (off Lodge St.)
Wellington M. Tur 1K 199
Wellington Pl. Roch 5D 204
Wellington Pl. Walt D 6N 135
Wellington Rd. Ash R 8E 114
Wellington Rd. B'brn 5K 139
Wellington Rd. Blac 8B 88
Wellington Rd. Lanc 2L 29
Wellington Rd. Todm 1L 165
Wellington Rd. Tur 1J 199
Wellington St. Acc 3B 142
Wellington St. Barn 3M 77
Wellington St. B'brn 2L 139
Wellington St. Chor 5E 174
Wellington St. Clay M 7M 121
Wellington St. Gt Har 5J 121
Wellington St. K'ham 4L 111
Wellington St. Lyth A 4C 130
Wellington St. Miln 7K 205
Wellington St. Nels 1H 105
Wellington St. Pres 9G 114
Wellington St. Roch 4C 204
Wellington St. South 8G 167
Wellington Ter. More 3B 22
Well i' th' La. Roch 8D 204
Well La. Bar 6L 207
Well La. Brins 8A 156
Well La. Cast 6G 9
Well La. Hut R 6C 8
Well La. Lar 5J 65
Well La. Todm 2L 165
Well La. War 5B 12
Well La. Yeal C 8B 6
Wellogate Gdns. Blac 3D 108
Well Orchard. Bam B 2D 154
Wellow Pl. Lyth A 3J 129
Wells Clo. Heat O 6B 22
Wells Clo. T Clev 1G 62
Wells Fold Clo. Clay W 6E 154
Wells St. Has 4G 161
Wells St. Pres 8M 115
Well St. Pad 9G 103
Well St. Rish 7H 121
Well St. Roch 8D 204
Well St. Todm 3L 165
Well St. Waterf 4D 162
Well St. N. Ram 4H 181
Well St. W. Ram 9G 180 (off Holt St. W.)
Well Ter. Clith 2M 81
Welsby Rd. Ley 7G 153
Welwyn Av. South 7E 186
Welwyn Pl. T Clev 2E 62
Wembley Av. Blac 2E 88
Wembley Av. Pen 3E 134
Wembley Av. Poul F 8L 63
Wembley Rd. T Clev 8H 55
Wemyss Clo. Hey 9K 21
Wendover Rd. Poul F 5G 63
Wenlock Clo. Hor 7D 196
Wenning Av. Ben 7L 19
Wenning Av. Liv 9D 216
Wenning Ct. More 6F 22
Wenning Pl. Lanc 6J 23
Wenning St. Nels 3K 105
Wennington. 5F 18
Wennington Rd. South 6M 167
Wennington Rd. Wray 8E 18
Wensley Av. Fltwd 3E 54
Wensley Clo. Burn 6C 124
Wensleydale Av. Blac 3G 88
Wensleydale Clo. Liv 9A 216
Wensleydale Clo. T Clev 3K 63
Wensley Dri. Acc 2C 142
Wensley Dri. Lanc 5K 23
Wensley Fold. 4K 139
Wensley Pl. Rib 5N 115
Wensley Rd. B'brn 4J 139
Wensley Way. Roch 7E 204
Wentcliffe Dri. Earby 3E 78
Wentworth Av. Bury 9G 200
Wentworth Av. Fltwd 5D 54
Wentworth Av. Ins 2G 93
Wentworth Clo. Pen 2D 134
Wentworth Clo. South 9C 186
Wentworth Ct. K'ham 5M 111
Wentworth Cres. More 6B 22
Wentworth Dri. Brough 7F 94
Wentworth Dri. Eux 1N 173
Wentworth Dri. T Clev 3J 63
Wentworth M. St A 2G 129
Wentworth Pl. Brough 7F 94
Werneth Clo. Pen 7J 135
Wervin Rd. Liv 9J 223
Wervin Way. Liv 9H 223
Wescoe Clo. Orr 6H 221
Wesham. 2L 111
Wesham Hall Clo. Wesh 3M 111
Wesham Hall Rd. Wesh 3M 111
Wesleyan Row. Clith 3L 81
Wesley Clo. Ben 6L 19
Wesley Clo. Roch 2E 204
Wesley Ct. Fltwd 8H 41
Wesley Ct. Tot 6D 200
Wesley Dri. Hey 9L 21
Wesley Gro. Burn 2B 124
Wesley Ho. Tot 6D 200
Wesley Pl. Bacup 6J 163
Wesley St. Bam B 8B 136
Wesley St. B'brn 1N 139
Wesley St. Brier 4F 104
Wesley St. Brom X 5G 198
Wesley St. Chu 2M 141
Wesley St. Osw 3L 141
Wesley St. Pad 1J 123
Wesley St. Roch 2E 204 (off Rhodes St.)
Wesley St. Sab 2E 102
Wesley St. South 7H 167
Wesley St. Tot 6D 200
Wesley St. Wig 7N 221
Wesley Ter. Bacup 8L 145
Wessex Clo. Acc 9D 122
Wessex Rd. Wig 2N 221
West Av. Barn 2M 77
West Av. Ing 3D 114
West Av. Roch 2F 204
West Bank. Chor 6E 174
Westbank Av. Blac 2G 108
W. Bank Av. Lyth A 5L 129
West Beach. Lyth A 5M 129
Westborough Clo. Hey 7L 21
Westbourne. Ross 7F 160
Westbourne Av. Blac 9C 88
Westbourne Av. Burn 5B 124
Westbourne Av. W Grn 6G 111
Westbourne Av. S. Burn 6C 124
Westbourne Ct. Kno S 8K 41
Westbourne Dri. Lanc 9H 23
Westbourne Gdns. South 1D 186
Westbourne Pl. Lanc 8H 23
Westbourne Rd. Chor 8D 174
Westbourne Rd. Kno S 8K 41
Westbourne Rd. Lanc 9G 23
Westbourne Rd. M'ton 5M 27
Westbourne Rd. South 1D 186
Westbourne Rd. T Clev 7C 54
Westbourne Rd. War 6N 11
West Bradford. 7L 73
W. Bradford Rd. Clith 8M 73
W. Bradford Rd. Wadd 8H 73
Westbrook Cres. Ing 5D 114
Westbury Av. Wig 9N 221
Westbury Clo. Burn 8J 105
Westbury Clo. T Clev 4C 62
Westbury Gdns. B'brn 4C 140
Westby. 5D 110
Westby Av. Blac 4E 108
Westby Ct. Poul F 9K 63
Westby Gro. Fltwd 8H 41
Westby Pl. Ash R 8C 114
Westby Rd. Lyth A 9E 108
Westby Rd. West 3C 110
Westby St. Lyth A 5A 130
Westby Way. Poul F 9K 63
West Cliff. Pres 2H 135
Westcliffe. Gt Har 3H 121
West Cliffe. Lyth A 5B 130
Westcliffe Dri. Blac 3E 88
Westcliffe Dri. More 6A 22
Westcliffe Ho. Roch 1G 205
Westcliffe Rd. Bolt 7F 198
Westcliffe Rd. South 9E 166
Westcliffe Wlk. Nels 3H 105
W. Cliff Ter. Pres 2H 135 (in two parts)
W. Close Av. High 5L 103
West Clo. Rd. Barn 1M 77
Westcombe Dri. Bury 9H 201
Westcote St. Dar 9B 158
Westcott Clo. Bolt 9L 199
Westcott Dri. Wig 7M 221
West Ct. T Clev 7C 54
West Cres. Acc 9A 122
West Cres. Brough 7F 94
Westcroft. Much H 4J 151
Westdene. Parb 2M 211
West Dri. Bury 8K 201 (in three parts)
West Dri. Ins 2G 92
West Dri. Lanc 6H 23
West Dri. Ley 4N 153
West Dri. T Clev 9D 54
West Dri. Wesh 2K 111
West Dri. Whal 3G 100
West Dri. W. T Clev 9D 54
West End. 3J 141 (Accrington)
West End. 4A 22 (Morecambe)
West End. Gt Ecc 6M 65
West End. Pen 2D 134
Westend Av. Cop 4N 193
W. End Bus. Pk. Osw 3H 141
W. End La. W'ton 2G 130
W. End Rd. More 4N 21
W. End Ter. South 7G 167
Westerdale Dri. Banks 1G 168
Westerham Clo. Bury 6H 201
Westerlong. Lea 8A 114
Western Av. Burn 5C 124
Western Ct. Bacup 7G 162
Western Dri. Ley 6G 152
Western Rd. Bacup 7G 162
Westfield. Los H 8K 135
Westfield. Nels 1H 105
Westfield Av. Blac 1F 88
Westfield Av. Fltwd 2E 54
Westfield Av. Read 9C 102
Westfield Av. Stain 3H 89
Westfield Clo. Roch 4K 203
Westfield Ct. T Clev 8H 55
Westfield Dri. Bolt S 3L 15
Westfield Dri. Hogh 7F 136
Westfield Dri. Ley 6G 153
Westfield Dri. Rib 5N 115
Westfield Dri. W'ton 3L 131
Westfield Dri. W Brad 6L 73
Westfield Gro. More 4A 22
West Fld. Rd. Barn 10F 52
Westfield Rd. Blac 8D 88
Westfields. Crost 4L 171
Westfield Villa. Whal 3F 100
Westfield Wlk. Liv 8G 222
West Gdns. Bacup 7F 162 (off West Vw.)
Westgate. Barn 3L 77
Westgate. Burn 3C 124
Westgate. Fltwd 9D 40
Westgate. Ful 4G 115
Westgate. Ley 7J 153
Westgate. More 5A 22
Westgate. Read 9B 102
Westgate. Skel 2H 219
Westgate. Whitw 7M 183
Westgate Av. More 6B 22
Westgate Av. Ram 3F 200
Westgate Cvn. Pk. More 6A 22
Westgate Clo. Whitw 7M 183
Westgate Dri. Orr 6G 221
Westgate Ind. Est. Uph 3H 219
Westgate La. I'ton 1M 19
Westgate Pk. Rd. More 5C 22
Westgate Rd. Lyth A 5C 108
Westgate Trad. Cen. Burn 3D 124 (off Wiseman St.)
West Gillibrands. 3G 218
Westgrove Av. Bolt 7E 198
W. Hall La. Whit 9C 8
Westham St. Lanc 9L 23
Westhaven Cres. Augh 2H 217
Westhead. 8C 210
Westhead Av. Liv 8L 223
Westhead Clo. Liv 9M 223
Westhead Rd. Crost 4L 171

Wildoaks Dri.—Wood Hey Gro.

Wildoaks Dri. T Clev 3K 63
Wilds Bldgs. Roch 6G 205
Wild's Pas. L'boro 1H 205
(New Rd.)
Wild's Pas. L'boro 4N 185
(Todmorden Rd.)
Wilds Pl. Ram 9G 181
Wildwood Clo. Ram 1F 200
Wilfield St. Burn 3C 124
Wilford St. Blac 3E 88
Wilfred Dri. Bury 9N 201
(off Huntley Mt. Rd.)
Wilfred St. Acc 4B 142
Wilfred St. Brom X 6G 198
Wilkesley Av. Stand 4N 213
Wilkie Av. Burn 7C 124
Wilkin Bri. Clith 3L 81
Wilkinson Av. Blac 6E 88
Wilkinson Mt. Earby 2E 78
(off Aspen La.)
Wilkinson Mt. Earby 3E 78
(off Cowgill St.)
Wilkinson Rd. Bolt 8D 198
Wilkinson St. Burn 7H 105
Wilkinson St. Dunn 4N 143
Wilkinson St. Has 3G 160
Wilkinson St. High 5L 103
Wilkinson St. Los H 8L 135
Wilkinson St. Nels 8G 85
Wilkinson Way. Pre 8M 41
Wilkin Sq. Clith 3L 81
Willacy La. Catf 7J 93
Willacy Pde. Hey 7L 21
Willard Av. Bil 8G 221
Willaston Av. Black 3J 85
Willbutts La. Roch 5N 203
William Griffiths Ct. B'brn 6J 139
(off Mill Hill Bri. St.)
William Henry St. Pres 9M 115
William Henry St. Roch 9D 204
William Herbert St. B'brn 2N 139
William Hopwood St. B'brn 4A 140
William Roberts Av. Liv 8H 223
Williams Av. More 2G 22
Williams La. Ful 2M 115
Williamson Rd. Lanc 8L 23
Williams Pl. Nels 2K 105
Williams Rd. Burn 9F 104
William St. Acc 1B 142
William St. Bacup 7N 163
William St. B'brn 6M 139
William St. Blac 3E 88
William St. Brier 4F 104
William St. Carn 7A 12
William St. Chor 8E 174
William St. Clay M 8N 121
William St. Col 7B 86
William St. Dar 6A 158
William St. Earby 3E 78
William St. Hor 9B 196
William St. Hur 1G 205
William St. L'boro 9K 185
William St. Los H 8K 135
William St. Nels 2J 105
William St. Ram 5H 181
William St. Roch 7C 204
William St. Whitw 5N 183
William Young Clo. Pres 7M 115
Willington Clo. Bury 6H 201
Willis Rd. B'brn 6G 139
Willis St. Burn 4C 124
Willoughby Av. T Clev 1D 62
Willoughby St. B'brn 2M 139
Willow Av. Kirkby 7H 223
Willow Av. Ross 3M 161
Willowbank. Blac 4J 89
Willow Bank. Dar 9A 158
Willowbank. Lyth A 1E 128
Willow Bank. Todm 1L 165
Willow Bank. W'head 9N 209
Willowbank Av. Blac 4E 108
Willow Bank La. Dar 6N 157
Willow Brook. Acc 2A 142
Willow Brook. Hals 3B 208
Willowbrook Dri. Shev 5L 213
Willow Clo. And 5K 195
Willow Clo. Barfd 1F 104
Willow Clo. Clay M 6L 121
Willow Clo. Fort 2M 45
Willow Clo. Hogh 7G 136
Willow Clo. Los H 8K 135
Willow Clo. Pres 4D 134
Willow Clo. T Clev 2K 63
Willow Coppice. Lea 6B 114
Willow Ct. T Clev 2K 63
Willow Cres. Burs 7D 190
Willow Cres. Frec 3M 131
Willow Cres. Ley 4N 153
Willow Cres. Rib 7N 115
Willowcroft Dri. Hamb 2A 64
Willow Dale. T Clev 2K 63
Willowdene. T Clev 2E 62
Willowdene Clo. Brom X 5F 198
Willow Dri. Barr 2K 101
Willow Dri. Char R 2N 193
Willow Dri. Frec 3M 131
Willow Dri. Gars 3N 59
Willow Dri. Poul F 2K 89
Willow Dri. Skel 2J 219
Willow Dri. W Grn 5H 111
Willow End. Burs 9D 190
Willowfield. Clay W 4E 154
Willowfield Chase. Hogh 6K 137
Willowfield Rd. Hey 9M 21
Willow Grn. Ash R 9D 114
Willow Grn. Orm 7L 209
Willow Grn. Ruf 2E 190
Willow Grn. South 2B 168
Willow Gro. Blac 1G 88
Willow Gro. Form 8A 206
Willow Gro. Goos 4N 95
Willow Gro. Hamb 1A 64
Willow Gro. Lanc 8M 23
Willow Gro. More 2F 22
Willow Gro. South 7L 167
Willow Gro. W Brad 5K 73
Willow Hey. Brom X 6J 199
Willow Hey. Liv 3D 222
Willow Hey. Skel 2K 219
Willowhey. South 2M 167
Willow Hey. Tar 8E 150
Willow La. Lanc 9G 23
Willow Lodge. Lyth A 1J 129
Willowmead Pk. Mos S 7E 110
Willowmead Way. Roch 3L 203
Willow Mill. Cat 3H 25
Willow Mt. B'brn 6N 119
Willow Pk. Osw 6J 141
Willow Pl. Elsw 1L 91
Willow Ri. L'boro 2J 205
Willow Rd. Chor 4G 174
Willow Rd. Ley 9C 152
Willows Av. Lyth A 5L 129
Willows Av. T Clev 2E 62
Willows Cotts. Miln 6H 205
Willows La. Acc 3N 141
Willows La. K'ham 4L 111
Willows La. Roch 7G 205
Willows Pk. La. L'rdge 2K 97
Willows, The. Cop 5A 194
Willows, The. Lyth A 5L 129
Willows, The. Maw 3N 191
Willows, The. Mel B 6D 118
Willows, The. South 8F 166
(off Beechfield Gdns.)
Willows, The. Whitw 9N 183
(off Tonacliffe Rd.)
Willow St. Acc 2A 142
Willow St. B'brn 1A 140
Willow St. Burn 3C 124
Willow St. Clay M 6L 121
Willow St. Dar 6N 157
Willow St. Fltwd 9G 40
Willow St. Gt Har 5J 121
Willow St. Has 4G 161
Willow St. Ross 7C 162
Willow Tree Av. Brough 7G 94
Willow Tree Av. Ross 5K 161
Willow Tree Cres. Ley 6G 152
Willow Tree Gdns. T Clev 2K 63
Willow Trees Dri. B'brn 9K 119
Willow Wlk. Skel 8M 211
Willow Way. New L 9C 134
Wills Av. Liv 9B 216
Willsford Av. Liv 7G 222
Willshaw Rd. Blac 1B 88
Willy La. C'ham 9H 37
Wilmar Rd. Ley 5M 153
Wilmcote Gro. South 9B 186
Wilmers. L'boro 4N 185
Wilmore Clo. Col 6N 85
Wilmot Rd. Rib 6A 116
Wilmslow Av. Bolt 8E 198
Wilpshire. 4N 119
Wilpshire Banks. Wilp 5N 119
Wilpshire Golf Course. 4A 120
Wilpshire Rd. Rish 5D 120
Wilsham Rd. Orr 6H 221
Wilson Clo. Tar 8D 150
Wilson Clo. Todm 9K 147
Wilson Dri. Elsw 1M 91
Wilson Gro. Hey 8K 21
Wilson Sq. T Clev 4C 62
Wilson St. B'brn 6L 139
Wilson St. Clith 4K 81
Wilson St. Foul 2A 86
Wilson St. Hor 9B 196
Wilson St. Roch 5C 204
Wilton Clo. Lanc 4L 23
Wilton Gro. Pen 4D 134
Wilton Pde. Blac 3B 88
Wilton Pl. Ley 6L 153
Wilton Rd. Bolt 8E 198
Wilton Rd. Shev 6K 213
Wilton St. Barfd 8H 85
Wilton St. Bolt 9F 198
Wilton St. Brier 5F 104
Wilton St. Burn 9F 104
Wilton Ter. Roch 5B 204
Wiltshire Av. Burn 2N 123
Wiltshire Dri. Has 7G 161
Wiltshire M. Cot 4A 114
Wiltshire Pl. Wig 5M 221
Wilvere Ct. T Clev 4C 62
Wilvere Dri. T Clev 3C 62
Wilworth Cres. B'brn 8M 119
Wimberley Banks. B'brn 1N 139
(off Wimberley St.)
Wimberley Gdns. B'brn 2M 139
Wimberley Pl. B'brn 2M 139
Wimberley St. B'brn 2M 139
Wimbledon Av. T Clev 5D 62
Wimbledon Ct. T Clev 5D 62
(off Wimbledon Av.)
Wimbledon Dri. Roch 8A 204
Wimborne Rd. Orr 3K 221
Wimbourne Pl. Blac 3A 108
Wimbrick Clo. Orm 8J 209
Wimbrick Cres. Orm 9J 209
Winby St. Roch 9D 204
Wincanton Dri. Bolt 6D 198
Winchcombe Rd. T Clev 4E 62
Winchester Av. Acc 1B 142
Winchester Av. Ain 7C 222
Winchester Av. Blac 9D 88
Winchester Av. Chor 2G 194
Winchester Av. Lanc 3M 29
Winchester Av. More 2D 22
Winchester Clo. Bury 6H 201
Winchester Clo. Heat O 6B 22
Winchester Clo. Orr 4J 221
Winchester Dri. Poul F 5G 63
Winchester Rd. Bil 9G 221
Winchester Rd. Pad 3J 123
Winchester St. B'brn 5A 140
Winckley Ct. Pres 1J 135
Winckley Gdns. Pres 1J 135
Winckley Rd. Clay M 7M 121
Winckley Rd. Pres 2G 135
Winckley Sq. Pres 1J 135
Winckley St. Pres 1J 135
Winder Gth. Over K 9G 12
Winder La. Fort 4M 45
Windermere Av. Acc 8C 122
Windermere Av. Burn 8E 104
Windermere Av. Clith 4J 81
Windermere Av. Col 5C 86
Windermere Av. Far 4K 153
Windermere Av. Fltwd 4D 54
Windermere Av. More 4D 22
Windermere Clo. B'brn 2N 139
Windermere Ct. More 4D 22
(off Windermere Av.)
Windermere Cres. South 1C 206
Windermere Dri. Adl 4K 195
Windermere Dri. Dar 4C 158
Windermere Dri. Kirkby 6J 223
Windermere Dri. Mag 9D 216
Windermere Dri. Rainf 9K 219
Windermere Dri. Ram 7H 181
Windermere Dri. Rish 8G 120
Windermere Rd. Bacup 4L 163
Windermere Rd. Blac 1C 108
Windermere Rd. Bolt S 4L 15
Windermere Rd. Carn 1B 16
Windermere Rd. Chor 7G 174
Windermere Rd. Ful 5M 115
Windermere Rd. Lanc 8M 23
Windermere Rd. Liv 7A 214
Windermere Rd. Orr 3J 221
Windermere Rd. Pad 9H 103
Windermere Rd. Pres 8C 116
Windermere Sq. Lyth A 7F 108
Windermere St. Roch 3C 204
Windfield Clo. Liv 4M 223
Windflower Dri. Ley 5A 154
Windgate. Much H 5J 151
Windgate. Skel 3K 219
Windgate. Tar 1E 170
Windgate Fold. Tar 1E 170
Windham Pl. Lanc 5G 22
Windham St. Roch 2F 204
Windhill La. Rim 5L 75
Windholme. Lanc 6G 22
Windle Ash. Liv 9B 216
Windle Clo. Blac 5B 108
Windmill Animal Farm. 1N 189
Windmill Av. K'ham 5A 112
Windmill Av. Orm 7L 209
Windmill Cvn. Pk. Blac 1L 109
Windmill Clo. Liv 5K 223
Windmill Clo. Stain 5L 89
Windmill Ct. Lanc 4L 29
Windmill Ct. Roch 7E 204
Windmill Heights. Uph 3D 220
Windmill La. Brin 9K 137
Windmill Pl. Blac 3F 108
Windmill Rd. Uph 4C 220
Windmill St. Roch 7E 204
Windmill Vw. Wesh 3M 111
Windrows. Skel 2K 219
Windrush Av. Ram 3F 200
Windrush, The. Roch 1N 203
Windsor Av. Adl 7H 195
Windsor Av. Ash R 7E 114
Windsor Av. Blac 1B 108
Windsor Av. Chu 9N 121
Windsor Av. Clith 4J 81
Windsor Av. Helm 6F 160
Windsor Av. Lanc 2M 29
Windsor Av. L'rdge 3H 97
Windsor Av. More 5N 21
Windsor Av. New L 7D 134
Windsor Av. Pen 5F 134
Windsor Av. Ross 6C 162
Windsor Av. T Clev 1H 63
Windsor Clo. B'brn 5B 140
Windsor Clo. Burs 1C 210
Windsor Clo. Chor 7D 174
Windsor Clo. G'mnt 4F 200
Windsor Clo. Read 8C 102
Windsor Ct. Poul F 8L 63
Windsor Ct. South 1E 186
Windsor Dri. Brins 7N 155
Windsor Dri. Ful 3G 115
Windsor Gdns. Gars 5M 59
Windsor Gro. More 5A 22
Windsor Lodge. Ans 4K 129
Windsor Pk. Rd. Liv 7D 222
Windsor Pl. Barn 1A 78
Windsor Pl. Fltwd 8H 41
Windsor Rd. Ans 4K 129
Windsor Rd. B'brn 3E 140
(Blackburn Rd.)
Windsor Rd. B'brn 2J 139
(Revidge Rd.)
Windsor Rd. Blac 3H 89
Windsor Rd. Brom X 6G 198
Windsor Rd. Chor 7D 174
Windsor Rd. Chor & E'ston 7F 172
Windsor Rd. Dar 4N 157
Windsor Rd. Gars 5M 59
Windsor Rd. Gt Har 4K 121
Windsor Rd. K'ham 4L 111
Windsor Rd. Lyth A 3G 128
Windsor Rd. Mag 1B 222
Windsor Rd. More 5N 21
Windsor Rd. South 8K 167
Windsor Rd. Todm 1K 165
Windsor Rd. Uph 3D 220
Windsor Rd. Walt D 5N 135
Windsor St. Acc 2B 142
Windsor St. Burn 3A 124
Windsor St. Col 6B 86
Windsor St. Nels 3K 106
Windsor St. Roch 8D 204
Windsor Ter. Fltwd 8H 41
Windsor Ter. Miln 7H 205
Windsor Ter. Roch 6F 204
Windy Bank. Col 6B 86
Windycroft. Brom X 5H 199
Windy Harbour Cvn. Pk. Sing 6E 64
Windy Harbour La. Brom X 5H 199
Windy Harbour La. Todm 7L 147
Windy Harbour Rd. Sing 7F 64
Windy Harbour Rd. South 6E 186
Windy Hill. Ben 6N 19
Windyhill. Lanc 8K 23
Windy St. Chip 5G 70
Winery La. Walt D 3M 135
Winewall. 7F 86
Winewall La. Traw 6E 86
Winewall Rd. Col 6E 86
Wingate Av. More 5C 22
Wingate Av. T Clev 3D 62
Wingate Pl. T Clev 3D 62
Wingate Rd. Kirkby 6L 223
Wingates. Pen 5F 134
Wingate-Saul Rd. Lanc 8J 23
Wingate St. Roch 4J 203
Wingate Wlk. Liv 7L 223
Wingfield Vs. L'boro 7M 185
Wingrove Rd. Fltwd 2F 54
Winifred Av. Bury 9D 202
Winifred La. Augh 2F 216
Winifred St. Blac 6B 88
Winifred St. Ram 9G 181
Winmarleigh. 9J 45
Winmarleigh Rd. Ash R 8E 114
Winmarleigh Rd. Lanc 5L 29
Winmarleigh St. B'brn 4C 140
Winmarleigh Wlk. B'brn 4B 140
Winmoss Dri. Liv 5L 223
Winnipeg Clo. B'brn 9J 119
Winnipeg Pl. Blac 8D 62
Winscar Wlk. Poul F 8H 63
Winsford Cres. T Clev 3C 62
Winsford Dri. Roch 8K 203
Winsford Wlk. Burn 4N 123
Winsham Clo. Liv 9K 223
Winslow Av. Poul F 6H 63
Winslow Clo. Pen 6H 135
Winsor Av. Ley 7L 153
Winstanley. 8N 221
Winstanley Gro. Blac 5C 88
Winstanley Rd. Orr 7H 221
Winster Clo. Hogh 4G 136
Winster Ct. Clay M 7L 121
Winster Ho. Wig 4M 221
Winster Pk. Lanc 6G 22
Winster Pl. Blac 9K 89
Winsters, The. Skel 2K 219
Winster Wlk. Lanc 6G 22
Winston Av. Lyth A 2H 129
Winston Av. Roch 7J 203
Winston Av. T Clev 1F 62
Winston Cres. South 3L 187
Winston Rd. B'brn 1L 139
Winterburn Av. Bolt 7H 199
Winterburn La. E'tn 1M 53
Winterburn Rd. B'brn 9K 139
Winterbutlee Gro. Todm 6K 165
Winterbutlee Rd. Todm 6K 165
Winter Gap La. Loth 4L 79
Winter Gardens. 5B 88
Winter Gdns. Arc. More 3A 22
Winter Hey La. Hor 9C 196
Winter Hill Clo. Pres 2E 116
Winterley Dri. Acc 8D 122
Winterton Rd. Dar 5A 158
Winthorpe Av. More 4D 22
Winton Av. Blac 9G 88
Winton Av. Ful 3J 115
Winton Av. Wig 6N 221
Winton St. L'boro 9L 185
Winward Clo. Lwr D 1N 157
Wirral Dri. Wig 9M 221
Wiseman Clo. More 4C 22
Wiseman St. Burn 3C 124
Wisp Hill Gro. Halt 1C 24
Wisteria Dri. Lwr D 9A 140
Wiswell. 3M 101
Wiswell Clo. Burn 8J 105
Wiswell Clo. Ross 3M 161
Wiswell La. Whal 4K 101
Witham Clo. Stand 3N 213
Witham Rd. Skel 2G 219
Withens New Rd. Todm 4N 165
(in two parts)
Withens Rd. Liv 8C 216
Witherslack Clo. More 5B 22
Withers St. B'brn 4N 139
Withgill Fold. W'gll 5D 80
Within Grove. 8C 122
Within Gro. Acc 8C 122
Withington La. Hesk 3H 193
Withins Fld. Liv 8A 214
Withins La. Liv 4F 214
Withnell. 6B 156
Withnell Fold. 4L 155
Withnell Fold. Withn 4L 155
Withnell Fold Old Rd. Brins 5N 155
Withnell Gro. Chor 5G 175
Withnell Rd. Blac 1B 108
Withy Ct. Ful 6H 115
Withy Gro. Clo. Bam B 7B 136
Withy Gro. Cres. Bam B 7B 136
Withy Gro. Rd. Bam B 7B 136
Withy Pde. Ful 5H 115
Withy Trees Av. Bam B 8B 136
Withy Trees Clo. Bam B 7B 136
Witley Rd. Roch 6E 204
Witney Av. B'brn 8F 138
Wittlewood Dri. Acc 8A 122
Witton. 5J 139
Witton Av. Fltwd 3E 54
Witton Country Pk. & Vis. Cen. 5G 139
Witton Gro. Fltwd 3E 54
Witton Pde. B'brn 5K 139
Witton St. Pres 9L 115
Witton Way. Rainf 3K 225
Woborrow Rd. Hey 9K 21
Woburn Clo. Acc 5D 142
Woburn Clo. Miln 7H 205
Woburn Grn. Ley 5L 153
Woburn Rd. Blac 3C 88
Woburn Way. Catt 1A 68
Wold, The. H'pey 3J 175
Wolfenden Grn. Ross 7D 162
Wollaton Dri. South 2M 187
Wolseley Clo. Ley 7K 153
Wolseley Pl. Pres 1K 135
Wolseley Rd. Pres 3H 135
Wolseley St. B'brn 7L 139
Wolseley St. Lanc 8L 23
Wolseley St. Miln 9L 205
Wolsey Clo. T Clev 9E 54
Wolsley Rd. Blac 9B 88
Wolsley Rd. Fltwd 9F 40
Wolstenholme. 4G 202
Wolstenholme Av. Bury 7L 201
Wolstenholme Coalpit La. Roch 3F 202
Wolstenholme La. Roch 3G 202
(in two parts)
Wolverton. Skel 3K 219
Wolverton Av. Blac 9B 62
Wolvesey. Roch 7B 204
Woodacre La. Scor 1A 60
Woodacre Rd. Rib well
Woodale Laithe. Barfd 8G 85
Woodale Rd. Clay W 3D 154
Wood Bank. Pen 5F 134
Wood Bank. Ross 9E 160
Woodbank Av. Dar 5M 157
Woodbank Dri. Bury 9H 201
Woodbank Rd. L'boro 2K 205
Woodberry Clo. Liv 4L 223
Woodbine Gdns. Burn 2N 123
Woodbine Pas. L'boro 9K 185
(off William St.)
Woodbine Rd. B'brn 2J 139
Woodbine Rd. Burn 3A 124
Woodbine St. Roch 8D 204
(in two parts)
Woodbine St. E. Roch 8E 204
Woodbine Ter. Todm 7E 146
Woodbridge Gdns. Roch 3N 203
Woodbrook Dri. Wig 7N 221
Woodburn Clo. B'brn 9H 119
Woodburn Dri. Bolt 9B 198
Woodbury Av. B'brn 6L 139
Woodbury Av. Fence 3B 104
Woodchat Ct. Chor 9B 174
Wood Clo. Arns 1F 4
Wood Clo. Liv 8J 223
Wood Clo. R'lee 6E 84
Woodclose Cvn. Pk. K Lon 6F 8
Wood Clough Flats. Brier 5E 104
Woodcock Clo. Roch 6K 203
Woodcock Clo. T Clev 7G 54
Woodcock Est. Los H 1L 153
Woodcock Fold. E'ston 7F 172
Woodcock Hill Rd. Pleas 5C 138
Woodcock La. Char R 1H 193
Woodcock's Ct. Pres 1J 135
Woodcote Clo. Liv 6M 223
Woodcott Bank. Bolt 9E 198
Woodcourt Av. Burn 6B 124
Woodcrest. Wilp 4N 119
Woodcroft. Shev 6H 213
Woodcroft. Skel 3K 219
Woodcroft Av. Ross 2L 161
Woodcroft Clo. Pen 6F 134
Woodcroft St. Ross 2L 161
Wooded Clo. Bury 8L 201
Wood End. Burn 7D 104
Wood End. Pen 7F 134
Woodend Av. Mag 3B 222
Woodend La. Ward 8G 185
Wood End Rd. Clay W 4C 154
Woodfall. Chor 5D 174
Woodfield. Bam B 1E 154
Woodfield Av. Acc 5C 142
Woodfield Av. Blac 8B 88
Woodfield Av. Roch 3B 204
Woodfield Rd. Blac 8B 88
Woodfield Rd. Chor 5E 174
Woodfield Rd. Orm 9J 209
Woodfield Rd. T Clev 2K 63
Woodfield St. Todm 1K 165
(off Buckley Vw.)
Woodfield Ter. Brier 5G 104
Woodfield Vw. Whal 5J 101
Wood Fold. Brom X 7J 199
Woodfold Clo. Mel B 6D 118
Woodfold La. Cabus 8N 45
Woodfold Pl. B'brn 3J 139
Woodford Copse. Chor 7B 174
Woodford St. Wig 5L 221
Woodgate. Whi L 6F 22
Woodgate Av. Bury 9B 202
Woodgate Hill. 9B 202
Woodgate Hill Rd. Bury 9A 202
(in two parts)
Woodgates Rd. B'brn 3F 138
Woodgreen. Ley 5H 153
Woodgreen. Wesh 2N 111
Wood Grn. Dri. T Clev 3F 62
Woodgrove Rd. Burn 6F 124
Woodhall Clo. Bury 8J 201
Woodhall Cres. Hogh 4G 136
Woodhall Gdns. Hamb 1B 64
Woodhart La. E'ston 9F 172
Woodhead Clo. Ram 1H 201
Woodhead Clo. Ross 6E 162
Woodhead Rd. Read 8C 102
Woodhey. 2F 200
Wood Hey Gro. Roch 1B 204

Woodhey Rd.—Zion Ter.

Woodhey Rd. Ram 2F 200
Woodheys Rd. L'boro 3K 205
Woodhill. 9H 201
Woodhill Av. More 5A 22
Woodhill Clo. More 5A 22
Woodhill Fold. 9J 201
Woodhill Fold. Bury 9J 201
Woodhill Ho. More 4A 22
Woodhill La. More 4A 22
Woodhill Rd. Bury 9J 201
Woodhill St. Bury 9J 201
Wood House. 4B 50
Wood Ho. Ct. Todm 1N 165
Woodhouse Dri. Wig 9N 213
Woodhouse Farm Cotts. Roch 3H 203
Woodhouse Gro. Pres 1H 135
Woodhouse Gro. Todm 2N 165
Woodhouse La. Roch 3H 203
Wood House La. Slai 3A 50
Woodhouse La. Wig 1N 221 (in two parts)
Woodhouse Rd. T Clev 3L 63
Woodhouse Rd. Todm 2N 165
Woodhouse St. Burn 5F 124
Woodhurst Dri. Stand 3N 213
Woodland. Brins 8A 156
Woodland Av. Bacup 2K 163
Woodland Av. Scar 6E 188
Woodland Av. T Clev 1H 63
Woodland Clo. Hamb 2C 64
Woodland Clo. W Grn 6G 111
Woodland Cres. Pre 7N 41
Woodland Dri. Clay M 4M 121
Woodland Dri. Poul F 1L 89
Woodland Dri. Stand 2N 213
Woodland Grange. Pen 5G 135
Woodland Gro. Blac 6E 88
Woodland Gro. Eger 3D 198
Woodland Gro. Pen 3E 134
Woodland Mt. Bacup 7G 162
Woodland Pl. Lwr D 9N 139
Woodland Rd. Mell 6F 222
Woodland Rd. Roch 3N 203
Woodlands. Roch 2F 204
Woodlands Av. Bam B 6C 136
Woodlands Av. B'brn 7F 138
Woodlands Av. K'ham 4L 111
Woodlands Av. Pen 5G 135
Woodlands Av. Rib 7A 116
Woodlands Av. Roch 7L 203
Woodlands Av. Todm 1L 165
Woodlands Clo. Newt 6D 112
Woodlands Clo. Orm 8M 209
Woodlands Clo. South 6K 167
Woodlands Clo. W Brad 5K 73
Woodlands Ct. Lyth A 4K 129
Woodlands Cres. Brtn 5E 94
Woodlands Dri. Ful 1H 115
Woodlands Dri. Hey 6M 21
Woodlands Dri. Ley 6J 153
Woodlands Dri. Shev 8J 213
Woodlands Dri. Silv 7G 5
Woodlands Dri. W'ton 3H 131
Woodlands Dri. Wesh 2N 111
Woodlands Dri. W Brad 5K 73
Woodlands Dri. Whal 5J 101
Woodlands Gro. Bury 9G 200
Woodlands Gro. Dar 5L 157
Woodlands Gro. Grims 9G 96
Woodlands Gro. Hey 6M 21
Woodlands Gro. Pad 1G 122
Woodlands Mdw. Chor 2E 194
Woodlands Pk. Whal 5J 101
Woodlands Rd. Lanc 4L 23
Woodlands Rd. Lyth A 4K 129
Woodlands Rd. Miln 8H 205
Woodlands Rd. Nels 2K 105
Woodlands Rd. Ram 4J 181
Woodlands, The. Ash R 8B 114
Woodlands, The. Bury 8J 201
Woodlands, The. Gars 4M 59
Woodlands, The. Old L 4C 100
Woodlands, The. South 8C 186
Woodland St. Roch 3D 204
Woodlands Vw. Over K 1F 16
Woodlands Vw. Ram 8H 181
Woodlands Vw. Roch 5F 204
Woodlands Way. Brtn 4E 94
Woodlands Way. Longt 8K 133
Woodland Ter. Bacup 3K 163
Woodland Vw. Bacup 3K 163
Woodland Vw. Brom X 5H 199
Woodland Vw. Gt Har 3J 121
Wood La. Form & Liv 2J 215
Wood La. Hesk 1G 193
Wood La. Lath 8H 191
Wood La. Maw 9A 172
Wood La. Parb 2A 212
Wood Lark Dri. Chor 9B 174
Wood Lea. Todm 8H 147
Wood Lea Bank. Ross 7D 162 (off Wood Lea Rd.)
Woodlea Chase. Dar 3C 178
Woodlea Clo. South 1C 168
Woodlea Gdns. Brier 5H 105
Woodlea Rd. B'brn 4B 140
Woodlea Rd. Ley 7J 153
Wood Lea Rd. Ross 7C 162
Woodlee Rd. Hesk B 5D 150
Woodleigh Clo. Liv 6A 216
Woodley Av. Acc 4B 142
Woodley Av. T Clev 2K 63
Woodley Pk. Rd. Skel 8M 211
Woodley Rd. Liv 4B 222
Woodman Cote. Chor 4D 174
Woodman Dri. Bury 7K 201
Woodman La. Burr 9F 8
Woodmoss La. Scar 2C 188
Woodnook. 4A 142
Wood Nook. Ross 9M 143
Woodnook Rd. App B 4H 213
Wood Pk. Rd. Blac 9E 88
Woodpecker Hill. Burn 4A 124 (off Nightingale Cres.)
Woodplumpton. 8B 94
Woodplumpton La. Brough 7E 94
Woodplumpton Rd. Burn 7D 124
Woodplumpton Rd. Ful & Ash R 5E 114
Wood Plumpton Rd. Wood 6B 94
Woodridge Av. T Clev 3C 62
Wood Road. 4H 201
Wood Rd. La. Bury 3H 201
Woodrow. Skel 3J 219
Woodrow Dri. Newb 3K 211
Woodruff Clo. T Clev 7F 54
Woodrush. More 2F 22
Woodrush Rd. Stand L 9N 213
Woods Brow. Bald 4M 117
Wood's Brow. K Grn 4B 98
Woods Clo. Hask 8N 207
Woodsend Clo. B'brn 8A 140
Woodsfold. 4J 93
Woods Grn. Pres 3H 135
Woodside. Chor & Eux 3M 173
Woodside. Far 3M 153
Woodside. Has 5H 161
Woodside. Miln 8M 205
Woodside Av. Clay W 6D 154
Woodside Av. Ful 5H 115
Woodside Av. New L 9C 134
Woodside Av. Rib 6A 116
Woodside Av. Rish 9F 120
Woodside Av. South 1B 206
Woodside Clo. Acc 8E 122
Woodside Clo. Uph 3F 220
Woodside Cres. Ross 6B 162
Woodside Dri. Blac 5G 88
Woodside Dri. Ram 9F 180
Woodside Gro. B'brn 8H 139
Woodside Pk. Cvn. Pk. Pre 3B 56
Woodside Pl. Chor 1G 195
Woodside Rd. Acc 9D 122 (Bolton Av., in two parts)
Woodside Rd. Acc 8E 122 (Sutton Cres.)
Woodside Rd. S'stne 8D 102
Woodside Ter. Nels 2G 105
Woodside Way. Clay M 5M 121
Woodside Way. Liv 5L 223
Wood's La. Eag H 5E 58
Woods La. Wood 3J 93
Woodsley St. Burn 4N 123
Woods Pas. L'boro 9J 185
Woods, The. Roch 9N 203
Woodstock Av. T Clev 3J 63
Woodstock Clo. Los H 8M 135
Woodstock Cres. B'brn 8F 138
Woodstock Dri. South 5F 186
Woodstock Dri. Tot 6C 200
Woodstock Gdns. Blac 2B 108
Woodstock St. Roch 4N 203
Wood St. Blac 5B 88 (in two parts)
Wood St. Brier 5F 104
Wood St. Burn 1E 124
Wood St. Col 7B 86
Wood St. Dar 5B 158 (Alexandra Rd.)
Wood St. Dar 6N 157 (Vale Rd.)
Wood St. Fltwd 4E 54
Wood St. Gt Har 4L 121
Wood St. Hap 5H 123
Wood St. Hor 9D 196
Wood St. Lanc 8K 23
Wood St. L'boro 9L 185
Wood St. Lyth A 2E 128
Wood St. Osw 3L 141
Wood St. Poul I 8M 63
Wood St. Ram 9G 180
Wood St. Roch 9M 205 (Huddersfield Rd.)
Wood St. Roch 7D 204 (Oldham Rd.)
Wood St. Todm 1L 165
Wood Ter. Chat 7D 74
Wood Top. 6K 161
Wood Top Av. Roch 8K 203
Woodvale. 1B 206
Woodvale. Dar 6N 157
Woodvale. Ley 7D 152
Woodvale Airfield. 4A 206
Woodvale Ct. Banks 1F 168
Woodvale Rd. South 2C 206
Wood Vw. B'brn 7G 139
Wood Vw. Heyw 9G 202
Wood Vw. Shev 6L 213
Wood Vw. Stalm 5B 56
Woodville Rd. B'brn 1A 140
Woodville Rd. Brier 4F 104
Woodville Rd. Chor 6E 174
Woodville Rd. Hth C 4H 195
Woodville Rd. Pen 6G 134
Woodville Rd. W. Pen 6F 134
Woodville St. Far 4L 153
Woodville St. Lanc 8L 23
Woodville Ter. Dar 9B 158
Woodville Ter. Lyth A 5M 129
Woodward Clo. Bury 8L 201
Woodward Rd. Know I 6A 224
Woodway. Ful 5F 114
Woodwell La. Silv 1G 10
Wookey Clo. Ful 3N 115
Wooley La. Acc 5E 142
Woolfold. 9G 201
Woolfold Trad. Est. Bury 9H 201
Woolman Rd. Blac 6C 88
Woolwich St. B'brn 3B 140
Woone La. Clith 5K 81
Worcester Av. Acc 1N 141
Worcester Av. Gars 5M 59
Worcester Av. Lanc 2M 29
Worcester Av. Ley 7L 153
Worcester Pl. Chor 1G 195
Worcester Rd. B'brn 3C 140
Worcester Rd. Blac 7F 88
Worcester St. Bury 9J 201
Worchester Gdns. Cot 4A 114
Worden Clo. Ley 8J 153
Worden La. Ley 8K 153
Worden La. Withn 4N 155
Worden Rd. Ash R 6G 114
Wordsworth Av. Bil 9G 221
Wordsworth Av. Blac 8H 89
Wordsworth Av. Bolt S 4L 15
Wordsworth Av. Lyth A 4C 130
Wordsworth Av. Orr 5J 221
Wordsworth Av. Pad 2K 123
Wordsworth Av. T Clev 1F 62
Wordsworth Av. W'ton 2K 131
Wordsworth Clo. Orm 6J 209
Wordsworth Clo. Osw 4J 141
Wordsworth Cres. L'boro 3J 205
Wordsworth Dri. Gt Har 4H 121
Wordsworth Gdns. Dar 6B 158
Wordsworth Pl. Walt D 6N 135
Wordsworth Rd. Acc 5N 141
Wordsworth Rd. Col 6A 86
Wordsworth St. Brclf 8K 105
Wordsworth St. Burn 3A 124
Wordsworth St. Hap 5H 123
Wordsworth Ter. Chor 4F 174
Wordsworth Way. Roch 7J 203
Wordworth Ct. Lyth A 4J 129
Workshop Rd. Hey 5L 27
Worrall St. Roch 3A 204
Worsicks Cotts. Sing 1D 90
Worsley Av. Blac 2C 108
Worsley Clo. Kno S 8K 41
Worsley Clo. Wig 6L 221
Worsley Ct. Osw 4L 141
Worsley Grn. Wig 6L 221
Worsley Ho. Fltwd 2E 54
Worsley Pl. Roch 6E 204
Worsley Rd. Lyth A 3J 129
Worsley St. Acc 4C 142
Worsley St. Ris B 9F 142
Worsley St. Roch 6E 204
Worsley St. Tot 6D 200
Worsley St. Wig 6L 221
Worsthorne. 4M 125
Worston. 1C 82
Worston Clo. Acc 4M 141
Worston Clo. Ross 3M 161
Worston La. Gt Har 3L 121
Worston Pl. B'brn 3J 139
Worston Rd. Chat 9B 74
Worswick Cres. Ross 5M 161
Worthalls Rd. Read 8C 102
Worthing Clo. South 2F 186
Worthing Rd. Ing 5D 114
Worthington Rd. Blac 5G 109
Worthy St. Chor 7G 174
Wragby Clo. Bury 8J 201
Wraith St. Dar 7A 158
Wrampool. 5N 43
Wrangling, The. 5L 139
Wrath Clo. Bolt 8H 199
Wray. 8E 18
Wray Ct. Lanc 4J 23
Wray Cres. Ley 9C 152
Wray Cres. W Grn 5H 111
Wray Gro. T Clev 3D 62
Wray Pl. Roch 7F 204
Wrayton. 3F 18
Wraywood Ct. Fltwd 3C 54
Wrea Green. 5G 111
Wrekin Dri. Liv 8D 222
Wren Av. Pen 3H 135
Wrenbury Clo. Wig 5L 221
Wrenbury Dri. Bolt 7F 198
Wrenbury Dri. Roch 9F 204
Wren Clo. Orr 2L 221
Wren Clo. Poul F 7G 63
Wren Clo. T Clev 3J 63
Wren Dri. Bury 9N 201
Wren Grn. Roch 7E 204
Wren Gro. Blac 8E 88
Wrennalls La. E'ston 1D 192
Wren St. Burn 3A 124
Wren St. Nels 2K 105
Wren St. Pres 8L 115
Wrightington. 9E 192
Wrightington Bar. 6J 193
Wrights Fold. Ley 7M 153
Wrights Ter. South 2H 187
Wright St. Bacup 9K 145
Wright St. Chor 6G 174
Wright St. Hor 9C 196
Wright St. South 7H 167
Wright St. Wesh 3L 111
Wright St. W. Hor 9C 196 (off Julia St.)
Wrigley Pl. L'boro 2J 205
Wrigleys Clo. Liv 7A 206
Wrigleys La. Liv 7A 206
Wrigley's Sq. Roch 5C 204
Written Stone La. L'rdge 1N 97
Wroxham Clo. Burn 8H 105
Wroxham Clo. Bury 8J 201
Wroxton Clo. T Clev 4F 62
Wuerdle. 2H 205
Wuerdle Clo. Roch 1H 205
Wuerdle Farm Way. Roch 1H 205
Wuerdle Pl. Roch 1H 205
Wuerdle St. Roch 1H 205
Wycherley Rd. Roch 3M 203
Wychnor. Ing 2E 114
Wycollar Clo. Acc 4B 142
Wycollar Dri. B'brn 2H 139
Wycollar Rd. B'brn 2H 139
Wycoller. 8K 87
Wycoller Av. Burn 4H 125
Wycoller Country Pk. & Vis. Cen. 8K 87
Wycoller Rd. Traw 7G 86
Wycombe Av. Blac 3B 108
Wyfordby Av. B'brn 1G 139
Wyke Cop Rd. South 1C 188
Wykeham Gro. Roch 4M 203
Wykeham Rd. Lyth A 4A 130
Wyke La. South 6B 168
Wyke Wood La. South 6E 168
Wyllin Rd. Liv 8M 223
Wymott. 9C 152
Wymundsley. Chor 5B 174
Wyndene Clo. L'rdge 2L 97
Wyndene Gro. Frec 2N 131
Wyndham Gdns. Blac 3D 108
Wyndham Pl. More 2F 22
Wynnstay Av. Liv 8C 216
Wynnwood Av. Blac 1C 88
Wynotham St. Burn 8F 104
Wyre Av. K'ham 4N 111
Wyre Bank. St M 4F 66
Wyre Chalet Pk. Poul F 7C 64
Wyre Clo. Gt Ecc 6A 66
Wyre Clo. More 6F 22
Wyre Ct. Fltwd 1E 54
Wyre Cres. Dar 4L 157
Wyredale Rd. Lyth A 9C 108
Wyre Estuary Country Pk. 9M 55
Wyrefields. Poul I 8N 63
Wyre Gro. Blac 7C 88
Wyre La. Gars 3N 59
Wyre Rd. T Clev 5L 63
Wyresdale Av. Acc 9N 121
Wyresdale Av. Blac 7D 62
Wyresdale Av. Hey 7M 21
Wyresdale Av. Poul F 8J 63
Wyresdale Av. South 1K 187
Wyresdale Ct. Fltwd 1F 54
Wyresdale Ct. Lanc 9M 23
Wyresdale Cres. Glas D 2C 36
Wyresdale Cres. Rib 5N 115
Wyresdale Cres. Scor 6B 46
Wyresdale Dri. Ley 8L 153
Wyresdale Gdns. Lanc 9M 23
Wyresdale Rd. Kno S 8K 41
Wyresdale Rd. Lanc 9L 23
Wyresdale Rd. Quer 3C 30
Wyreside. 3K 65
Wyre Side. Kno S 8K 41
Wyreside Clo. Gars 4N 59
Wyreside Dri. Hamb 1A 64
Wyre St. Ash R 8F 114
Wyre St. Fltwd 1F 54
Wyre St. Pad 1J 123
Wyre St. St A 1G 128
Wyre St. Wesh 3L 111
Wyre Va. Pk. Gars 3M 59
Wyre Vw. Kno S 7L 41
Wytham St. Pad 2J 123
Wythburn Av. B'brn 8F 138
Wythburn Clo. Burn 1N 123
Wythorpe Cft. More 4B 22
Wyvern Way. Poul F 6J 63

Y

Yardley Rd. Know I 9A 224
Yare St. Ross 7D 162
Yarlside. 8D 52
Yarlside La. Brac 8D 52
Yarmouth Av. Has 5H 161
Yarm Pl. Burn 3E 124
Yarraville St. Ross 5M 161
Yarrow Av. Liv 9E 216
Yarrow Clo. Crost 4M 171
Yarrow Clo. Roch 8C 204
Yarrow Clo. Withn 6B 156
Yarrow Ga. Chor 8G 174
Yarrow Gro. Hor 9C 196
Yarrow Pl. Ley 7G 153
Yarrow Rd. Chor 7G 175
Yarrow Rd. Ley 7G 153
Yarrow Valley Pk. 3C 194
Yarrow Wlk. More 6B 22
Yarwell. Roch 5B 204 (off Spotland Rd.)
Yates Fold. B'brn 6N 139
Yates St. Blac 4B 88
Yates St. Chor 8D 174
Yates Ter. Bury 8K 201
Yeadon Gro. Chor 7C 174
Yeadon Way. Blac 1C 108
Yealand Av. Gigg 2N 35
Yealand Av. Hey 1L 27
Yealand Clo. Roch 7M 203
Yealand Conyers. 1B 12
Yealand Dri. Lanc 3L 29
Yealand Gro. Carn 8B 12
Yealand Redmayne. 7B 6
Yealand Rd. Yeal C 1B 12
Yealand Storrs. 6N 5
Yellow Hall. 7D 78
Yellow Hall. Kel 7D 78
Yellow Ho. La. South 8H 167
Yenham Rd. Over 6B 28
Yeoman's Clo. Miln 6J 205
Yeovil Ct. Pres 8N 115
Yerburgh Rd. Mel 7F 118
Yewbarrow Clo. Burn 9A 104
Yew Ct. Fltwd 3C 54
Yew Ct. Roch 3E 204
Yewdale. Shev 6L 213
Yewdale. Skel & S'way 2L 219 (in three parts)
Yewdale Av. Hey 1L 27
Yewdale Gdns. Roch 9M 203
Yew Grn. Wesh 2N 111 (off Mowbreck La.)
Yewlands Av. Bam B 7B 136
Yewlands Av. Ful 3H 115
Yewlands Av. Ley 6K 153
Yewlands Cres. Ful 3H 115
Yewlands Dri. Burn 7F 104
Yewlands Dri. Ful 3H 115
Yewlands Dri. Gars 3N 59
Yewlands Dri. Ley 6J 153
Yew St. B'brn 1A 140
Yew St. Bury 9A 202
Yew Tree Av. Eux 2M 173
Yew Tree Av. Grims 8E 96
Yewtree Clo. Chor 2E 194
Yew Tree Clo. Clay D 3M 119
Yew Tree Clo. Gars 4M 59
Yew Tree Clo. Newt 6D 112
Yew Tree Ct. Todm 7K 165
Yew Tree Dri. B'brn 9G 119
Yew Tree Dri. L Bent 6K 19
Yew Tree Dri. Osw 5M 141
Yew Tree Gdns. Silv 9G 4
Yew Tree Grn. Liv 6G 223
Yewtree Gro. Los H 9K 135
Yew Tree Gro. Ross 7L 161
Yew Tree La. Bolt 8G 198
Yew Tree Rd. Blac 1G 89
Yew Tree Rd. Orm 5K 209
Yew Trees Av. Rib 5C 116
York. 1D 120
York Av. Fltwd 1E 54
York Av. Ful 5H 115
York Av. Has 7F 160
York Av. Roch 7L 203
York Av. South 9G 167
York Av. T Clev 1D 62
York Clo. Clay M 6M 121
York Clo. Form 6A 206
York Clo. Ley 8H 153
York Clo. Walt D 5N 135
York Cres. B'brn 6N 119
York Dri. Frec 7N 111
York Dri. Gt Ecc 6A 66
York Dri. Ram 1F 200
Yorke St. Burn 4D 124
York Fields. Barn 3M 77
York Gdns. South 9G 166
York Gro. Gars 5M 59
York Ho. Pres 1K 135
York La. Lang 1C 120
York Mnr. Liv 9A 206
York Pl. Acc 1A 142
York Pl. Adl 5J 195
York Pl. More 3B 22
York Pl. Todm 2L 165 (off Bond St.)
York Rd. B'brn 4C 120
York Rd. Blac 7B 62
York Rd. Brier 5F 104
York Rd. Form 9A 206
York Rd. Lanc 2L 29
York Rd. Lyth A 3F 128
York Rd. Mag 3C 222
York Rd. South 1F 186
Yorkshire St. Acc 4B 142
Yorkshire St. Bacup 4K 163
Yorkshire St. Blac 7B 88
Yorkshire St. Burn 3E 124 (in two parts)
Yorkshire St. Hun 7D 122
Yorkshire St. Nels 2J 105
Yorkshire St. Roch 6C 204 (in three parts)
Yorkshire St. E. More 4N 21
Yorkshire St. W. More 4M 21
York St. Acc 1A 142
York St. Bacup 2K 163
York St. Barn 2M 77
York St. B'brn 5M 139
York St. Blac 7B 88
York St. Chor 7F 174
York St. Chu 2L 141
York St. Clith 2M 81
York St. Col 6B 86
York St. Gt Har 4K 121
York St. Nels 2K 105
York St. Osw 5J 141
York St. Rish 8H 121
York St. Roch 7E 204
York St. Ross 9M 143
York St. Todm 1L 165
York Ter. B'brn 8E 138
York Ter. South 6J 167
York Vw. Live 1J 157
Young Av. Ley 6M 153
Young St. B'brn 6J 139
Young St. Ram 8G 181

Z

Zama St. Ram 1F 200
Zebudah St. B'brn 6K 139
Zechariah Brow. B'brn 6J 119
Zedburgh. Roch 5B 204 (off Spotland Rd.)
Zetland Pl. Roch 5E 204
Zetland St. Pres 1M 135
Zetland St. South 7K 167
Zion Rd. B'brn 9A 120
Zion St. Bacup 4L 163
Zion St. Col 7A 86
Zion Ter. Roch 4J 203

HOSPITALS and HOSPICES
covered by this atlas.

N.B. Where Hospitals and Hospices are not named on the map, the reference
given is for the road in which they are situated.

ABRAHAM ORMEROD DAY HOSPITAL 2L **165**
Burnley Rd.
TODMORDEN
Lancashire
OL14 7BY
Tel: 01706 817911

ACCRINGTON VICTORIA COMMUNITY HOSPITAL 1A **142**
Haywood Rd.
ACCRINGTON
Lancashire
BB5 6AS
Tel: 01254 263555

ASHWORTH HOSPITAL 9G **216**
Parkbourn
LIVERPOOL
L31 1HW
Tel: 0151 4730303

BILLINGE HOSPITAL 9G **221**
Upholland Rd.
Billinge
WIGAN
Lancashire
WN5 7ET
Tel: 01942 244000

BIRCH HILL HOSPITAL 9G **185**
Union Rd.
ROCHDALE
Lancashire
OL12 9QB
Tel: 01706 377777

BLACKBURN ROYAL INFIRMARY 6L **139**
Bolton Rd.
BLACKBURN
BB2 3LR
Tel: 01254 263555

BRIAN HOUSE (HOSPICE) 9F **62**
Within Trinity - the Hospice in the Fylde
Low Moor Rd.
BLACKPOOL
FY2 0BG
Tel: 01253 358881

BURNLEY GENERAL HOSPITAL 8G **104**
Casterton Av.
BURNLEY
Lancashire
BB10 2PQ
Tel: 01282 425071

BURY GENERAL HOSPITAL 8L **201**
Walmersley Rd.
BURY
BL9 6PG
Tel: 0161 764 6081

CALDERSTONES 3G **101**
Mitton Rd., Whalley
CLITHEROE
Lancashire
BB7 9PE
Tel: 01254 822121

CASTLEBERG HOSPITAL 3M **35**
Raines Rd., Giggleswick
SETTLE
North Yorkshire
BD24 0BN
Tel: 01729 823515

CHORLEY AND SOUTH RIBBLE DISTRICT GENERAL HOSPITAL
....4E **174**
Preston Rd.
CHORLEY
Lancashire
PR7 1PP
Tel: 01257 261222

CLIFTON HOSPITAL 3H **129**
Pershore Rd.
LYTHAM ST ANNES
Lancashire
FY8 1PB
Tel: 01253 306204

CLITHEROE COMMUNITY HOSPITAL 9N **73**
Chatburn Rd.
CLITHEROE
Lancashire
BB7 4JX
Tel: 01200 427311

DERIAN HOUSE (HOSPICE) 3D **174**
Chancery Rd.
CHORLEY
Lancashire
PR7 1DH
Tel: 01257 233300

DEVONSHIRE ROAD HOSPITAL 4D **88**
Devonshire Rd.
BLACKPOOL
FY3 8AZ
Tel: 01253 303364

EAST LANCASHIRE HOSPICE 7M **139**
Park Lee Rd.
BLACKBURN
BB2 3NY
Tel: 01254 342810

EUXTON HALL HOSPITAL 5M **173**
Wigan Rd.
Euxton
CHORLEY
Lancashire
PR7 6DY
Tel: 01257 276261

FAIRFIELD GENERAL HOSPITAL 9C **202**
Rochdale Old Rd.
Jericho
BURY
Lancashire
BL9 7TD
Tel: 0161 764 6081

FLEETWOOD HOSPITAL 8H **41**
Pharos St.
FLEETWOOD
Lancashire
FY7 6BE
Tel: 01253 306000

FULWOOD HALL HOSPITAL (C.H.G.) 4M **115**
Midgery La.
Fulwood
PRESTON
PR2 9SZ
Tel: 01772 704111

FYLDE COAST BUPA HOSPITAL 3F **88**
St Walburgas Rd.
BLACKPOOL
FY3 8BP
Tel: 01253 394188

GISBURNE PARK ABBEY HOSPITAL 8A **52**
Gisburn Park Est.
Gisburn
CLITHEROE
Lancashire
BB7 4HX
Tel: 01200 445693

GUILD PARK 6B **96**
Whittingham La.
Goosnargh
PRESTON
PR3 2JH
Tel: 01772 865531

HESKETH CENTRE, THE 5J **167**
51-55 Albert Rd.
SOUTHPORT
Merseyside
PR9 0LT
Tel: 01704 530940

HETTINGA HOUSE (HOSPICE) 6N **209**
Dark La.
Lathom
ORMSKIRK
Lancashire
L40 5TR
Tel: 01695 578713

LANCASTER & LAKELAND NUFFIELD HOSPITAL 9L **23**
Meadowside
LANCASTER
LA1 3RH
Tel: 01524 62345

LYTHAM HOSPITAL 5C **130**
Warton St.
LYTHAM ST ANNES
Lancashire
FY8 5EE
Tel: 01253 303953

ORMSKIRK AND DISTRICT GENERAL HOSPITAL 8M **209**
Wigan Rd.
ORMSKIRK
Lancashire
L39 2AZ
Tel: 01695 577111

PARKWOOD 5G **88**
East Park Dri.
BLACKPOOL
FY3 8PW
Tel: 01253 306824

PENDLE COMMUNITY HOSPITAL 1J **105**
Leeds Rd.
NELSON
Lancashire
BB9 9SZ
Tel: 01282 474900

PENDLESIDE HOSPICE 6E **104**
Colne Rd.
BURNLEY
Lancashire
BB10 2LW
Tel: 01282 440100

QUEENSCOURT HOSPICE 1M **187**
Town La.
SOUTHPORT
Merseyside
PR8 6RE
Tel: 01704 544645

QUEEN'S PARK HOSPITAL 6A **140**
Haslingden Rd.
BLACKBURN
BB2 3HH
Tel: 01254 263555

QUEEN VICTORIA HOSPITAL 3B **22**
Thornton Rd.
MORECAMBE
Lancashire
LA4 5NN
Tel: 01524 411661

RAMSBOTTOM COTTAGE HOSPITAL 9G **181**
Nuttall La.
Ramsbottom
BURY
BL0 9JZ
Tel: 01706 823123

RENACRES HALL HOSPITAL 8B **188**
Renacres La., Halsall
ORMSKIRK
Lancashire
L39 8SE
Tel: 01704 841133

RIBBLETON HOSPITAL 7B **116**
Miller Rd.
Ribbleton
PRESTON
PR2 6LS
Tel: 01772 401600

RIBCHESTER COMMUNITY HOSPITAL 4A **98**
Ribchester Rd., Ribchester
PRESTON
PR3 3XD
Tel: 01772 782216

RIDGE LEA HOSPITAL 7N **23**
Quernmore Rd.
LANCASTER
LA1 3JR
Tel: 01524 586200

ROCHDALE INFIRMARY 4B **204**
Whitehall St.
ROCHDALE
Lancashire
OL12 0NB
Tel: 01706 377777

ROSSALL HOSPITAL 4C **54**
Westway
Rossall
FLEETWOOD
Lancashire
FY7 8JH
Tel: 01253 303800

ROSSENDALE GENERAL HOSPITAL 5J **161**
Haslingden Rd.
ROSSENDALE
Lancashire
BB4 6NE
Tel: 01706 215151

ROSSENDALE HOSPICE 6J **161**
Cribden Ho.
Rossendale General Hospital
Haslingden Rd.
ROSSENDALE
Lancashire
BB4 6NE
Tel: 01706 240084

ROYAL LANCASTER INFIRMARY 9K **23**
Ashton Rd.
LANCASTER
LA1 4RP
Tel: 01524 65944

Hospitals & Hospices

ROYAL PRESTON HOSPITAL 3H **115**
Sharoe Green La. N., Fulwood
PRESTON
PR2 9HT
Tel: 01772 716565

ST CATHERINE'S HOSPICE 9M **135**
Lostock La., Lostock Hall
PRESTON
PR5 5XU
Tel: 01772 629171

ST JOHN'S HOSPICE 4K **23**
Slyne Rd.
LANCASTER
LA2 6ST
Tel: 01524 382538

SHAROE GREEN HOSPITAL 5J **115**
Sharoe Green La. S., Fulwood
PRESTON
PR2 8DU
Tel: 01772 716565

SOUTHPORT & FORMBY DIST. GEN. HOSP. & CHRISTIANA
    HARTLEY MATERNITY WARD 1L **187**
Town La.
SOUTHPORT
Merseyside
PR8 6PN
Tel: 01704 547471

SOUTHPORT GENERAL INFIRMARY 9K **167**
Scarisbrick New Rd.
SOUTHPORT
Merseyside
PR8 6PH
Tel: 01704 547471

SOUTH SHORE HOSPITAL 4C **108**
Stony Hill Av.
BLACKPOOL
FY4 1HX
Tel: 01253 306100

BEARDWOOD BMI HOSPITAL, THE 2H **139**
Preston New Rd.
BLACKBURN
BB2 7AE
Tel: 01254 507607

HIGHFIELD BMI HOSPITAL, THE 8B **204**
Manchester Rd.,
ROCHDALE
Lancashire
OL11 4LZ
Tel: 01706 655121

TRINITY - THE HOSPICE IN THE FYLDE 9F **62**
Low Moor Rd.
BLACKPOOL
FY2 0BG
Tel: 01253 358881

VICTORIA HOSPITAL (BLACKPOOL) 4G **89**
Whinney Heys Rd.
BLACKPOOL
FY3 8NR
Tel: 01253 300000

WESHAM PARK HOSPITAL 2L **111**
Derby Rd.
Wesham
PRESTON
PR4 3AL
Tel: 01253 303280

WRIGHTINGTON HOSPITAL 2G **213**
Hall La.
Appley Bridge
WIGAN
Lancashire
WN6 9EP
Tel: 01257 252211